PRINCIPLES OF QUANTUM ARTIFICIAL INTELLIGENCE

Quantum Problem Solving and Machine Learning

Second Edition

PRINCIPLES OF QUANTUM ARTIFICIAL INTELLIGENCE

Quantum Problem Solving and Machine Learning

Second Edition

Andreas Wichert

Instituto Superior Técnico - Universidade de Lisboa, Portugal & INESC-ID, Portugal

World Scientific

NEW JERSEY • LONDON • SINGAPORE • BEIJING • SHANGHAI • HONG KONG • TAIPEI • CHENNAI • TOKYO

Published by

World Scientific Publishing Co. Pte. Ltd.
5 Toh Tuck Link, Singapore 596224
USA office: 27 Warren Street, Suite 401-402, Hackensack, NJ 07601
UK office: 57 Shelton Street, Covent Garden, London WC2H 9HE

British Library Cataloguing-in-Publication Data
A catalogue record for this book is available from the British Library.

PRINCIPLES OF QUANTUM ARTIFICIAL INTELLIGENCE
Quantum Problem Solving and Machine Learning
Second Edition

ISBN 978-981-122-430-0 (hardcover)
ISBN 978-981-122-431-7 (ebook for institutions)
ISBN 978-981-122-432-4 (ebook for individuals)

For any available supplementary material, please visit
https://www.worldscientific.com/worldscibooks/10.1142/11938#t=suppl

for André

Preface

Artificial intelligence and quantum computation divide the subject into many major areas. Each of these areas are now so extensive and huge, that a major understanding of the core concepts that unite them is extremely difficult. This book is about the core ideas of artificial intelligence and quantum computation. They are united in new subarea of artificial intelligence: "Quantum Artificial Intelligence".

This unique compendium presents an introduction to problem solving, information theory, statistical machine learning, stochastic methods and quantum computation. It indicates how to apply quantum computation to problem solving, machine learning and and quantum-like models to decision making - the core disciplines of artificial intelligence.

The first edition of the book was based on the course "Information and Computation for Artificial Intelligence" in the years 2008 – 2012 at Department of Computer Science and Engineering, Instituto Superior Técnico, Technical University of Lisbon. Most of the chapters of the first edition were rewritten and extensive new materials were updated. New topics include quantum machine learning, quantum-like Bayesian networks and mind in Everett many-worlds.

My research in recent years has benefited from many discussions with Dr. Luís Tarrataca and Dr. Catarina Moreira. Especially I would like to thank Senior Editor Steven Patt at World Scientific for his support. Finally, I would like to thank my loving wife *Manuela*, without her encouragement the book would be never finished.

Andreas Wichert

Contents

Chapter 1

Introduction

Symbolical artificial intelligence is a field of computer science that is highly related to quantum computation. At first glance, this statement appears to be a contradiction. However, the artificial intelligence framework, such as search and production system theory, allows an elegant description of a quantum computer model that is capable of quickly executing programs.

1.1 Artificial Intelligence

Artificial intelligence (AI) is a subfield of computer science that models the mechanisms of intelligent human behavior (intelligence). This approach is accomplished via simulation with the help of artificial artifacts, typically with computer programs on a machine that performs calculations. It should be noted that the machine does not need to be electronic. Indeed, Charles Babbage (1791-1871) sketched the first mechanical machine (a difference engine) for the calculation of certain values of polynomial functions [Hyman (1985)]. With the goal of mechanizing calculation steps, Babbage sketched the first model of a mechanical universal computer and called it an analytical engine. At the same time, Lady Ada Lovelance (1815-1852) thought about the computing power of such a machine. She argued that such a machine could only perform what it was told to do; such a machine could not generate new knowledge.

The term "artificial intelligence" itself was invented by the American computer scientist John McCarthy. It was used in the title of a conference that took place in the year 1956 at Dartmonth College in the USA. During this meeting, programs were presented that played chess and checkers, proved theorems and interpreted texts. The programs were thought to simulate human intelligent behavior. However, the terms "intelligence" and "intelligent human behavior" are not very well defined and understood. The definition of artificial intelligence leads to the paradox of a discipline whose principal purpose is its own definition.

A.M. Turing (1912-1954), in 1950, wrote the essay "Computing Machinery and Intelligence", in which he poses the question of how to determine whether a program is intelligent or not [Turing (1950)]. He defines intelligence as the reaction of an intelligent being to certain questions. This behavior can be tested by the so-called Turing test. A subject communicates over a computer terminal with two non-visible partners, a program and a human. If the subject cannot differentiate between the human and the program, the program is called intelligent. The questions posed can originate from any domain. However, if the domain is restricted, then the test is called a restricted Turing test. A restricted domain could be, for example, a medical diagnosis or the game of chess.

Human problem-solving algorithms are studied in Artificial Intelligence (AI). The key idea behind these algorithms is the symbolic representation of the domain in which the problems are solved. Symbols are used to denote or refer to something other than themselves, namely other things in the world (according to the, pioneering work of Tarski [Tarski (1944, 1956, 1995)]). They are defined by their occurrence in a structure and by a formal language which manipulates these structures [Simon (1991); Newell (1990)] (see Figure 1.1). In this context, symbols do not, by themselves, represent any utilizable knowledge. For example, they cannot be used for a definition of similarity criteria between themselves. The use of symbols in algorithms which imitate human intelligent behavior led to the famous physical symbol system hypothesis by Newell and Simon (1976) [Newell and Simon (1976)]: "The necessary and sufficient condition for a physical system to exhibit intelligence is that it be a physical symbol system." Symbols are not present in the world; they are the constructs of a human mind and simplify the process of representation used in communication and problem solving.

1.1.1 *Machine Learning*

There are some parallels between humans (animals) and machine learning. During learning, humans attempt to gain some knowledge, which involves some modification of behavioral tendencies by experience. Many of the techniques are derived from the efforts of psychologists and biologists to make more sense of human learning through computational models

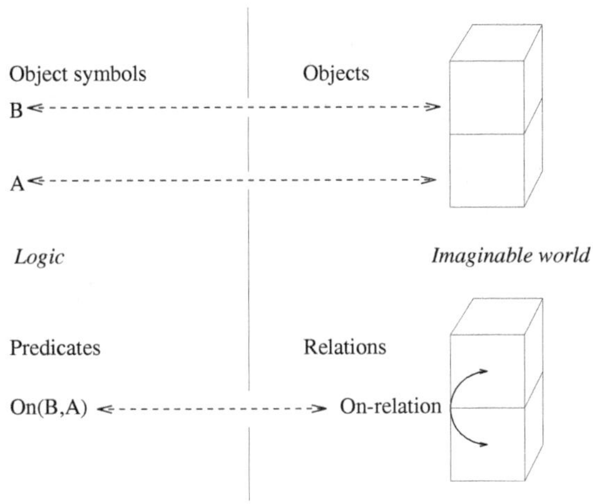

Fig. 1.1 Object represented by symbols and relation represented by predicate.

[Anderson (1995b)]. In machine learning a sub-symbolical or distributed representation is used. One form of distributed representation corresponds to a pattern that mirrors the way the biological sense organs describe the world. Perception organs sense the world by receptors. By the given order of the receptors, living organisms experience reality as a vector in which each dimension corresponds to a certain value in the receptor [Wichert (2009)]. One can measure the distance between two D dimensional vectors by a distance function like the the Euclidean distance function

$$d(\mathbf{x}, \mathbf{y}) = \|\mathbf{x} - \mathbf{y}\| = \sqrt{|x_1 - y_1|^2 + |x_2 - y_2|^2 + \cdots + |x_D - y_D|^2}.$$

We can describe objects by features. Let us imagine that we want to describe two species of a fish, the sea bass and the salmon, by some features (see Figure 1.2), [Duda *et al.* (2000)]. The process of choosing the correct features is called feature extraction. In our example, only two features are chosen since they can be inspected with the aid of a two-dimensional coordinate system. The two chosen features are width and lightness. In Figure 1.3, each salmon is represented by a dot and each sea bass by a cross. We attempt to separate the two classes by a line; we have some errors, but most examples are correctly separated. One of the most important machine learning algorithms, perceptron, attempts to determine (learn) this line from a given sample. Later, during classification, an unknown fish is described by a two-dimensional vector, and depending on which side of the separating line it falls, it is classified as either salmon or sea bass.

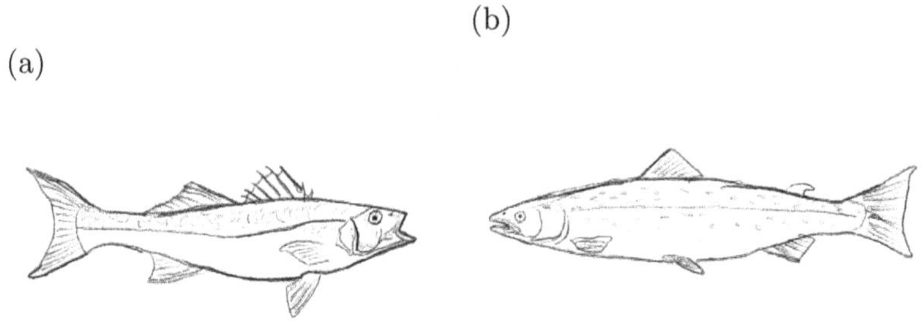

Fig. 1.2 (a) Sea bass and (b) salmon.

In machine learning, we can distinguish between supervised learning, as described in the preceding example and unsupervised learning. In supervised learning, the algorithm is presented with examples of inputs and their desired outputs. The goal is to learn a general rule that maps inputs to outputs. Supervised learning is frequently referred to as learning with a teacher because the desired outputs are indicated by a type of teacher. Consequently, unsupervised learning is referred to as learning without a teacher. In unsupervised learning, the algorithm groups information that is primarily represented by vectors into groups. The algorithm attempts to find the hidden structure of unlabeled data; clustering is an example of such an algorithm.

Deep artificial neural networks have many hidden layers usually trained by backpropagation. The models achieved tremendous results, and it is now common to identify artificial intelligence with deep learning and not with symbol manipulating systems. This results from the paradox of artificial intelligence as stated before in which the terms "intelligence" and "intelligent human behavior" are not very well defined and understood.

1.2 Motivation and Goals

Traditional AI is built around abstract algorithms and data structures that manipulate symbols. One of the important algorithms is the tree or graph search. Common forms of knowledge representation are symbolic rules and semantic nets. Traditional AI attempts to imitate human behavior without any relationship to physical reality, for example, in biological hardware.

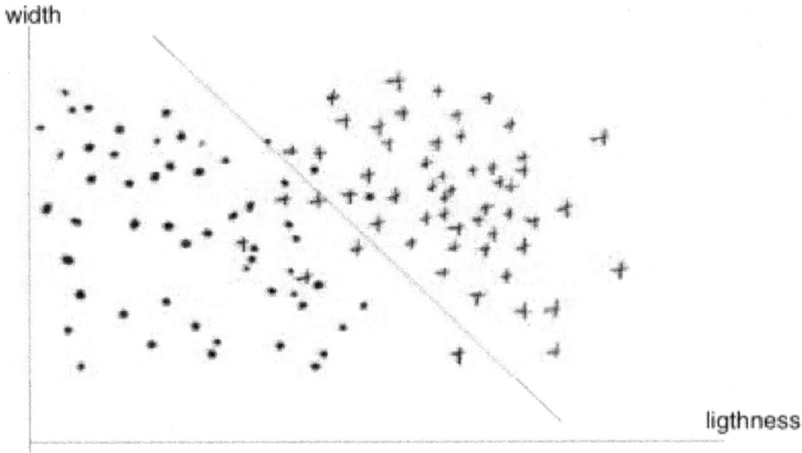

Fig. 1.3 In a sample, each salmon is represented by a dot and each sea bass by a cross. We separate the two classes by a line. Some errors are present, but most examples are correctly separated. Later, during classification, an unknown fish is described by a two-dimensional vector, and depending on which side of the separating line it falls, it is classified as either salmon or sea bass.

Sub-symbolical processing, on the other hand, belongs to biology-inspired AI, which involves methods such as behavioral systems or neural networks and statistical machine learning. Could the physical nature, as described by quantum physics, also lead to algorithms that imitate human behavior? What are the possibilities for the realization of artificial intelligence by means of quantum computation? Computational algorithms that are inspired by this physical reality are described by quantum computation. We will answer questions such as why and how to use quantum algorithms in artificial intelligence.

Questions that appear to be quite simple, such as: what are random numbers and how can we generate them, cannot be answered by traditional computer science. The widely used pseudo random generators are based on deterministic procedures and do not generate randomness; instead, they generate pseudo-randomness. Pseudo random generators are related to deterministic chaos sequences, which are described by mathematical chaos theory. Chaotic patterns can arise from very simple mathematics. While the results can be similar to true randomness, the output patterns are generated by deterministic rules. Chaotic patterns differ from most deterministic systems because any small change made to their variables can result in unpredictable changes to the system behavior.

In this book, we introduce quantum computation and its application to AI. Based on information science, we will illustrate the general principles that govern information processing and information structures. Artificial intelligence (AI) can be dividing into different areas: symbolical artificial intelligence, machine learning, cognitive psychology and philosophy. We demonstrate how quantum computation and quantum physics contribute to each of these subareas.

Quantum algorithms for AI have been proposed by [Tarrataca and Wichert (2011b,a, 2012b, 2013b)], including a quantum tree search algorithm and a quantum production system.

Linear algebra-based quantum machine learning is based on the HHL quantum algorithm for solving linear equations, quantum PCA, and quantum kernels. Quantum annealing is demonstrated on a Boltzmann machine and deep belief networks. Quantum cognition leads to quantum Bayesian networks and quantum-like evolution models. Finally, we describe probabilities and the mind in the Everett many-worlds theory.

1.3 Guide to the Reader

This book is about some core ideas of artificial intelligence and quantum computation and is composed of four sections: the first is on classical computation and the second section is on quantum computation. In the first section, we introduce the basic principles of computation, representation and problem solving. Quantum physics is based on information theory and probability theory. We present both theories and indicate their relationships to artificial intelligence by associative memory and Bayesian networks. In the second section, we introduce the principles of quantum computation and its mathematical framework. We present two principles on which quantum computation is based, the discrete Fourier transform and Grover's algorithm. Based on these principles, we introduce the iterative quantum tree search algorithm that speeds up the search. In the next step we introduce a quantum production system on which a universal quantum computer model is based. In the third section, quantum machine learning is explained from two perspectives, linear algebra-based quantum machine learning (e.g., the HHL quantum algorithm for solving linear equations) and quantum annealing for a Boltzmann machine and deep belief networks. The fourth section deals with quantum cognition and quantum-like models. Finally, the fifth section discusses the philosophical question of quantum computation and the multiverse. Readers who want to develop a general understanding of the quantum computation mathematical framework should read the second section, beginning with the chapter "Introduction to Quantum Physics?. Sections that go into more detail are marked by a star "∗? and can be skipped on the first reading.

1.4 Content

1.4.1 *Classical computation*

Computation - Chapter 2 The Entscheidungsproblem is presented, and the Turing machine is introduced. The proof of the Entscheidungsproblem is based on Cantor's diagonal argument and Gödelization. The Universal Turing machine is an abstract model of a computer. Computational complexity theory addresses questions regarding which problems can be solved in a finite amount of time on a computer. The Church-Turing thesis states that any algorithmic process can be simulated on a Turing machine. Two classes of practical computers are presented: analog and digital computers.

Problem Solving - Chapter 3 In the first step, the knowledge representation framework is introduced: rules, logic-based operators, frames and categorical representations. In the next step, production systems are introduced. A production system is a model of human problem solving. It is composed of long-term memory and working memory, which is also called short-term memory. We distinguish between deduction systems and reaction systems. Planning can be performed more easily by reaction systems in which the premise specifies the conditions that must be satisfied; in this way, the condition that specifies an action can be undertaken. An 8-puzzle example is presented. There is an assumption that the distance between states in the problem space is related to the distance between the sub-symbols that represent the states in sub-symbolical problem-solving. Sub-symbolical problem-solving takes advantage of the geometric nature of the world.

Information - Chapter 4 Information theory is highly related to mathematical probability theory and thermodynamics. Entropy is a measure of the disorder of the configuration of states and can be described by a dice model. The Maxwell paradox identifies information with a negative measure of entropy. The ideal entropy represents the minimal number of optimal questions that must be addressed to know the result of an experiment. We will indicate the relationships between information and hierarchical structures and measurement. In the section on information and memory, we will introduce a biologically inspired model of associative memory. The Information and storage capacity of the model is high, given that the binary representation is sparse. Finally, a deduction system based on associative memory is presented.

Reversible Algorithms - Chapter 5 Bennett (1973) showed that irreversible overwriting of one bit causes at least $k \cdot T \cdot log2$ joules of energy dissipation, where k is Boltzmann's constant and T is the absolute temperature. Bennett also indicated that this lower bound can be ignored when using reversible computation. Reversible computing is a model of computing in which the computational process is reversible. Reversible Boolean gates and circuits are described.

Probability - Chapter 6 Probability theory is built around Kolmogorov's axioms. For a joint distribution of n possible variables, the exponential growth of combinations being true or false becomes an intractable problem for large n. There are two possible solutions to this problem, Naïve Bayes and Bayesian networks. Naïve Bayes is related to counting and categorization. For the unobservable variables, the Bayesian networks are based on the law of total probability. A Markov chain is a mathematical system that undergoes transitions described by a stochastic matrix. A stochastic matrix evolution that occurs when describing the evolution of a physical system is usually non-reversible. A vector representation of events for the possible worlds approach is introduced. In the vector based framework for probabilities a state represents events in a n-dimensional vector space by a unit-length vector in the norm l_1. By replacing the l_1 norm by the Euclidean l_2 norm we introduce quantum probabilities.

1.4.2 *Quantum computation*

Introduction to Quantum Physics - Chapter 7 The unitary deterministic evolution represented by the Schrödinger equation and two interpretations of quantum mechanics are presented. We indicate the difference between stochastic Markov evolution and unitary evolution. The mathematical framework of quantum theory is based on linear algebra in Hilbert space. The relationships between the unitary operators represented by unitary matrices and the Schrödinger equation and the Hamiltonian are described by a spectral representation. A 2-state quantum system is described by a two-dimensional Hilbert space. Such a 2-state quantum system corresponds to a qubit. A register is composed of several qubits and is defined by the tensor product. Shannon entropy of a superposition of qubits measures the distribution of the probabilities. It describes the departure of the state from a basis state (eigenstate). For a basis state, there is no uncertainty during the measurement. The higher the entropy is, the higher the uncertainty during the measurement.

Computation with Qubits - Chapter 8 A unitary operator on a qubit is called a unary quantum gate. An operation on several qubits can be represented by unitary matrices. The matrix representation of serial and parallel operations is composed of either a product or a tensor operation between the matrices. A reversible circuit of m bits corresponds to a unitary mapping. A reversible circuit can be represented by a unitary permutation matrix or by quantum Boolean gates. The Deutsch algorithm exploits the superposition of qubits that are generated by Hadamard gates; the Deutsch algorithm is more powerful than any other classical algorithm and determines whether an unknown function of one bit is constant or not by calling the function one time. A classical algorithm requires two calls. The Deutsch Jozsa algorithm generalizes the working principle even to a more powerful algorithm for a function of m bits.

Periodicity - Chapter 9 The Fourier transform changes a signal from the time domain to the frequency domain. The discrete Fourier transform changes discrete time-based or space-based data into frequency-based data. The discrete Fourier transform (DFT) can be seen as a linear transform represented by a unitary matrix F. This unitary matrix F also defines the quantum Fourier transform (QFT). The decomposition of the matrix is described by the fast Fourier transform (FFT). The QFT decomposition is equivalent to the FFT. The QFT period algorithm determines the period of a periodic function in polynomial time and is the basis of Shor's Algorithm for the factorization of numbers in polynomial time. An alternative approach is described in Kitaev's phase estimation algorithm, which determines the eigenvalue for a unitary operator and an eigenvector.

Search - Chapter 10 We want to find x for which $f(x) = 1$, $x = \xi$. This task is equivalent to a decision problem with a binary answer $1 = yes$ and $0 = no$ and the instance x. There is a lower bound for a quantum search on a quantum computer using a quantum oracle. The possible speedup is quadratic; $NP - complete$ problems remain $NP - complete$. The search is described by Grover's algorithm and is based on the Householder reflection. In the case, the number of the solutions is unknown, we can apply a quantum counting algorithm. The generate-and-test method is a simple AI paradigm that can directly benefit from Grover's algorithm.

Quantum Problem-Solving - Chapter 11 Problem-solving can be modeled by a production system that implements a search algorithm. The search defines a problem space and can be represented as a tree. In an uninformed search, no additional information about the states is given. A heuristic search is based on a heuristic function $h(\nu)$ that estimates the cheapest cost from the node ν to the goal. However, inventing heuristic functions is difficult. An alternative approach is that of the quantum tree search algorithm. Using Grover's algorithm, we search through all possible paths and verify, for each path, whether it leads to the goal state. We present the iterative quantum tree search, which is the basis of the quantum production system. We explain the principles of Tarrataca's quantum production system on a trivial example, the 3-puzzle. Finally, we present a universal quantum computer model that is capable of more quickly executing programs. The corresponding principles can be integrated into the unified theories of human cognition.

1.4.3 *Quantum machine learning*

Grover's Algorithm and the Input Problem - Chapter 12 The input and the destruction problem are introduced. The amplitude distribution of a quantum state is initialized by reading N data points. This cost can dominate the complexity of an algorithm. A quantum memory can be queried only once because of its collapse during the measurement (destruction). We present a quantum algorithm based on Wilshaw's associative memory that efficiently prepares the data. The idea is to generate quantum superposition from the classical data where the reading cost is negligible.

Statistical Machine Learning - Chapter 13 In unsupervised learning, algorithm groups input information that is primarily represented by vectors into groups without additional information. The algorithm attempts to find the hidden structure of unlabeled data; principal component analysis is an example of such algorithm. In supervised learning, the algorithm is presented with example inputs and their desired outputs, and the goal is to obtain a general rule that maps inputs and outputs. We describe the principal component analysis, linear and logistic regression, backpropagation algorithm, support vector machines, and kernel machines.

Linear Algebra-based Quantum Machine Learning - Chapter 14 Linear algebra-based quantum machine learning is based on quantum gates that describe quantum basic linear algebra subroutines. These subroutines exhibit theoretical exponential speedups compared to classical counterparts and are essential for machine learning. The quantum algorithm for linear systems of equations is one of the main fundamental algorithms expected to provide a speedup compared to classical counterparts. The algorithm is also called the HHL algorithm and is based on Kitaev's phase algorithm. We describe the quantum principal component analysis (qPCA) and the quantum random access memory (qRAM). We introduce quantum kernels and indicate quantum advantage kernels.

Stochastic Methods - Chapter 15 We introduce the Hopfield and Ising models and describe the finite temperature dynamics. The stochastic dynamics of the Ising model can be described by Gibbs sampling. The metropolis algorithm is a modified Monte Carlo method; it is referred to as the Markov chain Monte Carlo. The rate of convergence of the Markov chain of the Gibbs sampling or the Metropolis algorithm to thermal equilibrium is extremely slow at very low temperatures. For improved computational efficiency, we operate the stochastic system at high temperature (where convergence to equilibrium is fast) and then maintain the system at equilibrium as the temperature is slowly lowered. Simulated annealing is named by analogy to real annealing that a real metallurgist does by slowly cooling the sample. The Boltzmann machine is a stochastic Hopfield network with hidden units. It is a stochastic binary machine whose composition consists of stochastic neurons in states 1 or 0. The learning process in the Boltzmann machine is very slow, particularly when the number of hidden units used in the machine is large. A restricted Boltzmann machine (RBM) has connections only between visible and hidden units to simplify inference and learning. A deep belief network (DBN) is a generative graphical model or, alternatively, a class of deep neural networks composed of multiple layers of latent variables (hidden units) with connections between the layers but not between units within each layer. It can be viewed as a composition of restricted Boltzmann machines. Deep belief networks, which are also called deep neural networks (DNN) (Hinton, 2006), capture higher-level representations of input features.

Adiabatic Quantum Computation and Quantum Annealing - Chapter 16 Adiabatic quantum computation is an alternative approach to quantum computation. It is based on the time evolution of a quantum system. Adiabatic quantum computation is a polynomial equivalent to the quantum gate model. Adiabatic quantum computation and quantum annealing are frequently used interchangeably; however, there are some distinctions. Adiabatic quantum computation refers to a universal model that solves any Turing-compatible problems that run in an adiabatically closed system without interference from the environment. Quantum annealing solves optimization problems. In simulated annealing, the neighborhoods remain the same throughout the search. The temperature determines the probability of moving out of a local minimum. In the beginning, the temperature is high, and the probability of moving out of a minimum is high. Then, it is slowly reduced until the probability of moving out of a minimum is zero. The disordering Hamiltonian introduces quantum fluctuations in quantum annealing. The transverse field coefficient, which is also called the tunneling coefficient, controls the passage of the solution landscape by quantum tunneling. We introduce the D-Wave quantum annealer. An alternative approach for a Boltzmann machine or deep belief network is to estimate model expectations by a quantum annealer such as D-Wave. Variational algorithms are related to the adiabatic quantum computation; however, they are based on discrete unitary evolution. A variational quantum eigensolver is a hybrid algorithm based on a quantum device and a classical algorithm to estimate the ground state of a system.

1.4.4 *Quantum-like models*

Quantum Cognition - Chapter 17 Quantum cognition uses a mathematical quantum theory to model cognitive phenomena. It is assumed that the computation itself is performed on a classical computer and not on a quantum computer. In a quantum world, the brain is considered to be a classical computer. The quantum probabilities, when observed, correspond to classical probability theory. If not observed, the state of a system is described by a complex vector with a length of one. Two equivalent states represent the same state when a measurement is performed, but they can behave differently during the unitary evolution. Humans, when making decisions, violate the law of total probability. The violation can be explained as a quantum interference. We introduce the law of balance and quantum-like Bayesian networks.

Quantum-like Evolution - Chapter 17 Evolutionary dynamics have traditionally been studied in the context of homogeneous populations. Population structures are modeled by arranging individuals on a graph in which each vertex represents an individual. Their evolutionary behavior is modeled by Markov chains described by a stochastic matrix. An important question is whether more generalizable probabilistic models can be found using quantum probabilities. Quantum-like evolution is l_2 norm preserving in which the matrix does not need to be unitary. By coding the phase of the input vector into the phase of the balanced phase matrix, we can simulate the unitary evolution. The phase that describes the matrix is dynamically updated. Quantum-like evolution can simulate either unitary evolution by coding the phase of the input vector into the phase of the balanced phase matrix, a Markov chain, or an alternative evolution that can lead to fixed, periodic, or chaotic behavior, which results in strange oscillations.

1.4.5 *Quantum philosophy*

Quantum Computation and the Multiverse - Chapter 18 The Everett many-worlds theory views reality as a many-branched tree in which every possible quantum outcome is realized. The modern version of the wave-function collapse is based on decoherence and leads to the multiverse interpretation of quantum mechanics. Following a controversial suggestion by David Deutsch that decision theory can solve the problem of probabilities in the Everett many-worlds, we suggest that the probabilities are induced by Shannon's entropy that measures the uncertainty of events. We argue that a relational person prefers certainty to uncertainty due to the fundamental biological principle of homeostasis. Then, we redefine free will as the concept of identity in a deterministic universe. Causality is related to a meaningful explanation. For impossible explanations, causality does not exist, and the identity of the self breaks. Personal identities can exist only in meaningful causal worlds. We are one person described by the meaningful path in the multiverse that is correlated with our free choices.

Conclusion- Chapter 20 In classical physics, randomness does not exist; in quantum physics, it cannot be explained. In addition to randomness, quantum computation cannot offer any noncomputable schema such as that claimed by the quantum mind or the quantum consciousness hypothesis. However, quantum cognition assumes that the brain is a classical computer in a quantum world. Because a wave function can be present at the macro scale, predictions, such as the hidden inference, are based on von Neumann probabilities and not on the classical probability theory.

Chapter 2

Computation

2.1 Entscheidungsproblem

David Hilbert, one of the most famous German mathematicians (see Figure 2.1), attended a banquet in 1934, and he was seated next to the new minister of education, Bernhard Rust [Reid (1996)]. Rust asked, "How is

Fig. 2.1 David Hilbert (1862 - 1943) one of the most famous German mathematicians.

mathematics in Göttingen now that it has been freed of the Jewish influence?" Hilbert replied, "Mathematics in Göttingen? There is really none any more." David Hilbert died in 1943. On his tombstone, at Göttingen, one can read his epitaph:

- Wir müssen wissen (We have to know)
- Wir werden wissen (We shall know!)

At the International Congress of Mathematicians in Paris in 1900, he put forth an influential list of 23 unsolved problems in mathematics. Hilbert's 23rd problem became known as the Entscheidungsproblem. Hilbert's Entscheidungsproblem is formulated as the following question:

- Is there a general algorithm to determine whether a mathematical conjecture is true or false?

It was commonly believed that there was no such thing as an unsolvable problem. However, Alonzo Church and Alan Turing discovered independently, around 1936, that a general solution to the Entscheidungsproblem is impossible. They showed that it is impossible to decide algorithmically whether statements in arithmetic are true or false. This result is now known as Church's Theorem or the Theorem Church-Turing Theorem.

Alonzo Church created the method for defining recursive functions λ-calculus [Church (1936a)], [Church (1936b)], [Church (1941)] and Alan Turing created a simple model called the Turing machine [Turing (1936)] (see Figure 2.2). The Turing machine constitutes an infinitely long tape that is divided into a sequence of cells. In each cell, a certain symbol can be written and later read by a head. The head can move along the tape and exist in one state of a finite set of internal states. A set of rules specifies a new state given the current state and the symbol being read. The new state determines in which direction the head must move and if it must write or read a symbol. For each state, only one rule describes one action. Turing realized that one could encode the transformation rules of any specific Turing machine T as some pattern of symbols on the tape that fed into a special Turing machine U. U had the effect of reading in the pattern, specifying the transformation rules for T and then simulating T. Any algorithmic process can be simulated on a Turing machine U. Entscheidungsproblem corresponds to the halting problem. Whether a program will halt or run forever can be determined and is based on the given program with a finite input. We will sketch the proof, assuming a common computer model and not the Turing machine, to make the explanation easier.

The proof uses a technique called reduction ad absurdum, in which we assume the truth of the opposite of what we want to prove and then derive

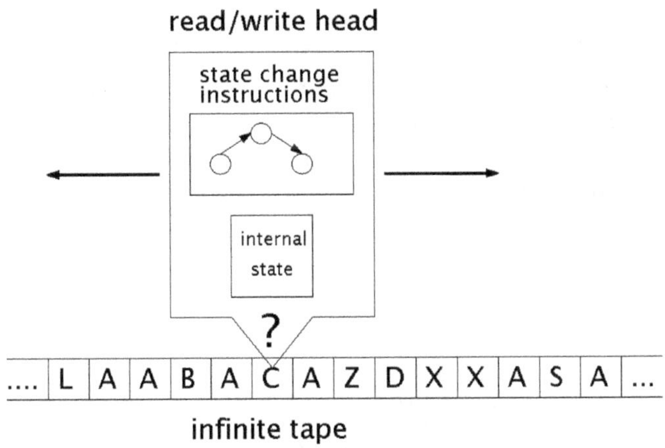

Fig. 2.2 The Turing machine constitutes an infinitely long tape that is divided into a sequence of cells. In each cell, a certain symbol can be written and later read by a head. The head can move along the tape and exist in one state of a finite set of internal states. A set of rules specifies a new state given the current state and the symbol being read. The new state determines in which direction the head must move and if it must write or read a symbol. For each state, only one rule describes one action.

a logical contradiction. The proof is based on Cantor's diagonal argument and a form of coding in which a function or a program can be represented by a number. This form of coding is called Gödelization. It allows self-reference, which means that the code of the program that is represented by a number can form an input to the program. The program can make statements about itself.

2.1.1 *Cantor's diagonal argument*

Cantor's diagonal argument indicates that there is no bijection between infinite sets and natural numbers [Lewis and Papadimitriou (1981)]. Natural numbers are countably infinite, and infinite sets are uncountably infinite. Suppose that infinite sets are represented by binary infinite strings, and we list all of the sets in a table. This list is infinitely long, and we can write each entry as an infinitely long binary string. It is possible to build a new infinite binary string in such a way that its first element is different from the first element of the first infinite binary string in the list, its second element is different from the second element of the second infinite binary sting in the list, and so on. In general, its nth element is different from the nth element of the nth infinite binary string in the list. The new infinite binary string corresponds to the diagonal elements of the list in which its element is zero if the diagonal element is one and is zero if the diagonal element is one. The procedure can be repeated many times; the infinite list of infinite sets is never complete, and the set of all infinite sets is uncountable. It should be noted that to deny the Cantor's diagonal argument implicates the rejection of infinity. Because the size of the power set is 2^n, it follows from Cantor's diagonal argument

$$\lim_{n\to\infty} n < \lim_{n\to\infty} 2^n.$$

2.1.2 *Reductio ad absurdum*

Using Gödelization, we can represent a program with binary numbers. A binary number can be easily mapped to a binary string. A program can be infinite because the Turing machine has an infinite tape [Lewis and Papadimitriou (1981)]. As previously observed, we cannot list all of the infinite programs. Suppose that the program is finite. The program and the finite input are encoded as a pair of positive binary numbers. Is there a program that solves the halting problem? Let us suppose that such a program exists and that it is using a self-referent function $halt(x)$. The binary number x is its representation using the Gödelization principle. The function $halt(x)$ returns a one if the corresponding program represented by the binary number x with the input x halts and otherwise returns a zero.

$$halt(x) = \begin{cases} 1 \; program \; x \; halts \; on \; input \; x \\ 0 \; otherwise \end{cases}$$

Using the modified diagonal argument we define the program with the name "Diagonal"

```
Diagonal(x)
{
 if halt(x)=0 then halt;
 else loop forever;
}
```

The program "Diagonal" is represented by the binary number u. Does the program Diagonal(u) halt? If yes, then we have a contradiction to the definition of $halt(x)$. If it does not halt, then there is also a contradiction to the definition of $halt(x)$. From the contradiction, it would follow that there is no program that solves the halting problem.

2.2 Complexity Theory

The elegant way of modeling a computer by a Turing machine leads us to computational complexity theory. Computational complexity theory addresses the questions of which problems can be solved in a finite amount of time on a computer. Time is the most important resource during computation besides space and energy. Space and energy are negligible when using the Turing machine because the Turing machine itself is composed of infinitely long tape and does not require any energy resources [Lewis and Papadimitriou (1981)]. To simplify the analysis of the correspondence to time, special computational problems are investigated, namely decision problems.

2.2.1 *Decision problems*

A decision problem is a computational problem with instances formulated as a question with a binary "yes" or "no" answer. An example is the question of whether a certain number n is a prime number. Most problems can be converted into a decision problem. A problem is easy if a certain Turing machine can determine the instances related to the input for the answer "yes" in polynomial time. Otherwise, we state that the problem is hard. The relationship to the size of the input accounts for the reading time of the input. It should not influence the time complexity. A number is usually represented by the base $B > 1$, which means that k digits can represent B^k different numbers. In other words, the hierarchical organized structure of the numbers exponentially speeds up the reading time of a deterministic Turing machine. This relationship is not valid for a unary representation in which the input size is equivalent to the numbers that can be represented.

2.2.2 *P and NP*

The formal definition for easy problems represented by P is as follows: The set of all decision problems that have instances that are solvable in polynomial time using a deterministic Turing machine. In a deterministic Turing machine, all of the transitions are described by some fixed rules [Lewis and Papadimitriou (1981)]. An example for an easy problem is multiplication $x \times b = c$, where x is the instance and the values b and c are given; determine x so that the answer to the question is $x \times 7 = 28$

is yes. On the other hand, it is thought that the factoring determines the integers for which the product is equal to for a given number d; for example, integers a, b with $a \times b = d$ is not in P, which indicates that it is hard. The class NP is the set of all decision problems that have instances that are solvable in polynomial time using a non-deterministic Turing machine. In a non-deterministic Turing machine, in contrast to a deterministic Turing machine, for each state, several rules with different actions can be applied.

Non-deterministic Turing machine branches into many copies that are represented by a computational tree in which there are different computational paths. The class NP corresponds to a non-deterministic Turing machine that guesses the computational path that represents the solution. By doing so, it guesses the instances of the decision problem. In the second step, a deterministic Turing machine verifies whether the guessed instance leads to a "yes" answer. It is easy to verify whether a solution is valid or not. This statement does not mean that finding a solution is easy. Clearly, the class $P \subseteq NP$ is known, and it follows that $NP \neq P$ or $NP = P$; however, other relationships are not known. The class $NP - complete$ is present if the problem is in NP and every other problem in NP can be reduced to the class $NP - complete$.

It was not obvious that an $NP - complete$ problem exists. Cook-Levin described the first example of an $NP - complete$ problem, the satisfiability problem. Until recently, thousands of other problems are known to be $NP - complete$, including the well-known traveling salesman and Hamiltonian cycle problem [Cormen *et al.* (2001)].

The structure of $NP - complete$ problems is equivalent to a computational tree of a non-deterministic Turing machine in which all different computational paths must be searched by a deterministic Turing machine. A simple algorithm for solving $NP - complete$ problems by a deterministic Turing machine is to perform an iterative search for all possible instances.

- The formal definition for NP is as follows: a deterministic Turing machine verifies whether an instance (ticket) leads to a "yes" answer in polynomial time.
- The formal definition of an $NP - complete$ problem is as follows: The problem is NP and the problem is $NP - hard$. $NP - hard$ means that every other problem in NP can be reduced to it in polynomial time.

2.3 Church-Turing Thesis

The definition of P and NP should not depend upon the currently used computational model. The following is stated in the Church-Turing thesis: Any algorithmic process can be simulated on a Turing machine. The extended Church-Turing Thesis, which is also called the strong Church-Turing thesis, states that everything that can be computed in a certain amount of time on any physical computer can be also be computed on a Turing machine with a polynomial slowdown. In other words, any reasonable algorithmic process can be simulated on a Turing machine, with the possibility of a polynomial slowdown, in the number of steps required to run the simulation. The problems in P are precisely those for which a polynomial-time solution is the best possible, in any physically reasonable model of computation.

The hypothesis that the universe is equivalent to a Turing machine, which is related to the Church-Turing thesis, is similar to that stated in digital physics. However, Richard Feynman observed in the early eighties that it did not appear possible for a Turing machine to simulate certain quantum physical processes without incurring an exponential slowdown. This fact would contradict the strong Church-Turing thesis, which led Feynman to ask whether a quantum system can be simulated on an imaginary quantum computer.

2.3.1 *Church-Turing-Deutsch principle*

In 1985, David Deutsch [Deutsch (1985)] (see Figure 2.3) reformulated the Church-Turing thesis based on the observation of Richard Feynman in physical terms: "Every finitely realizable physical system can be perfectly simulated by universal computing machine operating by finite means." The Turing machine was replaced by the universal computing machine which operates by finite means.

2.4 Computers

The Turing machine is a theoretical mathematical model, not a practical engineering model of a computer. There are two distinct classes of practical computers, analog and digital computers.

Fig. 2.3 David Elieser Deutsch, the "father" of quantum computing.

2.4.1 *Analog computers*

An analog computer represents information by analog means, such as voltage. In such a computer, information is represented by a voltage wave and the algorithm is represented by an electrical circuit. Such a circuit is composed of resistors and capacitors that are connected together. An algorithm represents a mathematical model of a physical system, which can be described, for example, by specific differential equations. In the first step, the mathematical model is determined. Then, a block diagram that models the analogous system is developed. This model defines the electrical components that specify the computation. The input and output of the computation are voltage waves that can be observed by an oscilloscope. The represented values are usually less accurate than digitally represented values. The results of each computation can vary due to external influences. For this reason, each result of the computation is unique. The exact value cannot be reproduced without an error. This type of noise, which results from an external influence, makes it impossible to recompute the output of chaotic deterministic functions. Even making the smallest change to the initial condition can cause the results to greatly diverge. It is important to note that analog computers are not covered by the Church-Turing thesis because they cannot be simulated by a Turing machine; however, analog computers are covered by the Church-Turing-Deutsch principle because they correspond to a computing machine that operates by finite means. Analog computers were popular in the 1950s (see Figure 2.4).

Fig. 2.4 a The AKAT-1 was an analog computer constructed by the Polish pioneer in computing Jacek Karpiński at the Polish Academy of Science's Institute of Automatics in 1959. AKAT-1 was the world's first transistor differential analyzer. In the drawing his team is shown.

However, analog computers fell into decline with the advent of the development of the microprocessor, which led to the development of digital computers.

2.4.2 *Digital computers*

A digital computer is a device that processes information that is represented in discrete means such as symbols. Usually, the symbols are represented in binary form. Modern digital computers are based on digital circuits. In a digital circuit, the information is represented by binary digits. Due to a digital representation, the exact values of each computation can be reproduced without any error. The computation can be repeated, and the result remains the same (this scenario is not the case with analog computers). Binary digits are represented by the minimal unit of information, the bit. The binary information is manipulated by Boolean digital circuits. Emil Post has proven the complete sets of truth functions. It follows that they can be computed using Boolean circuits, which are composed of Boolean gates and represent Boolean logic, which operates on bits [Cormen *et al.* (2001)]. An algorithm can be described by a circuit. The construction of a circuit requires the exact knowledge of the values that must be computed. For this reason, a circuit is not an algorithmic device; by itself, it does not correspond to a universal Turing machine. The Halting problem cannot by represented by a circuit.

2.4.3 *Von Neumann architecture*

The ENIAC (Electronic Numerical Integrator And Computer) was one of the first Turing-complete universal digital computers that was capable of being programmed. John von Neumann learned in 1945 of the ENIAC Project and described this model in a technical report called "First Draft of a Report on the EDVAC" [von Neumann (1945)]. The model become known as the Van Neumann architecture [Aspray (1990)]. This technology is composed of five main concepts:

- An arithmetic logic unit (ALU) unit that is capable of performing both arithmetic and logic operations on the data.
- A control unit (CU) that interprets an instruction retrieved from the memory and that selects alternative courses of action based on the results of the previous operations.
- Main memory stores both data and instructions and read-write random-access memory (RAM).
- Secondary memory represents the external mass storage.
- Input and output mechanisms.

In modern computers, the ALU and the CU are parts of the central processing unit (CPU) that are represented by a single silicon chip called a microprocessor. The subsystem called a bus transfers the data between the random-access memory, the CPU, and the input and output (see Figure 2.5). Most modern computers are based on the von Neumann architecture.

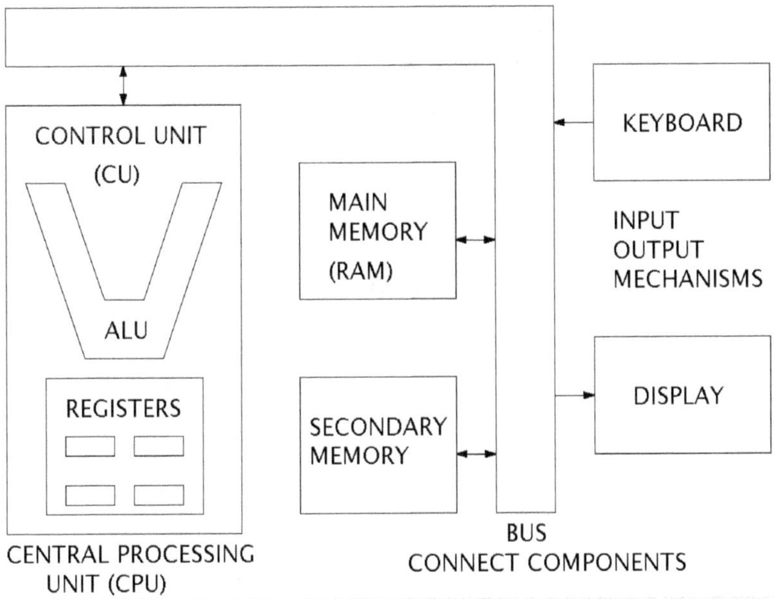

Fig. 2.5 The Van Neumann architecture. In modern computers, the ALU and the CU are parts of the central processing unit (CPU) that are represented by a single silicon chip called a microprocessor. The subsystem called a bus transfers the data between the random-access memory, the CPU, and the input and output.

Chapter 3

Problem Solving

It is quite certain for the cognitive psychologist that the human computational model is not at all based on the Van Neumann architecture. Instead, they propose that the human computational model is based on production systems. A production system is a mathematical as well as a practical model that can be realized as a computing machine. Production systems are closely related to the approach taken by Markov algorithms [Markov (1954)], and similar to these approaches, production systems are equivalent in power to a Turing machine [Turing (1936)]. A Turing machine can also be easily simulated by a production system. The production system is a model of actual human problem-solving behavior [Newell and Simon (1972); Anderson (1983); Klahr and Waterman (1986); Newell (1990)].

3.1 Knowledge Representation

Production systems are composed of if-then rules that are also called productions. A rule contains several "if" patterns and one or more "then" patterns. A pattern in the context of rules is an individual predicate, which can be negated together with arguments. A rule can establish a new assertion by the "then" part (its conclusion) whenever the "if" part (its premise) is true. Productions can be represented by rules or logic-based operators. Alternative sub-symbolical representation is based on categorial representation. Binary vector representation is the basis of the quantum production systems.

3.1.1 *Rules*

A rule [Winston (1992); Russell and Norvig (1995); Luger and Stubblefield (1998)] contains several "if" patterns and one or more "then" patterns. A pattern in the context of rules is an individual predicate which can be negated together with arguments. The rule can establish a new assertion by the "then" part, the conclusion whenever the "if" part, the premise, is true. When variables become identified with values they are bound to these values. Whenever the variables in a pattern are replaced by values, the pattern is said to be instantiationed. Here is an example of rules with a variable x:

- $\underbrace{\text{If (flies(x)} \vee \text{feathes(x))} \wedge \text{lays eggs(x)}}_{premise}$ then $\underbrace{\text{bird(x)}}_{conclusion}$
- If bird(x) $\wedge$ swims(x) then penguin(x)
- If bird(x) $\wedge$ sings(x) then nightinagle(x)

The following assertions are present:

- feathers(Pit)
- lays eggs(Pit)
- swims(Pit)
- flies(Airbus)

Pit is a bird because the premise of the first rule is true when x is bound to Pit. Because bird(Pit), the premise of the second rule is true and Pit is a penguin.

3.1.2 *Logic-based operators*

Logical representation is motivated by philosophy and mathematics [Kurzweil (1990); Tarski (1995); Luger and Stubblefield (1998)]. Predicates are functions that map objects' arguments into true or false values. They describe the relation between objects in a world which is represented by symbols. Whenever a relation holds with respect to some objects, the corresponding predicate is true when applied to the corresponding object symbols.

Predicates can be negated by the function $\neg$ (not) and combined by the logical connectives $\vee$ (disjunction), $\wedge$ (conjunction) and the implies ($\rightarrow$) operator. $\neg$, $\vee$, $\wedge$, and $\rightarrow$ determine the predicate's value. To signal that an expression is universally true, the universal quantifier and a variable standing for possible objects is used.

$$\forall \text{ x[Feathers(x)} \rightarrow \text{Bird(x)]}.$$
An Object having feathers is a bird.

Some expressions are true only for some objects. This is represented by an existential quantifier and a variable.

$$\exists \text{ x[Bird(x)]}.$$
There is at least one object which is a bird.

An interpretation is an accounting of the correspondence between objects and object symbols and between relations and predicates. An interpretation can be only either true or false. These are some basic ideas about representation in predicate calculus, which is a subset of formal logic. A world state can be described including properties and relations using predicate calculus. This kind of description can be used to define operators like those used in the STRIPS computer science approach (see Figure 3.1) [Fikes and Nilsson (1971); Nilsson (1982); Givan and Dean (1997)].

ontable(A).
ontable(C).
on(B,A).
clear(B).
clear(C).
gripping().

Using the block examples, four operations "pickup", "putdown", "stack" and "unstack" can be defined [Nilsson (1982)]: [1]

$$pickup(x) \begin{cases} P : gripping() \wedge clear(x) \wedge ontable(x) \\ A : gripping(x) \\ D : ontable(x) \wedge gripping() \end{cases}$$

$$putdown(x) \begin{cases} P : gripping(x) \\ A : ontable(x) \wedge gripping() \wedge clear(x) \\ D : gripping(x) \end{cases}$$

[1]The expressions are always universally true, and therefore the universal quantifier is omitted.

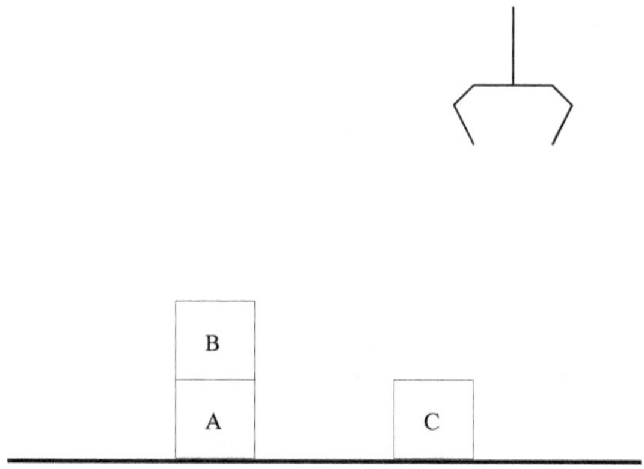

Fig. 3.1 ABC block world.

$$stack(x,y)\begin{cases} P: gripping(x) \wedge clear(x) \\ A: on(x,y) \wedge gripping() \wedge clear(x) \\ D: clear(y) \wedge gripping(x) \end{cases}$$

$$unstack(x,y)\begin{cases} P: gripping() \wedge clear(x) \wedge on(x,y) \\ A: gripping(x) \wedge clear(y) \\ D: on(x,y) \wedge gripping() \end{cases}$$

Each of the operators is represented as triples of description. The first element is the precondition, the world state that must be met for an operator to be applied. It can be true or false when variables become identified with the values, which describe the state. The second element is the additions to the state description that are a result of applying the operator. The last element is the items that are removed from the state description to create a new state when the operator is applied. These operators obey the frame axiom since they specify what is true in one state of the world and what exactly has changed by performing some action by an operator. The problem of specifying which part of the description should change and which should not is called the frame problem [Winston (1992)].

ontable(A).
clear(A)
ontable(C).
clear(C).
gripping(B).

The state after the operator *pickup(B)* was applied to the state of Figure 3.1 (see Figure 3.2).

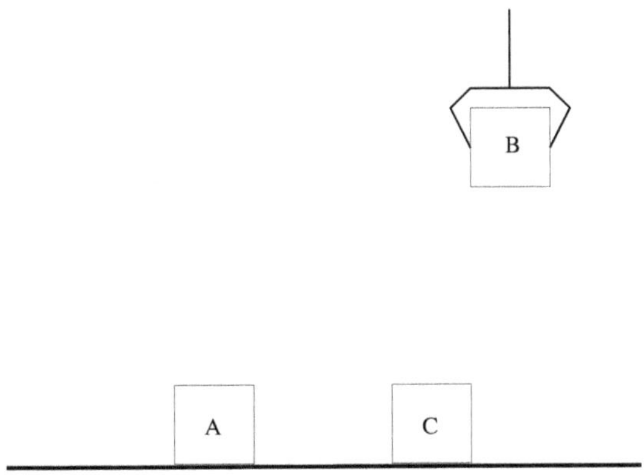

Fig. 3.2 The state after the operator *pickup(B)* was applied to the state of Figure 3.1.

3.1.3 *Frames*

Frames describe individual objects and entire classes [Minsky (1975, 1986); Winston (1992)] and can be used to represent states of the world. They are composed of slots which can be either attributes, which describe the classes or object, or links to other frames. With the aid of links, a hierarchy can be represented in which classes or objects are parts of more general classes. In this taxonomic representation, frames inherit attributes of the more general classes (see Figure 3.3). Frames can be viewed as generalization of semantic nets. They are psychologically motivated and were popularized in computer science by Marvin Minsky. One important result of the frame theory is the object-oriented approach in programming.

3.1.4 *Categorial representation*

Humans divide the world into categories so that they can make sense of it [Smith (1995)]. The categorization task consists of the determination if an object belongs to a category [Osherson (1995); Lakeoff (1987)]. Objects can be described by a set of discrete features, such as red, round and

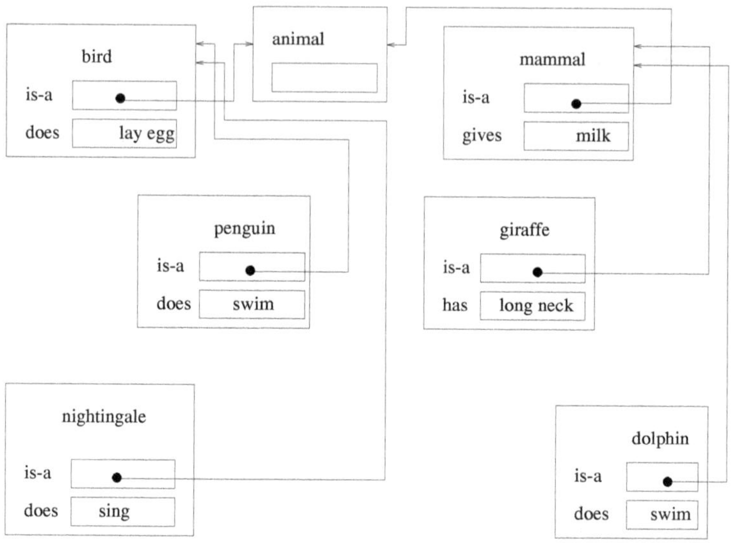

Fig. 3.3 Taxonomic frame representation of some animals.

sweet [Tversky (1977); McClelland and Rumelhart (1985)]. The similarity between them can be defined as a function of the features they have in common [Osherson (1995); Sun (1995); Goldstone (1999); Gilovich (1999)]. The contrast model of Tversky [Tversky (1977)] is one well known model in cognitive psychology [Smith (1995); Opwis and Plötzner (1996)] which describes the similarity between two objects which are described by their features. Rather than relying on prototypical features, picture categorization often relies on detailed shape representation [Smith *et al.* (1978); Murphy and Brownell (1985); Smith (1995)]. Objects and scenes can be represented by binary pictures which are normalized for size and orientation [Feldman (1985)]. Similarity between the objects or scenes is measured by the amount of shared area between the overlaid patterns [Biederman and Ju (1988); Kurbat *et al.* (1994); Smith and Sloman (1994)]. Categorial representation represents the basis of sub-symbolical representation.

3.1.5 *Binary vector representation*

Binary vectors can represent discrete features. A one represents a discrete feature at the corresponding position of a binary vector, its absence is denoted by a zero. The feature set A, B, C, D, E, F, G, H, I, J, K is represented by a binary vector of dimension 11. The presence of features C and E is represented by the binary vector [0 0 1 0 1 0 0 0 0 0 0]. Binary vectors can represent transitions between states. The first binary vector describes the state which should be present before the transition (the premise). The second binary vector describes the world state after the transition (the conclusion).

3.2 Production System

Human problem solving can be described by a problem-behavior graph constructed from a protocol of the person talking aloud, mentioning considered moves and aspects of the situation. According to the resulting theory, searching whose state includes the initial situation and the desired situation (goal) in a problem space [Newell (1990); Anderson (1995b)]. This process can be described by the production system theory. The production system in the context of classical Artificial Intelligence and Cognitive Psychology is one of the most successful computer models of human problem solving. The production system theory describes how to form a sequence of actions, which lead to a goal, and offers a computational theory of how humans solve problems [Anderson (1995b)]. A production system is composed of [Brownston *et al.* (1985); Luger and Stubblefield (1998)] (see Figure 3.4):

- Set of rules. These rule are also called productions. The set of rules models the human long-term memory.
- Working memory. This memory contains a description of the state in a problem solving process. The state is described using predicate calculus and is simply called a pattern. Whenever a premise is true, the conclusions of the rules change the contents of the working memory. The working memory models the human short-term memory.
- Recognize-act cycle. The current state of the problem-solving process is maintained as a set of patterns in the working memory. Working memory is initialized with the initial state description. The patterns in working memory are matched against the premise of the rules. The premise of the rules that match the patterns in working memory produces a set, which is called the conflict set. One of the rules of this set is chosen and the conclusion of the rule changes the content of the working memory. This process is denoted as firing of the rule. This recognize-cycle is repeated on

the modified working memory until a desired state is reached or no rules can be fired. The recognize-act cycle models the current focus of attention triggering one of the set of permanent skills. This, in turn, changes the focus of attention.

Conflict resolution chooses a rule from the conflict set for firing. There are different conflict resolution strategies, such as choosing a random rule from the set, or selecting a rule by some certain function. In a pure production system which was proposed as a formal theory of computation [Post (1943)] the system halts if no production can fire in a state.

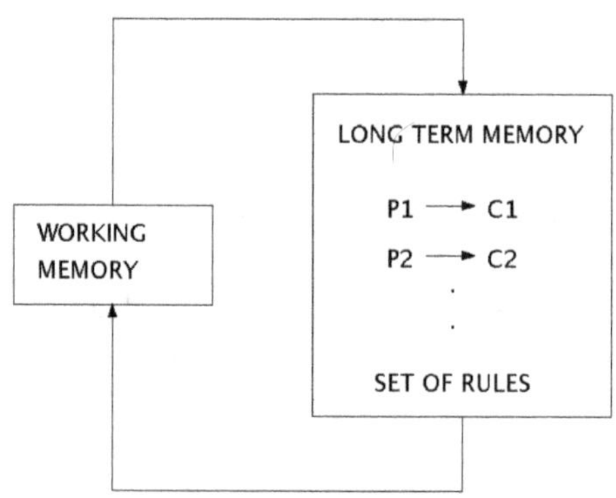

Fig. 3.4 A production system is composed of the long term memory and the working memory also called short term memory. This recognize-cycle is repeated on the modified working memory until a desired state is reached or no rules can be fired.

3.2.1 *Deduction systems*

Problems without side effects of actions can be described by deduction systems which are a subgroup of production systems [Winston (1992)]. In deduction systems the premise specifies combinations of assertions, by which a new assertion of the conclusion is directly deduced. This new assertion is added to the working memory. Deduction systems do not need strategies for conflict resolution because every rule presumably produces reasonable assertions and there is no harm in firing all triggered rules. Deduction systems may chain together rules in a forward direction, from assertions to conclusions, or backward from hypotheses to premises. During backward chaining it is ensured that all features are properly focused. Backward chaining is used if no features are present. If all features are given, forward chaining is used to prevent wasting of time pursuing hypotheses, which are not specified by the features. The chained rules describe the complete problem space which can be represented by a graph [Quillian (1968); Shastri (1988)]. Examples of deduction systems are semantic nets, diagnostic systems and expert systems. Simple if then rules can be represented by a knowledge base. We present a compendium of six rules concerning problems with the oil of a car expert system:

(1) oil lamp lights during driving round a bend **or** oil lamp lights during braking **then** cable of the oil pressure lamp is loose
(2) driving round a bend **and** problems with oil **then** oil lamp lights during driving round a bend
(3) braking **and** problems with oil **then** oil lamp lights during braking
(4) oil lamp goes out after some time **and** problems with oil **and** during idling **then** oil pressure too low
(5) problems with oil **and** during idling **then** oil level too low
(6) oil lamp lights up **then** problems with oil

For clarity we can replace the names of features and categories by symbols, each symbol representing a name, for example B representing "oil lamp lights during driving round a bend":

(1) $B \vee C$ then A
(2) $D \wedge F$ then B
(3) $E \wedge F$ then C
(4) $H \wedge F \wedge I$ then G
(5) $F \wedge I$ then J
(6) K then F

The representation of the logical relationship defined by these rules requires an extension to the basic graph model known as AND/OR graph [Luger and Stubblefield (1998)]. We can represent the set of rules (for example describing an ontology) by a directed AND/OR graph. In Figure 3.5 we see the representation of the six rules. During the deduction a subgraph is constructed. The deduction system is a simple model. It is not practical therefore to use it for planning, as planning is mostly described by fewer rules, but it characterizes a much bigger problem space. Dynamical representation of the problem space is suitable instead of static for reaction systems.

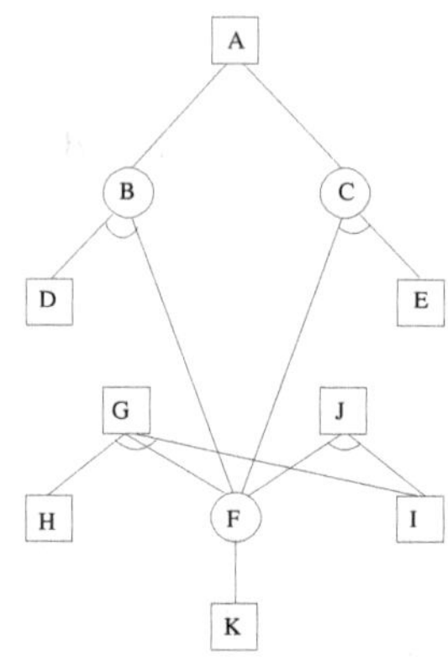

Fig. 3.5 Representation of six rules by a directed AND/OR graph. The 'and' rules are indicated by an arc between the links connecting the nodes indicating the manifestations.

3.2.2 *Reaction systems*

Problems with side effects of actions like planning can be resolved by reaction systems [Winston (1992)]. Reaction systems are a subgroup of production systems. The premise specifies the conditions that must be true before the action described in the conclusion can be taken. Reaction systems need strategies for conflict resolution. We will call the reaction systems simply "production system" if no confusion with a deduction system is possible.

3.2.3 *Conflict resolution*

Conflict resolution strategies are often specified by general provisions [Jackson (1999)]:

- chose randomly a rule;
- a rule should be not allowed to fire more than once on the same data;
- rules that have used more recent data are preferred;
- rules that have a greater number of patterns in the premise are preferred.

Rules also can be evaluated by a heuristic function. There are two different kinds of heuristic functions:

- the probability that the function is on the best path;
- the distance or difference between a given state and the desired state.

It is difficult to define heuristic functions, though frequently features can be picked out which describe the distance to the goal [Russell and Norvig (1995)]. The other possibility is the reuse of solutions to solved problems to indicate which rule to use.

3.2.4 *Human problem-solving*

In systems which model human behavior and in practical applications, backtracking to a previous state of working memory is allowed. By allowing backtracking and the exclusion of loops, a search from the initial state to the desired state is executed. The search defines a problem space and can be represented as a tree. However, it may not reach the desired goal either because the branches are infinite, or because after backtracking to the initial state no rule can fire. A problem is described by the productions in the long term memory, by the initial state, and by the desired state. The solution to the problem is represented by a set of the productions which successively change the state from the initial state to the desired state. One of the best-known cognitive models, based on the production system, is SOAR. The SOAR state, operator and result model was developed to explain human problem-solving behavior [Newell (1990)]. It is a hierarchical production system in which the conflict-resolution strategy is treated as another problem to be solved. All satisfied instances of rules are executed in parallel in a "temporary" mode. After the temporary execution, the best rule is chosen to take action. The decision takes place in the context of a stack of earlier decisions. Those decisions are rated utilizing preferences and added to the stack by chosen rules. Preferences are determined together with the rules by an observer using knowledge about a problem.

3.2.5 *Example*

The 8-puzzle is composed of eight numbered movable tiles in a 3×3 frame. One cell of the frame is empty; as a result, tiles can be moved around to form different patterns. The goal is to find a series of moves of tiles into the blank space that changes the board from the initial configuration to a desired configuration (see Figure 3.6). The production of long-term memory can be specified by four productions [Luger and Stubblefield (1998)]:

- *If* the empty cell is not on the top edge, *then* move the empty cell up;
- *If* the empty cell is not on the left edge, *then* move the empty cell left;
- *If* the empty cell is not on the right edge, *then* move the empty cell

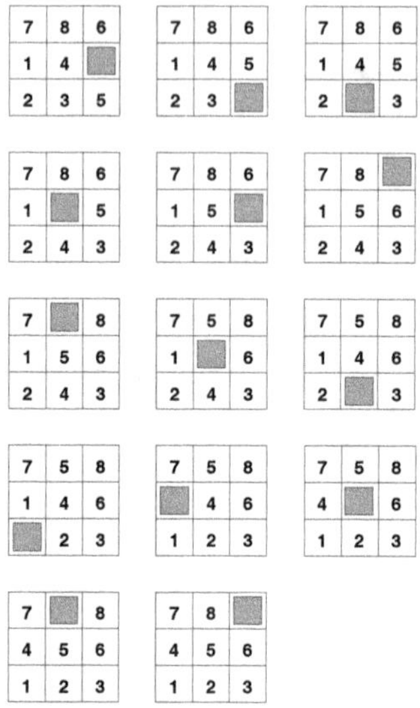

Fig. 3.6 The first pattern (upper left) represents the initial configuration and the last (low right) the desired configuration. The series of moves describe the solution to the problem.

right;
- *If* the empty cell is not on the bottom edge, *then* move the empty cell down.

The control strategy for the search would be

- halt when goal is in the working memory;
- chose a random production;
- do not allow loops.

3.3 Sub-Symbolic Models of Problem-Solving

Perception-oriented representation is an example of sub-symbolical representation, such as the representation of numbers by the Oksapmin tribe of Papua New Guinea. The Oksapmin tribe of Papua New Guinea counts by associating a number with the position of the body [Lancy (1983)]. The sub-symbolical representation often corresponds to a pattern that mirrors the way the biological sense organs describe the world. Vectors represent patterns. A vector is only a sub-symbol if there is a relationship between the vector and the corresponding similarity of the represented object or state in the real world through sensors or biological senses. Feature-based representation is an example of sub-symbolical representation.

Living organisms experience the world as a simple Euclidian geometrical world. The actual perception of the world and manipulation in the world by living organisms lead to the invention or recreation of an experience that, at least in some respects, resembles the experience of actually perceiving and manipulating objects in the absence of direct sensory stimulation [Wichert (2009)].

This kind of representation is called sub-symbolic. Sub-symbolic representation implies heuristic functions. The assumption that the distance between states in the problem space is related to the similarity between the sub-symbols representing the states is only valid in simple cases. However, simple cases represent the majority of exiting problems in domain. Sense organs sense the world by receptors which a part of the sensory system and the nervous system.

According to the production system theory (reaction systems), we can define a geometrically-based problem-solving model as a production system operating on vectors of fixed dimensions. Instead of rules, we use associations and vectors represent the states. Our goal is to form a sequence of associations, which lead to a desired state represented by a vector, from an initial state represented by a vector. Each association changes some parts of the vector. In each state, several possible associations can be executed, but only one has to be chosen. Otherwise, conflicts in the representation of the state would occur. To perform these operations, we divided a vector representing a state into sub-vectors. An association recognizes some sub-vectors in the vector and exchanges them for different sub-vectors. It is composed of a precondition of fixed arranged α sub-vectors and a conclusion [Wichert (2009)], [Wichert (2013)].

3.3.1 *Proto logic*

The manipulation of the states is described by simple proto logic, which verifies if a subset of symbols is present in a certain set of symbols. Suppose a vector is divided into α sub-vectors with $\alpha > \beta$. A production recognizes β different sub-vectors and exchanges them for β different sub-vectors. Let $\alpha = 7$ objects that were recognized in the visual scene. The seven visual objects are indicated at a certain position of the scene by symbols A, B, C, D, E, F and G. The task of proto logic is to identify a precondition formed by visual objects represented by the set B, C, G, $\beta = 3$. Each of the symbols B, C, G is checked for presence in the set that represents the scene. It is verified if a set representing a precondition is a subset of the set representing a scene. *Proto logic operates on sets. It verifies whether a subset is present in a certain set* [Wichert (2013)]. The task of proto logic is trivial when working with sets. For an associative memory the direct access to the stored information is not present, a solution to this problem is described in [Wichert (2011)].

3.3.2 *Binding problem*

The "binding problem" determines how to connect together all physically separated fragments of a complex object so that they can be processed as a whole in sub-symbolical representation [Miikkulainen (1993); Kurfess (1997); Wennekers (1999); Hummel (1999)]. For example, a red block is obviously a different object then a blue block. The fragments in this example are the form and the color. Sub-vectors representing different fragments can be concatenated to a sub-vector representing the object [Wichert (2011)].

3.3.3 *Icons*

Out of several possible associations, we chose the one, which modifies the state in such a way that it becomes more similar to the desired state according to the Euclidean distance [Wichert (2009)] (see Figure 3.7).

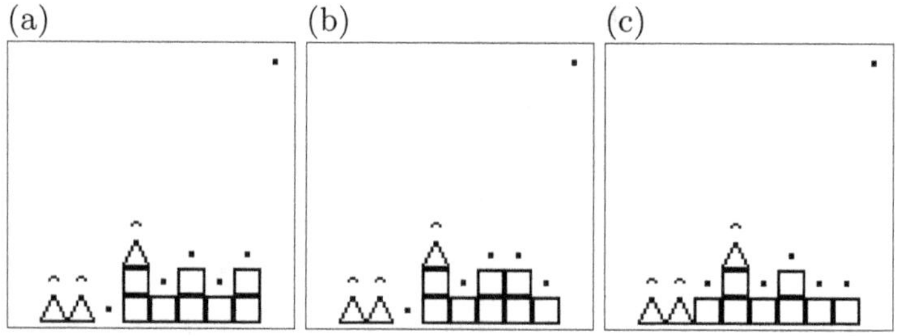

Fig. 3.7 The Euclidean distance between the corresponding vectors can compute the distance between the icons. The distance between the states in the problem space is actually related to the distance between the icons representing the states. Euclidian distance of state (a) and state (c) is smaller than the distance between state (b) and (c). The distance in the problem space as well between state (a) and state (c) is smaller than the distance between state (b) and (c).

With the aid of this heuristic hill climbing is performed. Each element represents an object. Objects are represented by some dimensions of the space and form a sub-space by themselves.

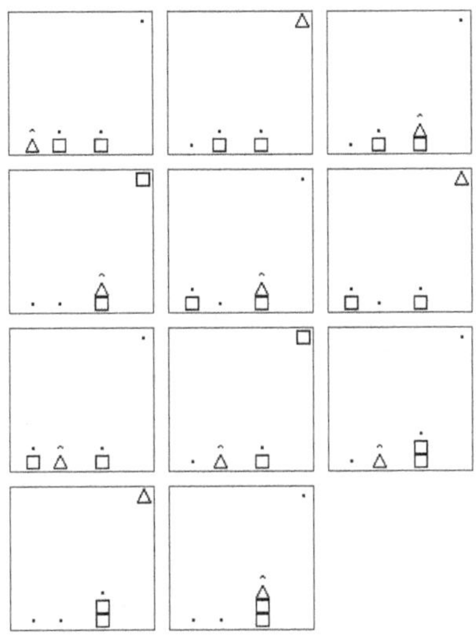

Fig. 3.8 The simplest method corresponds to a random choice, and does not offer any advantage over simple symbolical representation. An example of visual planning of the tower building task of three blocks using the random choice is shown. The upper left pattern represents the initial state; the bottom right pattern, the desired state.

The example of Figure 3.8 and Figure 3.9 consists of the task of building a tower from a collection of blocks [Nilsson (1982)]. A robot arm can stack, unstack, and move the blocks within a plane on three different positions at a table. There are two different classes of blocks: cubes and pyramids. While additional blocks may be stacked on top of a cube, no other blocks may be placed on top of a pyramid. The robot arm, which is represented in the upper right corner, has a gripper that can grasp any available block. It can move the block to eight different positions on the tabletop or place it on top of another cube [Wichert (2001, 2005a)].

The computation can be improved by a simple and universal heuristics function, which takes into account the relationship between the vector and the corresponding similarity of the represented states (see Figure 3.8 and Figure 3.9). The heuristics function makes a simple assumption that the distance between the states in the problem space is related to the similarity

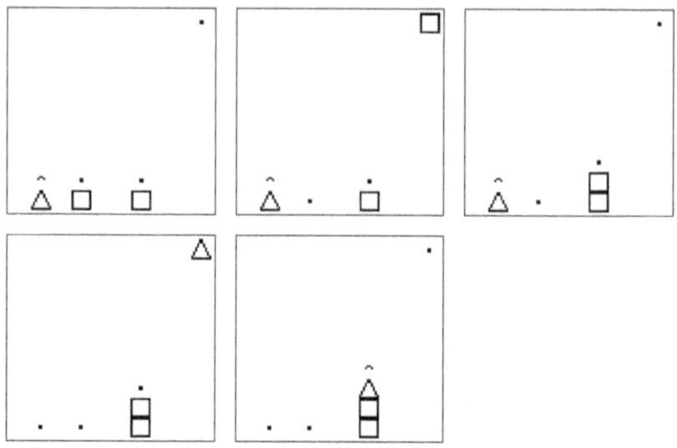

Fig. 3.9 An example of visual planning of the tower building task of three blocks using hill climbing shown. The upper left pattern represents the initial state; the bottom right pattern, the desired state.

of the vectors representing the states. This becomes more obvious with the growth of objects that can be manipulated (see Figure 3.10).

3.3.4 *Euclidian geometry of the world*

The similarity between the corresponding vectors can indicate the distance between the sub-symbols representing the state. Empirical experiments in popular problem-solving domains of Artificial Intelligence, like robot in a maze, block world or 8-puzzle indicated that the distance between the states in the problem space is actually related to the similarity between the images representing the states [Wichert (2001); Wichert *et al.* (2008); Wichert (2009)].

Sub-symbolical problem solving takes advantage of the geometric nature of the world. The assumption that the distance between states in the problem space is related to the distance between the sub-symbols representing the states is only valid in simple cases. For example, our simple heuristics and the resulting hill climbing cannot overcome problems in which one cannot perform either of the necessary first actions without undoing them at a later stage. These kinds of problems are very often called anomalies, such as the "Sussman anomaly" [Sussman (1975)].

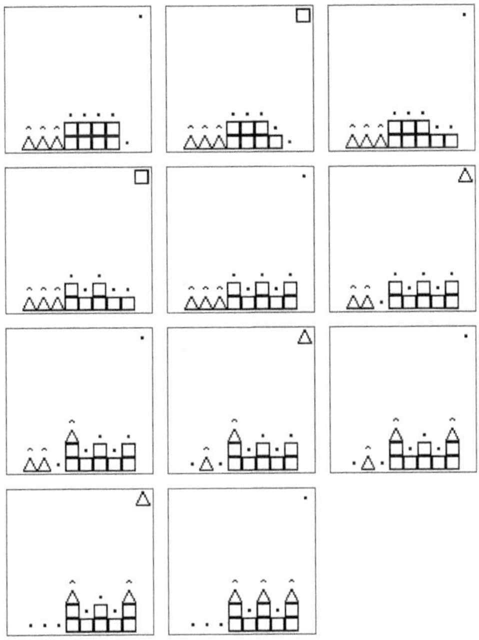

Fig. 3.10 An example of visual planning of the tower building task of eleven blocks using hill climbing shown. The upper left pattern represents the initial state; the bottom right pattern, the desired state.

Chapter 4

Information

4.1 Information and Thermodynamics

Information can be presented in a variety of forms that differ from one another: natural language, symbols, acoustic speech and pictures [Resnikoff (1989)] (see Figure 4.1).

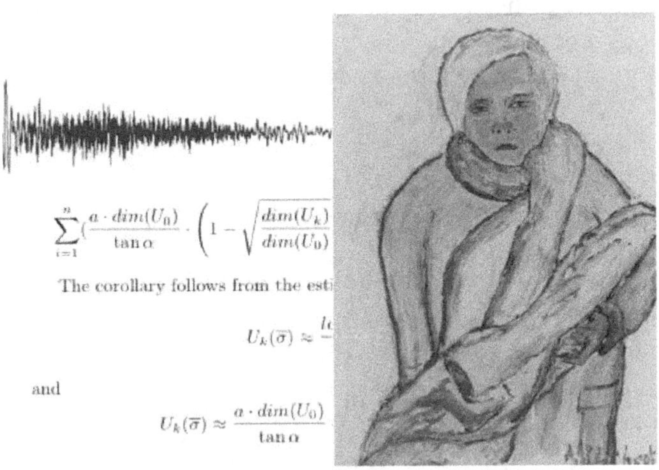

Fig. 4.1 Information can be presented in a variety of forms which differ from one another: natural language, symbols, acoustic speech, pictures.

Information appeared as a unifying scientific concept before the invention of the first computers. Information does not concern the substance and the forces of the physical world [Stonier (1990)]. Information is what remains after one abstracts from the material aspects of physical reality. Information theory is highly related to mathematical probability theory and thermodynamics. A thermodynamic description similar to information is not a description of a physical property and relationships, but rather, this description is a fundamental property. Thermodynamic relations might remain valid for all physical theories that can describe an aspect of reality. They link physical entities to their organization and to their informational structure. Thermodynamics is the study of the collective behavior of entities on a macroscopic scale and uses statistics to describe microscopic states of entities. The microscopic behavior corresponds to the motion of the entities; on a macroscopic scale, this behavior is represented by the temperature, pressure, and volume of physical systems such as a gas or a fluid. The statistical description gives us freedom of abstraction [Maxwell (2001)]. It was James Clerk Maxwell, (1831 – 1879), a Scottish mathematician, who was one of the first to recognize the connection between thermodynamic quantities that are associated with gas, such as temperature, and the statistical descriptions of the molecules. We do not need to specify each entity as a molecule or specify its exact speed or position. It is sufficient to describe the statistical behavior of specific molecules. The three laws of thermodynamics describe the processes that are involved in the transport of heat. They are some of the most important laws of physics.

- Conservation of energy (first law of thermodynamics): The change in the internal energy of a closed thermodynamic system is equal to the sum of the amount of heat energy supplied to the system and the work performed on the system.
- The second law deals with entropy. Entropy is a measure of disorder of the configuration of the states of the atoms or other particles, which make up the system. The total entropy of any isolated thermodynamic system tends to increase over time, approaching a maximum value.
- Third law of thermodynamics: absolute zero temperature As a system asymptotically approaches the absolute zero of the temperature, all processes virtually cease and the entropy of the system asymptotically approaches a minimum value. The entropy of all systems and of all states of a system is zero at absolute zero.

"A physical system that is made up of many, many tiny parts will have microscopic details to its physical behavior that are not easy to observe. There are various microscopic states the system can have, each of which is defined by the state of motion of every one of its atoms, for instance." a

Table 4.1 Each of the two die can have one out of six microstates.

macrostate	(die1, die2)	number of microstates
2	1,1	1
3	1,2;2,1	2
4	1,3; 2,2; 3,1	3
5	1,4; 2,3; 3,2; 4,1	4
6	1,5; 2,4; 3,3; 4,2; 5,1	5
7	1,6; 2,5; 3,4; 4,3; 5;2, 5,1	6
8	2,6; 3,5; 4,4; 5,3; 6,2	5
9	3,6; 4,5; 5,4; 6,3	4
10	4,6; 5,5; 6,4	3
11	5,6; 6,5	2
12	6,6	1

quote from Matt McIrvin.[1] We can choose to measure a physical system at the macroscopic level. Macroscopic properties such as density or pressure are the result of microscopic properties. A macroscopic property can be realized by different microscopic states. Macroscopic states are not static, but they continuously change corresponding to the motion of atoms or molecules. Statistical mechanics describes this motion by some random parameters, whereby each atom is moving randomly from a macroscopic viewpoint. A set of atoms is described by a distribution of random variables that express the random movements.

4.1.1 *Dice model*

Suppose that we have two dice; the macrostate is the total of the two dice, and the microstate corresponds to the number on each of the die. There are six ways to get a total of 7 from the microstates of the two dice but only one way to get a total of 2 or 12. For this reason, throwing two dice to sum a total of seven is more likely to occur; a sum of seven is six times more likely to occur than two or twelve. Each die can have one out of six microstates. The number of microstates of the whole system of two dice is $6 \times 6 = 36$, the number of possible microstates is multiplied together. The number of different macrostates adds, for example, $(6+6)-1=11$. We must subtract a one because the smallest macrostate is two and not one (see Table 4.1). For four dice the number of microstates is already $6 \times 6 \times 6 \times 6 = 1296$. In general, when several systems are combined into a larger system, the number of possible microstates of each system is multiplied, and the number of macrostates is added. For n fair dice,

[1] Matt McIrvin physics- group posting.

the total number of possible microstates is at a maximum at a macrostate value of $3.5 \times n$. The value corresponds to the median of the Gaussian distribution. The median of a finite list of microstates can be found by arranging all of the microstates from the lowest value that represents a macrostate to the highest value of a macrostate and picking the middle value (see Table 4.1). The value of $3.5 \times n$ can be derived for n dice, as follows; the median is also represented as follows,

$$\frac{min + max}{2} \tag{4.1}$$

for n dice it follows:

$$\frac{n + n \cdot 6}{2} = n \cdot 3.5. \tag{4.2}$$

If we shake n dice in a bag and measure the uppermost faces, and we repeat the experiment, the dice will converge rapidly on the value (the "macrostate") for which the number of ways to make the value from individual dice ("microstates") is at a maximum. By performing this action, we model an isolated system, the second law of thermodynamics. We model the thermal fluctuations by "shaking" the bag. The macroscopically measurable quantities converge to the values that have the largest number of microstates. It appears that the basis of the time direction, as expressed by the second law of thermodynamics, is a type of Gaussian randomness.

4.1.2 *Entropy*

When several systems are combined into a larger system, the number of possible microstates of each system are multiplied. This operation leads to a very large number, which becomes intractable very quickly. A solution to this problem is to use the logarithms of numbers; in this case, the log of the product is the sum of the logs. In statistical thermodynamics, Boltzmann's equation relates the entropy S of an ideal gas to the *number of microstates*, where W corresponds to a given macrostate [Boltzman (1995)]. We add the number of microstates when we put systems together by taking the logarithm. The result indicates the relationship between entropy and the number of ways that the atoms or molecules of a thermodynamic system can be arranged. Entropy corresponds to the number of ways that the microstate can rearrange itself without affecting the macrostate. In the equation, k is Boltzmann's constant, which is equal to 1.38062×10^{-23} joule/kelvin.

$$S = k \cdot \log \cdot W \tag{4.3}$$

The Second Law states that isolated systems tend toward an equilibrium macrostate with as large total entropy as possible corresponding to the largest number of microstates. For example, atoms moving around in a gas possess a large number of possible microstates. This number is less for a crystalline structure and, finally, it is one at $0K$, where all microstates become identical.

4.1.3 *Maxwell paradox and information*

In 1929, Leó Szilárd explained the thermodynamic Maxwell paradox by identifying information with the negative measure of entropy [Szilárd (1929)]. Suppose that we have two chambers that are separated by a common partition, which could be removed to permit the objects in one to move freely to the other. One chamber contains gas and the other chamber contains nothing; on the removal of the partition, the gas will rapidly diffuse and fill the empty chamber (see Figure 4.2). Reverse evidence of this

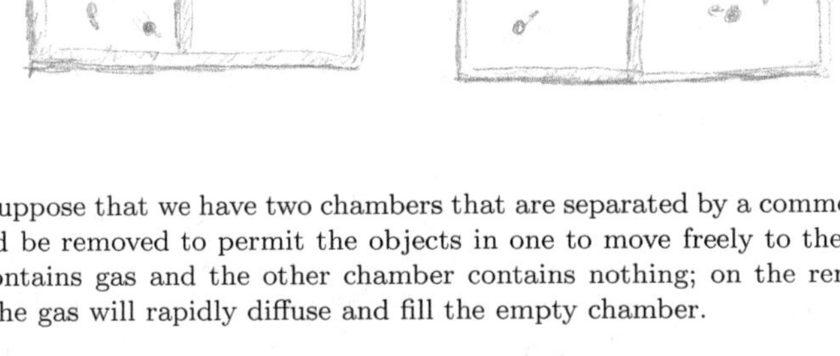

Fig. 4.2 Suppose that we have two chambers that are separated by a common partition, which could be removed to permit the objects in one to move freely to the other. One chamber contains gas and the other chamber contains nothing; on the removal of the partition, the gas will rapidly diffuse and fill the empty chamber.

sequence mostly does not occur because an isolated systems tends toward an equilibrium macrostate that corresponds to the largest number of microstates that are present when the gas is diffused over the two chambers. Thinking in terms of the dice model, the probability of reverse evidence approaches zero but is never equal to zero. In the paradox, there is a demon that observes the gas molecules. Between the chambers, there is a small door. The demon can open and close the small door, passing only one molecule into a chamber. When a molecule in its random motion heads toward the door of the chamber, it opens the door, briefly permitting the molecule to pass into the other chamber. Soon there will be more molecules in one chamber than the other. Because the demon requires almost no energy to operate the door, the process decreases the entropy, which is a contradiction to the second law of thermodynamics. Szilard's explanation is the following: to perform this task, the demon must be very well informed about the position and velocity of the molecules that approached the door. Only with this information can he judge when and for how long the door should be opened to pass a molecule through and into the chamber without allowing any molecules to pass in the opposite direction. As the demon's information about the distribution of the gas increases, the entropy of the gas decreases.

4.1.4 *Information theory*

Instead of a demon that operates a door between two chambers, let us imagine a simple experiment, for example, throwing a fair coin [Topsoe (1974)]. Before we perform the experiment, we do not know what will be the result; we are uncertain about the outcome. We measure the uncertainty by the entropy of the experiment. The experiment starts at t_0 and ends at t_1. At t_0, we have no information about the results of the experiment, and at t_1, we have all of the information, so that the entropy of the experiment is 0. We can describe an experiment by probabilities. For the outcome of the flip of an honest coin, the probability for a head or tail is 0.5, $p = (0.5, 0.5)$. How can we define entropy? A person A knows the outcome, but person B does not. Person B could ask A about the outcome of the experiment. If the question is of the most basic nature, then we could measure the minimal number of optimally required questions B must pose to know the result of the experiment. A most basic question corresponds to the smallest information unit that could correspond to a yes or no answer. The smallest information unit is called a binary digit, or bit. For a fair coin, we pose just one question, for example, is it a tail?

For a card game, to determine if a card is either red, clubs or spades, we have a different number of possible questions. If the card is red, then we need only one question. However, in the case in which the card is not red, we need another question to determine whether it is a spade or a club. The probability of being red is 0.5, of clubs 0.25 and spades 0.25, $p = (0.5, 0.25, 0.25)$. If the card is red, then we need only one question (with probability 0.5). For clubs and spades, we need two questions. In the meantime, we must ask $1 \cdot 0.5 + 2 \cdot 0.25 + 2 \cdot 0.25$ questions, which would result in 1.5 questions. Thus, we must measure the mean number of optimal questions. For four cards, of which one is the joker, the probability of a joker is 0.25 and of the other cards $1 - 0.25 = 0.75$, $p = (0.25, 0.75)$. In the meantime, we must ask $1 \cdot 0.25 + 1 \cdot 0.75$ questions to determine if the card is a joker or not. This approach results in one question. Given n cards, of which one is the joker, the probability of a joker is $1/n$ and of the other cards is $1 - 1/n$. In the meantime, we must ask $1 \cdot 1/n + 1 \cdot (1 - 1/n)$ questions to determine if the card is a joker or not. This approach results in one question that is independent of the size of n. How could it be that the result is independent of the size of n? It appears that something is missing in our definition. Our result is correct for one independent experiment; however, for several experiments, the mean number of questions is lower. We define the real entropy for one experiment as $H_0(F^1)$, for two experiments as $H_0(F^2)$, and for k experiments as $H_0(F^k)$. Here, we have the mean number of questions for the first experiment, the second, and the third to the kth experiment. The mean number of questions for one experiment in the sequence of k experiments is $1/k \cdot H_0(F^k)$.

For four cards of which one is the joker the probability of a joker is 0.25 and of other cards $1 - 0.25 = 0.75$ The real entropy for one experiment is $H_0(F^1)$:

$$H_0(F^1) = 1 \cdot 0.75 + 1 \cdot 0.25 = 1$$

$$\frac{H_0(F^1)}{1} = 1$$

The binary search tree corresponding to one experiment is represented in the Figure 4.3.

The hierarchy of the probabilities for two experiments is shown in Table 4.2 and the resulting binary search tree is represented in the Figure 4.4. The real entropy for two experiments is $H_0(F^2)$:

$$H_0(F^2) = 1 \cdot 0.75 \cdot 0.75 + 2 \cdot 0.75 \cdot 0.25 + 3 \cdot 0.25 \cdot 0.75 + 3 \cdot 0.25 \cdot 0.25$$

$$H_0(F^2) = 1.6875$$

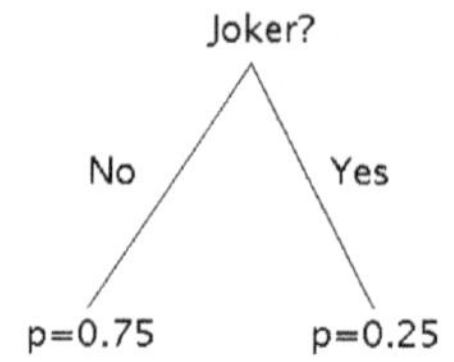

Fig. 4.3 For four cards of which one is the joker the probability of a joker is 0.25 and of other cards $1-0.25=0.75$, $p=(0.25,0.75)$. In the mean we have to ask $1\cdot 0.25+1\cdot 0.75$ questions to determine to determine if the card is a joker or not. The real entropy for one experiment as $H_0(F^1)$.

Table 4.2 Hierarchy of the probabilities for two experiments.

results	probability
card, card	$0.75\cdot 0.75$
joker, card	$0.25\cdot 0.75$
card, joker	$0.75\cdot 0.25$
joker, joker	$0.25\cdot 0.25$

$$\frac{H_0(F^2)}{2}=0.84375$$

The hierarchy of the probabilities for three experiments is shown in Table 4.3 and the resulting binary search tree is represented in the Figure 4.5. The real entropy for two experiments is $H_0(F^3)$:

$$H_0(F^3)=1\cdot 0.42188+3\cdot 0.14062+3\cdot 0.14062+3\cdot 0.14062+$$

$$+5\cdot 0.046875+5\cdot 0.046875+5\cdot 0.046875+5\cdot 0.015625$$

$$H_0(F^3)=2.4688$$

$$\frac{H_0(F^3)}{3}=0.82292$$

Does the sequence $h_k:=\frac{H_0(F^k)}{k}$, with the values $\{1,0.84375,0.82292,...\}$ for $k=1,2,3,..$ have a limit for $\lim_{k\to\infty} h_k$?
It has. The limit is defined as

$$H(F):=\lim_{k\to\infty}\frac{H_0(F^k)}{k}\leq H_0(F) \tag{4.4}$$

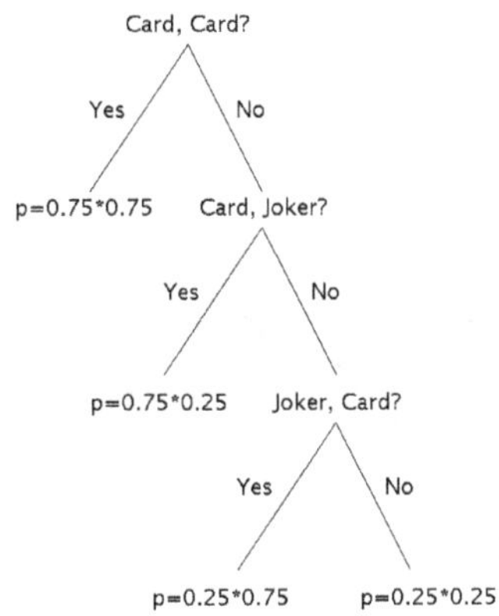

Fig. 4.4 The real entropy for two experiments as $H_0(F^2)$.

Table 4.3 Hierarchy of the probabilities for three experiments.

results	probability
card, card, card	$0.75 \cdot 0.75 \cdot 0.75$
card, card, joker	$0.75 \cdot 0.75 \cdot 0.25$
card, joker, card	$0.75 \cdot 0.25 \cdot 0.75$
joker. card card	$0.25 \cdot 0.75 \cdot 0.75$
joker, joker, card	$0.25 \cdot 0.25 \cdot 0.75$
joker, card, joker	$0.25 \cdot 0.75 \cdot 0.25$
card, joker, joker	$0.75 \cdot 0.25 \cdot 0.25$
joker, joker, joker	$0.25 \cdot 0.25 \cdot 0.25$

it is called the ideal entropy, it converges to [Shannon (1948)]

$$H(F) = -\sum_i p_i \log_2 p_i. \tag{4.5}$$

In our case it is simply

$$H(F) = -0.25 \cdot \log_2 0.25 - 0.75 \cdot \log_2 0.75 = 0.81128.$$

The ideal entropy indicates the minimal number of optimal questions that B must pose to know the result of the experiment on A [Shannon (1948)], [Topsoe (1974)]. Suppose that A repeated the experiment an infinite number of times. The ideal entropy is the essential information obtained by taking out the redundant information that corresponds to the ideal distribution to which the results converge. An experiment is described by the

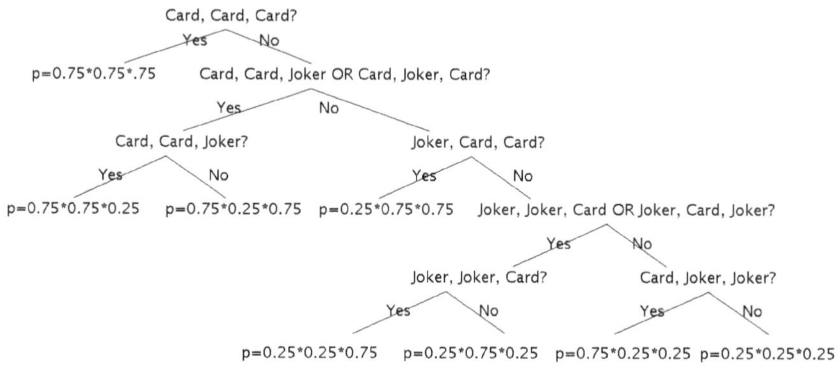

Fig. 4.5 The real entropy for two experiments as $H_0(F^3)$.

probabilities $p = (p_1, p_2, ..., p_n)$. Does the distribution of these probabilities have an effect on the ideal entropy? It turns out that the ideal entropy is maximal in the case in which all probabilities are equal, which means that $p = (1/n, 1/n..., 1/n)$. In this case, the maximal ideal entropy is

$$H(F) = -\sum_i p_i \log_2 p_i = -\log_2 1/n = \log_2 n \tag{4.6}$$

in which n describes the number of states. For $2^{16} = 65536$ states that present with the equal probability $1/65536$, the optimal number of questions is 16, which corresponds to 16 bits. If we suppose the letters of the alphabet (26 of them) occur with equal probability in a message, then the average information content per letter in a message is

$$H(F) - \sum_i^{26} 1/26 \cdot \log_2 1/26 = \log_2 26 = 4.7004 \; bit.$$

A word of five letters has an average information content of $5 \cdot \log_2 6 = 23.502$ bits. However, in a real human language, the average information content per letter is much lower because the distribution is not equal [Topsoe (1974)]. Some letters are more frequent than others; an e is more frequent than an x. We say that events that seldom happen, for example, the letter x in a message, have a higher surprise. Surprise is inversely related to probability. The larger the probability that we receive a character, the less surprised we are. A message over events that are not equally distributed has less information than a message over events that are equally distributed, but that message allows a higher surprise. The large is the probability that we receive a message, the lower is the degree that we are surprised. Surprise of a message m_i is defined as the inverse probability

$$s_i = \frac{1}{p(m_i)}. \tag{4.7}$$

Information is defined as

$$I_i = log_2(s_i) = -log_2(p(m_i)) \tag{4.8}$$

Probabilities are multiplied and information is summed. The theoretical minimum average number of bits that are required to transmit (represent) information is known as ideal entropy or the Shannon entropy. With n as the number of different messages m_i and $p(m_i)$ as the probability of occurrence of the symbol, the theoretical minimum average number of bits is computed using Shannon's formula of entropy

$$H(F) = -\sum_i^n p(m_i) \cdot \log_2 p(m_i) = -\sum_i p_i \log_2 p_i. \tag{4.9}$$

The relationship between $\log_2$ and any other base b involves multiplication by a constant,

$$\log_2 x = \frac{log_b x}{log_b 2} = \frac{log_{10} x}{log_{10} 2}. \tag{4.10}$$

The equation $H(F) = \log_2 n$ is very similar to Boltzmann's equation, in which W *number of microstates* corresponds to a given macrostate. It follows, then, that the *number of microstates* is evenly distributed, and each microstate has the same probability of appearance. There are, however, two differences between the two equations. Boltzmann's equation includes Boltzmann's constant, and it uses log instead of $\log_2$. Instead of measuring the information in bits (yes/no questions) it measures the information in nepit (nat), which is based on Euler's number $e = 2.7182818...$ (sometimes also called Napier's constant). Euler's number is irrational and cannot be attributed to any questions. However, in the next section, we indicate that Euler's number is the ideal number that minimizes the depth of an idealistic search tree.

4.2 Hierarchical Structures

The principles of hierarchical organization appear in nature, for example, the structure of matter itself is hierarchically organized, including elementary particles, atomic nuclei, atoms, and molecules [Resnikoff (1989)]. The idea of hierarchical structures is based on the decomposition of a hierarchy into simpler parts. One of the greatest inventions of human civilization is the possibility of representing numbers by a hierarchically organized structure, which was begun approximately 5000 years ago by the Sumerian and Akkadian civilizations and later popularized by the Babylonians. An ancient way to denote a positive whole number is a sequence of marks used for counting. A requirement for the sequence is to provide a way to write down the next mark. An example is the arrangement of a number as a set of similar strokes; however, this representation takes up a large amount of space. This type of representation is called the unary numeral system. Positional notation is itself a hierarchical organized structure in which the whole number is mapped to positional notation to a certain base. For a unary numeral system, the base is one, and no hierarchy is present. For base $B > 1$ (a whole number), the hierarchy for a number N corresponds to determining the largest integer k such that $B^k \leq N$, where k indicates the number of digits that correspond to the depth of the hierarchy for the basis B. B^k represents the number of possible numbers that can be represented by the corresponding hierarchy. In the next step, k questions for each layer of the hierarchy must be answered to indicate which combination out of the B^k possible numbers is present. Each question has B possible answers, which correspond to the digits $B-1, B-2, .., 0$. The first question is: what is the leading digit n_k of the base B representing N, $n_k \cdot B^k \leq N$. The next question asks about the digit,

$$n_{k-1} \cdot B^{k-1} \leq N - n_k \cdot B^k. \tag{4.11}$$

The following questions ask about the digit

$$n_{k-2} \cdot B^{k-2} \leq N - n_k \cdot B^k - n_{k-1} \cdot B^{k-1} \tag{4.12}$$

and so forth.

For a binary base, the hierarchical structure corresponds to the ideal Entropy in which all of the probabilities of occurrences of the numbers are equal. Each question receives a reply of either yes or no. For each base, each question has B possible answers. This representation is related to a tree in computer science that has a constant branching factor of B. However, there are some differences; the nodes are organized in levels, the root of the tree corresponds to the level 0, and each node at each level has B children, which means that, at each level k, there are B^k nodes. A has the highest level L, and there are $B^L = N$ leaves that correspond to the N represented objects. For N objects and the number of levels L, the branching factor B

is equal to

$$B = N^{\frac{1}{L}}. \tag{4.13}$$

For each level k there are

$$N(K) = B^k = N^{\frac{1}{L}} \tag{4.14}$$

nodes with $N(L) = L$. For a search of an object out of N at each level, B questions must be answered. The costs are $B \cdot log(N)/(log(B)$. Is there a B for which the cost becomes minimal? If we suppose that the tree is an ideal tree in which the branching factor can be an irrational number, then the solution is easy

$$cost = B \cdot \frac{\log(N)}{\log(B)} \tag{4.15}$$

$$0 = \frac{\partial cost}{\partial B} = \frac{\log(N)}{\log(B)} - \frac{\log(N)}{\log(B)^2}$$

with the solution

$$B = e = 2.7182818...$$

which corresponds to Euler's number. The closest whole number is three, followed by two. Euler's number minimizes the cost of an idealistic search tree; it is the minimal mean number of questions that must be answered. The minimal value of the number of questions corresponds to the essential information represented by nepit (nat) in the Boltzmann's equation. We assumed that we can answer all of the questions. Suppose that we cannot. In this case, we do not know which path to follow, and we must perform a search. Either we chose the path (answer to a question) randomly, or we perform a blind search, or we get a hint of which path (which answer) is right. In computer science, the hint is expressed by a heuristic function that rates the value's different paths according to how far the paths are from the goal object.

4.2.1 *Example of a taxonomy*

One of the most effective ways to structure knowledge is the taxonomic arrangement of the information that represents it [Resnikoff (1989)]. In 1887 Professor Harry Govier Seeley grouped all dinosaurs into the Saurischia and Ornithischia groups according to their hip design [Haines (1999)]. In Figure 4.6 and we 4.7 can see some examples of the two categories [Wichert (2000)].

Fig. 4.6 Stenonychosaurus is an example if the category Saurischia.

Fig. 4.7 Stegosaurus. is an example if the category Ornithischia.

The saurischian were divided later into two subgroups: the carnivorous, bipedal theropods and the plant-eating, mostly quadruped sauropodomorphs. The ornithischians were divided into the subgroups birdlike ornithopods, armored thyreophorans, and margginoncephalia. The subgroups can be divided into suborders and then into families and finally into genus. The genus includes the species. It must be noted that in this taxonomy many relations are only guesswork, and many paleontologists have different ideas about how the taxonomy should look [Lambert (1983, 1993)] (see Figure 4.8).

4.3 Information and Measurement

Numbers are used in two fundamentally different ways. Either they can describe measurements of observed phenomena or they are used for mathematical calculations. Numbers that are attached to an observed magnitude represent the gained information. A real number a will be represented as decimal expansions of the form

$$a = a_{-N} \cdots a_{-1} a_0 . a_1 a_2 \cdots \tag{4.16}$$

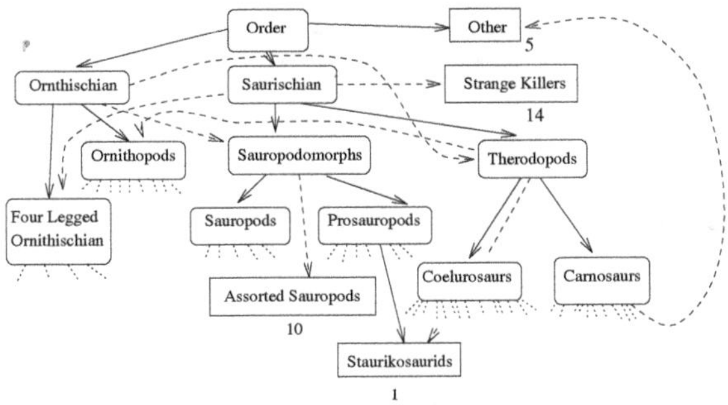

Fig. 4.8 Taxonomy of dinosauria. The number written below the rectangular boxes represents the categories which are not divided, the species. Uncertain categories are represented by dotted arrows.

it is a shorthand of notation of

$$a = a_{-N}10^N + \cdots + a_{-1}10 + a_0 10^0 + a_1 10^{-1} + a_2 10^{-2} + \cdots . \tag{4.17}$$

Increasingly precise variants of the measurement yield to least significant digit (right one) in the decimal expansion. How much additional information is provided by increasing the process of measurement? The measurement of a quantity Ξ is made. Its numerical value is h with infinitely many digits. The measurement provides a range of values in which h will be contained. Suppose the measurement provides numbers x_1 and y_1 with [Resnikoff (1989)]

$$x_1 < h < y_1, \tag{4.18}$$

(see Figure 4.9). In terms of decimal expansion, the measurement has

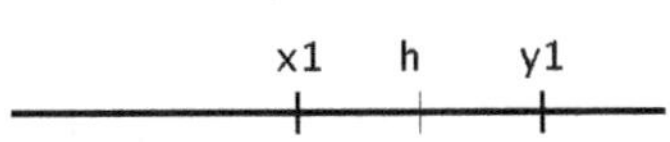

Fig. 4.9 The measurement provides numbers x_1 and y_1 with $x_1 < h < y_1$.

determined a certain fixed numbers of the expansion of h. The second measurement is done with a greater precision x_2 and y_2 with

$$x_1 < x_2 < h < y_2 < y_1, \tag{4.19}$$

(see Figure 4.10). The gain of information after the second measurement can be expressed by

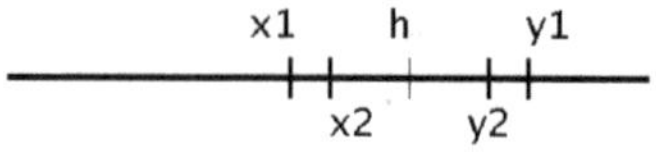

Fig. 4.10 The second measurement is done with a greater precision x_2 and y_2 with $x_1 < x_2 < h < y_2 < y_1$.

$$I_{10} = \log_{10}\left(\frac{y_1 - x_1}{y_2 - x_2}\right) = \log_{10}(y_1 - x_1) - \log_{10}(y_2 - x_2) \tag{4.20}$$

with $\log_{10}(y_2 - x_2)$ being approximately number of digits in decimal expansion. The information can be measured in different units, for example binary digit expansion is

$$I_2 = \log_2\left(\frac{y_1 - x_1}{y_2 - x_2}\right) = \log_2(y_1 - x_1) - \log_2(y_2 - x_2). \tag{4.21}$$

The Equation 4.20 represents the information, which depends only on the endpoints x and y of the measurement of the interval. It does not depend on

- the choice of the zero point
$$I(x + b, y + b) = I(x, y)$$
- nor the scale
$$I(x \cdot a, y \cdot a) = I(x, y).$$

4.3.1 *Information measure I*

We determine the function I which satisfies both conditions [Resnikoff (1989)]. With $b = -x$ we get

$$I(x, y) = I(x + b, y + b) = I(0, y - x) \tag{4.22}$$

and with $a = \frac{1}{x}$ we get

$$I(x, y) = I(a \cdot x, a \cdot y) = I\left(1, \frac{y}{x}\right). \tag{4.23}$$

If we apply $a = \frac{1}{y-x}$ to Equation 4.22 we get

$$I(x, y) = I(0, y - x) = I(a \cdot 0, a \cdot (y - x)) = I(0, 1) = constant \tag{4.24}$$

One measurement results always in a constant gain. Information gain does not depend on the results of one measurement described by x and y. Suppose that I is a function of 3 variables x, y, z which were the results of a measurement (see Figure 4.11). The function does not depend on

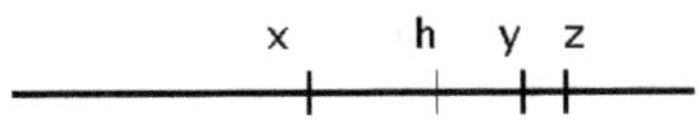

Fig. 4.11 I is a function of 3 variables x, y, z which were the results of a measurement.

- the choice of the zero point

$$I(x+b, y+b, z+b) = I(x, y, z)$$

- nor the scale

$$I(x \cdot a, y \cdot a, z \cdot a) = I(x, y, z).$$

Setting $b = -x$ and $a = \frac{1}{y}$ we get

$$I(x, y, z) = I(x+b, y+b, z+b) = I(0, y-x, z-x) \tag{4.25}$$

$$I(x, y, z) = I(a \cdot x, a \cdot y, a \cdot z) = I\left(\frac{x}{y}, 1, \frac{z}{y}\right) \tag{4.26}$$

Combining this two results together we get

$$I(x, y, z) = I\left(0, 1, \frac{z-x}{y-x}\right). \tag{4.27}$$

Information measurement which yields the numbers x, y, z can be expressed as a function of the ratio of the difference $z-x$ to the difference $y-x$. This ratio corresponds to two measurements for h with $x < y < z$ (see Figure 4.11):

- first with the bounds $x < h < z$,
- second with the bounds $x < h < y$.

We can preform a third measurement h with $x < w < y < z$, see Figure 4.12. The information content of the second measurement relative to the

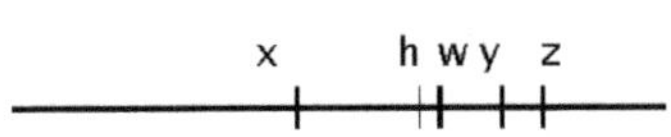

Fig. 4.12 x, y, z, w describe two measurements for h with $x < w < y < z$.

first one is

$$I(x, y, z) = I\left(0, 1, \frac{z-x}{y-x}\right) \tag{4.28}$$

and the information content of the third measurement relative to the second one is

$$I(x,y,z) = I\left(0,1,\frac{y-x}{w-x}\right). \tag{4.29}$$

The information content of the third measurement relative to the first should remain unchanged

$$I\left(0,1,\frac{z-x}{w-x}\right) = I\left(0,1,\frac{z-x}{y-x}\right) + I\left(0,1,\frac{y-x}{w-x}\right). \tag{4.30}$$

We simplify

$$I\left(\frac{z-x}{w-x}\right) = I\left(\frac{z-x}{y-x}\right) + I\left(\frac{y-x}{w-x}\right) \tag{4.31}$$

with

$$t := z-x, \quad u := y-x, \quad v := w-x$$

$$I\left(\frac{t}{v}\right) = I\left(\frac{t}{u}\right) + I\left(\frac{u}{v}\right) \tag{4.32}$$

and with

$$s := \frac{1}{v}, \quad u := 1$$

$$I(s \cdot t) = I(t) + I(s). \tag{4.33}$$

I must be a Logarithm with respect to chosen base, for $\log_2$

$$I(s) = \log_2 s \tag{4.34}$$

and

$$I\left(\frac{z-x}{w-x}\right) = \log_2\left(\frac{z-x}{w-x}\right) \tag{4.35}$$

represent the gain of information in bits. The general case is the one of the two measurements, with the first measurement $x < h < z$ and second one is a more precise measurement $u < h < v$ with $x < u < v$ (see Figure 4.13). Additivity of the information function I provides

$$I\left(\frac{z-x}{z-u}\right) + I\left(\frac{z-u}{v-u}\right) = I\left(\frac{z-x}{v-u}\right) \tag{4.36}$$

- First term is the information increment obtained by narrowing the estimate $x < h < z$ to $u < h < z$ where $x < u$.
- Second term is the information increment gained by narrowing the estimate $u < h < z$ to $u < h < v$ where $v < z$.
- Sum as in formation gained by passing from the estimate $x < h < z$ to the more precise estimate $u < h < v$.

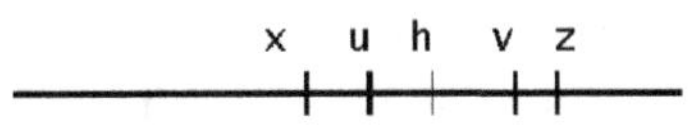

Fig. 4.13 The general case is the one of the two measurements, with the first measurement $x < h < z$ and second one is a more precise measurement $u < h < v$ with $x < u < v$.

4.3.2 *Nature of information measure*

Information measure is relative [Resnikoff (1989)]:

- The information remains unchanged when each of the variables is increased by a value or multiplied by a constant.
- A single measurement does not provide information.

Information gained from the measurement of an interval must always be considered relative to some prior measurement. This prior measurement can be represented by a pre defined scale representing the first measurement, like defined by the metric system.

4.3.3 *Measurement of angle*

In a circle a measurement is represented by an angle α and a more exact one by the angle β with $\alpha > \beta$ (see Figure 4.14). The information gain is

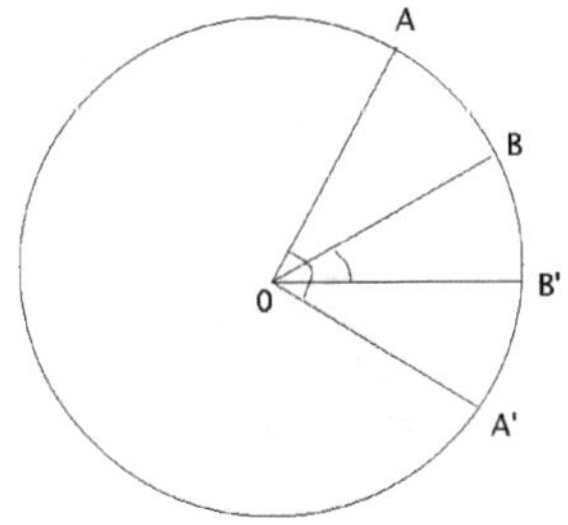

Fig. 4.14 In a circle a measurement is represented by two angles.

$$I\left(\frac{\alpha}{\beta}\right) = \log_2\left(\frac{\alpha}{\beta}\right) \tag{4.37}$$

bits. The angle measure of a direction must lie between 0 and $2 \cdot \pi$ With a priori knowledge $\alpha = 2 \cdot \pi$ only one measurement β is required [Resnikoff (1989)]

$$I\left(\frac{2 \cdot \pi}{\beta}\right) = \log_2\left(\frac{2 \cdot \pi}{\beta}\right). \tag{4.38}$$

For a straight line $\beta = \pi$ and the information content is

$$I(\pi) = \log_2\left(\frac{2 \cdot \pi}{\pi}\right) = 1 \ bit. \tag{4.39}$$

The observed direction lies in one half-of the planes. Smaller angles correspond to greater information, $I(\pi/2) = 2 \ bits, \quad I(\pi/4) = 3 \ bits.$

4.3.4 *Information and contour*

A contour is subdivided into short segments of equal length. Each segmenting point can be thought as the vertex of an angle formed with two neighboring points [Resnikoff (1989)]. Associated with that angle is its measure of information gain. In a simple example there are three points P, Q, R (see Figure 4.15). We move on a line from P to Q. The corresponding information is 1 bit. The information gain passing from one straight line to the next is

$$I\left(\frac{\pi}{\pi}\right) = 0 \ bits$$

since the angle remains unchanged. When the right angle at vertex Q is reached, there is a positive gain of information

$$I\left(\frac{\pi}{\pi/2}\right) = 1 \ bits.$$

At the next step, passing from right angle to the straight angle there is an information loss

$$I\left(\frac{\pi/2}{\pi}\right) = -1 \ bits.$$

In the example the right angle is where the contour changes its direction. Corners yield the greatest information, more strongly curved points yield more information.

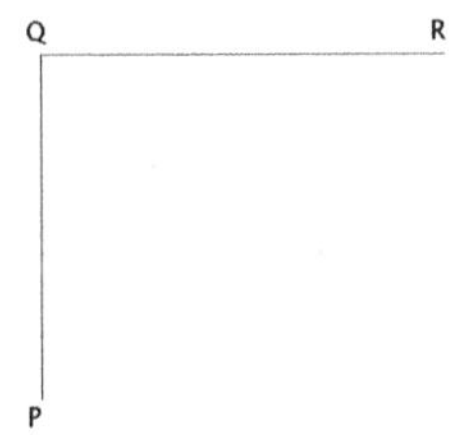

Fig. 4.15 There are three points P, Q, R.

4.4 Information and Memory

"Human memory is based on associations with the memories it contains. Just a snatch of well-known tune is enough to bring the whole thing back to mind. A forgotten joke is suddenly completely remembered when the next-door neighbor starts to tell it again. This type of memory has previously been termed content-addressable, which means that one small part of the particular memory is linked - associated -with the rest." Cited from [Brunak and Lautrup (1990)], page 104.

Associative memory models human memory [Palm (1990); Churchland and Sejnowski (1994); Fuster (1995); Squire and Kandel (1999)]. The associative memory and sub-symbolic distributed representation incorporate the following abilities in a natural way [Palm (1982); Hertz *et al.* (1991); Anderson (1995b); Kohonen (1989)]:

- The ability to correct faults if false information is given.
- The ability to complete information if some parts are missing.
- The ability to interpolate information. In other words, if a sub-symbol is not currently stored the most similar stored sub-symbol is determined.

The Lernmatrix, or Wilshaw's associative memory also simply called "associative memory", was developed by Steinbuch in 1958 as a biologically inspired model from the effort to explain the psychological phenomenon of conditioning [Steinbuch (1961, 1971)]. Later this model was studied under biological and mathematical aspects mainly by Willshaw [Willshaw *et al.* (1969)] and Palm [Palm (1982, 1990)].

Associative memory is composed of a cluster of units. Each unit represents a simple model of a real biological neuron. The Lernmatrix was invented by Steinbuch, whose goal was to produce a network that could use a binary version of Hebbian learning to form associations between pairs of binary vectors, for example each one representing a cognitive entity. Each unit is composed of binary weights, which correspond to the synapses and dendrites in a real neuron (see Figure. 4.16).

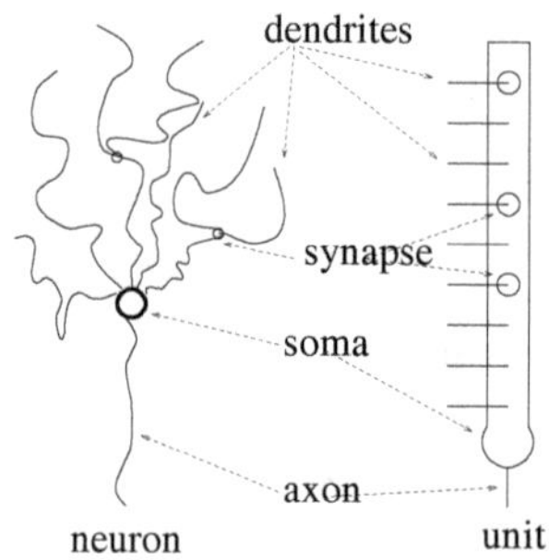

Fig. 4.16 A unit is an abstract model of a biological neuron [McClelland and Kawamoto (1986); Palm (1990); Hertz *et al.* (1991); OFTA (1991); Schwenker (1996)].

They are described by $w_{ij} \in \{0,1\}$ in Figure 4.17. T is the threshold of the unit. The Lernmatrix is simply called *associative memory* if no confusion with other models is possible [Anderson (1995a); Ballard (1997)].

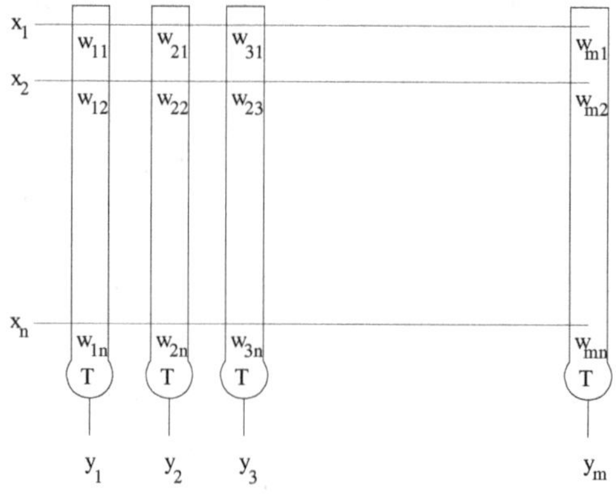

Fig. 4.17 The Lernmatrix is composed of a set of units which represent a simple model of a real biological neuron. The unit is composed of weights, which correspond to the synapses and dendrites in the real neuron. In this Figure they are described by $w_{ij} \in \{0,1\}$ where $1 \leq i \leq m$ and $1 \leq j \leq n$. T is the threshold of the unit.

The patterns, which are stored in the Lernmatrix, are represented by binary vectors. The presence of a feature is indicated by a 'one' component of the vector, its absence through a 'zero' component of the vector. A pair of these vectors is associated and this process of association is called learning. The first of the two vectors is called the *question vector* and the second, the *answer vector*. After learning, the question vector is presented to the associative memory and the answer vector is determined by the retrieval rule.

Learning Initially, no information is stored in the associative memory. Because the information is represented in weights, all unit weights are initially set to zero. In the learning phase, pairs of binary vector are associated. Let $\mathbf{x}$ be the question vector and $\mathbf{y}$ the answer vector, the learning rule is:

$$w_{ij}^{new} = \begin{cases} 1 & if \;\; y_i \cdot x_j = 1 \\ w_{ij}^{old} & \text{otherwise.} \end{cases} \tag{4.40}$$

This rule is called the binary Hebbian rule [Palm (1982)]. Every time a pair of binary vectors is stored, this rule is used.

Retrieval In the *one-step* retrieval phase of the associative memory, a fault tolerant answering mechanism recalls the appropriate answer vector for a question vector $\mathbf{x}$. The retrieval rule for the determination of the answer vector $\mathbf{y}$ is:

$$y_i = \begin{cases} 1 & \sum_{j=1}^{n} w_{ij} x_j = T \\ 0 & \text{otherwise} \end{cases} \tag{4.41}$$

where T is the threshold of the unit. The threshold T is set to the number of "one" components in the question vector $\mathbf{x}$, $T := |\mathbf{x}|$. It is quite possible that no answer vector is determined (zero answer vector). This happens when the question vector has a subset of components that was not correlated with the answer vector. A solution to this problem is the soft threshold strategy. In this strategy, the threshold is set to the maximum sum:

$$T := \max_i \left\{ \sum_{j=1}^{n} w_{ij} x_j \right\} = \max_i \left\{ \sum_{j=1}^{n} w_{ij} \wedge x_j \right\} \tag{4.42}$$

and the retrieval rule for the determination of the answer vector $\mathbf{y}$ is:

$$y_i = \begin{cases} 1 & \sum_{j=1}^{n} w_{ij} x_j \geq T \\ 0 & \text{otherwise.} \end{cases} \tag{4.43}$$

This retrieval is called:

- association provided that the answer vector represents the reconstruction of the disturbed question vector;
- hetero-assocation if both vectors are different.

Example In Figure 4.18 the vector pair $\mathbf{x}_1 = (1,0,0,0,1)$ and $\mathbf{y}_1 = (0,1,1,1,0)$ is learned. The corresponding binary weights of the associated pair are indicated by a black square. In the next step the vector pair $\mathbf{x}_2 = (0,1,1,0,1)$ and $\mathbf{y}_2 = (1,1,0,0,1)$ is learned. The corresponding binary weights of the associated pair are indicated by a black circle. In third step the retrieval phase is preformed. The question vector $\mathbf{x}_* = (0,1,0,0,1)$ differs by one bit to the learned question vector $\mathbf{x}_2 = (0,1,1,0,1)$. The threshold T is set to the number of "one" components in the question vector $\mathbf{x}_*$, $T = 2$. The retrieved vector is the vector $\mathbf{y}_2 = (1,1,0,0,1)$ that was stored. A backward projection can be preformed in the fourth step. The synaptic matrix is a transpose of the matrix W, which is used for the forward projection. The similarity between the stored vector pair and the presented can be computed.

Storage capacity For an estimation of the asymptotic number L of vector pairs $(\vec{x}, \vec{y})$ that can be stored in an associative memory before it begins to make mistakes in the retrieval phase, it is assumed that both vectors have the same dimension n. It is also assumed that both vectors are composed of k ones, which are equally likely to be in any coordinate of the vector. In this case it was shown [Palm (1982); Hecht-Nielsen (1989); Sommer (1993)] that the optimum value for k is approximately

$$k \doteq \log_2(n/4). \tag{4.44}$$

For example for a vector of the dimension n=1000000 only $k = 18$ ones should be used to code a pattern according to the Equation 4.44. For an optimal value for k according to the Equation 4.44 with ones equally distributed over the coordinates of the vectors, approximately L vector pairs can be stored in the associative memory [Palm (1982); Hecht-Nielsen (1989)]. L is approximately

$$L \doteq (\ln 2)(n^2/k^2). \tag{4.45}$$

This value is much greater than n. The estimate of L is very rough because Equation 4.45 is only valid for very large networks. Equation 4.45 does not apply for networks of reasonable size, however the capacity increase is still considerable. For realistic values please consult Table 2 in [Knoblauch *et al.* (2010)]. Small deviation from the logarithmic sparseness reduces the

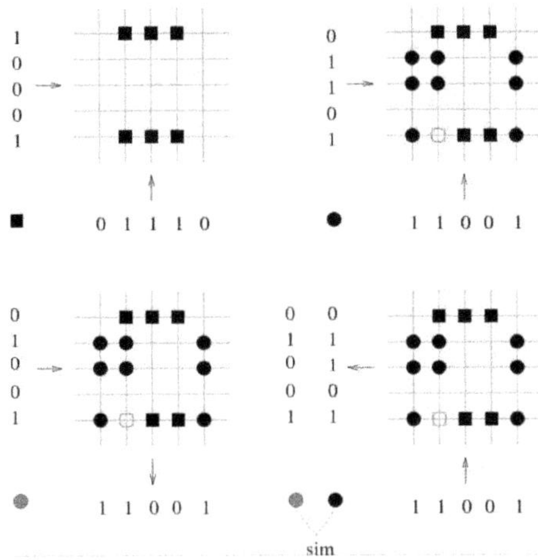

Fig. 4.18 The vector pair $\mathbf{x}_1 = (1, 0, 0, 0, 1)$ and $\mathbf{y}_1 = (0, 1, 1, 1, 0)$ is learned. The corresponding binary weights of the associated pair are indicated by a black square. In the next step the vector pair $\mathbf{x}_2 = (0, 1, 1, 0, 1)$ and $\mathbf{y}_2 = (1, 1, 0, 0, 1)$ is learned. The corresponding binary weights of the associated pair are indicated by a black circle. In third step the retrieval phase is preformed. The question vector $\mathbf{x}_* = (0, 1, 0, 0, 1)$ differs by one bit to the learned question vector $\mathbf{x}_2 = (0, 1, 1, 0, 1)$. The threshold T is set to the number of "one" components in the question vector $\mathbf{x}_*$, $T = 2$. The retrieved vector is the vector $\mathbf{y}_2 = (1, 1, 0, 0, 1)$ that was stored. A backward projection can be preformed in the fourth step. The synaptic matrix is a transpose of the matrix W, which is used for the forward projection. The similarity between the stored vector pair and the presented can be computed.

network capacity. It is very difficult to find coding schemas that represent the information by logarithmic sparse codes [Knoblauch *et al.* (2010)].

It should be noted that the Lernmatrix system allows high capacity and fast access when working in parallel, each unit represents a neuron that performs calculations. On a conventional Von Neumann architecture, compressed look-up tables are more efficient [Knoblauch *et al.* (2010)]. However a Von Neuman architecture is not biologically plausible.

Information and storage capacity We indicate a sketch of a proof for Equation 4.44 and 4.45 [Hecht-Nielsen (1989)]. There are $C(n, k)$ different binary vectors of the dimension n with k ones,

$$C(n, k) = \frac{n!}{(n-k)! \cdot k!} \tag{4.46}$$

for example

$$C(3, 2) = \frac{3!}{(1)! \cdot 2!} = 3,$$

$$(1, 1, 0), \quad (1, 0, 1), \quad (0, 1, 1).$$

We can determine for each vector the probability the presence of a one

$$p_{C(n,k)} = \frac{1}{C(n,k)}. \tag{4.47}$$

The entropy of L vectors is

$$H(F) = -\sum_i p_i \log_2 p_i = -L \cdot p_{C(n,k)} \log_2 p_{C(n,k)} \tag{4.48}$$

and we can rewrite it as

$$H(F) = L \cdot \frac{1}{C(n,k)} \log_2 C(n,k). \tag{4.49}$$

The self-information or the information content associated with the outcome of a random variable ω_i is defined as

$$I(\omega_i) = -\log_2 P(\omega_i). \tag{4.50}$$

The information content of L vectors is

$$I = -L \cdot \log_2 p_{C(n,k)} = L \cdot \log_2 C(n,k) = L \cdot \log_2 \left(\frac{n!}{(n-k)! \cdot k!} \right). \tag{4.51}$$

We want to maximize the information I in correspondence to the size of the associative memory n,

$$Maximize \longrightarrow \frac{I}{n^2}. \tag{4.52}$$

Depending on the size n, we have to find optimal values for k and L.

- We need to determine the probability p after storing L binary vectors in the associative memory, that a weight w_{ij} at a certain position (ij) is one.
- We need to determine the probability $p-1$ after storing L binary vectors in the associative memory, that a weight w_{ij} at a certain position (ij) is zero.

The probability p depends on the probability $1 - p$. For L pairs the probability that a weight is zero is

$$(1-p) = \left(\frac{n^2 - k^2}{n^2} \right)^L \tag{4.53}$$

since the probability of a sequence of n independent events is its product. For L pairs the probability that a weight is one is

$$p = 1 - \left(1 - \frac{k^2}{n^2} \right)^L. \tag{4.54}$$

We try to determine the probability of obtaining an extra 1 during recall of $\mathbf{y}_q$. We know that the vector $\mathbf{x}_q$ has k ones and the probability of a weight being 1 is p. Let us demand that the number of wrong ones on each $\mathbf{y}_q$ vector recall be 1. The product of $(n-k)$, the number of 0 in $\mathbf{y}_q$ and the probability of each 0 being wrongly set to one (p^k) will be equal to one

$$1 = (n-k) \cdot p^k. \tag{4.55}$$

Combining the Equations 4.54 and 4.55 yields

$$(n-k) \cdot \left(1 - \left(1 - \frac{k^2}{n^2}\right)^L\right)^k = 1, \tag{4.56}$$

$$1 - \left(1 - \frac{k^2}{n^2}\right)^L = (n-k)^{-\frac{1}{k}}, \tag{4.57}$$

$$\left(1 - \frac{k^2}{n^2}\right)^L = 1 - (n-k)^{-\frac{1}{k}}, \tag{4.58}$$

$$L \cdot \log\left(1 - \frac{k^2}{n^2}\right) = \log\left(1 - (n-k)^{-\frac{1}{k}}\right), \tag{4.59}$$

$$L = \frac{\log\left(1 - (n-k)^{-\frac{1}{k}}\right)}{\log\left(1 - \frac{k^2}{n^2}\right)}. \tag{4.60}$$

Combining the Equations 4.51

$$I = L \cdot \log_2 C(n,k) = \frac{\log\left(1 - (n-k)^{-\frac{1}{k}}\right)}{\log\left(1 - \frac{k^2}{n^2}\right)} \cdot \log_2\left(\frac{n!}{(n-k)! \cdot k!}\right) \tag{4.61}$$

and

$$\log_2\left(\frac{n!}{(n-k)! \cdot k!}\right) = \log_2(n!) - \log_2((n-k)!) - \log_2(k!). \tag{4.62}$$

We can use the logarithmic version of Sterling‘s formula. The Sterling‘s formula is given by

$$\log(n!) = \frac{n+1}{2} \cdot \log(n) - n + \frac{1}{2} \cdot \log(2 \cdot \pi), \tag{4.63}$$

$$\log_2(n!) = \frac{n+1}{2} \cdot \log_2(n) \cdot log(2) - n + \frac{1}{2} \cdot \log_2(2 \cdot \pi) \cdot \log(2),$$

$$\log_2(n!) = \frac{n+1}{2} \cdot \log_2(n) \cdot log(2) - n + 0.92. \tag{4.64}$$

All together yields

$$I = L \cdot \log_2 C(n,k) = \frac{1}{\log(2)} \cdot \left(\frac{\log\left(1-(n-k)^{-\frac{1}{k}}\right)}{\log\left(1-\frac{k^2}{n^2}\right)} \right) \cdot$$

$$\left(n + \frac{1}{2} \cdot (log(n) - log(n-k)) + k \cdot log(n-k) - \log(k) \cdot \left(k + \frac{1}{2}\right) - 0.92 \right) \tag{4.65}$$

Using computer simulation we can determine the corresponding values k that maximize I

$$Maximize \longrightarrow \frac{I}{n^2}$$

depending on n, $n = 10^2, 10^3, \cdots, 10^{100}$, see Figure 4.19. We find the

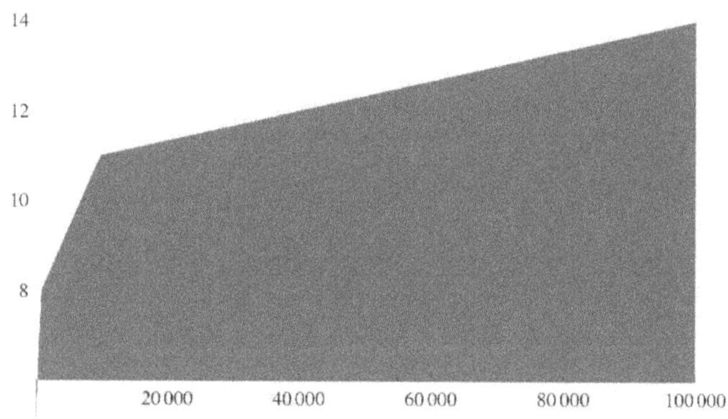

Fig. 4.19 Values k that maximizes I for $n = 10^2, 10^3, 10^4, 10^5$.

optimum value for k to be

$$k \doteq \log_2(n) - 2 = \log_2(n/4) \tag{4.66}$$

and

$$L \doteq (\ln 2)(n^2/k^2).$$

Substituting Equation 4.66 into Equation 4.65 we get the upper bound for large n

$$I = n^2 \log 2 = n^2 \cdot 0.693 \tag{4.67}$$

the asymptotic capacity is 69.31 percent with allowed error rate of one additional one per $\mathbf{y}_q$ as expressed by Equation 4.55. This capacity is only valid for sparse equally distributed ones [Palm (1982)].

Weight matrix diagram The diagram of the weight matrix illustrates the weight distribution which results from the distribution of the stored patterns [Marcinowski (1987); Freeman (1994)]. Useful associative properties result from equally distributed weights over the whole weight matrix. Clusters in the diagram indicate strong correlation between parts of stored patterns. The load of the associative memory is indicated by the percentage of weights which are not zero. A high percentage indicates an overload and the loss of its associative properties. Figure 4.20 represents a diagram of a high loaded matrix with equally distributed weights.

Structure of weight matrix The structure of the weight matrix indicates the elementary blocks which compose an associative memory. It is represented by the frequency of different sum values of the weights of rows or columns [Marcinowski (1987)]. The sum over column i is,

$$\mu_i = \sum_{j=1}^{n} w_{ij}$$

The μ_i are sorted with a new index $\pi = \iota(i)$,

$$\mu_1 \leq \mu_2 \leq \mu_3 \leq \mu_\pi \leq \ldots \leq \ldots \leq \mu_m.$$

The number ζ of groups with different μ values and the number of their elements is determined,

$$\underbrace{\mu_1 = \mu_2 = \mu_3}_{\tau_1=3} < \underbrace{\mu_\pi = \ldots}_{\tau_2} < \underbrace{\ldots = \mu_m.}_{\tau_\zeta}$$

This can be represented as a procedure:

$\Phi = 1$
$\tau_\Phi = 1$
FOR $\pi = 1$ TO m-1 STEP 1
DO
IF $\mu_\pi = \mu_{\pi+1}$ THEN $\tau_\Phi = \tau_\Phi + 1$
ELSE DO $\Phi = \Phi + 1$; $\tau_\Phi = 1$ OD
OD
$\zeta = \Phi$.

The ζ sorted different τ_Φ values are represented by a diagram. The x axis represents the $\Phi \in [1, 2, \ldots, \zeta]$ values and y axis the corresponding frequency of sum values τ_Φ. The relationship between the x axis ordinate and corresponding value μ_π is represented additionally, for example, by an additional plot. If the associative memory performs hetroassocative recalls, the associative matrix is not symmetric and the diagrams for the sum of rows and columns are different. The sum over row j is

$$\mu_j = \sum_{i=1}^{n} w_{ij}.$$

There are n μ_j values (see Figure 4.17). In Figure 4.21 the structure of the weight matrix of Figure 4.20 is represented. The plot illustrates that the weight matrix is composed of approximately 300 elementary blocks which represent a nearly gausian correlation between the stored pattern parts. Figure 4.20 shows the distribution results of the ten randomly set ones in the 2000 dimensional, 20000 learned vector pairs.

4.5 Sparse code for Sub-symbols

Usually suboptimal sparse codes are used. An example of a suboptimal sparse code is the representation of words by context-sensitive letter units [Wickelgren (1969, 1977); Rumelhart and McClelland (1986); Bentz *et al.* (1989)]. The ideas for the used robust mechanism come from psychology and biology [Wickelgren (1969, 1977); Rumelhart and McClelland (1986); Bentz *et al.* (1989)]. Each letter in a word is represented as a triple, which consists of the letter itself, its predecessor, and its successor. For example, six context-sensitive letters encode the word *desert*, namely: *_de, des, ese, ser, ert, rt_*. The character "_" marks the word beginning and ending. Because the alphabet is composed of 26+1 characters, 27^3 different context-sensitive letters exist. In the 27^3 dimensional binary vector each position corresponds to a possible context-sensitive letter, and a word is represented by indication of the actually present context-sensitive letters.

A set of features can be represented by a binary vector and represent a category. A position in the corresponding vector corresponds to a feature. To be sparse, the set of features that describes a category compared to the dimension of the vector has to be sufficiently small. This is because, of all possible features, only some should define categories. This can be achieved by sparsification based on unary sub-vector representation.

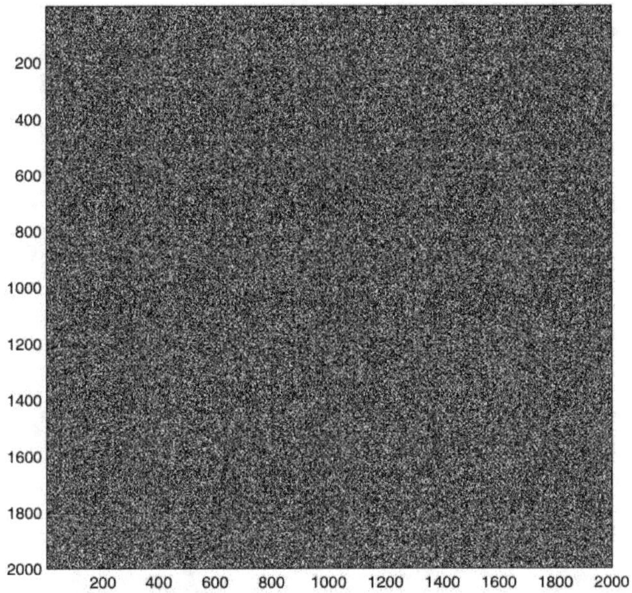

Fig. 4.20 The weight matrix after learning of 20000 test patterns, in which ten ones were randomly set in a 2000 dimensional vector represents a high loaded matrix with equally distributed weights. This example shows that weight matrix diagram often contains nearly no information. Information about the weight matrix can be extracted by the structure of weight matrix. (White color represents wights.)

4.5.1 *Sparsification based on unary sub-vectors*

A binary representation of a number h would require a vector of length $d = \lfloor log_2 h+1 \rfloor$. However if we represent the number h in unary, we require$h$ positions. One unary representation of $h \neq 0$ is a string of $h-1$ zeros with a one at h-th postion [Wichert (2013)]. A binary number of length d is represented by a unary number of 2^d positions, which is exponential in the size of input. A binary vector $\mathbf{x}$ of dimension t is split into f distinct sub vectors of dimension $p = dim(t/f)$. The binary sub vectors $u_i(\mathbf{x})$ of dimension $p = dim(t/f)$ are represented as unary vectors of dimension 2^p :

$$\mathbf{x} = \underbrace{x_1, , x_2, \cdots, x_p}_{u_1(\mathbf{x})}, \cdots, \underbrace{x_{m-p+1}, \cdots, x_m}_{u_f(\mathbf{x})} \tag{4.68}$$

The resulting binary vector is composed out of the unary vectors and has the dimension $f \cdot 2^p$. In the following example a binary vector of dimension

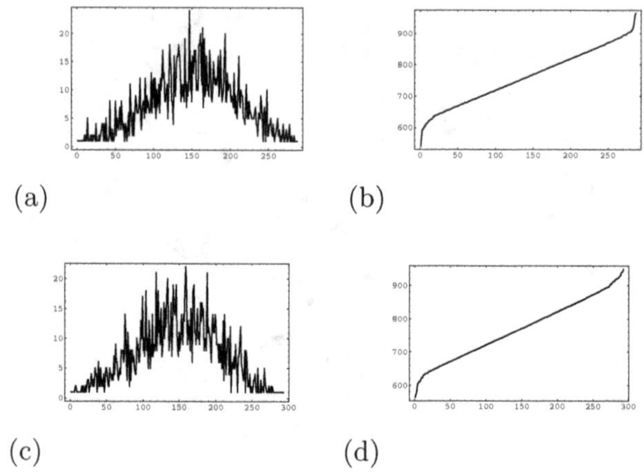

Fig. 4.21 38% of synapses of associative memory are not zero. (a) The frequency of different sum values of columns. (b) The corresponding sum values of columns. (c) The frequency of different sum values of rows. (d) The corresponding sum values of rows.

6 is split into 2 distinct sub vectors of dimension 3. The binary sub vectors $u_i(\mathbf{x})$ of dimension 3 are represented as unary vectors of dimension 2^3 :

$$\mathbf{x} = \underbrace{1,0,1}_{u_1(1,0,1)}, \underbrace{0,0,1}_{u_2(0,0,1)} \tag{4.69}$$

$$u_1(1,0,1) = (0,0,0,0,1,0,0,0); \quad (h=5)$$

$$u_2(0,0,1) = (1,0,0,0,0,0,0,0); \quad (h=1)$$

$$u(\mathbf{x}) = (0,0,0,0,1,0,0,0,1,0,0,0,0,0,0,0), \tag{4.70}$$

resulting in a new vector of dimension $16 = 2*2^3$ with 2 ones. The resulting vector is more sparse, however some information related to correlation is lost [Wichert (2013)]. These ideas are related to the Wilshaw model of associative memory with local inhibition [Shim *et al.* (1990)] and [Kropff and Treves (2005)].

4.6 Deduction Systems and Associative Memory

In this section we will present a straightforward transformation from symbolic rules into a representation by associative memory. We will indicate that deduction systems may be represented by an associative memory with feedback connections [Wichert (2005b)], [Wichert (2006)], [Wichert (2012)]. Binary vectors can represent features. A 'one' represents a feature at the corresponding position of a binary vector; its absence is denoted by a 'zero'. The feature set $A, B, C, D, E, F, G, H, I, J, K$ (defined in the preceding section) is represented by a binary vector of dimension 11, no distinction between categories and features is made. The presence of features C and E is represented by the binary vector [0 0 1 0 1 0 0 0 0 0 0].

The associative memory represents the long-term memory of our deduction system in which the rules are stored. In the initialization phase of the associative memory, no information is stored. Because the information is represented in the weights, they are all initially set to zero. In the learning phase, binary vector pairs are associated. In the first vector $\mathbf{x}$ we store the feature set; the category itself is indicated by the second vector $\mathbf{y}$. For example, the rule $D \wedge F$ then B is represented in the vectors $x = [0\ 0\ 0\ 1\ 0\ 1\ 0\ 0\ 0\ 0\ 0]$ and $y = [0\ 1\ 0\ 0\ 0\ 0\ 0\ 0\ 0\ 0\ 0]$.

We demonstrate this procedure with the example that was introduced in the section about the deduction systems (see Section 3.2.1). For clarity we can replace the names of features and categories by symbols, each symbol representing a name, for example B representing "oil lamp lights during driving round a bend":

(1) $B \vee C$ then A
(2) $D \wedge F$ then B
(3) $E \wedge F$ then C
(4) $H \wedge F \wedge I$ then G
(5) $F \wedge I$ then J
(6) K then F

In Figure 4.22 we see the associative memory after learning of the six rules. The 'or' rules are indicated by a one in the threshold. For example, the 'or' rule $B \vee C$ then A is represented by the first unit, and the rule $D \wedge F$ then B is represented by the second unit (see Figure 4.22).

After learning the categories can be determined by the inference with the aid of associative memory. The present features represented by the question vector $\mathbf{x}$ are presented to the associative memory and the categories are identified by the retrieval rule which determines the answer vector $\mathbf{y}$ with the aid of the following adapted retrieval rule:

$$y_i = \mu(z_i) \tag{4.71}$$

with

$$z_i = \frac{\sum_{j=1}^{n} w_{ij} x_j - 1}{\sum_{j=1}^{n} w_{ij}} \tag{4.72}$$

and

$$\mu(z_i) = \begin{cases} 1 \; if \begin{cases} z_i > 0 & \text{for or rules} \\ z_i = 1 & \text{for and rules} \end{cases} \\ 0 \; else \end{cases} \tag{4.73}$$

The short-term memory, which is initialized with the initial state description, is represented by the row buffer (short-term memory) on the left side of the associative memory, see Figure 4.22. The features of the short-term memory are presented to the associative memory, which determines the categories by using the retrieval rule to perform an inference step. The determined categories are transported from the buffer below the units (column buffer) via the feedback connections to the short-term memory. The short-term memory is updated and the procedure is repeated until the short-term memory does not change, i.e. the number of features in it does not grow.

The features 'oil lamp lights up' and 'braking' are present (represented in our symbol notation by K and E). The short-term memory is initialized with $/K, E/$ (see Figure 4.23 (i)). In the first inference step, F is deduced; the short-term memory is now $/K, E, F/$ (see Figure 4.23 (ii)). The features of the short-term memory are presented to the associative memory and, in the following inference, C and F are deduced (see Figure 4.23 (iii)). The short-term memory is then updated to $/K, E, F, C/$. In the next inference steps, C, F and A are deduced. A is deduced, because $A \Rightarrow B \vee C$ is an 'or' rule as indicated by the threshold value of the corresponding unit (see Figure 4.23 (iv)). The inference procedure is completed because no new features are determined in the following inference step. In our example the category A would correspond to "the cable of the oil pressure lamp is loose."

The representation of directed AND/OR graphs by associative memory with feedback are summarized in the following points:

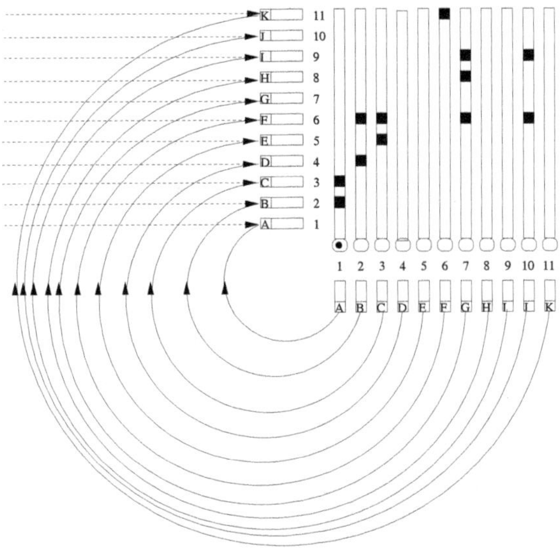

Fig. 4.22 The architecture of our inference system is composed of associative memory with feedback connections [Palm (1990); Palm *et al.* (1992)]. The rule $B \vee C$ then A is represented by the first unit; that it is an 'or' rule is indicated by a one in its threshold (represented in this Figure by a black dot). The associative memory forms the long-term memory; the short-term memory that is initialized with the initial state description is represented by the row buffer on the left side of the associative memory. The features of the short-term memory are presented to the associative memory, which determines the categories by using the retrieval rule. The determined categories are transported from the buffer below the units (column buffer) via the feedback connections to the short-term memory.

- The inference in the AND/OR graphs corresponds to breadth-first search.
- The number of cycles performed by the associative memory with the feedback correspond to the maximum depth of the represented graphs.
- The directed AND/OR graph can contain cycles, because only new, not yet present disorders are added to the short term memory, and the feedback is done until the number of features in the short term memory does not grow.
- The number of represented disorders is correlated with the size of the associative memory; this number is only limited by the size of the expandable associative memory.

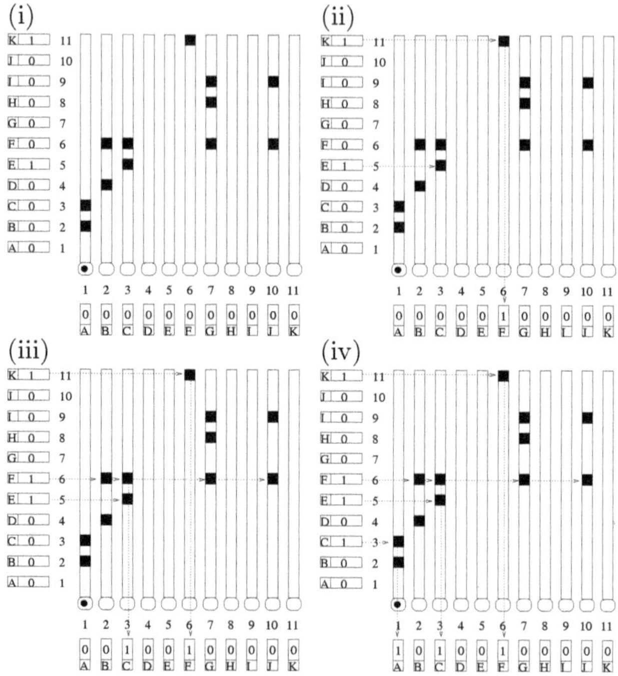

Fig. 4.23 (i) The features 'oil lamp lights up' and 'braking' are represented in our symbol notation by K and E respectively. The short-term memory is initialized with $/K, E/$. (ii) In the first inference step, F is deduced. The activation of the units is indicated by the buffer below the units and should be not confused with the 'or' rule indication of a one in the threshold (represented by a black dot). iii) The short-term memory is now $/K, E, F/$. The features of the short-term memory are presented to the associative memory, and C and F are deduced in the following inference. (iv) The short-term memory is now updated to $/K, E, F, C/$. In the next inference step, C, F and A are deduced. A is deduced, because $A \Rightarrow B \vee C$ is an 'or' rule as indicated by the threshold value *one* of the corresponding unit (represented by a black dot.

4.6.1 *Taxonomic knowledge organization*

For clarity, rules should be arranged in groups [Aikins (1986); Kahn *et al.* (1987)] that define taxonomy. A module could represent a group, each feature is indicated by a name in the context of a module and each module is represented by an associative memory [Wichert (2012)] (see Figure 4.24).

Each module (see Figure 4.24) could correspond to a different area of the human brain. How can we link this different areas of the brain? For example, 5 modules would be represented by 5 associative memories. From the 5 associative memories, we can compose a global associative memory by

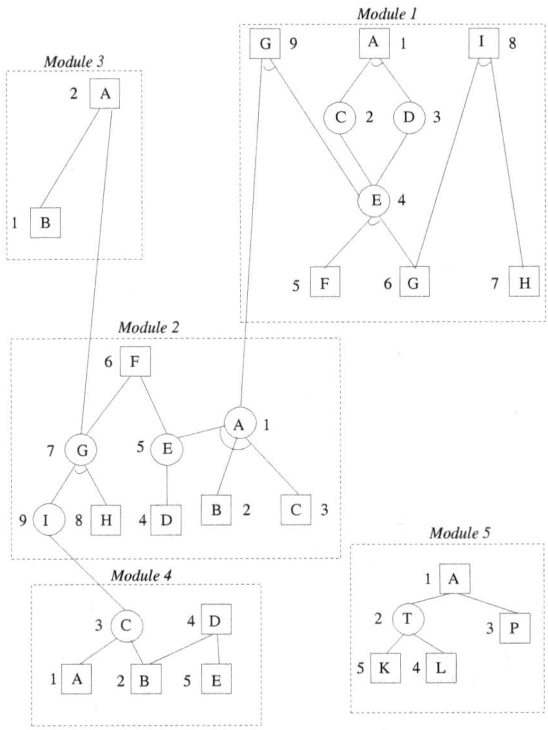

Fig. 4.24 Representation of 16 rules arranged in five modules by two directed AND/OR graphs. A name and a number in the context of a module indicate each feature. Each module is represented by an associative memory. The number of a feature indicates the position in the corresponding vector. A disorder that is defined in a certain module can cause a manifestation in other modules. This relation corresponds to connections between modules. The 'and' rules are indicated by an arc between the links connecting the nodes, which indicate the manifestations.

the arrangement on the diagonal. An associative memory of the dimension 30 evolves in which local feature addresses are translated into global feature addresses (see Figure 4.25). In this global context, connections between modules can be easily indicated by weights outside the modules, in the column of the first module and the row to the second module (connection from the first module to the second module). In Figure 4.25 we can see three connections between the modules corresponding to our rule base [Wichert (2012)].

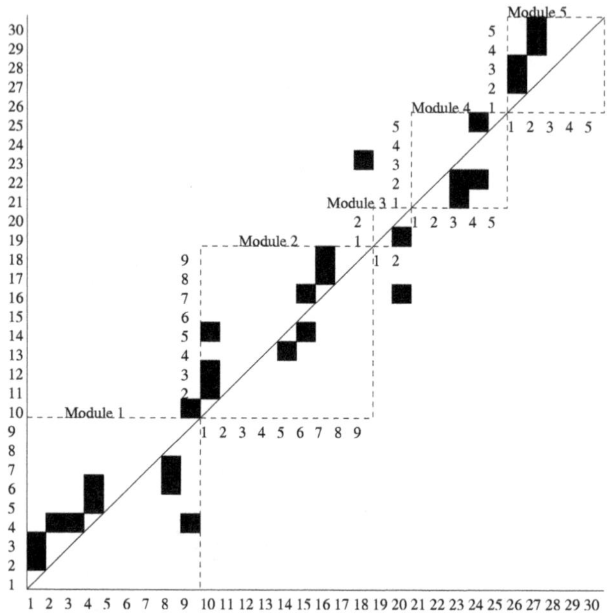

Fig. 4.25 The five modules are represented by five associative memories. By arranging them diagonal, we compose a global associative memory. An associative memory of dimension 30 evolves. In this global context, connections between modules can be easily indicated by weights depicted outside the modules. Connection from the first to the second module is indicated by the weights in the column of the first module and the row of the second module. In this Figure we can see three connections between the modules.

Chapter 5

Reversible Algorithms

5.1 Reversible Computation

Energy is negligible when using the Turing machine model, because the Turing machine itself constitutes an infinitely long tape and does not require any energy resources. However, what is the relation between energy and information that is processed by a Turing machine? In the thermodynamic Maxwell paradox, there is a demon that observes the gas molecules. Between the chambers, there is a small door. The demon can open and close the small door, passing only one molecule into a chamber. The negative of the demon's entropy increments as the measure of the quantity of the information that it has used. Information increments when entropy decrements. The information must be stored in a demon's memory. Given the fact that the memory is finite, the demon must erase some information. The erasing of information increases the entropy represented by energy. Bennett (1973) showed [Bennett (1973)] that irreversible overwriting of one bit causes at least $k \cdot T \cdot log2$ joules of energy dissipation, where k is Boltzmann's constant and T is the absolute temperature. Bennett also indicated that this lower bound can be ignored when using reversible computation. Reversible computing is a model of computing in which the computational process is reversible. For example, a NOT gate is reversible in the sense that one can infer the output from the input. However, neither the AND or OR gates are reversible in the sense that one cannot infer the output from the input. For example, $(1\ AND\ 0) = (0\ AND\ 1) = (0\ AND\ 0) = 0$ [Bennett (1982)]. Reversibility is obtained by Bennett by the storage of all of the computational steps. A three-tape Turing machine is used, with an input tape, history tape and output tape. The computation is performed on the input tape, and all steps are stored on the history tape. Without the history tape, the computational history would be forgotten. When the computation stops, the results are copied to the output tape, and the computation is run backward to erase the history tape for feature usage. Any Turing machine can be simulated by a reversible Turing machine [Bennett (1988)], [Bennett (1989)]. For a reversible production system, the sequence of productions at each step must be remembered. This requirement is usually met for any production system. A computation of a production system is specified by the initial and the goal state, the set of productions. The solution is represented by the sequence of productions at each step.

5.2 Reversible Circuits

5.2.1 *Boolean gates*

The sets of truth functions can be computed using Boolean circuits, which are composed of Boolean gates. An algorithm can be described by such a circuit; however, the AND and OR gates are not reversible; each one of them erases one bit and generates approximately $k \cdot T \cdot log2$ joules of energy dissipation [Landauer (1961)], [Landauer (1992)]. During the computation, information is lost; however, at the same time, the entropy grows [Landauer (1992)], [Bennett (2003)]. For this reason, processors generate waste heat and must be cooled to keep them within permissible operating temperature limits. A solution to the generation of waste heat is reversible Boolean gates. However, reversible Boolean gates require additional *waste* bits.

5.2.2 *Reversible Boolean gates*

To make a circuit reversible, we must make each of the gates reversible. A necessary condition for a reversible gate is that of a bijective transition function with m inputs and m outputs. No injective transition function can be used, if n is the input and m the output; if $n > m$, then some information is lost. Such a bijective function is a permutation of m inputs and m outputs. For m bits, there are $c = 2^m$ different combinations. For c different combinations, there are $c!$ possible permutations between the input and output. A reversible gate is such a permutation. For the NOT gate, there are two possible combinations of one bit, $c = 2^1$. Either the bit is 1 or 0. There are also two possible permutations, which means two different gates, which are both reversible. One gate is the identity gate, and the other gate is the NOT gate. Both of them are reversible. For the

Table 5.1 Truth table of the Toffoli gate.

	inputs	outputs	
dec.	x_1, x_2, x_3	y_1, y_2, y_3	dec.
0	0,0,0	0,0,0	0
1	0,0,1	0,0,1	1
2	0,1,0	0,1,0	2
3	0,1,1	0,1,1	3
4	1,0,0	1,0,0	4
5	1,0,1	1,0,1	5
6	*1,1,0*	*1,1,1*	*7*
7	*1,1,1*	*1,1,0*	*6*

identity gate, the input is equal to the output. For gates with two bits, there are altogether four combinations of two bits, $c = 2^2$ and $24 = 4!$ possible permutations, which means 24 different gates. However, none of the 24 gates solves the AND or OR problem.

5.2.3 *Toffoli gate*

The AND gate can be only computed by a reversible gate, which operates on three bits. On there bits, $c = 2^3$ and $40320 = 8!$ possible permutations. One of the possible permutations corresponds to the truth table of the Toffoli gate [Toffoli (1980a)], [Toffoli (1980b)], [Toffoli (1980c)] Each value of Table 5.1 corresponds to three input bits x_1, x_2, x_3 and three output bits y_1, y_2, y_3. The permutation is defined by the exchange of the values $1, 1, 0$ with $1, 1, 1$ (decimal $6, 7$).

The Toffoli gate does not change the first input bits x_1 and x_2. The operation is described by the following mapping on three input bits x_1, x_2, x_3 with $\mathbf{B} = \{0, 1\}$

$$T : \mathbf{B}^3 \to \mathbf{B}^3 :, T(x_1, x_2, x_3) = (x_1, x_2, (x_1 \wedge x_2) \oplus x_3)$$

A Toffoli gate is a universal reversible gate it performs following operations.

- It computes the AND operation, the ancilla (fixed) bit x_3 is set to 0

$$T : \mathbf{B}^3 \to \mathbf{B}^3 :, T(x_1, x_2, 0) = (x_1, x_2, x_1 \wedge x_2)$$

- It computes the NOT operation on x_3

$$T : \mathbf{B}^3 \to \mathbf{B}^3 :, T(1, 1, x_3) = (1, 1, \neg x_3)$$

- It computes the $NAND$ operation, the ancilla (fixed) bit x_3 is set to 1

$$T : \mathbf{B}^3 \to \mathbf{B}^3 :, T(x_1, x_2, 1) = (x_1, x_2, \neg(x_1 \wedge x_2)$$

- It computes the $FANOUT$ operation (the value of bit x_2 is copied into x_3)

$$T : \mathbf{B}^3 \rightarrow \mathbf{B}^3 :, T(1, x_2, 0) = (1, x_2, x_2)$$

The OR operation follows from the De Morgan's laws

$$x_1 \vee x_2 = \neg(\neg x_1 \wedge, \neg x_2)$$

Because $NAND$ and $FANOUT$ are together universal, we can implement any reversible circuit using the Toffoli gate.

5.2.4 *Circuit*

A reversible circuit can be built using Toffoli gates and NOT gates. This construct represents a permutation on m bits, defining an injective mapping $\mathbf{B}^m \rightarrow \mathbf{B}^m$. Out of m bits, several bits act as control bits (ancilla bits) and others are not changed during the computation. For each AND operation, one ancilla bit is required. A reversible circuit performs a permutation of the input bits. The output is a permutation of the input bits. Each reversible circuit can be represented by a permutation matrix. As stated before, a circuit is not an algorithmic device; by itself, it does not correspond to a universal reversible Turing machine. This arrangement also applies to any reversible circuit.

Chapter 6

Probability

6.1 Kolmogorovs Probabilities

Probability theory is built around Kolmogorov's axioms [Kolmogorov (1933)], see Figure 6.1.

Fig. 6.1 A quotation attributed to Andrey Kolmogorov: "Every mathematician believes that he is ahead of the others. The reason none state this belief in public is because they are intelligent people."

All probabilities are between 0 and 1. For any event a,

$$0 \leq p(a) \leq 1$$

and

$$p(true) = 1, \quad p(false) = 0.$$

To each sentence, a numerical degree of belief between 0 and 1 is assigned, which provides a way of summarizing the uncertainty. The last axiom expresses the probability of disjunction and is given by

$$p(a \vee b) = p(a) + p(b) - p(a \wedge b)$$

Where do these numerical degrees of belief come from?

- Humans can believe in a subjective viewpoint, which can be determined by some empirical psychological experiments. This approach is a very subjective way to determine the numerical degree of belief. This approach is called Bayesian.
- For a finite sample we can estimate the true fraction. We count the frequency of an event in a sample. We do not know the true value because we cannot access the whole population of events. This approach is called frequentist.
- It appears that the true values can be determined from the true nature of the universe, for example, for a fair coin, the probability of heads is 0.5. This approach is related to the Platonic world of ideas. However, we can never verify whether a fair coin exists.

6.1.1 *Conditional probability*

The degree of belief $p(a)$ is attached to an event a before any evidence about the nature of the sentence is obtained; we call this probability the prior (before) probability. Arising from the frequentist approach, one can determine the probability of an event a by counting. If Ω is the set of all possible events, $p(\Omega) = 1$, then $a \in \Omega$. The cardinality determines the number of elements of a set, $card(\Omega)$ is the number of elements of the set Ω, $card(a)$ is the number of elements of the set a and

$$p(a) = \frac{card(a)}{card(\Omega)}. \tag{6.1}$$

Now we can define the posterior probability, the probability of a after the evidence b is obtained

$$p(a|b) = \frac{card(a \wedge b)}{card(b)}.$$

The posterior probability is also called the conditional probability. From

$$p(a \wedge b) = \frac{card(a \wedge b)}{card(\Omega)} \tag{6.2}$$

and

$$p(b) = \frac{card(b)}{card(\Omega)} \tag{6.3}$$

we get

$$p(a|b) = \frac{p(a \wedge b)}{p(b)} \tag{6.4}$$

and

$$p(b|a) = \frac{p(a \wedge b)}{p(a)}. \tag{6.5}$$

The Bayes' rule follows from both equations

$$p(b|a) = \frac{p(a|b) \cdot p(b)}{p(a)}. \tag{6.6}$$

6.1.2 *Law of total probability*

For mutually exclusive events $b_1, ..., b_n$ with

$$\sum_{i=1}^{n} p(b_i) = 1 \tag{6.7}$$

the law of total probability is represented by

$$p(a) = \sum_{i=1}^{n} p(a) \wedge p(b_i) = \sum_{i=1}^{n} p(a, b_i) = \sum_{i=1}^{n} p(a|b_i) \cdot p(b_i) \tag{6.8}$$

The two rules of probability are called:

- the sum rule

$$p(x) = \sum_{y} p(x, y)$$

- the product rule

$$p(x, y) = p(y|x) \cdot p(x) = p(x|y) \cdot p(y)$$

For binary events there are two states: true or false. In other words, for any event a there is an event $\neg a$ which corresponds to the event that a does not occur. Binary events are described by binary variables. For binary events,

$$p(x) + p(\neg x) = 1, \; p(y) + p(\neg y) = 1, \tag{6.9}$$

where the law of total probability is represented by

$$p(y) = p(y, x) + p(y, \neg x) \tag{6.10}$$

$$p(y) = p(y|x) \cdot p(x) + p(y|\neg x) \cdot p(\neg x).$$

and

$$p(\neg y) = p(\neg y, x) + p(\neg y, \neg x), \tag{6.11}$$

6.1.3 *Bayes' rule*

The Bayes' rule was discovered by Thomas Bayes (1702-1761). Bayes rule can be used to determine the prior total probability $p(h_i)$ of hypothesis h_i to given data D. For example, what is the probability that some illness is present?

- $p(D|h_i)$ is the probability that a hypothesis h_i generates the data D. $p(D|h_i)$ can be easily estimated. For example, what is the probability that some illness generates some symptoms?
- The probability that an illness is present given certain symptoms, can be then determined by the Bayes rule
$$p(h_i|D) = \frac{p(D|h_i) \cdot p(h_i)}{p(D)} = \frac{p(D, h_i)}{p(D)}. \tag{6.12}$$

The most probable hypothesis h_i out of a set of possible hypothesis $h_1, h_2, \cdots$ given some present data is according to the Bayes rule
$$p(h_i|D) = \frac{p(D|h_i) \cdot p(h_i)}{p(D)}. \tag{6.13}$$
We notice that $p(h_i|D)$ and $p(D, h_i)$ are related in a linear manner
$$p(h_i|D) \propto p(D|h_i) \cdot p(h_i). \tag{6.14}$$
To determine the maximum a posteriori (MAP) hypothesis h_{MAP} we maximize
$$h_{MAP} = \arg\max_{h_i} \frac{p(D|h_i) \cdot p(h_i)}{p(D)}. \tag{6.15}$$
The maximization is independent of $p(D)$, it follows
$$h_{MAP} = \arg\max_{h_i} p(D|h_i) \cdot p(h_i). \tag{6.16}$$
If assume $p(h_i) = p(h_\gamma)$ for all h_i and h_γ, then can further simplify, and choose the maximum likelihood (ML) hypothesis
$$h_{ML} = \arg\max_{h_i} p(D|h_i). \tag{6.17}$$

6.1.3.1 *Bayesian Interpretation*

In the Bayesian (or epistemological) interpretation, probability measures a "degree of belief." Bayes' rule then links the degree of belief in a proposition before and after accounting for evidence [Bishop (2006)]. For example it is believed in certain value of $p(h_i)$ (without knowing the exact value) of each hypothesis and
$$\frac{p(D, h_i)}{p(D)} = \frac{p(D|h_i) \cdot p(h_i)}{p(D)}.$$
represents the support D provides for h_i.

6.1.3.2 *Frequentist Interpretation*

In the frequentist interpretation, probability measures a "proportion of outcomes." For example $p(h_i)$ is determined trough some data as well as $p(D)$.

6.1.3.3 *Example*

Cancer screening aims to detect cancer before symptoms appear. This may involve for example a blood tests. Suppose a result of one test is positive. The test is secure because in 99 percent of the cases the test returns a correct positive result ($= positive$) in which a rare form of cancer is actually present. Should the doctor tell the patient, that he has cancer?

The test has correct negative result ($= n$) in 99 percent of the cases when rare form of cancer is not present. It is also known that 0.001 of the entire population have rare form of cancer ($h_1 = c$).

$$p(cancer) = 0.001, \quad p(\neg cancer) = 0.999,$$

$$p(positive|cancer) = 0.99, \quad p(negative|cancer) = 0.01,$$

$$p(positive|\neg cancer) = 0.01, \quad p(negative|\neg cancer) = 0.99.$$

We determine h_{map} according to the linear relation

$$posterior \propto likelihood \times prior$$

$$p(cancer|positive) \propto p(positive|cancer) \cdot p(cancer) = 0.99 \cdot 0.001$$

$$p(\neg cancer|positive) \propto \cdot p(positive|\neg cancer) \cdot p(\neg cancer) \cdot 0.01 \cdot 0.999$$

it follows

$$h_{map} = \neg cancer$$

We can determine $p(positive)$ by the law of total probability

$$p(positive) = p(positive|cancer) + p(positive|\neg cancer)$$

In frequentist approach we would determine $p(cancer)$ through some data, for example some statistics of a country. However this can be problematic since the value becomes very general or cannot be determined. In the Bayesian approach we would set a belief value for the probability of $p(cancer)$ asking the patient if he smokes. This can be as well quite problematic, since the belief value do not need to be correct, it can be biased by some preconceptions. An example of such a preconception is a photo on a CV that can result in subjective preconceptions about the candidate.

6.1.4 *Expectation*

The arithmetic mean most commonly used is

$$\mu = \overline{x} = \frac{1}{n} \sum_{i=1}^{n} x_i. \tag{6.18}$$

It is the set of observed data is defined as being equal to the sum of the numerical values of each and every observation divided by the total number of observations. For a random variable X with a finite number of finite outcomes $x_1, x_2, x_3, \cdots, x_n$ occurring with probabilities $p_1, p_2, p_3, \cdots, p_n$ with

$$1 = \sum_{i=1}^{n} p_i,$$

the expectation of X is defined as

$$\mathbb{E}(X) = \sum_{i=1}^{n} p_i \cdot x_i. \tag{6.19}$$

Usually a random variable is denoted with a capital letter. Another important operations involving probabilities is that of finding weighted averages of functions. The average value of some function $f(x)$ under a probability distribution $p(x)$ is called the expectation of $f(x)$

$$\mathbb{E}(f) = \int p(x) f(x) dx,$$

$$\mathbb{E}(f) = \sum_{x} p(x) f(x). \tag{6.20}$$

For a finite number n of points the expectation can be approximated (similar or equal) as a

$$\mathbb{E}(f) \simeq \frac{1}{n} \sum_{i=1}^{n} f(x_i). \tag{6.21}$$

A conditional expectation with respect to a conditional distribution is given by

$$\mathbb{E}(f|y) = \sum_{x} p(x|y) f(x). \tag{6.22}$$

The variance of $f(x)$ is defined by

$$var[f] = \mathbb{E}\left[(f(x) - \mathbb{E}[f(x)])^2 \right] \tag{6.23}$$

and provides a measure of how much variability there is in $f(x)$ around its mean value $\mathbb{E}[f(x)]$.

6.1.5 *Joint distribution*

The joint distribution for n possible variables is described by 2^n possible combinations. The probability distribution $d_1 \times d_2 \times \cdots \times d_n$ corresponds to a vector of length 2^n. For a joint distribution of n possible variables, the exponential growth of combinations being true or false becomes an intractable problem for large n. For

$$p(h_i|d_1, d_2, d_3, .., d_n) = \frac{(d_1, d_2, d_3, ..., d_n|h_i) \cdot p(h_i)}{p(d_1, d_2, d_3, ..., d_n)} \tag{6.24}$$

all $2^n - 1$ possible combinations must be known. There are two possible solutions to this problem.

- The first solution is the decomposition of large probabilistic domains into weakly connected subsets via conditional independence,

  $$p(d_1, d_2, d_3, ..., d_n|h_i) = \prod_{j=1}^{n} p(d_j|h_i). \tag{6.25}$$

  This approach is known as the Naïve Bayes assumption and is one of the most important developments in the recent history of Artificial Intelligence. It assumes that a single cause directly influences a number of events, all of which are conditionally independent,

  $$h_{map} = \arg\max_{h_i} \prod_{j=1}^{n} p(d_j|h_i) \cdot p(h_i). \tag{6.26}$$

  However, this conditional independence is very restrictive. Often, it is not present in real life events. Dependence between some events is always present.
- Bayesian networks represent the second and more realistic solution. Bayesian networks can describe a probability distribution of a set of variables by combining conditional independence assumptions with conditional probabilities. Unlike the Naïve Bayes assumption, which states that all of the variables are conditionally independent given the value of the target variable, Bayesian networks enable these conditional independence assumptions to be applied to subsets of variables, providing a model with fewer constraints than the Bayes assumption [Mitchell (1997)].

6.1.6 *Naïve Bayes and counting*

The Naïve Bayes approach is related to simple counting if we follow the frequentist approach. For maximum a posteriori hypothesis h_{map}

$$h_{map} = arg \max_{h_i} \prod_{j=1}^{n} p(d_j|h_i) \cdot p(h_i) = arg \max_{h_i} \prod_{j=1}^{n} p(d_j \wedge h_i) \tag{6.27}$$

Ω is a set of all possible events

$$p(h_i) = \frac{card(h_i)}{card(\Omega)} \tag{6.28}$$

and

$$p(d_j|h_i) = \frac{card(d_j \wedge h_i)}{card(h_i)}, \tag{6.29}$$

$$h_{map} = argmax_{h_i} \prod_{j=1}^{n} \frac{card(d_j \wedge h_i)}{card(h_i)} \cdot \frac{card(h_i)}{card(\Omega)}. \tag{6.30}$$

Because Ω is a set of all possible events it does not play a role in the process maximization of h_{map}

$$h_{map} = argmax_{h_i} \prod_{j=1}^{n} card(d_j \wedge h_i) \tag{6.31}$$

we can apply *log*

$$h_{map} = argmax_{h_i} \log\left(\prod_{j=1}^{n} card(d_j \wedge h_i)\right), \tag{6.32}$$

$$h_{map} = argmax_{h_i} \sum_{j=1}^{n} \log\left(card(d_j \wedge h_i)\right). \tag{6.33}$$

For the process of maximization h_{map} we can simply write

$$h_{map} = argmax_{h_i} \sum_{j=1}^{n} card(d_j \wedge h_i). \tag{6.34}$$

The result is related to categorial representation based the contrast model of Tversky [Tversky (1977)].

6.1.7 *Counting and categorization*

An object is judged to belong to a verbal to the extent that its features are predicted by the verbal category [Osherson (1987)]. The sets of prototypical features defines a category. If Ca is a category and B the features set, so only $Ca \cap B$ features are considered [Wichert (1998)], [Wichert (2000)]. Then

$$card(Ca \wedge B) = |Ca \cap B|, \tag{6.35}$$

we normalize the result, in our case we normalize to the interval $[-1, 1]$ and define the $Sim(Ca, B)$ function as

$$Sim(Ca, B) = \frac{2}{|Ca|} \cdot |Ca \cap B| - 1 \quad \in [-1, 1] \tag{6.36}$$

$|Ca|$ is the number of the prototypical features that define the category Ca. This function corresponds to the simplified normalized contrast model of Tversky [Tversky (1977)]

$$Sim(Ca, B) = \alpha|Ca \cap B| - \beta|Ca - B| \tag{6.37}$$

in which only $Ca \cap B$ features are considered

$$Sim(Ca, B) = \alpha|Ca \cap B| - \beta(|Ca - (Ca \cap B)| \tag{6.38}$$

it is supposed that the similarity value should be from the interval $[-1, 1]$ so $\alpha = 1/|Ca|$ and $\beta = 1/|Ca|$ and

$$Sim(Ca, B) = \frac{|Ca \cap B|}{|Ca|} - \frac{|(Ca - (Ca \cap B)|}{|Ca|}. \tag{6.39}$$

The present features are counted and normalized so that the value can be compared. For example, the category **bird** is defined by the following features: flies, sings, lays eggs, nests in trees, eats insects. The category **bat** is defined by the following features: flies, gives milk, eat insects. The following features are present: flies and gives milk.

$$Simc(\mathbf{bird}, present features) = \frac{1}{5} - \frac{4}{5} = \frac{2}{5} \cdot 1 - 1 = -\frac{3}{5}, \tag{6.40}$$

$$Simc(\mathbf{bat}, present features) = \frac{2}{3} - \frac{1}{3} = \frac{2}{3} \cdot 2 - 1 = \frac{1}{3}. \tag{6.41}$$

Features that discriminate among relevant facts should have a higher salience than those that do not [Smith (1995)]. The features of an equal salience have a unary representation, they can only be represented as existent or nonexistent. A category that is described as a set of features can be present with different grades of vagueness corresponding to the cardinal number of the set. A set of features that describes a category can be sometimes divided into subsets that represent some subcategories. Each feature can be also regarded as a kind of subcategory. If this subcategory cannot be described by other features, but, nevertheless, should have the properties of variable salience and vagueness, it is described by invisible features. To each feature a number of invisible features is assigned dependent on its salience. An example of two old sayings from country folklore:

(1) If it is April and it snows much then probably the apple harvest will be bad.
(2) If it is April and it rains a lot and it is very cold then the vintage will be good.

The number of invisible features as determined by the observer:

- **April** is represented by one invisible feature, as it can be present or absent.
- **snows much** is described by two invisible features because the observer thinks that it has a higher salience than **April**. It can be either present, maybe present, or absent.
- The observer thinks that **rains a lot** has the same salience as **snows much**.
- The observer thinks that **very cold** has the greatest salience, as it is described by three invisible features. It can be either present, maybe present, maybe absent or absent.

With this approach hierarchical categorization can be preformed in analogy to the Naïve Bayes approach. Categories can be divided into subcategories, so that a taxonomy can be constructed and represented by an acyclic graph. The nodes in this graph correspond to categories and the links indicate the "is a subcategory" relation between them. The process of the hierarchical categorization can be performed by moving from more general categories to more specific categories until the desired categories are reached. Several expert systems were build based on this approach [Wichert (2000)], [Wichert (2004)].

6.2 Bayesian Network

For binary events there are two states: true or false. In other words, for any event a there is an event $\neg a$ which corresponds to the event that a does not occur. Binary events are described by binary variables. For binary events,

$$p(x) + p(\neg x) = 1, \quad p(y) + p(\neg y) = 1, \tag{6.42}$$

where the law of total probability is represented by

$$p(y) = p(y,x) + p(y,\neg x) = p(y|x) \cdot p(x) + p(y|\neg x) \cdot p(\neg x) \tag{6.43}$$

and

$$p(\neg y) = p(\neg y,x) + p(\neg y,\neg x) = p(\neg y|x) \cdot p(x) + p(\neg y|\neg x) \cdot p(\neg x). \tag{6.44}$$

The relationship can be represented by a graph (see Figure 6.2) that indicates the influence between events x and y. If two events x and y are

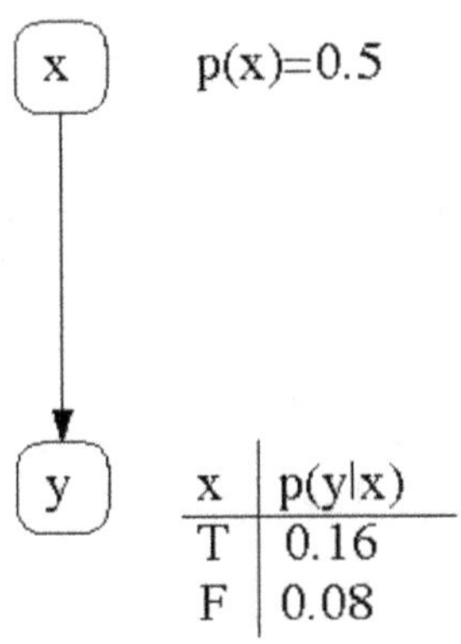

Fig. 6.2 The causal relation between events x and y represented by a direct graph of two nodes. Note that each node is followed by a conditional probability table that specifies the probability distribution of that node according to its parent node. This direct graph with two nodes representation corresponds to a simple Bayesian network.

independent, then the probability that events x and y both occur is

$$p(x,y) = p(x \wedge y) = p(x) \cdot p(y). \tag{6.45}$$

In this case the conditional probability is

$$p(x|y) = p(x). \tag{6.46}$$

If all n possible variables are independent, then

$$p(x_1, x_2, \cdots, x_n) = p(x_1) \cdot p(x_2) \cdot \cdots \cdot p(x_n) = \prod_{i=1}^{n} p(x_i) \tag{6.47}$$

In the case that not all variables are independent we can decompose the probabilistic domain into subsets via conditional independence. For a subset of dependent variables

$$p(x_1, x_2) = p(x_1|x_2) \cdot p(x_2) = p(x_2|x_1) \cdot p(x_1). \tag{6.48}$$

This follows from the Bayes' rule

$$p(x_1|x_2) = \frac{p(x_1, x_2)}{p(x_2)} = \frac{p(x_2|x_1) \cdot p(x_1)}{p(x_2)} \tag{6.49}$$

Two variables x_1 and x_2 are conditionally independent given x_3 if

$$p(x_1|x_2, x_3) = p(x_1|x_3). \tag{6.50}$$

Assuming x_2 and x_3 are independent, but x_1 is conditionally dependent given x_2 and x_3 then

$$p(x_1, x_2, x_3) = p(x_1|x_2, x_3) \cdot p(x_2) \cdot p(x_3). \tag{6.51}$$

Assuming x_4 is conditionally dependent given x_1 but independent of x_2 and x_3 then

$$p(x_1, x_2, x_3, x_4) = p(x_1|x_2, x_3) \cdot p(x_2) \cdot p(x_3) \cdot p(x_4|x_1). \tag{6.52}$$

This relationship between occurrence of events called causality is represented by conditional dependency.. The relationship can be represented by a graph (see Figure 6.3) that indicates the influence between events x_1, x_2, x_3 and x_4. In our example x_2 and x_3 cause x_1 and only then x_1 causes x_4. This kind of decomposition via conditional independence is modelled by Bayesian networks. Bayesian networks provide a natural representation for (causally induced) conditional independence. They represent a set of conditional independence assumptions by the topology of an acyclic directed graph and sets of conditional probabilities. In the network each variable is represented by a node and the links between them represent the conditional independence of the variable towards its non descendants and its immediate predecessors (see Figure 6.3). The corresponding network topology reflects our belief in the associated causal knowledge. Consider the well-known example of Judea Perl [Pearl (1989); Russell and Norvig (2010)]. "I am at work in Los Angeles, and neighbour John calls to say that the alarm of my house is ringing. Sometimes minor earthquakes set off the alarm. Is there a burglary?" Constructing a Bayesian network , should be easy because each variable is directly influenced by only a few other variables. In the example, there are four variables, namely, $Burglary(= x_2)$, $Earthquake(= x_3)$, $Alarm(= x_1)$ and $JohnCalls(= x_4)$. Due to simplicity, we ignore an additional variable $MaryCalls$ that was present in the original example. The corresponding network topology in Figure 6.3 reflects the following "causal" knowledge:

- A burglar can set the alarm on.
- An earthquake can set the alarm on.
- The alarm can cause John to call.

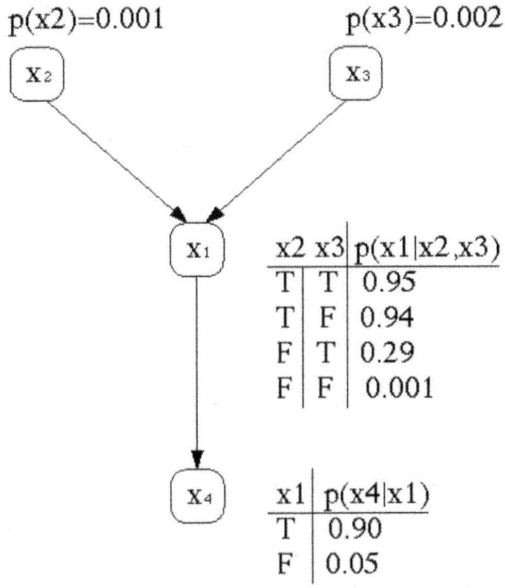

Fig. 6.3 A Bayesian network representing the causal relationship between events x_1, x_2, x_3 and x_4. The four variables can be associated with causal knowledge, in our example *Burglary*$(= x_2)$, *Earthquake*$(= x_3)$, *Alarm*$(= x_1)$ and *JohnCalls*$(= x_4)$.

Bayesian networks represent for each variable a conditional probability table which describes the probability distribution of a specific variable given the values of its immediate predecessors. A conditional distribution for each node x_i given its parents is

$$p(x_i|Parent_1(x_i), Parent_2(x_i), .., Parent_i(x_i))$$

with k representing the number of predecessor nodes (or parent nodes) of node x_i

$$p(x_1, .., x_n) = \prod_{i=1}^{n} p(x_i|Parent_1(x_i), Parent_2(x_i), .., Parent_i(x_i)). \quad (6.53)$$

Given the query variable x whose value has to be determined and the evidence variable e which is known and the remaining unobservable variables

y, we perform a summation over all possible y. In the following examples, for simplification the variables are binary and describe binary events. All possible values (true/false) of the unobservable variables y are determined according to the law of total probability

$$p(x|e) = \alpha \sum_y p(x,e,y) = \alpha \cdot (p(x,e,y) + p(x,e,\neg y)). \tag{6.54}$$

or

$$p(x|e) = \alpha \sum_y p(x,e,y) = \alpha \cdot (p(x,e|y) \cdot p(y) + p(x,e|\neg y) \cdot p(\neg y)). \tag{6.55}$$

with

$$\alpha = \frac{1}{p(e)} = \frac{1}{\sum_y p(x,e,y) + \sum_y p(\neg x,e,y)} \tag{6.56}$$

and

$$1 = \alpha \cdot \left(\sum_y p(x,e,y) + \sum_y p(\neg x,e,y) \right).$$

For the preceding example

$$p(x_4|x_1,x_2,x_3) = \alpha \cdot p(x_1|x_2,x_3) \cdot p(x_2) \cdot p(x_3) \cdot p(x_4|x_1) \tag{6.57}$$

for an unknown variable, for example x_3, we will use the notion X_3 to indicate that its value is unknown. We can then apply the law of total probability by making a summation over its values.

$$p(x_1,x_2,X_3,x_4) = p(x_1,x_2,x_3,x_4) + p(x_1,x_2,\neg x_3,x_4) \tag{6.58}$$

$$p(x_1,x_2,X_3,x_4) = p(x_2) \cdot p(x_4|x_1) \cdot \left(\sum_{x_3} p(x_1|x_2,x_3) \cdot p(x_3) \right). \tag{6.59}$$

$$p(x_4|x_1,x_2) = \alpha \cdot p(x_2) \cdot p(x_4|x_1) \cdot \left(\sum_{x_3} p(x_1|x_2,x_3) \cdot p(x_3) \right). \tag{6.60}$$

$$p(x_4|x_1,x_2) = \alpha \cdot p(x_2) \cdot p(x_4|x_1) \cdot (p(x_1|x_2,x_3) \cdot p(x_3) + p(x_1|x_2,\neg x_3) \cdot p(\neg x_3)) \tag{6.61}$$

with

$$\alpha = \frac{1}{p(x_1,x_2)} = \frac{1}{p(x_1,x_2,X_3,x_4) + p(x_1,x_2,X_3,\neg x_4)} \tag{6.62}$$

and

$$p(x_1, x_2) = p(x_1, x_2, X_3, x_4) + p(x_1, x_2, X_3, \neg x_4). \tag{6.63}$$

After calculating, we arrive at

$$p(x_4|x_1, x_2) = \frac{p(x_4|x_1, x_2)}{p(x_4|x_1, x_2) + p(\neg x_4|x_1, x_2)}. \tag{6.64}$$

For unknown variables x_1, x_3 indicated by X_1 andX_3, we apply the law of total probability.

$$p(X_1, x_2, X_3, x_4) = p(x_1, x_2, x_3, x_4) + p(\neg x_1, x_2, x_3, x_4)$$

$$+ p(x_1, x_2, \neg x_3, x_4) + p(\neg x_1, x_2, \neg x_3, x_4) \tag{6.65}$$

$$p(X_1, x_2, X_3, x_4) = p(x_2) \cdot \sum_{x_1} \left(p(x_4|x_1) \cdot \left(\sum_{x_3} p(x_1|x_2, x_3) \cdot p(x_3) \right) \right). \tag{6.66}$$

$$p(x_4|x_2) = \alpha \cdot p(x_2) \cdot (p(x_4|x_1) \cdot p(x_1|x_2, x_3) \cdot p(x_3)$$

$$+ p(x_4|x_1) \cdot p(x_1|x_2, \neg x_3) \cdot p(\neg x_3)$$

$$+ p(x_4|\neg x_1) \cdot p(\neg x_1|x_2, x_3) \cdot p(x_3) + p(x_4|\neg x_1) \cdot p(\neg x_1|x_2, \neg x_3) \cdot p(\neg x_3)) \tag{6.67}$$

with

$$\alpha = \frac{1}{p(x_2)} = \frac{1}{p(X_1, x_2, X_3, x_4) + p(X_1, x_2, X_3, \neg x_4)}. \tag{6.68}$$

6.2.1 *Example*

As indicated in Figure 6.3 determine the probability of x_1 given x_4 and x_5 are false and x_2 is unknown.

$$p(x_1|\neg x_4, \neg x_3) = \alpha \cdot p(x_1, \neg x_4, \neg x_3)$$

$$p(x_1, \neg x_4, \neg x_3) = \sum_{x_2} p(x_2) \cdot p(\neg x_3) \cdot p(x_1|x_2, \neg x_3) p(\neg x_4|x_1)$$

$$p(x_1, \neg x_4, \neg x_3) = p(\neg x_3) \cdot p(\neg x_4|x_1) \cdot \left(\sum_{x_2} p(x_2) \cdot p(x_1|x_2, \neg x_3) \right)$$

$$p(x_1, \neg x_4, \neg x_3) = p(\neg x_3) \cdot p(\neg x_4|x_1) \cdot (p(x_2) \cdot p(x_1|x_2, \neg x_3)$$

$$+p(\neg x_2)\cdot p(x_1|\neg x_2,\neg x_3))$$

$$p(x_1,\neg x_4,\neg x_3)=(1-0.002)\cdot(1-0.9)\cdot(0.001\cdot 0.94+(1-0.001)\cdot 0.001)$$

$$p(x_1,\neg x_4,\neg x_3)=0.000193512.$$

$$p(\neg x_1,\neg x_4,\neg x_3)=p(\neg x_3)\cdot p(\neg x_4|\neg x_1)\cdot(p(x_2)\cdot p(\neg x_1|x_2,\neg x_3)$$

$$+p(\neg x_2)\cdot p(\neg x_1|\neg x_2,\neg x_3))$$

$$p(\neg x_1,\neg x_4,\neg x_3)=(1-0.002)\cdot(1-0.05)$$

$$\cdot(0.00.1\cdot((1-0.94)+1-0.001)\cdot(1-0.001))$$

$$p(\neg x_1,\neg x_4,\neg x_3)=0.946205.$$

$$p(x_1|\neg x_4,\neg x_3)=\frac{p(x_1,\neg x_4,\neg x_3)}{p(x_1,\neg x_4,\neg x_3)+p(\neg x_1,\neg x_4,\neg x_3)}=0.000204472.$$

6.3 Mixed Distribution

Suppose that the variable d_1 represents whether a person likes mathematics or not. The truth-values are represented by 0 and 1, so $d_1=0$ means that the person does not like mathematics. The next variable d_2 represents whether the person studies philosophy or not, and d_3 represents if the person knows how to play chess or not. If we introduce positional notation for the variables, then $d_1,d_2,d_3=101$ would mean that the person likes mathematics and does not study philosophy and knows how to play chess. The probability of $p(d_1=1,d_2=0,d_3=1)$ is written in short as p_{101}. In this case, the distribution $d_1\times d_2\times d_3$ is represented by a vector of length 8 [Rieffel and Polak (2011)]:

$$\mathbf{p}=(p_{000},p_{001},p_{010},p_{011},p_{100},p_{101},p_{110},p_{111}). \tag{6.69}$$

Suppose that we do not know anything about a person; in this case, the probability distribution is a mixed distribution and is represented by the vector

$$\mathbf{p}=(1/8,1/8,1/8,1/8,1/8,1/8,1/8,1/8).$$

The vector p represents the mixed distribution on uncertainty before knowing the facts about the person. Every possible combination has the same probability. Before we know the facts, the distribution is mixed, with 2^3 states. After learning the fact that the person studies philosophy, $d_2 = 1$, we know for certain that four possible combinations are not present, namely those combinations in which $d_2 = 0$, which are $p_{000}, p_{001}, p_{100}$ and p_{101}. The mixed distribution represented by the vector $\mathbf{p}$ must be re-normalized,

$$\mathbf{p} = (0, 0, 1/4, 1/4, 0, 0, 1/4, 1/4).$$

After learning the fact that the person does like mathematics, $d_1 = 1$, the mixed distribution represented by the vector $\mathbf{p}$, must be re-normalized again

$$\mathbf{p} = (0, 0, 0, 0, 0, 0, 1/2, 1/2).$$

Finally, after learning that the person plays chess $d_3 = 1$, the mixed distribution becomes pure; in this case, there is no uncertainty that the vector $\mathbf{p}$ is a unary vector with a one at the position that corresponds to p_{111}

$$\mathbf{p} = (0, 0, 0, 0, 0, 0, 0, 1).$$

6.4 Markov Chains

A physical system is described by the state of the system. The state of the system can be represented by a vector $\mathbf{x}$. A single object can be described in classical mechanics by its position and momentum. Momentum is the product of the mass and velocity of an object. The corresponding vector is $\mathbf{x} = (x_1, x_2, x_3, p_1, p_2, p_3) \in R^6$, where (x_1, x_2, x_3) describes the position and (p_1, p_2, p_3) describes the momentum of the object. As the object moves, the state of the system changes over time $\mathbf{x}(t)$. Classical mechanics describes the time evolution of the state by the Hamiltonian equation of motion represented by differential equations [Hirvensalo (2004)], [Ross (2009)].

If we do not know the states of the system, we can attempt to describe the probability distribution of the system. We know that a system is in states $x_1, ..., x_n$ with probabilities $p_1, ..., p_n$ and that they sum up to 1. The probability distribution over state x_i is represented by the mixed state

$$p_1[x_1] + p_2[x_2] + ... + p_n[x_n]. \tag{6.70}$$

Tossing a fair coin with a head and a tail is represented by the mixed state

$$0.5[h] + 0.5[t].$$

The time evolution of a system is a non-deterministic procedure. It develops each state x_i into a distribution

$$p_{1i}[x_1] + p_{2i}[x_2] + ... + p_{ni}[x_n]$$

where p_{ij} is the probability that the system state x_i evolves into x_j. A simplification can be reached by using discrete time. Another simplification is the one-level dependence of the state, which is also called the Markov property. Each state is dependent on the preceding state. The discrete probabilistic time evolution represents a Markov chain that can be described by linear mapping. Transition probabilities between states are represented by conditional probabilities

$$p_{ij} = p(x_j(t+1)|x_i(t)). \tag{6.71}$$

We represent

$$p_1[x_1] + p_2[x_2] + ... + p_n[x_n]$$

by a stochastic vector

$$\mathbf{p} = (p_1, p_2, .., p_n).$$

For a state x_i the mapping is represented by

$$p_i' = p_{i1}p_1 + p_{i2}p_2 + ... + p_{ini}p_n. \tag{6.72}$$

The vector is defined by an $n \times n$ stochastic matrix $P = [p_{ij}]$ that is also called a Markov matrix or a stochastic matrix, and it has the following properties:

$$(i)\ p_{ij} \geq 0\ for\ 1 \leq i, j \leq n;$$

$$(ii) \sum_{i=1}^{n} p_{ij} = 1\ for\ 1 \leq j \leq n.$$

The probabilities are related by the linear mapping using the stochastic matrix P with

$$\begin{pmatrix} p_1' \\ p_2' \\ \vdots \\ p_n' \end{pmatrix} = \begin{pmatrix} p_{11} & p_{12} & \cdots & p_{1n} \\ p_{21} & p_{22} & \cdots & p_{2n} \\ \vdots & \vdots & \ddots & \vdots \\ p_{n1} & p_{n2} & \cdots & p_{nn} \end{pmatrix} \cdot \begin{pmatrix} p_1 \\ p_2 \\ \vdots \\ p_n \end{pmatrix}. \tag{6.73}$$

Because all the columns sum to one we are guaranteed that

$$p_1' + p_2' + .. + p_n' = p_1 + p_2 + .. + p_n. \tag{6.74}$$

A Markov chain is a mathematical system that undergoes transitions that are described by a stochastic matrix that moves from one stochastic vector to another [Markov (1954)]. The asymptotic behavior of Markov chains either converges to a fixed distribution or goes to a periodic sequence of distributions. Given that all of the entries of the stochastic matrix are larger than zero, which means that each state can be reached from another state, there is a fixed distribution $\mathbf{q}$. The distribution $\mathbf{q}$ is independent of the initial distribution $\mathbf{p}$. A fixed distribution is unchanged when it is transformed by P. The fixed distribution $\mathbf{q}$ is represented by the eigenvector of P, with the eigenvalue equal to 1.

$$\begin{pmatrix} q_1 \\ q_2 \\ \vdots \\ q_n \end{pmatrix} = \begin{pmatrix} p_{11} & p_{12} & \cdots & p_{1n} \\ p_{21} & p_{22} & \cdots & p_{2n} \\ \vdots & \vdots & \ddots & \vdots \\ p_{n1} & p_{n2} & \cdots & p_{nn} \end{pmatrix} \cdot \begin{pmatrix} q_1 \\ q_2 \\ \vdots \\ q_n \end{pmatrix} \tag{6.75}$$

because $\mathbf{q}$ is a probability vector, it follows that

$$\sum_{i=1}^{n} q_i = 1.$$

P describes the transition of the states of the weather, such as sunny, cloudy and rainy (see Figure 6.4). Each state of the weather can be reached from another state, and the prediction over several days is increasingly inaccurate. The prediction tends toward a steady state vector that represents the probabilities of sunny, cloudy and rainy, independent of the initial weather state. The information about the initial weather is lost and cannot be reconstructed. The evolution of a stochastic matrix does not lead to a loss of information if the matrix is orthogonal. An example orthogonal stochastic matrix is the permutation matrix. A permutation matrix is a square binary matrix that has exactly one entry 1 in each row and each column and is 0 elsewhere. As a consequence, each state cannot be reached from another state.

6.5 Vector-Based Framework for Probabilities

Vector-based framework is based on a possible world approach [Halpern (2003)] for probabilistic representation and computation. By representing

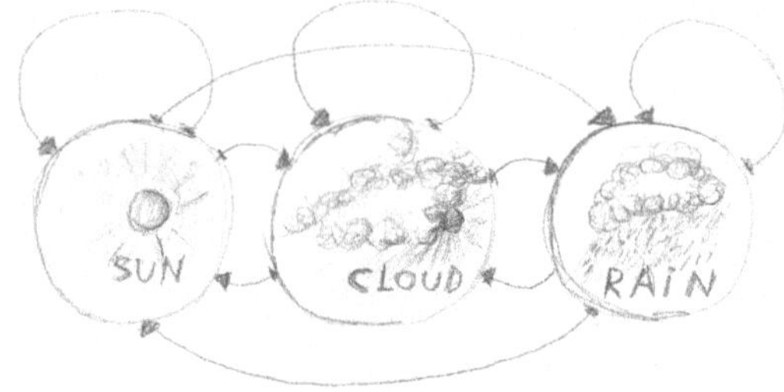

Fig. 6.4 Transition of for the states of the weather, such as sunny, cloudy and rainy represented by the symbol "sun","cloud" and "rain". Each state of the weather can be reached from another state.

the probabilities with this framework on a meta-level, we can embody logical sentences with absolutely certain truths. For example, the sentence ?All birds can fly? would be represented in first order logic as

$$\forall x\ [\mathrm{Bird(x)} \to \mathrm{Fly(x)}].$$
$$\text{An object } x \text{ corresponds to bird flies.}$$

and is either true or false. We can represent this sentence as a probabilistic sentence, "More than 70% of all birds fly? by the possible world approach. In seven of these worlds, the sentence would be true; in the remaining three worlds, the sentence would not be verified and would, consequently, be false [Halpern (2003)]. There is a straightforward probabilistic interpretation of this collection of sentences, namely, when one randomly selects a bird out of ten possible worlds, then the probability that the selected bird flies is 70%. Logic interpretation is valid in one world and is not valid in another. In this interpretation, a *world* can be identified by some time frame (or universe). For example, the statement *all swans are white* is valid in some time frame. At a later time frame, a black swan is discovered in the wild, and the previous statement is not valid anymore. For all time frames, the statement becomes *most swans are white.*

A related approach, called Markov logic network, has been proposed by [Richardson and Domingos (2006)] in which weights are attached to the first-order knowledge formula. The weights are learned by a machine learning algorithm. Our approach does not investigate learning but rather vector-based representation, which is motivated by quantum physics but operates using classical probabilities rather than quantum probabilities.

Relying on the frequentist approach, one can determine the probability of an event a by counting

$$p(a) = \frac{card(a)}{card(\Omega)}. \tag{6.76}$$

Relying on the possible world approach, we will reinterpret Ω as the finite number of possible worlds. Each event happens in one of the worlds. The probability of event a and event b appearing together in the same world is given by

$$p(a \land b) = \frac{card(a \land b)}{card(\Omega)}. \tag{6.77}$$

The cardinality determines the number of elements of a set that represents the corresponding world. Correspondingly $card(b)$ is the number of elements of the worlds where event b appears. Table 6.1 represents four different events D, C, B, A in six different worlds. We will use the upper case letters to indicate that an event is a random variable and lower case letter to indicate the realizations of a random variable (in this case, binary random variables that can either be true or false). Moreover, the presence of an event in a wold is indicated by 1 and the absence by 0. In worlds 5 and 6 represented in Table 6.1, no event is present. Taking into account

Table 6.1 Representation of four events D, C, B and A in six worlds.

world	D	C	B	A
1	0	0	1	1
2	0	1	1	1
3	1	0	0	0
4	1	0	0	0
5	0	0	0	0
6	0	0	0	0

the representation of the events in Table 6.1, the probability of the event b is given by

$$p(b) = \frac{2}{6}. \tag{6.78}$$

And the probability of $a \land b \land c$ is

$$p(a \land b \land c) = \frac{1}{6}. \tag{6.79}$$

and also (with negation $\neg a$ indicating that an event is not present)

$$p(\neg a \land \neg b \land \neg c \land \neg d) = \frac{2}{6} = \frac{1}{3}. \tag{6.80}$$

6.5.1 *Vector based representation framework*

In this section, we introduce a compressed vector representation of events for the possible worlds approach that is motivated by quantum physics. The orthogonal basis of the vector is is defined by all different worlds. Paul Dirac introduced the following notation for a vector **mw** as a shorthand notation for a column vector

$$|mw\rangle := \mathbf{mw}$$

and the representation of the table 6.1 becomes

$$|mw\rangle = \frac{1}{6} \cdot |0011\rangle + \frac{1}{6} \cdot |0111\rangle + \frac{2}{6} \cdot |1000\rangle + \frac{2}{6} \cdot |0000\rangle. \tag{6.81}$$

with the orthonormal basis of a sixteen dimensional vector space, which indicates all possible combinations of events that are defined by the four different events D, C, B, A. For example $|0011\rangle$ corresponds to the presence of the event a and b and the absence of the event c and d in the first row of Table 6.1. This corresponds to a possible worlds register of m events in a vector space of dimension $n = 2^m$.

$$|0000\rangle = \begin{pmatrix} 1 \\ 0 \\ 0 \\ 0 \\ 0 \\ 0 \\ 0 \\ 0 \\ 0 \\ 0 \\ 0 \\ 0 \\ 0 \\ 0 \\ 0 \\ 0 \end{pmatrix}, |0001\rangle = \begin{pmatrix} 0 \\ 1 \\ 0 \\ 0 \\ 0 \\ 0 \\ 0 \\ 0 \\ 0 \\ 0 \\ 0 \\ 0 \\ 0 \\ 0 \\ 0 \\ 0 \end{pmatrix}, |0010\rangle = \begin{pmatrix} 0 \\ 0 \\ 1 \\ 0 \\ 0 \\ 0 \\ 0 \\ 0 \\ 0 \\ 0 \\ 0 \\ 0 \\ 0 \\ 0 \\ 0 \\ 0 \end{pmatrix}, \cdots, |1111\rangle = \begin{pmatrix} 0 \\ 0 \\ 0 \\ 0 \\ 0 \\ 0 \\ 0 \\ 0 \\ 0 \\ 0 \\ 0 \\ 0 \\ 0 \\ 0 \\ 0 \\ 1 \end{pmatrix}.$$

A state represents events in a n-dimensional vector space is defined by an orthonormal basis

$$|x_1\rangle, |x_2\rangle, \cdots |x_n\rangle$$

and is represented as a vector in the compact notation

$$\frac{\omega_1}{\Omega} \cdot |x_1\rangle + \frac{\omega_2}{\Omega} \cdot |x_2\rangle + \cdots + \frac{\omega_n}{\Omega} \cdot |x_n\rangle \tag{6.82}$$

or in the vector notation

$$\begin{pmatrix} \frac{\omega_1}{\Omega} \\ \frac{\omega_2}{\Omega} \\ \cdots \\ \frac{\omega_n}{\Omega} \end{pmatrix} \tag{6.83}$$

with

$$0 \leq \frac{\omega_i}{\Omega}, \quad \sum_{i=1}^{n} \frac{\omega_i}{\Omega} = 1 \Leftrightarrow \sum_{i=1}^{n} \omega_i = \Omega$$

where Ω represents the number of distinct worlds and ω_i represents the frequency of a certain world as described by the basis vector. The probability of presence of the world i is ω_i/Ω. It means that the vector is a unit-length vector in the norm l_1, with the l_1 norm being

$$\|\mathbf{x}\|_1 = |x_1| + |x_2| + \cdots + |x_n| \tag{6.84}$$

and is represented as a unit-length vector in the norm l_1

$$\|\mathbf{mw}\|_1 = \left|\frac{\omega_1}{\Omega}\right| + \left|\frac{\omega_2}{\Omega}\right| + \cdots + \left|\frac{\omega_n}{\Omega}\right| = 1. \tag{6.85}$$

6.5.2 *Conditional independence*

From this possible world approach representation by vector spaces, one can define probability functions such as conditional independence. If we assume two events with $p(a) = 0.5$ and $p(b) = 0.5$ are independent, it follows that

$$p(a \wedge b) = p(a) \cdot p(b) = 0.25. \tag{6.86}$$

The representation of $|mw\rangle$ by random variables is defined as

$$DCBA := |mw\rangle = \frac{1}{6} \cdot |0011\rangle + \frac{1}{6} \cdot |0111\rangle + \frac{2}{6} \cdot |1000\rangle + \frac{2}{6} \cdot |0000\rangle. \tag{6.87}$$

One should note that the the order of the representation of the events is a matter of agreement, we could as well represent $|mw\rangle$ as

$$ABCD := |mw\rangle = \frac{1}{6} \cdot |1100\rangle + \frac{1}{6} \cdot |1110\rangle + \frac{2}{6} \cdot |0001\rangle + \frac{2}{6} \cdot |0000\rangle \tag{6.88}$$

or any other permutation of the arrangement of events. We will follow the representational agreement $DCBA$. We can represent the event A as a vector of dimension two

$$A = \frac{1}{2} \cdot |0\rangle + \frac{1}{2} \cdot |1\rangle$$

with

$$\neg a = \frac{1}{2} \cdot |0\rangle, \quad \text{and} \quad a = \frac{1}{2} \cdot |1\rangle$$

and the basis

$$|0\rangle = \begin{pmatrix} 1 \\ 0 \end{pmatrix}, \quad |1\rangle = \begin{pmatrix} 0 \\ 1 \end{pmatrix}. \tag{6.89}$$

The event B as

$$B = \frac{1}{2} \cdot |0\rangle + \frac{1}{2} \cdot |1\rangle$$

with the same basis. The register of two independent events is represented as a direct product (also called Kronecker product) of A and B

$$BA = B \otimes A = \left(\frac{1}{2} \cdot |0\rangle + \frac{1}{2} \cdot |1\rangle\right) \cdot \left(\frac{1}{2} \cdot |0\rangle + \frac{1}{2} \cdot |1\rangle\right) \tag{6.90}$$

$$B \otimes A = \frac{1}{4} \cdot |00\rangle + \frac{1}{4} \cdot |10\rangle + \frac{1}{4} \cdot |01\rangle + \frac{1}{4} \cdot |11\rangle \tag{6.91}$$

with the new basis

$$|00\rangle = \begin{pmatrix} 1 \\ 0 \\ 0 \\ 0 \end{pmatrix}, |01\rangle = \begin{pmatrix} 0 \\ 1 \\ 0 \\ 0 \end{pmatrix}, |10\rangle = \begin{pmatrix} 0 \\ 0 \\ 1 \\ 0 \end{pmatrix}, |11\rangle = \begin{pmatrix} 0 \\ 0 \\ 0 \\ 1 \end{pmatrix}. \tag{6.92}$$

The probability of $p(a \wedge b)$ is $1/4$ since $a \wedge b$ corresponds to the dimension $|11\rangle$. The probability of $p(a)$ is $1/2$ since a corresponds to the dimension $|1\rangle$ that is present in $|01\rangle$ and $|11\rangle$. After observing event a the conditional probability $p(B|a)$ is given by

$$p(B|a) = \neg b|a + b|a = \frac{1}{2} \cdot |01\rangle + \frac{1}{2} \cdot |11\rangle \tag{6.93}$$

and $p(b|a)$ is given by

$$b|a = \frac{1}{2} \cdot |11\rangle. \tag{6.94}$$

$p(A|b)$ is given by

$$p(A|b) = \neg a|b + a|b = \frac{1}{2} \cdot |10\rangle + \frac{1}{2} \cdot |11\rangle \tag{6.95}$$

and $p(a|b)$ is given by

$$a|b = \frac{1}{2} \cdot |11\rangle. \tag{6.96}$$

6.5.3 *Dependency*

So far, we have defined conditional probabilities by the possible worlds approach representation under vector spaces. However, events are not always independent between each other. They can also be dependent (or correlated). Dependent events appear together: for two dependent events $p(a) = 0.5$ and $p(b) = 0.5$, one can consider $p(a \wedge b) = p(a) = p(b) = 0.5$. We can represent the event a as a vector of dimension two

$$A = \frac{1}{2} \cdot |0\rangle + \frac{1}{2} \cdot |1\rangle$$

and event b as

$$B = \frac{1}{2} \cdot |0\rangle + \frac{1}{2} \cdot |1\rangle$$

with the same basis. The register of two dependent events is represented as a direct sum of a and b

$$B \oplus A = \left(\frac{1}{2} \cdot |0\rangle + \frac{1}{2} \cdot |1\rangle\right) \oplus \left(\frac{1}{2} \cdot |0\rangle + \frac{1}{2} \cdot |1\rangle\right). \tag{6.97}$$

$$B \oplus A = \left(\frac{1}{2} \cdot |0\rangle \oplus \frac{1}{2} \cdot |0\rangle\right) + \left(\frac{1}{2} \cdot |1\rangle \oplus \frac{1}{2} \cdot |1\rangle\right) \tag{6.98}$$

$$BA = B \oplus A = \frac{1}{2} \cdot |00\rangle + \frac{1}{2} \cdot |11\rangle \tag{6.99}$$

The position of the element in the register indicated a possible event, in our case the first position corresponds to the event A and the second to the event B.

6.5.4 *Partial dependency**

There is also the case where events can share some degree of dependency. In other words, partial dependent can events appear together but not always will. For example, assume that events $p(b) = 0.5$ and $p(\neg a) = 1/3$ have a probability of appearing together of $p(\neg a \wedge \neg b) = p(\neg a) = 1/3$. We can represent the event B as a vector of dimension two

$$B = \frac{1}{2} \cdot |0\rangle + \frac{1}{2} \cdot |1\rangle$$

and event A as

$$A = \frac{1}{3} \cdot |0\rangle + \frac{2}{3} \cdot |1\rangle$$

with the same basis. The register of two dependent events is represented as a Kronecker sum of B and A

$$B \oplus A = \left(\frac{1}{2} \cdot |0\rangle + \frac{1}{2} \cdot |1\rangle\right) \oplus \left(\frac{1}{3} \cdot |0\rangle + \frac{2}{3} \cdot |1\rangle\right). \tag{6.100}$$

The register of two correlated events are represented as a Kronecker sum of B and A, however it is necessary to convert each fraction to an equivalent fraction with the same denominator

$$\frac{1}{2} + \frac{1}{3} = \frac{3}{6} + \frac{2}{6}$$

$$BA = B \oplus A = \left(\frac{3}{6} \cdot |0\rangle + \frac{3}{6} \cdot |1\rangle\right) \oplus \left(\frac{2}{6} \cdot |0\rangle + \frac{4}{6} \cdot |1\rangle\right). \tag{6.101}$$

with

$$B \oplus A = \left(\frac{2}{6} \cdot |0\rangle + \frac{1}{6} \cdot |0\rangle + \frac{3}{6} \cdot |1\rangle\right) \oplus \left(\frac{2}{6} \cdot |0\rangle + \frac{3}{6} \cdot |1\rangle + \frac{1}{6} \cdot |1\rangle\right). \tag{6.102}$$

$$B \oplus A = \left(\frac{2}{6} \cdot |0\rangle \oplus \frac{2}{6} \cdot |0\rangle\right) + \left(\frac{3}{6} \cdot |1\rangle \oplus \frac{3}{6} \cdot |1\rangle\right) + \left(\frac{1}{6} \cdot |0\rangle \oplus \frac{1}{6} \cdot |1\rangle\right) \tag{6.103}$$

$$B \oplus A = \frac{2}{6} \cdot |00\rangle + \frac{3}{6} \cdot |11\rangle + \frac{1}{6} \cdot |01\rangle. \tag{6.104}$$

6.5.5 *Bayes' rule**

With the definition of dependency, we can define the Bayes' rule under the possible worlds approach representation by vector spaces. Let A and B be two random variables representing two events, an event A is present together with an event B, $A \wedge B$, for

$$A = \frac{1}{2} \cdot |0\rangle + \frac{1}{2} \cdot |1\rangle \tag{6.105}$$

and

$$B|\neg a = \frac{1}{2} \cdot |00\rangle + \frac{1}{2} \cdot |10\rangle \tag{6.106}$$

$$B|a = \frac{1}{4} \cdot |01\rangle + \frac{3}{4} \cdot |11\rangle. \tag{6.107}$$

In order to build the representation BA, we will consider the following vector representation.

$$A : a = \begin{pmatrix} 1 \\ 0 \end{pmatrix} \text{ and } \neg a = \begin{pmatrix} 0 \\ 1 \end{pmatrix} \tag{6.108}$$

So, from Equation 6.108, the event A comprises one occurrence of a and one occurrence of $\neg a$. In other words,

$$card(a) = 1 \quad \text{and} \quad card(\neg a) = 1$$

Taking into account the Equation 6.106, since $B|\neg a$ is given by 1 occurrence of event $b|\neg a$ and one occurrence of event $\neg b|\neg a$, then we can represent event $B|\neg a$ see Table 6.2 In the same way, taking into account Equation 6.107,

Table 6.2 $B|\neg a$.

world	B	A
1	1	0
2	0	0

since $B|a$ is given by 1 occurrence of the event $\neg b|a$ and three occurrences of the event $b|a$, then we can represent the event see Table 6.3. The event

Table 6.3 $B|\neg a$.

world	B	A
1	0	1
2	1	1
3	1	1
4	1	1

$B|\neg a$ occurs twice, while the event $B|a$ occurs four times. In other words,

$$card(B|\neg a) = 2 \quad \text{and} \quad card(B|a) = 4$$

The fraction corresponding to the event A with $card(\neg a)/card(a)$ has to be equivalent to the fraction $card(B|\neg a)/card(B|a)$,

$$\frac{card(\neg a)}{cad(a)} \to \frac{1}{1} \equiv \frac{2 \cdot \alpha}{4 \cdot \beta} \leftarrow \frac{card(B|\neg a)}{card(B|a)}, \tag{6.109}$$

which becomes equivalent if we set $\alpha = 2$ and $\beta = 1$. We renormalize by multiplying the Equation 6.106 by $2 = \alpha$ and get

$$B|\neg a = \frac{2}{4} \cdot |00\rangle + \frac{2}{4} \cdot |10\rangle \tag{6.110}$$

and

$$B|a = \frac{1}{4} \cdot |01\rangle + \frac{3}{4} \cdot |11\rangle. \tag{6.111}$$

It follows the representation of BA (see Table 6.4)

$$BA = \frac{1}{8} \cdot |01\rangle + \frac{3}{8} \cdot |11\rangle + \frac{2}{8} \cdot |00\rangle + \frac{2}{8} \cdot |10\rangle. \tag{6.112}$$

Table 6.4 Representation of events B and A.

world	B	A
1	0	0
2	0	0
3	1	0
4	1	0
5	0	1
6	1	1
7	1	1
8	1	1

Our approach corresponds to the Bayes's rule with normalization, with

$$ba = \frac{3}{8} \cdot |11\rangle \Rightarrow a|b = \alpha \cdot \frac{3}{8} \cdot |11\rangle \Rightarrow p(a|b) = \alpha \cdot \frac{3}{8}$$

$$b\neg a = \frac{2}{8} \cdot |10\rangle \Rightarrow \neg a|b = \alpha \cdot \frac{2}{8} \cdot |10\rangle \Rightarrow$$

$$\neg\, a|b = \alpha \cdot \frac{2}{8} \cdot |10\rangle \Rightarrow p(\neg a|b) = \alpha \cdot \frac{2}{8}.$$

It follows with $\alpha = \frac{8}{5}$

$$1 = a|b + \neg a|b = \frac{8 \cdot 3}{5 \cdot 8} \cdot |11\rangle + \frac{8 \cdot 2}{5 \cdot 8} \cdot |10\rangle = \frac{3}{5} \cdot |11\rangle + \frac{2}{5} \cdot |10\rangle = 1.$$

Computing using probabilities and applying normalization by the Bayes's rule we would get the same results in the following way:

$$p(a|b) = p(b|a) \cdot p(a) = \alpha \cdot \frac{3}{4} \cdot \frac{1}{2} =$$

$$p(a|b) = \alpha \cdot \frac{3}{8} = \frac{3}{5}$$

$$p(\neg a|b) = p(b|\neg a) \cdot p(\neg a) = \alpha \cdot \frac{1}{2} \cdot \frac{1}{2} =$$

$$p(\neg a|b) = \alpha \cdot \frac{1}{4} = \frac{2}{5}.$$

6.5.6 *Bayesian networks**

Given the preceding example with

$$BA = \frac{1}{8} \cdot |01\rangle + \frac{3}{8} \cdot |11\rangle + \frac{2}{8} \cdot |00\rangle + \frac{2}{8} \cdot |10\rangle, \tag{6.113}$$

we extended it into a simple Bayesian network

$$C|\neg b = \frac{1}{2} \cdot |00\rangle + \frac{1}{2} \cdot |10\rangle \tag{6.114}$$

and

$$C|b = \frac{1}{3} \cdot |01\rangle + \frac{2}{3} \cdot |11\rangle. \tag{6.115}$$

The corresponding Bayesian network is represented in the Figure 6.5. Despite its simplicity, the Bayesian network generalises all required computational steps. We can determine the probability of event B from the vector

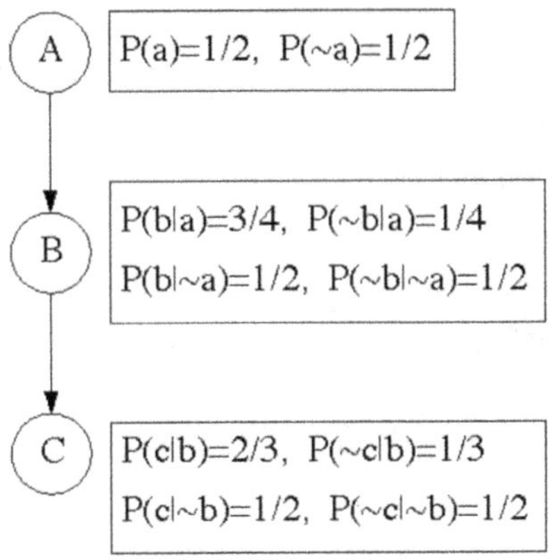

Fig. 6.5 A Bayesian network representing the causal relation between events C, B, A.

representation BA (Equation 6.113) as

$$B = \left(\frac{2}{8} + \frac{1}{8}\right) \cdot |0\rangle + \left(\frac{2}{8} + \frac{3}{8}\right) \cdot |1\rangle =$$

$$B = \frac{3}{8} \cdot |0\rangle + \frac{5}{8} \cdot |1\rangle.$$

We can then build the representation of the full joint probability CBA. Again, event b occurs three times in eight and event $\neg b$ occurs five times in eight. This means:

$$card(\neg b) = 3 \quad \text{and} \quad card(b) = 5$$

So, the fraction corresponding to the event B with $card(\neg b)/card(b)$ is

$$\frac{card(\neg b)}{card(b)} = \frac{3}{5}$$

We can apply the same procedure to find $card(C|B)$. From the state in Equation 6.114, we can see that event $\neg b$ occurs twice. And when considering the state in Equation 6.115, we can see that event b occurs three times. This means that

$$card(C|\neg b) = 2 \quad \text{and} \quad card(c|b) = 3$$

So, the fraction corresponding to the event $C|B$ with $card(C|\neg b)/card(C|b)$ is

$$\frac{card(C|\neg b)}{card(C|b)} = \frac{2}{3}$$

The fraction of the cardinality $card(\neg b)/card(b)$ has to be equivalent to the fraction $card(C|\neg b)/card(C|b)$,

$$\frac{card(\neg b)}{card(b)} \rightarrow \frac{3}{5} \equiv \frac{2 \cdot \alpha}{3 \cdot \beta} \leftarrow \frac{card(C|\neg b)}{card(C|b)} \tag{6.116}$$

which becomes equivalent for $\alpha = 9$ and $\beta = 10$. We renormalise by multiplying the Equations 6.114, 6.115 by $\alpha = 9$ and $\beta = 10$

$$C|\neg b = \frac{9}{18} \cdot |00\rangle + \frac{9}{18} \cdot |10\rangle \tag{6.117}$$

and

$$C|b = \frac{10}{30} \cdot |01\rangle + \frac{20}{30} \cdot |11\rangle. \tag{6.118}$$

and

$$CB = \frac{9}{48} \cdot |00\rangle + \frac{9}{48} \cdot |10\rangle + \frac{10}{48} \cdot |01\rangle + \frac{20}{48} \cdot |11\rangle. \tag{6.119}$$

Applying this notion of cardinality recursively, one can obtain the state CBA, which results in

$$CBA = \frac{6}{48} \cdot |000\rangle + \frac{3}{48} \cdot |001\rangle + \frac{6}{48} \cdot |100\rangle +$$

$$\frac{3}{48} \cdot |101\rangle + + \frac{4}{48} \cdot |010\rangle + \frac{6}{48} \cdot |011\rangle +$$

$$\frac{8}{48} \cdot |110\rangle + \frac{12}{48} \cdot |111\rangle. \tag{6.120}$$

For all events being true,

$$cba = \frac{12}{48} \cdot |111\rangle \Rightarrow p(a,b,c) = \frac{12}{48} = \frac{3}{4}.$$

Using probability notation

$$p(a,b,c) = \frac{1}{2} \cdot \frac{3}{4} \cdot \frac{2}{3} \cdot = \frac{6}{12} = \frac{3}{4}.$$

In the next step we want to determine the probability of the event a being true, event b is unknown and c is true, namely what is the probability of $p(a|c)$? First we project with c being true and preform the corresponding normalization

$$BA = \frac{6}{29} \cdot |00\rangle + \frac{3}{29} \cdot |01\rangle + \frac{8}{29} \cdot |10\rangle + \frac{12}{29} \cdot |11\rangle.$$

and

$$Ba = \frac{3}{29} \cdot |01\rangle + \frac{12}{29} \cdot |11\rangle \Rightarrow p(a|c) = \frac{15}{29}$$

Using the law of total probability and Bayes's rule with normalisation the computation is

$$p(A|c) = \alpha \sum_b (p(A,b,c) =$$

$$p(A|c) = \alpha \cdot p(A) \cdot \sum_b (p(b|A) \cdot p(c|b))$$

and

$$p(a|c) = \alpha \cdot p(a) \cdot (p(b|a) \cdot p(c|b) +$$

$$p(\neg b|a) \cdot p(c|\neg b))$$

$$p(a|c) = \alpha \cdot \frac{1}{2} \cdot \left(\frac{3}{4} \cdot \frac{2}{3} + \frac{1}{4} \cdot \frac{1}{2}\right) = \alpha \cdot \frac{5}{16}$$

and

$$p(\neg a|c) = \alpha \cdot p(\neg a) \cdot (p(b|\neg a) \cdot p(c|b) +$$

$$p(\neg b|\neg a) \cdot p(c|\neg b))$$

$$p(\neg a|c) = \alpha \cdot \frac{1}{2} \cdot \left(\frac{1}{2} \cdot \frac{2}{3} + \frac{1}{2} \cdot \frac{1}{2}\right) = \alpha \cdot \frac{7}{24}.$$

By normalisation it is

$$1 = p(a|c) + p(\neg a|c) = \alpha \cdot \left(\frac{5}{16} + \frac{7}{24}\right)$$

and

$$p(a|c) = \frac{\frac{5}{16}}{\left(\frac{5}{16} + \frac{7}{24}\right)} = \frac{15}{29}.$$

In the end, the possible worlds approach requires the same number of entries as the full joint distribution (which represents all possible state combinations and grows exponentially large with the number of random variables). However, the computation is faster than the inference of probabilities by Bayesian Networks, since the operations correspond to projection over evidence values and addition over the unknown values.

6.5.7 *Embodiment of representational framework*

The proposed meta-level approach is advantageous compared to more standard approaches because it allows us to embody any representation framework. It separates the knowledge from algebra, which deals with uncertainty. By representing probabilities on a meta-level, we can embody logical sentences with absolutely certain truths. Through this representation, we were able to redefine probabilistic notions such as conditional independence, dependency, and partial dependency. Under the frequentist many worlds approach, conditional independence can be represented as the direct product between two events. Dependency can be represented as the sum of a direct product between events. Finally, partial dependency can be represented as a Kronecker sum between events. With the help of these notions, one can represent more complex probabilistic formalisms, such as Bayes' rule, and extend it to Bayesian networks. Bayesian networks can be represented and interpreted by simple vector operations.

Logic interpretation is valid in one world and not valid in another one. In this interpretation, a *world* can be identified by some time frame (or universe). For example, the statement *all swans are white*, is valid in some time frame. At a later time frame, a black swan is discovered in the wild, and the previous statement is not valid anymore. For all time frames, the statement becomes *most swans are white.*

6.5.8 *From vector based framework to quantum physics*

In the vector-based framework for probabilities, a state represents events in a n-dimensional vector space, which is defined by an orthonormal basis and is represented as a unit-length vector in the norm l_1

$$\frac{\omega_1}{\Omega} \cdot |x_1\rangle + \frac{\omega_2}{\Omega} \cdot |x_2\rangle + \cdots + \frac{\omega_n}{\Omega} \cdot |x_n\rangle = 1$$

and

$$\|\mathbf{mw}\|_1 = \left|\frac{\omega_1}{\Omega}\right| + \left|\frac{\omega_2}{\Omega}\right| + \cdots + \left|\frac{\omega_n}{\Omega}\right| = 1.$$

In quantum physics the unit-length vector is computed in the in the norm l_2 instead of the norm l_1

$$\|\mathbf{x}\|_2 = \sqrt{(|x_1|^2 + |x_2|^2 + \cdots + |x_n|^2)} \tag{6.121}$$

with

$$\|\mathbf{mw}\|_2 = \sqrt{\left|\frac{\omega_1}{\Omega}\right|^2 + \left|\frac{\omega_2}{\Omega}\right|^2 + \cdots + \left|\frac{\omega_n}{\Omega}\right|^2}$$

$$\|\mathbf{mw}\|_2 = \left|\frac{\omega_1}{\Omega}\right|^2 + \left|\frac{\omega_2}{\Omega}\right|^2 + \cdots + \left|\frac{\omega_n}{\Omega}\right|^2 = 1. \tag{6.122}$$

By replacing the l_1 norm by the Euclidean l_2 norm in the classical probability theory (Kolmogorov probabilities), we obtain quantum mechanics [Aaronson (2004)] with all the corresponding laws.

Chapter 7

Introduction to Quantum Physics

7.1 Unitary Evolution

Physical measurements have an intrinsically probabilistic character. Repetitions of an observation using the same experimental apparatus with the same initial conditions will generally yield different measurements of the observed variable. Statistical laws govern the totality of large observations. An object can be described in classical mechanics by a vector $\mathbf{x} = (x_1, x_2, x_3, p_1, p_2, p_3) \in R^6$, which describes its position (x_1, x_2, x_3) and its momentum (p_1, p_2, p_3). The changes in the position and the momentum of the object over time are described by the Hamiltonian equation of motion

$$\frac{d}{dt}x_i = \frac{\partial}{\partial p_i}H, \frac{d}{dt}p_i = \frac{\partial}{\partial x_i}H. \tag{7.1}$$

The state of the object is described by the Hamiltonian function

$$H = H(x_1, x_2, x_3, p_1, p_2, p_3).$$

The wavefunction in quantum mechanics, if unobserved, evolves in a smooth and continuous way according to the Schrödinger equation, which is related to the Hamiltonian equation of motion. This equation describes a linear superposition of different states at time t, which is represented by the vector $\mathbf{x}$(t),

$$i \cdot h \cdot \frac{d}{dt}\mathbf{x}(t) = H \cdot \mathbf{x}(t) \tag{7.2}$$

with $i = \sqrt{-1}$ and h being the Planck's constant. For simplification we set $h = 1$. H is the Hamiltonian operator, which is related to the total energy of the system. A general solution of the Schroedinger equation (for the time-independent Hamiltonian) represents the unitary evolution with

$$\mathbf{x}(t) = e^{-i \cdot t \cdot H} \cdot \mathbf{x}(0) = U_t \cdot \mathbf{x}(0) \tag{7.3}$$

where $U_t = e^{-i \cdot t \cdot H}$ is the evolutionary operator, which can be represented by a unitary matrix. Unitary evolution is deterministic and reversible. The vector $\mathbf{x}(t)$ describes the probability of the presence of certain states. A dimension represents each state, and the value of the vector is related to the probability of the state being present. However, measurements always find the physical system to be in a definite state, which does something to the wavefunction represented by the vector $\mathbf{x}(t)$. This something is not explained by quantum theory.

7.1.1 *Schrödinger's cat paradox*

The best known example of this type kind of this 'something' is the Schrödinger's cat paradox [Schrödinger (1935)]. "When I hear about Schrödinger's cat, I reach for my gun," is a quote from Stephen Hawking. In our description of the paradox we will replace the cat with a rabbit...

A rabbit is apparently evolving into a superposition of two states that can be characterized as an alive rabbit and a dead rabbit. A Geiger counter measures the decay of a radioactive substance. There is a fifty percent chance that, in a given time frame, decay is measured. The Geiger counter is connected to a device that kills the rabbit, if decay is measured. Because the rabbit and the Geiger counter are in a closed room, we do not know whether the rabbit is dead or alive. Each of these possibilities is associated with a specific fifty percent probability. The rabbit is in a superposition state, and the two states are "really" present at the same time. A measurement always finds either an alive rabbit or a dead rabbit with a probability of fifty percent.

7.1.2 *Interpretations of quantum mechanics*

As long as we make no measurements, there are no random effects. The behavior of the system is strictly deterministic. The randomness is only present during the measurement. Randomness is an effect of measurement. Different interpretations of quantum mechanics propose different solutions of the measurement problem. We present the two most influential explanations:

- The most popular interpretation, the Copenhagen interpretation, claims that quantum mechanics is a mathematical tool that is used in the calculation of probabilities and has no physical existence; all other questions are metaphysical. This popular unscientific interpretation delayed for many years the development of quantum computation [Heisenberg (1949)].

- The many-worlds theory led to the development of the first quantum algorithms; this approach is less popular due to some philosophical difficulties. The many-worlds theory views reality as a many-branched tree in which every possible quantum outcome is realized [Everett (1959)], [Byrne (2007)]. The subjective appearance of the wave function collapse is explained by the mechanism of quantum decoherence. Every possible outcome to every event exists in its own world. In one world, randomness exists, but not in the universe (multiverse) that describes all possible worlds [Deutsch (1997)].

7.2 Quantum Mechanics

A bit can be represented by the state of a simple 2-state quantum system such as the spin state of a particle. When measured, the spin is always in one of two possible states: spin-up or spin-down. A quantum mechanical description of a physical system is related to a probabilistic representation; it is described by a vector in Hilbert space. This description extends the two- or three-dimensional Euclidean space into spaces that have any finite or infinite number of dimensions. In such a space, the Euclidean norm is induced by the inner product

$$\|\mathbf{x}\| = \sqrt{\langle \mathbf{x}|\mathbf{x}\rangle}. \tag{7.4}$$

A basis of n dimensional Hilbert space H_n is chosen. A 2-state system is described by a two dimensional Hilbert space H_2. For the basis

$$\mathbf{e}_1 = \begin{pmatrix} 1 \\ 0 \end{pmatrix}, \mathbf{e}_2 = \begin{pmatrix} 0 \\ 1 \end{pmatrix} \tag{7.5}$$

the system is described by a vector $\mathbf{x}$ with complex numbers ω_1, ω_2 that represent the amplitude of each dimension

$$\mathbf{x} = \omega_1 \cdot \mathbf{e}_1 + \omega_2 \cdot \mathbf{e}_2 = \begin{pmatrix} \omega_1 \\ \omega_2 \end{pmatrix}. \tag{7.6}$$

The probabilities are real numbers between 0 and 1. The probability that the system is in e_1 and e_2 is $|\omega_1|^2$ and $|\omega_2|^2$. This is because the product of complex number with is conjugate is always a real number

$$\omega^* \cdot \omega = (x - y \cdot i) \cdot (x + y \cdot i) = x^2 + y^2 = |\omega|^2. \tag{7.7}$$

The vector representing a state is normalized. Its length is one. The amplitudes correspond to the probability with

$$|\omega_1|^2 + |\omega_2|^2 = 1.$$

Paul Dirac introduced the following notation for a vector $\mathbf{x}$ describing a state

$$|x\rangle = \omega_1 \cdot |e_1\rangle + \omega_2 \cdot |e_2\rangle = \omega_1 \cdot |x_1\rangle + \omega_2 \cdot |x_2\rangle = \begin{pmatrix} \omega_1 \\ \omega_2 \end{pmatrix} \tag{7.8}$$

with

$$|e_1\rangle = |x_1\rangle, |e_2\rangle = |x_2\rangle.$$

It is a shorthand notation for a column vector. Related to the scalar product $\langle x|x\rangle$ row vector are $\langle x|$ "bra" and and column vectors are $|x\rangle$ "kets" from bra(c)kets. A state vector is just a particular instance of a ket vector. It is specified by a particular choice of basis and refers to observable that can have some system properties.

Operators represented by a square matrix give mathematical description how something changes in the quantum world. For a 2-state quantum system an operator that acts on the memory register would be represented by a 2×2 dimensional unitary matrix. In Unitary matrices, its conjugate transpose is equal to its inverse.

$$U^* = U^{-1}. \tag{7.9}$$

7.2.1 *Stochastic Markov evolution and unitary evolution*

To indicate the difference to a Markov chain we introduce the example of a quantum coin, a system with two basis states 0 and 1 with

$$|0\rangle = \begin{pmatrix} 1 \\ 0 \end{pmatrix}, |1\rangle = \begin{pmatrix} 0 \\ 1 \end{pmatrix}. \tag{7.10}$$

The mapping is represented as

$$|0\rangle \to \frac{1}{\sqrt{2}} \cdot |0\rangle + \frac{1}{\sqrt{2}} \cdot |1\rangle \tag{7.11}$$

and

$$|1\rangle \to \frac{1}{\sqrt{2}} \cdot |0\rangle - \frac{1}{\sqrt{2}} \cdot |1\rangle. \tag{7.12}$$

The corresponding operator is indicated by the following unitary matrix,

$$W = \begin{pmatrix} \frac{1}{\sqrt{2}} & \frac{1}{\sqrt{2}} \\ \frac{1}{\sqrt{2}} & -\frac{1}{\sqrt{2}} \end{pmatrix} = \frac{1}{\sqrt{2}} \cdot \begin{pmatrix} 1 & 1 \\ 1 & -1 \end{pmatrix}. \tag{7.13}$$

If the system starts in state $|0\rangle$ and undergoes the time evolution, the probability of observing 0 or 1 is $\left|\frac{1}{\sqrt{2}}\right|^2 = \frac{1}{2}$. If we do not preform a measurement and repeat the mapping, the probability of observing 0 becomes 1 and observing 1 becomes zero. This is due to the fact, that the amplitudes of $|1\rangle$ cancel each other. This effect is called destructive interference and cannot occur in the probability distribution since all its coefficients are non-negative real numbers.

Stochastic Markov evolution The behavior of a fair coin can be modeled by a Markov chain described by a stochastic matrix. The behavior of the system is independent from initial distribution $\mathbf{p}$. The information about the initial state is lost. The fixed distribution is reached after one step.

$$\begin{pmatrix} \frac{1}{2} \\ \frac{1}{2} \end{pmatrix} = \begin{pmatrix} \frac{p_1+p_2}{2} \\ \frac{p_1+p_2}{2} \end{pmatrix} = \begin{pmatrix} \frac{1}{2} & \frac{1}{2} \\ \frac{1}{2} & \frac{1}{2} \end{pmatrix} \cdot \begin{pmatrix} p_1 \\ p_2 \end{pmatrix}. \tag{7.14}$$

If constantly observed the quantum coin has the same behavior as a fair coin described by a stochastic matrix. The probability of being in one of the states is 0.5. Each time the coin is tossed the "random" effect is observed.

Unitary evolution During unitary evolution of a (not observed) quantum coin the information about the initial state is not lost, the system is reversible and deterministic. Each of the two state is present. The loss of information about its history occurs during the measurement.

In the next section we demonstrate the relation between the unitary matrices and evolutionary operator $U_t = e^{-i \cdot t \cdot H}$.

7.3 Hilbert Space

A norm describes the length of the vector, it is a function given a vector space V that maps a vector into a real number with

$$\|\mathbf{x}\| \geq 0, \quad and \quad \|\mathbf{x}\| = 0 \quad for \quad \mathbf{x} = 0 \quad only,$$

with α scalar

$$\|\alpha \cdot \mathbf{x}\| = |\alpha| \cdot \|\mathbf{x}\|,$$

$$\|\mathbf{x} + \mathbf{y}\| \leq \|\mathbf{x}\| + \|\mathbf{y}\|.$$

The l_p norm is defined as the following (for $p = 2$ it is the Euclidean norm):

$$\|\mathbf{x}\|_p = (|x_1|^p + |x_2|^p + \cdots + |x_n|^p)^{\frac{1}{p}} \tag{7.15}$$

For $p = 2$ it is the Euclidean norm. Only in a Hilbert space a scalar product induces the norm l_2

$$\|\mathbf{x}\| = \sqrt{\langle \mathbf{x}|\mathbf{x}\rangle}$$

A scalar product exists in l_2 but not in l_1 space or any other l_p space. The inner product is defined as by the inner product (scalar product)

$$\langle x|y\rangle = \langle y|x\rangle^*$$

$$\langle x|x\rangle \geq 0, \langle x|x\rangle = 0 \Leftrightarrow x = 0$$

$$\langle x|c_1 \cdot y + c_2 \cdot z\rangle = c_1 \cdot \langle x|y\rangle + c_2 \cdot \langle x|z\rangle$$

with

$$x, y, z \in H_n, c_1, c_2 \in C.$$

Amplitude distribution corresponds to a unit-length vector of a finite dimensional Hilbert space over complex numbers of dimension n denoted as H_n. With a fixed basis we will use the the coordinate representation that will induce the inner product by

$$\langle x|y\rangle = x_1^* \cdot y_1 + x_2^* \cdot y_2 + \cdots + x_n^* \cdot y_n$$

and the Euclidean vector norm. It is a vector space with and Euclidean norm. It is known that if quantum mechanics is altered by replacing the $_2$ norm with another l_p norm, then there does not exist any non-trivial linear norm-preserving maps [Aaronson (2004)]. Only in Hilbert space a general unitary operator is defined

$$U^* \cdot U = U \cdot U^* = I$$

with I being the identity matrix

$$I = \begin{pmatrix} 1 & 0 & 0 & \cdots & 0 \\ 0 & 1 & 0 & \cdots & 0 \\ \vdots & \vdots & & \ddots & \vdots \\ 0 & 0 & 0 & \cdots & 1 \end{pmatrix}. \tag{7.16}$$

If W is a subspace of a V, then the orthogonal complement of W is also a subspace of V. The orthogonal complement $W^\perp$ is the set of vectors

$$W^\perp = \{\mathbf{y} \in V | \langle \mathbf{y}|\mathbf{x}\rangle = 0 \;\; \mathbf{x} \in V\} \tag{7.17}$$

and ach vector $\mathbf{x} \in V$ can be represented as $\mathbf{x} = \mathbf{x}_W + \mathbf{x}_{W^\perp}$ with $\mathbf{x}_W \in W$ and $\mathbf{x}_{W^\perp} \in W^\perp$. The mapping $P \cdot \mathbf{x} = \mathbf{x}_W$ is an orthogonal projection. Such projection is always a linear transformation and can be represented by a projection matrix P. The matrix is self-adjoint $P = P^*$ with $P = P^2$. An orthogonal projection can never increase a norm

$$\|P \cdot \mathbf{x}\|^2 = \|\mathbf{x}_W\|^2 \leq \|\mathbf{x}_W\|^2 + \|\mathbf{x}_{W^\perp}\|^2 = \|\mathbf{x}_W + \mathbf{x}_{W^\perp}\|^2 = \|\mathbf{x}\|^2. \quad (7.18)$$

P can be generated by the normalized vector $|x\rangle$ indicating the direction of the bisecting line

$$|x\rangle = \frac{1}{\sqrt{n}} \cdot |x_1\rangle + \frac{1}{\sqrt{n}} \cdot |x_2\rangle + \cdots + \frac{1}{\sqrt{n}} \cdot |x_n\rangle = \begin{pmatrix} \frac{1}{\sqrt{n}} \\ \vdots \\ \frac{1}{\sqrt{n}} \end{pmatrix} \quad (7.19)$$

and the row representation

$$\langle x| = \left(\frac{1}{\sqrt{n}}, \frac{1}{\sqrt{n}}, \cdots, \frac{1}{\sqrt{n}} \right). \quad (7.20)$$

The projection matrix is

$$P = |x\rangle\langle x| = \begin{pmatrix} \frac{1}{n} & \frac{1}{n} & \cdots & \frac{1}{n} \\ \frac{1}{n} & \frac{1}{n} & \cdots & \frac{1}{n} \\ \vdots & \vdots & \ddots & \vdots \\ \frac{1}{n} & \frac{1}{n} & \cdots & \frac{1}{n} \end{pmatrix}. \quad (7.21)$$

The projection P computes for each dimension described by the fixed basis, for example $|x_i\rangle = |e_i\rangle$, the mean value of all dimensions. An example of such a projection in the two dimensional Hilbert space is the stochastic matrix describing the behavior of a fair coin.

7.3.1 *Spectral representation**

A linear mapping $H_n \to H_n$ is called an operator. An operator A is self-adjoint if

$$\langle x|A \cdot y\rangle = \langle A^* \cdot x|y\rangle. \quad (7.22)$$

which can be as well written as

$$\langle x|A|y\rangle = \langle A^*|x\rangle|y\rangle.$$

For a fixed basis a matrix can represent an operator. A self-adjoint operator is represented by a Hermitian matrix $A^* = A$ with $a_{ij} = \overline{a_{ji}}$. For real values the Hermitian matrix is a symmetrical matrix with $A^T = A$.

Hermitian matrices have real eigenvalues and corresponding eigenvectors are orthogonal. From the definition of eigenvalues and eigenvectors

$$A \cdot |x\rangle = \lambda \cdot |x\rangle \tag{7.23}$$

consequently

$$\lambda^* \cdot \langle x|x\rangle = \langle \lambda \cdot x|x\rangle = \langle A \cdot x|x\rangle = \langle x|A \cdot x\rangle = \lambda \cdot \langle x|x\rangle.$$

The eigenvectors of different eigenvalues $\lambda_1 \neq \lambda_2$ are orthogonal,

$$\lambda_1 \cdot \langle x_1|x_2\rangle = \langle A \cdot x_1|x_2\rangle = \langle x_1|A \cdot x_2\rangle = \lambda_2 \cdot \langle x_1|x_2\rangle$$

hence the two different eigenvectors are orthogonal

$$\lambda_1 \cdot \langle x_1|x_2\rangle = \lambda_2 \cdot \langle x_1|x_2\rangle \Rightarrow \langle x_1|x_2\rangle = 0.$$

A Hermitian matrix can be represented by a sum of projections of its orthonormal eigenvectors (normalized eigenvectors) $x_1, \cdots, x_n$ weighted by its eigenvalues. The projections are defined by the matrix $|x_i\rangle\langle x_i|$ with $|x_i\rangle\langle x_i| = (|x_i\rangle\langle x_i|)^2$. The set of the eigenvalues is called the spectrum and the corresponding representation a spectral representation

$$A = \lambda_1 \cdot |x_1\rangle\langle x_1| + \lambda_2 \cdot |x_2\rangle\langle x_2| + \cdots + \lambda_n \cdot |x_n\rangle\langle x_n|. \tag{7.24}$$

The function $e^{i \cdot A}$ with a self-adjoint operator A is unitary

$$e^{i \cdot A} = e^{i \cdot \lambda_1} \cdot |x_1\rangle\langle x_1| + e^{i \cdot \lambda_2} \cdot |x_2\rangle\langle x_2| + \cdots + e^{i \cdot \lambda_n} \cdot |x_n\rangle\langle x_n|. \tag{7.25}$$

An operator U is unitary, if $U^* = U^{-1}$,

$$\left(e^{i \cdot A}\right)^* = \left(e^{i \cdot A}\right)^{-1}, \tag{7.26}$$

$$\left(e^{i \cdot A}\right)^{-1} = e^{-i \cdot \lambda_1} \cdot |x_1\rangle\langle x_1| + e^{-i \cdot \lambda_2} \cdot |x_2\rangle\langle x_2| + \cdots + e^{-i \cdot \lambda_n} \cdot |x_n\rangle\langle x_n|. \tag{7.27}$$

This representation is similar to the evolutionary operator $U_t = e^{-i \cdot t \cdot H}$ for $t = 1$ and $A = H$ is the Hamiltonian operator that is related to the total energy of the system. Mathematical description in a quantum world is given by operators represented by a unitary square matrix. For example the unitary matrix that describes the quantum coin is

$$W = \frac{1}{\sqrt{2}} \cdot \begin{pmatrix} 1 & 1 \\ 1 & -1 \end{pmatrix}. \tag{7.28}$$

What is the relation between a unitary matrix and the evolutionary operator? For simplicity we omit the minus sign and write instead of U^* simply

$$W = U = e^{i \cdot H}.$$

What is the corresponding Hamiltonian operator? A unitary operator U is not self-adjoint, the Matrix is unitary but not Hermitian. However it can be decomposed into two self-adjoint operators. As shown before each self-adjoint operators has a spectral representation

$$U = \frac{1}{2} \cdot (R + i \cdot I) \tag{7.29}$$

with

$$R = \frac{1}{2} \cdot (U + U^*), \quad I = \frac{1}{i \cdot 2} \cdot (U + U^*).$$

R and I are Hermitian matrices and their spectral representation is

$$R = \lambda_1 \cdot |x_1\rangle\langle x_1| + \lambda_2 \cdot |x_2\rangle\langle x_2| + \cdots + \lambda_n \cdot |x_n\rangle\langle x_n|$$

and

$$I = \mu_1 \cdot |x_1\rangle\langle x_1| + \mu_2 \cdot |x_2\rangle\langle x_2| + \cdots + \mu_n \cdot |x_n\rangle\langle x_n|.$$

U can be written as

$$U = (\lambda_1 + i \cdot \mu_1) \cdot |x_1\rangle\langle x_1| + \cdots + (\lambda_n + i \cdot \mu_n) \cdot |x_n\rangle\langle x_n|. \tag{7.30}$$

How can we represent U as $U = e^{i \cdot H}$?
For all eigenvalues of U

$$\langle x|x\rangle = \langle x|U \cdot U^* x\rangle = \langle U \cdot x|U \cdot x\rangle = \langle \lambda \cdot x|\lambda \cdot x = |\lambda|^2 \cdot \langle x|x\rangle$$

the absolute value is 1

$$1 = |\lambda_i + \mu_i|$$

all values of λ_i and μ_i are real values from the interval $[-1, 1]$. Therefore there exist a value θ_i for each i with

$$\lambda_i = \cos\theta_i, \quad \mu_i = \sin\theta_i, \tag{7.31}$$

and because $e^{i \cdot x} = \cos x + i \cdot \sin x$

$$\lambda_i + i \cdot \mu_i = \cos\theta_i + i \cdot \sin\theta_i, \tag{7.32}$$

$$\mu_i = e^{i \cdot \theta_i}. \tag{7.33}$$

We can now represent any unitary operator U by the spectral representation

$$U = e^{i \cdot H} = e^{i \cdot \theta_1} \cdot |x_1\rangle\langle x_1| + e^{i \cdot \theta_2} \cdot |x_2\rangle\langle x_2| + \cdots + e^{i \cdot \theta_n} \cdot |x_n\rangle\langle x_n|. \tag{7.34}$$

with the corresponding Hamilton operator H

$$H = \theta_1 \cdot |x_1\rangle\langle x_1| + \theta_1 \cdot |x_2\rangle\langle x_2| + \cdots \theta_n \cdot |x_n\rangle\langle x_n|. \tag{7.35}$$

Example The unitary matrix that describes the quantum coin

$$W = \frac{1}{\sqrt{2}} \cdot \begin{pmatrix} 1 & 1 \\ 1 & -1 \end{pmatrix}$$

is as well Hermitian with $W^T = W$. Because of this the two eigenvalues are real, -1 and 1 . The corresponding eigenvectors are

$$|x_1\rangle = \frac{1}{\sqrt{4 - 2 \cdot \sqrt{2}}} \cdot \begin{pmatrix} 1 - \sqrt{2} \\ 1 \end{pmatrix}$$

and

$$|x_2\rangle = \frac{1}{\sqrt{4 + 2 \cdot \sqrt{2}}} \cdot \begin{pmatrix} 1 + \sqrt{2} \\ 1 \end{pmatrix}.$$

The Hermitian matrix W can be represented by the spectral representation

$$W = 1 \cdot |x_1\rangle\langle x_1| - 1 \cdot |x_2\rangle\langle x_2| \tag{7.36}$$

with

$$|x_1\rangle\langle x_1| = \begin{pmatrix} \frac{1-\sqrt{2}}{4} & \frac{-\sqrt{2}}{4} \\ \frac{-\sqrt{2}}{4} & \frac{1+\sqrt{2}}{4} \end{pmatrix}$$

and

$$|x_2\rangle\langle x_2| = \begin{pmatrix} \frac{1+\sqrt{2}}{4} & \frac{\sqrt{2}}{4} \\ \frac{\sqrt{2}}{4} & \frac{1-\sqrt{2}}{4} \end{pmatrix}.$$

We can now represent unitary operator W as (evolutionary operator) since

$$1 = e^{i \cdot 0}, \quad -1 = e^{i \cdot \pi}$$

$$U = e^{i \cdot H} = e^{i \cdot 0} \cdot |x_1\rangle\langle x_1| + e^{i \cdot \pi} \cdot |x_2\rangle\langle x_2| = |x_1\rangle\langle x_1| + e^{i \cdot \pi} \cdot |x_2\rangle\langle x_2| \tag{7.37}$$

with the corresponding Hamilton operator H

$$H = 0 \cdot |x_1\rangle\langle x_1| + \pi \cdot |x_2\rangle\langle x_2|. \tag{7.38}$$

A unitary matrix can be represented by the evolutionary operator with the Hamilton operator H.

7.4 Quantum Time Evolution

Quantum time Evolution is described by Schrödinger equation, its solution represents the unitary evolution described by the unitary operator U_t. The unitary operator is determined by the requirements for the time-evolution mapping

$$\mathbf{x}(t) = U_t \cdot \mathbf{x}(0).$$

Suppose U_t is a time-evolution mapping, then the following requirements should be fulfilled [Hirvensalo (2004)]

- U_t should preserve the norm,

  $$\|U_t \cdot \langle x|\| = \|\langle x|\|.$$

  The length of a vector is always one, before and after the mapping. It determines the probability of the presence of certain states represented by its dimensions. The vector itself describes the probability distribution.
- The mapping U_t is linear

  $$U_t \cdot (\lambda_1 \cdot |x_1\rangle + \cdots + \lambda_n \cdot |x_n\rangle) = U_t \cdot \lambda_1 \cdot |x_1\rangle + \cdots + U_t \cdot \lambda_n \cdot |x_n\rangle.$$

  For the basis

  $$|e_1\rangle = |x_1\rangle, |e_2\rangle = |x_2\rangle, \cdots, |e_n\rangle = |x_n\rangle$$

  the linearity corresponds to simple matrix operation

  $$U \cdot \begin{pmatrix} \lambda_1 \\ \lambda_2 \\ \vdots \\ \lambda_n \end{pmatrix} = U \cdot \begin{pmatrix} \lambda_1 \\ 0 \\ \vdots \\ 0 \end{pmatrix} + U \cdot \begin{pmatrix} 0 \\ \lambda_2 \\ \vdots \\ 0 \end{pmatrix} + \cdots + U \cdot \begin{pmatrix} 0 \\ 0 \\ \vdots \\ \lambda_n \end{pmatrix}.$$

- For all t_1 and t_2

  $$U_{t_2+t_1} = U_{t_2} U_{t_1}.$$

- The time evolution must be smooth. Even if we are interested in the state of the system a discrete time points, the evolution should be smooth and continuous

  $$\lim_{t \to t_0} U_t \cdot \mathbf{x}(0) = \lim_{t \to t_0} \mathbf{x}(t) = \mathbf{x}(t_0).$$

Only a unitary operator can satisfy the first three requirements. It can be represented by a unitary matrix and by the evolutionary operator with the Hamilton self-adjoint operator H. If U_t satisfies all four requirements, there exists self-adjoint operator H with a relation to time t

$$U_t = e^{-i \cdot t \cdot H}$$

and

$$\mathbf{x}(t) = e^{-i \cdot t \cdot H} \cdot \mathbf{x}(0) = U_t \cdot \mathbf{x}(0).$$

The time evolution is continuous and reversible, however we will represent an algorithm as a sequence of one-length vectors in discrete time steps

$$t_0 \to t_1 \to t_2 \to t_3 \to \cdots$$

as

$$|x\rangle \to U_1 \cdot |x\rangle \to U_2 \cdot U_1 \cdot |x\rangle \to U_3 \cdot U_2 \cdot U_1 \cdot |x\rangle \to \cdots$$

This representation is motivated by the first and second requirement.

7.5 Compound Systems

A 2-state quantum system is described by a two dimensional Hilbert space H_2,

$$|x_1\rangle = \begin{pmatrix} 1 \\ 0 \end{pmatrix}, |x_2\rangle = \begin{pmatrix} 0 \\ 1 \end{pmatrix} \tag{7.39}$$

is described by a vector $|x\rangle$ with complex numbers ω_1, ω_2 that represent the amplitude of each dimension.

$$|x\rangle = \omega_1 \cdot |x_1\rangle + \omega_2 \cdot |x_2\rangle = \begin{pmatrix} \omega_1 \\ \omega_2 \end{pmatrix}. \tag{7.40}$$

Such a 2-state quantum system corresponds to a qubit with the basis

$$|0\rangle = |x_1\rangle, \quad |1\rangle = |x_2\rangle.$$

The qubit is described by a vector $|x\rangle$ with complex numbers ω_1, ω_2 that represent the amplitude of each dimension

$$|x\rangle = \omega_0 \cdot |0\rangle + \omega_1 \cdot |1\rangle. \tag{7.41}$$

The vector has length one with

$$|\omega_0|^2 + |\omega_1|^2 = 1 \to \||x\rangle\| = 1.$$

The unitary matrix W performs the following mapping in the ket notation

$$W \cdot |0\rangle = W \cdot 1 \cdot |0\rangle + W \cdot 0 \cdot |1\rangle = \frac{1}{\sqrt{2}} \cdot |0\rangle + \frac{1}{\sqrt{2}} \cdot |1\rangle$$

with the vector notation

$$\frac{1}{\sqrt{2}} \cdot \begin{pmatrix} 1 & 1 \\ 1 & -1 \end{pmatrix} \cdot \begin{pmatrix} 1 \\ 0 \end{pmatrix} = \begin{pmatrix} \frac{1}{\sqrt{2}} \\ \frac{1}{\sqrt{2}} \end{pmatrix}.$$

Applying W again results in

$$W \cdot \left(\frac{1}{\sqrt{2}} \cdot |0\rangle + \frac{1}{\sqrt{2}} \cdot |1\rangle \right) = W \cdot \frac{1}{\sqrt{2}} \cdot |0\rangle + W \cdot \frac{1}{\sqrt{2}} \cdot |1\rangle = |0\rangle$$

with the vector notation

$$\frac{1}{\sqrt{2}} \cdot \begin{pmatrix} 1 & 1 \\ 1 & -1 \end{pmatrix} \cdot \begin{pmatrix} \frac{1}{\sqrt{2}} \\ \frac{1}{\sqrt{2}} \end{pmatrix} = \begin{pmatrix} 1 \\ 0 \end{pmatrix}.$$

How can we represent a register composed of two qubits? Such a register would represent 2^2 possible states and would be represented in a Hilbert space H_4. The first qubit is represented by a two dimensional Hilbert space H_2,

$$|x\rangle = \omega_0 \cdot |0\rangle + \omega_1 \cdot |1\rangle = \begin{pmatrix} \omega_0 \\ \omega_1 \end{pmatrix}$$

and the second as

$$|y\rangle = \omega_0 \cdot |0\rangle + \omega_1 \cdot |1\rangle = \begin{pmatrix} \omega_0 \\ \omega_1 \end{pmatrix}.$$

The register of two qubits is represented as a direct product of $|x\rangle$ and $|y\rangle$

$$|x\rangle \otimes |y\rangle = |x\rangle|y\rangle = |xy\rangle = \begin{pmatrix} \omega_0 \\ \omega_1 \end{pmatrix} \otimes \begin{pmatrix} \omega_0 \\ \omega_1 \end{pmatrix} = \begin{pmatrix} \omega_0 \cdot \omega_0 \\ \omega_0 \cdot \omega_1 \\ \omega_1 \cdot \omega_0 \\ \omega_1 \cdot \omega_1 \end{pmatrix} = \begin{pmatrix} \omega_0 \\ \omega_1 \\ \omega_2 \\ \omega_3 \end{pmatrix} \tag{7.42}$$

or

$$|xy\rangle = (\omega_0 \cdot |0\rangle + \omega_1 \cdot |1\rangle) \otimes (\omega_0 \cdot |0\rangle + \omega_1 \cdot |1\rangle)$$

$$|xy\rangle = \omega_0 \cdot |00\rangle + \omega_1 \cdot |01\rangle + \omega_2 \cdot |10\rangle + \omega_3 \cdot |11\rangle \tag{7.43}$$

with the new basis

$$|00\rangle = \begin{pmatrix} 1 \\ 0 \\ 0 \\ 0 \end{pmatrix}, |01\rangle = \begin{pmatrix} 0 \\ 1 \\ 0 \\ 0 \end{pmatrix}, |10\rangle = \begin{pmatrix} 0 \\ 0 \\ 1 \\ 0 \end{pmatrix}, |11\rangle = \begin{pmatrix} 0 \\ 0 \\ 0 \\ 1 \end{pmatrix}. \tag{7.44}$$

A register of three qubits represents 2^3 different states represented in a Hilbert space H_8.

$$|xyz\rangle = |x\rangle \otimes |y\rangle \otimes |z\rangle =$$

$$\omega_0 \cdot |00\rangle + \omega_1 \cdot |001\rangle + \omega_2 \cdot |010\rangle + \omega_3 \cdot |011\rangle +$$

$$+\omega_4 \cdot |100\rangle + \omega_5 \cdot |001\rangle + \omega_6 \cdot |110\rangle + \omega_7 \cdot |111\rangle. \tag{7.45}$$

A quantum register of length m represents m qubits in a Hilbert space of dimension $n = 2^m$. A state in a n-dimensional Hilbert space H_n is defined by an orthonormal basis

$$|x_1\rangle, |x_1\rangle, \cdots |x_n\rangle$$

and is represented as a unit-lengt vector

$$\omega_1 \cdot |x_1\rangle + \omega_2 \cdot |x_2\rangle + \cdots + \omega_n \cdot |x_n\rangle$$

that determines the probability of distribution of the states. Each dimension correspond to a possible combination. The state is in a basis state $|x_i\rangle$ with a probability $|\omega_i|^2$.

The compund system of the Hilbert space H_n and a w-dimensional Hilbert space H_w defined by a orthonormal basis $|y_1\rangle, |y_1\rangle. \cdots |y_w\rangle$ is defined by the tensor product

$$H_{n \cdot w} = H_n \otimes H_w \tag{7.46}$$

According to this definition we can apply an operator on two qubits as

$$W \cdot (\omega_0 \cdot |0\rangle + \omega_1 \cdot |1\rangle) \otimes W \cdot (\omega_0 \cdot |0\rangle + \omega_1 \cdot |1\rangle) =$$

$$\left(W \cdot \begin{pmatrix} \omega_0 \\ \omega_1 \end{pmatrix}\right) \otimes \left(W \cdot \begin{pmatrix} \omega_0 \\ \omega_1 \end{pmatrix}\right) \tag{7.47}$$

$$(W \otimes W) \cdot (\omega_0 \cdot |0\rangle + \omega_1 \cdot |1\rangle) \otimes (\omega_0 \cdot |0\rangle + \omega_1 \cdot |1\rangle) = (W \otimes W) \cdot \begin{pmatrix} \omega_0 \\ \omega_1 \\ \omega_2 \\ \omega_3 \end{pmatrix} \tag{7.48}$$

it follows

$$\left(W \cdot \begin{pmatrix} \omega_0 \\ \omega_1 \end{pmatrix}\right) \otimes \left(W \cdot \begin{pmatrix} \omega_0 \\ \omega_1 \end{pmatrix}\right) = (W \otimes W) \cdot \begin{pmatrix} \omega_0 \\ \omega_1 \\ \omega_2 \\ \omega_3 \end{pmatrix}. \tag{7.49}$$

The tensor product between matrix is defined as

$$A \otimes B = \begin{pmatrix} a_{11} \cdot B & a_{12} \cdot B \\ a_{21} \cdot B & a_{22} \cdot B \end{pmatrix} = \begin{pmatrix} a_{11} \cdot b_{11} & a_{11} \cdot b_{12} & a_{12} \cdot b_{11} & a_{12} \cdot b_{12} \\ a_{11} \cdot b_{21} & a_{11} \cdot b_{22} & a_{12} \cdot b_{21} & a_{12} \cdot b_{22} \\ a_{21} \cdot b_{11} & a_{21} \cdot b_{12} & a_{22} \cdot b_{11} & a_{22} \cdot b_{12} \\ a_{21} \cdot b_{21} & a_{21} \cdot b_{22} & a_{22} \cdot b_{21} & a_{22} \cdot b_{22} \end{pmatrix}.$$

For example $W \otimes W$ is

$$W \otimes W = \frac{1}{\sqrt{2}} \cdot \begin{pmatrix} 1 & 1 \\ 1 & -1 \end{pmatrix} \otimes \frac{1}{\sqrt{2}} \cdot \begin{pmatrix} 1 & 1 \\ 1 & -1 \end{pmatrix} = \frac{1}{2} \cdot \begin{pmatrix} 1 & 1 & 1 & 1 \\ 1 & -1 & 1 & -1 \\ 1 & 1 & -1 & -1 \\ 1 & -1 & -1 & 1 \end{pmatrix}.$$

7.6 Density Matrix

A state $|x\rangle$ ($\|x\| = 1$) in a Hilbert space H_n can be represented by the corresponding density matrix $P = |x\rangle\langle x|$ with,

$$|x\rangle\langle x| = \begin{pmatrix} x_1 \\ x_2 \\ \vdots \\ x_n \end{pmatrix} \cdot (x_1^*, x_2^*, \cdots, x_n^*) = \begin{pmatrix} |x_1|^2 & x_1 \cdot x_2^* & \cdots & x_1 \cdot x_n^* \\ x_2 \cdot x_1^* & |x_2|^2 & \cdots & x_2 \cdot x_n^* \\ \vdots & \vdots & \ddots & \vdots \\ x_n \cdot x_1^* & x_1 \cdot x_n^* & \cdots & |x_n|^2 \end{pmatrix} \tag{7.50}$$

A density matrix P has following properties

- P is a Hermitian matrix with $P^* = P$.
- P represents a self-adjoint operator P.
- P has a spectral representation.
- P is a projection with $P = P^2$, because $|x\rangle\langle x| = ||x\rangle\langle x||^2$.
- P is a linear combination of one-dimensional projections.
- The trace of P, $Tr(P) = 1$ with $Tr(P) = \sum_{i=1}^{n} |x_i|^2$.

7.7 Mixed states

Quantum states that can be represented by a vector in a Hilbert space are called pure states or a regular state. For a pure state, the $|x\rangle$ state is known exactly. A pure state can be a basis sate (eigenstate), or it can be in a superposition. When our knowledge of a system is incomplete, we say that the system is in an impure state, i.e., it is a probabilistic mixture of different pure states in the ensemble. It cannot be represented by a vector.

The probabilistic mixture of pure states is described by the density matrix P. A pure state can be also recast as a density matrix P; thus, pure states can be represented as a subset of the more general mixed states. For a pure state P

$$Tr(P^2) = 1$$

and for a mixed state P

$$Tr(P^2) < 1.$$

The von Neumann entropy $S(P)$ quantifies the departure of the system from a pure state. It codifies the degree of mixing of the state describing a given finite system. For the density matrix P, the Von Neumann entropy is defined as

$$S(P) = -Tr(P \cdot \log P), \tag{7.51}$$

with a logarithm of matrix $Q = \log P$, where Q is a matrix with $P = e^Q$. With the spectral decomposition of the self-adjoint operator P, the von Neumann entropy can be easily computed without using the logarithm of the matrix,

$$P = \lambda_1 \cdot |x_1\rangle\langle x_1| + \lambda_2 \cdot |x_2\rangle\langle x_2| + \cdots + \lambda_n \cdot |x_n\rangle\langle x_n|$$

with

$$S(P) = -\sum_{i=1}^{n}(\lambda_i \cdot \log \lambda_i) \tag{7.52}$$

and

$$1 = \sum_{i=1}^{n} \lambda_i.$$

In quantum computing, mixed states (opposite to quantum information) do not play any role. All states are pure in superposition, or they correspond to a basis state.

7.8 Shannon entropy

The representation of a pure state $|x\rangle$ by a vector of complex amplitudes depends on the orthonormal basis. For the orthonormal basis $|x_1\rangle = \mathbf{e}_1, |x_2\rangle = \mathbf{e}_2, \cdots, |x_n\rangle = \mathbf{e}_n$

$$|x\rangle = \omega_1 \cdot |x_1\rangle| + \omega_2 \cdot |x_2\rangle + \cdots + \omega_n \cdot |x_n\rangle$$

In other words, it codifies the degree of superposition of the state describing a given finite system we can assume that

$$H = -\sum_{i=1}^{n} |\omega_i|^2 \cdot \log_2 |\omega_i|^2. \tag{7.53}$$

States equal to a basis are called basis states or eigenstates . A basis state corresponds to a one-dimensional projection with one $|\omega| = 1$. Otherwise the states are in superposition. The Shannon entropy of a basis state is zero, $0 = 1 \cdot \log 1$. The Shannon entropy of a superposition measures the distribution of the probabilities represented by the probabilities $|\omega_i|^2$. It describes the departure of the state from a basis state with a maximal value when all $|\omega_i|^2$ are equal.

$$H = -\sum_{i=1}^{n} \frac{1}{n} \cdot \log_2 \frac{1}{n} = \log_2 n \tag{7.54}$$

We represent a state by a sequence of m qubits by a $n = 2^m$ dimensional vector in H_n Hilbert space. In this case the maximal value of the Shannon entropy is

$$H = \log_2 n = \log_2 2^m = m. \tag{7.55}$$

Before the measurement of a state $|x\rangle$ we are uncertain about the outcome. We measure the uncertainty by the entropy. After the measure the state is basis, the Shannon entropy is zero, $0 = 1 \cdot \log 1$. The measurement is a random process described by distributions of probabilities represented by $|\omega_i|^2$.

7.9 Measurement

After a unitary information processing starting form an initial basis state the result of the algorithm is determined by the measurement. The measurement corresponds to the collapse of the state vector, a projection into a basis state. The projection is not reversible and it is not consistent with the unitary time evolution. For a state represented by a unit-lenght vector

$$\omega_1 \cdot |x_1\rangle + \omega_2 \cdot |x_2\rangle + \cdots + \omega_n \cdot |x_n\rangle$$

in a n-dimensional Hilbert space $|x_k\rangle$ is observed. After the measurement (observation) the state is in a basis state

$$1 \cdot |x_k\rangle.$$

7.9.1 *Measuring a compound system*

The state of the system is projected to the subspace that corresponds to the observed state and the vector representing the state is renormalized to the unit length. An observable describes a subspace for some dimensions with a special case of one dimension. A part of the system can be observed by a projection in a subspace with a dimension higher one. The compound system of n-dimensional Hilbert space $|x\rangle \in H_n$ and a w-dimensional Hilbert space $|y\rangle \in H_w$ defined by a orthonormal basis $|xy\rangle \in H_{n \cdot w}$. A state of the system is represented as

$$|xy\rangle = \sum_{i=1}^{n} \sum_{j=1}^{w} \omega_{ij} |x_i\rangle |y_j\rangle. \tag{7.56}$$

For example

$$|xy\rangle = \sum_{i=1}^{2} \sum_{j=1}^{2} \omega_{ij} |x_i\rangle |y_j\rangle =$$

$$= \omega_{11} \cdot |x_1\rangle|y_1\rangle + \omega_{12} \cdot |x_1\rangle|y_2\rangle + \omega_{21} \cdot |x_2\rangle|y_1\rangle + \omega_{22} \cdot |x_2\rangle|y_2\rangle.$$

For simplicity we use the following notation for a qubit register

$$|xy\rangle = \omega_0 \cdot |00\rangle + \omega_1 \cdot |01\rangle + \omega_2 \cdot |10\rangle + \omega_3 \cdot |11\rangle$$

The probability of observing x_k is $\sum_{j=1}^{w} |\omega_{kj}|^2$. If we observe x_k, the system after the observation is projected into

$$|xy\rangle = \frac{1}{\sqrt{\sum_{j=1}^{w} |\omega_{kj}|^2}} \sum_{j=1}^{w} \omega_{kj} |x_k\rangle |y_j\rangle.$$

Suppose the two qubits are in the following state

$$\sqrt{0.25} \cdot |00\rangle + \sqrt{0.25} \cdot |01\rangle + \sqrt{0.25} \cdot |10\rangle + \sqrt{0.25} \cdot |11\rangle = \begin{pmatrix} \frac{1}{2} \\ \frac{1}{2} \\ \frac{1}{2} \\ \frac{1}{2} \end{pmatrix}.$$

The observed first qubit is $|0\rangle$. The probability of the observation is

$$|\omega_{00}|^2 + |\omega_{01}|^2 = |\omega_0|^2 + |\omega_1|^2 = |\sqrt{0.25}|^2 + |\sqrt{0.25}|^2 = 0.25 + 0.25 = 0.5$$

the system after the observation is projected into

$$\frac{\sqrt{0.25} \cdot |00\rangle + \sqrt{0.25} \cdot |01\rangle}{\sqrt{0.5}} = \sqrt{0.5} \cdot |00\rangle + \sqrt{0.5} \cdot |01\rangle = \begin{pmatrix} \sqrt{\frac{1}{2}} \\ \sqrt{\frac{1}{2}} \\ 0 \\ 0 \end{pmatrix}.$$

7.9.2 Observables

Observables are the things that are measured. They are some kind of machines with an input and output. The input is a state vector and the output represents the result represented by a real number. Observables can measure the input from different perspectives by rotating the coordinate system. Different perspectives can lead to different results. In quantum computing the coordinate system is fixed and the observables play a less important role. However observables motivate some models in quantum cognition. They lead to the Heisenberg uncertainty principle and to the quantum tunneling effect. Quantum tunneling plays an important role in quantum machine learning and quantum biology. In quantum physics observables are linear self-adjoint operators represented by a Hermitian matrix $A^* = A$ with $a_{ij} = \overline{a_{ji}}$. For real values the Hermitian matrix is a symmetrical matrix with $A^T = A$. Hermitian matrices have real eigenvalues and the corresponding eigenvectors are orthogonal (see spectral representation)

$$A \cdot |x\rangle = \lambda \cdot |x\rangle$$

with eigenvalue λ and eigenvector $|x\rangle$. To indicate that the eigenvalue λ_i corresponds to an eigenvector one writes

$$A \cdot |\lambda_i\rangle = \lambda_i \cdot |\lambda_i\rangle \tag{7.57}$$

with λ_i being the eigenvalue and $|\lambda_i\rangle$ being the corresponding eigenvector.

- For a state represented by a unit-length vector $|x\rangle$ the observable A rotates the state into a $|y\rangle$

$$|y\rangle = A \cdot |x\rangle \tag{7.58}$$

  After the measurement the state is in the eigenstate $|\lambda_i\rangle$ (it collapses to the basis state of A). The distinguishable states are the orthogonal vectors that define the coordinate system of the measurable operator A. They are the basis states of the coordinate system of the observable.
- The result of the measurement are the real eigenvalues λ_i of the operator that represent the observable. The state for which the result of a measurement λ_i corresponds to the eigenvector $|\lambda_i\rangle$. If the system is in the eigenstate $|\lambda_i\rangle$ then the measurement is λ_i since

$$\lambda_i \cdot |\lambda_i\rangle = A \cdot |\lambda_i\rangle.$$

- If $|x\rangle$ is the state vector of the system and the observable A is measured, the probability of the observable λ_i is

$$p(\lambda_i) = \langle x|\lambda_i\rangle\langle\lambda_i|x\rangle = |\langle x|\lambda_i\rangle|^2 \tag{7.59}$$

since the the inner product is not always positive or real and $\langle x|\lambda_i\rangle\langle\lambda_i|x\rangle$ is always positive and real and can be identified with probability.

If λ_1 and λ_2 are two unequal eigenvalues of an observable, then the corresponding eigenvectors are orthogonal. However if two eigenvalues are equal the corresponding eigenvectors can be orthogonal as well. For example the observable

$$A = \begin{pmatrix} 1 & 0 \\ 0 & -1 \end{pmatrix} \tag{7.60}$$

has the eigenvalues

$$\lambda_1 = 1, \quad \lambda_2 = -1$$

and the corresponding eigenvectors are

$$|\lambda_1\rangle = \begin{pmatrix} 1 \\ 0 \end{pmatrix}, \quad |\lambda_2\rangle = \begin{pmatrix} 0 \\ 1 \end{pmatrix}.$$

The observable represented by the identity matrix

$$B = \begin{pmatrix} 1 & 0 \\ 0 & 1 \end{pmatrix} \tag{7.61}$$

has equal eigenvalues

$$\lambda_1 = 1, \quad \lambda_2 = 1$$

and the corresponding eigenvectors are

$$|\lambda_1\rangle = \begin{pmatrix} 1 \\ 0 \end{pmatrix}, \quad |\lambda_2\rangle = \begin{pmatrix} 0 \\ 1 \end{pmatrix}.$$

7.9.2.1 *Example*

Fo the state vector

$$|x\rangle = \frac{1}{\sqrt{2}} \cdot |0\rangle + \frac{1}{\sqrt{2}} \cdot |1\rangle$$

acting with A gives

$$A \cdot |x\rangle = \frac{1}{\sqrt{2}} \cdot |0\rangle - \frac{1}{\sqrt{2}} \cdot |1\rangle.$$

After measuring the result is either in $\lambda_1 = 1$ leaving the system in the state

$$|\lambda_1\rangle = |0\rangle = \begin{pmatrix} 1 \\ 0 \end{pmatrix}$$

or $\lambda_1 = -1$ leaving the system in the state

$$|\lambda_2\rangle = |1\rangle = \begin{pmatrix} 0 \\ 1 \end{pmatrix}.$$

7.9.3 *Expectation values*

An average of all possible eigenvalue for the observable A is defined as

$$\langle A\rangle = \sum_{i=1}^{n} \lambda_i \cdot p(\lambda_i). \tag{7.62}$$

We can represent a quantum state $|x\rangle$ by a vector of the length one by the orthonormal basis of A

$$|x\rangle = \sum_{i=1}^{n} \alpha_i \cdot |\lambda_i\rangle \tag{7.63}$$

with

$$A \cdot |x\rangle = \sum_{i=1}^{n} \alpha_i \cdot A \cdot |\lambda_i\rangle = \sum_{i=1}^{n} \alpha_i \cdot \lambda_i \cdot |\lambda_i\rangle \tag{7.64}$$

since for eigenvectors

$$A \cdot |\lambda_i\rangle = \lambda_i \cdot |\lambda_i\rangle.$$

With

$$\langle\lambda_i| \cdot A = \lambda_i \cdot \langle\lambda_i|$$

we get

$$\langle x| \cdot A = \sum_{i=1}^{n} \alpha_i^* \cdot A \cdot \langle\lambda_i| = \sum_{i=1}^{n} \alpha_i^* \cdot \lambda_i \cdot \langle\lambda_i|. \tag{7.65}$$

Since the eigenvectors are orthonormal

$$\langle\lambda_i|\lambda_i\rangle = 1$$

and

$$\alpha_i^* \cdot \alpha_i = p(\lambda_i)$$

we get with

$$\langle x|A \cdot x\rangle = \langle x|A|x\rangle = \langle A\rangle = \sum_{i=1}^{n} (\alpha_i^* \cdot \alpha_i) \cdot \lambda_i = \sum_{i=1}^{n} \lambda_i \cdot p(\lambda_i). \tag{7.66}$$

We have a rule for computing the averages. When we preform many measurements the result converge to the average of the eigenvalue. We call the value $\langle A\rangle$ the expected value of observable A in state x. Each eigenvalue corresponds to the collapse on the eigenstate (basis state of the observable).

7.9.4 *Uncertainty*

For two observable A and B there is a basis of state-vectors $|\lambda_i, \mu_j\rangle$ that are the same eigenvectors of both observables with

$$A \cdot |\lambda_i, \mu_j\rangle = \lambda_i \cdot |\lambda_i, \mu_j\rangle$$

$$B \cdot |\lambda_i, \mu_j\rangle = \mu_j \cdot |\lambda_i, \mu_j\rangle$$

and

$$A \cdot B \cdot |\lambda_i, \mu_j\rangle = A \cdot \mu_j \cdot |\lambda_i, \mu_j\rangle = \lambda_i \cdot \mu_j \cdot |\lambda_i, \mu_j\rangle.$$

Since the eigenvalues are real numbers they are commutative,

$$A \cdot B \cdot |\lambda_i, \mu_j\rangle = B \cdot A \cdot |\lambda_i, \mu_j\rangle = \lambda_i \cdot \mu_j \cdot |\lambda_i, \mu_j\rangle = \mu_j \cdot \lambda_i \cdot |\lambda_i, \mu_j\rangle. \quad (7.67)$$

or

$$A \cdot B \cdot |\lambda_i, \mu_j\rangle - B \cdot A \cdot |\lambda_i, \mu_j\rangle = 0$$

$$(A \cdot B - B \cdot A) \cdot |\lambda_i, \mu_j\rangle = 0$$

$$(A \cdot B - B \cdot A) = 0$$

The commutator between two operators (observables) A and B is defined as

$$[A, B] := A \cdot B - B \cdot A \quad (7.68)$$

with

$$[A, B] = 0 \Longleftrightarrow A \cdot B = B \cdot A. \quad (7.69)$$

We can write in a shorter way

$$[A, B] \cdot |\lambda_i, \mu_j\rangle = 0.$$

If two observables commute, then there is a complete simultaneous eigenvectors of two observables. Two observables can be simultaneously measured if they commute. However usually matrix multiplication is not commutative

$$A \cdot B \neq B \cdot A \Longleftrightarrow [A, B] \neq 0. \quad (7.70)$$

7.9.5 *General Heisenberg's uncertainty principle**

The expected value of A is the ordinary average

$$\langle x|A|x\rangle = \langle A\rangle = \sum_{i=1}^{n}(\alpha_i^* \cdot \alpha_i) \cdot \lambda_i = \sum_{i=1}^{n} \lambda_i \cdot p(\lambda_i). \tag{7.71}$$

The uncertainty in A corresponds to the standard deviation by subtracting from it its expectation value

$$\overline{A} = A - \langle A\rangle \cdot I = A - \langle A\rangle \tag{7.72}$$

with I being the identity matrix (usually one does not write the identity matrix). The probability distribution of $\overline{A}$ is the same as of A, however its average is zero. For the eigenvalues a_i of A the eigenvalue of $\overline{A}$ is

$$\overline{a_i} = a_i - \langle A\rangle, \tag{7.73}$$

it is shifted so its average is zero. The square of standard deviation of A is defined as

$$(\Delta A)^2 = \sum_{i=1}^{n} \overline{a}_i^2 \cdot p(a_i) = \sum_{i=1}^{n} (a_i - \langle A\rangle)^2 \cdot p(a_i) = \langle x|\overline{A}^2|x\rangle. \tag{7.74}$$

If the expectation of A is zero, we do not need to shift and

$$(\Delta A)^2 = \sum_{i=1}^{n} a_i^2 \cdot p(a_i) = \langle x|A^2|x\rangle. \tag{7.75}$$

7.9.5.1 *Cauchy-Schwartz inequality*

With

$$\|\mathbf{y}\| = \sqrt{\langle \mathbf{y}|\mathbf{y}\rangle}, \quad \|\mathbf{z}\| = \sqrt{\langle \mathbf{z}|\mathbf{z}\rangle}$$

and

$$\|\mathbf{y}+\mathbf{z}\| = \sqrt{(\langle \mathbf{y}| + \langle \mathbf{z}|) \cdot ((\mathbf{y}| + \langle \mathbf{z}|)}$$

and the triangle inequality

$$\|\mathbf{y}\| + \|\mathbf{z}\| \geq \|\mathbf{y}+\mathbf{z}\|$$

we will arrive at the Heisenberg's uncertainty principle. We square the triangle inequality

$$\|\mathbf{y}\|^2 + |\mathbf{z}\|^2 \geq (\langle \mathbf{y}| + \langle \mathbf{z}|) \cdot ((\mathbf{y}| + \langle \mathbf{z}|)$$

$$\|\mathbf{y}\|^2 + |\mathbf{z}\|^2 + 2 \cdot \|\mathbf{y}\| \cdot |\mathbf{z}\| \geq \|\mathbf{y}\|^2 + |\langle \mathbf{y}|\mathbf{z}\rangle + \langle \mathbf{z}|\mathbf{y}\rangle| + \|\mathbf{z}\|^2$$

and we arrive at the Cauchy-Schwartz inequality

$$2 \cdot \|\mathbf{y}\| \cdot \|\mathbf{z}\| \geq |\langle \mathbf{y}|\mathbf{z}\rangle + \langle \mathbf{z}|\mathbf{y}\rangle|.$$

With two observables A and B we define

$$|\mathbf{y}\rangle = A \cdot |\mathbf{x}\rangle, \quad |\mathbf{z}\rangle = i \cdot B \cdot |\mathbf{x}\rangle \tag{7.76}$$

substituting it in Cauchy-Schwartz inequality leads to

$$2 \cdot \sqrt{\langle x|A^2|x\rangle \cdot \langle x|B^2|x\rangle} \geq |\langle x|AB|x\rangle - \langle x|BA|x\rangle| \tag{7.77}$$

with the minus sign resulting for i. Simplified with the notation of a commutator

$$2 \cdot \sqrt{\langle A^2\rangle \cdot \langle B^2\rangle} \geq |\langle x|[A, B]|x\rangle| \tag{7.78}$$

If the expectation of A and B is zero,

$$(\Delta A)^2 = \langle x|A^2|x\rangle = \langle A^2\rangle, \quad (\Delta B)^2 = \langle B^2\rangle$$

we write

$$\Delta A \cdot \Delta B \geq \frac{|\langle x|[A, B]|x\rangle|}{2}. \tag{7.79}$$

This the general uncertainty principle or the general version of Heisenberg uncertainty principle. If the expectation value is not zero then the uncertainty in A corresponds to the standard deviation by subtracting from it its expectation value. We do the same for the observable B with

$$\overline{A} = A - \langle A\rangle \cdot I, \quad \overline{B} = B - \langle B\rangle \cdot I.$$

Since

$$(\Delta A)^2 = \langle \overline{A}^2\rangle, \quad (\Delta B)^2 = \langle \overline{B}^2\rangle \tag{7.80}$$

as well

$$[A, B] = [\overline{A}, \overline{B}] \tag{7.81}$$

we arrive at the same Equation 7.79. In the Equation 7.79 on the left side we indicate the uncertainties of the two observables A and B in a state $|x\rangle$.

Example Suppose we have a large number of quantum systems in the state $|x\rangle$. If we measure the observable A on some and the observable B on others, then the standard deviation $\Delta(A)$ and $\Delta(B)$ will satisfy the Equation 7.79. For example the observable A is [Nielsen and Chuang (2000)]

$$A = \begin{pmatrix} 0 & 1 \\ 1 & 0 \end{pmatrix} \tag{7.82}$$

and

$$B = \begin{pmatrix} 0 & -i \\ i & 0 \end{pmatrix} \tag{7.83}$$

with

$$[A, B] = \begin{pmatrix} 0 & 1 \\ 1 & 0 \end{pmatrix} \cdot \begin{pmatrix} 0 & -i \\ i & 0 \end{pmatrix} - \begin{pmatrix} 0 & -i \\ i & 0 \end{pmatrix} \cdot \begin{pmatrix} 0 & 1 \\ 1 & 0 \end{pmatrix}$$

$$[A, B] = \begin{pmatrix} 2i & 0 \\ 0 & -2i \end{pmatrix}$$

then

$$\Delta(A)\Delta(B) \geq \frac{\left| \langle 0| \begin{pmatrix} 2i & 0 \\ 0 & -2i \end{pmatrix} |0\rangle \right|}{2} = 1 \tag{7.84}$$

$\Delta(A)$ and $\Delta(B)$ must be grater than 0 since their product needs to be greater equal to one.

Time-frequency information of a signal The uncertainty principle was originally applied to the momentum and location of moving particles. The uncertainty principle can also be applied to the classical time-frequency information of a signal. It is not possible to know the exact time-frequency representation of a signal. In short-time Fourier transform (STFT), the signal is divided into small segments. In each segment, the Fourier transform determines the frequency representation of the signal. The size of the window defines the time representation of the signal. The uncertainty principle of STFT is related to the width of the window function that is used.

- Narrow window: good time resolution, poor frequency resolution.
- Wide window: good frequency resolution, poor time resolution.

In classical physics, a possible solution exists. This solution is the multi resolution analysis of the signal, as described by the wavelet transform. The analysis is "repeated" several times. Each time, a different size (scale) of the window is used.

7.9.6 *Heisenberg's uncertainty principle**

A state-vector that is expressed as an integral rather then a sum is continuous and corresponds to a wave function $\psi(a, b, c, \cdots)$ with the observables $A, B, C, \cdots$ basis vectors $|a, b, c, \cdots\rangle$ and the eigenvalues $a, b, c, \cdots$. The probability of the commuting observables $a, b, c, \cdots$ is

$$p(a, b, c, \cdots) = \psi^*(a, b, c, \cdots)\psi(a, b, c, \cdots). \tag{7.85}$$

A particle is described by a wave function $\psi(x)$ that indicates its position x and the inverse Fourier transform $\tilde{\psi}(p)$ of its momentum p

$$\psi(x) = \frac{1}{\sqrt{2 \cdot \pi}} \int dpe^{\frac{ipx}{h}} \tilde{\psi}(p) \tag{7.86}$$

and the Fourier transform

$$\tilde{\psi}(p) = \frac{1}{\sqrt{2 \cdot \pi}} \int dpe^{\frac{-ipx}{h}} \psi(x) \tag{7.87}$$

with two observables for position X and momentum P. For a position x the function is multiplied with the value x, the particle is located at the point x, it is zero elsewhere

$$X\psi(x) = x\psi(x). \tag{7.88}$$

The momentum corresponds to the derivative with $-i$ to make the operator Hermitian and the Planck's constant h for the correct relation

$$P\psi(x) = -ih\frac{d\psi(x)}{dx}. \tag{7.89}$$

For two measurments

$$XP\psi(x) = -ihx\frac{d\psi(x)}{dx} \tag{7.90}$$

and

$$PX\psi(x) = -ihx\frac{d(x\psi(x))}{dx} = -ihx\frac{d\psi(x)}{dx} - ih\psi(x) \tag{7.91}$$

with

$$[X, P]\psi(x) = XP\psi(x) - PX\psi(x) = ih\psi(x) \tag{7.92}$$

The general uncertainty principle is given by

$$\Delta X \cdot \Delta P \geq \frac{|\langle x|[X, P]|x\rangle|}{2}$$

$$\Delta X \cdot \Delta P \geq \frac{|ih\langle \Psi|\Psi\rangle|}{2}. \tag{7.93}$$

since $\langle\Psi|\Psi\rangle = 1$

$$\Delta X \cdot \Delta P \geq \frac{h}{2}. \tag{7.94}$$

The Heisenberg's uncertainty principle is applied to the momentum and location of moving particles and is represented by where x is the position and p the momentum of a particle and h the Planck constant. It represents the relation between

$$\Delta(x)\Delta(p) \approx h \tag{7.95}$$

the position uncertainty times the momentum uncertainty.

7.9.7 *Quantum tunneling*

The relation

$$\Delta(x)\Delta(p) \approx h \tag{7.96}$$

is also valid for energy E and time t

$$\Delta(E)\Delta(t) \approx h. \tag{7.97}$$

This arrangement contradicts the first law of thermodynamics, which is the conservation of energy, where the sum of the amount of energy of a system remains constant. In quantum physics, there is uncertainty between the energy E and the time t.

$$\Delta(E) \approx \frac{h}{\Delta(t)}. \tag{7.98}$$

This uncertainty means that some energy can be borrowed, to overcome some mountain and go out of a minimum as long as we repay it in the time interval [Hey and Walters (2003)]

$$\Delta(t) \approx \frac{h}{\Delta(E)}. \tag{7.99}$$

Quantum tunneling allows classical energy barriers to be be overcome to some extend by the time-energy uncertainty. A particle cam tunnel through a region in which the potential energy function exceeds the total energy of the particle. The wave function has some probability of tunneling through a barrier rather than over it.

7.9.7.1 *Quantum biology*

In 1963, Per-Olov Lowdin proposed proton tunneling as a mechanism for DNA mutation and a new field of study called quantum biology. Electron tunneling in biological systems in proteins was first reported in Marcus 85. Enzymes may use quantum tunneling to transfer electrons for long distances. In photosynthesis electron tunneling plays an important role. In some enzymes quantum effects may contribute to enzymatic catalysis. It has been suggested that phonon tunneling of an electron between two receptor plays an essential role in olfaction, the sense of smell.

7.10 Observables in Quantum Computing

In quantum computing the coordinate system is fixed and the observables do not rotate the coordinate system. The eigenstates correspond to the basis states, the eigenvectors to the basis of the system. The measurement is preformed by an observable. A Hilbert space H_n can be represented as a collection of orthogonal subspaces

$$H_n = E_1 \oplus E_2 \oplus \ldots \oplus E_f \tag{7.100}$$

with $f \leq n$. Each subspace has a different label and is represented by a real number

$$\lambda_1, \lambda_2, \cdots, \lambda_2 \tag{7.101}$$

Instead seeing the spaces we see the labels with the aid of the observables. The input to the observable is a state $|x\rangle$ and the output is a label λ_i indicating the measured subspace E_i. A state $|x\rangle$ can be represented with $|x_i\rangle \in E_i$ as

$$\omega_1 \cdot |x_1\rangle + \omega_2 \cdot |x_2\rangle + \cdots + \omega_f \cdot |x_f\rangle.$$

For one dimensional subspaces

$$H_n = E_1 \oplus E_2 \oplus \ldots \oplus E_n$$

the value $|\lambda_k\rangle$ is observed with a probability $\|\omega_k \cdot |x_k\rangle\|^2 = |\omega_k|^2$. The input to the observable is a state $|x\rangle$ and the output is a label λ_k indicating the basis state $|x_k\rangle$. It means that after the measurement the system is in the basis state $|x_k\rangle$.

Another description is through a projection into a subspace. A subspace defines a projection P_{E_k}. Because a projection is self-adjoint $P_{E_k} = P_{E_k}^*$ and $P_{E_k} = P_{E_k}^2$ the probability of observing λ_k is

$$\langle x|P_{E_k} \cdot x\rangle = \langle x|P_{E_k}^2 \cdot x\rangle = \langle P_{E_k} \cdot x|P_{E_k} \cdot x\rangle = \|\omega_k \cdot |x_k\rangle\|^2 = |\omega_k|^2 \tag{7.102}$$

and the resulting value is

$$\frac{1}{\sqrt{\langle x | P_{E_k} \cdot x \rangle}} \cdot P_{E_k} \cdot |x\rangle = 1 \cdot |x_k\rangle.$$

Finally a state can be represented by the corresponding density matrix P with a corresponding spectral decomposition. The projection in the orthogonal subspace E_k is described by the projection matrix $|x_k\rangle\langle x_k|$ and the corresponding probability is λ_k. We can represent this probability as

$$\langle x|x_k\rangle\langle x_k|x\rangle = p(\lambda_k)$$

and the resulting value of the projection is

$$\frac{1}{\sqrt{\langle x|x_k\rangle\langle x_k|x\rangle}} |x_k\rangle\langle x_k| \cdot |x\rangle = 1 \cdot |x_k\rangle.$$

All three different descriptions represent the same fact through different formalisms. An observation corresponds to a non-reversible projection onto one or several basis states.

Since $\lambda_k \to |x_k\rangle$ we well write $|x_k\rangle$ instead of λ_k to indicate that the system is in the state $|x_k\rangle$.

7.11 Randomness

Randomness can be defined by numbers in a sequence [Williams and Clearwatter (1997)]. A random number alone does not exist. A sequence of random numbers must correspond to some distribution, and there should be no correlation among the numbers in the sequence. For example, the following sequence, which represents the toss of a fair coin 0, 1, is not random,

$$0, 1, 0, 1, 0, 1, 0, 1, 0, 1, 0, 1, 0, 1, 0, 1, 0, 1$$

because a correlation between 0 and 1 is present. Classical physics is deterministic. Because of that, no true randomness exists in its context. Some facts could appear to be random. However, this arrangement is only the case because some essential information is missing.

7.11.1 *Deterministic chaos*

A sequence could look random even though it is generated by a simple nonlinear deterministic equation. Such behavior is called deterministic chaos. The logistic map is defined by a dynamical nonlinear difference equation

$$x_{t+1} = r \cdot x_t \cdot (1 - x_t) \tag{7.103}$$

with with some constant r. The rule generates a sequence

$$x_0, x, x_2, x_3, x_4, \cdots$$

that depending on the value r.

For $x_0 = 0.1$ and $r = 3.2$ the equation converges to a period (see Figure 7.1). However, for values that are approximately in $[3.5699, 4]$, the

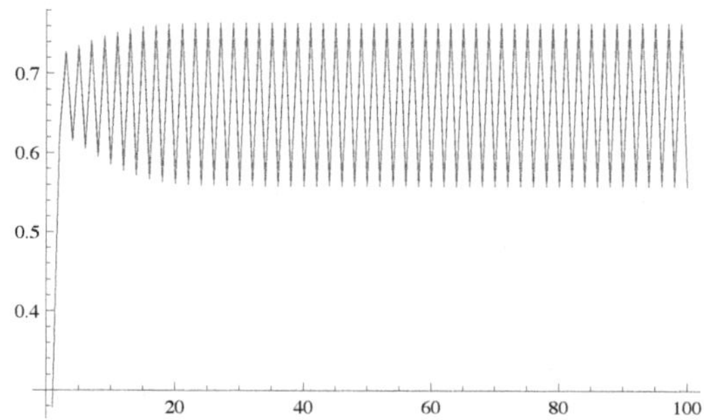

Fig. 7.1 For $x_0 = 0.1$ and $r = 3.2$ the logistic map converges to a period.

sequence does not converge to any pattern. A minimal change of x_0 leads to a different sequence (see the values $x_0 = 0.1$ and $r = 3.98$ represented in Figure 7.2 and the values $x_0 = 0.101$ and $r = 3.98$ in Figure 7.3).

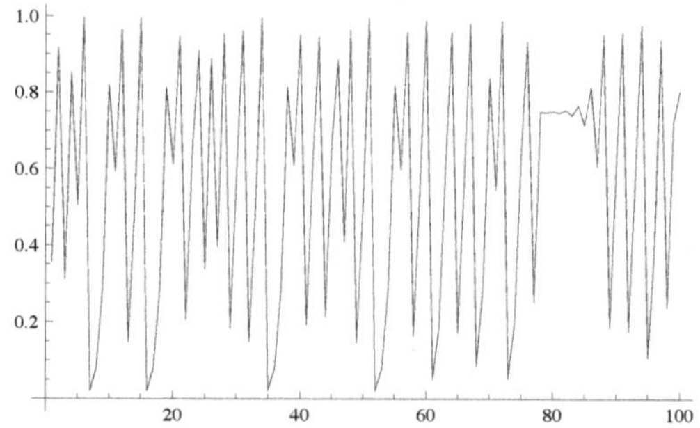

Fig. 7.2 For $x_0 = 0.1$ and $r = 3.98$ the logistic map behaves chaotically, it appears random.

There is no randomness in classical physics and in the resulting equations that describe it, in spite of the fact that a behavior can be generated

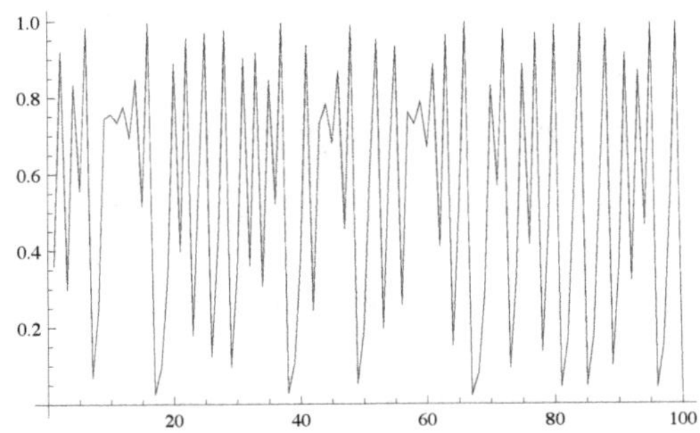

Fig. 7.3 The logistic map is sensitive to the initial condition. For $x_0 = 0.101$ and $r = 3.98$ it behaves diferently as the sequence with initial condition or $x_0 = 0.1$.

that is highly unpredictable due to our lack of information. For example, in the logistic equation, exact knowledge of the initial condition is required.

7.11.2 *Kolmogorov complexity*

Kolmogorov complexity is defined as the shortest program that can produce its output. It is a measure of the amount of innate randomness of a sequence. In the case of deterministic chaos, the randomness is low. It can be described by a very short program, such as in the case of the logistic map, by an equation together with the values of x_0 and r. Randomness is defined by the Kolmogorov complexity. The larger the shortest program that generates the sequence is, the more random it is. However, we cannot determine whether a sequence can be represented by a short program. The problem is related to the halting problem [Gardner (1979)]. We cannot generate a truly random sequence using a Turing machine.

7.11.3 *Humans and random numbers*

Randomness could be nature's way to avoid complexity. A decision could be chosen randomly, where no knowledge is present and planning is not possible. How well can people generate random sequences? It was indicated in one experiment that humans cannot generate true binary random sequences. Hagelbarger asked subjects to create a binary random sequence, and the sequence was analyzed for correlations by a computer program. The program attempted to predict the next symbol in the sequence and achieved a $55 - 60$ percent accuracy. For a random sequence, the accuracy should be approximately 50 percent [Shannon (1953)].

7.11.4 *Randomness in quantum physics*

Quantum physics is the only source of true randomness. Randomness can be generated by a quantum computing device that simulates a quantum coin. A quantum coin is defined by the unitary matrix

$$W = \frac{1}{\sqrt{2}} \cdot \begin{pmatrix} 1 & 1 \\ 1 & -1 \end{pmatrix}$$

and by the mapping

$$W \cdot |0\rangle = \frac{1}{\sqrt{2}} \cdot |0\rangle + \frac{1}{\sqrt{2}} \cdot |1\rangle \tag{7.104}$$

or

$$W \cdot |1\rangle = \frac{1}{\sqrt{2}} \cdot |0\rangle - \frac{1}{\sqrt{2}} \cdot |1\rangle. \tag{7.105}$$

The corresponding operator is indicated by the following unitary matrix,

$$W = \begin{pmatrix} \frac{1}{\sqrt{2}} & \frac{1}{\sqrt{2}} \\ \frac{1}{\sqrt{2}} & -\frac{1}{\sqrt{2}} \end{pmatrix} = \frac{1}{\sqrt{2}} \cdot \begin{pmatrix} 1 & 1 \\ 1 & -1 \end{pmatrix}. \tag{7.106}$$

After the mapping, a measurement is preformed. The probability of observing 0 or 1 is $\left|\frac{1}{\sqrt{2}}\right|^2 = \frac{1}{2}$. True randomness is present during the measurement; it is an effect of the measurement represented by the collapse. The collapse itself is not explained by quantum theory. Using a quantum coin, we can generate a true random binary sequence. It is easy to combine the results from a quantum coin to generate a random integer in the range 0 to 2^{n-1}. Later, we will see how to generate a true random quantum dice using QFT.

Chapter 8

Computation with Qubits

8.1 Computation with one Qubit

A unitary operator on a qubit is called an unary quantum gate. It is described by a unitary matrix of the dimension 2×2. For the qubit with the basis

$$|0\rangle = \begin{pmatrix} 1 \\ 0 \end{pmatrix}, |1\rangle = \begin{pmatrix} 0 \\ 1 \end{pmatrix}$$

the quantum not gate $M_\neg$ does the not operation on a qubit

$$M_\neg|0\rangle = |1\rangle, M_\neg|1\rangle = |0\rangle$$

and is represented by the unitary matrix

$$M_\neg = \begin{pmatrix} 0 & 1 \\ 1 & 0 \end{pmatrix}. \tag{8.1}$$

The not operation can be written using $XOR = \oplus$ for $x \in \mathbf{B}^1$

$$M_\neg|x\rangle = |x \oplus 1\rangle$$

$$M_\neg|0\rangle = |0 \oplus 1\rangle = |0\rangle, \quad M_\neg|1\rangle = |1 \oplus 1\rangle = |1\rangle.$$

The square root of the not gate $M_\neg = \sqrt{M_\neg} \cdot \sqrt{M_\neg}$ is represented by the unitary matrix

$$\sqrt{M_\neg} = \begin{pmatrix} \frac{1+i}{2} & \frac{1-i}{2} \\ \frac{1-i}{2} & \frac{1+i}{2} \end{pmatrix} \tag{8.2}$$

with

$$\begin{pmatrix} \frac{1+i}{2} & \frac{1-i}{2} \\ \frac{1-i}{2} & \frac{1+i}{2} \end{pmatrix} \cdot \begin{pmatrix} \frac{1+i}{2} & \frac{1-i}{2} \\ \frac{1-i}{2} & \frac{1+i}{2} \end{pmatrix} = \begin{pmatrix} 0 & 1 \\ 1 & 0 \end{pmatrix} \tag{8.3}$$

and it is unitary because

$$\begin{pmatrix} \frac{1+i}{2} & \frac{1-i}{2} \\ \frac{1-i}{2} & \frac{1+i}{2} \end{pmatrix} \cdot \begin{pmatrix} \frac{1-i}{2} & \frac{1+i}{2} \\ \frac{1+i}{2} & \frac{1-i}{2} \end{pmatrix} = \begin{pmatrix} 1 & 0 \\ 0 & 1 \end{pmatrix} \tag{8.4}$$

with

$$M_\neg|0\rangle = \frac{1+i}{2} \cdot |0\rangle + \frac{1-i}{2} \cdot |1\rangle$$

and

$$M_\neg|1\rangle = \frac{1-i}{2} \cdot |0\rangle + \frac{1+i}{2} \cdot |1\rangle.$$

The probability of measuring $|0\rangle$ and $|1\rangle$ is 0.5, because

$$\left|\frac{1-i}{2}\right|^2 = \left|\frac{1+i}{2}\right|^2 = \frac{1}{2}.$$

$-\sqrt{M_\neg}$ has the same behavior with

$$M_\neg = -\sqrt{M_\neg} \cdot -\sqrt{M_\neg}.$$

The identity gate preforms no operation on a qubit, it is defined as the identity matrix

$$I_1 = \begin{pmatrix} 1 & 0 \\ 0 & 1 \end{pmatrix}. \tag{8.5}$$

The square root of the identity matrix is the identity I matrix is I and $-I$

$$-I_1 = \begin{pmatrix} -1 & 0 \\ 0 & -1 \end{pmatrix}. \tag{8.6}$$

$-I_1$ changes the sign of the amplitude but not the probabilities. The introduced unitary matrix W maps a basis state in a superposition.

$$|0\rangle \rightarrow \frac{1}{\sqrt{2}} \cdot |0\rangle + \frac{1}{\sqrt{2}} \cdot |1\rangle$$

$$|1\rangle \rightarrow \frac{1}{\sqrt{2}} \cdot |0\rangle - \frac{1}{\sqrt{2}} \cdot |1\rangle$$

The probability of measuring $|0\rangle$ and $|1\rangle$ is 0.5. The matrix W is called Walsh, Hadarmad or Hamarad Walsh, matrix.

8.2 Computation with m Qubit

The register of m qubits is represented as a direct product of m qubits. It defines $n = 2^m$ dimensional Hilbert space H_n with an orthonprmal basis $|x_1\rangle, |x_1\rangle, \cdots |x_n\rangle$. For example four qubits define a 16 dimensional Hilbert space H_{16} with the basis

$$|0000\rangle = \begin{pmatrix} 1\\0\\0\\0\\0\\0\\0\\0\\0\\0\\0\\0\\0\\0\\0\\0 \end{pmatrix}, |0001\rangle = \begin{pmatrix} 0\\1\\0\\0\\0\\0\\0\\0\\0\\0\\0\\0\\0\\0\\0 \end{pmatrix}, |0010\rangle = \begin{pmatrix} 0\\0\\1\\0\\0\\0\\0\\0\\0\\0\\0\\0\\0\\0\\0 \end{pmatrix}, \cdots, |1111\rangle = \begin{pmatrix} 0\\0\\0\\0\\0\\0\\0\\0\\0\\0\\0\\0\\0\\0\\1 \end{pmatrix}. \tag{8.7}$$

It is difficult to simulate more than few of tens bits on an ordinary computer because the dimension of the Hilbert space grows exponentially in relation to the number of represented qubits. For example sixteen qubits are represented by a 65536 dimensional Hilbert space H_{65536}.

The Hadarmad matrix W on one qubit has the dimension 2×2 is also called a Hadamard gate and is indicated as W_1. A Hadarmad operator for m qubits W_m is represented by a $2^m \times 2^m$ dimensional matrix built by a direct product of m W_1 matrices. The complexity of the operator W_m corresponds to m Hadamard gates W_1.

$$W_m = \bigotimes^m W_1 = W_1 \otimes W_1 \cdots \otimes W_1 \tag{8.8}$$

The Hadamard matrix is also called the Hadamard transform and can be defined recursively with $W_0 = 1$ and

$$W_m = \frac{1}{\sqrt{2}} \cdot \begin{pmatrix} W_{m-1} & W_{m-1} \\ W_{m-1} & -W_{m-1} \end{pmatrix} \tag{8.9}$$

with W_3

$$W_3 = W_1 \otimes W_1 \otimes W_1$$

$$W_3 = \frac{1}{\sqrt{2}} \cdot \begin{pmatrix} W_2 & W_2 \\ W_2 & -W_2 \end{pmatrix} = \frac{1}{\sqrt{2^3}} \cdot \begin{pmatrix} 1 & 1 & 1 & 1 & 1 & 1 & 1 & 1 \\ 1 & -1 & 1 & -1 & 1 & -1 & 1 & -1 \\ 1 & 1 & -1 & -1 & 1 & 1 & -1 & -1 \\ 1 & -1 & -1 & 1 & 1 & -1 & -1 & 1 \\ 1 & 1 & 1 & 1 & -1 & -1 & -1 & -1 \\ 1 & -1 & 1 & -1 & -1 & -1 & -1 & 1 \\ 1 & 1 & -1 & -1 & -1 & -1 & 1 & 1 \\ 1 & -1 & -1 & 1 & -1 & 1 & 1 & -1 \end{pmatrix}.$$

The Hadamard operator W_m maps m qubits $|z\rangle$ representing a basis state in a Hilbert space H_{2^m} with $z \in B^m$

$$W_m|z\rangle = \frac{1}{\sqrt{2^m}} \sum_{x \in B^m} (-1)^{\langle z|x\rangle} \cdot |x\rangle \tag{8.10}$$

with a scalar product ($\langle z|x\rangle$) over the binary field with two elements corresponding to the bits 0 and 1. The multiplication of two bits is equal to the AND operation with

$$0 \cdot 0 = 0 \wedge 0 = 0, \quad 0 \cdot 1 = 0 \wedge 1 = 0, \quad 1 \cdot 0 = 1 \wedge 0 = 0, \quad 1 \cdot 1 = 1 \wedge 1 = 1$$

and the addition is equal to the XOR operation $\oplus$

$$0 + 0 = 0 \oplus 0 = 0, \quad 0 + 1 = 0 \oplus 1 = 1,$$

$$1 + 0 = 1 \oplus 0 = 1, \quad 1 + 1 = 1 \oplus 1 = 0.$$

For the state zero represented by m qubits

$$|0\rangle^{\otimes^m} = |0\rangle|0\rangle|0\rangle \cdots |0\rangle = \begin{pmatrix} 1 \\ 0 \\ \vdots \\ 0 \\ 0 \end{pmatrix}$$

the Hadamard operator W_m maps a basis state into a superposition of all possible states with no negative sign,

$$W_m|0\rangle^{\otimes^m} = \frac{1}{\sqrt{2^m}} \sum_{x \in B^m} |x\rangle. \tag{8.11}$$

For example

$$W_3|0\rangle^{\otimes^3} = W_3|000\rangle = \frac{1}{\sqrt{2^3}} \sum_{x \in B^3} |x\rangle$$

$$W_3|000\rangle =$$

$$= \frac{1}{\sqrt{2^3}} (|000\rangle + |001\rangle + |000\rangle + |010\rangle + |011\rangle + |100\rangle + |101\rangle + |111\rangle).$$

It can be expressed as

$$W_3|000\rangle = W_1|0\rangle \otimes W_1|0\rangle \otimes W_1|0\rangle = \left(\frac{|0\rangle + |1\rangle}{\sqrt{2}}\right) \cdot \left(\frac{|0\rangle + |1\rangle}{\sqrt{2}}\right) \cdot \left(\frac{|0\rangle + |1\rangle}{\sqrt{2}}\right)$$

and

$$W_3 \cdot W_3|000\rangle = |000\rangle.$$

This is because $W_m = W_m^*$ so that $I_m = W_m \cdot W_m$. The basis states $|11\rangle$ is maped into

$$W_2|11\rangle = W_1|1\rangle \otimes W_1|1\rangle = \left(\frac{|0\rangle - |1\rangle}{\sqrt{2}}\right) \cdot \left(\frac{|0\rangle - |1\rangle}{\sqrt{2}}\right)$$

$$W_2|11\rangle = \frac{1}{2} \cdot (|00\rangle - |01\rangle - |10\rangle + |11\rangle).$$

A Walsh matrix is a square matrix of the dimension power of two. It has the property that the scalar product of any two different rows or columns is zero. The vectors that represent the matrix are orthogonal. In Hadamard transform the vectors that represent the matrix are orthonormal. We indicate the matrix by W_m for m qubits (because of Walsh), not to be confused with the Hilbert space H_n of the dimension n with the relation $n = 2^m$.

8.3 Matrix Representation of Serial and Parallel Operations

A serial computation corresponds to a multiplication of matrices that represent the gates. The multiplication of matrices is usually not commutative, for example $W_1 \cdot M_\neg \neq M_\neg W_1$

$$\begin{pmatrix} \frac{1}{\sqrt{2}} & \frac{1}{\sqrt{2}} \\ \frac{1}{\sqrt{2}} & -\frac{1}{\sqrt{2}} \end{pmatrix} \cdot \begin{pmatrix} 0 & 1 \\ 1 & 0 \end{pmatrix} \neq \begin{pmatrix} 0 & 1 \\ 1 & 0 \end{pmatrix} \cdot \begin{pmatrix} \frac{1}{\sqrt{2}} & \frac{1}{\sqrt{2}} \\ \frac{1}{\sqrt{2}} & -\frac{1}{\sqrt{2}} \end{pmatrix}$$

$$\begin{pmatrix} \frac{1}{\sqrt{2}} & \frac{1}{\sqrt{2}} \\ -\frac{1}{\sqrt{2}} & \frac{1}{\sqrt{2}} \end{pmatrix} \neq \begin{pmatrix} \frac{1}{\sqrt{2}} & -\frac{1}{\sqrt{2}} \\ \frac{1}{\sqrt{2}} & \frac{1}{\sqrt{2}} \end{pmatrix}$$

it means

$$W_1 \cdot M_\neg \cdot |0\rangle = W_1 \cdot |1\rangle = \frac{|0\rangle - |1\rangle}{\sqrt{2}}$$

and

$$M_\neg \cdot W_1 \cdot |0\rangle = M_\neg \cdot \left(\frac{|0\rangle + |1\rangle}{\sqrt{2}} \right)$$

$$= \frac{M_\neg \cdot |0\rangle + M_\neg \cdot |1\rangle}{\sqrt{2}} = \frac{|1\rangle + |0\rangle}{\sqrt{2}} = \frac{|0\rangle + |1\rangle}{\sqrt{2}}$$

it follows

$$M_\neg \cdot W_1 \cdot |0\rangle = W_1 \cdot |0\rangle.$$

Only the multiplication with the identity matrix and the inverse matrix are commutative operations. Parallel operations correspond to the direct product, also called the tensor product or Kronecker product when dealing with matrices. For example with

$$M_\neg \otimes I_1 \otimes W_1 \cdot |000\rangle = (M_\neg \cdot |0\rangle) \otimes (I_1 \cdot |0\rangle) \otimes (W_1 \cdot |0\rangle) =$$

$$|10\rangle \cdot \frac{|0\rangle + |1\rangle}{\sqrt{2}} = \frac{|100\rangle + |101\rangle}{\sqrt{2}}$$

in vector representation as

$$\left(\begin{pmatrix} 0 & 1 \\ 1 & 0 \end{pmatrix} \cdot \begin{pmatrix} 1 \\ 0 \end{pmatrix} \right) \otimes \left(\begin{pmatrix} 1 & 0 \\ 0 & 1 \end{pmatrix} \cdot \begin{pmatrix} 1 \\ 0 \end{pmatrix} \right) \otimes \left(\begin{pmatrix} \frac{1}{\sqrt{2}} & \frac{1}{\sqrt{2}} \\ \frac{1}{\sqrt{2}} & -\frac{1}{\sqrt{2}} \end{pmatrix} \cdot \begin{pmatrix} 1 \\ 0 \end{pmatrix} \right) =$$

$$\begin{pmatrix} 0 & 0 & 0 & 0 & \frac{1}{\sqrt{2}} & \frac{1}{\sqrt{2}} & 0 & 0 \\ 0 & 0 & 0 & 0 & \frac{1}{\sqrt{2}} & -\frac{1}{\sqrt{2}} & 0 & 0 \\ 0 & 0 & 0 & 0 & 0 & 0 & \frac{1}{\sqrt{2}} & \frac{1}{\sqrt{2}} \\ 0 & 0 & 0 & 0 & 0 & 0 & \frac{1}{\sqrt{2}} & -\frac{1}{\sqrt{2}} \\ \frac{1}{\sqrt{2}} & \frac{1}{\sqrt{2}} & 0 & 0 & 0 & 0 & 0 & 0 \\ \frac{1}{\sqrt{2}} & -\frac{1}{\sqrt{2}} & 0 & 0 & 0 & 0 & 0 & 0 \\ 0 & 0 & \frac{1}{\sqrt{2}} & \frac{1}{\sqrt{2}} & 0 & 0 & 0 & 0 \\ 0 & 0 & \frac{1}{\sqrt{2}} & -\frac{1}{\sqrt{2}} & 0 & 0 & 0 & 0 \end{pmatrix} \cdot \begin{pmatrix} 1 \\ 0 \\ 0 \\ 0 \\ 0 \\ 0 \\ 0 \\ 0 \end{pmatrix} = \begin{pmatrix} 0 \\ 0 \\ 0 \\ 0 \\ \frac{1}{\sqrt{2}} \\ \frac{1}{\sqrt{2}} \\ 0 \\ 0 \end{pmatrix}.$$

Matrices representing quantum operators can be decomposed, for example

$$W_4 = W_2 \otimes W_2 = W_1 \otimes W_1 \otimes W_1 \otimes W_1.$$

There are however matrices representing quantum operators that can be not decomposed with some serious consequences.

8.4 Entangelment

The following operator M_{CNOT} s unitary and defends an injective mapping on two qubits that is reversible

$$M_{CNOT}|00\rangle = |00\rangle, \quad M_{CNOT}|01\rangle = |01\rangle,$$

$$M_{CNOT}|10\rangle = |11\rangle, \quad M_{CNOT}|11\rangle = |10\rangle.$$

The operator M_{CNOT} is called a controlled not gate. The first qubit counting from the left is not changed. The second qubit is only flipped in the case that the first qubit is 1. In this case a NOT operation on the second qubit is executed. The control not gate can as well perform the fan-out operation. For this operation the second qubit has to be zero. In this case the value of the first qubit is copied into the second one. The M_{CNOT} can be represented by a matrix

$$M_{CNOT} = \begin{pmatrix} 1\,0\,0\,0 \\ 0\,1\,0\,0 \\ 0\,0\,0\,1 \\ 0\,0\,1\,0 \end{pmatrix}. \tag{8.12}$$

M_{CNOT} cannot be expressed as a tensor product of 2×2 matrices. Suppose we start with the state $|00\rangle$ and map the first qubit bit into the superposition using the Hadamard gate

$$W_1 \otimes I \cdot |00\rangle = (W_1 \cdot |0\rangle) \otimes |0\rangle = \frac{|0\rangle + |1\rangle}{\sqrt{2}} \otimes |0\rangle = \frac{|00\rangle + |10\rangle}{\sqrt{2}}.$$

To this state represented by the two qubit we apply M_{CNOT} gate

$$M_{CNOT} \cdot \left(\frac{|00\rangle + |10\rangle}{\sqrt{2}} \right) = \frac{M_{CNOT} \cdot |00\rangle + M_{CNOT} \cdot |10\rangle}{\sqrt{2}} = \frac{|00\rangle + |11\rangle}{\sqrt{2}}.$$

A register of two qubit is decomposable if it can be represented as a direct product of two qubits. For example the state

$$\frac{|00\rangle + |01\rangle + |10\rangle + |11\rangle}{2} = \left(\frac{|0\rangle + |1\rangle}{\sqrt{2}} \right) \otimes \left(\frac{|0\rangle + |1\rangle}{\sqrt{2}} \right)$$

is decomposable. In vector notation it is represented as

$$\begin{pmatrix} \frac{1}{2} \\ \frac{1}{2} \\ \frac{1}{2} \\ \frac{1}{2} \end{pmatrix} = \begin{pmatrix} \frac{1}{\sqrt{2}} \\ \frac{1}{\sqrt{2}} \end{pmatrix} \otimes \begin{pmatrix} \frac{1}{\sqrt{2}} \\ \frac{1}{\sqrt{2}} \end{pmatrix}.$$

However the state of two qubits

$$\frac{|00\rangle + |11\rangle}{\sqrt{2}} \tag{8.13}$$

is not decomposable. We preform a proof by contradiction. From the assumption that the state is decomposable follows a contradiction,

$$\frac{|00\rangle + |11\rangle}{\sqrt{2}} = (a_o \cdot |0\rangle + a_1|1\rangle) \otimes (b_o \cdot |0\rangle + b_1|1\rangle) = \tag{8.14}$$

$$= a_0 \cdot b_0 \cdot |00\rangle + a_0 \cdot b_1 \cdot |01\rangle + a_1 \cdot b_0 \cdot |10\rangle + a_1 \cdot b_1 \cdot |11\rangle$$

$$\rightarrow \quad a_0 \cdot b_0 = \frac{1}{\sqrt{2}}, \quad a_0 \cdot b_1 = 0, \quad a_1 \cdot b_0 = 0, \quad a_1 \cdot b_1 = \frac{1}{\sqrt{2}}$$

that is a contradiction.

A state that is not decomposable is called entangled. If two qubits are entangled in a state $\frac{|00\rangle+|11\rangle}{\sqrt{2}}$, then observing one of them will result in either $|0\rangle$ or $|1\rangle$ with probability $\frac{1}{2}$. However, it is not possible to observe a different value on the other, non-observed qubit. Both qubits behave as one unit and are called an *ebit*. There are four known *ebits*:

$$\frac{|00\rangle + |11\rangle}{\sqrt{2}}, \quad \frac{|00\rangle - |11\rangle}{\sqrt{2}}, \quad \frac{|01\rangle + |10\rangle}{\sqrt{2}}, \quad \frac{|01\rangle - |10\rangle}{\sqrt{2}}. \tag{8.15}$$

Once either qubit of an ebit is measured, the states of both particles become definite. Experiments have shown that this correlation can remain even if the qubits are separated over a distance of several kilometers. Quantum collapse during measurement is a non-local force. A non-local interaction is not limited by the speed of light, and its strength is not mediated with distance. This arrangement conflicts with Einstein's Theory of Special Relativity, which states that nothing can travel faster than light. The conflict is resolved by the fact that one cannot use an ebit to send any information. If two qubits of an ebit are separated over a distance in two places, A and B, and there are no other means of communication, then measuring the qubit on place A determines the outcome on place B, but at place B, the outcome is unknown. Measuring at place B is a random process without the knowledge of the results of place A. More than two qubits can be entangled. The GHZ (Greenberger-Horne-Zeilinger) state is entangled over M qubits with $M > 2$

$$\frac{|0\rangle^{\otimes M} + |1\rangle^{\otimes M}}{\sqrt{2}}. \tag{8.16}$$

For $M = 3$

$$\frac{|000\rangle + |111\rangle}{\sqrt{2}}.$$

The entanglement can arise during a computation that uses quantum gates due to the nature of the M_{CNOT} gate. During a computation, a part of the system can be observed by a projection, and the vector that represents the state is renormalized to the unit length. However, if an entanglement is present, then the observed part determines the rest of the state. In contrast to the conventional register, several qubits in a quantum register can form an entity, such as an ebit. Extra care must be taken when a part of the system is measured. A register is used to indicate if the computation is terminated, $|1\rangle$ for terminated and $|0\rangle$ for not terminated. If we measure $|1\rangle$, then we are done. If we measure $|0\rangle$, then we must start all of the computation from the beginning due to entanglement. There is no entanglement between two qubits of a state if

$$\sum_i \omega_i \cdot |x_i\rangle|y_i\rangle = \left(\sum_i \omega_i \cdot |x_i\rangle\right) \otimes |y_i\rangle$$

that is only valid if $|y_i\rangle = |y_j\rangle$ for all i and j. The states

$$\sum_i \omega_i \cdot |x_i\rangle|y_i\rangle, \qquad \sum_i \omega_i \cdot |x_i\rangle$$

behave differently.

8.5 Quantum Boolean Circuits

A reversible circuit that is composed of m bits corresponds to a unitary mapping that represents a permutation on m bits, defining an injective mapping $\mathbf{B}^m \to \mathbf{B}^m$. A unitary permutation matrix can represent this unitary mapping. A more elegant method is to map the reversible circuit into the quantum Boolean gates. Such a mapping allows us to determine the complexity of the circuit by the number of gates. The following quantum gates are Boolean quantum gates: the identity gate I, the NOT gate and the control not gate M_{CNOT}. The control not gate performs the essential fan-out operation. What is missing are the AND and OR operations. These operations can be represented by the universal reversible Toffoli gate (see chapter "Reversible Algorithms"). A reversible Toffoli gate is a unitary mapping. It defines a quantum gate on three qubits and can be represented by a unitary matrix M in Hilbert space H_8

$$M = \begin{pmatrix} I_1 & 0 & 0 & 0 \\ 0 & I_1 & 0 & 0 \\ 0 & 0 & I_1 & 0 \\ 0 & 0 & 0 & M_\neg \end{pmatrix} = \begin{pmatrix} 1&0&0&0&0&0&0&0 \\ 0&1&0&0&0&0&0&0 \\ 0&0&1&0&0&0&0&0 \\ 0&0&0&1&0&0&0&0 \\ 0&0&0&0&1&0&0&0 \\ 0&0&0&0&0&1&0&0 \\ 0&0&0&0&0&0&0&1 \\ 0&0&0&0&0&0&1&0 \end{pmatrix}. \tag{8.17}$$

The unitary matrix M can be decomposed into several ways using non Boolean quantum gates. However each decomposition involves the M_{CNOT}, indicating that an entanglement may arise when applying a quantum Toffoli gate. With the basis of three qubits of the Hilbert space H_8

$$|000\rangle = \begin{pmatrix} 1\\0\\0\\0\\0\\0\\0\\0 \end{pmatrix}, |001\rangle = \begin{pmatrix} 0\\1\\0\\0\\0\\0\\0\\0 \end{pmatrix}, |010\rangle = \begin{pmatrix} 0\\0\\1\\0\\0\\0\\0\\0 \end{pmatrix}, |011\rangle = \begin{pmatrix} 0\\0\\0\\1\\0\\0\\0\\0 \end{pmatrix},$$

$$|100\rangle = \begin{pmatrix} 0\\0\\0\\0\\1\\0\\0\\0 \end{pmatrix}, |101\rangle = \begin{pmatrix} 0\\0\\0\\0\\0\\1\\0\\0 \end{pmatrix}, |110\rangle = \begin{pmatrix} 0\\0\\0\\0\\0\\0\\1\\0 \end{pmatrix}, |111\rangle = \begin{pmatrix} 0\\0\\0\\0\\0\\0\\0\\1 \end{pmatrix}$$

the mapping of the reversible $T(x_1, x_2, x_3) = (x_1, x_2, (x_1 \wedge x_2) \oplus x_3)$ corresponds to the unitary mapping

$$M \cdot |xyz\rangle = M \cdot |x\rangle|y\rangle|z\rangle = |x\rangle|y\rangle|(x \wedge y) \oplus z\rangle. \tag{8.18}$$

For the AND operation, the ancilla bit z is set to 0

$$M \cdot |x\rangle|y\rangle|0\rangle = |x\rangle|y\rangle|(x \wedge y)\rangle. \tag{8.19}$$

The four bit conjunction $x \wedge y \wedge z \wedge v$ requires three quantum Toffoli gates and three additional qubits that are zero. The input:

$$|x\rangle|y\rangle|0\rangle|z\rangle|0\rangle|v\rangle|0\rangle.$$

First quantum Toffoli gate

$$(M \cdot |x\rangle|y\rangle|0\rangle) \otimes (I_4| \cdot |z\rangle|0\rangle|v\rangle|0\rangle) = |x\rangle|y\rangle|x \wedge y\rangle|z\rangle|0\rangle|v\rangle|0\rangle.$$

Second quantum Toffoli gate

$$(I_2 \cdot |x\rangle|y\rangle) \otimes (M \cdot |x \wedge y\rangle|z\rangle|0) \otimes (I_2 \cdot |v\rangle|0\rangle)$$
$$= |x\rangle|y\rangle|x \wedge y\rangle|z\rangle|x \wedge y \wedge z\rangle|v\rangle|0\rangle.$$

Third quantum Toffoli gate

$$(I_4 \cdot |x\rangle|y\rangle|x \wedge y\rangle|z\rangle) \otimes (M \cdot |x \wedge y \wedge z\rangle|v\rangle|0\rangle)$$
$$= |x\rangle|y\rangle|x \wedge y\rangle|z\rangle|x \wedge y \wedge z\rangle|v\rangle|x \wedge y \wedge z \wedge v\rangle.$$

The circuit corresponds to the following unitary mapping

$$((I_4 \otimes M)\,(I_2 \otimes M \otimes I_2) \cdot (M \otimes I_4)) \cdot |xy0z0v0\rangle$$

with the result

$$|x\rangle|y\rangle|x \wedge y\rangle|z\rangle|x \wedge y \wedge z\rangle|v\rangle|x \wedge y \wedge z \wedge v\rangle.$$

The third and the fifth qubit are usually not required for further computation because the result is represented in the output qubit seven. However they are entangled with the output qubit. It is not possible to reset them to zero. Instead they are un-computed. Because $M^{-1} = M$ we recompute the first and the second quantum Toffoli gate after determining the result. The steps are reversed, it follows

$$((I_2 \otimes M \otimes I_2) \cdot (M \otimes I_4) \cdot (I_4 \otimes M)\,(I_2 \otimes M \otimes I_2) \cdot (M \otimes I_4)) \cdot |xy0z0v0\rangle$$
$$= |x\rangle|y\rangle|0\rangle|z\rangle|0\rangle|v\rangle|x \wedge y \wedge z \wedge v\rangle = |xy0z0v(x \wedge y \wedge z \wedge v)\rangle.$$

The OR operation is represented by the unitary mapping according to the De Morgan's laws

$$((I_2 \otimes M_{NOT}) \cdot M \cdot (M_{NOT} \otimes M_{NOT} \otimes I_1)) \cdot |xy0\rangle = xy(x \vee y)\rangle.$$

For each quantum Boolean AND, OR operation a naïve implementation requires an ancilla bit. These bits can be reused for further computation only by reversing the preceding steps. The complexity of the circuit corresponds to the number of used quantum gates. A quantum circuit represents a permutation in Hilbert space and is not an algorithmic device. The computation does not alter the distribution of the amplitudes; the Shannon entropy remains unchanged during the execution of the quantum Boolean gates. The probability of measuring certain states is the same before and after the computation; by itself, it does not offer any advantage over the classical computation.

8.6 Deutsch Algorithm

The Hadamard gate changes the Shannon entropy before and after the computation; it performs an operation that goes beyond the Boolean truth operations. It maps a state with zero Shannon entropy to a superposition with maximal entropy. The Deutsch algorithm [Deutsch and Jozsa (1992)] exploits the superposition of qubits generated by Hadamard gates and is more powerful than any classical algorithm. It determines if an unknown function $f : \mathbf{B}^1 \to \mathbf{B}^1 : f(x) = y$ of one bit is constant or not by calling the function one time. A classical algorithm requires two calls. A constant function on one bit is either $f(x) = 1$ or $f(x) = 0$. A non constant function is either the identity function $f(0) = 0$ and $f(1) = 1$ or the flip function $f(0) = 1$ and $f(1) = 0$. The condition of the function being constant $f(0) = f(1)$ implies that the XOR operation $\oplus$ is $f(0) \oplus f(1) = 0$ is zero. On the other hand if the function is not constant $f(0) \neq f(1)$ implies that the XOR operation $\oplus$ is $f(0) \oplus f(1) = 1$ is one. We can define a unitary operator U_f that acts on the two qubits

$$U_f \cdot |xy\rangle = |x\rangle|f(x) \oplus y\rangle.$$

U_f can be implemented by a quantum Boolean circuit including C_{NOT} gate. There are four different cases, for $f(x) = 0$ with the identity mapping

$$i)\ \ U_f|00\rangle = |0\rangle|0 \oplus 0\rangle = |00\rangle, \ \ U_f|01\rangle = |01\rangle,$$
$$U_f|10\rangle = |10\rangle, \ \ U_f|11\rangle = |11\rangle$$

for $f(x) = 1$ with the permutation of all elements.

$$ii)\ \ U_f|00\rangle = |0\rangle|1 \oplus 0\rangle = |01\rangle, \ \ U_f|01\rangle = |00\rangle,$$
$$U_f|10\rangle = |11\rangle, \ \ U_f|11\rangle = |10\rangle$$

and for a non constant function, $f(x) = x$ corresponds to a permutation of two elements.

$$iii)\ \ U_f|00\rangle = |0\rangle|0 \oplus 0\rangle = |00\rangle, \ \ U_f|01\rangle = |01\rangle,$$
$$U_f|10\rangle = |11\rangle, \ \ U_f|11\rangle = |10\rangle$$

and $f(x) = \neg x$ with a permutation of two elements as well

$$vi)\ \ U_f|00\rangle = |0\rangle|1 \oplus 0\rangle = |01\rangle, \ \ U_f|01\rangle = |00\rangle,$$
$$U_f|10\rangle = |10\rangle, \ \ U_f|11\rangle = |11\rangle.$$

There are two classes:

- No permutation *i*) or permutation of all elements *ii*) indicates that the function is constant.
- Permutation of two elements *iii*), *iv*) indicates that the function is non constant.

The Algorithm to determine if $f(x)$ is constant or not is composed of four steps. In the first step of the algorithm we build a superposition of two qubits

$$W2 \cdot |01\rangle = W_1 \cdot |0\rangle \otimes W_1 \cdot |1\rangle = \left(\frac{|0\rangle + |1\rangle}{\sqrt{2}}\right) \otimes \left(\frac{|0\rangle - |1\rangle}{\sqrt{2}}\right) =$$

$$W2 \cdot |01\rangle = \frac{1}{2} \cdot (|00\rangle - |01\rangle + |10\rangle - |11\rangle).$$

In the second step we apply the U_f, gate.

$$U_f \cdot W2 \cdot |01\rangle = U_f \left(\frac{1}{2} \cdot (|00\rangle - |01\rangle + |10\rangle - |11\rangle)\right)$$

$$= \frac{1}{2} \cdot (U_f \cdot |00\rangle - U_f \cdot |01\rangle + U_f \cdot |10\rangle - U_f \cdot |11\rangle).$$

There are four possible outcomes. For constant function

$$i) \quad = \frac{1}{2} \cdot (|00\rangle - |01\rangle + |10\rangle - |11\rangle) = \left(\frac{|0\rangle + |1\rangle}{\sqrt{2}}\right) \otimes \left(\frac{|0\rangle - |1\rangle}{\sqrt{2}}\right),$$

$$ii) \quad = \frac{1}{2} \cdot (|01\rangle - |00\rangle + |11\rangle - |10\rangle) = \frac{1}{2} \cdot (-|00\rangle + |01\rangle - |10\rangle + |11\rangle)$$

$$= \left(\frac{-|0\rangle - |1\rangle}{\sqrt{2}}\right) \otimes \left(\frac{|0\rangle - |1\rangle}{\sqrt{2}}\right) = -\left(\frac{|0\rangle + |1\rangle}{\sqrt{2}}\right) \otimes \left(\frac{|0\rangle - |1\rangle}{\sqrt{2}}\right),$$

and for non constant function

$$iii) \quad = \frac{1}{2} \cdot (|00\rangle - |01\rangle + |11\rangle - |10\rangle) = \frac{1}{2} \cdot (|00\rangle - |01\rangle|10\rangle + |11\rangle)$$

$$= \left(\frac{|0\rangle - |1\rangle}{\sqrt{2}}\right) \otimes \left(\frac{|0\rangle - |1\rangle}{\sqrt{2}}\right),$$

$$iv) \quad = \frac{1}{2} \cdot (|01\rangle - |00\rangle + |10\rangle - |11\rangle) = \frac{1}{2} \cdot (-|00\rangle + |01\rangle + |10\rangle - |11\rangle)$$

$$\left(\frac{-|0\rangle + |1\rangle}{\sqrt{2}}\right) \otimes \left(\frac{|0\rangle - |1\rangle}{\sqrt{2}}\right) = -\left(\frac{|0\rangle - |1\rangle}{\sqrt{2}}\right) \otimes \left(\frac{|0\rangle - |1\rangle}{\sqrt{2}}\right).$$

In the third step a Hadamard gate is applied to the first qubit

$$(W_1 \otimes I_1) \cdot U_f \cdot W2 \cdot |01\rangle. \tag{8.20}$$

There are four possible outcomes,

$$i) \quad |0\rangle \otimes \left(\frac{|0\rangle - |1\rangle}{\sqrt{2}}\right),$$

$$ii) \quad -|0\rangle \otimes \left(\frac{|0\rangle - |1\rangle}{\sqrt{2}}\right),$$

$$iii) \quad |1\rangle \otimes \left(\frac{|0\rangle - |1\rangle}{\sqrt{2}}\right),$$

$$vi) \quad -|1\rangle \otimes \left(\frac{|0\rangle - |1\rangle}{\sqrt{2}}\right).$$

In the fourth step the first qubit (that is in the basis state) is measured. It is $|0\rangle$ if the function is constant, otherwise $|1\rangle$.

Even the Deutsch algorithm is more powerful than any classical algorithm, it determines a unknown function of one bit by calling it only one time, it needs three serial steps before a measurement can take place. In the next section we generalize the working principle of the algorithm even to a more powerful algorithm.

8.7 Deutsch Jozsa Algorithm

It determines if a unknown function $f : \mathbf{B}^m \to \mathbf{B}^1 : f(x) = y$ of m bit is constant or a balanced function. In constant function of m bits for all possible $n = 2^m$ inputs the output is either 0 or 1 [Deutsch and Jozsa (1992)]. In a balanced function half of the $n = 2^m$ input values output 0 the other half output 1. A set of the input values x of the size 2^m is mapped into two subsets called 0 and 1 each of the size $2^m/2 = 2^{m-1}$. Such a two subsets could be the subset of even and odd numbers. A classical algorithm has to call the function $2^{m-1}+1$ times in the worst case, since in the worst case the output is 2^{m-1} times 0. If in the next call it is 0 then the function is constant, otherwise it is guaranteed to be balanced. The Deutsch Jozsa algorithm needs three serial steps before a measurement can take place. We define a unitary operator U_f that acts on the $m+1$ qubits with $x \in B^m$ and $y \in B^1$

$$U_f \cdot |x\rangle|y\rangle = |x\rangle|f(x) \oplus y\rangle.$$

The Algorithm to determine if $f(x)$ is constant or balanced is composed of four steps. In the first step of the algorithm we build a superposition of $m+1$ qubits

$$W_{m+1} \cdot |0^{\otimes m}\rangle|1\rangle = W_m \cdot |0^{\otimes n}\rangle \otimes W_1 \cdot |1\rangle = \frac{1}{\sqrt{2^n}} \sum_{x \in B^m} |x\rangle \otimes \left(\frac{|0\rangle - |1\rangle}{\sqrt{2}}\right).$$

The first m qubits represent a superposition over all possible states with a positive amplitude, in the last qubit one amplitude of the two possible states is negative. In the second step we apply the U_f, operator,

$$U_f \cdot W_{m+1} \cdot |0^{\otimes m}\rangle|1\rangle = U_f \cdot \left(\frac{1}{\sqrt{2^m}} \sum_{x \in B^m} |x\rangle \otimes \left(\frac{|0\rangle - |1\rangle}{\sqrt{2}} \right) \right)$$

$$= U_f \cdot \left(\frac{1}{\sqrt{2^{m+1}}} \sum_{x \in B^m} |x\rangle \otimes (|0\rangle - |1\rangle) \right)$$

$$= \frac{1}{\sqrt{2^{m+1}}} \cdot U_f \cdot \left(\sum_{x \in B^m} (|x\rangle|0\rangle - |x\rangle|1\rangle) \right)$$

$$= \frac{1}{\sqrt{2^{n+1}}} \cdot \sum_{x \in B^m} U_f \cdot (|x\rangle|0\rangle - |x\rangle|1\rangle)$$

$$= \frac{1}{\sqrt{2^{m+1}}} \cdot \sum_{x \in B^m} (U_f \cdot |x\rangle|0\rangle - U_f \cdot |x\rangle|1\rangle)$$

$$= \frac{1}{\sqrt{2^{m+1}}} \cdot \sum_{x \in B^m} U_f \cdot |x\rangle|0\rangle - \frac{1}{\sqrt{2^{m+1}}} \cdot \sum_{x \in B^m} U_f \cdot |x\rangle|1\rangle$$

$$= \frac{1}{\sqrt{2^{m+1}}} \cdot \sum_{x \in B^m} |x\rangle|f(x) \oplus 0\rangle - \frac{1}{\sqrt{2^{m+1}}} \cdot \sum_{x \in B^m} |x\rangle|f(x) \oplus 1\rangle.$$

There are three possible outcomes. For constant function

i) $$\frac{1}{\sqrt{2^{m+1}}} \cdot \sum_{x \in B^m} |x\rangle|0 \oplus 0\rangle - \frac{1}{\sqrt{2^{m+1}}} \cdot \sum_{x \in B^m} |x\rangle|0 \oplus 1\rangle$$

$$= \frac{1}{\sqrt{2^m}} \sum_{x \in B^m} |x\rangle \otimes \left(\frac{|0\rangle - |1\rangle}{\sqrt{2}} \right),$$

ii) $$\frac{1}{\sqrt{2^{m+1}}} \cdot \sum_{x \in B^m} |x\rangle|1 \oplus 0\rangle - \frac{1}{\sqrt{2^{m+1}}} \cdot \sum_{x \in B^m} |x\rangle|1 \oplus 1\rangle$$

$$= -\frac{1}{\sqrt{2^m}} \sum_{x \in B^m} |x\rangle \otimes \left(\frac{|0\rangle - |1\rangle}{\sqrt{2}} \right),$$

and for non constant function

$$iii)\ \frac{1}{\sqrt{2^{n+1}}} \cdot \Big(\sum_{f(x)=0} |x\rangle|0 \oplus 0\rangle - \sum_{f(x)=0} |x\rangle|0 \oplus 1\rangle$$

$$+ \sum_{f(x)=1} |x\rangle|1 \oplus 0\rangle - \sum_{f(x)=1} |x\rangle|1 \oplus 1\rangle\Big)$$

$$= \frac{1}{\sqrt{2^n}} \cdot \left(\sum_{f(x)=0} |x\rangle - \sum_{f(x)=1} |x\rangle \right) \oplus \left(\frac{|0\rangle - |1\rangle}{\sqrt{2}} \right)$$

$$= \frac{1}{\sqrt{2^n}} \sum_{x \in B^m} (-1)^{f(x)} \cdot |x\rangle \otimes \left(\frac{|0\rangle - |1\rangle}{\sqrt{2}} \right).$$

The result i), ii) can be as well represented by iii). The representation

$$\frac{1}{\sqrt{2^m}} \sum_{x \in B^m} (-1)^{f(x)} \cdot |x\rangle \otimes \left(\frac{|0\rangle - |1\rangle}{\sqrt{2}} \right) \tag{8.21}$$

is one of the most used notations in quantum computation. The value of the function $f(x)$ is encoded by $(-1)^{f(x)}$, the sign of the amplitude. The last qubit $\left(\frac{|0\rangle - |1\rangle}{\sqrt{2}} \right)$ is called auxiliary, or target bit and is ignored, so the Equation 8.21 is written as

$$\frac{1}{\sqrt{2^m}} \sum_{x \in B^m} (-1)^{f(x)} \cdot |x\rangle. \tag{8.22}$$

In the third step a Hadamard gate is applied to the first n qubits, the target qubit is ignored

$$(W_m \otimes I_1) \cdot U_f \cdot W_{m+1} \cdot |0^{\otimes n}\rangle|1\rangle \tag{8.23}$$

there are four possible outcomes,

$$i)\ |0^{\otimes n}\rangle \otimes \left(\frac{|0\rangle - |1\rangle}{\sqrt{2}} \right)$$

$$ii)\ -|0^{\otimes n}\rangle \otimes \left(\frac{|0\rangle - |1\rangle}{\sqrt{2}} \right)$$

$$iii)\ W_m \cdot \frac{1}{\sqrt{2^m}} \sum_{x \in B^m} (-1)^{f(x)} \cdot |x\rangle \otimes I_1 \cdot \left(\frac{|0\rangle - |1\rangle}{\sqrt{2}} \right)$$

$$= W_m \cdot \left(\frac{1}{\sqrt{2^m}} \sum_{x \in B^n} (-1)^{\langle z|x\rangle} \cdot |x\rangle \right) \otimes \left(\frac{|0\rangle - |1\rangle}{\sqrt{2}} \right) = |z\rangle \otimes \left(\frac{|0\rangle - |1\rangle}{\sqrt{2}} \right)$$

$$vi)\ W_m \cdot \frac{1}{\sqrt{2^m}} \sum_{x \in B^m} (-1)^{f(x)} \cdot |x\rangle \otimes I_1 \cdot \left(\frac{|0\rangle - |1\rangle}{\sqrt{2}} \right)$$

$$= W_m \cdot \left(\frac{-1}{\sqrt{2^m}} \sum_{x \in B^n} (-1)^{\langle z|x\rangle} \cdot |x\rangle \right) \otimes \left(\frac{|0\rangle - |1\rangle}{\sqrt{2}} \right) = -|z\rangle \otimes \left(\frac{|0\rangle - |1\rangle}{\sqrt{2}} \right).$$

The results i), ii), iii) and iv) can be represented as

$$\frac{1}{2^m} \sum_{z \in B^m} \sum_{x \in B^m} (-1)^{f(x)} \cdot |z\rangle \otimes \left(\frac{|0\rangle - |1\rangle}{\sqrt{2}} \right). \tag{8.24}$$

In the fourth step the first m qubits are measured. They are $|0^{\otimes m}\rangle$ if the function is constant, for a balanced function $|z\rangle \neq |0^{\otimes m}\rangle$. The algorithm determines as well the shape of the function $f(x)$. The shape is represented by the z row or column of the W_m matrix, in which either 1 represents the value zero of the function and -1 the value one or visa versa. Before the measurement this information is represented by the minus sign of the amplitude. The first n qubits are either $|z\rangle$ or $-|z\rangle$. After the measurement the m qubits are $|z\rangle$, the information about of the amplitude is lost, $|0^{\otimes m}\rangle$ is either the constant function $f(x) = 0$ or $f(x) = 1$. The Deutsch Jozsa algorithm is build on three serial steps. It maps a state with zero Shannon entropy to a superposition with maximal entropy, does the computation on this superposition and maps the result into a state with zero entropy. It provides three most important principles of quantum computation:

- The function $f(x)$ is represented by a quantum Boolean circuit.
- The properties of the function $f(x)$ are determined using the superposition principle and a generalized class of Fourier transform (The Hadamard transform).
- The values of the function $f(x)$ are encoded by $(-1)^{f(x)}$, the sign of the amplitude.

This principles are the basis for the two most revolutionary quantum algorithms, Shor's algorithm and Grover's algorithm. Before their introduction, some limitations of quantum computation are highlighted.

8.8 Amplitude Distribution

The register of m qubits is represented as a direct product of m qubits. It defines $n = 2^m$ dimensional Hilbert space H_n with an orthonormal basis

$|x_1\rangle, |x_1\rangle \cdots |x_n\rangle$ and a state is represented as a unit-lengt vector

$$|x\rangle = \omega_1 \cdot |x_1\rangle + \omega_2 \cdot |x_2\rangle + \cdots + \omega_n \cdot |x_n\rangle.$$

After the measurement, observation the state $|x\rangle$ is projected into a basis state

$$1 \cdot |x_k\rangle.$$

All the information about the amplitude distribution $\omega_1, \cdots, \omega_n$ of $|x\rangle$ is lost. Could we save this inform by coping the unit-length vector $|x\rangle$ to another state? Could we clone a state?

8.8.1 *Cloning*

To preform this task we define a copy machine. We chose one orthonormal basis state of the orthonormal basis, for example $|x_1\rangle$ and define a unitary copy operator that copies an state $|x\rangle \in H_n$ as

$$U_{copy}(|x\rangle, |x_1\rangle) = |x\rangle|x\rangle. \tag{8.25}$$

Does U_{copy} exist? For basis states U_{copy} is defined. It can be realized for example by M_{CNOT} with $|x_1\rangle = |0\rangle$ and $|x_2\rangle = |1\rangle$,

$$U_{copy}(|x_1\rangle, |x_1\rangle) = |x_1\rangle|x_1\rangle, \quad U_{copy}(|x_2\rangle, |x_1\rangle) = |x_2\rangle|x_2\rangle.$$

If the state is in a superposition

$$|x\rangle = \frac{|x_1\rangle + |x_2\rangle}{\sqrt{2}}$$

it implies that

$$U_{copy}(|x\rangle, |x_1\rangle) = |x\rangle|x\rangle = \left(\frac{|x_1\rangle + |x_2\rangle}{\sqrt{2}}\right) \otimes \left(\frac{|x_1\rangle + |x_2\rangle}{\sqrt{2}}\right) =$$

$$\frac{1}{2} \cdot (|x_1\rangle|x_1\rangle + |x_1\rangle|x_2\rangle + |x_2\rangle|x_1\rangle + |x_2\rangle|x_2\rangle).$$

Because of the linearity of U_{copy} it follows,

$$U_{copy}(|x\rangle, |x_1\rangle) = U_{copy}\left(\frac{|x_1\rangle + |x_2\rangle}{\sqrt{2}}, |x_1\rangle\right) =$$

$$U_{copy}(|x\rangle, |x_1\rangle) = U_{copy}\left(\frac{|x_1\rangle|x_1\rangle + |x_2\rangle|x_1\rangle}{\sqrt{2}}\right) =$$

$$\frac{U_{copy}(|x_1\rangle|x_1\rangle) + U_{copy}(|x_2\rangle|x_1\rangle)}{\sqrt{2}} = \frac{1}{\sqrt{2}} \cdot (|x_1\rangle|x_1\rangle + |x_2\rangle|x_2\rangle)$$

it leads to a contradiction. An operation that would produce a copy of an arbitrary quantum state is not possible, we cannot copy an unknown amplitude distribution of a state. For example we cannot copy an unknown qubit $\alpha \cdot |0\rangle + \beta \cdot |1\rangle$. The amplitude distribution is specified by the values of α and β. However we can copy the basis, $\alpha \cdot |0\rangle + \beta \cdot |1\rangle$ into the basis $\alpha \cdot |00\rangle + \beta \cdot |11\rangle$. The operator copy base U_{copy^*}

$$U_{copy^*}(\alpha \cdot |x_1\rangle + \beta \cdot |x_2\rangle, |x_1\rangle)$$

$$= U_{copy^*}(\alpha \cdot |x_1 x_1\rangle + \beta \cdot |x_2 x_1\rangle) = \alpha \cdot |x_1 x_1\rangle + \beta \cdot |x_2 x_2\rangle \tag{8.26}$$

exist, it can be realized by M_{CNOT}. U_{copy^*} does not change the entropy of the register, U_{copy} would change it.

8.8.2 *Teleportation*

It is possible to teleport a qubit from one location to another using an *ebit* [Bennett *et al.* (1993)]. The two qubits in an *ebit* behave as one unit, even if the qubits are separated. This nonlocal interaction is not limited by speed of light, not mediated by the distance. The qubit is transferred from one point to another without traversing the physical space. Suppose we have two qubits that are entangled in a state $\frac{|00\rangle+|11\rangle}{\sqrt{2}}$. We separate the two qubits of the *ebit* over a distance on two places A and B.

$$\frac{|0_A\rangle|0_B\rangle + |1_A\rangle|1_B\rangle}{\sqrt{2}}. \tag{8.27}$$

In the first step of the teleportation of the qubit $\alpha \cdot |0_A\rangle + \beta \cdot |1_A\rangle$ from the place A to the place B we interact with the corresponding *ebit*

$$(\alpha \cdot |0_A\rangle + \beta \cdot |1_A\rangle) \otimes \left(\frac{|0_A\rangle|0_B\rangle + |1_A\rangle|1_B\rangle}{\sqrt{2}}\right) \tag{8.28}$$

$$\frac{\alpha \cdot (|0_A\rangle|0_A\rangle|0_B\rangle + |0_A\rangle|1_A\rangle|1_B\rangle) + \beta \cdot (|1_A\rangle|0_A\rangle|0_B\rangle + |1_A\rangle|1_A\rangle|1_B\rangle)}{\sqrt{2}}. \tag{8.29}$$

After the interaction there are two qubits on the location A and on the location B. In the second step we apply the M_{CNOT} quantum gate to the first two qubits at the location A and on the location B we do noting

$$(M_{CNOT} \otimes I_1) \cdot \frac{1}{\sqrt{2}} \cdot (\alpha \cdot (|0_A\rangle|0_A\rangle|0_B\rangle + |0_A\rangle|1_A\rangle|1_B\rangle) +$$

$$\beta \cdot (|1_A\rangle|0_A\rangle|0_B\rangle + |1_A\rangle|1_A\rangle|1_B\rangle)) =$$

$$\frac{\alpha \cdot (|0_A\rangle|0_A\rangle|0_B\rangle + |0_A\rangle|1_A\rangle|1_B\rangle) + \beta \cdot (|1_A\rangle|1_A\rangle|0_B\rangle + |1_A\rangle|0_A\rangle|1_B\rangle)}{\sqrt{2}}. \tag{8.30}$$

This can be rewritten as

$$\frac{\alpha \cdot |0_A\rangle \otimes (|0_A\rangle|0_B\rangle + |1_A\rangle|1_B\rangle) + \beta \cdot |1_A\rangle \otimes (|1_A\rangle|0_B\rangle + |0_A\rangle|1_B\rangle)}{\sqrt{2}}. \tag{8.31}$$

In the third step we apply the W_1 quantum gate to the first qubit at the location A and on the location B we do noting.

$$(W_1 \otimes I_2) \cdot \frac{1}{\sqrt{2}} \cdot (\alpha \cdot |0_A\rangle \otimes (|0_A\rangle|0_B\rangle + |1_A\rangle|1_B\rangle) +$$

$$\beta \cdot |1_A\rangle \otimes (|1_A\rangle|0_B\rangle + |0_A\rangle|1_B\rangle)) =$$

$$\frac{1}{2} \cdot (\alpha \cdot (|0_A\rangle + 1_A\rangle) \otimes (|0_A\rangle|0_B\rangle + |1_A\rangle|1_B\rangle)$$

$$+\beta \cdot (|0_A\rangle - 1_A\rangle) \otimes (|1_A\rangle|0_B\rangle + |0_A\rangle|1_B\rangle)) =$$

$$\frac{1}{2} \cdot (\alpha \cdot |0_A\rangle 0_A\rangle|0_B\rangle + \alpha \cdot |0_A|1_A\rangle|1_B\rangle +$$

$$\alpha \cdot |1_A\rangle 0_A\rangle|0_B\rangle + \alpha \cdot |1_A|1_A\rangle|1_B\rangle +$$

$$\beta \cdot |0_A\rangle|1_A\rangle|0_B\rangle + \beta \cdot |0_A\rangle 0_A\rangle|1_B\rangle - \beta \cdot |0_A\rangle 1_A\rangle|0_B\rangle - \beta \cdot |0_A\rangle|0_A\rangle|1_B\rangle)$$

after rewriting the equation we get the following representation

$$\frac{1}{2} \cdot (|0_A\rangle|0_A\rangle \otimes (\alpha \cdot |0_B\rangle + \beta \cdot |1_B\rangle) + |0_A\rangle|1_A\rangle \otimes (\alpha \cdot |1_B\rangle + \beta \cdot |0_B\rangle) +$$

$$|1_A\rangle|0_A\rangle \otimes (\alpha \cdot |0_B\rangle - \beta \cdot |1_B\rangle) + |1_A\rangle|1_A\rangle \otimes (\alpha \cdot |1_B\rangle - \beta \cdot |0_B\rangle)).$$

In the fourth step a measurement of the first two qubits at the place A is done. There are four possible results; each of them has an equal probability of being measured.

$|\mathbf{00}\rangle$ is measured the state collapses at place B to

$$\alpha \cdot |0\rangle + \beta \cdot |1\rangle$$

at place B no correction is nesseascary, the qubit described by its amplitude distribution was teleported.

$|\mathbf{01}\rangle$ is measured the state collapses at place B to

$$\alpha \cdot |1\rangle + \beta \cdot |0\rangle$$

at place B a correction is necessary to reconstruct the teleported qubit. M_{NOT} gate is applied.

$$M_{NOT} \cdot (\alpha \cdot |1\rangle + \beta \cdot |0\rangle) = \alpha \cdot |0\rangle + \beta \cdot |1\rangle$$

$|\mathbf{10}\rangle$ is measured the state collapses at place B to

$$\alpha \cdot |0\rangle - \beta \cdot |1\rangle$$

at place B a correction is necessary to reconstruct the teleported qubit. Z gate is applied.

$$Z = \begin{pmatrix} 1 & 0 \\ 0 & -1 \end{pmatrix} \tag{8.32}$$

$$Z \cdot (\alpha \cdot |0\rangle - \beta \cdot |1\rangle) = \alpha \cdot |0\rangle + \beta \cdot |1\rangle$$

$|\mathbf{11}\rangle$ is measured the state collapses at place B to

$$\alpha \cdot |1\rangle - \beta \cdot |0\rangle$$

at place B a correction is necessary to reconstruct the teleported qubit. M_{NOT} gate and then the Z gate is applied.

$$Z \cdot M_{NOT} \cdot (\alpha \cdot |1\rangle - \beta \cdot |0\rangle) = \alpha \cdot |0\rangle + \beta \cdot |1\rangle.$$

This transformation is also called the Y gate

$$Y = Z \cdot M_{NOT} = \begin{pmatrix} 1 & 0 \\ 0 & -1 \end{pmatrix} \cdot \begin{pmatrix} 0 & 1 \\ 1 & 0 \end{pmatrix} = \begin{pmatrix} 0 & 1 \\ -1 & 0 \end{pmatrix}. \tag{8.33}$$

For the teleportation of qubits classical communication is required. To indicate how to reconstruct one qubit two bits have to be send over a classical channel, since one teleported qubit can take four different superpositions. It follows that an *ebit* cannot be used to send or teleport information, additionally a classical channel is required.

8.9 Geometric Operations

A unitary operator performs a rotation or a reflection of a state represented by a unit length vector in a Hilbert space. States may be equivalent if they differ only by the relative amplitudes, different states when measured are always equal.

Equivalent states Two equivalent states represent the same state when a measurement is preformed, but they can have behave differently during the unitary evolution. Two states $|x\rangle$ and $|y\rangle$ are equivalent $|x\rangle \equiv |y\rangle$ if

$$|x\rangle = e^{i\cdot\theta} \cdot |y\rangle \tag{8.34}$$

with

$$e^{i\cdot\theta} = \cos\theta + i \cdot \sin\theta. \tag{8.35}$$

For example $|0\rangle$ and $-|0\rangle$ are two equivalent states

$$|0\rangle \equiv -|0\rangle \Leftrightarrow |0\rangle = -e^{i\cdot\pi} \cdot |0\rangle \tag{8.36}$$

for $\theta = \pi$

$$e^{i\cdot\pi} = \cos\pi + i \cdot \sin\pi = -1.$$

Other examples are

$$|0\rangle \equiv i \cdot |0\rangle \Leftrightarrow |0\rangle = i \cdot e^{i\cdot(-\pi/2)} \cdot |0\rangle \tag{8.37}$$

for $\theta = -\pi/2$

$$e^{i\cdot(-\pi/2)} = \cos -\pi/2 + i \cdot \sin -\pi/2 = -i$$

and

$$|0\rangle \equiv \frac{|0\rangle + i \cdot |0\rangle}{\sqrt{2}} \Leftrightarrow |0\rangle = \frac{1+i}{\sqrt{2}} \cdot e^{i\cdot\pi/4} \cdot |0\rangle \tag{8.38}$$

for $\theta = -\pi/4$

$$e^{i\cdot(-\pi/4)} = \cos(-\pi/4) + i \cdot \sin(-\pi/4) = \frac{1-i}{\sqrt{2}}$$

$$\frac{1-i}{\sqrt{2}} \cdot \frac{1+i}{\sqrt{2}} = \frac{2}{2} = 1.$$

However the following two state is not equal nor not equivalent

$$\frac{|0\rangle + |1\rangle}{\sqrt{2}} \neq \frac{|0\rangle - |1\rangle}{\sqrt{2}}.$$

They are the reflection of each other.

Reflection An example of a reflection operator is the Z operator

$$Z = \begin{pmatrix} 1 & 0 \\ 0 & -1 \end{pmatrix}.$$

It preforms a reflection on the basis defined by $|0\rangle$. The Z gate is a special case of the phase gate

$$P = \begin{pmatrix} 1 & 0 \\ 0 & e^{i \cdot \theta} \end{pmatrix} \tag{8.39}$$

with $\theta = \pi$. A phase gate alters the relative amplitudes but represents the same state value when a measurement is preformed and can be used together with the M_{NOT} gate

$$\begin{pmatrix} e^{i \cdot \theta} & 0 \\ 0 & e^{i \cdot \theta} \end{pmatrix} = \begin{pmatrix} 1 & 0 \\ 0 & e^{i \cdot \theta} \end{pmatrix} \cdot \begin{pmatrix} 0 & 1 \\ 1 & 0 \end{pmatrix} \cdot \begin{pmatrix} 1 & 0 \\ 0 & e^{-i \cdot \theta} \end{pmatrix}. \tag{8.40}$$

Rotation A rotation by an angle α is represented by the unitary operator R

$$R = \begin{pmatrix} \cos\alpha & -\sin\alpha \\ \sin\alpha & \cos\alpha \end{pmatrix}. \tag{8.41}$$

It can be shown that a unitary transformation is a rotation of $n = 2^m$ Hilbert space [Rieffel and Polak (2011)].

Changing the basis In data analysis the Karhunen-Loève transformation rotates the coordinate system in such a way that the covariance matrix is diagonal, means each dimension is uncorrelated. In quantum computation a unitary transformation is equivalent to a change of the basis.

Closure relation For a basis an orthonormal basis

$$|x_1\rangle, |x_1\rangle. \cdots |x_n\rangle$$

the identity operator is represented as

$$\sum_{i=1}^{n} |x_i\rangle\langle x_i|. \tag{8.42}$$

With the inner product

$$\langle x|x_i\rangle = \omega_i$$

an state $|x\rangle$ can be represented as

$$|x\rangle = I \cdot |x\rangle = \left(\sum_{i=1}^{n} |x_i\rangle\langle x_i| \right) |x\rangle = \sum_{i=1}^{n} |x_i\rangle\langle x_i|x\rangle = \sum_{i=1}^{n} \omega_i \cdot |x_i\rangle. \tag{8.43}$$

An operator A can be represented using the closure relation as

$$A = I \cdot A \cdot I = \left(\sum_{i=1}^{n} |x_i\rangle\langle x_i| \right) \cdot A \cdot \left(\sum_{j=1}^{n} |x_j\rangle\langle x_j| \right) = \sum_{i,j} \langle x_i|A \cdot |x_j\rangle \cdot |x_i\rangle\langle x_j| \tag{8.44}$$

with $a_{ij} = \langle x_i|A \cdot |x_j\rangle$ being the number of the operator matrix A at row i and column j for the base $|x_1\rangle, |x_1\rangle. \cdots |x_n\rangle$. For a different orthonormal basis

$$|y_1\rangle, |y_1\rangle. \cdots |y_n\rangle$$

the operator A is represented as $a'_{ij} = \langle y_i|A \cdot |y_j\rangle$

$$A' = \begin{pmatrix} \langle y_1|A \cdot |y_1\rangle & \langle y_1|A \cdot |y_2\rangle & \cdots & \langle y_1|A \cdot |y_n\rangle \\ \langle y_2|A \cdot |y_1\rangle & \langle y_2|A \cdot |y_2\rangle & \cdots & \langle y_2|A \cdot |y_n\rangle \\ \vdots & \vdots & \ddots & \vdots \\ \langle y_n|A \cdot |y_1\rangle & \langle y_n|A \cdot |y_2\rangle & \cdots & \langle y_n|A \cdot |y_n\rangle \end{pmatrix}. \tag{8.45}$$

The change of the basis $|x_i\rangle$ to $y_i\rangle$ is represented by the operator U

$$U = \begin{pmatrix} \langle y_1|x_1\rangle & \langle y_1|x_2\rangle & \cdots & \langle y_1|x_n\rangle \\ \langle y_2|x_1\rangle & \langle y_2|x_2\rangle & \cdots & \langle y_2|x_n\rangle \\ \vdots & \vdots & \ddots & \vdots \\ \langle y_n|x_1\rangle & \langle y_n|x_2\rangle & \cdots & \langle y_n|x_n\rangle \end{pmatrix}. \tag{8.46}$$

A vector $|x\rangle$ is changed to the basis $|y_i\rangle$ by the basis change

$$|x'\rangle = U \cdot |x\rangle \tag{8.47}$$

$|x'\rangle$ is the same vector as $|x\rangle$ represented in the basis $|y_i\rangle$. This method is also called the *unitary transformation*. If we apply an operator A to $|x\rangle$ and represent the result in the basis $|y_i\rangle$ we do the following operation

$$|z\rangle = U \cdot A \cdot |x\rangle = U \cdot A \cdot U^* \cdot U \cdot |x\rangle. \tag{8.48}$$

The operator A is represented in the new basis as

$$A' = U \cdot A \cdot U^*. \tag{8.49}$$

In the following example in H_2 we change from the basis

$$|0\rangle = \begin{pmatrix} 1 \\ 0 \end{pmatrix}, \quad |1\rangle = \begin{pmatrix} 0 \\ 1 \end{pmatrix}$$

to the Hadarmad basis

$$|+\rangle = \begin{pmatrix} \frac{1}{\sqrt{2}} \\ \frac{1}{\sqrt{2}} \end{pmatrix}, \quad |-\rangle = \begin{pmatrix} \frac{1}{\sqrt{2}} \\ \frac{-1}{\sqrt{2}} \end{pmatrix}.$$

The change of the basis $|0\rangle, |1\rangle$ to $|+\rangle, |-\rangle$ is represented by the operator U

$$U = \begin{pmatrix} \langle +|0\rangle & \langle +|1\rangle \\ \langle -|0\rangle & \langle -|1\rangle \end{pmatrix} = \begin{pmatrix} \frac{1}{\sqrt{2}} & \frac{1}{\sqrt{2}} \\ \frac{1}{\sqrt{2}} & \frac{-1}{\sqrt{2}} \end{pmatrix} = W_1. \tag{8.50}$$

The M_{NOT} gate

$$M_{NOT} = \begin{pmatrix} 0 & 1 \\ 1 & 0 \end{pmatrix}$$

is represented in the basis $|+\rangle, |-\rangle$ as

$$M'_{NOT} = U \cdot M_{NOT} \cdot U^* = \begin{pmatrix} \frac{1}{\sqrt{2}} & \frac{1}{\sqrt{2}} \\ \frac{1}{\sqrt{2}} & \frac{-1}{\sqrt{2}} \end{pmatrix} \cdot \begin{pmatrix} 0 & 1 \\ 1 & 0 \end{pmatrix} \cdot \begin{pmatrix} \frac{1}{\sqrt{2}} & \frac{1}{\sqrt{2}} \\ \frac{1}{\sqrt{2}} & \frac{-1}{\sqrt{2}} \end{pmatrix} = \begin{pmatrix} 1 & 0 \\ 0 & -1 \end{pmatrix}. \tag{8.51}$$

A base change corresponds to the unitary transformation.

In quantum physics there are two models:

- The Heisenberg picture, the state vectors are time-independent, the basis change in time.
- The Schrödinger picture, the states evolve in time, the basis does not change in time.

Both approaches are similar and depend on observer. Either he is inside the coordinate system or outside. Either the sun is rotating around the earth, or the earth is rotating around the sun. In quantum computation the Schrödinge picture is used.

Chapter 9

Periodicity

9.1 Fourier Transform

A way to solve a problem is to transform it into some other problem, for which a solution is known. Transformations are applied to signals to obtain further information from the signal that is not readily available in the raw signal. One such transformation is the Fourier transform. Many signals are represented in the time domain, and some additional information is present in the frequency content. A Fourier transform maps the signal from the time domain to the frequency domain. The frequency is the number of occurrences of a repeating event per unit time. The period is the duration of one cycle of an event, and the period is the reciprocal of the frequency f. For example, if we count 40 events in two seconds, then the frequency is

$$\frac{40}{2\ s} = \frac{20}{1\ s} = 20\ \frac{1}{s} = 20\ hertz$$

then the period is

$$T = p = \frac{1}{20} s.$$

A repeated event can be a rotation, oscillation, or a periodic wave. For periodic waves, one period corresponds to the time in which a full cycle of a wave passes. A cycle is represented by the wavelength. The velocity v of the wave is represented by the wavelength λ divided by the period p. Because the frequency f is the inverse of the period, we can represent the velocity as

$$v = \frac{\lambda}{p} = \lambda \cdot f \tag{9.1}$$

and the frequency as

$$f = \frac{1}{T} = \frac{1}{p} = \frac{v}{\lambda}. \tag{9.2}$$

If something changes rapidly, then we say that it has a high frequency. If it does not change rapidly, i.e., it changes smoothly, we say that it has a low frequency. The Fourier transform changes a signal from the time domain $x(t) \in \mathbf{C}$ to the frequency domain $X(f) \in \mathbf{C}$. The representation of the signal $x(t)$ in the frequency domain $X(f)$ is the frequency spectrum. This representation has the amplitude or phase plotted versus the frequency. In a wave, the amplitude describes the magnitude of change and the phase of the fraction of the wave cycle that has elapsed relative to the origin. The complex number $X(f)$ conveys both the amplitude and phase of the frequency f. The absolute value $|X(f)|$ represents the amplitude of the frequency f. The phase is represented by the argument of $X(f)$, $arg(X(f))$. For a complex number

$$z = x + i \cdot y = |z| \cdot e^{i \cdot \theta} \tag{9.3}$$

θ is the phase

$$\theta = arg(z) = tan^{-1}\left(\frac{y}{x}\right) \tag{9.4}$$

and

$$|z| = \sqrt{x^2 + y^2} \tag{9.5}$$

phase is an angle (radians), and that negative phase corresponds to positive time delay of the wave. For example if we shift the cosines function by the angle θ

$$\cos(x) \to \cos(x - \theta)$$

the phase of the cosines wave is shifted. It follows as well that

$$\sin(x) = \cos(x - \pi/2). \tag{9.6}$$

The Fourier transform of $x(t)$ is

$$X(f) = \int_{-\infty}^{\infty} x(t) \cdot e^{-2 \cdot \pi \cdot i \cdot t \cdot f} dt \tag{9.7}$$

t stands for time and f for frequency. The signal $x(t)$ is multiplied with an exponential term at some certain frequency f, and then integrated over all times. The frequency spectrum of a real valued signal is always symmetric, since the symmetric part is exactly a mirror image of the first part the second part is usually not shown. The inverse Fourier transform of $X(f)$ is

$$x(t) = \int_{-\infty}^{\infty} X(f) \cdot e^{2 \cdot \pi \cdot i \cdot t \cdot f} df. \tag{9.8}$$

9.2 Discrete Fourier Transform

The discrete Fourier transforms discrete time-based or space-based data into the frequency sequency-based data. Given a seqience α

$$\alpha_t : [1, 2, \cdots, n] \to C. \tag{9.9}$$

The discrete Fourier transform produces a sequence ω:

$$\omega_f : [1, 2, \cdots, n] \to C. \tag{9.10}$$

The discrete Fourier transform of $\alpha(t)$ is

$$\omega_f = \frac{1}{\sqrt{n}} \cdot \sum_{t=1}^{n} \alpha_t \cdot e^{-2\cdot\pi\cdot i\cdot(t-1)\cdot\frac{(f-1)}{n}} \tag{9.11}$$

its wave frequency is $\frac{(f-1)}{n}$ events per sample. The inverse discrete Fourier transform of ω_f is

$$\alpha_t = \frac{1}{\sqrt{n}} \cdot \sum_{f=1}^{n} \omega_f \cdot e^{2\cdot\pi\cdot i\cdot(t-1)\cdot\frac{(f-1)}{n}}. \tag{9.12}$$

Discrete Fourier transform (DFT) can be seen as a linear transform F talking the column vector α to a column vector ω

$$\omega = F \cdot \alpha \tag{9.13}$$

$$\begin{pmatrix} \omega_1 \\ \omega_2 \\ \vdots \\ \omega_n \end{pmatrix} = F \cdot \alpha$$

$$= \frac{1}{\sqrt{n}} \cdot \begin{pmatrix} e^{-2\cdot\pi\cdot i\cdot(0)\cdot\frac{(0)}{n}} & e^{-2\cdot\pi\cdot i\cdot(0)\cdot\frac{(1)}{n}} & \cdots & e^{-2\cdot\pi\cdot i\cdot(0)\cdot\frac{(n-1)}{n}} \\ e^{-2\cdot\pi\cdot i\cdot(1)\cdot\frac{(0)}{n}} & e^{-2\cdot\pi\cdot i\cdot(1)\cdot\frac{(1)}{n}} & \cdots & e^{-2\cdot\pi\cdot i\cdot(1)\cdot\frac{(n-1)}{n}} \\ \vdots & \vdots & \ddots & \vdots \\ e^{-2\cdot\pi\cdot i\cdot(n-1)\cdot\frac{(0)}{n}} & e^{-2\cdot\pi\cdot i\cdot(n-1)\cdot\frac{(1)}{n}} & \cdots & e^{-2\cdot\pi\cdot i\cdot(n)\cdot\frac{(n-1)}{n}} \end{pmatrix} \cdot \begin{pmatrix} \alpha_1 \\ \alpha_2 \\ \vdots \\ \alpha_n \end{pmatrix} \tag{9.14}$$

and the inverse discrete Fourier transform (IDFT) can be seen as a linear transform IF talking the column vector ω to a column vector α

$$\alpha = IF \cdot \omega \tag{9.15}$$

$$\begin{pmatrix} \alpha_1 \\ \alpha_2 \\ \vdots \\ \alpha_n \end{pmatrix} = \frac{1}{\sqrt{n}} \cdot \begin{pmatrix} e^{2\cdot\pi\cdot i\cdot(0)\cdot\frac{(0)}{n}} & e^{2\cdot\pi\cdot i\cdot(0)\cdot\frac{(1)}{n}} & \cdots & e^{2\cdot\pi\cdot i\cdot(0)\cdot\frac{(n-1)}{n}} \\ e^{2\cdot\pi\cdot i\cdot(1)\cdot\frac{(0)}{n}} & e^{2\cdot\pi\cdot i\cdot(1)\cdot\frac{(1)}{n}} & \cdots & e^{2\cdot\pi\cdot i\cdot(1)\cdot\frac{(n-1)}{n}} \\ \vdots & \vdots & \ddots & \vdots \\ e^{2\cdot\pi\cdot i\cdot(n-1)\cdot\frac{(0)}{n}} & e^{2\cdot\pi\cdot i\cdot(n-1)\cdot\frac{(1)}{n}} & \cdots & e^{2\cdot\pi\cdot i\cdot(n)\cdot\frac{(n-1)}{n}} \end{pmatrix} \cdot \begin{pmatrix} \omega_1 \\ \omega_2 \\ \vdots \\ \omega_n \end{pmatrix}. \tag{9.16}$$

The the matrix F can be represented as a Vandermonde matrix using the nth root of unity. An nth root of unity is a complex number ζ satisfying the equation

$$\zeta^n = 1 \tag{9.17}$$

with $n = 1, 2, 3, \cdots, n-1$ being a a positive integer, for example

$$\zeta_n = e^{-2\cdot\pi\cdot i\cdot\frac{1}{n}} = \cos\left(2\cdot\pi\cdot\frac{1}{n}\right) - i\cdot\sin\left(2\cdot\pi\cdot\frac{1}{n}\right) \tag{9.18}$$

with exponential of the complex number

$$e^{i\cdot x} = \cos(x) + i\cdot\sin(x) \tag{9.19}$$

and

$$e^{-i\cdot x} = \cos(x) - i\cdot\sin(x). \tag{9.20}$$

With $\zeta_n = e^{-2\cdot\pi\cdot i\cdot\frac{1}{n}}$ the matrix F can be represented as

$$F = \frac{1}{\sqrt{n}} \cdot \begin{pmatrix} \zeta_n^{(0)\cdot(0)} & \zeta_n^{(0)\cdot(1)} & \cdots & \zeta_n^{(0)\cdot(n-1)} \\ \zeta_n^{(1)\cdot(0)} & \zeta_n^{(1)\cdot(1)} & \cdots & \zeta_n^{(1)\cdot(n-1)} \\ \vdots & \vdots & \ddots & \vdots \\ \zeta_n^{(n-1)\cdot(0)} & \zeta_n^{(n-1)\cdot(1)} & \cdots & \zeta_n^{(n-1)\cdot(n-1)} \end{pmatrix}. \tag{9.21}$$

A Vandermonde matrix V is a matrix with the terms of a geometric progression in each row

$$V = \begin{pmatrix} 1 & \gamma_1 & \gamma_1^2 & \gamma_1^3 & \cdots & \gamma_1^{(n-1)} \\ 1 & \gamma_2 & \gamma_2^2 & \gamma_2^3 & \cdots & \gamma_2^{(n-1)} \\ 1 & \gamma_3 & \gamma_3^2 & \gamma_3^3 & \cdots & \gamma_3^{(n-1)} \\ \vdots & \vdots & \ddots & \vdots & \vdots & \vdots \\ 1 & \gamma_n & \gamma_n^2 & \gamma_n^3 & \cdots & \gamma_n^{(n-1)} \end{pmatrix}. \tag{9.22}$$

F is a Vandermonde matrix, it can be represented as

$$F = \frac{1}{\sqrt{n}} \cdot \begin{pmatrix} 1 & 1 & 1 & 1 & \cdots & 1 \\ 1 & \zeta_n & \zeta_n^2 & \zeta_n^3 & \cdots & \zeta_n^{(n-1)} \\ 1 & \zeta_n^2 & \zeta_n^4 & \zeta_n^6 & \cdots & \zeta_n^{2\cdot(n-1)} \\ 1 & \zeta_n^3 & \zeta_n^6 & \zeta_n^9 & \cdots & \zeta_n^{3\cdot(n-1)} \\ \vdots & \vdots & \ddots & \vdots & \ddots & \vdots \\ 1 & \zeta_n^{(n-1)} & \zeta_n^{2\cdot(n-1)} & \zeta_n^{3\cdot(n-1)} & \cdots & \zeta_n^{(n-1)\cdot(n-1)} \end{pmatrix}. \tag{9.23}$$

The matrix F, also called DFT matrix is unitary

$$F^{-1} = F^{*} = IF. \tag{9.24}$$

Because F is unitary it implies that the length of a vector is preserved as stated in Parseval's theorem

$$\|\omega\| = \|F \cdot \alpha\| = \|\alpha\|. \tag{9.25}$$

9.2.1 *Example*

We generates a list with $256 = 2^8$ elements containing a periodic signal α_t with Gaussian random noise from the interval $[-0.5, 0.5]$.

$$\alpha_t = sin\left(\frac{50 \cdot t \cdot 2 \cdot \cdot \pi}{256}\right) + noise.$$

The represented data looks random (see Figure 9.1).

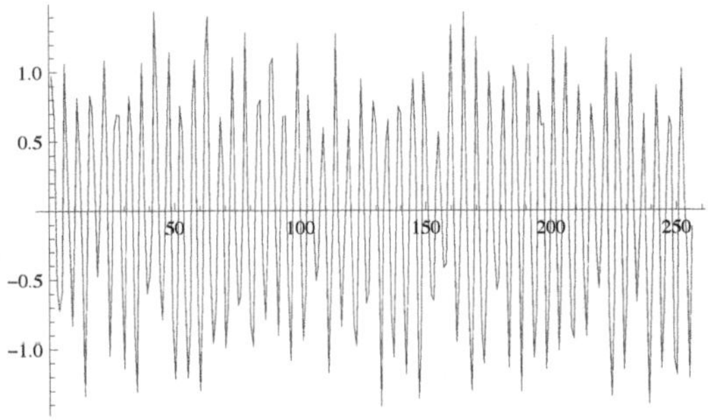

Fig. 9.1 A periodic signal α_t with with Gaussian random noise.

The discrete Fourier transform ω_f of the real valued signal α_t is symmetric. It shows a strong peak at 50+1 and a symmetric peak at 256−50+1 representing the frequency component of the signal α_t (see Figure 9.2). The zero frequency term represents the DC average and appears at position 1 instead at the position 0.

A filter that reduces Gaussian noise based on DFT removes frequencies with low amplitude of ω_f and performs inverse discrete Fourier transform.

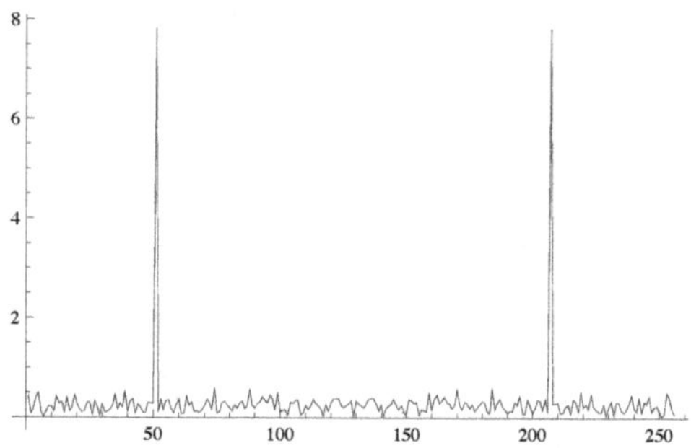

Fig. 9.2 The discrete Fourier transform ω_f . It shows a strong peak at $50+1$ and a symmetric peak at $256-50+1$ representing the frequency component of the signal α_t. The zero frequency term represents the DC average and appears at position 1 instead at the position 0.

9.3 Quantum Fourier Transform

For $n = 2^m$ F performs a Quantum Fourier Transform (QFT) on a state $|x\rangle$ of m qubits in a n-dimensional Hilbert space H_n

$$|x\rangle = \alpha_1 \cdot |x_1\rangle + \alpha_2 \cdot |x_2\rangle + \cdots + \alpha_n \cdot |x_n\rangle.$$

The QFT is defined as

$$|y\rangle = F_m \cdot |x\rangle \tag{9.26}$$

with

$$|y\rangle = \omega_1 \cdot |x_1\rangle + \omega_2 \cdot |x_2\rangle + \cdots + \omega_n \cdot |x_n\rangle$$

and inverse QFT is defined as

$$|x\rangle = IF_m \cdot |y\rangle = F_m^* \cdot |y\rangle. \tag{9.27}$$

For one qubit $m = 1$, $n = 2$

$$\zeta_2 = e^{-2\cdot\pi\cdot i\cdot\frac{1}{2}} = e^{-\pi\cdot i} = e^{\pi\cdot i} = -1$$

and the QFT F_1 is

$$F_1 = \frac{1}{\sqrt{2}} \cdot \begin{pmatrix} 1 & 1 \\ 1 & \zeta_2 \end{pmatrix} = \frac{1}{\sqrt{2}} \cdot \begin{pmatrix} 1 & 1 \\ 1 & -1 \end{pmatrix} = W_1. \tag{9.28}$$

F_1 is just a Hadamard transform W_1 of one qubit in Hilbert space H_2. A Hadamard transform of m qubits in Hilbert space H_n with $n = 2^m$ is equivalent to a multidimensional two size discrete Fourier transforms F_1

$$W_m = \bigotimes^m W_1 = \bigotimes^m F_1 = F_1 \otimes F_1 \cdots \otimes F_1. \tag{9.29}$$

For two qubits $m = 2$, $n = 4$

$$\zeta_4 = e^{-2\cdot\pi\cdot i\cdot\frac{1}{4}} = e^{-\cdot\pi\cdot i\cdot\frac{1}{2}} = -i$$

and the QFT F_2 is

$$F_2 = \frac{1}{\sqrt{4}} \cdot \begin{pmatrix} 1 & 1 & 1 & 1 \\ 1 & \zeta_4 & \zeta_4^2 & \zeta_4^3 \\ 1 & \zeta_4^2 & \zeta_4^4 & \zeta_4^6 \\ 1 & \zeta_4^3 & \zeta_4^6 & \zeta_4^9 \end{pmatrix} = \frac{1}{2} \cdot \begin{pmatrix} 1 & 1 & 1 & 1 \\ 1 & -i & -1 & i \\ 1 & -1 & 1 & -1 \\ 1 & i & -1 & -i \end{pmatrix} \tag{9.30}$$

and the inverse QFT IF_2 is

$$IF_2 = F_2^* = \frac{1}{2} \cdot \begin{pmatrix} 1 & 1 & 1 & 1 \\ 1 & i & -1 & -i \\ 1 & -1 & 1 & -1 \\ 1 & -i & -1 & i \end{pmatrix}. \tag{9.31}$$

For three qubits $m = 3$, $n = 8$

$$\zeta_8 = e^{-2\cdot\pi\cdot i\cdot\frac{1}{8}} = e^{-\pi\cdot i\cdot\frac{1}{4}} = \frac{1-i}{\sqrt{2}}$$

$$F_3 = \frac{1}{\sqrt{8}} \cdot \begin{pmatrix} 1 & 1 & 1 & 1 & 1 & 1 & 1 & 1 \\ 1 & \zeta_8^1 & \zeta_8^2 & \zeta_8^3 & \zeta_8^4 & \zeta_8^5 & \zeta_8^6 & \zeta_8^7 \\ 1 & \zeta_8^2 & \zeta_8^4 & \zeta_8^6 & \zeta_8^8 & \zeta_8^{10} & \zeta_8^{12} & \zeta_8^{14} \\ 1 & \zeta_8^3 & \zeta_8^6 & \zeta_8^9 & \zeta_8^{12} & \zeta_8^{15} & \zeta_8^{18} & \zeta_8^{21} \\ 1 & \zeta_8^4 & \zeta_8^8 & \zeta_8^{12} & \zeta_8^{16} & \zeta_8^{20} & \zeta_8^{24} & \zeta_8^{28} \\ 1 & \zeta_8^5 & \zeta_8^{10} & \zeta_8^{15} & \zeta_8^{20} & \zeta_8^{25} & \zeta_8^{30} & \zeta_8^{35} \\ 1 & \zeta_8^6 & \zeta_8^{12} & \zeta_8^{18} & \zeta_8^{24} & \zeta_8^{30} & \zeta_8^{36} & \zeta_8^{42} \\ 1 & \zeta_8^7 & \zeta_8^{14} & \zeta_8^{21} & \zeta_8^{28} & \zeta_8^{35} & \zeta_8^{42} & \zeta_8^{49} \end{pmatrix} \tag{9.32}$$

$$F_3 = \frac{1}{\sqrt{8}} \cdot \begin{pmatrix} 1 & 1 & 1 & 1 & 1 & 1 & 1 & 1 \\ 1 & e^{-\pi\cdot i\cdot\frac{1}{4}} & -i & e^{-\pi\cdot i\cdot\frac{3}{4}} & -1 & e^{\pi\cdot i\cdot\frac{3}{4}} & i & e^{\pi\cdot i\cdot\frac{1}{4}} \\ 1 & -i & -1 & i & 1 & -i & -1 & i \\ 1 & e^{-\pi\cdot i\cdot\frac{3}{4}} & i & e^{-\pi\cdot i\cdot\frac{1}{4}} & -1 & e^{\pi\cdot i\cdot\frac{1}{4}} & i & e^{\pi\cdot i\cdot\frac{3}{4}} \\ 1 & -1 & 1 & -1 & 1 & -1 & 1 & -1 \\ 1 & e^{\pi\cdot i\cdot\frac{3}{4}} & -i & e^{\pi\cdot i\cdot\frac{1}{4}} & -1 & e^{-\pi\cdot i\cdot\frac{1}{4}} & i & e^{-\pi\cdot i\cdot\frac{3}{4}} \\ 1 & i & -1 & -i & 1 & i & -1 & -i \\ 1 & e^{\pi\cdot i\cdot\frac{1}{4}} & i & e^{\pi\cdot i\cdot\frac{3}{4}} & -1 & e^{-\pi\cdot i\cdot\frac{3}{4}} & -i & e^{-\pi\cdot i\cdot\frac{1}{4}} \end{pmatrix}. \tag{9.33}$$

The first row of F_3 is the DC average of the amplitude of the input state when measured, the following rows represent the AC (difference) of the input state amplitudes. The QFT operation on the state $|x\rangle$ is

$$\begin{pmatrix} \omega_1 \\ \omega_2 \\ \omega_3 \\ \omega_4 \\ \omega_5 \\ \omega_6 \\ \omega_7 \\ \omega_8 \end{pmatrix} = \frac{1}{\sqrt{8}} \cdot \begin{pmatrix} 1 & 1 & 1 & 1 & 1 & 1 & 1 & 1 \\ 1 & \frac{1-i}{\sqrt{2}} & -i & \frac{-1-i}{\sqrt{2}} & -1 & \frac{-1+i}{\sqrt{2}} & i & \frac{1+i}{\sqrt{2}} \\ 1 & -i & -1 & i & 1 & -i & -1 & i \\ 1 & \frac{-1-i}{\sqrt{2}} & -i & \frac{1-i}{\sqrt{2}} & -1 & \frac{1+i}{\sqrt{2}} & i & \frac{-1+i}{\sqrt{2}} \\ 1 & -1 & 1 & -1 & 1 & -1 & 1 & -1 \\ 1 & \frac{-1+i}{\sqrt{2}} & -i & \frac{1+i}{\sqrt{2}} & -1 & \frac{1-i}{\sqrt{2}} & i & \frac{-1-i}{\sqrt{2}} \\ 1 & i & -1 & -i & 1 & i & -1 & -i \\ 1 & \frac{1+i}{\sqrt{2}} & -i & \frac{-1+i}{\sqrt{2}} & -1 & \frac{-1-i}{\sqrt{2}} & i & \frac{1-i}{\sqrt{2}} \end{pmatrix} \cdot \begin{pmatrix} \alpha_1 \\ \alpha_2 \\ \alpha_3 \\ \alpha_4 \\ \alpha_5 \\ \alpha_6 \\ \alpha_7 \\ \alpha_8 \end{pmatrix} \tag{9.34}$$

F_3 can be represented as a sum of a real and imaginary matrix.

$$F3 = \frac{1}{\sqrt{8}} \cdot \begin{pmatrix} 1 & 1 & 1 & 1 & 1 & 1 & 1 & 1 \\ 1 & \frac{1}{\sqrt{2}} & 0 & \frac{-1}{\sqrt{2}} & -1 & \frac{-1}{\sqrt{2}} & 0 & \frac{1}{\sqrt{2}} \\ 1 & 0 & -1 & 0 & 1 & 0 & -1 & 0 \\ 1 & \frac{-1}{\sqrt{2}} & 0 & \frac{1}{\sqrt{2}} & -1 & \frac{1}{\sqrt{2}} & 0 & \frac{-1}{\sqrt{2}} \\ 1 & -1 & 1 & -1 & 1 & -1 & 1 & -1 \\ 1 & \frac{-1}{\sqrt{2}} & 0 & \frac{1}{\sqrt{2}} & -1 & \frac{1}{\sqrt{2}} & 0 & \frac{-1}{\sqrt{2}} \\ 1 & 0 & -1 & 0 & 1 & 0 & -1 & 0 \\ 1 & \frac{1}{\sqrt{2}} & 0 & \frac{-1}{\sqrt{2}} & -1 & \frac{-1}{\sqrt{2}} & 0 & \frac{1}{\sqrt{2}} \end{pmatrix} \tag{9.35}$$

$$+\frac{1}{\sqrt{8}} \cdot \begin{pmatrix} 0 & 0 & 0 & 0 & 0 & 0 & 0 & 0 \\ 0 & \frac{-i}{\sqrt{2}} & -i & \frac{-i}{\sqrt{2}} & 0 & \frac{i}{\sqrt{2}} & i & \frac{i}{\sqrt{2}} \\ 0 & -i & 0 & i & 0 & -i & 0 & i \\ 0 & \frac{-i}{\sqrt{2}} & -i & \frac{-i}{\sqrt{2}} & 0 & \frac{i}{\sqrt{2}} & i & \frac{-i}{\sqrt{2}} \\ 0 & 0 & 0 & 0 & 0 & 0 & 0 & 0 \\ 0 & \frac{i}{\sqrt{2}} & -i & \frac{i}{\sqrt{2}} & 0 & \frac{-i}{\sqrt{2}} & i & \frac{-i}{\sqrt{2}} \\ 0 & i & 0 & -i & 0 & i & 0 & -i \\ 0 & \frac{i}{\sqrt{2}} & -i & \frac{i}{\sqrt{2}} & 0 & \frac{-i}{\sqrt{2}} & i & \frac{-i}{\sqrt{2}} \end{pmatrix}. \tag{9.36}$$

The first row measures the DC, the second row fractional frequency of the amplitude of the input state of $1/8$, the third of $1/4 = 2/8$, the fourth of $3/8$, the fifth of $1/2 = 4/8$, the sixth of $5/8$, the seventh of $3/4 = 6/8$ and the eighth of $7/8$ or equivalently the fractional frequency of $-1/8$. The resulting frequency of the amplitude vector of the state $|y\rangle$ for a real valued amplitude vector α of the state $|x\rangle$ is symmetric, $|\omega_2| = |\omega_8|$, $|\omega_3| = |\omega_7|$ and $|\omega_4| = |\omega_6|$.

9.4 FFT

The Hadamard transform H_m is composed of multidimensional two size discrete Fourier transforms F_1, it is a subset of DFT [Cormen *et al.* (2001)]. DFT F_m is related to the Hadamard transform but cannot be decomposed as a tensor product of 2×2 matrices. Any operator can be represented by single qubit gates together with M_{CNOT} gates, however their number can grow exponential in the number if qubits [Rieffel and Polak (2011)]. An efficient decomposition is represented by the fast Fourier transform (FFT). Carl Friedrich Gauss invented the FFT algorithm around 1805. However because the corresponding article was written in Latin it did not gain any popularity. FFT was several times rediscovered and it was made popular by J. W. Cooley and J. W. Tukey in 1965 [Cormen *et al.* (2001)]. The original algorithm is limited to the DFT matrix of the size $2^m \times 2^m$, power of two. Variants of the algorithm for the case in which the size of the matrix is not power of two exist. The original algorithm decomposes F_m recursively.

$$F_{m+1} = \frac{1}{\sqrt{2}} \cdot \begin{pmatrix} I_m & D_m \\ I_m & -D_m \end{pmatrix} \cdot \begin{pmatrix} F_m & 0 \\ 0 & F_m \end{pmatrix} \cdot R_{m+1} \tag{9.37}$$

with the permutation matrix R_m given that $n = 2^m$

$$R_m = \begin{pmatrix} r_{11} & \cdots & r_{1n} \\ \vdots & \ddots & \vdots \\ r_{n1} & \cdots & r_{nn} \end{pmatrix} \tag{9.38}$$

with

$$r_{ab} = \begin{cases} 1 & if \quad 2 \cdot a - 1 = b \\ 1 & if \quad 2 \cdot a - n = b \\ 0 & else \end{cases} \tag{9.39}$$

and the diagonal matrix with $n \cdot 2 = 2^{m+1}$

$$D_m = \begin{pmatrix} \zeta_{n\cdot 2}^0 & 0 & \cdots & 0 \\ 0 & \zeta_{n\cdot 2}^1 & \cdots & 0 \\ \vdots & \vdots & \ddots & \vdots \\ 0 & 0 & \cdots & \zeta_{n\cdot 2}^{n-1} \end{pmatrix}. \tag{9.40}$$

For example F_2 is decomposed with

$$D_1, \zeta_4 = e^{-2\cdot\pi\cdot i\cdot\frac{1}{4}} \to D_1 = \begin{pmatrix} e^{-\cdot\pi\cdot i\cdot\frac{0}{2}} & 0 \\ 0 & e^{-\cdot\pi\cdot i\cdot\frac{1}{2}} \end{pmatrix} = \begin{pmatrix} 1 & 0 \\ 0 & -i \end{pmatrix} \tag{9.41}$$

and

$$R_2 = \begin{pmatrix} 1\,0\,0\,0 \\ 0\,0\,1\,0 \\ 0\,1\,0\,0 \\ 0\,0\,0\,1 \end{pmatrix} \tag{9.42}$$

it follows

$$F_2 = \frac{1}{\sqrt{2}} \cdot \begin{pmatrix} 1 & 0 & 1 & 0 \\ 0 & 1 & 0 & -i \\ 1 & 0 & -1 & 0 \\ 0 & 1 & 0 & i \end{pmatrix} \cdot \frac{1}{\sqrt{2}} \cdot \begin{pmatrix} 1 & 1 & 0 & 0 \\ 1 & -1 & 0 & 0 \\ 0 & 0 & 1 & 1 \\ 0 & 0 & 1 & -1 \end{pmatrix} \cdot \begin{pmatrix} 1\,0\,0\,0 \\ 0\,0\,1\,0 \\ 0\,1\,0\,0 \\ 0\,0\,0\,1 \end{pmatrix} \tag{9.43}$$

$$F_2 = \frac{1}{2} \cdot \begin{pmatrix} 1 & 1 & 1 & 1 \\ 1 & -i & -1 & i \\ 1 & -1 & 1 & -1 \\ 1 & i & -1 & -i \end{pmatrix}. \tag{9.44}$$

The complexity of the FFT algorithm that decomposes F_m recursively is $O(n \cdot m)$.

9.5 QFT Decomposition

The Hadamard transform W_m can be decomposed into a tensor product of m 2×2 matrices representing W_1

$$W_m = \bigotimes^m W_1 = W_1 \otimes W_1 \cdots \otimes W_1$$

so that the quantum complexity is $O(m)$ [Rieffel and Polak (2011)]. F_m cannot be decomposed as a tensor product of 2×2 matrices. Using the decomposition of the FFT algorithm and decomposing the corresponding matrices by the tensor product a quantum complexity of $O(m^2) = O(m \cdot m)$ can be achieved. The decomposition performs m steps. In each step is represented by a product of three unitary matrices. They can be decomposed at the step k into k tensor products. It folows

$$m + (m-1) + (m-2) + \cdots + 1 = \frac{m \cdot (m-1)}{2} = O(m^2). \tag{9.45}$$

The permutation matrix R_m is unitary and can be decomposed into a tensor product of m swap operators S preforming a swap operation on one qubit states $|x\rangle$ and $|y\rangle$,

$$S|xy\rangle = |yx\rangle \tag{9.46}$$

with

$$S|00\rangle = |00\rangle, \quad S|01\rangle = |10\rangle, \quad S|10\rangle = |01\rangle, \quad S|11\rangle = |11\rangle$$

and the matrix representation

$$S = \begin{pmatrix} 1\,0\,0\,0 \\ 0\,0\,1\,0 \\ 0\,1\,0\,0 \\ 0\,0\,0\,1 \end{pmatrix}. \tag{9.47}$$

The following matrix can be recursively decomposed

$$\begin{pmatrix} F_m & 0 \\ 0 & F_m \end{pmatrix} = I_1 \otimes F_m \tag{9.48}$$

and

$$\frac{1}{\sqrt{2}} \cdot \begin{pmatrix} I_m & D_m \\ I_m & -D_m \end{pmatrix} = (W_1 \cdot |0\rangle\langle 0|\cdot) \otimes I_m + (W_1 \cdot |1\rangle\langle 1|\cdot) \otimes D_m \tag{9.49}$$

with

$$D_m = D_{m-1} \otimes \begin{pmatrix} 1 & 0 \\ 0 & \zeta_{n\cdot 2} \end{pmatrix}. \tag{9.50}$$

9.5.1 *QFT quantum circuit**

We can rewrite the recursive decomposition into a "kind" of tensor product using the binary representation of $|x\rangle, |y\rangle$. This representation is popular, however it not a real tensor decomposition. The QFT on a state $|x\rangle$ of m qubits in a n-dimensional Hilbert space $H_n = H_{2^m}$ can be represented as [Kaye *et al.* (2007)]

$$|y\rangle = F_m \cdot |x\rangle = \frac{1}{\sqrt{n}} \sum_{y \in B^m} e^{-2\cdot\pi\cdot i\cdot \frac{y}{n}\cdot x} \cdot |y\rangle. \tag{9.51}$$

It is just the discrete Fourier transform of $\alpha(t)$ in the bra-ket notation

$$\omega_f = \frac{1}{\sqrt{n}} \cdot \sum_{t=1}^{n} \alpha_t \cdot e^{-2\cdot\pi\cdot i\cdot \frac{(f-1)}{n}\cdot(t-1)}.$$

The binary representation of x of m bits is given by

$$x = x_m \cdot 2^{m-1} + x_{m-1} \cdot 2^{m-2} + \cdots + x_2 \cdot 2^1 + x_1 \cdot 2^0 \tag{9.52}$$

and of y by

$$y = y_m \cdot 2^{m-1} + y_{m-1} \cdot 2^{m-2} + \cdots + y_2 \cdot 2^1 + y_1 \cdot 2^0. \tag{9.53}$$

We can represent the multiplication of

$$e^{\frac{-2\cdot\pi\cdot i\cdot y\cdot x}{n}} = e^{\frac{-2\cdot\pi\cdot i\cdot y\cdot x}{2^m}}$$

$$= e^{\frac{-2\cdot\pi\cdot i\cdot(y_m\cdot 2^{m-1}+\cdots 1+y_1\cdot 2^0\cdot x)\cdot\cdot(x_m\cdot 2^{m-1}\cdots+x_2\cdot 2^1+x_1\cdot 2^0)}{2^m}} \tag{9.54}$$

$$= e^{\frac{-2\cdot\pi\cdot i\cdot(y_m\cdot 2^{m-1}\cdot(x_m\cdot 2^{m-1}\cdots+x_2\cdot 2^1+x_1\cdot 2^0)+\cdots+y_1\cdot 2^0\cdot(x_m\cdot 2^{m-1}\cdots+x_2\cdot 2^1+x_1\cdot 2^0))}{2^m}}. \tag{9.55}$$

Because

$$e^{-2\cdot\pi\cdot i\cdot(a+b+c)} = e^{(-2\cdot\pi\cdot i\cdot a)+(-2\cdot\pi\cdot i\cdot b)+(-2\cdot\pi\cdot i\cdot c)}$$

$$= e^{(-2\cdot\pi\cdot i\cdot a)}\cdot e^{(-2\cdot\pi\cdot i\cdot b)}\cdot e^{(-2\cdot\pi\cdot i\cdot c)}$$

and $e^{-2\cdot\pi\cdot i}$ is a nth root of unity

$$e^{-2\cdot\pi\cdot i\cdot n} = 1, \quad n \in N_0 = \{0,1,2,3,\cdots\}.$$

we can ignore in

$$e^{\frac{-2\cdot\pi\cdot i\cdot(y_m\cdot 2^{m-1}\cdot(x_m\cdot 2^{m-1}\cdots+x_2\cdot 2^1+x_1\cdot 2^0)+\cdots+y_1\cdot 2^0\cdot(x_m\cdot 2^{m-1}\cdots+x_2\cdot 2^1+x_1\cdot 2^0))}{2^m}}$$

the terms divisible by $n = 2^m$. For example

$$e^{-2\cdot\pi\cdot i\cdot(1+\frac{1}{2}+2)} = e^{(-2\cdot\pi\cdot i\cdot 1)}\cdot e^{(-2\cdot\pi\cdot i\cdot\frac{1}{2})}\cdot e^{(-2\cdot\pi\cdot i\cdot 3)} = 1\cdot e^{(-2\cdot\pi\cdot i\cdot\frac{1}{2})}\cdot 1 = -1.$$

It follows that

$$e^{\frac{-2\cdot\pi\cdot i\cdot y\cdot x}{2^m}}$$

$$= e^{-2\cdot\pi\cdot i\cdot\left(y_m\cdot\frac{x_1}{2^1}+y_{m-1}\cdot\left(\frac{x_2}{2^1}+\frac{x_1}{2^2}\right)+y_{m-2}\cdot\left(\frac{x_3}{2^1}+\frac{x_2}{2^2}+\frac{x_1}{2^3}\right)+\cdots+y_1\cdot\left(\frac{x_m}{2^1}+\frac{x_{m-1}}{2^2}+\cdots+\frac{x_1}{2^m}\right)\right)} \tag{9.56}$$

using the binary fraction notation for binary numbers

$$e^{\frac{-2\cdot\pi\cdot i\cdot y\cdot x}{2^m}}$$

$$= e^{-2\cdot\pi\cdot i\cdot(y_m\cdot 0.x_1+y_{m-1}\cdot 0.x_2x_1+y_{m-2}\cdot 0.x_3x_2x_1+\cdots+y_1\cdot 0.x_mx_m\ {}_1x_{m-2}\cdots x_2x_1)} \tag{9.57}$$

binary fractions are represented as

$$0.x_mx_m\ {}_1x_{m-2}\cdots x_2x_1 = \frac{x_m}{2^1}+\frac{x_{m-1}}{2^2}+\cdots+\frac{x_1}{2^m}.$$

So the QFT can be factored into the tensor product of m single-qubit operations,

$$|y\rangle = F_m\cdot|x\rangle = \frac{1}{\sqrt{n}}\sum_{y\in B^m} e^{-2\cdot\pi\cdot i\cdot\frac{y}{n}\cdot x}\cdot|y\rangle =$$

$$\frac{1}{\sqrt{n}} \cdot \left(\sum_{y_m \in \{0,1\}} e^{-2 \cdot \pi \cdot i \cdot y_m \cdot 0.x_1} \right) \cdot \left(\sum_{y_{m-1} \in \{0,1\}} e^{-2 \cdot \pi \cdot i \cdot y_{m-1} \cdot 0.x_2 x_1} \right) \cdots$$

$$\cdots \left(\sum_{y_1 \in \{0,1\}} e^{-2 \cdot \pi \cdot i \cdot y_1 \cdot 0.x_m \cdots x_2 x_1} \right) \quad (9.58)$$

$$= \frac{1}{\sqrt{n}} \cdot \left(|0\rangle + e^{-2 \cdot \pi \cdot i \cdot 0.x_1} \cdot |1\rangle \right) \otimes \left(|0\rangle + e^{-2 \cdot \pi \cdot i \cdot 0.x_2 x_1} \cdot |1\rangle \right) \otimes \cdots \quad (9.59)$$

$$\otimes \left(|0\rangle + e^{-2 \cdot \pi \cdot i \cdot 0.x_m \cdots x_2 x_1} \cdot |1\rangle \right).$$

The representation involeves the input in the tensor decomposition. For example the equivalent decomposition of the the Hadamard matrix would involve the input to determine the sign,

$$W_m = \frac{1}{\sqrt{n}} \cdot \left(|0\rangle + (-1)^{x_m} \cdot |1\rangle \right) \otimes \left(|0\rangle + (-1)^{x_{m-1}} \cdot |1\rangle \right) \otimes \cdots$$

$$\otimes \left(|0\rangle + (-1)^{x_1} \cdot |1\rangle \right)$$

if the corresponding input is zero the sign is positive, if it is one the sign is negative. The product of m single-qubit operations of the QFT allows us to define a quantum circuit. The circuit will use a controlled phase gate CR_k that performs following mapping on two qubits

$$CR_k|00\rangle = |00\rangle, \quad CR_k|01\rangle = |01\rangle,$$

$$CR_k|10\rangle = |10\rangle, \quad CR_k|11\rangle = e^{-2 \cdot \pi \cdot i \cdot / 2^k} \cdot |11\rangle.$$

The general phase gate is

$$P = \begin{pmatrix} 1 & 0 \\ 0 & e^{i \cdot \theta} \end{pmatrix}.$$

The phase gate R_k is

$$R_k = \begin{pmatrix} 1 & 0 \\ 0 & e^{-2 \cdot \pi \cdot i \cdot / 2^k} \end{pmatrix} \quad (9.60)$$

and the controlled phase gate CR_k is

$$CR_k = \begin{pmatrix} 1 & 0 & 0 & 0 \\ 0 & 1 & 0 & 0 \\ 0 & 0 & 1 & 0 \\ 0 & 0 & 0 & e^{-2 \cdot \pi \cdot i \cdot / 2^k} \end{pmatrix}. \quad (9.61)$$

We demonstrate the definition of the quantum circuit on F_2

$$F_2 = \frac{1}{\sqrt{4}} \cdot \left(|0\rangle + e^{-2\cdot\pi\cdot i\cdot 0.x_1} \cdot |1\rangle\right) \otimes \left(|0\rangle + e^{-2\cdot\pi\cdot i\cdot 0.x_2 x_1} \cdot |1\rangle\right) \tag{9.62}$$

on the input $|x_2 x_1\rangle$. We define the circuit recursively from the back. Because

$$e^{-2\cdot\pi\cdot i\cdot 0.x_1} = e^{-2\cdot\pi\cdot i\cdot \frac{x_1}{2}} = (-1)^{x_1}$$

it follows that

$$\frac{1}{\sqrt{2}} \cdot \left(|0\rangle + e^{-2\cdot\pi\cdot i\cdot 0.x_1} \cdot |1\rangle\right) = \frac{1}{\sqrt{2}} \cdot \left(|0\rangle + (-1)^{x_1} \cdot |1\rangle\right)$$

can be represented by

$$(I_1 \otimes W_1) \cdot |x_2 x_1\rangle.$$

The "first" operation can be represented as

$$\frac{1}{\sqrt{2}} \cdot \left(|0\rangle + e^{-2\cdot\pi\cdot i\cdot 0.x_2 x_1} \cdot |1\rangle\right) = \frac{1}{\sqrt{2}} \cdot \left(|0\rangle + e^{-2\cdot\pi\cdot i\cdot \frac{x_2}{2^1}} \cdot e^{-2\cdot\pi\cdot i\cdot \frac{x_1}{2^2}} \cdot |1\rangle\right)$$

and can be represented as

$$CR_1 \cdot (W_1 \otimes I_1) \cdot |x_2 x_1\rangle.$$

Together we get

$$(I_1 \otimes W_1) \cdot CR_2 \cdot (W_1 \otimes I_1) \cdot |x_2 x_1\rangle$$

$$= \frac{1}{\sqrt{4}} \cdot \left(|0\rangle + e^{-2\cdot\pi\cdot i\cdot 0.x_2 x_1} \cdot |1\rangle\right) \otimes \left(|0\rangle + e^{-2\cdot\pi\cdot i\cdot 0.x_1} \cdot |1\rangle\right) \tag{9.63}$$

The arrangement of the bits is is not correct. This is because the last qubit in the result uses the first input qubit and so on. To correct the order we have to apply swap gate S as defined for the FFT. The decomposition is given by

$$F_2 \cdot |x_2 x_1\rangle = S \cdot (I_1 \otimes W_1) \cdot CR_1 \cdot (W_1 \otimes I_1) \cdot |x_2 x_1\rangle. \tag{9.64}$$

or in matrix notation

$$F_2 = \frac{1}{2} \cdot \begin{pmatrix} 1 & 1 & 1 & 1 \\ 1 & -i & -1 & i \\ 1 & -1 & 1 & -1 \\ 1 & i & -1 & -i \end{pmatrix} = \begin{pmatrix} 1&0&0&0 \\ 0&0&1&0 \\ 0&1&0&0 \\ 0&0&0&1 \end{pmatrix} \cdot \left(\begin{pmatrix} 1&0 \\ 0&1 \end{pmatrix} \otimes \frac{1}{\sqrt{2}} \cdot \begin{pmatrix} 1 & 1 \\ 1 & -1 \end{pmatrix} \right)$$

$$\cdot \begin{pmatrix} 1&0&0&0 \\ 0&1&0&0 \\ 0&0&1&0 \\ 0&0&0&-i \end{pmatrix} \cdot \left(\frac{1}{\sqrt{2}} \cdot \begin{pmatrix} 1 & 1 \\ 1 & -1 \end{pmatrix} \otimes \begin{pmatrix} 1&0 \\ 0&1 \end{pmatrix} \right).$$

For F_3 we need to define phase gate on three qubits $|x_3x_2x_1\rangle$ and a swap operation of the first and last qubit. The swap operation is simply the swap of the value of x_1 with the value of x_2, of the value of x_2 with the value of x_3 and finally of the value of x_1 with the value of x_2,

$$(I_1 \otimes S) \cdot (S \otimes I_1) \cdot (I_1 \otimes S).$$

The phase gate on third qubit controlled by the second qubit is simply

$$CR_k \otimes I_1.$$

The phase gate on third qubit controlled by the first qubit is

$$(I_1 \otimes S) \cdot (CR_k \otimes I_1) \cdot (I_1 \otimes S)$$

$$F_3 = \frac{1}{\sqrt{8}} \cdot \left(|0\rangle + e^{-2\cdot\pi\cdot i\cdot 0.x_1} \cdot |1\rangle\right) \otimes \left(|0\rangle + e^{-2\cdot\pi\cdot i\cdot 0.x_2x_1} \cdot |1\rangle\right)$$

$$\otimes \left(|0\rangle + e^{-2\cdot\pi\cdot i\cdot 0.x_3x_2x_1} \cdot |1\rangle\right) \tag{9.65}$$

the decomposition is given by

$$[(I_1 \otimes S) \cdot (S \otimes I_1) \cdot (I_1 \otimes S)] \cdot [(I_2 \otimes W_1)] \cdot [(I_1 \otimes CR_1) \cdot (I_1 \otimes W_1 \otimes I_1)]$$

$$\cdot [(I_1 \otimes S) \cdot (CR_2 \otimes I_1) \cdot (I_1 \otimes S) \cdot (CR_1 \otimes I_1) \cdot (W_1 \otimes I_2)] \cdot |x_3x_2x_1\rangle.$$

The first term requires one Hadamard gate, the second one requires a Hadamard gate and a controlled phase gate. Each following term requires an additional controlled phase gate. Summing up

$$1 + 2 + 3 + \cdots (m-1) + m = \frac{m \cdot (m-1)}{2} = O(m^2).$$

9.6 QFT Properties

QFT is just a simple DFT represented by the DFT matrix. However one should take ***care*** of the fact that in quantum computing literature it is common that the QFT is defined as the inverse discrete Fourier transform (IDFT) and the inverse QFT as the DFT. QFT decomposition is motivated by FFT. The complexity of QFT is $O(m^2)$ that is exponentially less then $O(n \cdot m)$ of the classical FFT. The saving results from the possible tensor decomposition that can be computed in parallel. The main difference between DFT and QFT beside the time complexity is quite obvious. In QFT we cannot access the frequency domain of a signal represented by the amplitude distribution of the state $|y\rangle$. We can only gain some insight by repeated experiments, measurements. DFT can be defined for any dimension n, for example $n = 3$ or $n = 6$. With $n = 6$ we could define a quantum dice that cannot be represented by qubits. The basis of a 6 dimensional Hilbert space H_6 is

$$|I\rangle = \begin{pmatrix} 1 \\ 0 \\ 0 \\ 0 \\ 0 \\ 0 \end{pmatrix}, |II\rangle = \begin{pmatrix} 0 \\ 1 \\ 0 \\ 0 \\ 0 \\ 0 \end{pmatrix}, |III\rangle = \begin{pmatrix} 0 \\ 0 \\ 1 \\ 0 \\ 0 \\ 0 \end{pmatrix},$$

$$|IV\rangle = \begin{pmatrix} 0 \\ 0 \\ 0 \\ 1 \\ 0 \\ 0 \end{pmatrix}, |V\rangle = \begin{pmatrix} 1 \\ 0 \\ 0 \\ 0 \\ 1 \\ 0 \end{pmatrix}, |VI\rangle = \begin{pmatrix} 0 \\ 0 \\ 0 \\ 0 \\ 0 \\ 1 \end{pmatrix}. \tag{9.66}$$

The DFT for the basis in H_6 is F^6

$$\zeta_6 = e^{-2\cdot\pi\cdot i\cdot\frac{1}{6}} = e^{-\pi\cdot i\cdot\frac{1}{3}} = \frac{1 - i\cdot\sqrt{3}}{2}$$

$$F^6 = \frac{1}{\sqrt{6}} \cdot \begin{pmatrix} 1 & 1 & 1 & 1 & 1 & 1 \\ 1 & \zeta_6^1 & \zeta_6^2 & \zeta_6^3 & \zeta_6^4 & \zeta_6^5 \\ 1 & \zeta_6^2 & \zeta_6^4 & \zeta_6^6 & \zeta_6^8 & \zeta_6^{10} \\ 1 & \zeta_6^3 & \zeta_6^6 & \zeta_6^9 & \zeta_6^{12} & \zeta_6^{15} \\ 1 & \zeta_6^4 & \zeta_6^8 & \zeta_6^{12} & \zeta_6^{16} & \zeta_6^{20} \\ 1 & \zeta_6^5 & \zeta_6^{10} & \zeta_6^{15} & \zeta_6^{20} & \zeta_6^{25} \end{pmatrix} \tag{9.67}$$

$$F^6 = \frac{1}{\sqrt{6}} \cdot \begin{pmatrix} 1 & 1 & 1 & 1 & 1 & 1 \\ 1 & \frac{1-i\cdot\sqrt{3}}{2} & \frac{-1-i\cdot\sqrt{3}}{2} & -1 & \frac{-1+i\cdot\sqrt{3}}{2} & \frac{1+i\cdot\sqrt{3}}{2} \\ 1 & \frac{-1-i\cdot\sqrt{3}}{2} & \frac{-1+i\cdot\sqrt{3}}{2} & 1 & \frac{-1-i\cdot\sqrt{3}}{2} & \frac{-1+i\cdot\sqrt{3}}{2} \\ 1 & -1 & 1 & -1 & 1 & -1 \\ 1 & \frac{-1+i\cdot\sqrt{3}}{2} & \frac{-1-i\cdot\sqrt{3}}{2} & 1 & \frac{-1+i\cdot\sqrt{3}}{2} & \frac{-1-i\cdot\sqrt{3}}{2} \\ 1 & \frac{1+i\cdot\sqrt{3}}{2} & \frac{-1+i\cdot\sqrt{3}}{2} & -1 & \frac{-1-i\cdot\sqrt{3}}{2} & \frac{1-i\cdot\sqrt{3}}{2} \end{pmatrix}. \tag{9.68}$$

We can use F^6 to map the dice from a basis state in a superposition of maximal entropy

$$F^6|I\rangle = \frac{1}{\sqrt{6}}\cdot|I\rangle + |\frac{1}{\sqrt{6}}\cdot II\rangle + \frac{1}{\sqrt{6}}\cdot|III\rangle + \frac{1}{\sqrt{6}}\cdot|IV\rangle + \frac{1}{\sqrt{6}}\cdot|V\rangle + \frac{1}{\sqrt{6}}\cdot|VI\rangle.$$

We can define a register of m quantum dices using the tensor product, and map a base sate $|I\rangle$ in a superposition by

$$F_m^6 = \bigotimes^m F^6 = F^6 \otimes F^6 \cdots \otimes F^6. \tag{9.69}$$

We can define quantum computation on any base B besides qubits, base $B = 2$. The qubit representation as the bit representation is the most popular one.

9.7 The QFT Period Algorithm

QFT and F_m is used equivalently as W_m in the Deutsch Jozsa algorithm to determine the properties of the function $f(x)$. In Deutsch Jozsa algorithm the function must be balanced or constant. In the algorithm based on QFT the function $f(x)$ must be periodic. The determined property is the period of the function $f(x)$. We cannot use QFT to determine if a function is periodic or not. The QFT algorithm is built on three serial steps. It maps a state with zero Shannon entropy to a superposition with the maximal entropy, does the computation in this superposition and maps the result into a state with low entropy. It should be noted that the entropy is not zero and consequently the algorithm is probabilistic. The algorithms is build on three principles of quantum computation that are related to the Deutsch Jozsa algorithm,

- The function $f(x)$ is represented by a quantum Boolean circuit.
- The properties of the function $f(x)$ are determined using the superposition principle and QFT.
- The values of the function $f(x)$ are determined by measuring a compound system.

We represent the function $f(x)$ by a quantum Boolean circuit represented by a unitary operator U_f that acts on two registers of m qubits,

$$U_f \cdot |x\rangle|0^{\otimes m}\rangle = |x\rangle|f(x)\rangle$$

after the application of U_f the two registers are entangled. In the first step of the algorithm we build a superposition of m qubits

$$W_m \cdot |0^{\otimes m}\rangle|0^{\otimes m}\rangle = \frac{1}{\sqrt{2^m}} \sum_{x \in B^m} |x\rangle|0^{\otimes m}\rangle.$$

In the second step we apply the U_f operator

$$U_f \left(\frac{1}{\sqrt{2^m}} \sum_{x \in B^m} |x\rangle|0^{\otimes m}\rangle \right)$$

$$= \frac{1}{\sqrt{2^m}} \sum_{x \in B^m} U_f \cdot |x\rangle|0^{\otimes m}\rangle = \frac{1}{\sqrt{2^m}} \sum_{x \in B^m} |x\rangle|f(x)\rangle.$$

In the third step we measure the second register of the compound system [Shor (1994)], [Shor (1995)]. The state of the system is projected to the subspace that corresponds to the observed state and the vector representing the state is renormalized to the unit length. Because the function $f(x)$ is periodic, the new amplitude distribution is normalized and has the same period as $f(x)$. Before the measurement the amplitude distribution is at a constant value $\frac{1}{\sqrt{2^m}}$, it corresponding to the maximum entropy. The measured value γ corresponds to all k x_i values for which the periodic function is $\gamma = f(x_i)$. The function $\alpha(x)$ after the measurement is defined as

$$\alpha(x) = \begin{cases} \frac{1}{\sqrt{k}} & if \quad \gamma = f(x) \\ 0 & else \end{cases}. \tag{9.70}$$

After the measurement the state is represented as

$$\sum_{x \in B^m} \alpha(x) \cdot |x\rangle|\gamma\rangle.$$

In the fourth step we apply QFT that computes the discrete Fourier transform. The discrete Fourier transform of $\alpha(x)$ is $\omega(x)$. F_m s a linear transform talking the column vector α to a column vector ω

$$F_m \cdot \sum_{x \in B^m} \alpha(x) \cdot |x\rangle|\gamma\rangle = \sum_{x \in B^m} \omega(x) \cdot |x\rangle|\gamma\rangle.$$

In the fifth step we measure the first register. The measurement gives us a value v that is close to a multiple value of $\frac{n}{period}$. There are three possible cases:

Period r happens to be power of 2, the discrete Fourier transform gives exact multiplies

$$v = t \cdot \frac{n}{r} = t \cdot \frac{2^m}{r}. \tag{9.71}$$

In this case we can estimate r by several experiments if necessary

$$\frac{v}{2^m} = \frac{t}{r} \tag{9.72}$$

where the lowest term of $\frac{v}{2^m}$ will yield a fraction $\frac{t}{r}$ whose denominator is the period r.

Period r is not power of 2, the discrete Fourier transform gives approximate multiples

$$v \approx t \cdot \frac{n}{r} = t \cdot \frac{2^m}{r}. \tag{9.73}$$

In this case we can estimate r by continued finite fraction expansion of $\frac{v}{2^m}$ resulting in a unique fraction $\frac{p}{q}$ with $r \approx q$. For unique fraction $\frac{p}{q}$ of $\frac{v}{2^m}$ with $q < M$

$$\left| \frac{v}{2^m} - \frac{p}{q} \right| < \frac{1}{M^2}. \tag{9.74}$$

The fraction can be obtained by the following algorithm:

$$a_0 = \left\lfloor \frac{v}{2^m} \right\rfloor, \quad \epsilon_0 = \frac{v}{2^m} - a_0, \quad p_0 = a_0, \quad q_0 = 1$$

$$a_1 = \left\lfloor \frac{1}{\epsilon_0} \right\rfloor, \quad \epsilon_1 = \frac{1}{\epsilon_0} - a_0, \quad p_1 = a_1 \cdot a_0 + 1, \quad q_1 = a_1$$

$$a_i = \left\lfloor \frac{1}{\epsilon_{i-1}} \right\rfloor, \quad \epsilon_i = \frac{1}{\epsilon_{i-1}} - a_i, \quad p_i = a_i \cdot p_{i-1} + p_{i-2}, \quad q_i = a_i \cdot q_{i-1} + q_{i-2}.$$

We stop the algorithm with the output $\frac{p_i}{q_i}$ with $r \approx q_i$ if

$$q_i < M \leq q_{i+1}.$$

***f*(*x*) is a periodic block function,** the measured value γ in a block function corresponds to all k x_i values for which the periodic function is $\gamma = f(x_i)$. The amplitude function $\alpha(x)$ after the measurement has less or equal number of zeros with

$$n - k \leq k.$$

The $\frac{1}{\sqrt{k}}$ dominates the amplitude distribution. After the DFT the DC average of the amplitude dominates the distribution. The measured value will be with high probability $v = 1$, we cannot estimate the period. It is important to remember that the first row of DFT matrix F_m is the DC average of the amplitude of the input state. However during data analysis using mathematical software care has to to be taken because many DFT plot functions omit the DC component.

Fig. 9.3 Peter Williston Shor developed the Shor's algorithm, a quantum algorithm for factoring exponentially faster than the best currently-known algorithm running on a classical computer.

9.8 Factorization

The application of QFT gained popularity by Shor's algorithm for factorization of numbers in polynomial time [Shor (1994)], [Shor (1995)] (see Figure 9.3). The widely used RSA-public key cryptography scheme is secure. Its security corresponds to the difficulty in factoring large numbers on conventional computers. Shor's algorithm indicated how to do it on a quantum computer in polynomial time.

Number theory relates the period of a particular function to the factor of an integer. Given an integer number M to be factored, a function $f(x)_M$ is defined

$$f_M(x) = a^x \ mod \ M, \tag{9.75}$$

a is a randomly chosen coprime to M, means the greatest common divisor of a and M is 1. $f(x)_M$ is periodic. For a value a the period of a modulo M is r.

$$a^r = 1 \ mod \ M, \tag{9.76}$$

if r is an even number (r is dependent on a, if r is not even, chose different

a), then

$$\left(a^{\frac{r}{2}}\right)^2 = 1 \; mod \; M \tag{9.77}$$

$$\left(a^{\frac{r}{2}}\right)^2 - 1 = 0 \; mod \; M \Rightarrow \left(a^{\frac{r}{2}}\right)^2 - 1^2 = 0 \; mod \; M$$

$$\left(a^{\frac{r}{2}} - 1\right) \cdot \left(a^{\frac{r}{2}} + 1\right) = 1 \; mod \; M. \tag{9.78}$$

The product $\left(a^{\frac{r}{2}} - 1\right) \cdot \left(a^{\frac{r}{2}} + 1\right)$ is some integer multiple of M, because if we divide it by M the reminder is zero. A common factor between them can be efficiently determined by the greatest common divisor (gcd) Euclidean algorithm.

$$gcd\left(\left(a^{\frac{r}{2}} - 1\right), M\right), \quad gcd\left(\left(a^{\frac{r}{2}} + 1\right), M\right).$$

9.8.1 *Example*

In this example we will factor the number $M = 15$. We chose $a = 13$.

$$f_{15}(x) = 13^x \; mod \; 15.$$

We apply the $U_{f_{15}}$ operator

$$U_{f_{15}}\left(\frac{1}{\sqrt{2^8}} \sum_{x \in B^8} |x\rangle|0^{\otimes 8}\rangle\right) = \frac{1}{16} \sum_{x \in B^8} |x\rangle|f(x)\rangle.$$

In Figure 9.4 and 9.5 a superposition is indicated that is described by the amplitude of the second register. We measure the second register of the compound system. In our experiment the function $\alpha(x)$ of the first register after the measurement is defined as

$$\alpha(x) = \begin{cases} \frac{1}{\sqrt{64}} & if \quad 0.25 = f(x) \\ 0 & else \end{cases}. \tag{9.79}$$

We indicate the periodic block function $\alpha(x)$ of the first register in Figure 9.6 and 9.7. We apply QFT that computes the discrete Fourier transform in the first register (see Figure 9.8 and 9.9). The measurement gives us a value v that is close to a multiple value of $\frac{n}{period}$. We measure the first register. The measurement gives us a value $64+1$ that is close to a multiple value of $\frac{256}{period}$. In our experiment the period r happens to be power of 2. The zero frequency term represents the DC average and appears at position 1 instead at the position 0, so $v = 64$. It follows for the period r

$$r = \frac{256}{v} = \frac{256}{64}.$$

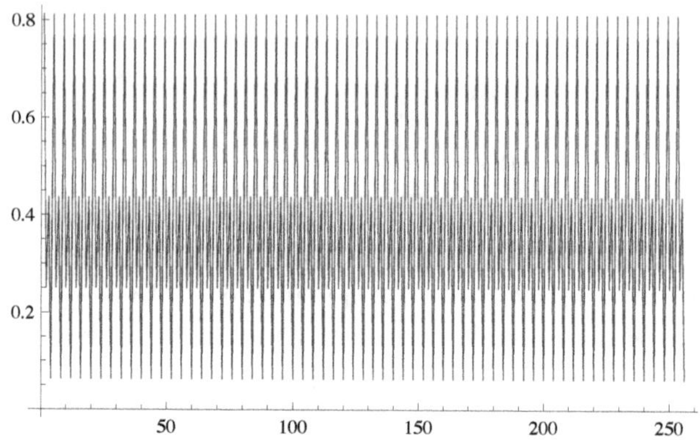

Fig. 9.4 The periodic signal $f_{15}(x) = 13^x \ mod \ 15$. It represents the superposition described by the amplitude of the second register.

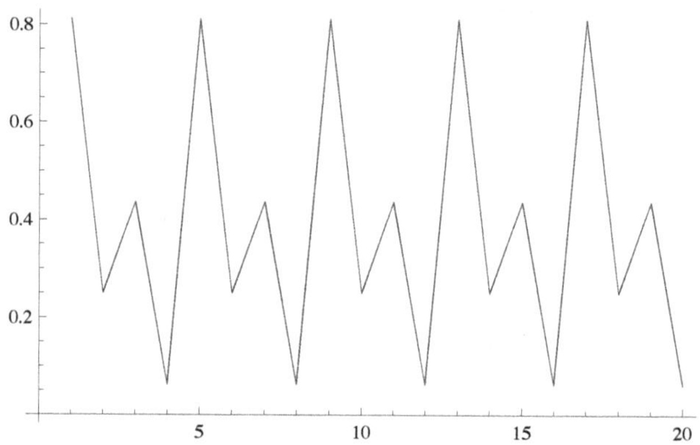

Fig. 9.5 The periodic signal $f_{15}(x) = 13^x \ mod \ 15$ in a higher resolution. We can recognize a period of four.

A common factor between them can be efficiently determined by the greatest common divisor (*gcd*) Euclidean algorithm,

$$gcd\left(\left(13^{\frac{4}{2}} - 1\right), 15\right) = 3, \quad gcd\left(\left(13^{\frac{4}{2}} + 1\right), 15\right) = 5.$$

The factors of 15 are 3 and 5. The algorithm is probabilistic and it can fail. Suppose the measurement gives us the value 1, in this case we have to repeat the whole procedure.

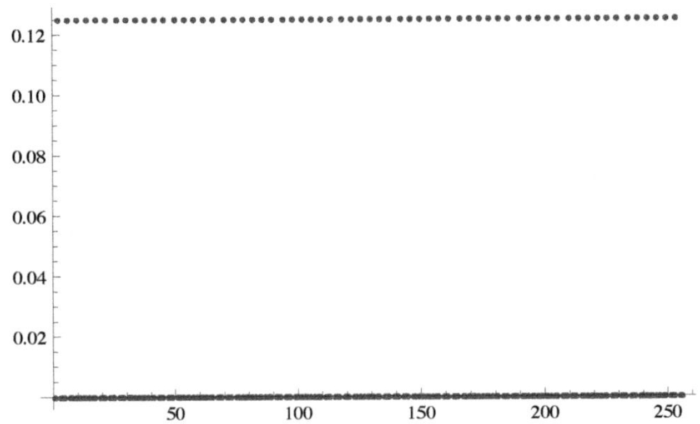

Fig. 9.6 The periodic block function $\alpha(x)$ of the first register.

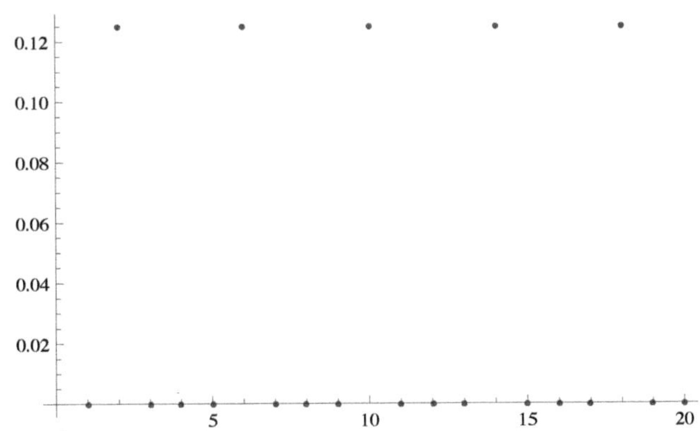

Fig. 9.7 The periodic block function $\alpha(x)$ of the first register in a higher resolution. We can recognize a period of four.

9.9 Kitaev's Phase Estimation Algorithm*

Given a unitary operator U on m qubits with an eigenvector $|u\rangle$ with an unknown eigenvalue $e^{2\cdot\pi\cdot i\cdot\theta}$ we want to determine the phase θ [Kitaev (1996)], [Kaye *et al.* (2007)]. For a complex number

$$z = x + i \cdot y = |z| \cdot e^{i\cdot\theta}$$

θ is the phase. if we apply U to $|u\rangle$ we get

$$U \cdot |u\rangle = e^{2\cdot\pi\cdot i\cdot\theta} \cdot |u\rangle \tag{9.80}$$

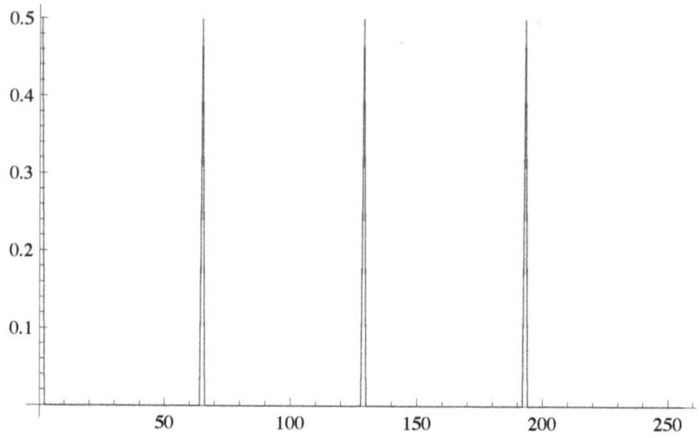

Fig. 9.8 DFT transform of the first register. It shows a strong peak at 1 and $64 + 1$, $2 \cdot 64 + 1 = 129$ and $3 \cdot 64 + 1 = 193$.

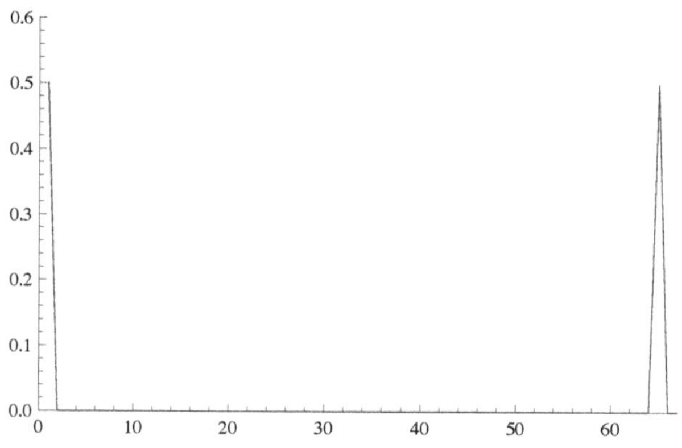

Fig. 9.9 DFT transform of the first register, higher resolution. The zero frequency term represents the DC average and appears at position 1 instead at the position 0.

if we apply U to $|u\rangle$ w times we get

$$U^w \cdot |u\rangle = U^{w-1} \cdot \left(e^{2\cdot\pi\cdot i\cdot\theta} \cdot |u\rangle\right) = \left(e^{2\cdot\pi\cdot i\cdot\theta}\right)^w \cdot |u\rangle = e^{2\cdot\pi\cdot i\cdot\theta\cdot w} \cdot |u\rangle. \quad (9.81)$$

However we will not gain any information, because $|u\rangle$ and $e^{2\cdot\pi\cdot i\cdot\theta\cdot w} \cdot |u\rangle$ are equivalent states, they represent the same state when a measurement is preformed. Instead of the unitary operator U^w we use the controlled U^w operator cU^w. If the control qubit is set then U^w is applied to the target qubits, otherwise not. The operator cU^w is unitary and defines an injective mapping on two qubits that is reversible

$$cU^w \cdot |0\rangle|u\rangle = |0\rangle|u\rangle, \quad cU^w \cdot |1\rangle|u\rangle = |1\rangle \left(e^{2\cdot\pi\cdot i\cdot\theta\cdot w} \cdot |u\rangle\right) = e^{2\cdot\pi\cdot i\cdot\theta\cdot w} \cdot |1\rangle|u\rangle.$$

So with $w = 2^j$

$$cU^{2^j} \cdot \left(\left(\frac{|0\rangle + |1\rangle}{\sqrt{2}}\right) \cdot |u\rangle\right) = \left(\frac{|0\rangle + e^{2\cdot\pi\cdot i\cdot\theta\cdot 2^j}|1\rangle}{\sqrt{2}}\right) \cdot |u\rangle.$$

The QFT is represented as a tensor product of m single-qubit operations. The inverse QFT can be factored into the tensor product of m single-qubit operations,

$$|y\rangle = IF_m \cdot |x\rangle = \frac{1}{\sqrt{n}} \sum_{y \in B^m} e^{2\cdot\pi\cdot i\cdot\frac{y}{n}\cdot x} \cdot |y\rangle$$

$$= \frac{1}{\sqrt{n}} \cdot \left(|0\rangle + e^{2\cdot\pi\cdot i\cdot 0.x_1} \cdot |1\rangle\right) \otimes \left(|0\rangle + e^{2\cdot\pi\cdot i\cdot 0.x_2x_1} \cdot |1\rangle\right) \otimes \cdots \tag{9.82}$$

$$\otimes \left(|0\rangle + e^{2\cdot\pi\cdot i\cdot 0.x_m\cdots x_2x_1} \cdot |1\rangle\right).$$

If we set $\theta = 0.x_m \cdots x_2x_1$ we can rewrite the equation as

$$|y\rangle = IF_m \cdot |x\rangle = \frac{1}{\sqrt{n}} \sum_{y \in B^m} e^{2\cdot\pi\cdot i\cdot y\cdot\theta} \cdot |y\rangle$$

$$= \frac{1}{\sqrt{n}} \cdot \left(|0\rangle + e^{2\cdot\pi\cdot i\cdot(\theta\cdot 2^{m-1})} \cdot |1\rangle\right) \otimes \left(|0\rangle + e^{2\cdot\pi\cdot i\cdot(\theta\cdot 2^{m-2})} \cdot |1\rangle\right) \otimes \cdots \tag{9.83}$$

$$\otimes \left(|0\rangle + e^{2\cdot\pi\cdot i\cdot(\theta\cdot 2^0)} \cdot |1\rangle\right).$$

For m control qubits we define $c_{j+1}U^{2^j}$ in the following way. For $j \in \{0, 1, 2, \cdots, m-1\}$ the control qubit $j+1$ of the m qubits is set then $c_{j+1}U^{2^j}$ is applied to the target $|u\rangle$, otherwise not. The initial state of the algorithm is

$$|0^{\otimes m}\rangle|u\rangle$$

with u being the eigenvector of U. In the first step of the algorithm we build a superposition of m control qubits

$$W_m \cdot |0^{\otimes m}\rangle|u\rangle = \frac{1}{\sqrt{2^m}} \sum_{x \in B^m} |x\rangle|u\rangle$$

$$= \frac{1}{\sqrt{n}} \cdot (|0\rangle + |1\rangle) \otimes (|0\rangle + |1\rangle) \otimes \cdots \otimes (|0\rangle + |1\rangle)\,|u\rangle. \tag{9.84}$$

In the second step we apply m $c_{j+1}U^{2^j}$ operators to the target $|u\rangle$

$$\prod_{j=0}^{m-1} c_{j+1}U^{2^j} \cdot \left(\frac{1}{\sqrt{2^m}} \sum_{x \in B^m} |x\rangle|u\rangle \right)$$

$$= IF_m \cdot |x\rangle|u\rangle = \frac{1}{\sqrt{n}} \sum_{y \in B^m} e^{2\cdot\pi\cdot i\cdot y\cdot\theta} \cdot |y\rangle|u\rangle$$

$$= \frac{1}{\sqrt{n}} \cdot \left(|0\rangle + e^{2\cdot\pi\cdot i\cdot(\theta\cdot 2^{m-1})} \cdot |1\rangle\right) \otimes \left(|0\rangle + e^{2\cdot\pi\cdot i\cdot(\theta\cdot 2^{m-2})} \cdot |1\rangle\right) \otimes \cdots \quad (9.85)$$

$$\otimes \left(|0\rangle + e^{2\cdot\pi\cdot i\cdot(\theta\cdot 2^0)} \cdot |1\rangle\right) \cdot |u\rangle$$

In the third step we apply QFT to the m control qubtis

$$F_m \cdot \left(\frac{1}{\sqrt{n}} \sum_{y \in B^m} e^{2\cdot\pi\cdot i\cdot y\cdot\theta} \cdot |y\rangle \right) \cdot |u\rangle$$

$$= F_m \cdot \left(\frac{1}{\sqrt{n}} \sum_{y \in B^m} e^{2\cdot\pi\cdot i\cdot\frac{y}{n}\cdot x} \cdot |y\rangle \right) \cdot |u\rangle = |x\rangle|u\rangle. \quad (9.86)$$

In the fourth step we measure the first register composed of m control qubtis and estimate θ

$$\theta = 0.x_m \cdots x_2 x_1 = \frac{x}{n} = \frac{x}{2^m}. \quad (9.87)$$

9.9.1 *Order finding**

It seem that with Kitaev's phase estimation algorithm we do not need to apply continued finite fraction expansion. But actually this is not the case. One big problem when using Kitaev's phase estimation algorithm is the determination of the eigenvector $|u\rangle$ of the unitary operator U. Usually this is non trivial and the computational costs are expensive. But for order finding (period estimation), there is an elegant way around the problem. For the unitary operator

$$U_a \cdot |x\rangle = |x \cdot a \ mod \ M\rangle, \ x \leq M \quad (9.88)$$

a is a coprime of M. Because $a^r = 1 \ mod \ M$ is a rth root of unity, it follows

$$U_a^r \cdot |x\rangle = |x \cdot a \ mod \ M\rangle = |x\rangle$$

that U_a^r is a rth root of unity operation, and U_a has the following eigenvector

$$|u_t\rangle = \frac{1}{\sqrt{r}} \sum_{x=0}^{r-1} e^{-2\cdot\pi\cdot i\cdot\frac{t}{r}\cdot x} \cdot |a^x \ mod \ M\rangle \tag{9.89}$$

in this case we can determine the eigenvalue

$$U_a \cdot |u_t\rangle = e^{2\cdot\pi\cdot i\cdot\frac{t}{r}} \cdot |u_t\rangle. \tag{9.90}$$

With the Kitaev's phase estimation algorithm we could determine $\frac{t}{r}$ and $r \approx q$ as before. Without knowing r in advance we cannot determine $|u_t\rangle$. However we can use the following relation

$$|a^x \ mod \ M\rangle = 1 \Leftrightarrow x = 0 \ mod \ r$$

it follows

$$\frac{1}{\sqrt{r}} \sum_{t=0}^{r-1} |u_t\rangle = |1\rangle \tag{9.91}$$

with this relation we can use Kitaev's phase estimation. In the first step of the algorithm we build a superposition of m control qubits and with $|u\rangle = |1\rangle$

$$W_m \cdot |0^{\otimes m}\rangle|1\rangle = \frac{1}{\sqrt{2^m}} \sum_{x \in B^m} |x\rangle|u\rangle$$

$$= \frac{1}{\sqrt{n}} \cdot (|0\rangle + |1\rangle) \otimes (|0\rangle + |1\rangle) \otimes \cdots \otimes (|0\rangle + |1\rangle)\, |1\rangle.$$

In the second step we apply m $c_{j+1}U^{2^j}$ operators to the target $|1\rangle = |u\rangle$. After applying QFT we get actually a superposition

$$\frac{1}{\sqrt{r}} \sum_{t=0}^{r-1} \left| \frac{t}{r} \right\rangle |u_t\rangle \tag{9.92}$$

after measuring the first register we can estimate $\frac{t}{r}$ and by continued finite fraction expansion $r \approx q$.

9.10 Unitary Transforms

Other unitary transforms beside DFT can be applied in quantum computation. Examples of such transforms are the Discrete Cosine Transform DCT and the Haar-Wavelet-Transform (HWT).

DCT corresponds to the sum of cosine functions oscillating at different frequencies with no imaginary number representation.

HWT The Haar transform analyzes the signal at different frequencies with different resolutions. The Haar-Wavelet-Transform (HWT) is represented by the unitary matrix (HW). For $n = 2^m$ HW_m performs a Quantum Haar-Wavelet-Transform on a state $|x\rangle$ of m qubits in a n-dimensional Hilbert space H_n.

$$HW_1 = W_1. \tag{9.93}$$

For tow qubits

$$HW_2 = \frac{1}{\sqrt{4}} \cdot \begin{pmatrix} 1 & 1 & 1 & 1 \\ 1 & 1 & -1 & -1 \\ \sqrt{2} & -\sqrt{2} & 0 & 0 \\ 0 & 0 & \sqrt{2} & -\sqrt{2} \end{pmatrix}. \tag{9.94}$$

For three qubits

$$HW_3 = \begin{pmatrix} \frac{1}{2\sqrt{2}} & \frac{1}{2\sqrt{2}} & \frac{1}{2\sqrt{2}} & \frac{1}{2\sqrt{2}} & \frac{1}{2\sqrt{2}} & \frac{1}{2\sqrt{2}} & \frac{1}{2\sqrt{2}} & \frac{1}{2\sqrt{2}} \\ \frac{1}{2\sqrt{2}} & \frac{1}{2\sqrt{2}} & \frac{1}{2\sqrt{2}} & \frac{1}{2\sqrt{2}} & -\frac{1}{2\sqrt{2}} & -\frac{1}{2\sqrt{2}} & -\frac{1}{2\sqrt{2}} & -\frac{1}{2\sqrt{2}} \\ \frac{1}{2} & \frac{1}{2} & -\frac{1}{2} & -\frac{1}{2} & 0 & 0 & 0 & 0 \\ 0 & 0 & 0 & 0 & \frac{1}{2} & \frac{1}{2} & -\frac{1}{2} & -\frac{1}{2} \\ \frac{1}{\sqrt{2}} & -\frac{1}{\sqrt{2}} & 0 & 0 & 0 & 0 & 0 & 0 \\ 0 & 0 & \frac{1}{\sqrt{2}} & -\frac{1}{\sqrt{2}} & 0 & 0 & 0 & 0 \\ 0 & 0 & 0 & 0 & \frac{1}{\sqrt{2}} & -\frac{1}{\sqrt{2}} & 0 & 0 \\ 0 & 0 & 0 & 0 & 0 & 0 & \frac{1}{\sqrt{2}} & -\frac{1}{\sqrt{2}} \end{pmatrix} \tag{9.95}$$

and $HW_3^{-1} = HW_3^T = HW_3^*$ is

$$HW_3^* = \begin{pmatrix} \frac{1}{2\sqrt{2}} & \frac{1}{2\sqrt{2}} & \frac{1}{2} & 0 & \frac{1}{\sqrt{2}} & 0 & 0 & 0 \\ \frac{1}{2\sqrt{2}} & \frac{1}{2\sqrt{2}} & \frac{1}{2} & 0 & -\frac{1}{\sqrt{2}} & 0 & 0 & 0 \\ \frac{1}{2\sqrt{2}} & \frac{1}{2\sqrt{2}} & -\frac{1}{2} & 0 & 0 & \frac{1}{\sqrt{2}} & 0 & 0 \\ \frac{1}{2\sqrt{2}} & \frac{1}{2\sqrt{2}} & -\frac{1}{2} & 0 & 0 & -\frac{1}{\sqrt{2}} & 0 & 0 \\ \frac{1}{2\sqrt{2}} & -\frac{1}{2\sqrt{2}} & 0 & \frac{1}{2} & 0 & 0 & \frac{1}{\sqrt{2}} & 0 \\ \frac{1}{2\sqrt{2}} & -\frac{1}{2\sqrt{2}} & 0 & \frac{1}{2} & 0 & 0 & -\frac{1}{\sqrt{2}} & 0 \\ \frac{1}{2\sqrt{2}} & -\frac{1}{2\sqrt{2}} & 0 & -\frac{1}{2} & 0 & 0 & 0 & \frac{1}{\sqrt{2}} \\ \frac{1}{2\sqrt{2}} & -\frac{1}{2\sqrt{2}} & 0 & -\frac{1}{2} & 0 & 0 & 0 & -\frac{1}{\sqrt{2}} \end{pmatrix}. \tag{9.96}$$

The first row of the HW_3 matrix measures the average value of the input vector multiplied by $\sqrt{2}$. The second row measures a low frequency component. The next two rows are sensitive to the first and second half of the input vector, respectively, which correspond to moderate frequency components. The remaining four rows are sensitive to the four sections of the input vector that correspond to high frequency components.

Interestingly The introduced unitary matrix W maps a basis state $|000\rangle$ in a superposition,

$$HW_3 \cdot |000\rangle = \frac{1}{2 \cdot \sqrt{2}} \cdot |000\rangle + \frac{1}{2 \cdot \sqrt{2}} \cdot |001\rangle + \frac{1}{2} \cdot |010\rangle + \frac{1}{\sqrt{2}} \cdot |100\rangle \quad (9.97)$$

where the distribution of the amplitudes does not corresponds to the maximal entropy.

Chapter 10

Search

10.1 Search and Quantum Oracle

For a function $f(x)$

$$f_\xi(x) = \begin{cases} 1 & if \quad x = \xi \\ 0 & else \end{cases} \tag{10.1}$$

we want to find x for which $f(x) = 1$, $x = \xi$. The task is equivalent to a decision problem with a binary answer $1 = yes$ and $0 = no$ and the instance x. We can describe by the function $f(x)$ $NP - complete$ problems. A problem is $NP - complete$, if it is in NP and every other problem in NP can be reduced to it. For NP a deterministic algorithm verifies if an instance (ticket) leads to a "yes" answer in polynomial time. The verification of an instance (ticket) is in polynomial time P and can be represented by a uniformly polynomial circuit, a circuit with a polynomial number of gates. If $f(x)$ is $NP - complete$ a quantum circuit U_f with a polynomial number of quantum gates can verify for a given instance x_{ticket} if $f(x_{ticket}) = 1, x_{ticket} = \xi$ or $f(x_{ticket}) = 0$. The search for ξ is based on the three principles of quantum computation:

- The function $f(x)$ is represented by a quantum Boolean circuit U_f.
- The properties of the function $f(x)$ are determined using the superposition principle and a some kind of unitary transform.
- The values of the function $f(x)$ are encoded by $(-1)^{f(x)}$, the sign of the amplitude.

Often $f(x)$ is represented by an abstract black box function and not by a quantum circuit. In this case U_f is a quantum oracle. The U_f quantum oracle or quantum circuit is a unitary operator that acts on the $m+1$ qubits with $x \in B^m$ and $y \in B^1$

$$U_f \cdot |x\rangle|y\rangle = |x\rangle|f(x) \oplus y\rangle.$$

The function $f(x)$, the solution is encoded by $(-1)^{f(x)}$, the sign of the amplitude. In correspondence with the Deutsch Jozsa algorithm we build a superposition of $m+1$ qubits

$$W_{m+1} \cdot |0^{\otimes m}\rangle|1\rangle = W_m \cdot |0^{\otimes m}\rangle \otimes W_1 \cdot |1\rangle = \frac{1}{\sqrt{2^m}} \sum_{x \in B^m} |x\rangle \otimes \left(\frac{|0\rangle - |1\rangle}{\sqrt{2}}\right)$$

and we apply the U_f, operator,

$$U_f \cdot W_{m+1} \cdot |0^{\otimes n}\rangle|1\rangle$$

$$= \frac{1}{\sqrt{2^{m+1}}} \cdot \sum_{x \in B^m} U_f \cdot |x\rangle|0\rangle - \frac{1}{\sqrt{2^{m+1}}} \cdot \sum_{x \in B^m} U_f \cdot |x\rangle|1\rangle$$

$$= \frac{1}{\sqrt{2^{m+1}}} \cdot \sum_{x \in B^m} |x\rangle|f(x) \oplus 0\rangle - \frac{1}{\sqrt{2^{m+1}}} \cdot \sum_{x \in B^m} |x\rangle|f(x) \oplus 1\rangle$$

$$= \frac{1}{\sqrt{2^{m+1}}} \cdot \left(\sum_{x \in B^m} |x\rangle|f(x) \oplus 0\rangle - \sum_{x \in B^m} |x\rangle|f(x) \oplus 1\rangle\right).$$

There are four possible cases:

$$U_f \cdot |x\rangle|0\rangle = |x\rangle|f(x) \oplus 0\rangle = |x\rangle|0\rangle,$$

$$U_f \cdot |x\rangle|1\rangle = |x\rangle|f(x) \oplus 1\rangle = |x\rangle|1\rangle,$$

$$U_f \cdot |\xi\rangle|0\rangle = |\xi\rangle|f(\xi) \oplus 0\rangle = |\xi\rangle|1\rangle,$$

$$U_f \cdot |\xi\rangle|1\rangle = |\xi\rangle|f(\xi) \oplus 1\rangle = |\xi\rangle|0\rangle.$$

It follows that

$$= \frac{1}{\sqrt{2^{m+1}}} \cdot \left(\sum_{x \neq \xi} |x\rangle|0\rangle + |\xi\rangle|1\rangle - \sum_{x \neq \xi} |x\rangle|1\rangle - |\xi\rangle|0\rangle\right)$$

$$= \frac{1}{\sqrt{2^{m+1}}} \cdot \left(\sum_{x \neq \xi} |x\rangle\left(|0\rangle - |1\rangle\right) + |\xi\rangle\left(|1\rangle - |0\rangle\right)\right)$$

$$= \frac{1}{\sqrt{n}} \sum_{x \in B^m} (-1)^{f(x)} \cdot |x\rangle \otimes \left(\frac{|0\rangle - |1\rangle}{\sqrt{2}}\right). \tag{10.2}$$

The value of the function $f(x)$ is encoded by $(-1)^{f(x)}$, in most cases again the auxiliary bit is ignored,

$$\frac{1}{\sqrt{2^m}} \sum_{x \in B^m} (-1)^{f(x)} \cdot |x\rangle = \frac{1}{\sqrt{n}} \sum_{x \in B^m} (-1)^{f(x)} \cdot |x\rangle. \tag{10.3}$$

For $m = 1$ we could use the Deutsch algorithm to decide if ξ exist, for $m = 2$ there exist the unitary operator described by the unitary matrix

$$S = \frac{1}{2} \cdot \begin{pmatrix} -1 & 1 & 1 & 1 \\ 1 & -1 & 1 & 1 \\ 1 & 1 & -1 & 1 \\ 1 & 1 & 1 & -1 \end{pmatrix} \tag{10.4}$$

with $I = S \cdot S^*$. We can determine $x = \xi$ by a simple approach. We apply the U_f operator and then the operator S,

$$(S \otimes I_1) \cdot U_f \cdot W_{2+1} \cdot |00\rangle|1\rangle = S \cdot \left(\frac{1}{\sqrt{4}} \sum_{x \in B^2} (-1)^{f(x)} \cdot |x\rangle \right) \otimes \left(\frac{|0\rangle - |1\rangle}{\sqrt{2}} \right) \tag{10.5}$$

$$(S \otimes I_1) \cdot U_f \cdot W_{2+1} \cdot |00\rangle|1\rangle = |\xi\rangle \otimes \left(\frac{|0\rangle - |1\rangle}{\sqrt{2}} \right) \tag{10.6}$$

and measure the first register and obtain $|\xi\rangle$ with probability 1. For example if $\xi = |10\rangle = 3$,

$$\frac{1}{2} \cdot \begin{pmatrix} -1 & 1 & 1 & 1 \\ 1 & -1 & 1 & 1 \\ 1 & 1 & -1 & 1 \\ 1 & 1 & 1 & -1 \end{pmatrix} \cdot \frac{1}{2} \cdot \begin{pmatrix} 1 \\ 1 \\ -1 \\ 1 \end{pmatrix} = \begin{pmatrix} 0 \\ 0 \\ 1 \\ 0 \end{pmatrix}. \tag{10.7}$$

Such a "spy" matrix S exist only for $m = 2$. Is it possible to get an exponential speed up for $m \gg 2$? To determine ξ for we would require only $O(m) = O(\log 2^m) = O(\log n)$ steps. This naïve hope can be not fulfilled.

10.2 Lower Bound $\Omega(\sqrt{n})$ for U_f-based Search*

If the operator U_f is represented by $O(m)$ gates, then we can get a speed up of maximum $O(\sqrt{n})$ steps, in fact $\Omega(\sqrt{n})$ is the lower bound. The proof for lower bound $\Omega(\sqrt{n})$ for U_f-based search is based on a sequence in a Hilbert space and the Euclidean norm properties of Hilbert space as well as the definition of the probabilities as normed squared amplitudes [Bennett *et al.* (1997)], [Boyer *et al.* (1998)]. Suppose we start with a state $|x\rangle$ of m qubits in a n-dimensional Hilbert space H_n

$$|x\rangle = \alpha_1 \cdot |x_1\rangle + \alpha_2 \cdot |x_2\rangle + \cdots + \alpha_n \cdot |x_n\rangle$$

and we are searching for one solution represented by the basis state $|\xi\rangle$ that corresponds to some basis of $|x\rangle$. We apply U_f which performs a phase shift to the amplitude of the corresponding basis, if $|x_i\rangle = |\xi\rangle$ then $-\alpha_i \cdot |x_i\rangle$. The Von Neumann Entropy is not changed by this operation. We will apply t times U_f and some arbitrary unitary operation A_t that would reduce the Von Neumann Entropy. The reduction is realized by changing the amplitude that indicates the solution together with the amplitudes of non solutions,

$$|x_t^\xi\rangle = A_t \cdot U_f \cdot A_{t-1} \cdot U_f \cdot \cdots \cdot A_1 \cdot U_f \cdot |x\rangle. \tag{10.8}$$

We will apply t times some arbitrary unitary operation A_t without indicating the solution by phase shift to the amplitude by U_f,

$$|x_t\rangle = A_t \cdot A_{t-1} \cdot \cdots \cdot A_1 \cdot |x\rangle. \tag{10.9}$$

We define a sequence a_t as the deviation after t steps between informed and uninformed evaluation of unitary operators on the a state $|x\rangle$

$$a_t = \| |x_t^\xi\rangle - |x_t\rangle \|^2 \tag{10.10}$$

with

$$\| |x_t\rangle \|^2 = \langle x_t | x_t \rangle.$$

The norm of difference between informed and uninformed evaluation is taken to the power of two, because the probabilities correspond to the normed amplitudes power two.

10.2.1 *Lower bound of a_t*

We suppose that an observation yields to the solution of the search with probability al least 0.5.

$$\| \langle \xi | x_t^\xi \rangle \|^2 \geq \frac{1}{2}. \tag{10.11}$$

We can rewrite a_t as

$$a_t = \| |x_t^\xi\rangle - |\xi\rangle + |\xi\rangle - |x_t\rangle \|^2 = \| \left(|x_t^\xi\rangle - |\xi\rangle \right) + (|\xi\rangle - |x_t\rangle) \|^2.$$

We define two sequences, the deviation after t steps between informed evaluation of unitary operators and the solution $|\xi\rangle$ with

$$a_t^+ = \| |x_t^\xi\rangle - |\xi\rangle \|^2$$

and the deviation after t steps between uninformed evaluation of unitary operators and the solution $|\xi\rangle$ with

$$a_t^- = \| |\xi\rangle - |x_t\rangle \|^2$$

Because of the inequality

$$\|\alpha + \beta\|^2 \geq \|\alpha\|^2 - 2 \cdot \|\alpha\| \cdot \|\beta\| + \|\beta\|^2$$

it follows that

$$a_t = \| \left(|x_t^\xi\rangle - |\xi\rangle \right) + (|\xi\rangle - |x_t\rangle) \|^2 \geq a_t^+ - 2 \cdot \sqrt{a_t^+} \cdot \sqrt{a_t^-} + a_t^- . \quad (10.12)$$

Using the two sequence we indicate a lower bound for a_t and $t \gg 1$

$$a_t \geq a_t^+ - 2 \cdot \sqrt{a_t^+} \cdot \sqrt{a_t^-} + a_t^- = \left(\sqrt{a_t^+} - \sqrt{a_t^-} \right)^2 \geq c. \quad (10.13)$$

With a_t^+ we indicate that in Hilbert space H_n a lower bound $c > 0$ exists

$$a_t^+ = \langle x_t^\xi | x_t^\xi \rangle - 2 \cdot \langle \xi | x_t^\xi \rangle + \langle \xi | \xi \rangle = 1 - 2 \cdot \langle \xi | x_t^\xi \rangle + 1. \quad (10.14)$$

The value of

$$2 \cdot \langle \xi | x_t^\xi \rangle$$

can be estimated. In the first step we notice that we can replace the state $\langle \xi |$ by an equivalent state

$$|\xi\rangle = e^{i \cdot \theta} \cdot |\xi\rangle.$$

Because of the Equation 10.11 for $t \gg 1$

$$2 \cdot \langle \xi | x_t^\xi \rangle = 2 \cdot |\langle \xi | x_t^\xi \rangle| \geq \frac{2}{\sqrt{2}} = \sqrt{2} \quad (10.15)$$

and

$$a_t^+ \leq 2 - \sqrt{2}. \quad (10.16)$$

For

$$a_t^- = \langle x_t | x_t \rangle - 2 \cdot \langle \xi | x_t \rangle + \langle \xi | \xi \rangle = 1 - 2 \cdot \langle \xi | x_t^\xi \rangle + 1 \quad (10.17)$$

with

$$2 \cdot \langle \xi | x_t \rangle = 2 \cdot |\langle \xi | x_t \rangle| \leq \frac{2}{\sqrt{n}} \quad (10.18)$$

it follows that

$$2 - \frac{2}{\sqrt{n}} \leq a_t^- \leq 2 \quad (10.19)$$

putting a_t+ and a_t^- together we get

$$a_t \geq \left(\sqrt{a_t^+} - \sqrt{a_t^-} \right)^2 \geq \left(\sqrt{2 - \sqrt{2}} - \sqrt{2} \right)^2 = c = 0.421002. \quad (10.20)$$

10.2.2 Upper bound of a_t

The deviation cannot grow faster as $O(t^2)$, this can be proven by induction. We prove that $4 \cdot \frac{t^2}{n} \geq a_t$. For $t = 0$

$$|x_0^\xi\rangle = |x\rangle$$

because no unitary operators were applied. The induction step is if $4 \cdot \frac{t^2}{n} \geq a_t$, then $4 \cdot \frac{(t+1)^2}{n} \geq a_{t+1}$ as well,

$$a_{t+1} = \|A_{t+1} \cdot U_f \cdot |x_t^\xi\rangle - A_{t+1} \cdot |x_t\rangle\|^2$$

$$a_{t+1} = \|A_{t+1} \cdot \left(U_f \cdot |x_t^\xi\rangle - |x_t\rangle\right) \|^2 \leq \||A_{t+1}\|^2 \cdot \|U_f \cdot |x_t^\xi\rangle - |x_t\rangle\|^2.$$

The norm for square matrices A in Hilbert space H_n is the Frobenius norm

$$\|A\|_F = \left(\sum_{i=1,j=1}^{n} |a_{ij} \right)^{\frac{1}{2}} = \sqrt{tr(A \cdot A^*)} \tag{10.21}$$

$\|A\|_2$ is also called the spectral norm. For unitary matrices A

$$\|A\|_F = \|A\|_2 = 1. \tag{10.22}$$

Because the matrix A_{t+1} is unitary it follows that

$$a_{t+1} = \||A_{t+1} \cdot \left(U_f \cdot |x_t^\xi\rangle - |x_t\rangle\right) \|^2 = \|U_f \cdot |x_t^\xi\rangle - |x_t\rangle\|^2$$

$$a_{t+1} = \||U_f \cdot \left(|x_t^\xi\rangle - |x_t\rangle\right) + (U_f - I_m) \cdot |x_t\rangle\|^2.$$

Note that if a solution exist the amplitude of the corresponding basis of $|x_t\rangle$ that is equal to $|\xi\rangle$ is $\langle\xi|x_t\rangle$, then

$$(U_f - I_m) \cdot |x_t\rangle = U_f \cdot |x_t\rangle - |x_t\rangle = -2 \cdot \langle\xi|x_t\rangle \cdot |\xi\rangle$$

and

$$-2 \cdot \|\langle\xi|x_t\rangle \cdot |\xi\rangle\| = -2 \cdot |\langle\xi|x_t\rangle|$$

also

$$\|U_f \cdot \left(|x_t^\xi\rangle - |x_t\rangle\right) \|^2 = \||x_t^\xi\rangle - |x_t\rangle\|^2$$

because

$$\|\alpha + \beta\|^2 \leq \|\alpha\|^2 + 2 \cdot \|\alpha\| \cdot \|\beta\| + \|\beta\|^2$$

it follows

$$a_{t+1} = \|U_f \cdot \left(|x_t^\xi\rangle - |x_t\rangle\right) - 2 \cdot \langle\xi|x_t\rangle \cdot |\xi\rangle\|^2$$

$$a_{t+1} \leq \||x_t^\xi\rangle - |x_t\rangle\|^2 + 4 \cdot \||x_t^\xi\rangle - |x_t\rangle t\| \cdot |\langle\xi|x_t\rangle| + 4 \cdot |\langle\xi|x_t\rangle|^2$$

$$a_{t+1} \leq a_t + 4 \cdot \sqrt{a_t} \cdot |\langle\xi|x_t\rangle| + 4 \cdot |\langle\xi|x_t\rangle|^2 \tag{10.23}$$

with

$$\langle\xi|x_t\rangle = |\langle\xi|x_t\rangle| \leq \frac{1}{\sqrt{n}} \tag{10.24}$$

it follows that

$$a_{t+1} \leq 4 \cdot \frac{t^2}{n} + 4 \cdot \sqrt{4 \cdot \frac{t^2}{n}} \cdot \frac{1}{\sqrt{n}} + \frac{4}{n} = 4 \cdot \frac{t^2}{n} + 4 \cdot \sqrt{4 \cdot \frac{t^2}{n^2}} + \frac{4}{n} \tag{10.25}$$

$$a_{t+1} \leq 4 \cdot \frac{t^2}{n} + 8 \cdot \frac{t}{n} + \frac{4}{n} = 4 \cdot \frac{(t+1)^2}{n} \tag{10.26}$$

and the induction step t to $t+1$ is concluded.

10.2.3 $\Omega(\sqrt{n})$

With the lower and upper bound of a_t we can estimate the lower bound of t. a_t grows quadratically,

$$4 \cdot \frac{t^2}{n} \geq a_t \geq c = 0.421002$$

it follows that

$$t \geq \sqrt{n \cdot \frac{c}{4}} = \sqrt{n} \cdot 0.324423. \tag{10.27}$$

The speed up of $O(\sqrt{n})$ compared to $O(n)$ is due to the definition of the probabilities as normed squared amplitudes. If the operator U_f is represented by $O(m)$ gates, then we can get a speed up of maximum $O(\sqrt{n})$ steps, in fact $\Omega(\sqrt{n})$ is the lower bound [Bennett *et al.* (1997)], [Boyer *et al.* (1998)], [Zalka (1999)]. This is the case when $f(x)$ is a $NP-$ *complete* problem. It follows that for U_f-based search using a quantum computer $NP-$ *complete* problems remain $NP-$ *complete*. Despite the fact the saving of $O(2^{\frac{m}{2}})$ compared to $O(2^m)$ is huge, $2^m \neq O(2^{\frac{m}{2}})$ means

$$\Theta(2^{\frac{m}{2}}) \neq \Theta(2^m). \tag{10.28}$$

For $2^m \neq O(2^{\frac{m}{2}})$ we assume there exist a constant c, that for certain value $m_0 > 0$

$$0 \leq 2^m \leq c \cdot 2^{\frac{m}{2}} \quad \forall m \geq m_0.$$

However such a constant does not exist because from

$$2^m = 2^{\frac{m}{2}} \cdot 2^{\frac{m}{2}} \leq c \cdot 2^{\frac{m}{2}}$$

follows the simple contradiction

$$2^{\frac{m}{2}} \leq c.$$

Does the result correspond to the reality? The answer is indicated by the quantum Grover's amplification algorithm [Grover (1996)] with the computational costs $\sqrt{n}$, [Grover (1997)], [Grover (1998a)], [Grover (1998b)], [Grover (1996)], [Grover (1996)]. The proof is based on a sequence in a Hilbert space and the Euclidean norm properties of Hilbert space as well as the definition of the probabilities as normed squared amplitudes [Bennett *et al.* (1997)], [Boyer *et al.* (1998)]. One could naïve hope that if the proof is related to the Hilbert space and the l_2 norm, that maybe for a l_p norm with $p > 2$ the cost would be related to

$$n^{\frac{1}{p}},$$

and for the infinity norm the cost would be constant. However it is known that if quantum mechanics is altered by replacing the 2 norm with another p norm, then there does not exist any non-trivial linear norm-preserving maps [Aaronson (2004)]. Only in a Hilbert space a scalar product induces the norm and only in Hilbert space a general unitary operator is defined. The naïve hope is in vain, we cannot reduce the cost.

10.3 Grover's Amplification

If the operator U_f is represented by $O(m)$ gates, then Grover's amplification algorithm implements exhaustive search in $O(\sqrt{n})$ steps in n-dimensional Hilbert space H_n [Grover (1996)], [Grover (1997)], [Grover (1998a)], [Grover (1998b)], [Grover (1996)], [Grover (1996)] (see Figure 10.1). It is as good as any possible quantum algorithm for exhaustive search due to the lower bound $\Omega(\sqrt{n})$ [Aharonov (1999)]. The algorithm is based on the Householder reflection of state $|x\rangle$ of m qubits with $n = 2^m$ [Zalka (1999)].

10.3.1 *Householder reflection*

Beside rotation and permutation the Householder reflection is an important class of unitary transformations (some times also called the elementary reflector). The Householder reflection reflects one vector $|x\rangle \in H_n$ to its

Fig. 10.1 Lov Kumar Grover originator of the Grover search algorithm .

negative and leaves invariant the orthogonal complement of this vectors. It is described by the Householder matrix Q_x With $\| |x\rangle \| = 1$ representing m qubits with $n = 2^m$

$$Q_x = I_m - 2 \cdot |x\rangle\langle x| \tag{10.29}$$

Q_x is unitary,

$$Q_x \cdot Q_x^* = (I_m - 2 \cdot |x\rangle\langle x|) \cdot (I_m - 2 \cdot |x\rangle\langle x|)^*$$

$$Q_x \cdot Q_x^* = I_m - 2 \cdot |x\rangle\langle x| - 2 \cdot |x\rangle\langle x| + 4 \cdot |x\rangle\langle x| \cdot |x\rangle\langle x|$$

$$Q_x \cdot Q_x^* = I_m - 4 \cdot |x\rangle\langle x| + 4 \cdot \langle x|x\rangle \cdot |x\rangle\langle x| = I_m$$

$\langle x|x\rangle = 1$ because $\| |x\rangle \| = 1$. With

$$P = |x\rangle\langle x|.$$

For example with

$$|x\rangle = \cos(\alpha) \cdot |x_1\rangle + \sin(\alpha) \cdot |x_2\rangle$$

we get

$$Q_x = \begin{pmatrix} 1 - 2 \cdot \cos^2 \cdot \alpha & -2 \cdot \cos\alpha \cdot \sin\alpha \\ -2 \cdot \cos\alpha \cdot \sin\alpha & 1 - 2 \cdot \sin^2 \alpha \end{pmatrix} = \begin{pmatrix} -\cos 2 \cdot \alpha & -\sin 2 \cdot \alpha \\ -\sin 2 \cdot \alpha & \cos 2 \cdot \alpha \end{pmatrix}. \tag{10.30}$$

It becomes clear with

$$Q_x \cdot |0\rangle = \begin{pmatrix} -\cos 2 \cdot \alpha \\ -\sin 2 \cdot \alpha \end{pmatrix}$$

and

$$Q_x \cdot |1\rangle = \begin{pmatrix} -\sin 2 \cdot \alpha \\ \cos 2 \cdot \alpha \end{pmatrix}$$

that Q_x is not a rotation by the angle $2 \cdot \alpha$

$$R_{2\alpha} = \begin{pmatrix} \cos 2 \cdot \alpha & -\sin 2 \cdot \alpha \\ \sin 2 \cdot \alpha & \cos 2 \cdot \alpha \end{pmatrix}.$$

It is a one dimensional reflection

$$S = \begin{pmatrix} -1 & 0 \\ 0 & 1 \end{pmatrix}$$

and a rotation by $R_{2\alpha}$

$$Q_x = R_{2\alpha} \cdot S.$$

10.3.2 *Householder reflection and the mean value*

Suppose P_m is generated by the normalized vector $|x\rangle$ indicating the direction of the bisecting line,

$$|x\rangle = \frac{1}{\sqrt{n}} \cdot |x_1\rangle + \frac{1}{\sqrt{n}} \cdot |x_2\rangle + \cdots + \frac{1}{\sqrt{n}} \cdot |x_n\rangle = \begin{pmatrix} \frac{1}{\sqrt{n}} \\ \vdots \\ \frac{1}{\sqrt{n}} \end{pmatrix} \tag{10.31}$$

or in qubit notation (binary)

$$|x\rangle = \frac{1}{\sqrt{2^m}} \cdot \sum_{y \in B^m} |y\rangle \tag{10.32}$$

then the projection matrix P_m is

$$P_m = |x\rangle\langle x| = \begin{pmatrix} \frac{1}{n} & \frac{1}{n} & \cdots & \frac{1}{n} \\ \frac{1}{n} & \frac{1}{n} & \cdots & \frac{1}{n} \\ \vdots & \vdots & \ddots & \vdots \\ \frac{1}{n} & \frac{1}{n} & \cdots & \frac{1}{n} \end{pmatrix} \tag{10.33}$$

it computes for each dimension described by the fixed basis he mean value of all dimensions.

$$\begin{pmatrix} \frac{\sum_{i=1}^n x_i}{n} \\ \frac{\sum_{i=1}^n x_i}{n} \\ \vdots \\ \frac{\sum_{i=1}^n x_i}{n} \end{pmatrix} = \begin{pmatrix} \frac{1}{n} & \frac{1}{n} & \cdots & \frac{1}{n} \\ \frac{1}{n} & \frac{1}{n} & \cdots & \frac{1}{n} \\ \vdots & \vdots & \ddots & \vdots \\ \frac{1}{n} & \frac{1}{n} & \cdots & \frac{1}{n} \end{pmatrix} \cdot \begin{pmatrix} x_1 \\ x_2 \\ \vdots \\ x_n \end{pmatrix} \tag{10.34}$$

we get

$$Q_x = I_m - 2 \cdot P_m. \tag{10.35}$$

For each dimension the Householder reflection in the direction of the bisecting line computes the following mapping,

$$x_i^{new} = x_i^{old} - 2 \cdot \frac{\sum_{i=1}^{n} x_i^{old}}{n}. \tag{10.36}$$

10.3.3 *Amplification*

Grover's amplification is based on $-Q_x$. It is a unitary operator with

$$G_m := -Q_x = -I_m + 2 \cdot P_m = 2 \cdot P_m - I_m \tag{10.37}$$

the mapping is defined as,

$$x_i^{new} = 2 \cdot \frac{\sum_{i=1}^{n} x_i^{old}}{n} - x_i^{old}. \tag{10.38}$$

Suppose only one amplitude of x_j is negative and the other one are positive. Then the corresponding amplitude grows with

$$x_j^{new} = 2 \cdot \frac{\sum_{i=1}^{n} x_j^{old}}{n} + x_i^{old} \tag{10.39}$$

the other x_i with $i \neq j$ diminish. With $j = 2$ we get

$$\begin{pmatrix} 2 \cdot \frac{\sum_{i=1}^{n} x_i}{n} - x_1 \\ 2 \cdot \frac{\sum_{i=1}^{n} x_i}{n} + x_2 \\ \vdots \\ 2 \cdot \frac{\sum_{i=1}^{n} x_i}{n} - x_n \end{pmatrix} = \begin{pmatrix} \frac{2}{n} - 1 & \frac{2}{n} & \cdots & \frac{2}{n} \\ \frac{2}{n} & \frac{2}{n} - 1 & \cdots & \frac{2}{n} \\ \vdots & \vdots & \ddots & \vdots \\ \frac{2}{n} & \frac{2}{n} & \cdots & \frac{2}{n} - 1 \end{pmatrix} \cdot \begin{pmatrix} x_1 \\ -x_2 \\ \vdots \\ x_n \end{pmatrix}. \tag{10.40}$$

Amplitude amplification is based on G_m and U_f. For a register of m qubits in a Hilbert space H_n we apply the U_f operator and then the operator G_m,

$$(G_m \otimes I_1) \cdot U_f \cdot W_{m+1} \cdot |0^{\oplus m}\rangle|1\rangle$$

$$= G_m \cdot \left(\frac{1}{\sqrt{n}} \sum_{x \in B^m} (-1)^{f(x)} \cdot |x\rangle \right) \otimes \left(\frac{|0\rangle - |1\rangle}{\sqrt{2}} \right) \tag{10.41}$$

with G_m

$$G_m = \begin{pmatrix} \frac{2}{n} - 1 & \frac{2}{n} & \cdots & \frac{2}{n} \\ \frac{2}{n} & \frac{2}{n} - 1 & \cdots & \frac{2}{n} \\ \vdots & \vdots & \ddots & \vdots \\ \frac{2}{n} & \frac{2}{n} & \cdots & \frac{2}{n} - 1 \end{pmatrix} \tag{10.42}$$

note that for $m = 2$, G_2 is equal to the "spy" matrix S

$$G_2 = S = \frac{1}{2} \cdot \begin{pmatrix} -1 & 1 & 1 & 1 \\ 1 & -1 & 1 & 1 \\ 1 & 1 & -1 & 1 \\ 1 & 1 & 1 & -1 \end{pmatrix} \tag{10.43}$$

the resulting state is $|\tau\rangle$

$$(G_m \otimes I_1) \cdot U_f \cdot W_{m+1} \cdot |0^{\oplus m}\rangle|1\rangle = |\tau\rangle \otimes \left(\frac{|0\rangle - |1\rangle}{\sqrt{2}} \right). \tag{10.44}$$

The state $|\tau\rangle$ has an amplitude distribution with a lower entropy as the state with the maximum entropy $\log n$ represented by the maximal superposition

$$|y\rangle = \frac{1}{\sqrt{n}} \sum_{x \in B^m} (-1)^{f(x)} \cdot |x\rangle.$$

With

$$|y\rangle = \begin{pmatrix} \frac{1}{\sqrt{n}} \\ \vdots \\ \frac{1}{\sqrt{n}} \\ -\frac{1}{\sqrt{n}} \\ \frac{1}{\sqrt{n}} \\ \vdots \\ \frac{1}{\sqrt{n}} \end{pmatrix} = \frac{(-1)^{f(x)}}{\sqrt{n}} \cdot \begin{pmatrix} 1 \\ \vdots \\ 1 \\ 1 \\ 1 \\ \vdots \\ 1 \end{pmatrix} = \frac{(-1)^{f(x)}}{\sqrt{n}} \cdot |\mathbf{1}\rangle \tag{10.45}$$

the new amplitude distribution is computed by

$$G_m \cdot |y\rangle = (2 \cdot P_m - I_m) \cdot |y\rangle = 2 \cdot P_m \cdot |y\rangle - I_m \cdot |y\rangle.$$

First two times the average amplitude is computed. The amplitude values for non solution are $\frac{1}{\sqrt{n}}$ and for one marked solution $-\frac{1}{\sqrt{n}}$, it follows

$$2 \cdot P_m \cdot |y\rangle = A \cdot |\mathbf{1}\rangle = \frac{2}{n} \cdot \left(n \cdot \frac{1}{\sqrt{n}} - \frac{1}{\sqrt{n}} + \left(-\frac{1}{\sqrt{n}} \right) \right) \cdot |\mathbf{1}\rangle \tag{10.46}$$

$$A \cdot |\mathbf{1}\rangle = \frac{2}{n} \cdot \left((n-1) \cdot \frac{1}{\sqrt{n}} - \frac{1}{\sqrt{n}} \right) \cdot |\mathbf{1}\rangle \tag{10.47}$$

$$A = \frac{2}{\sqrt{n}} \cdot \left(1 - \frac{2}{n} \right) = \frac{2 \cdot n - 4}{n^{\frac{3}{2}}} \tag{10.48}$$

and the amplitude distribution is

$$G_m \cdot |y\rangle = A \cdot |\mathbf{1}\rangle - I_m \cdot |y\rangle.$$

The amplitude of the state $|\tau\rangle$ indicating the solution in the dimension i is

$$\tau_i = A + \frac{1}{\sqrt{n}} = \frac{3 \cdot n - 4}{n^{\frac{3}{2}}} = \frac{3}{\sqrt{n}} - \frac{4}{n \cdot \sqrt{n}} \tag{10.49}$$

and the non solution in the dimension j with $j \neq i$

$$\tau_j = A - \frac{1}{\sqrt{n}} = \frac{n-4}{n^{\frac{3}{2}}} = \frac{1}{\sqrt{n}} - \frac{4}{n \cdot \sqrt{n}}. \tag{10.50}$$

For $n = 4$ $\tau_i = 1$ and $\tau_j = 0$, for $n = 2^8$ $\tau_i = 0.186523$ and $\tau_j = 0.0615234$. The probability of measuring the solution depending on the size n is

$$p(solution) = \left| \frac{3}{\sqrt{n}} - \frac{4}{n \cdot \sqrt{n}} \right|^2 \tag{10.51}$$

and non solution

$$p(non\ solution) = \left| \frac{1}{\sqrt{n}} - \frac{4}{n \cdot \sqrt{n}} \right|^2. \tag{10.52}$$

In the Figure 10.2 we indicated the probability of measuring the solution and non solution for $4 \leq n \leq 16$ and in the Figure 10.3 for $2^8 \leq n \leq 2^{16}$. For more than 4 qubits the probability of measuring a solution will be below 0.5. The probability can be increased by the iterative amplification.

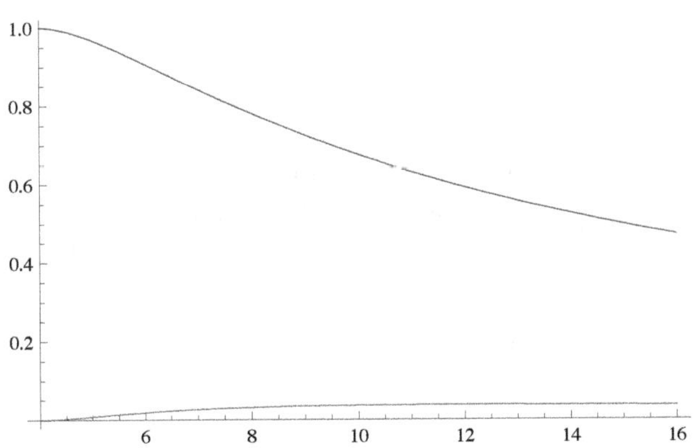

Fig. 10.2 The probability of measuring the solution and non solution for $4 \leq n \leq 16$. The x-axis indicates n and the y-axis the probability. Top curve is the probability of the solution, down curve the probability of the non solution.

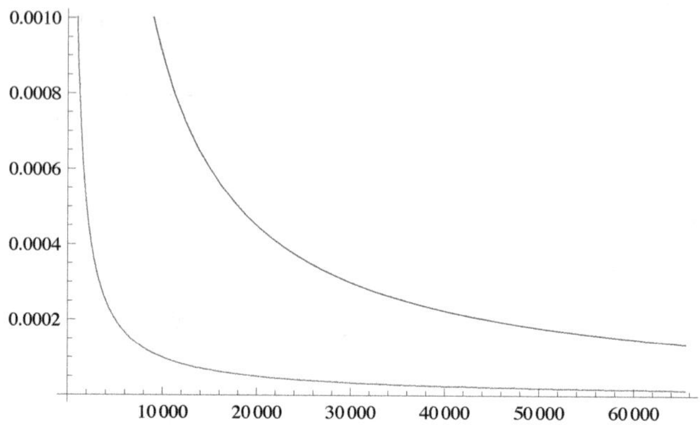

Fig. 10.3 The probability of measuring the solution and non solution for $2^8 \leq n \leq 2^{16}$. The x-axis indicates n and the y-axis the probability. Top curve is the probability of the solution, down curve the probability of the non solution.

10.3.4 *Iterative amplification*

With the definition

$$\Gamma_m := (G_m \otimes I_1) \cdot U_f \tag{10.53}$$

the resulting state is $|\tau\rangle$. We describe several amplifications by

$$\left(\prod_{t=1}^{r} \Gamma_m\right) \cdot W_{m+1} \cdot |0^{\oplus m}\rangle|1\rangle = \Gamma_m \cdot \Gamma_m \cdot \cdots \cdot \Gamma_m \cdot W_{m+1} \cdot |0^{\oplus m}\rangle|1\rangle$$

$$= |\tau\rangle \otimes \left(\frac{|0\rangle - |1\rangle}{\sqrt{2}}\right).$$

How many iterations do we need to preform, or what is the suitable value for r? The probability of seeing one solution should be as close as possible to 1 and r should be as small as possible. Suppose that the function $f(x)$ has k solutions with $n \gg k \geq 1$,

$$f_\xi(x) = \begin{cases} 1 & if \quad x = \xi_i \;\; i \in \{1, 2, \cdots, k\} \\ 0 & else \end{cases} \tag{10.54}$$

we want to find x for which $f(x) = 1$. All the preceding steps can be easily extended to this more general case. The amplitude for the solution at the iteration t will be indicated by α_t non solution by β_t. For $t = 0$ before the first iteration of Γ_m

$$\alpha_0 = \frac{1}{\sqrt{n}} \tag{10.55}$$

$$\beta_0 = \frac{1}{\sqrt{n}}. \tag{10.56}$$

In the first iteration Γ_m two times the average amplitude is computed, the amplitude values for non solution are $\frac{1}{\sqrt{n}}$ and for one marked solution $-\frac{1}{\sqrt{n}}$, it follows

$$A = \frac{2}{n} \cdot \left(n \cdot \frac{1}{\sqrt{n}} - \frac{k}{\sqrt{n}} - \frac{k}{\sqrt{n}}\right) = \frac{2}{n} \cdot \left((n-k) \cdot \frac{1}{\sqrt{n}} - \frac{k}{\sqrt{n}}\right) \tag{10.57}$$

$$A = \frac{2}{n} \cdot ((n-k) \cdot \beta_0 - k \cdot \alpha_0). \tag{10.58}$$

The amplitude of the solution is

$$\alpha_1 = A + \frac{1}{\sqrt{n}} = A + \alpha_0 = \frac{2}{n} \cdot ((n-k) \cdot \beta_0 - k \cdot \alpha_0) + \alpha_0, \tag{10.59}$$

$$\alpha_1 = \frac{1}{n} \cdot (\alpha_0 \cdot (n - 2 \cdot k) + \beta_0 \cdot (2 \cdot n - 2 \cdot k),$$

$$\alpha_1 = \alpha_0 \cdot (1 - \frac{2 \cdot k}{n}) + \beta_0 \cdot (2 - \frac{2 \cdot k}{n}), \tag{10.60}$$

and the non solution

$$\beta_1 = A - \frac{1}{\sqrt{n}} = A - \beta_0 = \frac{2}{n} \cdot ((n-k) \cdot \beta_0 - k \cdot \alpha_0) - \beta_0, \tag{10.61}$$

$$\beta_1 = -\alpha_0 \cdot \frac{2 \cdot k}{n} + \beta_0 \cdot (1 - \frac{2 \cdot k}{n}). \tag{10.62}$$

We can describe the evolution of the amplitudes in time t by two coupled recurrence equations. They represent a discrete dynamical system of two difference equations

$$\alpha_{t+1} = \alpha_t \cdot \left(1 - \frac{2 \cdot k}{n}\right) + \beta_t \cdot \left(2 - \frac{2 \cdot k}{n}\right) \tag{10.63}$$

$$\beta_{t+1} = -\alpha_t \cdot \frac{2 \cdot k}{n} + \beta_t \cdot \left(1 - \frac{2 \cdot k}{n}\right). \tag{10.64}$$

We can indicate the states of a system in three dimensional phase space of α_t, β_t and t with the boundary condition of $\alpha_0 = \beta_0 = \frac{1}{\sqrt{n}}$ (see Figure 10.4). It represents a periodic orbit in time. The projected orbit in the two dimensional subspace α_t, β_t represents an ellipse (see Figure 10.5). The ellipse is determined by the values of n and k (see Figure 10.6). The projected orbit in two dimensional subspace of amplitude and time t represents two sine waves, periodic functions described by α_t and β_t (see Figure 10.7).

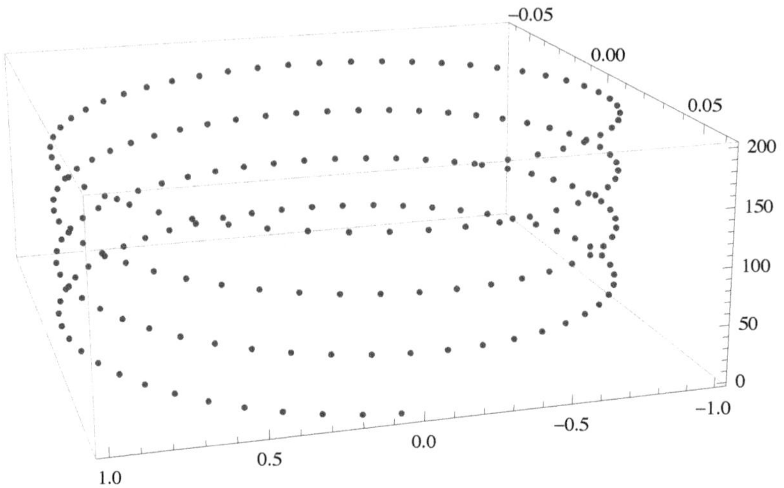

Fig. 10.4 Phase space ofα_t, β_t and t with the boundary condition of $\alpha_0 = \beta_0 = \frac{1}{\sqrt{n}}$. The values are $n = 256$, $k = 1$ and $1 \leq t \leq 200$. The x-axis indicates α_t, the y-axis β_t and the z-axis t.

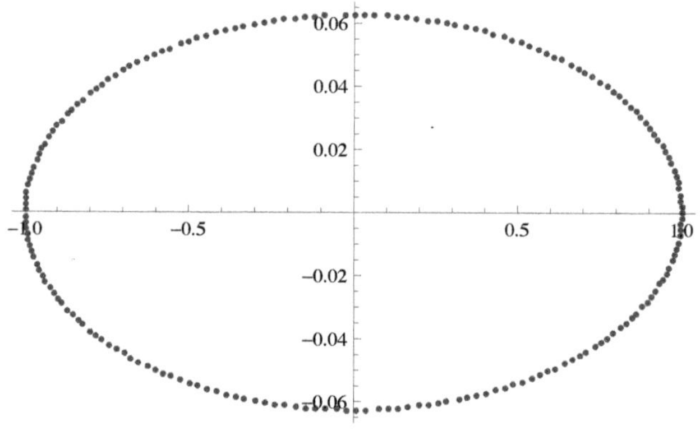

Fig. 10.5 The projected orbit in the two dimensional subspace α_t, β_t with the boundary condition of $\alpha_0 = \beta_0 = \frac{1}{\sqrt{n}}$. The values are $n = 256$, $k = 1$ and $1 \leq t \leq 200$. The x-axis indicates α_t and the y-axis β_t.

The period is determined by the value of k and n. With $k = 1$ the peak amplitude is one (see Figure 10.8 and Figure 10.6). Such a linear and periodic system is usually described by sine and cosine equations. It should be

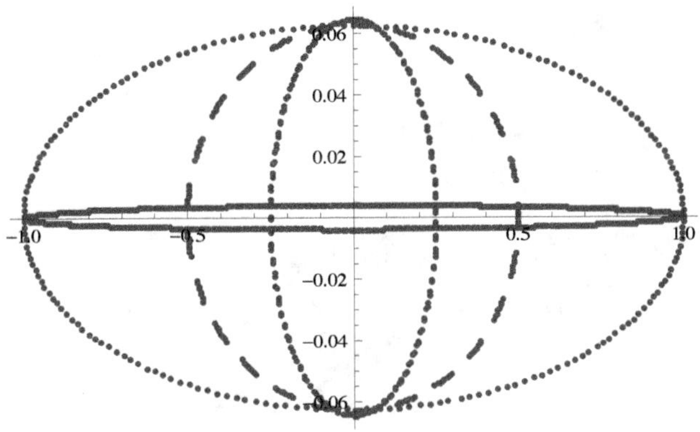

Fig. 10.6 The projected orbit in the two dimensional subspace α_t, β_t with the boundary condition of $\alpha_0 = \beta_0 = \frac{1}{\sqrt{n}}$. The x-axis indicates α_t, the y-axis β_t. The outer ellipse has the values $n = 256$, $k = 1$ as before, the two ellipses with diminishing x-axis radius corresponds to increased k values $k = 4$ and $k = 16$. For all three ellipses with $n = 256$, 200 iterations were done. In the fourth ellipse k is one and $n = 65536 = 2^{16}$, y-axis radius diminish. 1000 iterations were done.

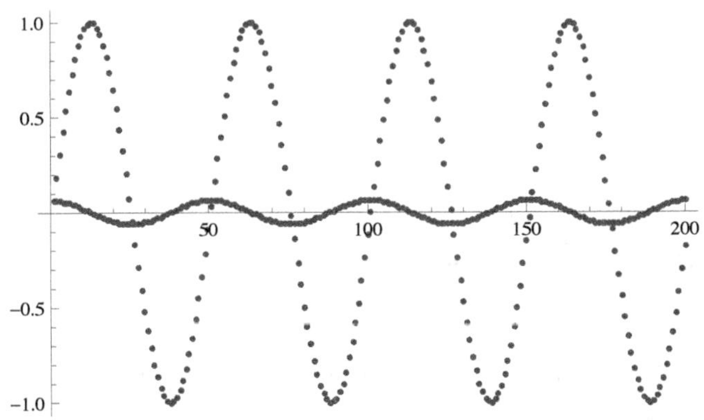

Fig. 10.7 The projected orbit in the two dimensional subspace of amplitude and time t represents a periodic function described by α_t (the dotted curve) and β_t (the continuous curve). The x-axis indicates t and the y-axis the amplitude. The values are $n = 256$, $k = 1$ and $1 \leq t \leq 200$.

noted that a cosine wave is a sine wave because of the phase-shift relation

$$\cos(\theta) = \sin\left(\theta + \frac{\pi}{2}\right).$$

The ellipse in a Cartesian system is represented by the equation

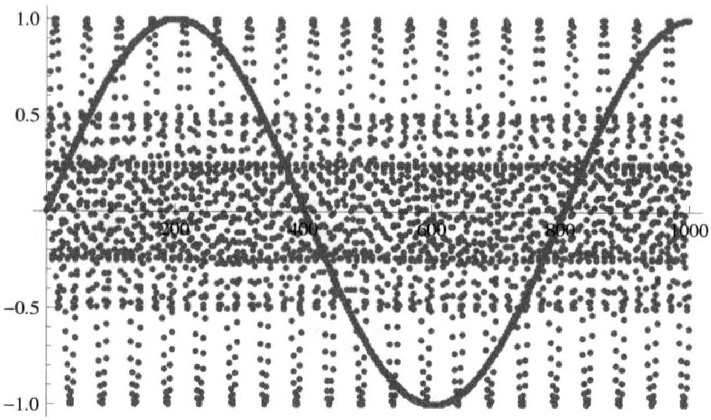

Fig. 10.8 The projected orbit in the two dimensional subspace of amplitude and time t The x-axis indicates t and the y-axis the amplitude. Four periodic functions represented by α_t with different periods are shown. The period is determined by the value of k and n. With $k = 1$ the peak amplitude is one. The greatest period corresponds to the values $k = 1$ and $n = 65536$. For $n = 256$ the period diminishes, for $k = 4$ and $k = 16$ the peak amplitude diminishes below one and the period diminishes even more. 1000 iterations were done.

$$\frac{x^2}{a^2} + \frac{y^2}{b^2} = 1. \tag{10.65}$$

Because α_t and β_t are real, following equation representing an ellipse is given by

$$k \cdot \alpha_t^2 + (n-k) \cdot \beta_t^2 = 1. \tag{10.66}$$

Using the the Pythagorean identity

$$\sin^2\theta + \cos^2\theta = 1$$

we can rewrite the equation representing the ellipse as

$$k \cdot \left(\sqrt{\frac{1}{k}} \cdot \sin\theta_t\right)^2 + (n-k) \cdot \left(\sqrt{\frac{1}{n-k}} \cdot \cos\theta_t\right)^2 = 1 \tag{10.67}$$

it follows that

$$\alpha_t = \sqrt{\frac{1}{k}} \cdot \sin\theta_t \quad \mathit{and} \quad \beta_t = \sqrt{\frac{1}{n-k}} \cdot \cos\theta_t \tag{10.68}$$

and we can rewrite the the two coupled recurrence equations as

$$\sqrt{\frac{1}{k}} \cdot \sin\theta_{t+1} = \sqrt{\frac{1}{k}} \cdot \sin\theta_t \cdot \left(1 - \frac{2 \cdot k}{n}\right) + \sqrt{\frac{1}{n-k}} \cdot \cos\theta_t \cdot \left(2 - \frac{2 \cdot k}{n}\right)$$

$$\sqrt{\frac{1}{n-k}} \cdot \cos\theta_{t+1} = -\sqrt{\frac{1}{k}} \cdot \sin\theta_t \cdot \frac{2\cdot k}{n} + \sqrt{\frac{1}{n-k}} \cdot \cos\theta_t \cdot \left(1 - \frac{2\cdot k}{n}\right)$$

simplified as

$$\sin\theta_{t+1} = \sin\theta_t \cdot \left(1 - \frac{2\cdot k}{n}\right) + \cos\theta_t \cdot \frac{2\cdot\sqrt{k}\cdot\sqrt{n-k}}{n} \tag{10.69}$$

$$\cos\theta_{t+1} = -\sin\theta_t \cdot \frac{2\cdot\sqrt{k}\cdot\sqrt{n-k}}{n} + \cos\theta_t \cdot \left(1 - \frac{2\cdot k}{n}\right). \tag{10.70}$$

Trigonometric simplification*

Because

$$-1 \leq \left(1 - \frac{2\cdot k}{n}\right) \leq 1$$

we can represent it as

$$\cos\omega = 1 - \frac{2\cdot k}{n}. \tag{10.71}$$

Because of the Pythagorean identity

$$\left(1 - \frac{2\cdot k}{n}\right)^2 + \left(\frac{2\cdot\sqrt{k}\cdot\sqrt{n-k}}{n}\right)^2 = 1$$

it follows that

$$\sin\omega = \frac{2\cdot\sqrt{k}\cdot\sqrt{n-k}}{n} \tag{10.72}$$

and we can rewrite again the the two coupled recurrence equations as

$$\sin\theta_{t+1} = \sin\theta_t \cdot \cos\omega + \cos\theta_t \cdot \sin\omega \tag{10.73}$$

$$\cos\theta_{t+1} = -\sin\theta_t \cdot \sin\omega + \cos\theta_t \cdot \cos\omega \tag{10.74}$$

Because of the trigonometric identities, addition and subtraction theorem, the two coupled recurrence equations with the boundary condition θ_0 are

$$\sin\theta_{t+1} = \sin(\theta_t + \omega) = \sin(\theta_0 + t\cdot\omega + \omega) \tag{10.75}$$

$$\cos\theta_{t+1} = \cos(\theta_t + \omega) = \cos(\theta_0 + t\cdot\omega + \omega) \tag{10.76}$$

and we can rewrite the recurrence equations into two simple equations

$$\alpha_t = \frac{1}{\sqrt{k}} \cdot \sin(\theta_0 + t\cdot\omega) \tag{10.77}$$

$$\beta_t = \frac{1}{\sqrt{n-k}} \cdot \cos(\theta_0 + t \cdot \omega). \tag{10.78}$$

With the boundary condition of $\alpha_0 = \beta_0 = \frac{1}{\sqrt{n}}$ and $\alpha_0 = \sqrt{\frac{1}{k}} \cdot \sin\theta_0$, $\beta_0 = \frac{1}{\sqrt{n-k}} \cdot \cos\theta_0$ it follows that

$$\sin^2\theta_0 = \frac{k}{n} \tag{10.79}$$

and

$$\cos^2\theta_0 = \frac{n-k}{n} = 1 - \frac{k}{n} \tag{10.80}$$

and because of the double angle formula

$$\cos(2 \cdot x) = 2 \cdot \cos^2 x - 1 = 1 - 2 \cdot \sin^2 x$$

and

$$\sin(2 \cdot x) = 2 \cdot \sin x \cdot \cos x$$

it follows that

$$\cos\omega = 1 - \frac{2 \cdot k}{n} = 1 - 2 \cdot \sin^2\theta_0 = \cos(2 \cdot \theta_0). \tag{10.81}$$

$$\sin\omega = \frac{2 \cdot \sqrt{k} \cdot \sqrt{n-k}}{n} = 2\sin\theta_0 \cdot \cos_0\theta_0 = \sin(2 \cdot \theta_0). \tag{10.82}$$

Using the trigonometric identities

$$\alpha_t = \frac{1}{\sqrt{k}} \cdot (\sin\theta_0 \cdot \cos(t \cdot \omega) + \cos\theta_0 \cdot \sin(t \cdot \omega)) \tag{10.83}$$

$$\beta_t = \frac{1}{\sqrt{n-k}} \cdot (-\sin\theta_0 \cdot \sin(t \cdot \omega) + \cos\theta_0 \cdot \cos(t \cdot \omega)) \tag{10.84}$$

the solution for the two difference equations representing the discrete dynamical with the boundary condition $\alpha_0 = \beta_0 = \frac{1}{\sqrt{n}}$ is represented by the two equations

$$\alpha_t = \frac{1}{\sqrt{k}} \cdot \sin(\theta_0 + t \cdot 2 \cdot \theta_0) = \frac{1}{\sqrt{k}} \cdot \sin(\theta_0 \cdot (2 \cdot t + 1)) \tag{10.85}$$

$$\beta_t = \frac{1}{\sqrt{n-k}} \cdot \cos(\theta_0 + t \cdot 2 \cdot \theta_0) = \frac{1}{\sqrt{n-k}} \cdot \cos(\theta_0 \cdot (2 \cdot t + 1)) \tag{10.86}$$

with

$$\theta_0 = \sin^{-1}\left(\sqrt{\frac{k}{n}}\right). \tag{10.87}$$

10.3.5 *Number of iterations*

The probability of seeing one solution should be as close as possible to 1 and the number of iterations r should be as small as possible. Because there are k solution, the probability of measuring a state that represents a solution is

$$k \cdot \alpha_t^2 = \sin^2(\theta_0 \cdot (2 \cdot t + 1)) = 1 \tag{10.88}$$

$$\theta_0 \cdot (2 \cdot t + 1) = \frac{\pi}{2} \tag{10.89}$$

after t^* iterations the probability of measuring a solution is nearly one

$$t^* := t = \frac{\pi}{4 \cdot \theta_0} - \frac{1}{2} = \frac{\pi}{4} \cdot \sqrt{\frac{n}{k}} - \frac{1}{2} = \frac{\pi}{4} \cdot \sqrt{\frac{2^m}{k}} - \frac{1}{2} \tag{10.90}$$

$$t^* = 0.785398 \cdot \sqrt{\frac{2^m}{k}} - 0.5. \tag{10.91}$$

For $k = 1$ and more than two qubits ($m > 2$, $n = 2^m$) the corresponding value is above the possible lower bound for U_f based search

$$t^* = \sqrt{n} \cdot 0.785398 - 0.5 > \sqrt{n} \cdot 0.324423. \tag{10.92}$$

The number of iterations r

$$\left(\prod_{t=1}^{r} \Gamma_m \right) \cdot W_{m+1} \cdot |0^{\oplus m}\rangle|1\rangle$$

is the largest integer not greater than t^*,

$$r = \lfloor t^* \rfloor = \left\lfloor \frac{\pi}{4} \cdot \sqrt{\frac{2^m}{k}} - \frac{1}{2} \right\rfloor. \tag{10.93}$$

The value of r depends on the relation of n versus k. For $n = 4$ and $k = 1$ we need only one rotation, we need as well only one rotation for

$$\frac{n}{4} = k$$

to find **one** of the k solutions. For 16 qubits and one solution, $k = 1$, $n = 65536 = 2^{16}$, $t^* = 200.562$. In this case we need two hundred rotations. The probability of measuring a state that represents a solution is nearly one. It is possible to adapt the iterations in such a way that the probability of finding a solution is exactly one. One changes θ_0 of the difference equations either in the last step or continuously so that the $r = t^* = \lfloor t^* \rfloor$ as proposed by Brassard [Brassard *et al.* (2000)], [Brassard *et al.* (1998)]. The resulting speed up remains quadratic. The iterative amplification algorithm requires the value of k in order to determine the number of iterations. We can determine the value of k by the quantum counting algorithm.

10.3.6 *Quantum counting*

Quantum counting algorithm is based on the QFT period algorithm to estimate the period of the sin wave period represented by the of the amplitude α_t or β_t [Brassard *et al.* (1998)]. [Brassard *et al.* (2000)] (see Figure 10.7). We define t iterations of amplification as

$$\Phi^t = \left(\prod_{t=1}^{t} \Gamma_m\right). \tag{10.94}$$

The state $|\tau\rangle$ has two different amplitudes representing solution and non solution. They define the two subspaces $|\tau_{solution}\rangle$ and $|\tau_{non}\rangle$ with

$$\Phi^t \cdot W_{m+1}|0^{\otimes m}\rangle|1\rangle = k \cdot \alpha_t \cdot |\tau_{solution}\rangle + (n-k) \cdot \beta_t \cdot |\tau_{non}\rangle \otimes \left(\frac{|0\rangle - |1\rangle}{\sqrt{2}}\right) \tag{10.95}$$

ignoring the auxiliary qubit, or target qubit we can write

$$\Phi^t \cdot W_m|0^{\otimes m}\rangle$$

$$= \sqrt{k}\cdot\sin(\theta_0\cdot(2\cdot t+1))\cdot|\tau_{solution}\rangle + \sqrt{(n-k)}\cdot\cos(\theta_0\cdot(2\cdot t+1))\cdot|\tau_{non}\rangle. \tag{10.96}$$

We define a unitary operator U_Φ that acts on two registers $|t\rangle$ and $|x\rangle$ and one auxiliary qubit,

$$U_\Phi \cdot |t\rangle|x\rangle \otimes \left(\frac{|0\rangle - |1\rangle}{\sqrt{2}}\right) = |t\rangle|\Phi^t|x\rangle \otimes \left(\frac{|0\rangle - |1\rangle}{\sqrt{2}}\right) \tag{10.97}$$

with

$$U_\Phi \cdot |t\rangle \otimes \left(\frac{1}{\sqrt{2^m}} \sum_{x \in B^m} |x\rangle\right) \otimes \left(\frac{|0\rangle - |1\rangle}{\sqrt{2}}\right)$$

$$= |t\rangle \otimes (k \cdot \alpha_t \cdot |\tau_{solution}\rangle + (n-k) \cdot \beta_t \cdot |\tau_{non}\rangle) \otimes \left(\frac{|0\rangle - |1\rangle}{\sqrt{2}}\right) \tag{10.98}$$

after the application of U_Ψ the two registers and the auxiliary qubit are entangled. In the first step of the algorithm we build a superposition of m qubits and μ qubits with $T = 2^\mu$ taking into account the auxiliary bit. The value of T can be estimated by the determination of the period of

$$\sin(\theta_0 \cdot (2 \cdot t + 1))$$

assuming $k = 1$. It follows that

$$W_\mu \cdot W_{m+1}|0^{\otimes \mu}\rangle|0^{\otimes m}\rangle|1\rangle =$$

$$= \left(\frac{1}{\sqrt{T}} \sum_{t \in B^{\mu}} |t\rangle \right) \otimes \left(\frac{1}{\sqrt{n}} \sum_{x \in B^{m}} |x\rangle \right) \otimes \left(\frac{|0\rangle - |1\rangle}{\sqrt{2}} \right).$$

In the second step we apply the U_{Φ} operator

$$U_{\Phi} \left(\frac{1}{\sqrt{T}} \sum_{t \in B^{\mu}} |t\rangle \right) \otimes \left(\frac{1}{\sqrt{n}} \sum_{x \in B^{m}} |x\rangle \right) \otimes \left(\frac{|0\rangle - |1\rangle}{\sqrt{2}} \right) =$$

$$\left(\frac{1}{\sqrt{T}} \sum_{t \in B^{\mu}} |t\rangle \right) \otimes (k \cdot \alpha_t \cdot |\tau_{solution}\rangle + (n-k) \cdot \beta_t \cdot |\tau_{non}\rangle) \otimes \left(\frac{|0\rangle - |1\rangle}{\sqrt{2}} \right). \tag{10.99}$$

In the third step we measure the second register of the compound system. As the result the state of the system is projected to the subspace that corresponds to the observed state and the vector representing the state is renormalized to the unit length. The result of the second register is either $f_{solution}(t) = \sin(\theta_0 \cdot (2 \cdot t + 1))$ or $f_{non}(t) = \cos(\theta_0 \cdot (2 \cdot t + 1))$. Both functions have the same period and will be represented as $f(t)$. The new amplitude distribution is normalized and has the same periodic period as $f(t)$. The following steps correspond to the QFT period algorithm as before.

10.4 Circuit Representation

Grover's amplification is based on $G_m = -Q_x$. and can be represented by $O(m)$ quantum gates The unitary operator Λ_m reverse the sign of $|0\rangle$

$$\Lambda_m \cdot |0\rangle = -|0\rangle$$

and for $|x\rangle \neq |0\rangle$

$$\Lambda_m \cdot |x\rangle = |x\rangle.$$

Λ_m can be implemented efficiently with $f_0(x)$

$$f_0(x) = \begin{cases} 1 & if \quad x = 0 \\ 0 & else \end{cases} \tag{10.100}$$

as

$$\frac{1}{\sqrt{n}} \sum_{x \in B^{m}} (-1)^{f_0(x)} \cdot |x\rangle \otimes \left(\frac{|0\rangle - |1\rangle}{\sqrt{2}} \right). \tag{10.101}$$

We can write

$$G_m = -Q_x = -I_m + 2 \cdot P_m = 2 \cdot P_m - I_m = -(W_m \cdot \Lambda_m \cdot W_m) \tag{10.102}$$

with the auxiliary qbit for the Λ_m operator representation it becomes

$$G_m = -(W_m \cdot \Lambda_m \cdot W_m) \otimes \left(\frac{|0\rangle - |1\rangle}{\sqrt{2}} \right) \tag{10.103}$$

neglecting the auxiliary qbit it follows that

$$W_m \cdot \Lambda_m \cdot W_m = \begin{pmatrix} 1-\frac{2}{n} & -\frac{2}{n} & \cdots & -\frac{2}{n} \\ -\frac{2}{n} & 1-\frac{2}{n} & \cdots & -\frac{2}{n} \\ \vdots & \vdots & \ddots & \vdots \\ -\frac{2}{n} & -\frac{2}{n} & \cdots & 1-\frac{2}{n} \end{pmatrix}. \tag{10.104}$$

The first row of W_m which is positive and can be represented as

$$\langle w| = \sum_{x \in B^m} \langle x|$$

By the operator Λ_m it becomes negative. $\langle w|$ it multiplies with the first column of W_m

$$|w\rangle = \sum_{x \in B^m} |x\rangle$$

the first column multiplied with the first row results in

$$|w\rangle\langle w| = P_m.$$

This value is subtracted from

$$I_m = W_m \cdot W_m$$

and replaced by $-|w\rangle\langle w|$

$$I_m - |w\rangle\langle w| - |w\rangle\langle w| = I_m - 2 \cdot |w\rangle\langle w| = I_m - 2 \cdot P_m. \tag{10.105}$$

Because $U_{f(0)}$ that represents $f_0(x)$ can be represented by $O(m)$ gates and all other operators are based on Hadamard operator W_m built by a direct product of m W_1 matrices, G_m can be represented by $O(m)$ quantum gates. Given the fact that the operator U_f is represented by $O(m)$ gates, then Grover's amplification algorithm implements exhaustive search in $O(\sqrt{n})$ steps in n-dimensional Hilbert space H_n.

10.5 Speeding up the Traveling Salesman Problem

A salesman must visit t cities; he must visit each city exactly once and finish at the city where his tour started. We call such a tour a valid tour. The costs of traveling from city i to city j are represented by c_{ij}. The costs do not need to be symmetrical $c_{ij} \neq c_{ji}$. The salesman wishes to conduct a valid tour that costs at most k. The traveling salesman problem (TSP) is the most popular $NP - complete$ problem. An instance (ticket) leads to a "yes" answer in polynomial time. Given a tour, we can verify whether the tour is valid, and the costs are below k in polynomial time.

We search through all possible orderings of the cities and verify, for each ordering, if the tour is valid and the costs are below k. A quantum circuit U_{TSP} with a polynomial number of quantum gates can verify, for a given tour, whether it is a solution. Because we can not reset to the input state, the circuit should recompute the output before applying the amplification step. For t cities, we can represent each city by $\lceil \log_2 t \rceil$ qubits, and a tour by a register of

$$m^* = t \cdot \lceil \log_2 t \rceil$$

qubits. We will examine all of the possible orderings of t cities with repetition for simplicity. Without repetitions, there are $t!$ possible orderings; with repetition,

$$t^t = 2^{t \log_2 t} = 2^m \tag{10.106}$$

with

$$m = t \cdot \log_2 t \leq m^*.$$

We apply the U_{TSP} operator,

$$\Gamma_m := (G_m \otimes I_1) \cdot U_{TSP} \tag{10.107}$$

determine the value of r by quantum counting

$$\left(\prod_{t=1}^{r} \Gamma_m \right) \cdot W_{m+1} \cdot |0^{\oplus m}\rangle|1\rangle = |\tau\rangle \otimes \left(\frac{|0\rangle - |1\rangle}{\sqrt{2}} \right) \tag{10.108}$$

and and determine the solution by the measurement of the register $|\tau\rangle$. The computing costs are

$$O(t^{\frac{t}{2}}) = O\left(\sqrt{2^m}\right) \tag{10.109}$$

with

$$t! \gg t^{\frac{t}{2}}.$$

Any $NP - complete$ problem can be solved in a similar way.

10.6 The Generate-and-Test Method

The generate-and-test method is a simple AI paradigm. This approach uses a generator and a tester. The generator produces all of the possible solutions, and the tester evaluates each possible solution to see whether it is the expected solution (see Figure 10.9).

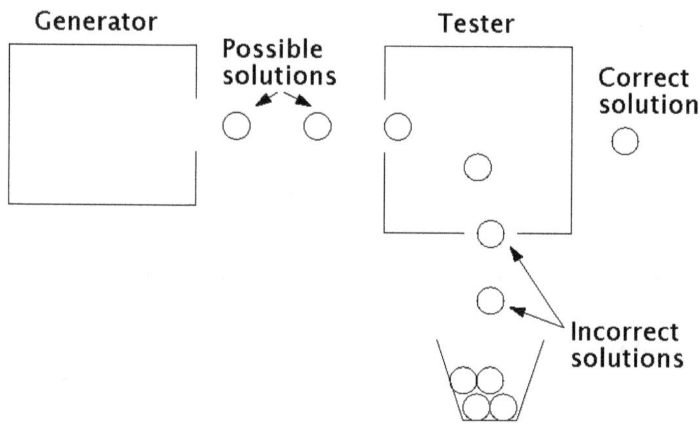

Fig. 10.9 The generate-and-test method.

This approach is mostly used to solve identification problems. The generator produces hypotheses that are tested. For some problems, the possible solutions can be represented by some points in the problem space. For other problems, the possible solutions can be represented by paths in the problem space. We can speed up the generate-and-test method by mapping the generator into a superposition and the tester into an oracle represented by a quantum circuit.

10.7 Quantum Walk

Related to Grover's algorithm and the quantum tree search algorithm is the quantum random walk on a graph ([Ambainis (2003)], [Kempe (2003)] and [Ambainis (2004)]). Indeed, Grover's algorithm can also be viewed as a quantum walk algorithm. A quantum random walk is an analog to the random walk. There are two types of random walk, namely, discrete- and continuous-time. We describe the discrete-time random walk on a lattice and the quantum random walk on a graph $G = (V, E)$.

10.7.1 *Random walk*

Randomness could be nature's way to avoid complexity when accomplishing certain tasks. A fly could choose the direction of its flight randomly. The insect flies for a time in a randomly chosen direction. Then, it randomly chooses another direction, and then, another random direction is chosen, and so forth. This process is an example of a random walk in three dimensions. We simplify the model by describing it as a discrete random walk on a three-dimensional lattice [Gaylord and Wellin (1995)]. At each point, the fly can choose to fly in six directions: up, down, north, south, west or east. Each random choice is made after a constant amount of time; the constant flight path intervals are of equal length. In Figure 10.10, we see a simulation of a lattice random walk in dimension three for 1000 steps. A two-dimensional lattice walk is represented in Figure 10.11. In the case that the random numbers are not generated by a quantum device the classical random walk is not true random but pseudo random.

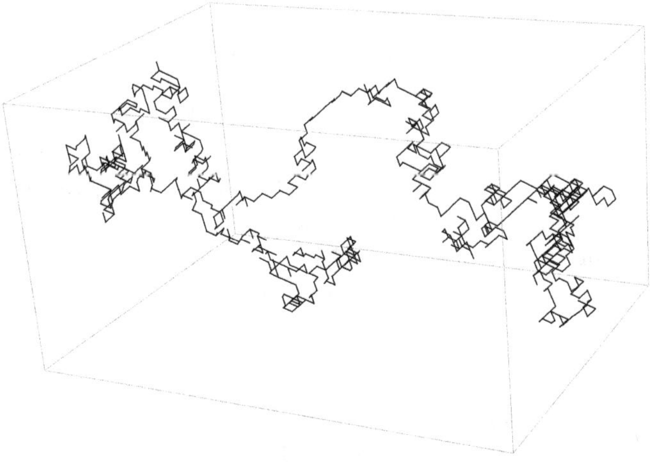

Fig. 10.10 Simulation of a lattice random walk in dimension three for 1000 steps.

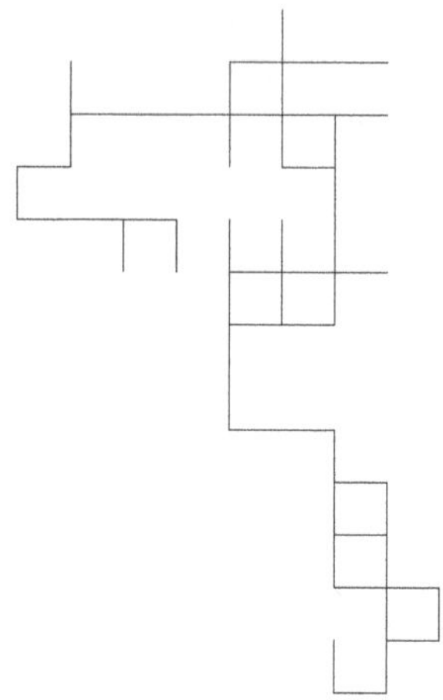

Fig. 10.11 Simulation of a lattice random walk in dimension two for 100 steps.

10.7.2 *Quantum insect*

In classical physics, randomness is not present. Suppose that a fly generates randomness by some quantum computing device that simulates the behavior of a quantum coin. In this case, a true random walk is present. Suppose that the fly is in a closed room and we do not know its position. The fly is evolving into a superposition of several states that can be characterized by its position. Each of the possible positions is associated with a specific probability. The "quantum fly" is in a superposition state. As long as we make no measurements, there are no random effects. The behavior of the system is strictly deterministic. The probability distribution represents the possible positions after several steps, and several measurements of the quantum fly and the classical fly will differ. This difference arises because the randomness in the quantum walk is present only during the measurement.

10.7.3 *Quantum walk on a graph*

The discrete-time quantum random walk on a graph $G = (V, E)$ can be described by a unitary operator U on Hilbert space

$$H = H_S \otimes H_C.$$

H_S represents the vertex of the graph and H_C describes the destination choice. The destination choice H_C is also called "coin space" [Shenvi *et al.* (2003)] because the choice in one dimension can be described by a quantum coin. U is composed of the operators S and C [Aharonov *et al.* (2001)],

$$U = S \cdot C.$$

A step of the quantum walk is represented by two operations [Childs (2011)]:

- Build a superposition over the neighbor states by operator C;
- Move the state to the new target destination by operator S.

A register represents a state

$$|jk\rangle = |j\rangle|k\rangle \Longleftrightarrow (j,k) \in E.$$

The neighbors of j are represented in the register $|k\rangle$ by the by operator C [Watrous (1998)], [Tarrataca and Wichert (2013a)],

$$C \cdot |j\rangle|k\rangle = |j\rangle \frac{1}{\sqrt{deg(j)}} \sum_{w:(j,w)\in E} |k \oplus w\rangle \tag{10.110}$$

with $deg(j)$ represents the degree of vertex j and $\sum_{m:(j,m)\in E} \frac{1}{deg(j)} = 1$. After applying the C operator the state of the system is moved from state $|j\rangle$ to state $|k\rangle$ for example by a simple permutation

$$S \cdot |j\rangle|k\rangle = |k\rangle|j\rangle \tag{10.111}$$

with the effect that the quantum random walk takes places on the edges of the graph.

10.7.4 *Quantum walk on one dimensional lattice*

The most simple graph is one dimensional lattice. The quantum walk is called the discrete walk on a line. A state is represented by a register

$$|n\rangle|0\rangle, \quad |n\rangle|1\rangle$$

with $n \in Z$ being an integer representing the position on the line and $|0\rangle$ and $|1\rangle$ being the state of the system. A step of the quantum walk is represented by two operations C and S [Ambainis (2003)]. The Hadamard coin is represented by the following unitary matrix

$$C := W_1 = \begin{pmatrix} \frac{1}{\sqrt{2}} & \frac{1}{\sqrt{2}} \\ \frac{1}{\sqrt{2}} & -\frac{1}{\sqrt{2}} \end{pmatrix} = \frac{1}{\sqrt{2}} \cdot \begin{pmatrix} 1 & 1 \\ 1 & -1 \end{pmatrix}. \tag{10.112}$$

The unitary S operator is defined as

$$S \cdot |n\rangle|0\rangle = |n-1\rangle|0\rangle, \quad S \cdot |n\rangle|1\rangle = |n+1\rangle|1\rangle. \tag{10.113}$$

Suppose we start in location $|0\rangle$ and the state $|0\rangle$.

$$S \cdot C \cdot |0\rangle|0\rangle = U \cdot |0\rangle|0\rangle = \frac{|-1\rangle|0\rangle + |1\rangle|1\rangle}{\sqrt{2}} \tag{10.114}$$

after one step the result is similar to classical random walk. After two steps

$$U \cdot U \cdot |0\rangle|0\rangle = \frac{|-2\rangle|0\rangle + |0\rangle 1\rangle + |0\rangle|0\rangle - |2\rangle|1\rangle}{2} \tag{10.115}$$

the probability of $n = 1$ is zero contrary to classical random walk. After three steps

$$U \cdot U \cdot U \cdot |0\rangle|0\rangle = \frac{|-3\rangle|0\rangle + |-1\rangle|1\rangle + 2 \cdot |-1\rangle|0\rangle - |1\rangle|0\rangle + |3\rangle|1\rangle}{2 \cdot \sqrt{2}} \tag{10.116}$$

the distribution is biased towards left because of the non-symmetric coin operator W_1. A symmetric unitary coin operator [Ambainis (2003)] would be represented by

$$C := \frac{1}{\sqrt{2}} \cdot \begin{pmatrix} 1 & i \\ i & 1 \end{pmatrix}. \tag{10.117}$$

In Figure 10.12 we see the comparison between the distribution of the classical random walk on a one dimensional lattice line and the quantum random walk with a symmetric coin operator. The quantum random walk propagates quadratically faster to the edges of the graph.

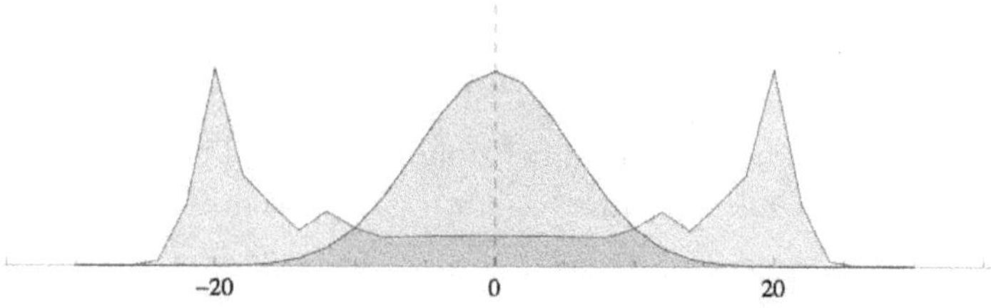

Fig. 10.12 Comparison between the distribution of the classical random walk on a one dimensional lattice and the quantum random walk with a symmetric coin operator after 50 steps [Hogg (2008)]. The walk starts at the origin. The classical walk has a peak near the origin, it corresponds to Gaussian distribution. The probability distribution for the quantum walk is approximately uniform near the origin and maximal near the edges of the graph.

10.7.5 *Quantum walk and search*

In quantum random walk the goal states are marked through an oracle operator as in the Grover's algorithm [Shenvi *et al.* (2003)]. To obtain for goal states with $n = |V|$ the complexity is $O(\sqrt{n})$. With the projection matrix P_m

$$P_m = |x\rangle\langle x| = \begin{pmatrix} \frac{1}{n} & \frac{1}{n} & \cdots & \frac{1}{n} \\ \frac{1}{n} & \frac{1}{n} & \cdots & \frac{1}{n} \\ \vdots & \vdots & \ddots & \vdots \\ \frac{1}{n} & \frac{1}{n} & \cdots & \frac{1}{n} \end{pmatrix} \tag{10.118}$$

we get Grover's amplification also called Grover's diffusion operator.

$$G_m = 2 \cdot P_m - I_m. \tag{10.119}$$

One can redefine the coin operator in order to perform Grover's diffusion operator [Moore and Russell (2001)]. The reformulated coin operator C is with $m := deg(j)$

$$C \cdot |j\rangle|k\rangle = |j\rangle \cdot \left(\frac{2}{\sqrt{m}} \cdot \sum_{w:(j,w)\in E} |k \oplus w\rangle\langle k| - I_m \right). \tag{10.120}$$

10.7.6 *Quantum walk for formula evaluation*

Quantum random walk can determine the properties of a graph by generating different distributions. Quantum walk algorithms for Boolean formula evaluation can evaluate a Boolean formula quadratically faster than any known classical algorithm. For a Boolean formula $f(x)$ to the input string $x_1, \neg x_1, \cdots, x_m, \neg x_m$. Boolean formula is $f(x) = 1$ otherwise $f(x) = 0$ [Farhi and Gutmann (1998)], [Childs *et al.* (2007)], [Ambainis (2007)], [Ambainis *et al.* (2007)]. However one should not neglect the cost of building the coin operators that represent the instanced formula. For example to speed up alpha-beta search by evaluating AND-OR formulas as used in games [Farhi *et al.* (2008)], [Cleve *et al.* (2008)], the instantiationed graph has to be determined dynamically during the performed search.

"We conclude by mentioning some open problems. Our algorithm needs to know the full structure of the formula beforehand to determine the coin's bias at each internal vertex...", cited from [Ambainis *et al.* (2007)].

Chapter 11

Quantum Problem-Solving

11.1 Symbols and Quantum Reality

Problem-solving can be modeled by a production system that implements a search algorithm. The search defines a problem space and can be represented as a tree. Because symbols do not by themselves represent any utilizable knowledge, additional heuristic functions are used to speed up the search. Without the use of heuristic functions, real-world problems become intractable because of the exponential growth of the leaves in the tree. A heuristic function is used that rates the value's different states according to how far they are from the desired state. A best-first search is that in which the best rule (according to a heuristic function of the conflict set) is chosen. The better the heuristic measure of the remaining distance to the desired state is, the faster the best-first search [Winston (1992)]. An example for a simple heuristic function is the simple assumption that the distance between the states in the problem space is related to the similarity of the vectors that represent the states. A vector corresponds to a pattern that mirrors the way that the biological sense organs describe the world and is called a sub-symbol. The argument as presented before indicates that the heuristic function results from the Euclidian geometry of the world as experienced by humans. Could physical nature as described by quantum physics also lead to a quantum heuristic? In the relation of sub-symbols to symbols, do quantum-symbols exist?

In quantum computation, there are two known principles to speed up the computation:

- The QFT can determine the period of a wave (periodic function) exponentially faster than any known classical algorithm. QFT is based on the unitary DFT matrix and FFT decomposition.

- Grover's algorithm can speed up the search quadratically. Grover's algorithm is based on the unitary Householder reflection, which is represented by a unitary matrix.

In a tree, we search for a leaf ξ. Using Grover's algorithm, we represent the corresponding search tree by a quantum Boolean circuit U_{tree}. What is the speedup in relation to the structure of the represented tree? We will investigate this question starting from classical tree search algorithms, which will lead us to the general model of a quantum computer, the Tarrataca's quantum production system.

11.2 Uninformed Tree Search

In an uninformed search, no additional information about the states is given. The search represented by a search tree is performed from an initial state through the following states until a goal state is reached. A search tree is represented by nodes and edges. Each node represents a state, and each edge represents a transition from one state to the following state. The initial state defines the root of the tree. From each state ν, either B_ν states can be reached or the state is a leaf. B_ν represents the branching factor of the node v. A leaf represents either the goal of the computation or an impasse when no valid transition to a succeeding state exists. In contrast to a real tree in computer science, the root of a tree structure is at the top of the tree and the leaves are at the bottom. Every node besides the root has a unique node from which it was reached, called the parent. The parent is the node above it and is connected by an edge. Each parent ν has B_ν children. The depth of a node ν is the number of edges to the root node. Nodes with the same depth k define the level k. For a tree with a constant branching factor B, each node at each level k has B children, and at each level k, there are $B \cdot k$ nodes [Nilsson (1982)], [Luger and Stubblefield (1993)], [Russell and Norvig (2010)].

Breadth-first search In a breadth-first search the root node (level $L = 0$) is expanded first. Then each children of the root at the level $L = 1$ are expanded, they become the parents of the children at the level $L = 2$. Then the procedure is repeated for the preceding levels until a goal is reached or all nodes are impasse states (see Figure 11.1). Breadth-first search performs a level wise search. All nodes at level L have to be visited before visiting a node at level $L + 1$. For a constant branching factor B B^m nodes are

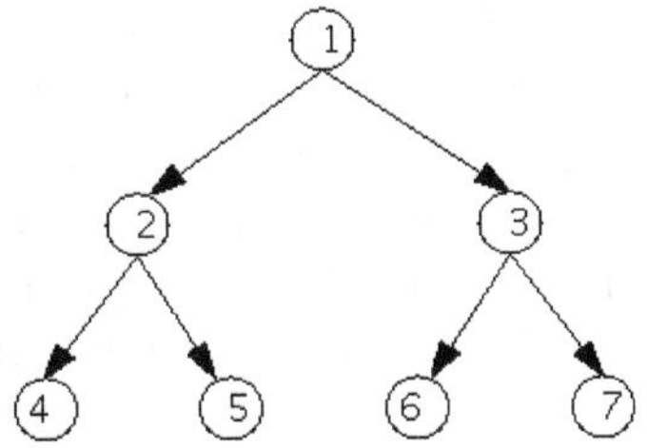

Fig. 11.1 In a breadth-first search the root node (level $L = 0$) is expanded first. Then each children of the root at the level $L = 1$ are expanded, they become the parents of the children at the level $L = 2$.

expanded at level m with $k = 0$ being the root. The total number of nodes at level m is represented by the geometric series

$$1 + B + B^2 + B^3 + \cdots + B^m = \sum_{i=0}^{m} B^i = \frac{1 - B^{m+1}}{1 - B} = O(B^m). \quad (11.1)$$

Every node that is generated has to be represented in memory and the number of nodes grows exponentially. The computing costs and the memory requirements are in worst case $O(B^m)$.

Depth-first search Progressive depending and local focusing leads to a depth-first search [Newell (1990)]. It always expands the deepest node in the search tree until a goal is reached or all nodes are impasse states (see Figure 11.2). An impasse is present when no valid transition to a

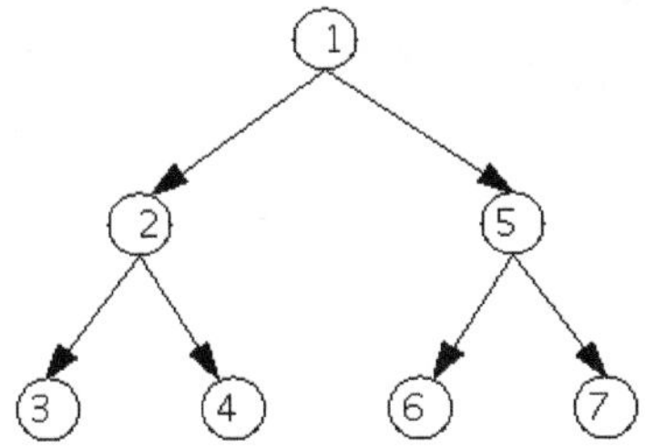

Fig. 11.2 Depth-first search always expands the deepest node in the search tree until a goal is reached or all nodes are impasse states.

succeeding state exists. In this case backtracking to the previous state is done. Another state can be chosen, if possible, or backtracking is repeated. In worst case the same number of nodes are visited as in breadth-first search. Commonly this number is less and the memory requirements are low compared to breadth-first search. Only a path from the root to the current node with the remaining unexpected sibling nodes for each node on the path have to be represented. If m is the maximum depth of the search tree and for a constant branching factor B the memory requirements are

$$B \cdot m + 1 \tag{11.2}$$

we add a one because the node at the depth m is a leaf or an impasse. The computing costs are in the worst case $O(B^m)$ and the memory requirements $B \cdot m = O(m)$. Depth-first search first search contrary to breadth-first search can fail in the case the maximum depth of the search tree converges to $m \to \infty$. A solution to this problem is the combination of both methods with the benefits of both of them.

Iterative deepening search In iterative deepening search we gradually increase the limit of the search from one, to two, three, four and continue to do it until a goal is found. For each limit m_k a depth-first search is performed from the root with m_k being the maximum depth of the search tree. During iterative deepening states are generated multiple times [Korf (1985)], [Russell and Norvig (2010)]. The time complexity of iterative deepening search is of the same order of magnitude as breadth-first search [Korf (1985)], as explained by Richard E. Korf: "Since the number of nodes on a given level of the tree grows exponentially with depth, almost all time is spent in the deepest level, even through shallower levels are generated an arithmetically increasing number of times." The paradox can be explained by the arithmetico-geometric sequence. The number of nodes for iterative deepening for each level starting with level zero (for simplicity) is given by

$$1$$

$$1 + B$$

$$1 + B + B^2$$

$$\cdots$$

to level m is given by

$$1 + B + B^2 + B^3 + \cdots + B^m$$

the costs C_m (total number of visited nodes) are represented by the arithmetic-geometric sequence that represent the sum of each iteration

$$C_m = (m+1) \cdot 1 + m \cdot B + (m-1) \cdot B^2 + (m-2) \cdot B^3 + \cdots + 1 \cdot B^m, \quad (11.3)$$

$$C_m = \sum_{i=0}^{m} (m+1-i) \cdot B^i. \quad (11.4)$$

With

$$C_m = \sum_{i=1}^{m+1} (m+1-(i-1)) \cdot B^{i-1}. \quad (11.5)$$

According to Riley[Riley *et al.* (2006)]

$$C_m - C_m \cdot B = C_m \cdot (1-B) = m+1-(2 \cdot m+1) \cdot B^{m+1} + \frac{B \cdot (1-B^m)}{(1-B)}, \quad (11.6)$$

$$C_m = \frac{m+1}{1-B} - \frac{(2 \cdot m+1) \cdot B^{m+1}}{1-B} + \frac{B \cdot (1-B^m)}{(1-B)^2}, \quad (11.7)$$

by simplifying this equation we arrive at

$$C_m = \frac{1 + m - B \cdot m - 2 \cdot B^{1+m} \cdot (1+m) + B^{2+m} \cdot (1 + 2 \cdot m)}{(B-1)^2} = O(B^m). \quad (11.8)$$

The computing costs are in the worst case $O(B^m)$ and the memory requirements $B \cdot m = O(m)$. It follows that we should use depth-first search if the depth of the solution is known, otherwise we should prefer iterative deepening over breadth-first search due to the low memory requirements.

Loops To speed up the search the formation of loops should be prohibited. By comparison with the sequence of carried out states loops can be prevented.

11.3 Heuristic Search

Heuristic search is based on a heuristic function $h(\nu)$ that estimates the cheapest cost from the node ν to the goal.

Greedy best-first search It expands the node ν that is closest to the goal according to a heuristic function $h(\nu)$. Out of the B children the node ν_i is chosen with

$$\min_{1\leq i\leq B}(h(\nu_i)). \tag{11.9}$$

Like depth-first search it follows a single path to the goal. It always expands the deepest node in the search tree according to $h(\nu)$ until a goal is reached or all nodes are impasse states. An impasse is present when no valid transition to a succeeding state exists. In this case backtracking to the previous state is done. Another state can be chosen that is closest to the goal, if possible, or backtracking is repeated. The computing costs are in the worst case $O(B^m)$ and the memory requirements $B \cdot m = O(m)$. However with a good heuristic function $h(\nu)$ the cost can be reduced considerably.

***A* search** It evaluates the nodes through a function $f(\nu)$ that estimates the cheapest solution that passes through the node ν. The function $f(\nu)$ is composed out of the heuristic function $h(\nu)$ and the function $g(\nu)$ that indicates the cheapest costs of reaching the node ν from the root node representing the initial state.

$$f(\nu) = g(\nu) + h(\nu).$$

As breadth-first search it keeps all evaluated nodes in memory. The computing costs and the memory requirements are in the worst case $O(B^m)$.

A^* search A^* search is equivalent to the A search with the constraint that the function $h(\nu)$ is an admissible heuristic, it never overestimates the cost to reach the goal. If $c(\nu)$ are the true cost to reach the goal it follows

$$h(\nu) \leq c(\nu).$$

In tree search it follows that the triangle inequality is valid with $c(\zeta, \nu)$ representing the true cost from node ζ to node ν

$$h(\zeta) \leq c(\zeta, \nu) + h(\nu). \tag{11.10}$$

A^* search is complete and optimal in a tree. In a graph search is not optimal and complete. In a graph search $h(\nu)$ must be consistent, means the triangle inequality must be valid. We have to discard the more expensive of any paths found. However "usually" all admissible heuristics in the graph search are consistent. A solution is found if it exists. A^* search is optimal, no other algorithm is guaranteed to expand fewer nodes. However the number of expanded nodes can grow exponential unless the error of estimates the cheapest cost from the node ν to the goal is extremely small

$$c(\nu) - h(\nu) \leq O(\log c(\nu)). \tag{11.11}$$

The computing costs and the memory requirements are in worst case $O(B^m)$.

11.3.1 *Heuristic functions*

We will demonstrate the principles of heuristic function $h(\nu)$ on the 8-puzzle example. Two common heuristics for this task are the number of misplaced tiles, and the "city-block distance" [Nilsson (1982); Pearl (1984); Luger and Stubblefield (1998)]. The first heuristic counts the number of misplaced tiles out of place in each state compared to the desired goal. However this heuristic fails to take into account all available information such as the distance the tiles must be moved. The "city-block distance" sums all the distances by which the tiles are out of place, with one count for each square a tile must be moved to reach a position of the desired state. The "city-block distance", also called the "Manhattan distance", is often better than the "number of misplaced tiles" (see Figure 11.3). Both heuristic functions are admissible.

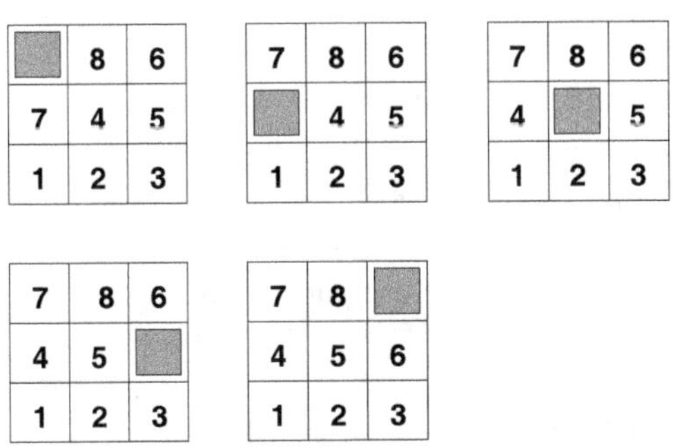

Fig. 11.3 The first pattern (upper left) represents the initial configuration and the last (low right) the desired configuration. The series of moves describe the solution to the problem using the "city-block distance" heuristic function.

11.3.2 *Invention of heuristic functions*

Euclidean geometry of the world The invention process can be inspired by the Euclidean geometry of the world as stated before. The Oksapmin tribe of Papua New Guinea counts by associating a number with the position of the body [Lancy (1983)]. This suggests a representation of numbers by bars at certain positions which can overlap. A bar at a certain position codes the magnitude of the number. The closeness or similarity of different numbers is determined by the overlap of the bar codes [Wichert *et al.* (2008)] (see Figure 11.4). In the 8-puzzle, each tile is defined by its

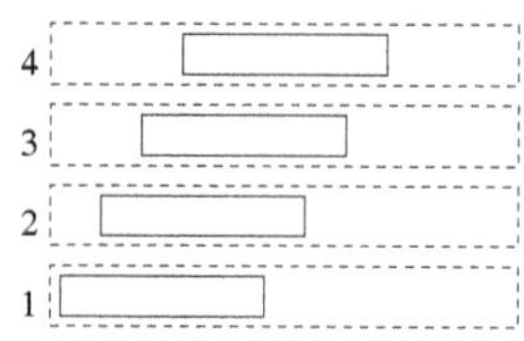

Fig. 11.4 A bar at a certain position codes the magnitude of the number. The closeness or similarity of different numbers is determined by the overlap of the bar codes.

corresponding coordinates. Two numbers can be represented by two bars (see fig 11.5). The amount of overlapping indicates the closeness of different tiles. The resulting function is equivalent to the city-block distance. The distance between a state and a desired state corresponds to the sum of distance by which the tiles are out of place. The closeness or similarity of a tile to the desired position of the tile is determined by the overlap of the two bar codes representing the tile (see Figure 11.6). The overlap corresponds to the distance by which the tile is out of place. The heuristic function emerged by a reasonable sub-symbolical representation of the states in the 8-puzzle world [Wichert *et al.* (2008)].

Symbolical problems Generally the invention of heuristic functions is difficult. In many applications there is no relation to the Euclidean geometry of the world. Examples are chemical structures or mathematical expressions as used in symbolical integration. One way to is to approximate a problem by a relaxed problem with fewer restrictions. For example in the relaxed version of the n-puzzle problem we assume we can move each tile to its position independently of moving the other tiles. The relaxed problem represents an admissible heuristic function of the problem. An optimal solution in the original problem $c(\nu)$ is also a solution in the

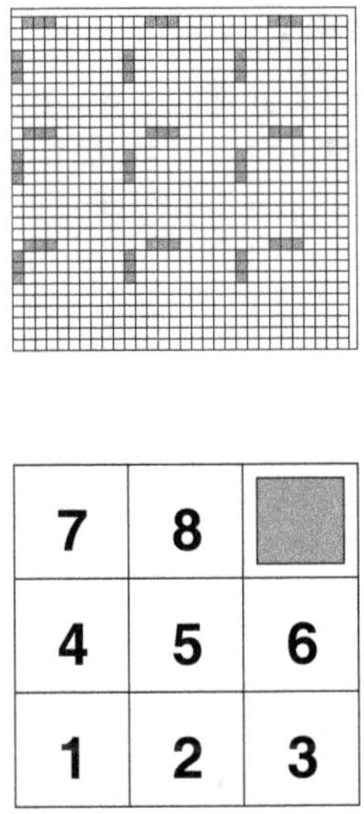

Fig. 11.5 The desired state for the task 8-puzzle and its representation by bars. The associative fields in which the objects are describe have a fixed dimension of ten times ten pixels. Because of this, excessive unused space is present.

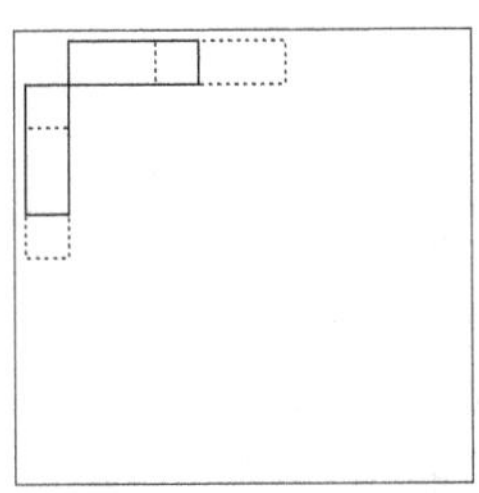

Fig. 11.6 The tile "1" at the position of the tile "6" (shown by dotted bars). The value of the city-block distance is three. The hamming distance between the patterns representing the tile "1" and "6" is also three.

relaxed problem. By the abolition of present restrictions the cost of the relaxed problem are less or equal to $c(\nu)$. Another way is to decompose the problem into sub-problems and to store all exact solution in a database and to use it to speed up the search using the solution of sub-problems or to extract the heuristic function by machine learning.

11.3.3 *Quality of heuristic*

A frequent used measure is the effective branching factor b. It is independent of the length of the optimal solution. It is related to the costs C_m represented by the number of generated nodes during A^* search [Nilsson (1982)], [Russell and Norvig (2010)]. It is represented by the geometric series (we do not omit level L=0 for simplicity)

$$C_m = 1 + b + b^2 + b^3 + \cdots + b^m = \sum_{i=0}^{m} b^i = \frac{1 - b^{m+1}}{1 - b}. \tag{11.12}$$

We cannot represent b as a function of m and C_m, however we can plot the values of C_m in dependence of b and m (see Figure 11.7). The exponential grow cost C_m can be only stopped in the case of fully informed search $b = 1$. A heuristic reduces the value of b. By doing so it extends the horizon of

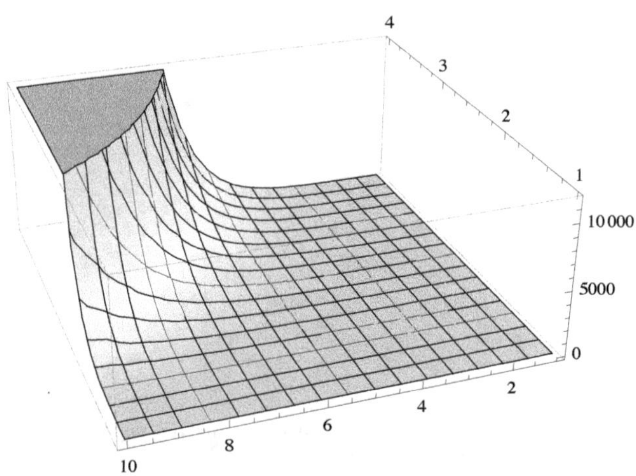

Fig. 11.7 Values of C_m in dependence of branching factor b (1-4) and depth m (1-10).

m of tractable C_m values. No classical universal heuristic function for all domains exist, for each domain a heuristic function has to be invented. This process in general is non trivial.

11.4 Quantum Tree Search

11.4.1 *Principles of quantum tree search*

There is a simple relation between a tree search and information theory. Suppose that we have a constant branching factor B and the depth of the tree is m. In this case, there are $B^m = n$ leaves. The goal of the search is to visit all of the leaves. The ideal entropy indicates the minimum number of optimal questions that describe the result of an experiment. The experiment represents n leaves of a search tree with equal probabilities $p = (1/n, 1/n..., 1/n)$. The maximal ideal Entropy is

$$H(F) = m = -\sum_i p_i \log_B p_i = \log_B n \tag{11.13}$$

and corresponds to the depth of the search tree. In the case of $B = 2$, each of the m questions has a reply of either "yes" or "no" and can be represented by a bit (see Figure 11.8). The m answers are represented by

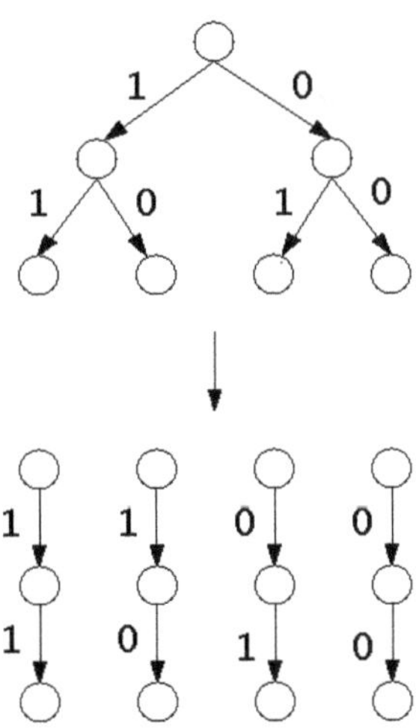

Fig. 11.8 Search tree for $B = 2$ and $m = 2$. Each question can be represented by a bit. Each binary number (11, 10, 01, 00) represents a path from the root to the leaf.

a binary register of length m. There are n different binary registers, which represent all of the possible binary numbers of length m. Each binary number represents a path from the root to a leaf. A path could contain loops, or an impasse could be present before a leaf is reached. However, for each goal, a certain binary number indicates the solution. For a constant branching factor $B > 2$, each question has B possible answers. The m answers can be represented by a base-B number with m digits. For example, with $B = 8$, the number is represented in an octal numeral system. Alternatively, the m answers can be represented by a binary register of length $m \cdot \lceil \log_2 B \rceil$.

Using Grover's algorithm, we search through all possible paths and verify, for each path, whether it leads to the goal state [Tarrataca and Wichert (2011b)]. A quantum circuit U_p with a polynomial number of quantum gates can verify whether each path corresponds to a sequence of productions that lead from the initial state to the goal state. Because we can not reset to the input state, the circuit should recompute the output before applying the amplification step. We apply the U_p operator with,

$$\mu = m \cdot \lceil \log_2 B \rceil \tag{11.14}$$

with the special case $\mu = m$ for constant branching factor $B = 2$, it follows

$$\Gamma_\mu := (G_\mu \otimes I_1) \cdot U_p \tag{11.15}$$

determine the value of r by quantum counting

$$\left(\prod_{t=1}^{r} \Gamma_\mu\right) \cdot W_{\mu+1} \cdot |0^{\oplus \mu}\rangle|1\rangle = |\tau\rangle \otimes \left(\frac{|0\rangle - |1\rangle}{\sqrt{2}}\right) \tag{11.16}$$

and and determine the solution by the measurement of the register $|\tau\rangle$. Because

$$\sqrt{B^m} \approx \sqrt{2^{m \cdot \lceil \log_2 B \rceil}} \tag{11.17}$$

it follows that the computing costs are

$$O\left(\sqrt{B^m}\right) = O\left(\sqrt{2^\mu}\right) = O\left(\sqrt{2^{m \cdot \lceil \log_2 B \rceil}}\right) \tag{11.18}$$

which is much less then uninformed tree search algorithms with

$$O\left(\sqrt{2^{m \cdot \lceil \log_2 B \rceil}}\right) = O\left(\sqrt{B^m}\right) \ll O(B^m) = O\left(2^{m \cdot \lceil \log_2 B \rceil}\right). \tag{11.19}$$

The effective branching factor for quantum tree search b_q is given by the equation

$$C_m = \frac{1 - b^{m+1}}{1 - b} \approx B^{\frac{m}{2}} \tag{11.20}$$

it follows that

$$b_q \approx \sqrt{2^{\lceil \log_2 B \rceil}} \geq \sqrt{B}. \tag{11.21}$$

11.4.2 *Iterative quantum tree search*

The presented algorithm is limited to a search of depth m. This constraint can be overcome by the quantum iterative deepening search. A quantum iterative deepening search is equivalent to the iterative deepening search [Tarrataca and Wichert (2012a)], [Tarrataca and Wichert (2013b)]. We gradually increase the limit of the search from one, to two, three, and four and continue to search until the goal is found. For each limit m, a quantum tree search is performed from the root, with m being the maximum depth of the search tree. The possible solutions are determined by a measurement. The time complexity of an iterative deepening search has the same order of magnitude as the quantum tree search. With

$$\beta := B^{\frac{1}{2}}$$

the computing costs for each level starting with level zero (for simplicity) are given by

$$O(1)$$

$$O(\beta) = O(B^{\frac{1}{2}})$$

$$O(\beta^2) = O(B^{\frac{2}{2}})$$

$$\cdots$$

to level m is given by

$$O(\beta^m) = O(B^{\frac{m}{2}})$$

the total costs of m_k iterations with m measurments are $O(B^{\frac{m}{2}}) = O\left(\sqrt{B^m}\right)$

$$O(1) + O(B^{\frac{1}{2}}) + O(B^{\frac{2}{2}}) + O(B^{\frac{3}{2}}) + \cdots + O(B^{\frac{m}{2}}) = O(B^{\frac{m}{2}}) = O\left(\sqrt{B^m}\right) \tag{11.22}$$

$$O\left(\sqrt{B^m}\right) = O\left(\sqrt{2^\mu}\right) = O\left(\sqrt{2^{m\cdot\lceil\log_2 B\rceil}}\right)$$

the equation is based on the geometric series

$$1+\beta+\beta^2+\beta^3+\cdots+\beta^m = \sum_{i=0}^{m} \beta^i = \frac{1-\beta^{m+1}}{1-\beta} = O(\beta^m) = O(B^{\frac{m}{2}}) \tag{11.23}$$

and the effective branching factor is equal to b_q as for quantum tree search.

11.4.3 *No constant branching factor*

Suppose the branching factor is not constant, in this case the tree search can be described by the effective branching factor. For uninformed tree search for a large number of instances (different initial and goal states) the effective branching factor converge to the averaged branching factor for uninformed tree search [Tarrataca and Wichert (2011b)]. For a not constant branching factor the quantum tree search the maximal branching factor B_{max} has to be used for the quantum tree search. For B_{max} the quantum algorithm using qubit representation is better then the classical tree search described by the effective branching factor b in the case

$$b > b_q. \tag{11.24}$$

If B_{max} is a power of two then

$$b > b_q = \sqrt{2^{\lceil \log_2 B_{max} \rceil}} = \sqrt{B_{max}} \tag{11.25}$$

otherwise

$$b > b_q = \sqrt{2^{\lceil \log_2 B_{max} \rceil}} > \sqrt{B_{max}} \tag{11.26}$$

for example $B_{max} = 9$, then

$$b_q = 4 = \sqrt{2^4} > 3 = \sqrt{9}.$$

and base-9 instead of qubit representation would be more economical. In production systems B_{max} corresponds often to the number of productions. In the 8-puzzle example there are four productions in the long term memory and $B_{max} = 4$ and $b_q = 2$. For blind search the effective branching factor is ≈ 2.8 [Russell and Norvig (2010)], the "city-block distance" heuristic effective branching factor is ≈ 1.24. However one should keep in mind that the invention of heuristic functions is difficult and the 8-puzzle is a well studied problem in the AI community [Nilsson (1982); Pearl (1984); Luger and Stubblefield (1998)]. Heuristic functions can fail. For example in instances of a problem in which one cannot perform the first necessary action without undoing them at a later stage, also called "Sussman anomaly" [Sussman (1975)]. Iterative quantum tree search never fails. This is because during the iterative amplifications of the Grover's algorithm one can adapt the iterations in such a way that the probability of finding a solution is exactly one.

11.5 Quantum Production System

The control structure of a production system (reaction system) can be defined in terms of an iterative quantum tree search [Tarrataca and Wichert (2012b)], [Tarrataca and Wichert (2011a)]. In an iterative quantum tree search, the limit is increased gradually in each step t. For each limit m_t, a quantum tree search is performed from the root, with m_t being the maximum depth of the search tree. With a maximal branching factor B_{max} and using the qubit representation, there are n_t different binary registers, which represent all of the possible binary numbers of length μ_t with

$$n_t = 2^{\mu_t} = 2^{m_t \cdot \lceil \log_2 B_{max} \rceil}. \tag{11.27}$$

The register is called a path descriptor κ_i^t for the iteration step t with $i \in \{1, 2, \cdots, n_t\}$. Each path descriptor κ_i^t represents a possible path from the root to the leaf. A path can be undefined. However, for each goal state, a corresponding κ_i^t exists. The quantum production system is deterministic and reversible because the search is determined by the path descriptor. No conflict resolution is needed. The circuit U_p^t verifies whether each path specified by the path descriptor κ_i^t corresponds to a sequence of productions that leads from the initial state to the goal state. The computation is described by the initial state, the goal state and the long-term memory. The long-term memory is composed of several productions. The productions define the circuit U_p^t. The result of the computation is represented by a path descriptor κ_i^t. After each iterative step t, Grover's algorithm is performed. If no goal at step t was reached, then the resulting path descriptor κ_i^t is randomly chosen. In a case in which the goal state can be reached by only one path at iteration t, the path descriptor κ_i^t is chosen deterministically by Grover's algorithm. The number of possible paths to a goal state can be determined by quantum counting.

11.6 Tarrataca's Quantum Production System

A formal definition of Tarrataca's quantum production system is based on the pure production system [Tarrataca and Wichert (2012b)]. We explain the principles of Tarrataca's quantum production system on a trivial example, the 3-puzzle. In the next step we generalize to n-puzzle and to general quantum production systems. The description is a simplified version of the one presented in [Tarrataca and Wichert (2011a)].

11.6.1 3-*puzzle*

The 3-puzzle is composed of three numbered movable tiles in a 2×2 frame (see Figure 11.9.

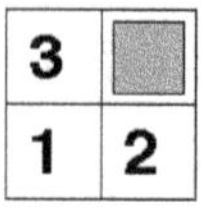

Fig. 11.9 The desired configuration of the 3-puzzle.

One cell of the frame is empty and because of this, tiles can be moved around to form different patterns. The goal is to find a series of moves of tiles into the blank space that changes the board from the initial configuration to a desired configuration). There are twelve possible configurations (see Figure 11.10). For any of this configuration only two movements are possible. The movement of the empty cell are either a clockwise or counter-clockwise movement.

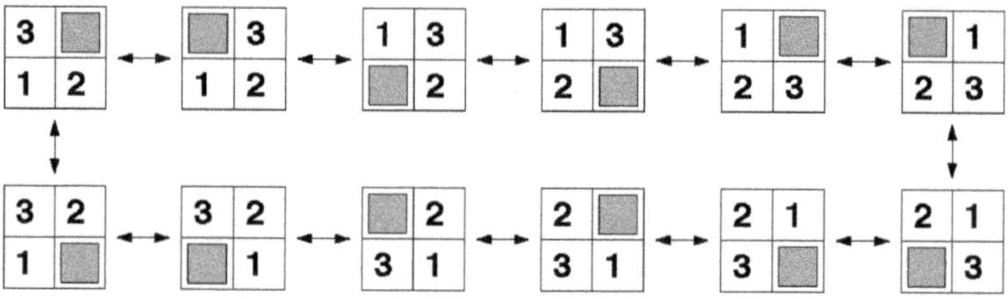

Fig. 11.10 There are twelve possible configurations. For any of this configuration only two movements are possible. The movement of the empty cell are either a clockwise or counter-clockwise movement.

The 3-puzzle is tractable and requires fewer qubits to encode. However the model can be generalized to any n-puzzle. The number of possible solvable configurations of the n-puzzle is

$$\frac{n!}{2}. \tag{11.28}$$

There are $n!$ different configurations, however only $n!/2$ are solvable by moving the empty tile according to the rules. The problem of finding the shortest solution is $NP-complete$.

In our example there are four different objects: 3 cells and one empty cell. Each object can be coded by two qubits (2^2) and a configuration of the four objects can be represented by a register of eight qubits $|x\rangle$. The control function of the quantum production system needs to fulfill two requirements [Tarrataca and Wichert (2011a)]:

- For a given board configuration and a production rule determine the new board configuration.
- To determine if the configuration is the goal configuration.

The function $g(x)$ determines if the configuration is the goal configuration

$$g(x) = g(\underbrace{x_1, x_2, x_3, x_4, x_5, x_6, x_7, x_8}_{board\ configuration}) = \begin{cases} 1 \text{ if goal board configuration} \\ 0 \text{ otherwise.} \end{cases} \tag{11.29}$$

Function $g(x)$ is represented by a unitary operator T. T acts on the $8+1$ qubits with $x \in B^8$ and $c \in B^1$

$$T \cdot |x\rangle|c\rangle = |x\rangle|f(x) \oplus c\rangle.$$

The new board configuration is determined by productions that are represented by the function p. There are four possible positions of the empty cell. The input of the function p is the current board configuration and a bit m that indicates whether the blank cell should perform a clockwise ($m = 1$) or counter-clockwise movement ($m = 0$). Together, there are 8 possible mappings, which are represented by 8 productions. There are four possible positions of the empty cell times two possible moves. For simplicity, we will represent the mappings of the function p by a unitary permutation matrix $L(1)$. For each mapping, the empty tile can have three different neighbors. It follows that, in total, there are $24 = 8 \times 3$ instantiationed rules. They correspond to permutations in the unitary permutation matrix $L(1)$. The matrix acts on the $8+1$ qubits with $m \in B^1$ and $x \in B^8$

$$L(1) \cdot |m\rangle|x\rangle = |m\rangle|\gamma\rangle.$$

The $L(1)$ matrix represents the long-term memory of our production system.

Decomposition An important open question is whether the permutation matrix $L(1)$ of dimension $512 = 2^9$ can be decomposed. It is possible to determine if a permutation is tensor decomposable and to chose an efficient tensor decomposition if present [Kolda and Bader (2009)]. An alternative less costly representation of the long-term memory can be realized by a uniformly polynomial circuit. The circuit is based on the truth table that describes the mappings of the function p.

In the case in which the system is not based on an iterative quantum tree search but instead is based on a quantum tree search, we should apply only the move of the blank cell if and only if the input board configuration is not a target board configuration. This process could be performed by including a reference to function g in the new function p's definition and can be described by a unitary operator.

The operator that describes the application of a single production rule for the 3-puzzle and a test condition in order to determine if the final board is a target configuration board is represented in B^{10} as

$$(I_1 \otimes T) \cdot (L(1) \otimes I_1) \cdot |m, x_1, x_2, x_3, x_4, x_5, x_6, x_7, x_8, c\rangle. \tag{11.30}$$

The operator that describes the application of a two production rules for the 3-puzzle and a test condition in order to determine if the final board is a target configuration board is represented with

$$L(2) \cdot |m_2, m_1\rangle|x\rangle = |m_2, m_1\rangle|\gamma\rangle$$

as

$$(I_2 \otimes T) \cdot (L(2) \otimes I_1) \cdot (L(2) \otimes I_1) \cdot |m_2, m_1, x_1, x_2, x_3, x_4, x_5, x_6, x_7, x_8, c\rangle$$

$$(I_2 \otimes T) \cdot (L(2) \otimes I_1)^2 \cdot |m_2, m_1, x_1, x_2, x_3, x_4, x_5, x_6, x_7, x_8, c\rangle. \tag{11.31}$$

The operator that describes the application of a t production rules for the 3-puzzle and a test condition in order to determine if the final board is a target configuration board is represented with

$$L(t) \cdot |m_t, \cdots, m_1\rangle|x\rangle = |m_t, \cdots, m_1\rangle|\gamma\rangle$$

and

$$|\kappa^t\rangle = |m_t, \cdots, m_1\rangle$$

as

$$(I_t \otimes T) \cdot (L(t) \otimes I_1)^t \cdot |\kappa^t, x_1, x_2, x_3, x_4, x_5, x_6, x_7, x_8, c\rangle. \tag{11.32}$$

In quantum computation it is not possible to reset the register $x_1, x_2, x_3, x_4, x_5, x_6, x_7, x_8$ to the pattern representing the initial state. Instead we un-compute the output back to the input before applying the amplification step of the Grover's algorithm. Because of the unitary evolution it follows that

$$(I_t \otimes T)^* \cdot ((L(t) \otimes I_1)^*)^t \cdot (I_t \otimes T) \cdot (L(t) \otimes I_1)^t \cdot \tag{11.33}$$

$$\cdot|\kappa^t, x_1, x_2, x_3, x_4, x_5, x_6, x_7, x_8, c\rangle = |\kappa^t, x_1, x_2, x_3, x_4, x_5, x_6, x_7, x_8, c\rangle$$

the computation can be undone. The result indicated in the qubit c and can saved into the qubit y by a controlled not gate M_{CNOT}. The computation is defined on B^{10+t} with

$$U_{3-puzzle} := (I_t \otimes T \otimes I_1)^* \cdot ((L(t) \otimes I_2)^*)^t \cdot$$

$$\cdot(I_{(9)+t} \otimes M_{CNOT}) \cdot (I_t \otimes T \otimes I_1) \cdot (L(t) \otimes I_2)^t \tag{11.34}$$

simplified as

$$U_{3-puzzle} \cdot |\kappa^t, x_1, x_2, x_3, x_4, x_5, x_6, x_7, x_8, c, y\rangle = U_{3-puzzle} \cdot |\kappa^t, x, c, y\rangle. \tag{11.35}$$

We apply the $U_{3-puzzle}$ operator,

$$\Gamma_T := (T_t \otimes I_{10}) \cdot U_{3-puzzle} \tag{11.36}$$

determine the value of r by quantum counting

$$\left(\prod_{t=1}^{r} \Gamma_T\right) \cdot ((W_t \cdot |0^{\oplus t}\rangle) \otimes |x\rangle \otimes |0\rangle \otimes (W_1 \cdot |1\rangle)) = \tag{11.37}$$

it follows

$$\left(\prod_{t=1}^{r} \Gamma_T\right) \cdot (W_t \otimes I_{10}) \cdot (I_{t+9} \otimes W_1) \cdot |0^{\oplus t}\rangle|x\rangle|0\rangle|1\rangle = |\kappa_i^t\rangle|x\rangle|0\rangle \otimes \left(\frac{|0\rangle - |1\rangle}{\sqrt{2}}\right) \tag{11.38}$$

and and determine the solution by the measurement of the register $|\kappa_i^t\rangle$ that represents the path descriptor. The 3-puzzle quantum production system highlighted the principles of quantum production systems. It does not give any true computational speed up due to the simplicity of the problem and due to the naïve implementation of the long term memory by a permutation matrix.

11.6.2 *Extending for any n-puzzle*

For n-puzzle there are $n+1$ different objects: n cells and one empty cell. Each object can be coded by $\rho = \lceil \log_2 n + 1 \rceil$ qubits and a configuration of $n+1$ objects can be represented by a register of $z := \rho \cdot (n+1)$ qubits $|x\rangle$.

The function $g(x)$ is represented a unitary operator T. T acts on the $z+1$ qubits with $x \in B^z$ and $c \in B^1$

$$T \cdot |x\rangle|c\rangle = |x\rangle|f(x) \oplus c\rangle.$$

The new board configuration is determined by the function p. The input of the function p is the current board configuration and two bits $m = m_1, m_2$ indicating whether the blank cell should perform move up ($m = 0 = |00\rangle$), down ($m = 1 = |01\rangle$), right ($m = 2 = |10\rangle$) or left ($m = 3 = |11\rangle$). The mappings of the function p between states can be described by a truth table and can represented as column permutations.

In the case the empty cell is in the corner only two movements are possible, the other one are not valid. In the case of not valid movement a halt bit flag h represented by one bit is set and no further production is applied. We move the blank cell if and only if the halt bit flag h is not set. The same applies for empty cell on the edge. In this case only three movements are possible. For 8-puzlle $B_{max} = 4$ and B_{avarge}

$$B_{avarge} = \frac{4 \cdot 1 + 2 \cdot 4 + 3 \cdot 4}{9} = 2.7778. \tag{11.39}$$

With growing value n B_{avarge} converges to B_{max}.

There are maximal $n+1$ possible positions of the empty cell. The empty cell can move either up, down, left or right or the halt bit flag is set. Together there $(4+1)$ actions and for $n+1$ positions there are $(n+1) \cdot 5$ possible mappings represented by $n \cdot 5 + 5$ permutations. In each combination the empty tile can have n different neighbors. It follows that in total there are $(n+1) \cdot 5 \cdot n = 5 \cdot n^2 + 5 \cdot n$ instantiationed productions. A 8-puzzle there would represented by 360 instantiationed productions.

The instantiationed productions are represented unitary permutation matrix $L(1)$. The matrix acts on the $z+3$ qubits with $m \in B^2$ and $x \in B^z$ and $h \in B^1$

$$L(1) \cdot |m\rangle|x\rangle|h\rangle = |m\rangle|\gamma\rangle|h'\rangle.$$

11.6.3 *Pure production system*

The pure production system model has no mechanism for recovering from an impasse [Post (1943)]. The system halts if no production can fire. It is composed of the set of productions L (the long term memory) and control system C. A pure production system is a sextuple:

$$(\Sigma, L, W, \gamma_i, \gamma_g, C) \tag{11.40}$$

with

- Σ is a finite alphabet;
- W is the working memory. It represents a state $\gamma \in \Sigma$.
- L is the long term memory. It is the set of B productions. A production p has the form $(precondition, conclusion) \in \Sigma$. The precondition is matched against the contents of the working memory. If the precondition is met then the conclusion is preformed and changes the contents of the working memory;
- $\gamma_i \in \Sigma$ is the initial state. The working memory is initialized with the initial state γ_i;
- $\gamma_g \in \Sigma$ is the goal state;
- δ is the control function of the form $\Sigma \to L \times \Sigma \times h$. It chooses a production and fires it or halts h.

If $C(\gamma) = (p, \gamma', h)$, then the working memory contains symbol γ. It is substituted by the the production p by γ' or the computation halts h. The computation halts if the goal state γ_g is reached or an an impasse is present (no production can be applied).

11.6.4 *Unitary control strategy*

A pure production system can be converted into a quantum production system by mapping the control strategy into a unitary control strategy represented by a unitary operator $L(t)$ on a register $|v_1\rangle$ [Tarrataca and Wichert (2012b)], [Tarrataca and Wichert (2013b)].

$$L(t) \cdot |v_1\rangle = |v_2\rangle.$$

$L(t)$ is used during the iterative quantum tree search to the limit t. The register $|v_1\rangle$ is determined by,

- $\mu = t \cdot \lceil \log_2 B_{max} \rceil$ maximal branching factor represents the path descriptor κ_i^t
- $\alpha = \lceil \log_2 |\Sigma| \rceil$, represents the number of bits required to encode the symbol set
- $\beta = \lceil \log_2 B \rceil$, represents the number of bits required to encode each one of the productions;

- η is a single bit used to encode h

The size of $|v_1\rangle$ is

$$\aleph := \mu + \alpha + \beta + \eta$$

qubits. $2^{\aleph}$ combinations can be represented. A combination can be represented by a one at a certain position of the vector. The corresponding unitary operator $L(t)$ is represented by a matrix of the dimension $2^{\aleph} \times 2^{\aleph}$. The matrix is sparse, it is populated primarily with zeros. It is possible to determine if a permutation is tensor decomposable and to chose an efficient tensor decomposition if present [Kolda and Bader (2009)]. Additionally we need a unitary operator T that determines if the state is the goal state γ_g. As indicated in the 3-puzzle example, the circuit should recompute the output before applying the amplification step of the Grover's algorithm.

11.7 A General Model of a Quantum Computer

In classical models such as the Turing machine, the end of a calculation is indicated by a halt state. An observer must check if the calculation halted. In a e quantum Turing machine, a halt flag can be non-trivially implemented due to entanglement and the collapse of the halt qubit after the measurement. A solution to this problem is a universal quantum Turing machine in [Bernstein and Vazirani (1993)], which does not incorporate into its definition the concept on non-termination. Myers in [Myers (1997)] argues that the models presented in [Deutsch (1985)] and [Bernstein and Vazirani (1993)] are not truly universal because they do not allow for non-terminating computation.

A quantum production system represents a general model of computation. This type of system is an alternative approach to the quantum Turing machine and allows an elegant description of the Halting problem through the iterative quantum tree search. It is possible to simulate classical universal models of computation such as the universal Turing machine by a quantum production system as shown in [Tarrataca and Wichert (2013b)]. This model can operate independently of whether the computation terminates or not. The quantum production system also provides the maximal speedup of $\sqrt{n}$ in the case where the Turing machine simulation allows for n multiple computational branches [Tarrataca and Wichert (2013b)].

A quantum computer based on a quantum production system would involve classical artificial intelligence programing languages such as OPS5

[Brownston *et al.* (1985)]. OPS5 programs are executed by matching working memory elements with productions in long-term memory [Forgy (1981)]. Such a programmer does not need to contend with quantum gates, nor is it required to address the principles of quantum computation. However, a strong artificial intelligence background is essential.

11.7.1 *Cognitive architecture*

Unified theories of cognition is a theory that attempts to unify all of the theories of the mind in a single framework. Allen Newell proposed the SOAR cognitive architecture [Laird *et al.* (1987)], [Newell (1990)], [Franklin (1997)]. SOAR is an architecture of the mind: a fixed structure underlying the flexible domain of cognitive processing as well as an architecture for intelligent agents. All of the problem solving activity is formulated as the selection and application of rules to a state to achieve a goal. In SOAR, the domain knowledge is divided into two categories:

- basic problem space knowledge represents legal moves that are represented by productions;
- control knowledge, such as, for example, heuristic functions and other control strategies.

With basic knowledge, SOAR can proceed to perform an unguided search using depth first. Resolving an impasse leads to learning. Impasses are given, for example, when

- two or more productions are chosen to fire;
- no production can fire;
- one chosen production is rejected by another.

The learning mechanism is called chunking. Chunking collapses the results of an impasse into a production that can then be fired if the same, or similar situation occurs again [Laird *et al.* (1986)]. Chunking is a psychological phenomenon that involves the association of expressions and the production of a new, single expression [Newell (1990)]. An extension of the proposed SOAR cognitive architecture by a quantum production system would lead to a hybrid architecture. The quantum production system would be invoked if an impasse were present. Such a hybrid approach would speed up the learning process without a need for domain-specific control knowledge (see Figure 11.11).

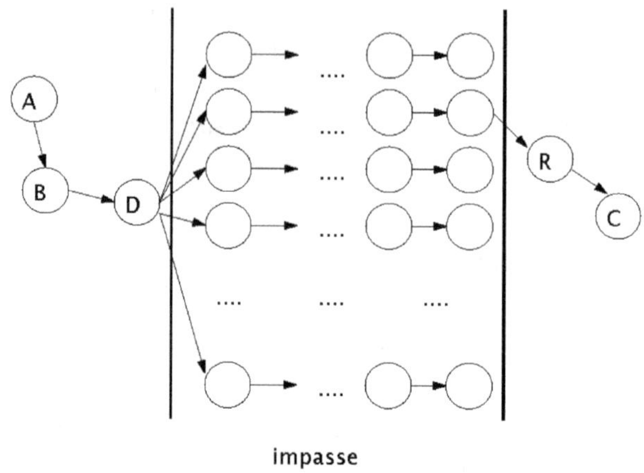

Fig. 11.11 An extension of the proposed SOAR cognitive architecture by a quantum production system would lead to a hybrid architecture. The quantum production system would be invoked if an impasse is present. Such an hybrid approach would speed up the learning process without the need of domain specific control knowledge.

11.7.2 *Representation*

The representation of the knowledge is the most important aspect. The unitary operator L that represents the long-term memory with the productions can be represented by a permutation matrix. It is possible to determine whether an abstract permutation is tensor decomposable and to choose an efficient tensor decomposition if present [Kolda and Bader (2009)].

The question of how to decompose L representing a real world problem is related to the question of how to decompose a problem into sub-problems. A problem solving strategy is given by breaking a problem up into a set of subproblems, solving each of the subproblems, and then composing a solution to the original problem from the solutions of the subproblems. How can we decompose a 15-puzzle into an 8-puzzle for example? This problem corresponds to the definition of a tensor product and the efficient implementation of a quantum production system to be the decomposition of L,

$$L = \begin{pmatrix} a_{11} \cdot B \; a_{12} \cdot B \\ a_{21} \cdot B \; a_{22} \cdot B \end{pmatrix} = A \otimes B.$$

Chapter 12

Grover's Algorithm and the Input Problem

12.1 Classical Input

Using Grover's algorithm, we could achieve a quadratic speed-up. For example, let us consider a range query vector $\mathbf{y}$ from a collection of N vectors,

$$\mathbf{x}_1, \mathbf{x}_2, \mathbf{x}_3, \cdots, \mathbf{x}_N$$

all vectors $\mathbf{x}_i$ that are ϵ-similar according to the distance function d are searched

$$d(\mathbf{x}_i, \mathbf{y}) < \epsilon. \tag{12.1}$$

Assuming that the collection of vectors is represented in a superposition, e.g., in $|\psi\rangle$, the cost to determine one possible ϵ-similar vector would be $O(\sqrt{N})$ using the quantum oracle described by Eq 12.1. The naïve assumption that the speed-up is quadratic is not realistic. Most quantum machine learning algorithms and quantum associative memories that are based on Grover's algorithm suffer from the input destruction problem (**ID problem**) [Aïmeur *et al.* (2013); Wittek (2014); Aaronson (2015)]:

- The input (reading) problem: The amplitude distribution of a quantum state is initialized by reading N data points. Although the existing quantum algorithm requires only $O(\sqrt{N})$ steps and is faster than the classical algorithms, N data points must be read. Hence, the complexity of the algorithm does not improve and is $O(N) = O(N) + O(\sqrt{N})$.
- The destruction problem: A quantum associative memory [Ventura and Martinez (1988, 2000); Tay *et al.* (2010)] for N data points for dimension m requires only m or fewer units (quantum bits). An operator which acts as an oracle [Tay *et al.* (2010)]. indicates the solution. In the next step, the Grover's algorithm performs the phase amplification. However, this memory can be queried only once because of the

collapse during measurement (destruction); hence, quantum associative memory does not have any advantages over classical memory.

The assumption that the speed-up is quadratic is not realistic in practice due to the ID problem; we are required to read N data points and can query only once because of the collapse during measurement (destruction). However, most quantum machine learning algorithms overcome this problem by the efficient preparation of data. The efficient preparation of data is present in quantum kernels and is possible for sparse data for the quantum algorithm for linear systems of equations (HHL). Quantum annealing does not suffer from the input problem. Before describing linear algebra-based quantum machine learning algorithms and quantum annealing, we provide an example of a quantum algorithm based on Wilshaw's associative memory that efficiently prepares the data. The idea is to generate quantum superposition from the classical data where the reading cost is negligible [Wichert (2016b)].

12.2 Quantum Binding in Context of Associative Memory

The visual (sub-symbolic) variable binding algorithm for Wilshaw's associative memory (Lernmatrix) involves intensive computation because it corresponds to a combinatorial problem [Wichert *et al.* (2008); Wichert (2011)]. We suggest some mechanisms based on quantum computation to reduce this high complexity and present a hybrid architecture from the quantum computation perspective. In the proposed architecture, different objects are mapped into superposition representing different combinations. Wilshaw's associative memory performs the familiarity discrimination task [Sacramento and Wichert (2012)] that can be efficiently represented by a quantum oracle. Grover's algorithm considerably improves the time complexity. The binding problem determines a method to connect all of the physically separated fragments of a complex object to enable them to be processed as a whole by an agent. For example, a red block is obviously a different object from a blue block. The binding problem can be divided into two subproblems: the segregation problem and the combination problem. The segregation problem involves the determination of a method to segregate the elements in an input such that they represent objects that can also be features. The combination problem involves the determination of the elements that represent an object or a category. In sub-symbolic binding, the elements are represented by sub-symbols. The sub-symbolic representation often corresponds to a pattern that mirrors the manner in which the biological sense organs describe the world. Patterns are represented by vectors. Thus, the vectors correspond to sub-symbols.

An example of a sub-symbolic binding problem is the definition of a category of objects in a visual scene [Wichert *et al.* (2008); Wichert (2011)] that is based on proto logic .

12.2.1 *Proto logic and associative memory*

Suppose 7 objects were recognized in the visual scene. We represent the 7 objects at various positions in the scene by the symbols A, B, C, D, E, F, G. The task is the identification of a category that is formed by the objects represented by the set B, C, G [Wichert *et al.* (2008); Wichert (2011, 2013)]. We determine whether each of the symbols B, C, G is present in the set that represents the scene. We also verify whether a set representing a category is a subset of the set representing a scene. This task is described by proto logic sets [Wichert (2013)]. Proto logic operates on sets; it verifies whether a subset is present in a certain set. The proto logic task seems trivial in the case of sets and symbols. However, if the category (set of sub-symbols) is stored in an associative memory, the task is non-trivial and is an example of the combination problem. The combination problem determines a method to combine individual objects or features into a single category. In an associative memory, we do not have **direct access** to the stored information.

An associative memory operates on vectors of fixed dimensions. Two of these vectors are always associated; this process of association is called learning. The first vector is called the address vector, and the second vector is called the retrieved vector. After the learning process, the address vector is presented to the associative memory, and the retrieved vector is determined. This process is called association. A distinction exists between heteroassociation and auto-association. An auto-association is present if the retrieved vector represents the reconstruction of the faulty address vector. A heteroassociation is present if the retrieved vector is different from the address vector. In our model, we store auto-associations, i.e., the address vector is the same as the retrieved vector. After a retrieved vector is determined, the similarity between the determined retrieved vector and the address vector is calculated. A greater similarity indicates a higher probability of the corresponding address vector being stored in the associative memory.

A set of objects (a category) is represented by a vector created by concatenating the sub-vectors that represent the objects. For N sub-vectors, the number of possible orderings of the corresponding sub-vectors is $N!$. To verify whether a set of M sub-vectors representing a category is a subset of the set of N sub-vectors representing a scene, the number of orderings is $L = \frac{N!}{(N-M)!}$ orderings [Wichert *et al.* (2008); Wichert (2009, 2011)]. For large values of N and M, the combination problem leads to a combinatorial explosion. A set of objects (a category) is represented by a vector created by concatenating the sub-vectors that represent the objects. For M sub-vectors, the number of possible orderings of the corresponding sub-vectors is $M!$. To verify whether a set of M sub-vectors representing a category is a subset of the set of N sub-vectors representing a scene, there are

$$L = Perm(N, M) = \frac{N!}{(N-M)!} \tag{12.2}$$

L possible orderings. For $N = 7$ and $M = 3$, we must pose $L = 210$ queries to the associative memory, as shown in Figure 12.1. The combination

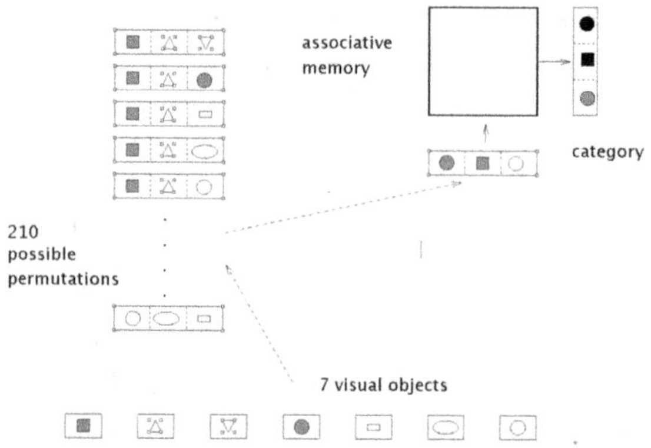

Fig. 12.1 In the retrieval phase L permutations are formed. Each permutation represents a address vector $\mathbf{x}_i$, $i \in \{1, \ldots, L\}$. Some of the address vectors represent a category, given that the determined retrieved vector is similar to the address vector.

problem leads to an combinatorial explosion for large N and M values, for example for $N = 100$ and $M = 4$ the value $9.41094 \cdot 10^7$. From the L permutations only the familiar patterns represent visual categories that were learned.

12.2.2 *Familiarity discrimination*

For the computation of the reliability of the the answer for the heteroassociation a backward projection of the associative memory is required [Wichert (2011)]. The backward projection corresponds to a bidirectional associative memory (BAM) [Kosko (1992)]. This time the learned matrix is cued with the retrieved vector and the best address vector is retrieved. Formally, $\mathbf{y}$ is the address vector, and the retrieved vector which should be determined is $\mathbf{x}^l$. The categorization rule for the determination of the retrieved vector $\mathbf{x}^l$ is:

$$x_j^l = \begin{cases} 1 & \sum_{i=1}^{m} w_{ij} y_i \geq T^* \\ 0 & \text{otherwise.} \end{cases} \tag{12.3}$$

This means that the synaptic matrix used is a transposition of the matrix which is used for the forward projection. T^* is the threshold of the unit. The threshold is set to the maximum sum $\sum_{j=1}^{m} w_{ij} y_j$:

$$T^* := \max_{1 \leq j \leq A} \left\{ \sum_{i=1}^{m} w_{ji} y_i \right\}. \tag{12.4}$$

Let $\mathbf{x}$ be the question vector and $\mathbf{y}$ the retrieved vector that was determined by the associative memory for example by a part of the associative memory. First, the vector $\mathbf{x}^l$ which belongs to the vector $\mathbf{y}$ is determined. These two vectors form together a vector pair $\mathbf{x}^l$ $\mathbf{y}$ which is stored in the associative memory. It was either created by learning, $\mathbf{x}^l$ and $\mathbf{y}$ were learned together, or created through overlap with other already learned vector pairs. The vector $\mathbf{x}^l$ is determined by a backward projection of the vector $\mathbf{y}$. In the second step, the similarity of the stored address vector $\mathbf{x}^l$ to the actually presented vector $\mathbf{x}$ is determined. The greater the similarity of the vector $\mathbf{x}^l$ to the vector $\mathbf{x}$, the more reliable the retrieved vector $\mathbf{y}$. We can measure the similarity by the Hamming distance function

$$d_1(\mathbf{x}, \mathbf{x}^l) = \|\mathbf{x} - \mathbf{x}^l\|_1 = |x_1 - x_1^l| + |x_2 - x_2^l| + \cdots + |x_m - x_m^l| \tag{12.5}$$

or by the scalar product

$$\langle \mathbf{x} | \mathbf{x}^l \rangle = \cos\omega \cdot \|\mathbf{x}\| \cdot \|\mathbf{x}^l\|, \tag{12.6}$$

that measure of the projection of one vector onto another.

For auto-association the task there is no need for a backward projection. In the case of auto-association $n = m$. We can measure the similarity by the scalar product with

$$y = W \cdot \mathbf{x} \tag{12.7}$$

and

$$\langle \mathbf{x} | \mathbf{y} \rangle \tag{12.8}$$

since W is symmetric with $n = m$. This is equivalent to the quadratic form

$$net = \mathbf{x}^\top \cdot W \cdot \mathbf{x} = \sum_{i=1}^{n} \sum_{j=1}^{n} w_{ij} \cdot x_i \cdot x_j. \tag{12.9}$$

The quadratic form can be as well be interpreted as the energy function [Sacramento and Wichert (2012)]

$$H = -\sum_{i=1}^{n} \sum_{j=1}^{n} w_{ij} \cdot x_i \cdot x_j. \tag{12.10}$$

In statistics and physics the energy function is called Hamiltonian. The threshold operation to determine similarity sim is applied to the scalar value net,

$$sim = \begin{cases} 1 & net =\geq t \\ 0 & \text{otherwise.} \end{cases} \tag{12.11}$$

with the threshold

$$t := T^2 \tag{12.12}$$

$sim = 1$ indicates that the question vector $\mathbf{x}$ was stored in the associative memory, $sim = 0$ that is was not. This operation called the familiarity discrimination, in familiarity discrimination there is no need per se to extract the whole answer pattern [Sacramento and Wichert (2012)]. In the following we will only preform auto-association.

12.2.3 *Visual scene coding*

The visual system recognizes objects in an image. It was suggested [Gross and Mishkin (1977)] that the brain includes two mechanisms for visual categorization [Posner and Raichle (1994)]: one for the representation of the object and the other for the representation of the localization [Kosslyn (1994)]. The first mechanism is called the *what* pathway and is located in the temporal lobe. The second mechanism is called the *where* pathway and is located in the parietal lobe. According to this division, the identity of a visual object can be coded apart from its location. A visual scene can be either represented by an image or by objects and their position in the visual field. Objects are represented by pictograms together with their

Fig. 12.2 **Category,** Category "tower" in the blockworld. Blocks can be placed in different positions and picked up and set down. There are two different classes of blocks: cubes and pyramids.

corresponding position in the image. This is a simple form of structured and compressed representation of a mental image.

The definition of a visual category is motivated by the verbal category definition that is a set of prototypical features [Osherson (1987)], such as red, round and sweet [Tversky (1977); McClelland and Rumelhart (1985)]. According to [Wichert (2001); Wichert *et al.* (2008); Wichert (2011, 2013)] the identity of an object can be represented by a binary pattern which is normalized for size and orientation. Its location in the x-axis is represented by a binary vector of the size of the abscissa of the pictogram representing the object. The location in the y-axis is likewise represented by a binary vector of the size of the coordinate of the pictogram representing the object. A binary bar of the size and position of the object in the pictogram of the state represents the location and size (see Fig 12.3) in each of those vectors. The three vectors that compose the cognitive entity are called associative fields. Each associative field is represented by a binary vector of a fixed dimension; each cognitive entity is formed by the concatenation of the associative fields [Wichert *et al.* (2008); Wichert (2011, 2013)]. A cognitive entity is represented by a binary vector formed by the concatenation of binary vectors which represent the three associative fields [Wichert (2001); Wichert *et al.* (2008); Wichert (2011, 2013)].

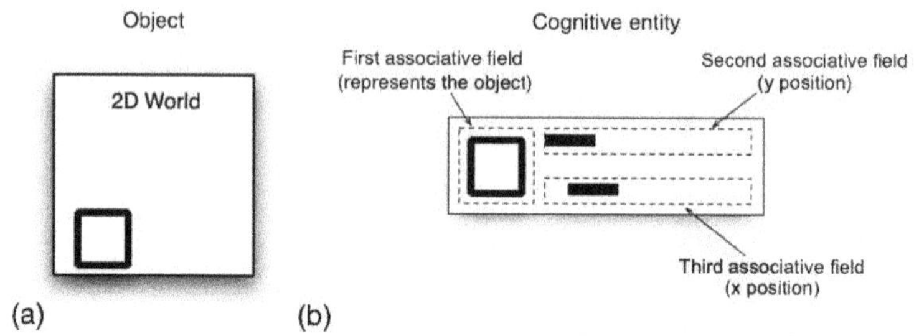

Fig. 12.3 **Representation of an object in a 2D world,** (a) 2D world. (b). The identity of an object is represented in the first associative field by a binary pattern which is normalized for size and orientation. Its location corresponding to the abscissa is represented by a binary vector in the second associative field. The location corresponding to the ordinate is likewise represented by a binary vector in the third associative field of the size of the ordinate of the pictogram representing the state. A binary bar of the size and position of the object in the pictogram of the state represents the location.

12.2.4 *Associations*

A cognitive entity is represented by a binary vector formed by the concatenation of binary vectors which represent the three associative fields. A visual category "tower" is represented in the blockworld as shown in Fig 12.2. It corresponds to a set of prototypical visual objects at certain position. The address and retrieved vectors are represented by a binary vector formed by the concatenation of three binary sub-vectors which represent the cognitive entities. Both the question and the answer vectors have dimension 900 because each cognitive entity is described by a binary vector of dimension 300 ($= p$). The representation of the category "tower":

```
0000110000
0000110000
0001001000
0001001000
0010000100
0010000100
0100000010
0100000010
1000000001
1111111111

0000000000000000000011111111110000000000000000000000000000000000000000000000000000000000000000000000

0000000000000000000000000000001111111111000000000000000000000000000000000000000000000000000000000000

1111111111
1000000001
1000000001
1000000001
1000000001
1000000001
1000000001
1000000001
1000000001
1111111111

0000000000111111111100000000000000000000000000000000000000000000000000000000000000000000000000000000
```

```
0000000000000000000000000000001111111111000000000000000000000000000000000000000000000000000000000000

1111111111
1000000001
1000000001
1000000001
1000000001
1000000001
1000000001
1000000001
1000000001
1111111111

1111111111000000000000000000000000000000000000000000000000000000000000000000000000000000000000000000

0000000000000000000000000000001111111111000000000000000000000000000000000000000000000000000000000000
```

Associations representing different positions of the category "tower" are learned by the associative memory and can be recognized later despite the presence of noise. Ten associations representing ten different positions of the category "tower" are learned by the associative memory. After learning is complete, a weight matrix of dimension $n = 900$ emerges; the weight matrix consists of three parts, each of size $p = 300$ and $n = 3 \cdot p = 3 \cdot 300$.

12.2.5 *Retrieval*

In the following example, we indicate the recognition of the category tower (Fig 12.2) from the pictogram in Fig 12.4 that is represented by nine different objects. To determine the visual category present, a familiar pattern is determined. During familiarity discrimination, there is no need to extract the entire answer pattern. The corresponding vector values of

$$720 = \frac{10!}{(10-3)!}$$

combinations are determined, and the category tower is identified from the noisy input by using Eqs 12.9 and 12.11 with threshold $t = 0.87$. After determining the correct input vector from the 720 possible combinations, the associative memory is queried, and the answer vector representing the category tower without noise is determined (see Fig 12.2).

12.2.6 *Quantum hybrid algorithm for sub-symbolic binding*

In our proposed hybrid approach, we will use Eqs 12.9 and 12.11 to build an oracle and Grover's algorithm to speed up the combination of Eq 12.2. By doing so, we can overcome the ID problem. After determining the correct input vector from all possible combinations, the classical associative memory is queried, and the answer vector representing the category is obtained.

Fig. 12.4 **Visual representation by a pictogram.** Visual representation of the world with nine different objects and with the category "tower" including noise. The state of the world is described by a pictogram of 100×100 pixels; the pictogram is represented by $N = 10$ cognitive entities, and the category tower is described by $M = 3$ cognitive entities.

To simplify the computational process, we can approximate L by permutations with repetition

$$P = N^M \tag{12.13}$$

where $P > L$. Based on this simplification, we develop a reversible circuit that generates all possible M permutations with repetitions of the N objects. The register $|x\rangle$ should represent the superposition of the N different objects that represent a visual scene; the read time would be $O(N)$. We start with the assumption $M = 1$. In this case, $P = N$, and the superposition corresponds to N objects. Each represented object is identified by a unique address with a value ranging from 1 to N. The task involves loading the corresponding representation of the object having a given address α into the register $|x\rangle$ by a reversible circuit. This task is equivalent to the process of initializing the amplitude distribution of a quantum state, as described in [Ventura and Martinez (1999); Rosenbaum and Perkowski (2009)]. However, instead of describing the distribution by using a quantum circuit, we load the required values from a given set by using a reversible circuit.

12.2.6.1 *Reversible load*

Each object is represented by a vector (of size p) describing the object, the corresponding address and a flag that is set to 0,

$$scene = (\mathbf{z}_1, address_1, flag_1), (\mathbf{z}_2, address_2, flag_2), \cdots, (\mathbf{z}_N, address_N, flag_N)$$

$$scene = (\mathbf{z}_1, 1, 0), (\mathbf{z}_2, 2, 0), \cdots, (\mathbf{z}_N, N, 0).$$

For a given address α, the corresponding address is determined, and the flag is set to one. This task can be performed by a reversible circuit by subtracting the given address α from the unique address, verifying whether the difference is zero and checking whether the result is zero. After this operation, the flag is equal to one. The loading operation is performed by the reversible circuit $load(\alpha, \mathbf{scene})$

$$\mathbf{x}_{address} = load(\alpha, \mathbf{scene}) =: (\mathbf{z}_1 \wedge flag_1) \vee (\mathbf{z}_2 \wedge flag_2) \vee \cdots \vee (\mathbf{z}_N \wedge flag_N).$$

using $N \cdot (N-1) \cdot p$ reversible gates. The reversible circuit corresponds to the reversible operator U_{load}

$$|\mathbf{x}_{address}\rangle |\alpha\rangle |\mathbf{scene}\rangle = U_{load} |0 \cdots 0\rangle |\alpha\rangle |\mathbf{scene}\rangle \tag{12.14}$$

that loads the object representation from *scene* to a given address α and the resulting waste bits into $|\mathbf{x}_{address}\rangle$. Each binary $\wedge$ and $\vee$ generates one waste bit due to the reversible implementation by a Toffoli gate.

12.2.6.2 *Superposition*

The superposition of the address is generated by a Hadamard gate with

$$\nu = 2^{\lceil log_2 N \rceil} \geq N \tag{12.15}$$

and

$$|\alpha^*\rangle := H_\nu \underbrace{|00 \cdots 0\rangle}_{\nu \text{ bits}} = \underbrace{\frac{1}{\sqrt{2^\nu}}}_{\text{amplitude}} \sum_{x=0}^{2^\nu - 1} \underbrace{|x\rangle}_{\nu \text{ bits}}. \tag{12.16}$$

In the case $\nu > N$ the scene is represented by $\nu - N$ additional waste objects.

12.2.6.3 *Parallel load*

We can perform a parallel loading of the corresponding representation of the object with a certain address represented in the superposition of addresses $|\alpha^*\rangle$ along with the resulting waste bits into the register $|\psi_{\mathbf{x}}\rangle$ by using the reversible operator U_{load}.

$$U_{load}|0\cdots 0\rangle|\alpha^*\rangle|\mathbf{scene}\rangle = U_{load}|0\cdots 0\rangle \otimes H_\nu|0\cdots 0\rangle|\mathbf{scene}\rangle \tag{12.17}$$

$$|\psi_{\mathbf{x}}\rangle|\alpha^*\rangle|\mathbf{scene}\rangle = U_{load}|0\cdots 0\rangle|\alpha^*\rangle|\mathbf{scene}\rangle \tag{12.18}$$

The register $|\psi_{\mathbf{x}}\rangle$ is in superposition because $|\alpha^*\rangle$ is in superposition. Further, it is entangled with the register $|\alpha^*\rangle$ that acts as a pointer to the values represented in $|\mathbf{scene}\rangle$. Because $|\mathbf{scene}\rangle$ is equal in each superposition, it is not entangled with $|\psi_{\mathbf{x}}\rangle$ and $|\alpha^*\rangle$.

12.2.6.4 *Tensor operation*

For $M > 1$ we simply tensor $|\psi_{\mathbf{x}}\rangle|\alpha^*\rangle$ M times

$$\underbrace{|\psi_{\mathbf{x}}\rangle|\alpha^*\rangle \otimes |\psi_{\mathbf{x}}\rangle|\alpha^*\rangle \otimes \cdots \otimes |\psi_{\mathbf{x}}\rangle|\alpha^*\rangle}_{M \text{ times}}|\mathbf{scene}\rangle \tag{12.19}$$

For simplicity we define

$$|\mathbf{x}^*\rangle := \underbrace{|\psi_{\mathbf{x}}\rangle|\alpha^*\rangle \otimes |\psi_{\mathbf{x}}\rangle|\alpha^*\rangle \otimes \cdots \otimes |\psi_{\mathbf{x}}\rangle|\alpha^*\rangle}_{M \text{ times}} \tag{12.20}$$

it follows

$$|\mathbf{x}^*\rangle|\mathbf{scene}\rangle = \underbrace{|\psi_{\mathbf{x}}\rangle|\alpha^*\rangle \otimes |\psi_{\mathbf{x}}\rangle|\alpha^*\rangle \otimes \cdots \otimes |\psi_{\mathbf{x}}\rangle|\alpha^*\rangle}_{M \text{ times}}|\mathbf{scene}\rangle. \tag{12.21}$$

The register $|\mathbf{x}^*\rangle$ represent P' superpositions of all possible objects M-permutations with repetition of the N objects as well as the entangled addresses and waste bits with

$$P' = \nu^M = 2^{\lceil log_2 N \rceil^M} \geq N^M. \tag{12.22}$$

The complexity of the operation is of size $O(N \cdot M)$.

12.2.7 *Quantum oracle for familiarity discrimination*

The quadratic form can be simplified because the input vector $\mathbf{x}$ and the weight matrix W are binary

$$net = \sum_{i=1}^{n} \sum_{j=i}^{n} w_{ij} \wedge x_i \wedge x_j. \tag{12.23}$$

This operation requires $2 \cdot n^2$ AND operations and n^2 full adder gates. A full adder is usually a component in a cascade of adders that adds together several bits, for example a four byte adder. A full adder adds two bits together with a bit carried in form another full adder. Its output is one bit together with the bit that is carried out to another full adder (overflow bit).

12.2.7.1 *Reversibles circuit for familiarity discrimination*

A reversible full adder can be build out of Toffoli gates. It itself can be represented as the Peres full adder gate [Islam *et al.* (2009)]. The Peres full adder gate does not change the first input bit x_1. The operation is described by the following mapping on three input bits x_1, x_2, x_3 with $\mathbf{B} = \{0, 1\}$

$$P : \mathbf{B}^4 \to \mathbf{B}^4 : P(x_1, x_2, x_3, x_4) = (y_1, y_2, y_3, y_4)$$

$$P(x_1, x_2, x_3, x_4) = (x_1, (x_1 \oplus x_2), (x_1 \oplus x_2 \oplus x_3), (x_1 \oplus x_2) \wedge x_3 \oplus x_1 \wedge x_2 \oplus x_4)$$

It computes the full adder operation with the ancilla (fixed) bit x_4 set to 0

$$P(x_1, x_2, x_3, 0) = (x_1, (x_1 \oplus x_2), \underbrace{(x_1 \oplus x_2 \oplus x_3)}_{\text{sum}}, \underbrace{((x_1 \oplus x_2) \wedge x_3 \oplus x_1 \wedge x_2)}_{\text{carry}})$$

bit number x_1 and x_2 are the operands and x_3 is the bit carried in from the previous less significant stage.

To determine if the question vector $\mathbf{x}$ was stored in the associative memory we subtract from the threshold *net* from t

$$sim = \begin{cases} 1 & (t - net) < 0 \\ 0 & \text{otherwise} \end{cases} \tag{12.24}$$

with the threshold

$$t := T^2. \tag{12.25}$$

A full subtractor can be designed using the same approach as that for an adder. Three bits are involved in performing the subtraction for each bit of the difference: the minuend x_1, the subtrahend x_2, and the borrow in from the previous (less significant) bit order position x_3. The full subtractor gate does not change the first input bit x_1. It performs the full subtractor operation with the ancilla (fixed) bit x_4 set to 0.

$$S(x_1, x_2, x_3, 0) = (x_1, (x_1 \oplus x_2), \underbrace{(x_1 \oplus x_2 \oplus x_3)}_{\text{subtraction}}, \underbrace{(\neg x_1 \wedge (x_2 \vee x_3) \vee x_2 \wedge x_3)}_{\text{borrowed bit}})$$

where bit numbers x_1 and x_2 are the operands, and x_3 is the borrowed bit. The value of sim can be determined from the borrow bit in the result; if the borrow bit is equal to one, then $sim = 1$, otherwise $sim = 0$. This operation requires n^2 full subtractor gates. The reversible familiarity discrimination is feasible because it requires $4 \cdot n^2$ reversible gates ($2 \cdot n^2$ and gates, n^2 full subtractor gates and n^2 full adder gates).

The reversible circuit corresponds to the reversible operator U_{Sim}. Permutation is a reversible operation; therefore, $|\mathbf{x}^*\rangle$ can be rearranged in such a way that the operator U_{Sim} accesses only the object representation. In addition to the object description, U_{Sim} requires the weight matrix representation as a binary vector $\mathbf{w}$. The results or the sums, $\wedge$ operations, subtraction operations and waste bits are mapped into the register $|\mathbf{result}\rangle$.

$$|\mathbf{result}\rangle|\mathbf{x}^*\rangle|\mathbf{scene}\rangle|\mathbf{w}\rangle = U_{Sim} \cdot |0\cdots 0\rangle|\mathbf{x}^*\rangle|\mathbf{scene}\rangle|\mathbf{w}\rangle \tag{12.26}$$

A single bit, the borrow bit, determines the familiarity discrimination and whether the subtraction is negative; if the borrow bit is equal to one, then $sim = 1$, otherwise $sim = 0$. We use a circuit U_{CNOT} composed of a controlled not gates to copy the result represented in the borrow bit into a single bit sim.

$$|sim\rangle|\mathbf{result}\rangle|\mathbf{x}^*\rangle|\mathbf{scene}\rangle|\mathbf{w}\rangle = U_{CNOT} \cdot |0\rangle|\mathbf{result}\rangle|\mathbf{x}^*\rangle|\mathbf{scene}\rangle|\mathbf{w}\rangle \tag{12.27}$$

In quantum computation it is not possible to reset value of the register $|\mathbf{result}\rangle$. Instead we un-compute the former operations of U_{Sim} by applying the U_{Sim}^{-1} operator.

$$|sim\rangle|0\cdots 0\rangle|\mathbf{x}^*\rangle|\mathbf{scene}\rangle|\mathbf{w}\rangle = U_{Sim}^{-1} \cdot |sim\rangle|\mathbf{result}\rangle|\mathbf{x}^*\rangle|\mathbf{scene}\rangle|\mathbf{w}\rangle \tag{12.28}$$

After these operations, the result of the familiarity operation is represented in the bit $|sim\rangle$, which is in the basis state $|1\rangle$ or $|0\rangle$. The registers $|sim\rangle$ and $|\mathbf{x}^*\rangle$ are entangled. The remaining registers $|\mathbf{scene}\rangle$, $|\mathbf{w}\rangle$ and $|0\cdots 0\rangle$ are not entangled because they are equal. We simplify the notation by defining the global operator U_F. The unitary operator U_F represents our quantum oracle that marks the solution by the bit sim; it is composed of the operators U_{Sim}, U_{CNOT} and U_{Sim}^{-1}. Its operation corresponds to

$$|sim\rangle|0\cdots 0\rangle|\mathbf{x}^*\rangle|\mathbf{scene}\rangle|\mathbf{w}\rangle = U_F \cdot |0\rangle|0\cdots 0\rangle|\mathbf{x}^*\rangle|\mathbf{scene}\rangle|\mathbf{w}\rangle. \tag{12.29}$$

12.2.8 *Grover's iteration*

The number of solutions (in our case, categories) can be determined efficiently by Quantum Fourier Transform [Brassard *et al.* (1998)], [Brassard *et al.* (2000)].

12.2.8.1 *One category present*

If one solution is present, Grover's amplification [Grover (1996)], [Grover (1997)], [Grover (1998a)], [Grover (1998b)], [Grover (1996)], [Grover (1996)] algorithm requires

$$O\left(\left(2^{\lceil log_2 N \rceil}\right)^{\frac{M}{2}}\right) \approx O\left(N^{\frac{M}{2}}\right) = O\left(\sqrt{N^M}\right) \tag{12.30}$$

applications of the quantum oracle [Brassard *et al.* (2000)], [Brassard *et al.* (1998)] U_F

$$|sim\rangle|0\cdots 0\rangle|\mathbf{x}^*\rangle|\mathbf{scene}\rangle|\mathbf{w}\rangle = U_F \cdot |0\rangle|0\cdots 0\rangle|\mathbf{x}^*\rangle|\mathbf{scene}\rangle|\mathbf{w}\rangle. \tag{12.31}$$

to determine the correct input vector representing a category that was stored in the associative memory with high probability. After determining the correct input vector, the classic Wilshaw's associative memory is queried, and the vector representing the category without noise is determined.

12.2.8.2 *Several categories present*

For r possible categories, only one category is determined with the cost.

$$O\left(\left(\frac{2^{\lceil log_2 N \rceil}}{r}\right)^{\frac{M}{2}}\right) \tag{12.32}$$

To determine all of the categories, the algorithm can be repeated several times until r different input vectors representing the categories are measured. An alternative approach would be to unlearn the associative memory specified by W from the already recognized category [Wichert (2002)].

12.2.9 *Cost Analysis*

The reversible load requires $N \cdot (N-1) \cdot p$ reversible gates and the reversible familiarity discrimination requires $4 \cdot n^2$ reversible gates with

$$4 \cdot n^2 = 4 \cdot (p \cdot M)^2.$$

Both operation are feasible and require the same number of gates as a classical application. The time complexity of the quantum hybrid algorithm for sub-symbolic binding is significant better then the classical (naïve) approach. For simplification of the computational process L is approximated by P permutations with repetition for one present category. The costs of the algorithm are

$$O\left(\sqrt{N^M}\right) = O\left(\sqrt{N^M}\right) + O(N \cdot M) \tag{12.33}$$

with

$$\left(2^{\lceil log_2 N \rceil}\right)^{\frac{M}{2}} << L = Perm(N, M) < N^M = P. \tag{12.34}$$

12.2.10 *Comparison*

Instead of being represented by units in superposition [Ventura and Martinez (1988, 2000); Tay *et al.* (2010)], the quantum associative memory is described by a quantum oracle for familiarity discrimination. The input represents permutations of visual objects by superposition. This architecture reduces the computational complexity and represents the relation between the associative memory and a quantum algorithm by a familiarity discrimination task. The proposed approach is a hybrid algorithm because after determining the correct input vector, the classic Wilshaw's associative memory is queried, and the vector representing the category without noise is determined.

Chapter 13

Statistical Machine Learning

In unsupervised learning, the algorithm groups input information that is primarily represented by vectors into groups without additional information. The algorithm attempts to find the hidden structure of unlabeled data; principal component analysis is an example of this algorithm. In supervised learning, the algorithm is presented with example inputs and their desired outputs, and the goal is to develop a general rule that maps inputs to outputs. Supervised learning is frequently referred to as learning with a teacher because the desired outputs are indicated by a specific type of teacher. Consequently, unsupervised learning is referred to learning without a teacher.

13.1 The Karhunen-Loève Transform

The Karhunen-Loève transform is a linear transform that maps possibly correlated variables into a set of values of linearly uncorrelated variables. This transformation is defined in such a way that the first principal component has the largest possible variance. The Karhunen-Loève transform is based on orthogonal basis functions determined by the covariance matrix. The covariance matrix measures the tendency of two features, x_i and x_j, to vary in the same direction. The covariance between features x_i and x_j is estimated for n vectors as

$$c_{ij} = \frac{\sum_{k=1}^{n}(x_{k,i} - \overline{x_i}) \cdot (x_{k,j} - \overline{x_j})}{n-1} \tag{13.1}$$

with $\overline{x_i}$ and $\overline{x_j}$ being the arithmetic mean of the two dimension features for the sample. The sample covariance has $n-1$ in the denominator rather than n due to Bessel's correction. For whole population we write n in the denominator. In computer science, the sample covariance is usually used.

Covariances are symmetric; $c_{ij} = c_{ji}$. The resulting covariance matrix C is symmetric and positive-definite,

$$C = \begin{pmatrix} c_{11} & c_{12} & \cdots & c_{1m} \\ c_{21} & c_{22} & \cdots & c_{2m} \\ \vdots & \vdots & \ddots & \vdots \\ c_{m1} & c_{m2} & \cdots & c_{mm} \end{pmatrix}. \tag{13.2}$$

A real matrix M is positive definite if $\mathbf{z}^\top \cdot M \cdot \mathbf{z}$ is positive for any non-zero column vector $\mathbf{z}$ of real numbers. A symmetric and positive-definite matrix can be diagonalized. It follows that

$$U^{-1} \cdot C \cdot U = \Lambda = diag(\lambda_1, \lambda_2, \cdots .\lambda_m) \tag{13.3}$$

U is an orthonormal matrix of the dimension $m \times m$,

$$U^\top \cdot U = I \tag{13.4}$$

$$U^\top \cdot C \cdot U = \Lambda = diag(\lambda_1, \lambda_2, \cdots .\lambda_m) \tag{13.5}$$

and

$$U \cdot \Lambda = C \cdot U. \tag{13.6}$$

There are m eigenvalues and eigenvectors with

$$(\lambda_i \cdot I - C) \cdot \mathbf{u}_i = 0 \tag{13.7}$$

and

$$C \cdot \mathbf{u}_i = \lambda_i \cdot \mathbf{u}_i \tag{13.8}$$

An eigenvector can have two directions, it is either $\mathbf{u}_i$ or $-\mathbf{u}_i$.

$$C \cdot (-\mathbf{u}_i) = \lambda_i \cdot (-\mathbf{u}_i) \tag{13.9}$$

The eigenvectors are always orthogonal, and their length is arbitrary. The normalized eigenvectors define the orthonormal matrix U of dimension $m \times m$. Each normalized eigenvector is a column of U with

$$U^\top \cdot U = I.$$

The matrix U defines the Karhunen-Loève transform. The Karhunen-Loève transform rotates the coordinate system in such a way that the new covariance matrix will be diagonal

$$\mathbf{y} = U^\top \cdot \mathbf{x} \tag{13.10}$$

The squares of the eigenvalues represent the variances along the eigenvectors.

13.1.1 *Principal component analysis*

Principal component analysis (PCA) is a technique that is useful for the compression of data. The purpose is to reduce the dimensionality of a data set by finding a new set of variables, smaller than the original set of variables, that nonetheless retains most of the sample's information. The first principal component corresponds to the normalized eigenvector with the highest variance. Uncorrelated features with higher variance, represented by λ_i, contain more information. In principal component analysis (PCA), the significant eigenvectors define the principal components. Accordingly to the Kaiser criterion, the eigenvectors whose eigenvalues are below 1 are discarded [de Sá (2001)]. Each of the s non-discarded eigenvectors is a column of the matrix W of dimension $s \times m$ with the linear mapping from $\mathbf{R}^m \rightarrow \mathbf{R}^s$,

$$\mathbf{z} = W^\top \cdot \mathbf{x} \tag{13.11}$$

with $dim(s) \leq dim(m)$. The resulting principal components are linear transformation of the original features.

13.2 Linear Regression

Multiple linear regression [Rao (1973)] represented as a linear combination

$$y = y(\mathbf{x}, \mathbf{w}) = w_0 + \sum_{j=1}^{D} w_j \cdot x_j = w_0 + \langle \mathbf{w} | \mathbf{x} \rangle \tag{13.12}$$

represented as a hyperplane (see Figure 13.1). Parameters w_j are values that control the behavior of the system. They are also called weights. The intercept term w_0 is often called the bias parameter of the affine transformation. The output of the transformation y is biased toward being w_0 in the absence of any input. This term is different from the idea of a statistical bias. The value y was can be named *net*

$$net = bias + \sum_{j=1}^{D} w_j \cdot x_j = w_0 + \sum_{j=1}^{D} w_j \cdot x_j$$

and we interpret the multiple linear regression as a linear artificial neuron. With a fixed value $x_0 = 1$ we can write as well

$$y = y(\mathbf{x}, \mathbf{w}) = \sum_{j=0}^{D} w_j \cdot x_j = \langle \mathbf{w} | \mathbf{x} \rangle = \mathbf{w}^T \cdot \mathbf{x}$$

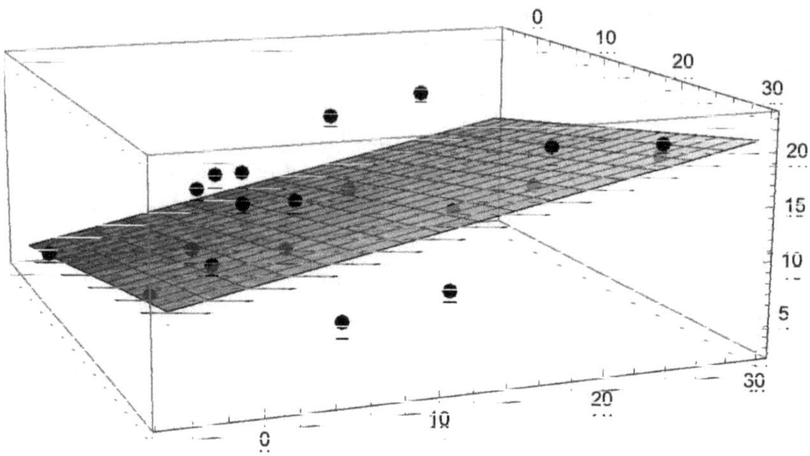

Fig. 13.1 A plane $y = y(\mathbf{w}) = w_0 + \sum_{j=1}^{2} w_j \cdot x_j$ is selected to find a best fit to a given data set.

13.2.1 *Design matrix*

Training set consists on N observations (sample)

$$X = (\mathbf{x}_1, \mathbf{x}_2, \cdots, \mathbf{x}_k, \cdots, \mathbf{x}_N)^T$$

together with the target values

$$\mathbf{t} = (t_1, t_2, \cdots, t_k, \cdots, t_N)^T.$$

The training set is represented by a data matrix with $x_{j,0} = 1$, also called design as

$$X = \begin{pmatrix} \mathbf{x}_1^T \\ \vdots \\ \mathbf{x}_k^T \\ \vdots \\ \mathbf{x}_N^T \end{pmatrix} = \begin{pmatrix} x_{1,0} & x_{1,1} & x_{1,2} & \cdots & x_{1,D} \\ x_{2,0} & x_{2,1} & x_{2,2} & \cdots & x_{2,D} \\ \vdots & \vdots & & \ddots & \vdots \\ x_{N,0} & x_{N,1} & x_{N,2} & \cdots & x_{N,D} \end{pmatrix} \tag{13.13}$$

with the linear mapping

$$\begin{pmatrix} y_1 \\ \vdots \\ y_k \\ \vdots \\ y_N \end{pmatrix} = \begin{pmatrix} 1 & x_{1,1} & x_{1,2} & \cdots & x_{1,D} \\ 1 & x_{2,1} & x_{2,2} & \cdots & x_{2,D} \\ \vdots & \vdots & & \ddots & \vdots \\ 1 & x_{N,1} & x_{N,2} & \cdots & x_{N,D} \end{pmatrix} \cdot \begin{pmatrix} w_0 \\ w_1 \\ \vdots \\ w_j \\ \vdots \\ w_D \end{pmatrix} \tag{13.14}$$

$$\mathbf{y} = X \cdot \mathbf{w} = \left(\mathbf{w}^T \cdot X^T\right)^T \tag{13.15}$$

13.2.2 *Squared-error*

The error between the predicted values y_k and the target t_k values is represented by the squared error (it is also called the squared loss, $L(\mathbf{w})$)

$$E(\mathbf{w}) = \sum_{k=1}^{N} (y(\mathbf{x}_k, \mathbf{w}) - t_k)^2 = \|\mathbf{t} - \mathbf{y}\|^2 = \left\| \begin{pmatrix} t_1 \\ \vdots \\ t_k \\ \vdots \\ t_N \end{pmatrix} - \begin{pmatrix} y_1 \\ \vdots \\ y_k \\ \vdots \\ y_N \end{pmatrix} \right\|^2 . \tag{13.16}$$

The error value depends on the choice of the parameters w_j represented by the vector $\mathbf{w}$.

13.2.3 *Closed-form solution*

A closed-form solution for $\mathbf{w}$ that minimises the error $E(\mathbf{w})$ exists with

$$\nabla E(\mathbf{w}) = 0. \tag{13.17}$$

and the gradient operator

$$\nabla = \left[\frac{\partial}{\partial w_1}, \frac{\partial}{\partial w_2}, \cdots, \frac{\partial}{\partial w_D}\right]^T$$

$$\nabla E(\mathbf{w}) = \left[\frac{\partial E}{\partial w_1}, \frac{\partial E}{\partial w_2}, \cdots, \frac{\partial E}{\partial w_D}\right]^T .$$

The sum-of-squares error function over all N training points

$$E(\mathbf{w}) = \sum_{k=1}^{N} \left(t_k - \mathbf{w}^T \cdot \mathbf{x}_k)\right)^2 = \sum_{k=1}^{N} \left(t_k - \mathbf{x}_k^T \cdot \mathbf{w})\right)^2 \tag{13.18}$$

and can be represented in the vector and matrix notation

$$E(\mathbf{w}) = \|\mathbf{t} - X \cdot \mathbf{w}\|^2 = (\mathbf{t} - X \cdot \mathbf{w})^T (\mathbf{t} - X \cdot \mathbf{w}). \tag{13.19}$$

We set the gradient to zero

$$\nabla E(\mathbf{w}) = \nabla \left((\mathbf{t} - X \cdot \mathbf{w})^T \cdot (\mathbf{t} - X \cdot \mathbf{w})\right) = 0 \tag{13.20}$$

and expand the equation to

$$\nabla \left(\mathbf{t}^T \cdot \mathbf{t} - 2 \cdot \mathbf{t}^T \cdot X \cdot \mathbf{w} + \mathbf{w}^T \cdot X^T \cdot X \cdot \mathbf{w}\right) = 0 \tag{13.21}$$

using the gradient rule

$$\nabla(a \cdot f(\mathbf{w}) + b \cdot g(\mathbf{w})) = a \cdot \nabla f(\mathbf{w}) + b \cdot \nabla g(\mathbf{w}), \quad a, b \in \mathbb{R}$$

we expand

$$\nabla\left(\mathbf{t}^T \cdot \mathbf{t}\right) - 2 \cdot \nabla\left(\mathbf{t}^T \cdot X \cdot \mathbf{w}\right) + \nabla\left(\mathbf{w}^T \cdot X^T \cdot X \cdot \mathbf{w}\right) = 0. \tag{13.22}$$

Using the gradient rules with $A = X^T \cdot X$ (A is symmetric)

$$\nabla\left((\mathbf{w}^T \cdot A \cdot \mathbf{w}\right) = 2 \cdot A \cdot \mathbf{w}$$

and

$$\nabla_w\left(\mathbf{t}^T \mathbf{w}\right) = \mathbf{t}$$

we simplify to

$$-2 \cdot X^T \cdot \mathbf{t} + 2 \cdot X^T \cdot X \cdot \mathbf{w} = 0$$

$$X^T \cdot \ \mathbf{t} - X^T \cdot X \cdot \mathbf{w} = 0$$

$$X^T \cdot \ \mathbf{t} = X^T \cdot X \cdot \mathbf{w} \tag{13.23}$$

and we get the closed-form solution for $\mathbf{w}$

$$\left(X^T \cdot X\right)^{-1} \cdot X^T \cdot \mathbf{t} = \mathbf{w}. \tag{13.24}$$

The matrix

$$X^\dagger = \left(X^T \cdot X\right)^{-1} \cdot X^T \tag{13.25}$$

$X^\dagger$ is the pseudo-inverse of X or as the Moore-Penrose matrix named after Roger Penrose and Eliakim Hastings Moore. When some features are linear combinations of the others, or when the number of features D is larger, the number N of examples $N < D$, then the matrix $X^T \cdot X$ is not invertible, it is said to be singular or degenerate. However, the Moore-Penrose pseudoinverse $X^\dagger$ is always defined; it is based on the SVD decomposition of the matrix X [Bishop (2006)].

13.3 Linear Regression and Linear Artificial Neuron

The multiple linear regression

$$y = y(\mathbf{x}, \mathbf{w}) = w_0 + \sum_{j=1}^{D} w_j \cdot x_j = w_0 + \langle \mathbf{w} | \mathbf{x} \rangle$$

corresponds to a linear artificial neuron, an artificial neuron without any activation function (or the activation function is the identity).

$$o_k = net_k = bias + \sum_{j=1}^{D} w_j \cdot x_j = w_0 + \sum_{j=1}^{D} w_j \cdot x_{j,k}$$

The training error for a training data set *Data* of N elements is given by

$$E(\mathbf{w}) = \frac{1}{2} \cdot \sum_{k=1}^{N} (t_k - o_k)^2 = \frac{1}{2} \cdot \sum_{k=1}^{N} \left(t_k - \sum_{j=0}^{D} w_j \cdot x_{k,j} \right)^2 \tag{13.26}$$

with an additional scaling value $\frac{1}{2}$ and with $x_{k,0} = 1$. This kind of error is also called squared error (sum-of-square error). We have seen that a closed-form solution that minimises the error $E(\mathbf{w})$ for $\mathbf{w}$ exists with

$$\nabla E(\mathbf{w}) = 0$$

with the the gradient operator

$$\nabla = \left[\frac{\partial}{\partial w_1}, \frac{\partial}{\partial w_2}, \cdots, \frac{\partial}{\partial w_D} \right]^T.$$

A non closed solution is based on the gradient descent. For $D = 1$ the training error is function of $\mathbf{w}$, with $\mathbf{w} = (w_0, w_1)$ we can represent all possible values as a two dimensional function, see Figure 13.2. The function corresponds to the error surface with one global minimum. The task of the algorithm is to determine the corresponding minimum. We can find the solution without the need to determine all possible $\mathbf{w}$ value combinations by an optimization algorithm, namely the gradient descent [Mitchell (1997)]. To find a minimum of a function $E(\mathbf{w})$ using gradient descent, one takes steps proportional to the negative of the gradient

$$-\nabla E(\mathbf{w}) = -\left(\frac{\partial E}{\partial w_0}, \frac{\partial E}{\partial w_1}, \cdots, \frac{\partial E}{\partial w_n} \right)^T \tag{13.27}$$

of the function at the current point. One starts the process at some randomly chosen point $\mathbf{w}^{initial}$ and modifies the weights if required with the learning rule

$$\mathbf{w}^{new} = \mathbf{w}^{old} + \Delta \mathbf{w} \tag{13.28}$$

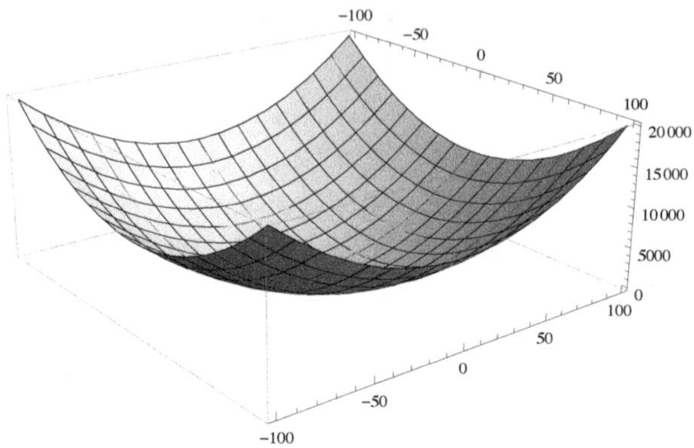

Fig. 13.2 The training error is function of $\mathbf{w}$, with $\mathbf{w} = (w_0, w_1)$ we can represent all possible values as a two dimensional function The x-axis represents w_0, the y-axis represents w_1 and the z-axis the value $E(\mathbf{w}) = E((w_0, w_1))$.The function corresponds to the error surface with a minimum. The task of the learning algorithm is to determine the corresponding minimum. The error surface as defined by $E(\mathbf{w})$ contains only one global minimum since it is convex.

with

$$w_j^{new} = w_j^{old} + \Delta w_j \tag{13.29}$$

and

$$\Delta \mathbf{w} = \eta \cdot (-\nabla E(\mathbf{w})) \tag{13.30}$$

with

$$\Delta w_j = -\eta \cdot \frac{\partial E}{\partial w_j}. \tag{13.31}$$

The weight vector $\mathbf{w}$ is moved by η within the direction that decrease $E(\mathbf{w})$, η is called the learning rate. For a sufficiently small η the algorithm will converge to a solution, because the error surface defined by $E(\mathbf{w})$ contains only one global minimum. For to large η the search could overstep the minimum in the error surface. The value

$$\frac{\partial E}{\partial w_j} = \frac{\partial}{\partial w_j} \frac{1}{2} \cdot \sum_{k=1}^{N} (t_k - o_k)^2 = \frac{1}{2} \cdot \sum_{k=1}^{N} \frac{\partial}{\partial w_j} (t_k - o_k)^2 \tag{13.32}$$

is given by

$$\frac{\partial E}{\partial w_j} = \frac{1}{2} \cdot \sum_{k=1}^{N} 2 \cdot (t_k - o_k) \cdot \frac{\partial}{\partial w_j} (t_k - o_k) \tag{13.33}$$

$$\frac{\partial E}{\partial w_j} = \sum_{k=1}^{N}(t_k - o_k) \cdot \frac{\partial}{\partial w_j}\left(t_k - \sum_{j=0}^{D} w_j \cdot x_{k,j}\right) \tag{13.34}$$

$$\frac{\partial E}{\partial w_j} = \sum_{k=1}^{N}(t_k - o_k) \cdot (-x_{k,j}) \tag{13.35}$$

$$\frac{\partial E}{\partial w_j} = -\sum_{k=1}^{N}(t_k - o_k) \cdot x_{k,j}. \tag{13.36}$$

The update rule for gradient decent is given by

$$\Delta w_j = \eta \cdot \sum_{k=1}^{N}(t_k - o_k) \cdot x_{k,j}. \tag{13.37}$$

also called gradient learning rule

$$w_j^{new} = w_j^{old} + \Delta w_j.$$

Since the error surface contains one global minimum the gradient descent converge to a weight vector with a global minimum error for a sufficiently small learning rate η. One starts the gradient descent with some small random values for each w_j. For the non linear continuous activation function

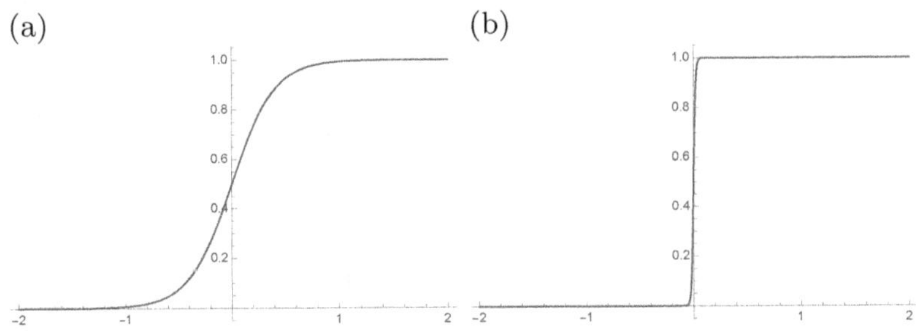

Fig. 13.3 (a) The function $\sigma(net)$ with $\alpha = 5$. (b) The function $\sigma(net)$ with $\alpha = 10$.

$\sigma()$ (sigmoid function),

$$\phi(net) := \sigma(net) = \frac{1}{1 + e^{(-\alpha \cdot net)}} \in [0, 1] \tag{13.38}$$

in which the value α determines its steepness, (see Figure, 13.3)

$$o_k = \sigma\left(\sum_{j=0}^{D} w_j \cdot x_{k,j}\right)$$

we can define as well the update rule for gradient decent with the differential

$$\sigma(x)' = \alpha \cdot \sigma(x) \cdot (1 - \sigma(x)) \tag{13.39}$$

and we get

$$\frac{\partial E}{\partial w_j} = -\alpha \cdot \sum_{k=1}^{N} (t_k - o_k) \cdot \sigma(net_k) \cdot (1 - \sigma(net_{k,})) \cdot x_{k,j}. \tag{13.40}$$

resulting in the update rule for gradient decent

$$\Delta w_j = \eta \cdot \alpha \sum_{k=1}^{N} (t_k - o_k) \cdot x_{k,j} \cdot o_k \cdot (1 - o_k) \tag{13.41}$$

$$w_j^{new} = w_j^{old} + \Delta w_j.$$

.

13.3.1 *Cross entropy loss function*

The sigmoid output unit use the linear input *net* and the sigmoid activation function to convert *net* into a probability value. Because of that it can be interpreted as logistic regression with two classes C_1 and C_2 with

$$\sigma(net) = \frac{1}{1 + e^{(-net)}} \in [0, 1]$$

$$p(C_1|\mathbf{x}) = \sigma\left(\sum_{j=0}^{N} w_j \cdot x_j\right) = \sigma\left(\mathbf{w}^T \cdot \mathbf{x}\right) \tag{13.42}$$

and

$$p(C_2|\mathbf{x}) = 1 - p(C_1|\mathbf{x}) \tag{13.43}$$

We can train

$$Data = \{(\mathbf{x}_1, t_1), (\mathbf{x}_2, t_2), \cdots,, (\mathbf{x}_N, t_N)\}, \quad t_k \in \{0, 1\}$$

the data efficiently taking into account our target values t_k are two values 0 an 1 representing two classes. The likelihood function can be written as the Bernoulli distribution [Bishop (2006)]

$$p(\mathbf{t}|\mathbf{w}) = \prod_{k=1}^{N} p(C_1|\mathbf{x}_k)^{t_k} \cdot (1 - p(C_1|\mathbf{x}_k))^{1-t_k} \tag{13.44}$$

with

$$o_k = p(C_1|\mathbf{x}_k) = \sigma\left(\mathbf{w}^T \cdot \mathbf{x}_k\right) = \sigma(net_k), \tag{13.45}$$

$$p(\mathbf{t}|\mathbf{w}) = \prod_{k=1}^{N} o_k^{t_k} \cdot (1 - o_k)^{1-t_k} \tag{13.46}$$

The error function or loss function can be defined by negative logarithm of the likelihood

$$E(\mathbf{w}) = -\log(p(\mathbf{t}|\mathbf{w})) = -\sum_{k=1}^{N} (t_k \log o_k + (1 - t_k)\log(1 - o_k)). \tag{13.47}$$

Such an error function is also called a loss function, it corresponds to the cross entropy error or cross entropy loss function with

$$\neg t_k = (1 - t_k)$$

$$H(t,p) = -\sum_{k=1}^{N} (t_k \cdot \log(p(C_1|\mathbf{x}_k)) + \neg t_k \cdot \log(p(C_2|\mathbf{x}_k)))$$

The gradient that minimizes the error (loss) function is given by

$$\frac{\partial E}{\partial w_j} = \frac{\partial}{\partial w_j}\left(-\sum_{k=1}^{N} (t_k \log o_k + (1 - t_k)\log(1 - o_k))\right) \tag{13.48}$$

with

$$\frac{\partial E}{\partial w_j} = -\sum_{k=1}^{N}\left(\frac{t_k}{o_k} + -\frac{(1-t_k)}{(1-o_k)}\right) \cdot \frac{\partial}{\partial w_j}(o_k) \tag{13.49}$$

$$\frac{\partial E}{\partial w_j} = \sum_{k=1}^{N}\left(\frac{(1-t_k)}{(1-o_k)} - \frac{t_k}{o_k}\right) \cdot \frac{\partial}{\partial w_j}(o_k) \tag{13.50}$$

$$\frac{\partial E}{\partial w_j} = \sum_{k=1}^{N}\left(\frac{(1-t_k)}{(1-o_k)} - \frac{t_k}{o_k}\right) \cdot (o_k \cdot (1-o_k)) \cdot \frac{\partial}{\partial w_j}\left(\sum_{j=0}^{D} w_j \cdot x_{k,j}\right) \tag{13.51}$$

$$\frac{\partial E}{\partial w_j} = \sum_{k=1}^{N}((1-t_k)\cdot(o_k)) - (t_k)\cdot(1-o_k)) \cdot \frac{\partial}{\partial w_j}\left(\sum_{j=0}^{D} w_j \cdot x_{k,j}\right) \tag{13.52}$$

$$\frac{\partial E}{\partial w_j} = \sum_{k=1}^{N}(o_k - t_k) \cdot \frac{\partial}{\partial w_j}\left(\sum_{j=0}^{D} w_j \cdot x_{k,j}\right) \tag{13.53}$$

$$\frac{\partial E}{\partial w_j} = \sum_{k=1}^{N}(o_k - t_k) \cdot x_{k,j} \tag{13.54}$$

$$\frac{\partial E}{\partial w_j} = -\sum_{k=1}^{N}(t_k - o_k) \cdot x_{k,j}. \tag{13.55}$$

The update rule for gradient decent is given by

$$\Delta w_j = \eta \cdot \sum_{k=1}^{N}(t_k - o_k) \cdot x_{k,j}. \tag{13.56}$$

In statistics the artificial neuron with sigmoid activation function is called logistic regression and the sigmoid function the logistic function. For an artificial neuron the sigmoid activation function indicates the output of the neuron, in logistic regression the output of the neuron would be either 1 (neuron fires) or 0 (neuron does not fire) and the output would indicate the probability that the artificial neuron fires.

13.4 Multiclass Linear Discriminant

For K artificial neurons with a continuous activation function ϕ an index t is used to identify the corresponding artificial linear neuron with

$$t \in \{1, 2, \cdots, K\}$$

to identify the weight vector $\mathbf{w}_t$ and the t the output o_t from the neuron.

$$o_t = \phi\left(\sum_{j=1}^{D} w_{t,j} \cdot x_j\right)$$

Training set consists on N observations (sample)

$$X = (\mathbf{x}_1, \mathbf{x}_2, \cdots, \mathbf{x}_k, \cdots, \mathbf{x}_N)^T$$

together with the target values (since t used as an index, we will use y_{kt} as indicating the target)

$$Y = (\mathbf{y}_1, \mathbf{y}_2, \cdots, \mathbf{y}_k, \cdots, \mathbf{y}_N)^T$$

represented as vectors of dimension K. During the training each neuron is trained individually withs its target value y_{kt}

$$y_{kt} \in \{0, 1\}, \quad \sum_{t=1}^{K} y_{kt} = 1$$

After training the prediction for an input pattern $\mathbf{x}$ is done. The 1-of K representation results in

$$p(C_s|\mathbf{x}) = \sigma(\mathbf{net})_s = \frac{\exp(net_s)}{\sum_{t=1}^{K}\exp(net_t)} \tag{13.57}$$

which is called the normalized exponential or softmax function with many interesting properties. It is the generalization of the logistic sigmoid with the activation net_s

$$net_s = \mathbf{w}_s^T \cdot \mathbf{x}$$

The softmax function is used in various multi class classification methods [Bishop (2006)], such as multinomial logistic regression (also known as softmax regression) with the prediction

$$\arg\max_s (\sigma(\mathbf{net})_s) = \arg\max_s \left(\mathbf{w}_s^T \cdot \mathbf{x}\right).$$

13.4.1 *Cross entropy loss function for Softmax*

Taking the error of the gradient function with respect to the vector $\mathbf{w}_j$ we obtain

$$\nabla_{\mathbf{w}_s} E(\mathbf{w}_1, \cdots, \mathbf{w}_K) = \sum_{k=1}^{N} (o_{ks} - y_{ks}) \cdot \mathbf{x}_k = -\sum_{k=1}^{N} (y_{ks} - o_{ks}) \cdot \mathbf{x}_k \quad (13.58)$$

again, it is the same as making the gradient sum-of-square error function for several artificial linear neurones. With

$$\sigma(net_{ks}) = \frac{\exp(net_{ks})}{\sum_{t=1}^{K} \exp(net_{kt})}$$

which is called the normalized exponential or softmax function. For simplification of the derivative function we drop the index k that indicates the k-th training pattern and we we get

$$\frac{\partial \sigma(net_s)}{\partial net_t} = \sigma(net_s) \cdot (I_{st} - \sigma(net_t)) = o_s \cdot (I_{st} - o_t)$$

means if $t = s$

$$\frac{\partial \sigma(net_s)}{\partial net_t} = \sigma(net_s) \cdot (1 - \sigma(net_s)) = o_s \cdot (1 - o_s)$$

if $t \neq s$

$$\frac{\partial \sigma(net_s)}{\partial net_t} = -\sigma(net_t) \cdot \sigma(net_s)) = -o_t \cdot o_s$$

with the Kronecker function

$$I_{st} = \delta_{st} = \begin{cases} 1, & \text{if } s = t \\ 0, & \text{otherwise.} \end{cases} \quad (13.59)$$

Taking the error of the gradient function with respect to net_j over all training patterns we get

$$E(\mathbf{w}) = -\sum_{k=1}^{N}\sum_{t=1}^{K} y_{kt} \cdot \log o_{kt} \tag{13.60}$$

$$\frac{\partial E}{\partial o_{kt}} = -\sum_{k=1}^{N}\sum_{t=1}^{K} \frac{y_{kt}}{o_{kt}}, \qquad \frac{\partial o_{kt}}{\partial net_s} = o_{kt} \cdot (I_{ts} - o_{ks}),$$

$$\frac{\partial E}{\partial net_s} = -\sum_{k=1}^{N}\sum_{t=1}^{K} \frac{y_{kt}}{o_{kt}} \cdot o_{kt} \cdot (I_{ts} - o_{ks}) \tag{13.61}$$

$$\frac{\partial E}{\partial net_s} = -\sum_{k=1}^{N}\sum_{t=1}^{K} (y_{kt} \cdot (I_{ts} - o_{ks}), \tag{13.62}$$

since

$$\sum_{t=1}^{K} y_{kt} = 1,$$

$$\frac{\partial E}{\partial net_s} = -\sum_{k=1}^{N} (y_{ks} - o_{ks}) \tag{13.63}$$

Since

$$net_{ks} = \sum_{j=1}^{D} w_{js} x_{kj}$$

we get for all N training patterns

$$\frac{\partial E}{\partial w_{js}} = -\sum_{k=1}^{N} (y_{ks} - o_{ks}) \cdot x_{kj} \tag{13.64}$$

with the learning rule

$$\Delta w_{js} = \eta \cdot \sum_{k=1}^{N} (y_{ks} - o_{ks}) \cdot x_{kj} \tag{13.65}$$

$$w_{js}^{new} = w_{js}^{old} + \Delta w_{js}.$$

This algorithm is called the logistic regression.

Fig. 13.4 Frank Rosenblatt (1928-1971) was an American psychologist notable for the invention of the perceptron.

13.4.2 *Limitations*

Logistic regression describes an algorithm for supervised learning that considers only linearly separable problems in which groups can be separated by a line or hyperplane. Logistic regression is based on the perceptron algorithm. The perceptron algorithm was invented in 1957 by Frank Rosenblatt [Rosenblatt (1962)] (see Figure 13.4). Seymour Aubrey Papert, published a book 1969 with the title "Perceptrons" [Minsky and Papert (1972)]. In the book, it was argued that perceptrons cannot model nonlinear functions such as the logical XOR operation (see Figure 13.5). Shortly after the book was published the research on artificial neural networks was stoped for the next 10 years

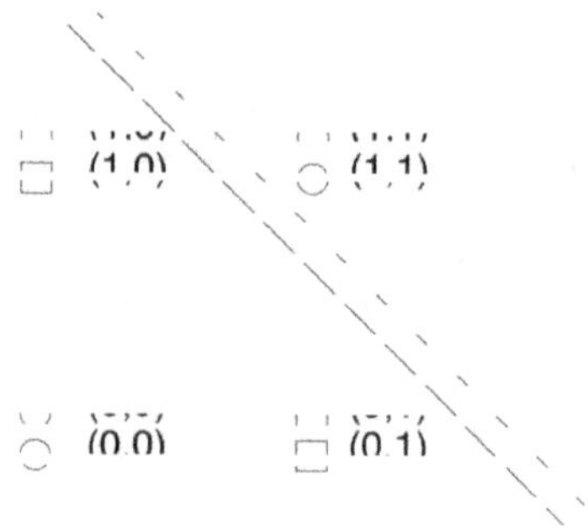

Fig. 13.5 "XOR" problem, there are two classes 0 and 1 as a result of the XOR operation. The class 0 results of the input $(0, 0)$ and $(1, 1)$ and the class 1 form the input $(0, 1)$ and $(1, 0)$. Bot classes cannot be separated by a line.

13.5 Networks with Hidden Nonlinear Layers

The limitations of logistic regression and perceptron do not apply to feed-forward networks with hidden nonlinear units. An example of a feed-forward network with one hidden layer is shown in Figure 13.6. The input pattern is represented by the five-dimensional vector $\mathbf{x}$; nonlinear hidden units compute the output V_1, V_2, V_3 and two output units compute the output o_1 and o_2. The units V_1, V_2, V_3 are referred to as hidden units because we cannot see their outputs and cannot directly perform error correction [Hertz *et al.* (1991)]. Feed-forward networks with hidden nonlinear units are universal approximators; they can approximate every bounded continuous function with an arbitrarily small error. Each Boolean function can be represented by a network with a single hidden layer. However, the representation may require an exponential number of hidden units. The hidden units should be nonlinear because multiple layers of linear units can only produce linear functions.

13.5.1 *Cross entropy error function*

Learning consists of minimizing the error (loss) function [Bishop (2006)],

$$E(\mathbf{w}) = -\sum_{k=1}^{N} y_k \log o_k$$

in which $y_{kt} \in \{0, 1\}$ and o_k corresponds to probabilities $(\sum_t y_{kt} = 1)$. The error surface is more steeply as the error surface defined by the squared

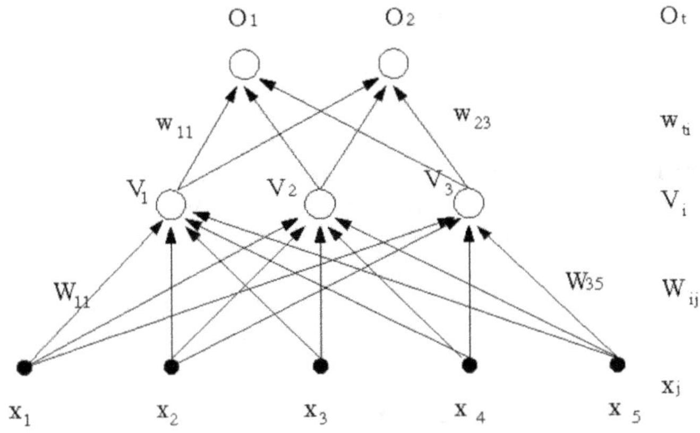

Fig. 13.6 The input pattern is represented by the five-dimensional vector $\mathbf{x}$; nonlinear hidden units compute the output V_1, V_2, V_3 and two output units compute the output o_1 and o_2. The units V_1, V_2, V_3 are referred to as hidden units because we cannot see their outputs and cannot directly perform error correction.

error

$$E(\mathbf{w}) = \frac{1}{2} \cdot \sum_{k=1}^{N} \sum_{t=1}^{2} (y_{kt} - o_{kt})^2$$

and the gradient converges faster. The cross entropy error function can be alternatively written as loss (cost) function with $\theta = \mathbf{w}$

$$L(\mathbf{x}, \mathbf{y}, \theta) = -\sum_{k=1}^{N} (y_k \log p(c_k|\mathbf{x}))$$

or as the loss function

$$J(\theta) = -\sum_{k=1}^{N} (y_k \log p(c_k|\mathbf{x})) = -\mathbb{E}_{x,y\sim p_{data}} \log p(c_k|\mathbf{x})$$

in which θ indicates the adaptive parameters of the model and $\mathbb{E}$ indicates the expectation. This notation is usually common in statistics.

13.5.2 *Backpropagation*

For output layer we use the softmax function with

$$\phi(net) = \frac{\exp(net_k)}{\sum_{j=1}^{K} \exp(net_j)}$$

and for the hidden units the sigmoid function

$$\phi(net) = \sigma(net) = \frac{1}{1 + e^{(-net))}}.$$

Using the sigmoid function we can reuse the results which we developed when we introduced the logistic regression. For simplification, we employ the notation in Figure 13.6. With the output unit

$$o_{k,t} = \phi\left(\sum_{i=0}^{3} w_{ti} \cdot V_{k,i}\right).$$

and

$$E(\mathbf{w}) = -\sum_{k=1}^{N}\sum_{t=1}^{2} y_{kt} \log o_{kt} = -\sum_{k=1}^{N}\sum_{t=1}^{2} y_{kt} \log \phi\left(\sum_{i=0}^{3} w_{ti} \cdot V_{k,i}\right) \quad (13.66)$$

we get the logistic regression given the target values $y_{kt} \in \{0,1\}$ and

$$\sum_{t=1}^{K} y_{kt} = 1$$

$$\frac{\partial E}{\partial w_{ti}} = -\sum_{k=1}^{N} (y_{kt} - o_{kt}) \cdot V_{k,i}. \quad (13.67)$$

If the hidden units use a continuous differentiable non linear activation function $\phi()$

$$V_{k,i} = \phi\left(\sum_{j=0}^{5} W_{ij} \cdot x_{k,j}\right).$$

we can define the training error for a training data set D_t of N elements with

$$E(\mathbf{w},\mathbf{W}) =: E(\mathbf{w}) = -\sum_{k=1}^{N}\sum_{t=1}^{2} (y_{kt} \cdot \log o_{kt}) \quad (13.68)$$

We apply the chain rule and make the distinction between the hidden and output units,

$$E(\mathbf{w},\mathbf{W}) = -\sum_{k=1}^{N}\sum_{t=1}^{2} \left(y_{kt} \cdot \log \phi\left(\sum_{i=0}^{3} w_{ti} \cdot V_{k,i}\right)\right)$$

$$E(\mathbf{w},\mathbf{W}) = -\sum_{k=1}^{N}\sum_{t=1}^{2} \left(y_{kt} \cdot \log \phi\left(\sum_{i=0}^{3} w_{ti} \cdot \phi\left(\sum_{j=0}^{5} W_{ij} \cdot x_{k,j}\right)\right)\right)$$

We know that

$$\frac{\partial E}{\partial w_{ti}} = -\sum_{k=1}^{N}(y_{kt} - o_{kt}) \cdot V_{k,i}. \tag{13.69}$$

For $\frac{\partial E}{\partial W_{ij}}$ we can use the chain rule and we obtain

$$\frac{\partial E}{\partial W_{ij}} = \sum_{k=1}^{N} \frac{\partial E}{\partial V_{ki}} \cdot \frac{\partial V_{ki}}{\partial W_{ij}}.$$

with

$$\frac{\partial E}{\partial V_{ki}} = -\sum_{k=1}^{N}\sum_{t=1}^{2}(y_{kt} - o_{kt}) \cdot w_{t,i}, \quad \frac{\partial V_{ki}}{\partial W_{ij}} = \phi'(net_{k,i}) \cdot x_{k,j}$$

it follows

$$\frac{\partial E}{\partial W_{ij}} = -\sum_{k=1}^{N}\sum_{t=1}^{2}(y_{kt} - o_{kt}) \cdot w_{t,i} \cdot \phi'(net_{k,i}) \cdot x_{k,j}. \tag{13.70}$$

We can reuse the computation that was used to determine Δw_{ti} as before

$$\Delta w_{ti} = \eta \cdot \sum_{k=1}^{N}(y_{kt} - o_{kt}) \cdot V_{k,i}.$$

and with

$$\delta_{kt} = (y_{kt} - o_{kt}) \tag{13.71}$$

we can write

$$\Delta w_{ti} = \eta \cdot \sum_{k=1}^{N} \delta_{kt} \cdot V_{k,i}. \tag{13.72}$$

With

$$\Delta W_{ij} = \eta \sum_{k=1}^{N}\sum_{t=1}^{2}(y_{kt} - o_{kt}) \cdot w_{t,i} \cdot \phi'(net_{k,i}) \cdot x_{k,j}$$

we can simplify (reuse the computation) to

$$\Delta W_{ij} = \eta \sum_{k=1}^{N}\sum_{t=1}^{2} \delta_{kt} \cdot w_{t,i} \cdot \phi'(net_{k,i}) \cdot x_{k,j}.$$

With

$$\delta_{ki} = \phi'(net_{k,i}) \cdot \sum_{t=1}^{2} \delta_{kt} \cdot w_{t,i} \tag{13.73}$$

we can simply to

$$\Delta W_{ij} = \eta \sum_{k=1}^{N} \delta_{ki} \cdot x_{k,j}. \tag{13.74}$$

13.5.3 *Computing power*

Feed-forward networks with hidden nonlinear units are universal approximators; they can approximate every bounded continuous function with an arbitrarily small error. According to the universality theorem, a neural network with a single hidden layer is capable of approximating any bounded continuous function [Cybenko (1989)], [Hornik *et al.* (1989)]. However, attempting to build a network with only one layer to approximate complex functions often requires a very large number of nodes [Hornik (1991)], [White (1992)]. It was also shown that each Boolean function can be represented by a network with a single hidden layer (nonlinear units), however, the representation may require an exponential number of hidden units [Bebis and Georgiopoulos (1994)].

13.6 Deep Learning and Backpropagation

Attempting to build a network with only one layer to approximate complex functions often requires a very large number of nodes. The immediate solution to this is to build networks with more hidden layers. In deep learning many hidden layers are used that reduce the training error on the validation set, see Figure 13.7. Empirical experiments indicate that "deep"

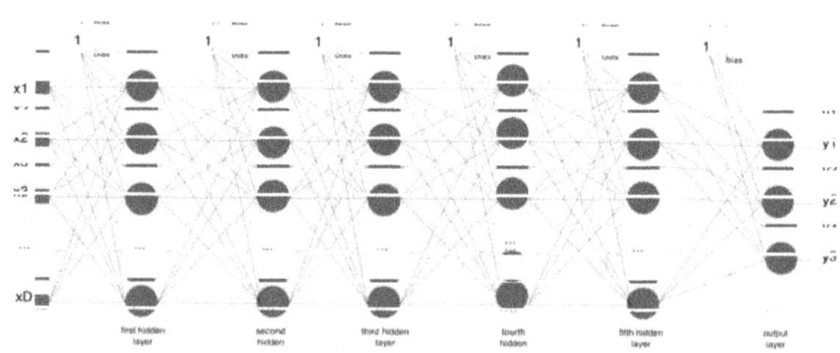

Fig. 13.7 A feed forward network with many hidden layers is called a deep network, in our example the network has five hidden layers. Depending on the training set more hidden layers can be used. Deep learning is a not a new algorithm, since it is usually trained by backpropagation. Different heuristics and methods are used with the aim of improving the results. The models achieved tremendous results due to computing power, and represent one of the most successful tools in engineering.

neural networks give better results then "fat" neural networks (see Figure

13.8). It seems that networks with many hidden layers have a different error landscape that is less prune to local minima [Goodfellow *et al.* (2016)]. However deep neural networks can overfit easier, since they have many more free parameter. In a "fat" neural networks there are many hidden neurons,

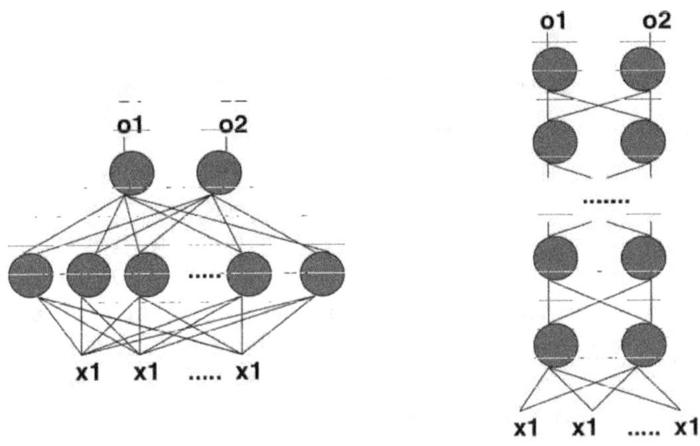

Fig. 13.8 Why should we use a "deep" neural network (right side) and not a "fat" neural network (left side)?

its many outputs represent a high dimensional vector that is classified by the output neurons. The high dimensionality of the vector influences negatively the classification of the output neurons during learning and generalization. It corresponds to the curse of dimensionality. Deep neural networks can ovoid the curse of dimensionality problem by constraining the number of hidden neurons.

13.6.1 *Overfitting*

The training data contains information about the regularities in the mapping from input to output, but it also contains noise. For example the target values (labels) may be unreliable. There is sampling error and a flexible architecture can model the sampling error really well. We cannot tell which regularities are real and which are caused by sampling error.

The smaller the $MSE(D_v)$ the better the hypothesis h describing the function f. We can define the mean squared error for the training data set

D_t

$$MSE_{Dt}(h) = \sum_{k=1}^{M} \frac{1}{M} \cdot \|\mathbf{y}_k - \mathbf{o}_k\|^2, \tag{13.75}$$

usually

$$MSE_{Dv}(h) > MSE_{Dt}(h).$$

If we have two hypothesis h_1 and h_2 with

$$MSE_{Dt}(h_1) < MSE_{Dt}(h_2), \quad MSE_{Dv}(h_1) > MSE_{Dv}(h_2). \tag{13.76}$$

then we say that the hypothesis h_1 overfits the training data set D_t, h_1 fits better the training examples than h_2, but performs more poorly over examples it didn't learn. It seems as h_1 learned by heart D_t and not the topological structure that describe the function f, on the other hand h_2 learned the corresponding structure and can generalize [Mitchell (1997)].

To overcome overfitting we can increase the size of the labeled data set, this is the best possible approach. Hoverer due to the cost of generating labeled data set often not possible. Another approach is the early stopping, one stops the learning before it overfits.

13.6.2 *Regularization*

To overcome overfitting one can use a model that has the right capacity, enough to model the true regularities and not enough to also model the spurious regularities. One can as well avoid overfitting through regularization. Regularization through weight-decay penalizes large weights using penalties or constraints on their squared values (l_2 regularization) or absolute values (l_1 regularization) [Haykin (2008)], [Goodfellow *et al.* (2016)].

13.6.2.1 l_2 *regularization*

$$\tilde{E}(\mathbf{w}) = \frac{1}{2} \cdot \sum_{k=1}^{N} (y_k - o_k)^2 + \frac{\lambda}{2} \|\mathbf{w}\|_2^2, \ \textit{or} \ \ \tilde{E}(\mathbf{w}) = -\sum_{k=1}^{N} y_k \log o_k + \frac{\lambda}{2} \|\mathbf{w}\|_2^2$$

$$\tilde{E}(\mathbf{w}) = E(\mathbf{w}) + \frac{\lambda}{2} \|\mathbf{w}\|_2^2 \tag{13.77}$$

$$\frac{\partial \tilde{E}}{\partial w_j} = \frac{\partial E}{\partial w_j} + \lambda \cdot w_j.$$

$$\Delta w_j = -\eta \left(\frac{\partial E}{\partial w_j} + \lambda \cdot w_j \right) = -\eta \left(\frac{\partial E}{\partial w_j} \right) - \eta\lambda \cdot w_j = -\eta \left(\frac{\partial E}{\partial w_j} \right) - \alpha \cdot w_j$$

13.6.2.2 l_1 *regularization*

$$\tilde{E}(\mathbf{w}) = \frac{1}{2} \cdot \sum_{k=1}^{N} (y_k - o_k)^2 + \lambda \cdot \|\mathbf{w}\|_1, \ or \ \tilde{E}(\mathbf{w}) = -\sum_{k=1}^{N} y_k \log o_k + \lambda \cdot \|\mathbf{w}\|_1$$

$$\tilde{E}(\mathbf{w}) = E(\mathbf{w}) + \lambda \|\mathbf{w}\|_1 \tag{13.78}$$

$$\frac{\partial \tilde{E}}{\partial w_j} = \frac{\partial E}{\partial w_j} + \lambda \cdot sign(w_j).$$

$$\Delta w_j = -\eta \left(\frac{\partial E}{\partial w_j} + \lambda \cdot sign(w_j) \right) = -\eta \left(\frac{\partial E}{\partial w_j} \right) - \eta\lambda \cdot sign(w_j)$$

$$\Delta w_j = -\eta \left(\frac{\partial E}{\partial w_j} \right) - \alpha \cdot sign(w_j)$$

13.6.3 *Second and first order optimization*

Optimization algorithms that use only the gradient, such as gradient descent, are called first-order optimization algorithms like

$$\mathbf{x}_{n+1} = \mathbf{x}_n - \eta \cdot \nabla f(\mathbf{x}_n).$$

Optimization algorithms that also use the Hessian matrix, such as Newton's method,

$$\mathbf{x}_{n+1} = \mathbf{x}_n - H_n^{-1} \cdot \nabla f(\mathbf{x}_n)$$

are called second-order optimization algorithms [Haykin (2008)], [Goodfellow *et al.* (2016)]. Newton's method converges quickly asymptotically and does not exhibit the zigzagging behavior that sometimes characterizes the method of steepest descent. Iteratively updating the approximation and jumping to the minimum of the approximation can reach the critical point much faster than gradient descent. When f($\mathbf{x}$) is a positive definite quadratic function, Newton's method consists of once to jump to the minimum of the function directly. However this useful property near a local minimum can be a harmful near a saddle point, a point of a function or surface which is a stationary point but not an extremum. Consider a continuously twice differentiable function $f(\mathbf{x})$.

$$f : \mathbb{R}^D \to \mathbb{R} : f(\mathbf{x}) = y$$

It maps the vector $\mathbf{x}$ into a real value. Then the Hessian matrix with respect to $\mathbf{x}$, written $\nabla^2 f(\mathbf{x})$ or simply as H is the $D \times D$ matrix of partial derivatives,

$$\nabla^2 f(\mathbf{x}) = \begin{pmatrix} \frac{\partial^2 f(\mathbf{x})}{\partial x_1^2} & \frac{\partial^2 f(\mathbf{x})}{\partial x_1 \partial x_2} & \cdots & \frac{\partial^2 f(\mathbf{x})}{\partial x_1 \partial x_D} \\ \frac{\partial^2 f(\mathbf{x})}{\partial x_2 \partial x_1} & \frac{\partial^2 f(\mathbf{x})}{\partial x_2 \partial x_2} & \cdots & \frac{\partial^2 f(\mathbf{x})}{\partial x_2 \partial x_D} \\ \vdots & \vdots & \ddots & \vdots \\ \frac{\partial^2 f(\mathbf{x})}{\partial x_D \partial x_1} & \frac{\partial^2 f(\mathbf{x})}{\partial x_D \partial x_2} & \cdots & \frac{\partial^2 f(\mathbf{x})}{\partial x_D^2} \end{pmatrix}. \tag{13.79}$$

By second-order Taylor series expansion we have

$$f(\mathbf{x}_{n+1}) \approx f(\mathbf{x}_n) + (\nabla f(\mathbf{x}_n))^T \cdot (\mathbf{x}_{n+1} - \mathbf{x}_n) + \frac{(\mathbf{x}_{n+1} - \mathbf{x}_n)^T H_n (\mathbf{x}_{n+1} - \mathbf{x}_n)}{2} \tag{13.80}$$

We can reformulate to

$$f(\mathbf{x}_{n+1}) - f(\mathbf{x}_n) \approx (\nabla f(\mathbf{x}_n))^T \cdot (\mathbf{x}_{n+1} - \mathbf{x}_n) + \frac{(\mathbf{x}_{n+1} - \mathbf{x}_n)^T H_n (\mathbf{x}_{n+1} - \mathbf{x}_n)}{2} \tag{13.81}$$

We minimize the resulting change with

$$0 = (\nabla f(\mathbf{x}_n))^T \cdot (\mathbf{x}_{n+1} - \mathbf{x}_n) + \frac{(\mathbf{x}_{n+1} - \mathbf{x}_n)^T H_n (\mathbf{x}_{n+1} - \mathbf{x}_n)}{2} \tag{13.82}$$

$$0 = (\nabla f(\mathbf{x}_n))^T + \frac{(\mathbf{x}_{n+1} - \mathbf{x}_n)^T H_n}{2} \tag{13.83}$$

we minimize when

$$0 = \nabla f(\mathbf{x}_n) + H_n (\mathbf{x}_{n+1} - \mathbf{x}_n) \tag{13.84}$$

$$(\mathbf{x}_{n+1} - \mathbf{x}_n) = -H_n^{-1} \cdot \nabla f(\mathbf{x}_n) \tag{13.85}$$

and we get the update rule as

$$\mathbf{x}_{n+1} = \mathbf{x}_n - H_n^{-1} \cdot \nabla f(\mathbf{x}_n). \tag{13.86}$$

This method is named after Sir Isaac Newton.

13.7 Support Vector Machines

In two class problem that is linear separable there are many decision boundaries can separate these two classes, see Figure 13.9. Which one of these

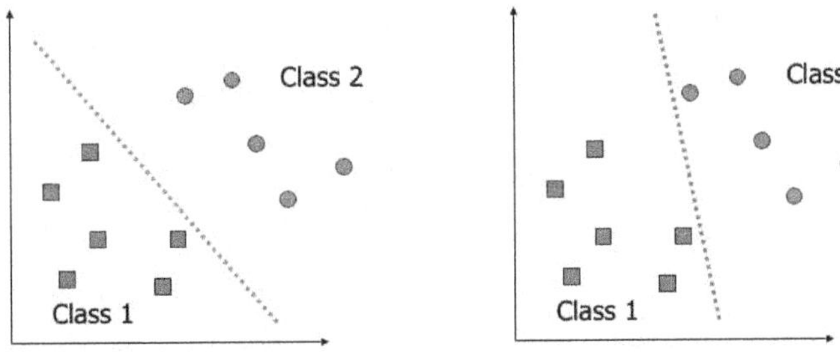

Fig. 13.9 In two class problem that is linear separable there are many decision boundaries can separate these two classes. Which one of these boundaries should we choose?

boundaries should we choose? A discriminant function for a perceptron is described

$$net = y(\mathbf{x}) = \mathbf{w}^T \cdot \mathbf{x} + w_0$$

The vector projection $\mathbf{x}$ on $\mathbf{w}$ of is defined as

$$proj_{\mathbf{w}}\mathbf{x} = \mathbf{x}^T \cdot \frac{\mathbf{w}}{\|\mathbf{w}\|} = \frac{\mathbf{w}^T \cdot \mathbf{x}}{\|\mathbf{w}\|} \tag{13.87}$$

also known as the vector component or vector resolution of $\mathbf{x}$ in the direction of $\mathbf{w}$. We want to find c such that the resulting vector $\mathbf{x} - c \cdot \mathbf{w}$ is orthogonal to $\mathbf{w}$. Two perpendicular (orthogonal) vectors have vector dot product of zero

$$(\mathbf{x} - c \cdot \mathbf{w})^T \cdot \mathbf{w} = 0 \tag{13.88}$$

$$\mathbf{x}^T \cdot \mathbf{w} - c \cdot \mathbf{w}^T \cdot \mathbf{w} = 0 \tag{13.89}$$

$$\frac{\mathbf{w}^T \cdot \mathbf{x}}{\|\mathbf{w}\|} = c \tag{13.90}$$

For the points on the decision surface

$$\mathbf{w}^T \cdot \mathbf{x} + w_0 = 0$$

it follows

$$\mathbf{w}^T \cdot \mathbf{x} = -w_0$$

we put is in the distance formula and we get

$$\frac{\mathbf{w}^T \cdot \mathbf{x}}{\|\mathbf{w}\|} = -\frac{w_0}{\|\mathbf{w}\|} = c \tag{13.91}$$

which is the distance from the origin to the decision surface.

Let $\mathbf{x}_p$ be the orthogonal projection of $\mathbf{x}$ onto the decision surface

$$y(\mathbf{x}_p) = \mathbf{w}^T \cdot \mathbf{x}_p + w_0 = 0$$

and we represent $\mathbf{x}$ as

$$\mathbf{x} = \mathbf{x}_p + r \cdot \frac{\mathbf{w}}{\|\mathbf{w}\|}. \tag{13.92}$$

Then

$$y(\mathbf{x}) = \mathbf{w}^T \cdot \left(\mathbf{x}_p + r \cdot \frac{\mathbf{w}}{\|\mathbf{w}\|} \right) + w_0$$

$$y(\mathbf{x}) = \mathbf{w}^T \cdot \mathbf{x}_p + w_0 + r \cdot \mathbf{w}^T \cdot \frac{\mathbf{w}}{\|\mathbf{w}\|} = 0 + r \cdot \|\mathbf{w}\| \tag{13.93}$$

$y(\mathbf{x})$ gives the distance of the point $\mathbf{x}$ to the decision surface with

$$r = \frac{y(\mathbf{x})}{\|\mathbf{w}\|}. \tag{13.94}$$

13.7.1 *Optimal hyperplane for linear separable patterns*

Given a training set $\{\mathbf{x}_i, t_i\}_{i=1}^N$, with $t_i \in \{-1, +1\}$ of linear separable patterns we have

$$\mathbf{w}^T \cdot \mathbf{x}_i + w_0 \geq 0, \quad for \;\; t_i = +1$$

$$\mathbf{w}^T \cdot \mathbf{x}_i + w_0 < 0, \quad for \;\; t_i = -1$$

with a hyperplane

$$\mathbf{w}^T \cdot \mathbf{x} + w_0 = \mathbf{w}^T \cdot \mathbf{x} + b = 0.$$

We want to find the parameters $\mathbf{w}_{opt}$ and b_{opt}

$$\mathbf{w}_{opt}^T \cdot \mathbf{x}_i + b_{opt} \geq 1, \quad for \;\; t_i = +1 \tag{13.95}$$

$$\mathbf{w}_{opt}^T \cdot \mathbf{x}_i + b_{opt} \leq 1, \quad for \;\; t_i = -1 \tag{13.96}$$

with a hyperplane

$$\mathbf{w}_{opt}^T \cdot \mathbf{x}_i + b_{opt} = 0, \tag{13.97}$$

since the patterns are linearly separable we can always rescale $\mathbf{w}_{opt}$ and b_{opt} correspondingly. The data points$\{\mathbf{x}_i, t_i\}$ for which

$$\mathbf{w}_{opt}^T \cdot \mathbf{x}_i + b_{opt} = \pm 1 \tag{13.98}$$

are called support vectors $\mathbf{x}^{(s)}$, That is why the algorithm is called support vector machine. All the remaining examples in the training sample are **irrelevant** for the determination of the hyperplane.

$$y(\mathbf{x}^{(s)}) = \mathbf{w}_{opt}^T \cdot \mathbf{x}^{(s)} + b_{opt} = \pm 1, \quad for \ \ t^{(s)} = \pm 1 \tag{13.99}$$

and

$$y(\mathbf{x}^{(s)}) = r \cdot \|\mathbf{w}_{opt}\| = \pm 1. \tag{13.100}$$

Since

$$r = \frac{y(\mathbf{x})}{\|\mathbf{w}\|}.$$

we get

$$r = \frac{y(\mathbf{x}^{(s)})}{\|\mathbf{w}_{opt}\|} = \begin{cases} \frac{1}{\|\mathbf{w}_{opt}\|} & \text{if} \quad t^{(s)} = +1 \\ \\ -\frac{1}{\|\mathbf{w}_{opt}\|} & \text{if} \quad t^{(s)} = -1 \end{cases} \tag{13.101}$$

We define now the optimum value ρ of the margin of separation between the two classes that constitute the training sample as

$$\rho = \frac{1}{\|\mathbf{w}_{opt}\|} + \left| -\frac{1}{\|\mathbf{w}_{opt}\|} \right| = \frac{2}{\|\mathbf{w}_{opt}\|} = 2 \cdot r \tag{13.102}$$

Maximizing the margin of separation between binary classes is equivalent to minimizing the Euclidean norm of the weight vector $\mathbf{w}$. The optimal hyperplanes unique in the sense that the optimum weight vector $\mathbf{w}_{opt}$ provides the maximum possible separation between positive and negative examples [Haykin (2008)].

13.7.2 *Quadratic optimization for finding the optimal hyperplane*

Good decision boundary means that the margin ρ should be large. The decision boundary should be as far away from the data of both classes as possible We need to maximize the margin ρ. For a training set $\{\mathbf{x}_i, t_i\}_{i=1}^N$, with $t_i \in \{-1, +1\}$ of linear separable patterns we want find the optimum values of the weight vector $\mathbf{w}$ and bias b such that they satisfy the constraints

$$\mathbf{w}^T \cdot \mathbf{x}_i + b \geq 1, \quad for \ \ t_i = +1$$

$$\mathbf{w}^T \cdot \mathbf{x}_i + b \leq 1, \quad for \ \ t_i = -1$$

expressed in a single line as

$$t_i \cdot \left(\mathbf{w}^T \cdot \mathbf{x}_i + b\right) \geq 1, \qquad for \ \ t_i = \pm 1 \tag{13.103}$$

and the weight vector $\mathbf{w}$ minimizes the cost function

$$\Phi(\mathbf{w}) = \frac{1}{2} \cdot \mathbf{w}^T \mathbf{w} = \frac{1}{2} \cdot \|\mathbf{w}\|^2 \tag{13.104}$$

with scaling factor $\frac{1}{2}$ that is introduced for convenience. This constrained optimization problem is called the primal problem and it is described by $\Phi(\mathbf{w})$ with the constraint of Equation 13.103. We note that

- the cost function $\Phi(\mathbf{w})$ is a convex function of $\mathbf{w}$,
- the constraints are linear in $\mathbf{w}$.

Because of this we may solve the constrained optimiyation problem by using the method of Lagrange multipliers with

$$J(\mathbf{w}, b, \alpha) = \frac{1}{2} \cdot \mathbf{w}^T \mathbf{w} - \sum_{i=1}^{N} \alpha_i \cdot \left(t_i \cdot \left(\mathbf{w}^T \cdot \mathbf{x}_i + b\right) - 1\right) \tag{13.105}$$

where α_i are called Lagrange multipliers. The solution to the constrained optimization problem is determined by the saddle point of the Lagrangian function $J(\mathbf{w}, b, \alpha)$, The saddle point has to be minimized with respect to $\mathbf{w}$ and b and maximized with respect to α. We get two conditions

$$\frac{\partial(\mathbf{w}, b, \alpha)}{\partial \mathbf{w}} = \mathbf{0}, \qquad \frac{\partial(\mathbf{w}, b, \alpha)}{\partial b} = 0 \tag{13.106}$$

leading to

$$\mathbf{w} = \sum_{i=1}^{N} \alpha_i \cdot t_i \cdot \mathbf{x}_i, \qquad \sum_{i=1}^{N} \alpha_i \cdot t_i = 0 \tag{13.107}$$

This solution is unique by virtue of the convexity of the Lagrangian, but not with respect of the Lagrange multipliers α_i. For the all constraints

$$t_i \cdot \left(\mathbf{w}^T \cdot \mathbf{x}_i + b\right) - 1 \neq 0$$

that are not satisfied as equalities, the corresponding multiplier α_i must be zero. The following Karush-Kuhn-Tucker conditions [Haykin (2008)] must be satisfied

$$\alpha_i \cdot \left(t_i \cdot \left(\mathbf{w}^T \cdot \mathbf{x}_i + b\right) - 1\right) = 0. \tag{13.108}$$

13.7.3 *Dual problem*

It is possible to construct another problem called the dual problem that has the same optimal value as the primal problem. If the primal problem has an optimal solution, the dual problem also has an optimal solution, and the corresponding optimal values are equal.
In order for $\mathbf{w}_{opt}$ to be an optimal primal solution and α_{opt} to be an optimal dual solution, it is necessary and sufficient that $\mathbf{w}_{opt}$ is feasible for the primal problem, and

$$\Phi(\mathbf{w}_{opt}) = J(\mathbf{w}_{opt}, b_{opt}, \alpha_{opt}) = \min_{\mathbf{w}} J(\mathbf{w}, b, \alpha) \tag{13.109}$$

We expand

$$J(\mathbf{w}, b, \alpha) = \frac{1}{2} \cdot \mathbf{w}^T \mathbf{w} - \sum_{i=1}^{N} \alpha_i \cdot \left(t_i \cdot \left(\mathbf{w}^T \cdot \mathbf{x}_i + b\right) - 1\right)$$

to

$$J(\mathbf{w}, b, \alpha) = \frac{1}{2} \cdot \mathbf{w}^T \mathbf{w} - \sum_{i=1}^{N} \alpha_i \cdot t_i \cdot \mathbf{w}^T \mathbf{x}_i - b \cdot \sum_{i=1}^{N} \alpha_i \cdot t_i + \sum_{i=1}^{N} \alpha_i, \tag{13.110}$$

because

$$\mathbf{w} = \sum_{i=1}^{N} \alpha_i \cdot t_i \cdot \mathbf{x}_i,$$

$$\mathbf{w}^T \mathbf{w} = \sum_{i=1}^{N} \alpha_i \cdot t_i \cdot \mathbf{w}^T \mathbf{x}_i = \sum_{i=1}^{N} \sum_{j=1}^{N} \alpha_i \cdot \alpha_j \cdot t_i \cdot t_j \cdot \mathbf{x}_i^T \mathbf{x}_j,$$

$$J(\mathbf{w}, b, \alpha) = \frac{1}{2} \cdot \sum_{i=1}^{N} \alpha_i \cdot t_i \cdot \mathbf{w}^T \mathbf{x}_i - \sum_{i=1}^{N} \alpha_i \cdot t_i \cdot \mathbf{w}^T \mathbf{x}_i - b \cdot \sum_{i=1}^{N} \alpha_i \cdot t_i + \sum_{i=1}^{N} \alpha_i \tag{13.111}$$

simplifying to

$$J(\mathbf{w}, b, \alpha) = -b \cdot \sum_{i=1}^{N} \alpha_i \cdot t_i + \sum_{i=1}^{N} \alpha_i - \frac{1}{2} \cdot \sum_{i=1}^{N} \alpha_i \cdot t_i \cdot \mathbf{w}^T \mathbf{x}_i \tag{13.112}$$

and substituting

$$\mathbf{w} = \sum_{i=1}^{N} \alpha_i \cdot t_i \cdot \mathbf{x}_i,$$

into the equation we get

$$J(\mathbf{w}, b, \alpha) = -b \cdot \sum_{i=1}^{N} \alpha_i \cdot t_i + \sum_{i=1}^{N} \alpha_i - \frac{1}{2} \cdot \sum_{i=1}^{N} \sum_{j=1}^{N} \alpha_i \cdot \alpha_j \cdot t_i \cdot t_j \cdot \mathbf{x}_i^T \mathbf{x}_j \quad (13.113)$$

Since the Lagrangian condition is

$$\sum_{i=1}^{N} \alpha_i \cdot t_i = 0,$$

and setting

$$Q(\alpha) = J(\mathbf{w}, b, \alpha)$$

we reformulate the constraint.

$$Q(\alpha) = \sum_{i=1}^{N} \alpha_i - \frac{1}{2} \cdot \sum_{i=1}^{N} \sum_{j=1}^{N} \alpha_i \cdot \alpha_j \cdot t_i \cdot t_j \cdot \mathbf{x}_i^T \mathbf{x}_j \quad (13.114)$$

with α_i being non negative.

13.7.3.1 *Training data*

Given the training sample $\{\mathbf{x}_i, t_i\}_{i=1}^{N}$, with $t_i \in \{-1, +1\}$ of linear separable patterns find the Lagrange multipliers $\{\alpha_i\}_{i=1}^{N}$ that maximize

$$Q(\alpha) = \sum_{i=1}^{N} \alpha_i - \frac{1}{2} \cdot \sum_{i=1}^{N} \sum_{j=1}^{N} \alpha_i \cdot \alpha_j \cdot t_i \cdot t_j \cdot \mathbf{x}_i^T \mathbf{x}_j$$

subject to constraints

$$\sum_{i=1}^{N} \alpha_i \cdot t_i = 0, \qquad \alpha_i \geq 0, \qquad i = 1, 2, \cdots, N.$$

The dual problem is cast entirely in terms of the training data by $\mathbf{x}_i^T \mathbf{x}_j$. The dual problem $\alpha_i \geq 0$ is satisfied with the inequality sign for all the support vectors for which the α's are nonzero, and with the equality sign for all the other data points in the training sample, for which the α's are all zero. The support vectors constitute a subset of the training sample, which means that the solution vector is sparse.

Having determined the optimum Lagrange multipliers $\alpha_{opt,i}$ (not equal zero) we may recover

$$\mathbf{w}_{opt} = \sum_{i=1}^{N} \alpha_{opt,i} \cdot t_i \cdot \mathbf{x}_i, \quad (13.115)$$

$$\mathbf{w}_{opt}^T \cdot \mathbf{x}_i + b_{opt} = \pm 1 \tag{13.116}$$

and

$$b_{opt} = 1 - \mathbf{w}_{opt}^T \cdot \mathbf{x}^{(s)}, \quad for \;\; t^{(s)} = 1 \tag{13.117}$$

since

$$b_{opt} = 1 - \left(\sum_{i=1}^{N} \alpha_{opt,i} \cdot t_i \cdot \mathbf{x}_i^T \right) \cdot \mathbf{x}^{(s)}, \;\; for \;\; t^{(s)} = 1.$$

Later we will see, how to determine the bias for a non optimal case.

13.8 Optimal Hyperplane for Non-separable Patterns

We allow "error" ξ_i in classification resulting in

$$t_i \cdot \left(\mathbf{w}^T \cdot \mathbf{x}_i + b \right) \geq 1 - \xi_i, \quad for \;\; i = 1, 2, \cdots, N \tag{13.118}$$

ξ_i are called the slack variables; they measure the deviation of a data point from the ideal condition of pattern separability.

- For $0 < \xi_i \leq 1$ the data point falls inside the region of separation, but on the correct side of the decision surface,
- For $\xi_i > 1$ falls on the wrong side of the separating hyperplane

Our goal is to find a separating hyperplane for which the misclassification error, averaged over the training sample, is minimized

The weight vector $\mathbf{w}$ minimizes the cost function

$$\Phi(\mathbf{w}, \xi) = \frac{1}{2} \cdot \mathbf{w}^T + C \cdot \sum_{i=1}^{N} \xi_i \tag{13.119}$$

with C controls the tradeoff between complexity of the machine and the number of non separable points. C may be viewed as an inverse regularization parameter.

- Large value indicates high confidence in the quality of the training sample.
- Small value indicates noisy training set, and less emphasis should therefore be placed on it.

Given the training sample $\{\mathbf{x}_i, t_i\}_{i=1}^{N}$, with $t_i \in \{-1, +1\}$ of linear separable patterns find find the parameters $\mathbf{w}$ and b with the constraint

$$t_i \cdot \left(\mathbf{w}^T \cdot \mathbf{x}_i + b\right) \geq 1 - \xi_i, \quad for \ \ i = 1, 2, \cdots, N \tag{13.120}$$

$$\xi_i \geq 0 \tag{13.121}$$

and such that the weight vector $\mathbf{w}$ and the slack variables ξ_i minimize the cost function $\Phi(\mathbf{w}, \xi)$.

13.8.1 *Dual problem*

We formulate the dual problem: Given the training sample $\{\mathbf{x}_i, t_i\}_{i=1}^{N}$, with $t_i \in \{-1, +1\}$ of linear separable patterns find the Lagrange multipliers $\{\alpha_i\}_{i=1}^{N}$ that maximize

$$Q(\alpha) = \sum_{i=1}^{N} \alpha_i - \frac{1}{2} \cdot \sum_{i=1}^{N} \sum_{j=1}^{N} \alpha_i \cdot \alpha_j \cdot t_i \cdot t_j \cdot \mathbf{x}_i^T \mathbf{x}_j \tag{13.122}$$

subject to constraints

$$\sum_{i=1}^{N} \alpha_i \cdot t_i = 0 \tag{13.123}$$

and a new constraint

$$0 \leq \alpha_i \leq C, \quad i = 1, 2, \cdots, N \tag{13.124}$$

where C is a user specified positive parameter. The one difference is that $0 \leq \alpha_i$ constraint is bounded by the value C, $0 \leq \alpha_i \leq C$, This is a quadratic-programming (QP) that can be solved by a QP solver. Later in the example XOR problem we indicate how to solve this problem by hand.

13.9 Support Vector Machine as a Kernel Machine

We will preform a nonlinear mapping of an input vector into a high-dimensional feature space that is hidden from both the input and output and construction of an optimal hyperplane for separating the features that were discovered before. Let $\mathbf{x}$ be a vector from the input space of the dimension D. and let $\{\phi_j(\mathbf{x})\}_{j=1}^{\infty}$ be a set of nonlinear functions, from D dimension to infinite dimension [Haykin (2008)]. The hyperplane is defined as

$$\sum_{j=1}^{\infty} w_j \cdot \phi_j(\mathbf{x}) + b = 0 \tag{13.125}$$

using vector notation

$$\mathbf{w}^T \cdot \Phi(\mathbf{x}) + b = 0. \tag{13.126}$$

with $\Phi(\mathbf{x})$ being a feature vector for infinite dimension and $\mathbf{w}$ is the wight vector. With N_s being the number of support vectors with the feature vector we can represent now the weights vector as

$$\mathbf{w} = \sum_{i=1}^{N_s} \alpha_i \cdot t_i \cdot \Phi(\mathbf{x}_i) \tag{13.127}$$

and the feature vector of infinite dimension

$$\Phi(\mathbf{x}_i) = \begin{pmatrix} \phi_1(\mathbf{x}_i) \\ \phi_2(\mathbf{x}_i) \\ \vdots \end{pmatrix} \tag{13.128}$$

we represent the decision surface as

$$\sum_{i=1}^{N_s} \alpha_i \cdot t_i \cdot \Phi^T(\mathbf{x}_i)\Phi(\mathbf{x}) = 0 \tag{13.129}$$

$\Phi^T(\mathbf{x}_i)\Phi(\mathbf{x})$ represents an inner product $\langle \Phi(\mathbf{x}_i) | \Phi(\mathbf{x}) \rangle$

$$k(\mathbf{x}, \mathbf{x}_i) = \Phi^T(\mathbf{x}_i)\Phi(\mathbf{x}) = \langle \Phi(\mathbf{x}_i) | \Phi(\mathbf{x}) \rangle \tag{13.130}$$

$$k(\mathbf{x}, \mathbf{x}_i) = \langle \Phi(\mathbf{x}_i) | \Phi(\mathbf{x}) \rangle = \sum_{j=1}^{\infty} \phi(\mathbf{x}_i) \cdot \phi(\mathbf{x}) \tag{13.131}$$

with $k(\mathbf{x}, \mathbf{x}_i)$ being the inner-product kernel. The kernel has two properties:

(1) The function $k(\mathbf{x}, \mathbf{x}_i)$ is symmetric about the center point $\mathbf{x}_i$ that is,

$$k(\mathbf{x}, \mathbf{x}_i) = k(\mathbf{x}_i, \mathbf{x})$$

and it attains its maximum value at the point $\mathbf{x} = \mathbf{x}_i$.

(2) The total volume under the surface of the function $k(\mathbf{x}, \mathbf{x}_i)$ is a constant.

And now comes the kernel trick.

13.9.1 *Kernel trick*

Specifying the kernel $k(\mathbf{x}, \mathbf{x}_i)$ is sufficient, we need never explicitly compute the weight vector $\mathbf{w}_{opt}$!

$$\sum_{j=1}^{\infty} w_j \cdot \phi_j(\mathbf{x}) + b = \sum_{i=1}^{N_s} \alpha_i \cdot t_i \cdot k(\mathbf{x}, \mathbf{x}_i) + b = 0 \tag{13.132}$$

Even though we assumed that the feature space could be of infinite dimensionality, defining the optimal hyperplane, consists of a finite number of terms that is equal to the number of training patterns used in the classifier. A support vector machine with a kernel is also referred to as a kernel machine.

For pattern classification, the machine is parametrized by an N-dimensional vector whose ith term is defined by the product $\alpha_i \cdot t_i$,

$$\mathbf{w}^T \cdot \Phi(\mathbf{x}) + b = \sum_{i=1}^{N} \alpha_i \cdot t_i \cdot \Phi^T(\mathbf{x}_i)\Phi(\mathbf{x}) + b = 0$$

$$\sum_{i=1}^{N} \alpha_i \cdot t_i \cdot k(\mathbf{x}, \mathbf{x}_i) + b = 0 \tag{13.133}$$

Kernel $k(\mathbf{x}_i, \mathbf{x}_j)$ needs to satisfy Mercer condition specified by Mercer's theorem [Haykin (2008)]. Mercer's theorem tells us only whether a candidate kernel is actually an inner-product kernel in some space and therefore admissible for use in a support vector machine, in this case the kernel is called the Mercer kernel. We may view $k(\mathbf{x}_i, \mathbf{x}_j)$ as the ij-th element of the $N \times N$ matrix

$$K = \begin{pmatrix} k(\mathbf{x}_1, \mathbf{x}_1) & k(\mathbf{x}_1, \mathbf{x}_2) & k(\mathbf{x}_1, \mathbf{x}_3) & \cdots & k(\mathbf{x}_1, \mathbf{x}_N) \\ k(\mathbf{x}_2, \mathbf{x}_1) & k(\mathbf{x}_2, \mathbf{x}_2) & k(\mathbf{x}_2, \mathbf{x}_3) & \cdots & k(\mathbf{x}_2, \mathbf{x}_N) \\ \vdots & \vdots & & \ddots & \vdots \\ k(\mathbf{x}_N, \mathbf{x}_1) & k(\mathbf{x}_N, \mathbf{x}_2) & k(\mathbf{x}_N, \mathbf{x}_3) & \cdots & k(\mathbf{x}_N, \mathbf{x}_N) \end{pmatrix} \tag{13.134}$$

A way to characterize Mercer kernels is to they give rise to positive matrices K [Haykin (2008)]. The matrix K is a nonnegative definite matrix called the kernel matrix; it is also referred to simply as the Gram with being nonnegative definite

$$\mathbf{a}^T K \mathbf{a} \geq 0.$$

for any real valued vector $\mathbf{a}$.

13.9.2 *Dual problem*

In the dual problem formulation we replace the scalar multiplication

$$\mathbf{x}_i^T \mathbf{x}_j = \langle \mathbf{x}_i | \mathbf{x}_j \rangle$$

by the kernel

$$k(\mathbf{x}_i, \mathbf{x}_j),$$

every thing else stays the same. Given the training sample $\{\mathbf{x}_i, t_i\}_{i=1}^N$, with $t_i \in \{-1, +1\}$ of linear separable patterns find the Lagrange multipliers $\{\alpha_i\}_{i=1}^N$ that maximize

$$Q(\alpha) = \sum_{i=1}^{N} \alpha_i - \frac{1}{2} \cdot \sum_{i=1}^{N} \sum_{j=1}^{N} \alpha_i \cdot \alpha_j \cdot t_i \cdot t_j \cdot k(\mathbf{x}_i, \mathbf{x}_j) \tag{13.135}$$

subject to constraints

$$\sum_{i=1}^{N} \alpha_i \cdot t_i = 0 \tag{13.136}$$

$$0 \leq \alpha_i \leq C, \quad i = 1, 2, \cdots, N \tag{13.137}$$

where C is a user specified positive parameter. A quadratic-programming (QP) solver can solve the maximization problem.

13.9.3 *Classification*

In order to classify data points, we evaluate the *sgn* that indicates us on which side of the decision boundary the query point is

$$o = sgn\left(\mathbf{w}^T \cdot \Phi(\mathbf{x}) + b\right)$$

with

$$sgn(net) = \begin{cases} 1 & \text{if} \quad net \geq 0 \\ -1 & \text{if} \quad net < 0 \end{cases},$$

$$o = sgn\left(\sum_{i=1}^{N_s} \alpha_i \cdot t_i \cdot \Phi(\mathbf{x}_i)^T \Phi(\mathbf{x}) + b\right) \tag{13.138}$$

using the kernel trick to avoid high or infinite dimension

$$o = sgn\left(\sum_{i=1}^{N} \alpha_i \cdot t_i \cdot k(\mathbf{x}, \mathbf{x}_i) + b\right) = sgn\left(\sum_{i=1}^{N_s} \alpha_i \cdot t_i \cdot k(\mathbf{x}, \mathbf{x}_i) + b\right)$$

with $N_s \ll N$ since for all not supported vectors $\alpha_i = 0$. The bias is given by

$$b = \frac{1}{N_s} \sum_{i=1}^{N_s} \left(t_i - \sum_{j=1}^{N_s} \alpha_j \cdot t_j \cdot k(\mathbf{x}_i, \mathbf{x}_j)\right). \tag{13.139}$$

13.9.3.1 *Example: XOR problem*

The XOR Problem is described by four vectors [Haykin (2008)], instead of 0 we will use (-1)

$$\mathbf{x}_1 = \begin{pmatrix} -1 \\ -1 \end{pmatrix}, \mathbf{x}_2 = \begin{pmatrix} 1 \\ 1 \end{pmatrix}, \mathbf{x}_3 = \begin{pmatrix} 1 \\ -1 \end{pmatrix}, \mathbf{x}_4 = \begin{pmatrix} 1 \\ 1 \end{pmatrix},$$

and the corresponding target of the two classes is indicated as

$$t_1 = -1, t_2 = 1, t_3 = 1, t_4 = -1.$$

We will use a polynomial kernel

$$k(\mathbf{x}_i, \mathbf{x}_j) = (1 + \mathbf{x}_i^T \mathbf{x}_j)^2$$

with

$$k(\mathbf{x}_i, \mathbf{x}_j) = 1 + x_{i1}^2 \cdot x_{j1}^2 + 2 \cdot x_{i1} \cdot x_{i2} \cdot x_{j1} \cdot x_{j2} + x_{i2}^2 \cdot x_{j2}^2 + 2 \cdot x_{i1} \cdot x_{j1} + 2 \cdot x_{i2} \cdot x_{j2}$$

with the feature vectors (not required, indeed for certain kernels the vector can have an infinite dimension)

$$\Phi(\mathbf{x}_i) = \begin{pmatrix} 1 \\ x_{i1}^2 \\ \sqrt{2} \cdot x_{i1} \cdot x_{i2} \\ x_{i2}^2 \\ \sqrt{2} \cdot x_{i1} \\ \sqrt{2} \cdot x_{i2} \end{pmatrix}, \quad \Phi(\mathbf{x}_j) = \begin{pmatrix} 1 \\ x_{j1}^2 \\ \sqrt{2} \cdot x_{j1} \cdot x_{j2} \\ x_{j2}^2 \\ \sqrt{2} \cdot x_{j1} \\ \sqrt{2} \cdot x_{j2} \end{pmatrix}$$

We obtain the Gram

$$K = \begin{pmatrix} k(\mathbf{x}_1,\mathbf{x}_1) & k(\mathbf{x}_1,\mathbf{x}_2) & k(\mathbf{x}_1,\mathbf{x}_3) & k(\mathbf{x}_1,\mathbf{x}_4) \\ k(\mathbf{x}_2,\mathbf{x}_1) & k(\mathbf{x}_2,\mathbf{x}_2) & k(\mathbf{x}_2,\mathbf{x}_3) & k(\mathbf{x}_2,\mathbf{x}_4) \\ k(\mathbf{x}_3,\mathbf{x}_1) & k(\mathbf{x}_3,\mathbf{x}_3) & k(\mathbf{x}_3,\mathbf{x}_3) & k(\mathbf{x}_4,\mathbf{x}_3) \\ k(\mathbf{x}_4,\mathbf{x}_1) & k(\mathbf{x}_4,\mathbf{x}_4) & k(\mathbf{x}_4,\mathbf{x}_3) & k(\mathbf{x}_4,\mathbf{x}_4) \end{pmatrix} = \begin{pmatrix} 9 & 1 & 1 & 1 \\ 1 & 9 & 1 & 1 \\ 1 & 1 & 9 & 1 \\ 1 & 1 & 1 & 9 \end{pmatrix}$$

The objective function for the dual form of optimization is

$$Q(\alpha) = \sum_{i=1}^{4} \alpha_i - \frac{1}{2} \cdot \sum_{i=1}^{4} \sum_{j=1}^{4} \alpha_i \cdot \alpha_j \cdot t_i \cdot t_j \cdot k(\mathbf{x}_i, \mathbf{x}_j)$$

$$Q(\alpha) = \alpha_1 + \alpha_2 + \alpha_3 + \alpha_4 - \frac{1}{2} \cdot (9\alpha_1^2 - 2\alpha_1\alpha_2 - 2\alpha_1\alpha_3 + 2\alpha_1\alpha_4$$

$$9\alpha_2^2 + 2\alpha_2\alpha_3 - 2\alpha_2\alpha_4 + 9\alpha_3^2 - 2\alpha_3\alpha_4 + 9\alpha_4^2)$$

We maximize the objective function $Q(\alpha)$ by determining the partial derivatives

$$\frac{\partial Q(\alpha)}{\partial \alpha_1} = 1 - 9 \cdot \alpha 1 + \alpha 2 + \alpha 3 - \alpha 4 = 0$$

$$\frac{\partial Q(\alpha)}{\partial \alpha_2} = 1 - +\alpha 1 - 9 \cdot \alpha 2 - \alpha 3 + \alpha 4 = 0$$

$$\frac{\partial Q(\alpha)}{\partial \alpha_3} = 1 + \alpha 1 - \alpha 2 - 9 \cdot \alpha 3 + \alpha 4 = 0$$

$$\frac{\partial Q(\alpha)}{\partial \alpha_4} = 1 - \alpha 1 + \alpha 2 + \alpha 3 - 9 \cdot \alpha 4 = 0$$

that lead to four equation that can be solve by

$$\begin{pmatrix} 9 & -1 & -1 & 1 \\ -1 & 9 & 1 & -1 \\ -1 & 1 & 9 & -1 \\ 1 & -1 & -1 & 9 \end{pmatrix} \cdot \begin{pmatrix} \alpha_1 \\ \alpha_2 \\ \alpha_3 \\ \alpha_4 \end{pmatrix} = \begin{pmatrix} 1 \\ 1 \\ 1 \\ 1 \end{pmatrix}$$

with the optimum values of the Lagrange multipliers

$$\alpha_{opt,1} = \alpha_{opt,2} = \alpha_{opt,3} = \alpha_{opt,4} = \frac{1}{8}$$

with all input vectors being support vectors. To compute the output

(1) we compute the bias

$$b = \frac{1}{4} \sum_{i=1}^{4} \left(t_i - \sum_{j=1}^{4} \alpha_j \cdot t_j \cdot k(\mathbf{x}_i, \mathbf{x}_j) \right), \tag{13.140}$$

$$b = \frac{1}{4} \left(\cdot \left(-1 - \frac{1}{8} \cdot (-9 + 1 + 1 - 1) \right) + \left(1 - \frac{1}{8} \cdot (-1 + 9 + 1 - 1) \right) + \right.$$

$$\left. \left(1 - \frac{1}{8} \cdot (-1 + 1 + 9 - 1) \right) + \left(-1 - \frac{1}{8} \cdot (-1 + 1 + 1 - 9) \right) \right) = 0.$$

In this case we had an optimum Lagrange multipliers $\alpha_{opt,i}$, se we could as well use the form

$$b_{opt} = 1 - \sum_{i=1}^{N} \alpha_{opt,i} \cdot t_i \cdot \cdot k(\mathbf{x}_i, \mathbf{x}^{(s)}), \quad for \ \ t^{(s)} = 1.$$

(2) then the output

$$o = sgn\left(\sum_{i=1}^{4} \alpha_i \cdot t_i \cdot k(\mathbf{x}, \mathbf{x}_i) + b\right). \tag{13.141}$$

For the query vector

$$\mathbf{x}_q = \begin{pmatrix} -1 \\ -1 \end{pmatrix}$$

we get

$$o = sgn\left(\frac{1}{8} \cdot (-9 + 1 + 1 - 1)\right) = sgn(-1) = -1$$

Since the feature vector $\Phi(\mathbf{x}_i)$ has a finite dimension, we can determine the hyperplane (line) by

$$\mathbf{w} = \sum_{i=1}^{4} \alpha_i \cdot t_i \cdot \Phi(\mathbf{x}_i)$$

$$\mathbf{w}_{opt} = \frac{1}{8}\left(-\phi(\mathbf{x}_1) + \phi(\mathbf{x}_2) + \phi(\mathbf{x}_3) - \phi(\mathbf{x}_4)\right)$$

and

$$\mathbf{w}_{opt} = \begin{pmatrix} 0 \\ 0 \\ -\frac{1}{\sqrt{2}} \\ 0 \\ 0 \\ 0 \end{pmatrix}.$$

With bias zero

$$\mathbf{w}_{opt}^T \cdot \Phi(\mathbf{x}) + 0 = 0$$

we get the hyperplane (line)

$$\left(0, 0, -\frac{1}{\sqrt{2}}, 0, 0, 0\right) \cdot \begin{pmatrix} 1 \\ x_1^2 \\ \sqrt{2} \cdot x_1 \cdot x_2 \\ x_2^2 \\ \sqrt{2} \cdot x_1 \\ \sqrt{2} \cdot x_2 \end{pmatrix} = -x_1 \cdot x_2 = 0.$$

13.10 Kernel Function

The kernel function is defined as

$$k(x,x') = \phi(x)^T \cdot \phi(x') = \sum_{i=1}^{M} \phi_i(x) \cdot \phi_i(x') \tag{13.142}$$

with basis function $\phi_i(x)$ [Bishop (2006)]. Consider a kernel function n a two dimensional space given by

$$k(\mathbf{x},\mathbf{z}) = (\mathbf{x}^T \cdot \mathbf{z})^2 = (x_1 \cdot z_1 + x_2 \cdot z_2)^2 = x_1^2 \cdot z_1^2 + 2 \cdot x_1 \cdot x_2 \cdot z_1 \cdot z_2 + x_2^2 \cdot z_2^2$$

$$k(\mathbf{x},\mathbf{z}) = (\mathbf{x}^T \cdot \mathbf{z})^2 = (x_1^2, \sqrt{2} \cdot x_1 \cdot x_2, x_2^2) \cdot (z_1^2, \sqrt{2} \cdot z_1 \cdot z_2, z_2^2)^T$$

$$k(\mathbf{x},\mathbf{z}) = (\mathbf{x}^T \cdot \mathbf{z})^2 = \phi(\mathbf{x})^T \cdot \phi(\mathbf{z})$$

with

$$\phi(\mathbf{x}) = (x_1^2, \sqrt{2} \cdot x_1 \cdot x_2, x_2^2)^T$$

A way to characterize Mercer kernels is to they give rise to positive matrices K [Haykin (2008)]. The matrix K is a nonnegative definite matrix called the kernel matrix; it is also referred to simply as the Gram with being nonnegative definite. However this condition tells us only whether a candidate kernel is actually an inner-product kernel in some space and therefore admissible for use in a support vector machine, however it says nothing about how to construct the functions. One powerful technique for constructing new kernels is to build them out of simpler kernels as building blocks.

13.10.1 *Gaussian kernel*

$$k(\mathbf{x},\mathbf{x'}) = \exp\left(-\frac{\|\mathbf{x}-\mathbf{x'}\|^2}{2 \cdot \sigma^2}\right)$$

with

$$\|\mathbf{x}-\mathbf{x'}\|^2 = \mathbf{x}^T \cdot \mathbf{x} + (\mathbf{x'})^T \cdot \mathbf{x'} - 2 \cdot \mathbf{x}^T \cdot \mathbf{x'}$$

and we get

$$k(\mathbf{x},\mathbf{x'}) = \exp\left(\frac{\mathbf{x}^T \cdot \mathbf{x}}{2 \cdot \sigma^2}\right) \cdot \exp\left(\frac{\mathbf{x}^T \cdot \mathbf{x'}}{\sigma^2}\right) \cdot \exp\left(\frac{\mathbf{x'}^T \cdot \mathbf{x'}}{2 \cdot \sigma^2}\right)$$

The feature vector that corresponds to the Gaussian kernel has infinite dimensionality

13.10.2 *Sigmoidal kernel*

A kernel function is the sigmoidal kernel given by

$$k(\mathbf{x}, \mathbf{x'}) = \tanh(a \cdot \mathbf{x}^T \cdot \mathbf{x'} + b) \tag{13.143}$$

whose Gram matrix in general is not positive semidefinite. This form of kernel has, however, been used in practice [Cortes and Vapnik (1995)], [Haykin (2008)], because it gives kernel expansions such as the support vector machine and it is similar to the one used in neural network models.

Chapter 14

Linear-Algebra Based Quantum Machine Learning

Linear algebra-based quantum machine learning is based on quantum gates that describe quantum basic linear algebra subroutines. These subroutines can exhibit theoretical exponential speed ups over the classical counterparts and are essential for machine learning. The quantum basic linear algebra subroutines represent a quantum coprocessor for extensive and nontractable computation routines in machine learning. Such 'mathematical' quantum coprocessor can be used with a conventional computer.

14.1 Quantum Algorithm for Linear Systems of Equations

The algorithm is one of the main fundamental algorithms expected to provide a speedup over their classical counterparts. In the honor of its inventors Aram Harrow, Avinatan Hassidim, and Seth Lloyd, it is called the HHL algorithm. HHL is going to be one of the most useful subroutines for any quantum machine learning algorithm because almost all machine learning uses some form of a linear system of equations. The algorithm has already been implemented in existing quantum computers/devices [Pan *et al.* (2014)].

14.1.1 *Motivation*

For an invertible complex matrix $n \times n$ A and a complex vector $\mathbf{b}$

$$A \cdot \mathbf{x} = \mathbf{b} \tag{14.1}$$

we want to find $\mathbf{x}$. If A is Hermitian $A^* = A$ (for real matrix $A^T = A$ then

$$U^* \cdot A \cdot U = \Lambda = diag(\lambda_1, \lambda_2, \cdots, \lambda_n) \tag{14.2}$$

and

$$A^{-1} = U \cdot \Lambda^{-1} \cdot U^* = U \cdot diag(\lambda_1^{-1}, \lambda_2^{-1}, \cdots, \lambda_n^{-1}) \cdot U^* \tag{14.3}$$

Where U is a orthonormal matrix composed of eigenvectors $\mathbf{u}_1, \mathbf{u}_!, \cdots \mathbf{u}_n$ and Λ represents the corresponding eigenvalues of A. We can assume A is Hermitian. In the case A is not Hermitian, we define

$$A' = \begin{pmatrix} 0 & A \\ A^* & 0 \end{pmatrix}, \quad \mathbf{b}' = \begin{pmatrix} 0 \\ b \end{pmatrix}, \quad \mathbf{x}' = \begin{pmatrix} x \\ 0 \end{pmatrix}. \tag{14.4}$$

and

$$A' \cdot \mathbf{x}' = \mathbf{b}'. \tag{14.5}$$

A can be represented by the spectral decomposition as

$$A = \lambda_1 \cdot |u_1\rangle\langle u_1| + \lambda_2 \cdot |u_2\rangle\langle u_2| + \cdots + \lambda_n \cdot |u_n\rangle\langle u_n|. \tag{14.6}$$

and

$$A^{-1} = \frac{1}{\lambda_1} \cdot |u_1\rangle\langle u_1| + \frac{1}{\lambda_2} \cdot |u_2\rangle\langle u_2| + \cdots + \frac{1}{\lambda_n} \cdot |u_n\rangle\langle u_n|. \tag{14.7}$$

It follows

$$A \cdot |u_j\rangle = \lambda_j |u_j\rangle \tag{14.8}$$

and writing $|b\rangle$ as a linear combination of the eigenvectors of A

$$|b\rangle = \sum_j |u_j\rangle\langle u_j|b\rangle \tag{14.9}$$

leads to

$$A \cdot |b\rangle = \sum_j \lambda_j |u_j\rangle\langle u_j|b\rangle \tag{14.10}$$

and

$$A^{-1} \cdot |b\rangle = \sum_j \lambda_j^{-1} |u_j\rangle\langle u_j|b\rangle. \tag{14.11}$$

14.1.2 *Constraints for matrix multiplication and inversion*

In quantum we can efficiently determine the eigenvectors and eigenvalues by the Kitaev's phase estimation algorithm and the Hamiltonian simulation [Harrow *et al.* (2009)]. We will compute

$$\mathbf{x} = A \cdot \mathbf{b} \tag{14.12}$$

or

$$\mathbf{x} = A^{-1} \cdot \mathbf{b} \tag{14.13}$$

with length one vectors, $|b\rangle$ represented by $\log_2 n$ qubits with

$$|b\rangle = \frac{\sum_{i=1}^{n} b_i |i\rangle}{\| \sum_{i=1}^{n} b_i |i\rangle \|} \tag{14.14}$$

and

$$|x\rangle = \frac{\sum_{i=1}^{n} x_i |i\rangle}{\| \sum_{i=1}^{n} x_i |i\rangle \|}. \tag{14.15}$$

With the constraints:

- The vectors $|b\rangle$, $|x\rangle$ have the length one in the l_2 norm.
- $|b\rangle$ has to be prepared efficiently with the cost $\log(n)$. For example being constant with $W_{\log_2 n} \cdot |0\rangle$.
- The matrix A is sparse.
- For the output we are interested in the global properties of $|x\rangle$ rather than the coefficients x_i. For example we can estimate the expectation value of an observable M

$$\langle M \rangle = \langle x | M | x \rangle. \tag{14.16}$$

We will use the shorthand notation (Bachmann-Landau notation) since it mostly used in the related literature with

$$\tilde{O}(f(n)) = O(f(n) poly(\log(f(n)))) = O(f(n) \log(f(n))^k) \tag{14.17}$$

for some k ignoring logarithmic factors. The point of that notation is to only show the important part of the asymptotic complexity. If the constraints are fulfilled then we can find the estimate $\langle x|M|x\rangle$ in $\tilde{O}(\log n)$. Gauss elimination requires $O(n^3)$ and approximate solution for a sparse matrix via conjugate gradient descent requires $\tilde{O}(n)$ [Reif (1998)]. Taking into account the constraints the HHL algorithm on a quantum computer is exponentially faster than any algorithm that solves linear systems on the classical computer [Harrow *et al.* (2009)].

14.1.3 *HHL algorithm in machine learning*

HHL algorithm is one of the most useful subroutines for any quantum machine learning algorithm because almost all machine learning algorithms involve matrix multiplication or some form of optimization in which a matrix is inverted. Many machine learning algorithms fulfill the required constraints. The HHL algorithm plays an essential role in the following algorithms:

- Optimization algorithms that also use the Hessian matrix, such as Newton's method, such as deep neural networks. Usually the computational complexity is often a major limitation of Newton's method. With the Hessian matrix H the update rule as

$$\mathbf{x}_{t+1} = \mathbf{x}_t - H_t^{-1} \cdot \nabla f(\mathbf{x}_t). \tag{14.18}$$

  Newton's method converges quickly asymptotically and does not exhibit the zigzagging behavior that sometimes characterizes the method of steepest descent. Iteratively updating the approximation and jumping to the minimum of the approximation can reach the critical point much faster than gradient descent.
- Support vector Machines, maximizing the objective function with the optimum values of the Lagrange multipliers.
- Linear Regression with

$$\left(X^T \cdot X\right)^{-1} \cdot X^T \cdot \mathbf{t} = \mathbf{w}. \tag{14.19}$$

In the firs step $X^T \cdot \mathbf{t}$ is computed, in the second step the matrix inversion $\left(X^T \cdot X\right)^{-1}$ is applied to the result of $X^T \cdot \mathbf{t}$. In next section we introduce the Hamiltonian simulation that forms a basic building block of the HHL algorithm.

14.1.4 *Hamiltonian simulation*

A general solution of the Schroedinger equation (for the time-independent Hamiltonian) represents the unitary evolution with

$$\mathbf{x}(t) = e^{-i \cdot t \cdot H} \cdot \mathbf{x}(0) = U_t \cdot \mathbf{x}(0) \tag{14.20}$$

where $U_t = e^{-i \cdot t \cdot H}$ is the evolutionary operator, which can be represented by a unitary matrix with H being a Hamiltonian operator represented by a Hermitian matrix. The process of implementing a given Hamiltonian evolution on quantum computer is called Hamiltonian simulation [Lloyd (1996)]

$$|x(t)\rangle = e^{-i \cdot t \cdot H} \cdot |x(0)\rangle = U_t \cdot |x(0)\rangle. \tag{14.21}$$

The challenge is due to the fact that the application of matrix exponentials are computationally expensive [Schuld and Petruccione (2018)]. The dimension of the Hilbert space grows exponentially with the number of qubits, and thus any operator will be of exponential dimension. Hamiltonian simulation is very closely related to the question of how to decompose a unitary operator. Finding reliable and accurate methods to compute the matrix exponential is difficult, and this is still a topic of considerable current research. Our goal is that given a Hamiltonian H and a quantum state $|x(0)\rangle$ we want to find an algorithm which implements the evolution efficiently so that the final state $|\tilde{x}(t)\rangle$ is close to the desired state $|x(t)\rangle$

$$\| |x(t)\rangle - |\tilde{x}(t)\rangle \| < \epsilon. \tag{14.22}$$

14.1.4.1 *Taylor series*

The exponential of H is given by the power series

$$e^H = \sum_{k=0}^{\infty} \frac{1}{k!} H^k \tag{14.23}$$

with $H^0 = I$ and

$$e^{-i \cdot t \cdot H} = \sum_{k=0}^{\infty} \frac{1}{k!} (-i \cdot t \cdot H)^k \,. \tag{14.24}$$

For practical implementations, the series has to be truncated

$$e^{-i \cdot t \cdot H} = \sum_{k=0}^{R} \frac{1}{k!} (-i \cdot t \cdot H)^k \tag{14.25}$$

where the bigger the R, the more accurate the simulation.

14.1.4.2 *Diagonalization*

If the matrix H is diagonal

$$H = \begin{pmatrix} a_1 & 0 & \dots & 0 \\ 0 & a_2 & \dots & 0 \\ \vdots & \vdots & \ddots & \vdots \\ 0 & 0 & \dots & a_n \end{pmatrix} \tag{14.26}$$

then its exponential can be obtained by exponentiating each entry on the main diagonal

$$e^H = \begin{pmatrix} e^{a_1} & 0 & \dots & 0 \\ 0 & e^{a_2} & \dots & 0 \\ \vdots & \vdots & \ddots & \vdots \\ 0 & 0 & \dots & e^{a_n} \end{pmatrix} \tag{14.27}$$

This result also allows one to exponentiate diagonalizable matrices. If

$$H = U \cdot D \cdot U^{-1} \tag{14.28}$$

and D is diagonal, then

$$e^H = U \cdot e^D \cdot U^{-1} \tag{14.29}$$

14.1.4.3 *Product formulas*

If the hamiltonian H can be written as

$$H = \sum_{k=1}^{L} H_k \tag{14.30}$$

and H_k commute,

$$[H_j, H_k] = 0, \quad for\ all\ j, k$$

then

$$e^{-i\cdot t\cdot H} = e^{-i\cdot t\cdot H_1} \cdot e^{-i\cdot t\cdot H_2} \cdot \cdots e^{-i\cdot t\cdot H_L} \quad for\ all\ t. \tag{14.31}$$

Tensor product: If the hamiltonian H_T that acts on two qubits without interaction we can write it as a sum of two Hamiltonians that each acts on one of the two qubits

$$H_T = H_1 \otimes I_1 + I_1 \otimes H_2 \tag{14.32}$$

then

$$[H_1 \otimes I_1, I_1 \otimes H_2] = 0$$

$$e^{-i\cdot t\cdot H} = e^{-i\cdot t\cdot H_1} \otimes e^{-i\cdot t\cdot H_2} = e^{-i\cdot t\cdot (H_1\otimes I_1)} \cdot e^{-i\cdot t\cdot (I_1\otimes H_2)} \quad for\ all\ t. \tag{14.33}$$

this case can be generalized to more than two qubits.

General case: For general case of non-commuting H_k

$$[H_j, H_k] \neq 0$$

$$e^{-i\cdot t\cdot H} \neq e^{-i\cdot t\cdot H_1} \cdot e^{-i\cdot t\cdot H_2} \cdot \cdots e^{-i\cdot t\cdot H_L} \quad for\ all\ t. \tag{14.34}$$

However for non-commuting H_k the following asymptotic Suzuki-Trotter formula (Lie product formula) is true for any real t.

$$e^{-i\cdot t\cdot H} = \lim_{m\to\infty} \left(e^{-i\cdot t\cdot H_1/m} \cdot e^{-i\cdot t\cdot H_2/m} \cdot \cdots e^{-i\cdot t\cdot H_L/m}\right)^m \tag{14.35}$$

or we can write equivalently

$$e^{-i\cdot t\cdot H} = e^{-i\cdot t\cdot H_1} \cdot e^{-i\cdot t\cdot H_2} \cdot \cdots e^{-i\cdot t\cdot H_L} + O(t^2) \tag{14.36}$$

For small t the factorization is approximately valid,

$$U_t = e^{-i\cdot t\cdot H} \approx e^{-i\cdot t\cdot H_1} \cdot e^{-i\cdot t\cdot H_2} \cdot \cdots e^{-i\cdot t\cdot H_L}. \tag{14.37}$$

If we want to simulate the Hamiltonian evolution on a quantum computer, we have to preform a sequence of small steps, the smaller there more often we need to preform the simulation. It follows that with big T and a Hermitian matrix A

$$A = \sum_{k=1}^{L} A_k, \quad \Delta t = \frac{1}{T}, \tag{14.38}$$

$$U_{\Delta t} = e^{2\cdot\pi\cdot i\cdot\Delta t\cdot A} \approx e^{2\cdot\pi\cdot i\cdot\Delta t\cdot A_1} \cdot e^{2\cdot\pi\cdot i\cdot\Delta t\cdot A_2} \cdot\cdots e^{2\cdot\pi i\cdot\Delta t\cdot A_L}, \tag{14.39}$$

and

$$U^t := e^{\frac{2\cdot\pi\cdot i\cdot A\cdot t}{T}} \approx e^{\frac{2\cdot\pi\cdot i\cdot A_1\cdot t}{T}} \cdot e^{\frac{2\cdot\pi\cdot i\cdot A_2\cdot t}{T}} \cdot\cdots e^{\frac{2\cdot\pi\cdot i\cdot A_L\cdot t}{T}}. \tag{14.40}$$

according to Masuo Suzuki [Suzuki (1985)]. Decomposition formulas of exponential operators and Lie exponentials with some applications to quantum mechanics and statistical physics [Lloyd (1996)].

14.1.4.4 *Sparse Hamiltonian*

Hamiltonian simulation can be implemented efficiently for large n if the hermitian matrix H is sparse. A $n \times n$ matrix H is s-sparse if it has at most s non-zero elements in each row and column. A $n \times n$ matrix H is s-sparse is sparse, if $s = O((\log(n))^k)$ for some constant k. The entries of a matrix H are efficiently row computable if, given the indices i, j, we can obtain the entries $H_{i,j}$ efficiently in $O(s)$ time, where s is the sparsity as defined above. The algorithm is then linear in s. Given such a unitary oracle access to an s-sparse Hermitian matrix H, then the cost of the Hamiltonian simulation are $\tilde{O}(\log(n)\cdot s^2\cdot t)$. For a sparse matrix H, there is a logarithmic dependency of n [Berry *et al.* (2006)].

14.1.4.5 *Hamiltonian simulation and quantum chemistry*

Hamiltonian simulation makes it possible to analyze the behavior of complex physical systems. In quantum chemistry, the evolution of large molecular Hamiltonians can be simulated from a determined initial state. Observable properties can be estimated and compared with the experimental results, leading to new predictions [O'Malley *et al.* (2016)].

14.1.5 *Eigenvalue estimation*

Given a unitary operator U with an eigenvector $|u\rangle$ with an unknown eigenvalue $e^{2\cdot\pi\cdot i\cdot\theta}$ Kitaev's phase algorithm can determine the phase θ [Kitaev

(1996)], [Kaye *et al.* (2007)].

$$U \cdot |u\rangle = e^{2\cdot\pi\cdot i\cdot\theta} \cdot |u\rangle. \tag{14.41}$$

With Hamiltonian simulation

$$U^t = e^{\frac{2\cdot\pi\cdot i\cdot A\cdot t}{T}} \approx e^{\frac{2\cdot\pi\cdot i\cdot A_1\cdot t}{T}} \cdot e^{\frac{2\cdot\pi\cdot i\cdot A_2\cdot t}{T}} \cdot \cdots \cdot e^{\frac{2\cdot\pi\cdot i\cdot A_L\cdot t}{T}} \tag{14.42}$$

and

$$U^t \cdot |u_j\rangle = e^{\frac{2\cdot\pi\cdot i\cdot\lambda_j}{T}}|u_j\rangle. \tag{14.43}$$

If

$$A|u_j\rangle = \lambda_j|u_j\rangle \tag{14.44}$$

then

$$U^t \cdot |u_j\rangle = e^{\frac{2\cdot\pi\cdot i\cdot A\cdot t}{T}}|u_j\rangle = e^{\frac{2\cdot\pi\cdot i\cdot\lambda_j}{T}}|u_j\rangle. \tag{14.45}$$

We define conditional Hamiltonian evolution operator

$$cU = \sum_{t=0}^{T-1} |t\rangle\langle t| \otimes U^t. \tag{14.46}$$

With $T = 4$ and $U^t = e^{\frac{2\cdot\pi\cdot i\cdot A\cdot t}{4}}$ we get,

$$U^0 = I, \quad U^1 = e^{\frac{2\cdot\pi\cdot i\cdot A\cdot 1}{4}}, \quad U^2 = e^{\frac{2\cdot\pi\cdot i\cdot A\cdot 2}{4}}, \quad U^3 = e^{\frac{2\cdot\pi\cdot i\cdot A\cdot 3}{4}}$$

and

$$cU = \sum_{t=0}^{3} |t\rangle\langle t| \otimes U^t =$$

$$= |00\rangle\langle 00| \otimes I + |01\rangle\langle 01| \otimes e^{\frac{\pi\cdot i\cdot A}{2}} + |10\rangle\langle 01| \otimes e^{\pi\cdot i\cdot A} + +|11\rangle\langle 11| \otimes e^{\frac{\pi\cdot i\cdot A\cdot 3}{3}}. \tag{14.47}$$

Knowing u_j with $m = \log_2 T$,

$$cU \cdot W_m(|0^{\otimes m}\rangle) \cdot |u_j\rangle = cU \cdot \sum_{t=0}^{n} \frac{1}{\sqrt{T}}|t\rangle|u_j\rangle \tag{14.48}$$

we preform the conditional Hamiltonian evolution

$$cU \cdot \sum_{t=0}^{n} \frac{1}{\sqrt{T}}|t\rangle|u_j\rangle = \frac{1}{\sqrt{T}} \sum_{t=0}^{T-1} e^{\frac{2\cdot\pi\cdot i\cdot\lambda_j}{T}}|t\rangle|u_j\rangle. \tag{14.49}$$

We apply QFT on the control qubits with $m = \log_2 T$,

$$F_m\left(\frac{1}{\sqrt{T}}\sum_{t=0}^{T-1} e^{\frac{2\cdot\pi\cdot i\cdot\lambda_j}{T}}|t\rangle\right)|u_j\rangle = \frac{1}{T}\sum_{k=0}^{T-1}\left(\sum_{t=0}^{T-1} e^{\frac{2\cdot\pi\cdot i\cdot(\lambda_j-k)}{T}}\right)|k\rangle|u_j\rangle \tag{14.50}$$

$$\alpha_{k|j} = \frac{1 - e^{\frac{2\cdot\pi\cdot i\cdot(\lambda_j - k)\cdot T}{T}}}{T \cdot \left(1 - e^{\frac{2\cdot\pi\cdot i\cdot(\lambda_j - k)}{T}}\right)} \tag{14.51}$$

$$F_m\left(\frac{1}{\sqrt{T}}\sum_{t=0}^{T-1} e^{\frac{2\cdot\pi\cdot i\cdot\lambda_j}{T}}|t\rangle\right)|u_j\rangle = \sum_{k=0}^{T-1}\alpha_{k|j}\cdot|k\rangle|u_j\rangle \tag{14.52}$$

In the eigenvalue estimation the first register is measured where is the binary representation $\lambda_j = k/T$. We do not measure the first register and relabel $|k\rangle$ with $|\tilde{\lambda}_{k|j}\rangle$ resulting in

$$F_m\left(\frac{1}{\sqrt{T}}\sum_{t=0}^{T-1} e^{\frac{2\cdot\pi\cdot i\cdot\lambda_j}{T}}|t\rangle\right)|u_j\rangle = \sum_{k=0}^{T-1}\alpha_{k|j}\cdot|\tilde{\lambda}_{k|j}\rangle|u_j\rangle \tag{14.53}$$

14.1.5.1 *Unknown eigenvector*

We do not need to know the eigenvector $|u_j\rangle$ of U. Since a quantum state $|b\rangle$ can be decomposed into an orthogonal basis

$$|b\rangle = \sum_j |u_j\rangle\langle u_j|b\rangle = \sum_j \beta_j|u_j\rangle \tag{14.54}$$

We represent $|b\rangle$ as

$$|b\rangle = \sum_i b_i|i\rangle \tag{14.55}$$

The accuracy of the approximation of this will depend far more critically on an accurate estimation of the eigenvalues that are close to 0 rather than those that are far from 0. so that rather than using 'bins' of fixed width for approximating the phases we specify variable 'bins' so that we can have vastly increased accuracy close to 0 phase [Harrow *et al.* (2009)]. We use a cost function which minimizes a penalty for not correct answers

$$|\psi_0\rangle = \sqrt{\frac{2}{T}}\sum_{t=0}^{T-1}\sin\frac{\pi\cdot(t+1/2)}{T}|t\rangle \tag{14.56}$$

and

$$cU\cdot|\psi_0\rangle|b\rangle = \sqrt{\frac{2}{T}}\sum_{j=1}^{n}\beta_j\left(\sum_{t=0}^{T-1} e^{\frac{2\cdot\pi\cdot i\cdot\lambda_j}{T}}\sin\frac{\pi\cdot(t+1/2)}{T}|t\rangle\right)|u_j\rangle \tag{14.57}$$

We apply QFT o the control qubits,

$$F_{\tilde{m}}\left(\sqrt{\frac{2}{T}}\sum_{j=1}^{n}\beta_j\left(\sum_{t=0}^{T-1} e^{\frac{2\cdot\pi\cdot i\cdot\lambda_j}{T}}\sin\frac{\pi\cdot(t+1/2)}{T}|t\rangle\right)\right)|u_j\rangle =$$

$$\sum_{j=1}^{n} \beta_j \sum_{k=0}^{T-1} \left(\sqrt{\frac{2}{T}} \sum_{t=0}^{T-1} e^{\frac{2\cdot\pi\cdot i\cdot(\lambda_j - k)}{T}} \sin \frac{\pi \cdot (t+1/2)}{T} \right) |k\rangle|u_j\rangle \tag{14.58}$$

with

$$\alpha_{k|j} = \left(\sqrt{\frac{2}{T}} \sum_{t=0}^{T-1} e^{\frac{2\cdot\pi\cdot i\cdot(\lambda_j - k)}{T}} \sin \frac{\pi \cdot (t+1/2)}{T} \right) \tag{14.59}$$

we get as before

$$\sum_{j=1}^{n} \beta_j \sum_{k=0}^{T-1} \alpha_{k|j} |k\rangle|u_j\rangle = \sum_{j=1}^{n} \beta_j \sum_{k=0}^{T-1} \alpha_{k|j} \cdot |\tilde{\lambda}_{k|j}\rangle|u_j\rangle \tag{14.60}$$

with the following relation, if $|\alpha_{k|j}|$ is large then $\lambda_j \approx \tilde{\lambda}_{k|j}$. By linearity

$$\sum_{j=1}^{n} \beta_j \sum_{k=0}^{T-1} \alpha_{k|j} \cdot |\tilde{\lambda}_{k|j}|u_j\rangle = \sum_{j=1}^{n} \sum_{k=0}^{T-1} \beta_j \cdot \alpha_{k|j} \cdot |\tilde{\lambda}_{k|j}\rangle|u_j\rangle \tag{14.61}$$

For each value j the values $\tilde{\lambda}_{k|j}$ approximate the true value λ_j. For simplicity we assume

$$\sum_{j=1}^{n} \beta_j \sum_{k=0}^{T-1} \alpha_{k|j} \cdot |\tilde{\lambda}_{k|j}|u_j\rangle \approx \sum_{j=1}^{n} \beta_j \cdot |\tilde{\lambda}_j\rangle|u_j\rangle. \tag{14.62}$$

14.1.6 *Rotation conditioned on the eigenvalue*

The controlled $R(\tilde{\lambda}^{-1})$ rotation extracts the eigenvalues and executes the rotation. The rotation is conditioned on the value the binary representation of the eigenvalue. For each binary value we will have a different operator. A rotation by an angle α is represented by the unitary operator R

$$R = \begin{pmatrix} \cos\alpha & -\sin\alpha \\ \sin\alpha & \cos\alpha \end{pmatrix}. \tag{14.63}$$

with the relation

$$\alpha = \arccos\left(\frac{C}{\tilde{\lambda}}\right) \tag{14.64}$$

with C being a constant of normalization. For each different value we will have a different rotation. To do this we add an auxiliary state $|0\rangle$

$$\sum_{j=1}^{n} \beta_j \cdot |\tilde{\lambda}_j\rangle|u_j\rangle|0\rangle \tag{14.65}$$

and preform the controlled rotation on the auxiliary state. We preform a conditioned rotation. For each eigenvalue indicates a special rotation we have

$$\sum_{j=1}^{n}\left(\beta_j \cdot |\tilde{\lambda}_j\rangle|u_j\rangle(|0\rangle)R(\tilde{\lambda}_j^{-1})\right) =$$

$$\sum_{j=1}^{n}\left(\beta_j \cdot |\tilde{\lambda}_j\rangle|u_j\rangle\left(\frac{C}{\tilde{\lambda}_j}|1\rangle + \sqrt{1-\frac{C^2}{\tilde{\lambda}_j^2}}|0\rangle\right)\right). \tag{14.66}$$

We uncompute the phase estimation procedure with $IF_m = F_m^*$, cU^* resulting in the state

$$|0\rangle\sum_{j=1}^{n}\left(\beta_j \cdot |u_j\rangle\left(\frac{C}{\tilde{\lambda}_j}|1\rangle + \sqrt{1-\frac{C^2}{\tilde{\lambda}_j^2}}|0\rangle\right)\right) =$$

$$|0\rangle\sum_{j=1}^{n}\left(C \cdot \frac{\beta_j}{\tilde{\lambda}_j}|u_j\rangle|1\rangle + \sqrt{1-\frac{C^2}{\tilde{\lambda}_j^2}} \cdot \beta_j|u_j\rangle|0\rangle\right). \tag{14.67}$$

It is

$$|x\rangle = A^{-1}|b\rangle = \sum_{j=1}^{n}\frac{\beta_j}{\tilde{\lambda}_j}|u_j\rangle \tag{14.68}$$

so by measuring the third auxiliary register with the result 0 we get

$$|0\rangle\sum_{j=1}^{n}\left(\sqrt{1-\frac{C^2}{\tilde{\lambda}_j^2}} \cdot \beta_j|u_j\rangle\right) \tag{14.69}$$

and with the result 1

$$C \cdot |0\rangle\sum_{j=1}^{n}\left(\frac{\beta_j}{\tilde{\lambda}_j}|u_j\rangle\right) \approx C \cdot |0\rangle|x\rangle. \tag{14.70}$$

We have to select the outcome of the measurement 1 modulo the constant factor for normalization. We can preform amplitude amplification to boost the success probability instead of measuring and post selecting.

14.1.7 *Rotation for matrix multiplication*

To compute

$$\mathbf{x} = A \cdot \mathbf{b} \tag{14.71}$$

The controlled $R(\tilde{\lambda})$ rotation extracts the eigenvalues and executes the rotation. For each eigenvalue indicates a special rotation we can have

$$\sum_{j=1}^{n} \left(\beta_j \cdot |\tilde{\lambda}_j\rangle |u_j\rangle (|0\rangle) R(\tilde{\lambda}_j) \right) =$$

$$\sum_{j=1}^{n} \left(\beta_j \cdot |\tilde{\lambda}_j\rangle |u_j\rangle \left(C \cdot \tilde{\lambda}_j |1\rangle + \sqrt{1 - C^2 \cdot \tilde{\lambda}_j^2} |0\rangle \right) \right). \tag{14.72}$$

We uncompute the phase estimation procedure with $IF_m = F_m^*$, cU^* resulting in the state

$$|0\rangle \sum_{j=1}^{n} \left(\beta_j \cdot |u_j\rangle \left(C \cdot \tilde{\lambda}_j |1\rangle + \sqrt{1 - C^2 \cdot \tilde{\lambda}_j^2} |0\rangle \right) \right) =$$

$$|0\rangle \sum_{j=1}^{n} \left(C \cdot \ \beta_j \cdot \tilde{\lambda}_j |u_j\rangle |1\rangle + \sqrt{1 - \ C^2 \cdot \tilde{\lambda}_j^2} \cdot \beta_j |u_j\rangle |0\rangle \right). \tag{14.73}$$

It is

$$|x\rangle = A|b\rangle = \sum_{j=1}^{n} \beta_j \cdot \tilde{\lambda}_j |u_j\rangle \tag{14.74}$$

so by measuring the third auxiliary register with the result 1

$$C \cdot |0\rangle \sum_{j=1}^{n} \left(\beta_j \cdot \tilde{\lambda}_j |u_j\rangle \right) \approx C \cdot |0\rangle |x\rangle \tag{14.75}$$

We have to select the outcome of the measurement 1 modulo the constant factor for normalization.

14.1.8 *Obtaining the solution*

Obtaining the required coefficient x_i from $|x\rangle$ would require at least n measurements, so the complexity of the algorithm would be $O(n)$ which problematic since the cost on a classical computer for an approximate solution for a sparse matrix via conjugate gradient descent are equivalent. Many applications are interested in the global properties of $|x\rangle$ rather than the coefficients x_i. For a sparse matrix and efficient preparation of $|b\rangle$ we can estimate the expectation value of an observable M

$$\langle x|M|x\rangle = \langle M\rangle = \sum_{i=1}^{n}(\alpha_i^* \cdot \alpha_i)\cdot\lambda_i = \sum_{i=1}^{n}\lambda_i \cdot p(\lambda_i). \tag{14.76}$$

efficiently with $\tilde{O}(\log(n))$. Many features describing the vector $|x\rangle$ can be extracted efficiently, like for example values in different parts. We can as well efficiently estimate if two solutions of two different equations are the same or not [Harrow *et al.* (2009)].

14.2 Quantum Principal Component Analysis

We represent the covariance matrix C corresponds to a the density matrix ρ since for N data points it can be represented as

$$\rho = \frac{1}{N}\sum_{i=1}^{N}|x_i\rangle\langle x_i| \tag{14.77}$$

where for each vector the mean value of the data set was subtracted. The density matrix exponential can guarantee efficiency for low rank Hamiltonians [Lloyd *et al.* (2014)]. The goal is to simulate

$$e^{i\cdot H_\rho t} \tag{14.78}$$

that encodes a non-sparse density matrix ρ and apply it to a quantum state σ represented by a density matrix. Simulating H_ρ is approximately equivalent to simulating a spares swap operator S, applying it to the state $\rho\otimes\sigma$ and taking a partial trace operator. Since S is sparse, it can be simulated efficiently. The swap operator swaps two qubits with respect to the basis $|00\rangle, |01\rangle, |10\rangle, |11\rangle$ is

$$S = \begin{pmatrix} 1\,0\,0\,0 \\ 0\,0\,1\,0 \\ 0\,1\,0\,0 \\ 0\,0\,0\,1 \end{pmatrix}. \tag{14.79}$$

The trace of a matrix is defined as the sum of diagonal elements

$$Tr(A) = \sum_i a_{ii} = \sum_i \langle e_i|A|e_i\rangle$$

with the basis e_i for A. The partial trace over A is

$$Tr_A(A\otimes B) = Tr(A)\cdot B \tag{14.80}$$

and over B is

$$Tr_B(A \otimes B) = A \cdot Tr(B) \tag{14.81}$$

The partial trace can be viewed as a quantum operation, with an operator O_{AB} on $A \otimes B$, the partial trace of O_{AB} with respect to B is

$$Tr_B(O_{AB}) = \sum_i \langle \beta_i | O_{AB} | \beta_i \rangle \tag{14.82}$$

with the basis $|\beta_i\rangle$ for B and

$$Tr_A(O_{AB}) = \sum_i \langle \alpha_i | O_{AB} | \alpha_i \rangle \tag{14.83}$$

with the basis $|\alpha_i\rangle$ for A. We approximate

$$e^{-i\rho t} \cdot \sigma \cdot e^{i\rho t} \approx Tr_P \left(e^{-iSt} \cdot (\rho \otimes \sigma) \cdot e^{-iSt} \right) \tag{14.84}$$

Since S is sparse, it can be simulated efficiently. For the Kitaev's phase estimation algorithm we use m examples of ρ with cU^m to prepare powers of

$$\left(e^{-iH_\rho t} \right)^m . \tag{14.85}$$

We preform the Kitaev's phase estimation algorithm resulting in the eigenvectors and eigenvalues. Using ρ as initial state, the quantum phase algorithm yields the density matrix:

$$\sum_j \lambda_j |u_j\rangle\langle u_j| \otimes |\tilde{\lambda}_j\rangle\langle \tilde{\lambda}_j| \tag{14.86}$$

We can measure a density matrix with projective measurement and it allows us to reveal features of the eigenvectors $|u_j\rangle$ and the eigenvalues $|\tilde{\lambda}_j\rangle$ of ρ. The time complexity using m copies and **ignoring** the preparation cost of (due to the input problem) the non sparse Hamiltonian ρ is $O(m \cdot \log(n))$ [Lloyd *et al.* (2014)]. The probability of measuring large eigenvalues or the features of the eigenvectors is high: Preforming z measurements with $z \ll m$ allows us to gain sufficient information about the principal components that describe the density matrix ρ. We can reduce the cost for m copies neglecting the preparation cost of the non sparse Hamiltonian to $O(\log(n))$ be the usage of $qRAM$ [Giovannetti *et al.* (2008)] that will be described in the next section. The classical cost of PCA are $O(n)$ using covariance-free computation.

14.2.1 *Measuring density matrix*

Projective measurement is defined by a set of measurement operators P_i one for each possible measurement outcome for the computational basis. For the basis $|0\rangle$, $|1\rangle$ we have the operators

$$P_0 = |0\rangle\langle 0| = \begin{pmatrix} 1 & 0 \\ 0 & 0 \end{pmatrix}, \quad P_1 = |0\rangle\langle 0| = \begin{pmatrix} 0 & 0 \\ 0 & 1 \end{pmatrix}.$$

With

$$\rho = \frac{1}{2} \cdot |0\rangle\langle 0| + \frac{1}{2} \cdot |1\rangle\langle 1| = \begin{pmatrix} \frac{1}{2} & 0 \\ 0 & \frac{1}{2} \end{pmatrix},$$

P_0 is the probability $p(|0\rangle)$ with measuring $|0\rangle$ and $p(|1\rangle)$ with measuring $|1\rangle$.

$$p(|0\rangle) = Tr(P_o \cdot \rho) = Tr\left(\begin{pmatrix} 1 & 0 \\ 0 & 0 \end{pmatrix} \cdot \begin{pmatrix} \frac{1}{2} & 0 \\ 0 & \frac{1}{2} \end{pmatrix}\right) = Tr\left(\begin{pmatrix} \frac{1}{2} & 0 \\ 0 & 0 \end{pmatrix}\right) = \frac{1}{2}.$$

14.3 Quantum Random Access Memory

A quantum random access memory copies basis stats [Giovannetti *et al.* (2008)], [Schuld and Petruccione (2018)]. A *qRAM* queries a register $|i\rangle$ and load the ith binary patter into the second register

$$|i\rangle|0\rangle \rightarrow |i\rangle|x^i\rangle, \tag{14.87}$$

with $|x^i\rangle$ being a basis state representing a binary vector. Such an operation can be executed in parallel with

$$\frac{1}{\sqrt{m}} \sum_{i=1}^{m} |i\rangle|0\rangle \rightarrow \frac{1}{\sqrt{n}} \sum_{i=1}^{m} |i\rangle|x^i\rangle, \tag{14.88}$$

with the time complexity **ignoring** the preparation cost of (due to the input problem) is $O(\log(m)$. Because of the collapse during measurement (destruction) the *qRAM* cannot be reused after the measurement.

14.3.1 *Amplitude coding*

If the collection of vectors is represented in a superposition, e.g., in $|\psi\rangle$, could we copy $|\psi\rangle$ before the measurement? An operation that would produce a copy of an arbitrary quantum state such as $|\psi\rangle$ is not possible; we cannot copy non-basis states because of the linearity of quantum mechanics. However we can to some extend simulate the copy of non-basis states using quantum Random Access Memories ($qRAM$), with the complexity $O(n\log(m))$ where n is the dimension of the resulting superposition vector. We a convert a basis state of m qubits $|x\rangle = |01\cdots 1\rangle$ of dimension 2^m in Hilbert space into a n dimensional superposition

$$|01\cdots 1\rangle\frac{1}{\sqrt{n}}\sum_{i=1}^{n}|i\rangle \rightarrow |01\cdots 1\rangle\sum_{i=1}^{n}\alpha_i|i\rangle. \tag{14.89}$$

We divide the binary vector of the dimension 2^m into v parts, each substring representing $code_i$ a real number with $n = 2^m/v$.

$$|01\cdots 1\rangle\frac{1}{\sqrt{n}}\sum_{i=1}^{n}|i\rangle \rightarrow |code_1 cod_2\cdots code_n\rangle\frac{1}{\sqrt{n}}\sum_{i=1}^{n}|i\rangle \tag{14.90}$$

We add an auxiliary state $|0^{\otimes n}\rangle$

$$|code_1\cdots code_n\rangle\frac{1}{\sqrt{n}}\sum_{i=1}^{n}|i\rangle \rightarrow |code_1\cdots code_n\rangle\frac{1}{\sqrt{n}}\sum_{i=1}^{n}|i\rangle|0^{\otimes n}\rangle \tag{14.91}$$

For each $code_i$ represents a binary representation of a fractional real number that is smaller than one

$$code_i = \alpha_i < 1.$$

For each $value_i$ we preform a controlled rotation $R(\alpha_i)$

$$\left(C\cdot\alpha_i|1\rangle + \sqrt{1 - C^2\cdot\alpha_i^2}|0\rangle\right)$$

and preform a measurement. By measuring the corresponding auxiliary register with the result 1 we know that the resulting state is correct. We repeat the procedure at least n times with the resulting state

$$|01\cdots 1\rangle\sum_{i=1}^{n}\alpha_i|i\rangle. \tag{14.92}$$

The resulting complexity of the routine is $O(n)$, which is the same as reading a classic information. However to read classically m vectors of dimension n the complexity is $O(n\cdot m)$, using $qRAM$ **ignoring** the preparation cost it is $O(n\log(m))$. The described routine is **non reversible** since it is based on measurement. We cannot map

$$|01\cdots 1\rangle\sum_{i=1}^{n}\alpha_i|i\rangle \nRightarrow |01\cdots 1\rangle\frac{1}{\sqrt{n}}\sum_{i=1}^{n}|i\rangle. \tag{14.93}$$

As a consequence we cannot copy an arbitrary quantum state. If the Equation 14.93 was valid, we could speed up the search exponentially using the

Grover's algorithm with the aid of some "spy". We divide the space of n possible solutions into two groups of size $n/2$ and preform Grover's amplification for one step for each subgroup. Then for each of the two groups we verify if the probability values changed using the Equation 14.93 indicating a solution. If yes, then the solution is in the corresponding group. By doing it recursively we would preform a tree search that is logarithmic.

14.4 Quantum Kernels

For a quantum state $|\phi(x)\rangle|$ and $|\phi(y)\rangle|$, the inner product of two such states is called a quantum kernel

$$k(x,y) = \langle\phi(x)|\phi(y)\rangle \tag{14.94}$$

with a inner product

$$\langle x|y\rangle = x^T \cdot y. \tag{14.95}$$

The absolute value of the inner product can be estimated by the swap test [Schuld and Petruccione (2018)].

14.4.1 *Swap test*

We estimate $\langle x|y\rangle$ using the swap test. Each state represents a normalized vector for the dimension n represented by $m = \log_2 n$ qubits. Note that the quantum $|x\rangle$ and $|y\rangle$ are of length one in the l_2 norm,

$$\langle x|x\rangle = \||x\rangle\|_2 = 1, \quad \langle y|y\rangle = \||y\rangle\|_2 = 1.$$

With an additional auxiliary qubit $|0\rangle$ generate the state

$$|0\rangle|x\rangle|y\rangle = |0,x,y\rangle$$

Apply Hadamard gate on the control qubit $|0\rangle$,

$$(W \otimes I_m \otimes I_m) \cdot |0\rangle|x,y\rangle = \frac{1}{\sqrt{2}} \cdot (|0,x,y\rangle + |1,x,y\rangle) \tag{14.96}$$

Apply controlled swap operator on $|x\rangle$ and $|y\rangle$ states which swaps $|x\rangle$ and $|y\rangle$

$$|x\rangle|y\rangle \rightarrow |y\rangle|x\rangle$$

providing that the control qubit is in state $|1\rangle$ with

$$\frac{1}{\sqrt{2}} \cdot (|0,x,y\rangle + |1,x,y\rangle) \rightarrow \frac{1}{\sqrt{2}} \cdot (|0,x,y\rangle + |1,y,x\rangle) \tag{14.97}$$

We apply another Hadamard gate on the control qubit

$$(W \otimes I_m \otimes I_m) \cdot \left(\frac{1}{\sqrt{2}} \cdot (|0,x,y\rangle + |1,y,x\rangle) \right) =$$

$$\frac{1}{2} \cdot |0\rangle \cdot (|x,y\rangle + |y,x\rangle) + \frac{1}{2} \cdot |1\rangle \cdot (|x,y\rangle - |y,x\rangle) \tag{14.98}$$

The probability of measuring the control qubit in state $|0\rangle$ is given by

$$p(|0\rangle) = \left| \frac{1}{2} \cdot \langle 0|0\rangle \cdot (|0,x,y\rangle + |1,y,x\rangle) + \frac{1}{2} \cdot \langle 0|1\rangle \cdot (|0,x,y\rangle - |1,y,x\rangle) \right|^2$$

$$p(|0\rangle) = \frac{1}{4} \cdot |(|x\rangle|y\rangle + |y\rangle|x\rangle)|^2$$

$$p(|0\rangle) = \frac{1}{4} \cdot (\langle y|y\rangle\langle x|x\rangle + \langle y|x\rangle\langle x|y\rangle + \langle x|y\rangle\langle y|x\rangle + \langle x|x\rangle\langle y|y\rangle)$$

$$p(|0\rangle) = \frac{1}{4} \cdot (1 + \langle y|x\rangle\langle x|y\rangle + \langle x|y\rangle\langle y|x\rangle + 1)$$

$$p(|0\rangle) = \frac{1}{2} + \frac{1}{4} \cdot (\langle y|x\rangle\langle x|y\rangle + \langle x|y\rangle\langle y|x\rangle)$$

$$p(|0\rangle) = \frac{1}{2} + \frac{1}{2}|\langle x|y\rangle|^2 \tag{14.99}$$

and

$$p(|1\rangle) = \frac{1}{2} - \frac{1}{2}|\langle x|y\rangle|^2 \tag{14.100}$$

with

$$|\langle x|y\rangle| \approx \sqrt{1 + 2 \cdot p(|0\rangle)} = \sqrt{1 - 2 \cdot p(|1\rangle)}. \tag{14.101}$$

The probability $p(|0\rangle) = 0.5$ means that the states $|x\rangle$ and $|y\rangle$ are orthogonal, whereas the probability $p(|0\rangle) = 1$ indicates that the states are identical. However we have to preform several measurements to estimate $(|0\rangle$ or $(|1\rangle$. It is difficult to estimate the exact value by measurement, but the procedure is efficient for the estimation of the raw similarity. Also note that since the vectors are normalized the the inner product corresponds to the angle φ between the vectors

$$0 \leq \cos\varphi = |\langle x|y\rangle| \leq 1 \tag{14.102}$$

and is usually called the cosine similarity. We can estimate the Euclidean distance as well, since the distance for normalized vectors is constrained to a unit sphere with

$$0 \leq \|\mathbf{x} - \mathbf{y}\|_2 \leq \sqrt{2}. \tag{14.103}$$

14.4.2 *Quantum advantage kernels*

A quantum computer can estimate a quantum kernel and the estimate can be used by a kernel method on a classical computer [Schuld and Petruccione (2018)]. This is because the exponential quantum advantage in evaluating inner products allows to estimate the quantum kernel machines directly in the higher dimensional space. If the result is impossible to be simulated on a classical computer then the kernel is classically intractable [Schuld and Killoran (2019)]. We can map

$$|\phi(x)\rangle \rightarrow |\phi(x)\rangle \otimes \cdots \otimes |\phi(x)\rangle = |\phi(x)\rangle^{\otimes m} \tag{14.104}$$

$$k(x,y) = \langle \phi(x)|\phi(y)\rangle \otimes \cdots \otimes \langle \phi(x)|\phi(y)\rangle = (\phi(\mathbf{x})^T \cdot \phi(\mathbf{y}))^m. \tag{14.105}$$

and the homogenous polynomial kernel

$$k(x,y) = \langle x|y\rangle \otimes \cdots \otimes \langle x|y\rangle = (\mathbf{x}^T \cdot \mathbf{y})^m. \tag{14.106}$$

We can implement such kernel efficiently using a quantum computer. To do it we have to analyaze the vectors $\phi(\mathbf{x})$ and $\phi(\mathbf{y})$ on a classical computer. For each vector we have to determine the rotation angle on a basis state $|0\rangle$ that we call $\theta_{\phi(x)}$ and $\theta_{\phi(y)}$ that correspond to the rotation $R(\theta_{\phi(x)})$ and $R(\theta_{\phi(y)})$. We prepare a state

$$|0\rangle|0\rangle^{\otimes m}|0\rangle^{\otimes m} \tag{14.107}$$

and preform the inverse rotation tensor m to reconstruct the original vectors

$$(I \otimes R(\theta_x^{-1})^{\otimes m} \otimes R(\theta_y^{-1})^{\otimes m}) \cdot |0\rangle|0\rangle^{\otimes m}|0\rangle^{\otimes m} = |0\rangle|\phi(x)\rangle^{\otimes m}|\phi(y)\rangle^{\otimes m}. \tag{14.108}$$

Then we do the swap test as described earlier with

$$|(\phi(\mathbf{x})^T|\phi(\mathbf{y}))^m| \approx \sqrt{1 + 2 \cdot p(|0\rangle)} = \sqrt{1 - 2 \cdot p(|1\rangle)}. \tag{14.109}$$

For large m such a procedure is not tractable on a classic computer [Schuld and Killoran (2019)]. The procedure does not suffer from the input problem.

14.5 Problems

Quantum kernels do not experience input problems. Other methods assume an efficient method for state preparation, which is possible for sparse data, which are common in machine learning. It is interesting to note that neurons in the brain use sparse representations.

By ignoring the input problem, which is the main bottleneck for data encoding, theoretical speed ups can be analyzed [Schuld and Killoran (2019)]. For example, we can assume that the data are already present in $qRAM$ [Biamonte *et al.* (2017)]. With quantum data, we can use Grover's algorithm for quadratic speed up over classical machine learning algorithms [Wittek (2014)]. The output problem is related to the destruction problem and the nature of the results. We do not have access to the exact values; rather, we estimate the expected values that describe the results.

Chapter 15

Stochastic Methods

15.1 Hopfield Model

The Hopfield model represents a model of the associative memory [Hopfield (1982)], [Hertz *et al.* (1991)]. In a Hopfield model n units units are connected to each other by the weights w_{ij}, The dynamic of the network are represented by

$$x_i = sgn(net_i) = sgn\left(\sum_{j=1}^{n} w_{ij} \cdot x_j\right) \tag{15.1}$$

with

$$net_i = \sum_{j=1}^{n} w_{ij} \cdot x_j$$

$$sgn(net) = \begin{cases} 1 & \text{if} \quad net \geq 0 \\ -1 & \text{if} \quad net < 0 \end{cases}.$$

Usually the units are updated asynchronously, updated them one at the time. For example at each time step, a random unit i is selected and updated. A set of N binary patterns of dimension n

$$\mathbf{x}_1, \mathbf{x}_2, \cdots, \mathbf{x}_N$$

with

$$x_{k,i} \in \{1, -1\}$$

(k identifies the training pattern and i the dimension) is stored using the Hebbian learning rule

$$w_{ij} = \frac{1}{n} \cdot \sum_{k=1}^{N} x_{k,i} \cdot x_{k,j} \tag{15.2}$$

with $w_{ij} = w_{ji}$ for all i, j and $w_{ii} = 0$ for all i. Patterns that the network uses for training (called retrieval states) become attractors of the system. After the training we start with some configuration $\mathbf{x}_{query}$ and the network will converge after several steps using the update rule to an attractor, see Figure 15.1. Convergence is generally assured. The attractors are the stored patterns, however sometimes the network will converge to spurious patterns (different from the training patterns).

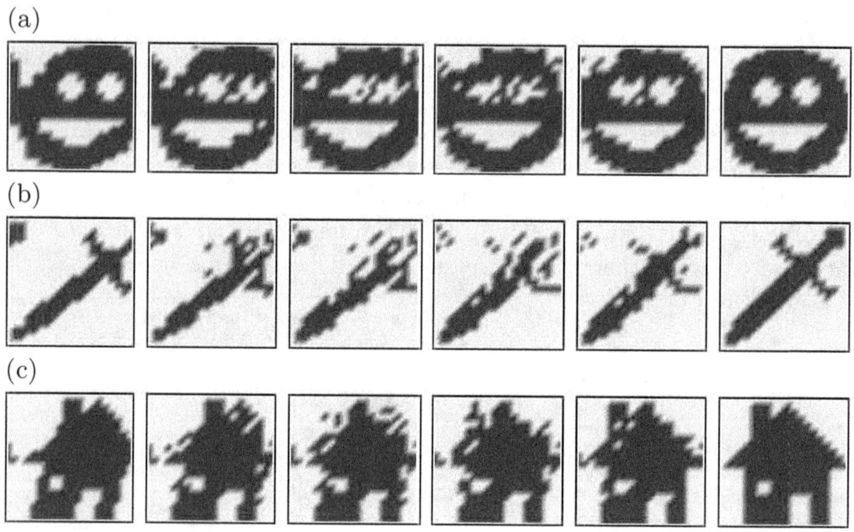

Fig. 15.1 Example how Hopfield networks restored distorted patterns. Three patterns were stored and recovered. (a) A smily, (b) a sword and (c) a house.

15.1.1 *Storage capacity*

The storage capacity of the model is

$$L = 0.138 \cdot n \tag{15.3}$$

which is much lower the the storage capacity of the (Lernmatrix) Willshaw's associative memory [Hertz *et al.* (1991)].

15.1.2 *Energy function*

One important property of the model is the idea of the energy function

$$H = -\frac{1}{2} \cdot \sum_{i=1}^{n} \sum_{j=1}^{n} w_{ij} \cdot x_i \cdot x_j. \tag{15.4}$$

The energy function describes the configuration of the system by a hilly "surface" In statistics and physics the energy function is called Hamiltonian [Hertz *et al.* (1991)]. The Hamiltonian always decrease (or remains constant) as the system evolves to its dynamical rule. Attractors are the local minima of the Hamiltonian (energy function). The dynamics of the system is similar to the motion of a particle on the hilly energy "surface" under the influence of gravity.

15.2 Ising Model

We can describe a magnetic material by a set of atomic magnets arranged on a regular lattice that represents the crystal structure of the material. We call the atomic magnets spins [Hertz *et al.* (1991)]. A simple model of spin 1/2 atoms is the Ising model. The spins represented by a variable s_i can point only into two different distinct directions that is oriented up $s_i = 1$ and down $s_i = -1$. The Ising model is related to the Hopfield associative memory in which a unit can fire $x_i = 1$ or be inactive $x_i = -1$. In magnetic field consist of the internal field produced by the spins and the external field h^{ext} that influences the spins. The coefficient w_{ij} measures the strength of the influence of spin. The influence is symmetric $w_{ij} = w_{ji}$ resulting in magnetic field

$$h_i = \sum_{j=1}^{n} w_{ij} \cdot s_j + h^{ext}. \tag{15.5}$$

At low temperatures the spin is updated by

$$s_i = sgn(h_i) = sgn\left(\sum_{j=1}^{n} w_{ij} \cdot s_j + h^{ext}.\right). \tag{15.6}$$

The updates are asynchronously or in random order. The energy function (Hamiltonian) is

$$H = -\frac{1}{2} \cdot \sum_{i=1}^{n} \sum_{j=1}^{n} w_{ij} \cdot s_i \cdot s_j - h^{ext} \cdot \sum_{i=1}^{n} s_i. \tag{15.7}$$

15.2.1 *Spin glass*

A spin glass is an Ising model without external field the model with the energy function (Hamiltonian)

$$H = -\frac{1}{2} \cdot \sum_{i=1}^{n} \sum_{j=1}^{n} w_{ij} \cdot s_i \cdot s_j. \tag{15.8}$$

Only nearest neighbor interactions similar to the Ising model. The spin glass is named from the n analogy between the magnetic disorder in a spin glass and the positional disorder of a conventional window glass. At low temperature the model is the same as Hopfield model.

15.2.2 *Finite temperature dynamics*

If the temperature is not very low thermal fluctuations tend to flip the spins randomly up and down. The thermal fluctuations become important at high temperature and decrease at low temperature and vanish at the absolute zero temperature. At high temperature the thermal fluctuations dominate the dynamics of the spin. The thermal fluctuations can be described by the Glauber dynamics that result in a stochastic rule

$$s_i = \begin{cases} +1 & \text{with probability } \; g(h_i) \\ -1 & \text{with probability } \; 1 - g(h_i). \end{cases} \tag{15.9}$$

The "Glauber" choice [Glauber (1963)] is represented by the sigmoid function

$$g(h) = \frac{1}{1 + e^{(-2 \cdot \beta \cdot h)}} \tag{15.10}$$

and

$$\beta = \frac{1}{k \cdot T} \tag{15.11}$$

where T is the absolute temperature and k the Boltzmann's constant, see Figure 15.2. It follows

$$g(-h) = 1 - g(h)$$

and the probability of spin s_i being 1 or -1

$$p(\pm s_i) = g(\pm h_i) = \frac{1}{1 + e^{(\mp 2 \cdot \beta \cdot h_i)}} \tag{15.12}$$

The temperature controls the steepness near $h = 0$.

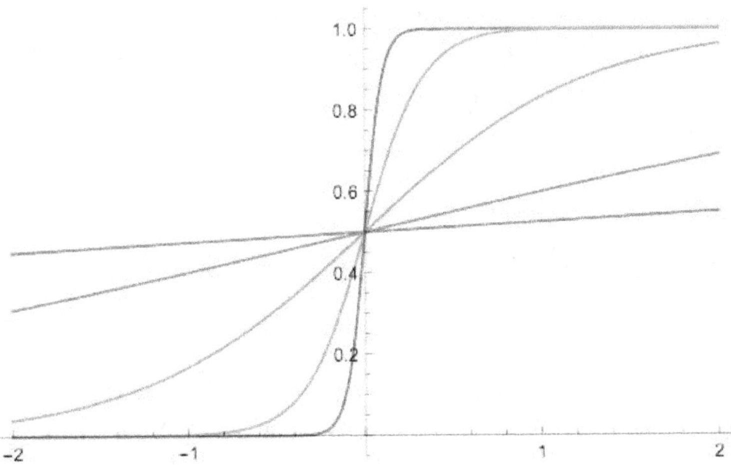

Fig. 15.2 The sigmoid function $g(h)$, for several values $\beta = 10$, $\beta = 3$, $\beta = 0.8$, $\beta = 0.2$ and $\beta = 0.05$. The temperature controls the steepness near $h = 0$, the bigger β, the more seep the function near $h = 0$. For $\beta = 0.05$. the function is nearly linear.

15.2.3 *Boltzmann-Gibbs distribution*

H_α denote the energy of the system when it is in state α. A fundamental result from the physics tells us that in thermal equilibrium each of the possible states α occurs with probability

$$p_\alpha = \frac{1}{Z} \cdot e^{\left(-\frac{H_\alpha}{k \cdot T}\right)} \tag{15.13}$$

and it is called the canonical distribution, or Boltzmann-Gibbs distribution, $e^{\left(-\frac{H_\alpha}{k \cdot T}\right)}$ is called the Boltzmann factor [Hertz *et al.* (1991)], [Haykin (2008)]. With

$$1 = \sum_\alpha p_\alpha$$

we get

$$Z = \sum_\alpha e^{\left(-\frac{H_\alpha}{k \cdot T}\right)} \tag{15.14}$$

the partition function that is the sum over all states, with Z because the German name *Zustadsumme*. It is derived from general assumptions about microscopic dynamics. We can compute the thermal average

$$\langle A \rangle = \sum_\alpha A_\alpha \cdot p_\alpha \tag{15.15}$$

that corresponds closely to the measured value of A. For a Hopfield network with probabilistic units and a bias b_i with the resulting energy function

$$H = -\frac{1}{2} \cdot \sum_{i=1}^{n} \sum_{j=1}^{n} w_{ij} \cdot x_i \cdot x_j - \sum_{i=1}^{n} b_i \cdot x_i \tag{15.16}$$

The partition function is over all possible stats, all 2^n combinations of $x_i = \pm 1$

$$Z = \sum_{x_1=\pm 1}^{n} \sum_{x_2=\pm 1}^{n} \cdots \sum_{x_n=\pm 1}^{n} \exp\left(\frac{\beta}{2} \cdot \sum_{i=1}^{n} \sum_{j=1}^{n} w_{ij} \cdot x_i \cdot x_j + \beta \cdot \sum_{i=1}^{n} b_i \cdot x_i \right) \tag{15.17}$$

where $\beta = 1/T$ since the temperature of a stochastic network is not related to physical temperature and we set $k = 1$. The average activation of unit i is

$$\langle x_i \rangle = \frac{1}{Z} \cdot \sum_{x_1=\pm 1}^{n} \cdots \sum_{x_n=\pm 1}^{n} x_i \cdot \exp\left(\frac{\beta}{2} \cdot \sum_{i=1}^{n} \sum_{j=1}^{n} w_{ij} \cdot x_i \cdot x_j + \beta \cdot \sum_{i=1}^{n} b_i \cdot x_i \right) \tag{15.18}$$

and we have to compute two times sum over all combinations. Knowing Z as a function of b_i we can simplify to

$$\langle x_i \rangle = \frac{1}{\beta \cdot Z} \cdot \frac{\partial Z}{\partial b_i} = T \cdot \frac{\partial}{\partial b_i} \cdot \log Z. \tag{15.19}$$

and we have to compute only one time the sum over all combinations.

15.2.4 *Free energy**

The Helmholtz free energy of a physical system, denoted by F, is defined

$$F = -T \cdot \log Z. \tag{15.20}$$

In the terms of free energy the average activation of unit i is

$$\langle x_i \rangle = -\frac{\partial F}{\partial b_i} = T \cdot \frac{\partial}{\partial b_i} \cdot \log Z \tag{15.21}$$

and

$$\langle x_i \cdot x_j \rangle = -\frac{\partial F}{\partial w_{ij}} = T \cdot \frac{\partial}{\partial w_{ij}} \cdot \log Z. \tag{15.22}$$

The minimum of the free energy of a stochastic system with respect to variables of the system is achieved at thermal equilibrium, at which point the system is governed by the Gibbs distribution [Hertz *et al.* (1991)], [Haykin (2008)].

15.2.4.1 *Free energy and entropy*

The average energy is

$$\langle H \rangle = \sum_{\alpha} p_\alpha \cdot H_\alpha \tag{15.23}$$

and

$$\langle H \rangle - F = \sum_{\alpha} p_i \cdot H_\alpha - (-T \cdot \log Z). \tag{15.24}$$

We know that

$$p_\alpha \cdot Z = \exp\left(-\frac{H_\alpha}{T}\right)$$

$$-\log(p_\alpha \cdot Z) = \frac{H_\alpha}{T}$$

$$H_\alpha = -T \cdot \log(p_\alpha \cdot Z). \tag{15.25}$$

We get the Equation

$$\langle H \rangle - F = \sum_{i} p_i \cdot (-T \cdot \log(p_\alpha \cdot Z)) - (-T \cdot \log Z) = \tag{15.26}$$

$$\langle H \rangle - F = -T \cdot \left(\sum_{\alpha} p_\alpha \cdot \log(p_\alpha \cdot Z) \; - \log Z \right) =$$

$$\langle H \rangle - F = -T \cdot \left(\sum_{\alpha} p_\alpha \cdot \log p_\alpha + \sum_{\alpha} p_\alpha \cdot \log Z - \log Z \right) =$$

$$\langle H \rangle - F = -T \cdot \left(\sum_{\alpha} p_\alpha \cdot \log p_\alpha + \log Z \cdot \sum_{\alpha} p_\alpha - \log Z \right) =$$

$$\langle H \rangle - F = -T \cdot \left(\sum_{\alpha} p_\alpha \cdot \log p_\alpha \right) \tag{15.27}$$

Apart from T the result is called Shannon's entropy indicated by $H(P)$ with

$$H(P) = \sum_{\alpha} p_\alpha \cdot \log p_\alpha \tag{15.28}$$

and the free energy of the system is represented as

$$F = \langle H \rangle - T \cdot H(P). \tag{15.29}$$

The entropy can be interpreted into two ways

- The width of the probability distribution p_α, the more state have noticeable probability, the larger $H(P)$. When If all K states have the same probability

$$H(P) = \log K. \tag{15.30}$$

We can interpret $e^{H(P)}$ as the number of different states even if not all probabilities are equal. It is the space of all possible configurations represented by α.

- The average amount of additional information to specify one state. The larger $H(P)$ the more uncertain the actual state α.

$$H(P) = \log_2 K. \tag{15.31}$$

is the number of bits needed to specify one choice of K alternatives.

15.2.5 *Stochastic dynamics*

Transition probability of flipping from s_i to $-s_i$ are represented as

$$W(s_i \to -s_i) = \frac{1}{1 + e^{(\beta \cdot \Delta H_i)}} \tag{15.32}$$

with

$$\Delta H_i = H(s_1, s_2, \cdots, -s_i, \cdots s_n) - H(s_1, s_2, \cdots, s_i, \cdots s_n) = 2 \cdot h_i \cdot s_i \tag{15.33}$$

resulting in the energy change from such a flip [Hertz *et al.* (1991)]. The transition probabilities $W(s_i \to -s_i)$ give us the stochastic sequence of state. In general the transition probabilities for the states α and α' are

$$W(\alpha \to \alpha').$$

However an arbitrary set can produce a limited cycle or a chaotic behavior instead of leading to a desirable thermal equilibrium. It is important to seek a condition on $W(\alpha \to \alpha')$ to guarantee equilibrium. In equilibrium the probability p_α of finding the system in statas α is given by the Boltzmann-Gibbs distribution. A sufficient condition for a thermal equilibrium is that the average number of transitions from α to α' and from α' to α be equal

$$p_\alpha \cdot W(\alpha \to \alpha') = p'_\alpha \cdot W(\alpha' \to \alpha) \tag{15.34}$$

and

$$\frac{W(\alpha \to \alpha')}{W(\alpha' \to \alpha)} = \frac{p'_\alpha}{p_\alpha} = e^{(-\beta \cdot \Delta H)} \tag{15.35}$$

with

$$\Delta H = H_{\alpha'} - H_{\alpha}.$$

This is called the principle of detailed balance. For

$$W(\alpha \to \alpha') = \frac{1}{1 + e^{(\beta \cdot \Delta H)}}, \quad W(\alpha' \to \alpha) = \frac{1}{1 + e^{(-\beta \cdot \Delta H)}}$$

with Boltzmann-Gibbs distribution

$$p_\alpha = \frac{1}{Z} \cdot e^{(-\beta H_\alpha)}, \quad p'_\alpha = \frac{1}{Z} \cdot e^{\left(-\beta H'_\alpha\right)}. \tag{15.36}$$

Also other rules are possible and also lead to the Boltzmann-Gibbs distribution. In simulating physical systems one often choses the Metropolis algorithm with

$$W(\alpha \to \alpha') = \begin{cases} 1 & \text{if} \quad \Delta H < 0 \\ e^{(-\beta H t)} & \text{otherwise} \end{cases}. \tag{15.37}$$

The stochastic dynamics are described by Monte Carlo methods. Monte Carlo methods are a broad class of computational algorithms that rely on repeated random sampling to obtain numerical results. The underlying concept is to use randomness to solve problems that might be deterministic in principle.

15.2.6 *Gibbs sampling*

The stochastic dynamics of the Ising model can be described by Gibbs sampling [Bishop (2006)]. Suppose that the system is in a state $\mathbf{s}$ and we have chosen an arbitrary coordinate i. We can then ignore the actual state of the spin s_i and ask for the conditional probability that this spin points upwards given all other spins.

$$h_i = \sum_{j=1, i \neq j}^{n} w_{ij} \cdot s_j + h^{ext} \tag{15.38}$$

with

$$p\left(s_i = 1 | \{s_j\}_{j \neq i}\right) = \frac{1}{1 + e^{(-2 \cdot \beta \cdot h_i)}}, \quad \beta = \frac{1}{k \cdot T}. \tag{15.39}$$

A single Gibbs sampling step now proceeds as follows:

- Randomly pick a coordinate i.
- Calculate the conditional probability $p = p\left(s_i = 1 | \{s_j\}_{j \neq i}\right)$.
- Draw a real number $\xi \in [0, 1]$ from the uniform distribution.

- If ξ is at most equal to p, set the spin at position i to $+1$, otherwise set it to -1.

The algorithm then starts with a randomly chosen state and subsequently applies a large number of Gibbs sampling steps. After some time, called the burn-in time, the states after each step then form the sample we are looking for represented by he equilibrium distribution.

15.2.6.1 *Markov chain Monte Carlo algorithm*

Gibbs sampling is a simple and widely applicable Markov chain Monte Carlo algorithm [Bishop (2006)]. It generates a Markov chain with the Gibbs distribution as the equilibrium distribution since during the evolution none of the conditional distributions be anywhere zero. Consider the distribution

$$p(\mathbf{x}) = p(x_1, x_2, \cdots, x_n)$$

from which we want to sample. We have chosen some initial state for the Markov chain. Each step of the Gibbs sampling procedure involves replacing the value of one of the variables by a value drawn from the distribution of that variable conditioned on the values of the remaining variables.

Gibbs Algorithm:

- Initialise

$$x_1, x_2, \cdots, x_n$$

- For $t = 1, 2, \cdots, T$:
  - sample $x_1^{(t+1)}$ and replace $x_1^{(t)}$
  $$x_1^{(t+1)} \sim p(x_1|x_2^{(t)}, x_3^{(t)}, \cdots, x_M^{(t)}),$$
  - sample $x_2^{(t+1)}$ and replace $x_2^{(t)}$
  $$x_2^{(t+1)} \sim p(x_2|x_1^{(t+1)}, x_3^{(t)}, \cdots, x_M^{(t)}),$$
  - ...
  $$\cdots\cdots\cdots,$$
  - sample $x_M^{(t+1)}$ and replace $x_M^{(t)}$
  $$x_M^{(t+1)} \sim p(x_M j|x_1^{(t+1)}, x_2^{(t+1)}, x_3^{(t+1)}, \cdots, x_{M-1}^{(t-1)},)$$

Gibbs sampling samples from the required distribution since the distribution $p(\mathbf{x})$ is an invariant of each of the Gibbs sampling steps individually. The Gibbs sampling procedure samples from the correct distribution. It converge to the equilibrium distribution since none of the conditional distributions be anywhere zero.

15.2.7 *Metropolis algorithm*

Metropolis algorithm is a modified Monte Carlo method, it is referred to as a Markov chain Monte Carlo [Metropolis *et al.* (1953)]. Metropolis proposed the following stochastic matrix that is composed on transition probabilities that describe the transition of states $W(\alpha \rightarrow \alpha')$ with

$$T_{ij} \geq 0, \quad T_{ij} = T_{ji}, \quad \sum_i T_{ij} = 1 \tag{15.40}$$

and is defined as

$$P_{ij} = \begin{cases} \begin{cases} T_{ij} & if \;\; p_i/p_j \geq 1 \\ T_{ij} \cdot p_i/p_j & if \;\; p_i/p_j < 1 \end{cases} & i \neq j \\ T_{jj} & i = j \end{cases} \tag{15.41}$$

With

$$\beta = \frac{1}{k \cdot T} \tag{15.42}$$

and Boltzmann-Gibbs distribution

$$p_i = \frac{1}{Z} \cdot e^{(-\beta H_i)}, \quad p_j = \frac{1}{Z} \cdot e^{(-\beta H_j)} \tag{15.43}$$

we get

$$P_{ij} = \begin{cases} \begin{cases} T_{ij} & if \;\; e^{(-\beta \cdot \Delta H)} \geq 1 \\ T_{ij} \cdot e^{(-\beta \cdot \Delta H)} & if \;\; e^{(-\beta \cdot \Delta H)} < 1 \end{cases} & i \neq j \\ T_{jj} & i = j \end{cases} \tag{15.44}$$

with

$$\Delta H = H_i - H_j.$$

A sufficient condition for a thermal equilibrium is that the average number of transitions from i to j and from j to i be equal with

$$P_{ij} \cdot p_j = (T_{ij} \cdot p_i/p_j) \cdot P_j = T_{ji} \cdot P_i = P_{ji} \cdot p_i.$$

The detailed balance holds for all i and j. The Metropolis algorithm states to accept a transition if the new configuration has a lower energy. Otherwise the algorithm says to accept the change that increase the energy but only with the probability $e^{(-\beta \cdot \Delta H)}$. A random value $\xi \in [0, 1]$ is generated. If $\xi < e^{(-\beta \cdot \Delta H)}$ then the transition is accepted. The acceptance depends on the temperature. With high temperature the probability of acceptance is high, with lowering the temperature the probability of acceptance diminishes.

15.3 Simulated Annealing

The rate of convergence of the Markov chain of the Gibbs sampling or the Metropolis algorithm to thermal equilibrium is extremely slow at very low temperatures. To improve computational efficiency, it is necessary to operate the stochastic system at high temperature where convergence to equilibrium is fast and then maintain the system at equilibrium as the temperature is slowly lowered. Simulated annealing is named by analogy to real annealing that real metallurgists do, i.e., slowly cooling the sample. The results are obtained at the true stable phase at low temperature [Hertz *et al.* (1991)]. Simulated annealing differs from conventional iterative optimization algorithms [Haykin (2008)].

(1) The algorithm does not need to get stuck in local minima because the transition out of a local minimum is possible when the system operates at a nonzero temperature.
(2) The global features of the final state of the system are seen at higher temperatures, while the fine details of the state appear at lower temperatures.

The Metropolis algorithm or Gibbs sampling is the basis for the simulated annealing process, during which the temperature T is slowly decreased. The simulated annealing process will converge to the configuration of minimal energy provided that the temperature does not decrease faster than logarithmically.

(1) The initial value T_0 of the temperature is chosen to be sufficiently high to ensure that virtually all proposed transitions are accepted by the simulated annealing algorithm.
(2) The changes made in the value of the temperature are small, and the decrement function can be defined linearly by

$$T_k = \alpha \cdot T_{k-1}, \qquad 0.8 \leq \alpha \leq 0.99.$$

We can define two phases of the decrement function, i.e., a fast decrease at the very high temperature to a certain temperature in the first phase followed by a very slow decrease in the second phase.
(3) At the final value of the temperature, the system is fixed, and annealing stops.

15.3.1 *Combinatorial optimization*

Simulated annealing is particularly well-suited for solving combinatorial optimization problems. The objective of combinatorial optimization is to minimize the cost function of a finite, discrete system that is characterized by a large number of possible solutions. We will present two examples, i.e., weighted matching and traveling salesmen problems [Hertz *et al.* (1991)].

Weighted matching problem: In the weighted matching problem, one has a set of N points with a distance d_{ij} between nodes i and j. We want to link the pairs of two nodes with each point linked exactly to each other in such a way that the total length of the links is minimized. This is actually not a hard problem, and fast polynomial algorithms are known. We will use this simple optimization problem to demonstrate how to formulate it as an Ising optimization problem. We will use 0/1 units. We assign n_{ij} with $i < j$ to each sites in the problem making $\frac{N \cdot (N-1)}{2}$ units. A possible solution of the problem is represented by the state of the system with $n_{ij} = 1$ if there is a link connecting point i and j and $n_{ij} = 0$ if there is not. The energy function has to deal with constraints.

- We have to minimize the total length of the links

$$L = \sum_{i<j} d_{ij} \cdot n_{ij}. \tag{15.45}$$

- With the constraint that each point should be connected to exactly one other point. We define

$$n_{ij} = n_{ji}, \qquad n_{ii} = 0$$

and

$$\sum_{i} n_{ij} = 1 \quad for\ all\ i. \tag{15.46}$$

We represent the constraint by a penalty term which is minimized when the constrained is satisfied resulting in the energy function

$$H = \sum_{i<j} d_{ij} \cdot n_{ij} + \frac{\gamma}{2} \sum_{i} \left(1 - \sum_{j} n_{ij} \right)^2 \tag{15.47}$$

Transition probability of flipping from n_{ij} to n'_{ij} are represented as

$$W(n_{ij} \rightarrow n'_{ij}) = \frac{1}{1 + e^{(\beta \cdot \Delta H_{ij})}} \tag{15.48}$$

with

$$\Delta H_{ij} = H(n'_{ij}) - H(n_{ij}) \tag{15.49}$$

resulting in the energy change from a flip $n_{ij} = 0$ and $n'_{ij} = 1$ or vice versa. The transition probabilities $W(n_{ij} \rightarrow n'_{ij})$ give us the stochastic sequence of state. The formulation is as well valid for ± 1 case.

Traveling salesmen problem: We can extend our approach to the NP-complete traveling salesmen problem. We have N points (or cities) with distances d_{ij} between them. We want to find a minimum closed tour that visit each city once and returns to its starting point. We will use N^2 units with n_{ia} to represent a possible solution with $n_{i,a} = 1$ if city i is the ath stop in the tour. The energy function has to deal with constraints.

- We have to minimize the total length of the closed tour

$$L = \frac{1}{2} \sum_{ij,a} d_{ij} \cdot n_{i,a} \cdot (n_{i,a+1} + n_{i,a-1}) \tag{15.50}$$

- with the constraint for every city i

$$\sum_{a} n_{i,a} = 1 \tag{15.51}$$

- and with the constraint for every stop a

$$\sum_{i} n_{i,a} = 1 \tag{15.52}$$

We represent the constraint by a penalty term which is minimized when the constrained is satisfied resulting in the energy function

$$H = \frac{1}{2} \sum_{ij,a} d_{ij} \cdot n_{i,a} \cdot (n_{i,a+1} + n_{i,a-1}) +$$

$$+\frac{\gamma}{2}\left(\sum_{a}\left(1 - \sum_{i} n_{i,a}\right)^2 + \sum_{i}\left(1 - \sum_{a} n_{i,a}\right)^2\right). \tag{15.53}$$

15.4 Boltzmann Machine

The Boltzmann machine is a stochastic Hopfield network with hidden units [Hinton and Sejnowski (1983)], [Ackley *et al.* (1985)], [Hinton and Sejnowski (1986)]. It is a stochastic binary machine whose composition consists of stochastic neurons in state 1 or state 0 (or 1 and -1). Boltzmann machine is the uses symmetric synaptic connections between its neurons. The synaptic connection form neuron i to j are

$$w_{ij} = w_{ji}, \quad for \quad all\ i, j$$

and

$$w_{ii} = 0, \quad for \quad all\ i$$

the use of a bias is permitted by using the weight $b_i = w_{i0}$ from a node $+1$. The stochastic neurons of the Boltzmann machine are divided into visible and hidden neurons. Visible neurons provide an interface between the network and the environment in which it operates. When a partial information-bearing vector is clamped onto a subset of the visible neurons, the network performs completion on the remaining visible neurons. By so doing, the network can perform pattern completion.

15.4.1 *Stochastic dynamics of the Boltzmann machine*

Assuming the network is composed of n units. Usually the units are updated asynchronously, updated them one at the time. For example at each time step, a random unit i is selected and updated with

$$net_i = \sum_{j=1}^{n} w_{ij} \cdot x_j + b_i = \sum_{j=1, j \neq i}^{n} w_{ij} \cdot x_j + b_i \tag{15.54}$$

with b_i being the bias. Unit i then turns on with a probability given by the sigmoid (logistic) function [Hinton and Sejnowski (1986)].:

$$p(x_i = 1) = \frac{1}{1 + e^{(-\beta \cdot net_i)}}, \qquad \beta = \frac{1}{T}. \tag{15.55}$$

The stochastic dynamics of Boltzmann machine can be described by Gibs sampling. Suppose that the system is in a state $\mathbf{x}$ and we have chosen an arbitrary coordinate i. We can then ignore the actual state of the unit x_i and ask for the conditional probability

$$p\left(x_i = 1 | \{x_j\}_{j \neq i}\right) = \frac{1}{1 + e^{(-\beta \cdot net_i)}}. \tag{15.56}$$

A single Gibbs sampling step now proceeds as follows:

- Randomly pick a coordinate i.
- Calculate the conditional probability $p = p\left(x_i = 1 | \{x_j\}_{j \neq i}\right)$.
- Draw a real number $\xi \in [0, 1]$ from the uniform distribution.
- If ξ is at most equal to p, set the spin at position i to $+1$, otherwise set it to -1.

Provided that the stochastic simulation is performed long enough, the network will reach thermal equilibrium at temperature T. The time taken to reach thermal equilibrium can be much too long. To overcome this difficulty, simulated annealing is used.

15.4.2 *Learning*

During the training phase of the network there are two phases to the operation of the Boltzmann machine [Hinton and Sejnowski (1986)]:

(1) Positive phase. In this phase, the network operates in its clamped condition under the direct influence of the training sample. The visible neurons are all clamped onto specific states determined by the environment.
(2) Negative phase. In this second phase, the network is allowed to run freely, and therefore with no environmental input. The states of the units are determined randomly. The probability of finding it in any particular global state depends on the energy function

A set of N binary patterns of dimension n

$$\mathbf{x}_1, \mathbf{x}_2, \cdots, \mathbf{x}_N$$

with (k identifies the training pattern and i the dimension)

$$x_{k,i} \in \{1, 0\}.$$

15.4.2.1 *Learning algorithm*

A learning is preformed over the whole training set of N vectors. Such learning is called the batch learning. It is often more efficient to learn over a sub sample of the training set, in this case the learning is called mini-batch usually with 10 to 100 training patterns.

- Initialize the weights and the bias with random numbers. With small random values chosen from a from a zero-mean Gaussian with a standard deviation of about 0.01.
- For $\tau = 1, 2, \cdots, \tau^{end}$:
  - Initialise:

$$pp_{ij} = 0, \quad pp_{i0} = 0, \quad pn_{ij} = 0, \quad pn_{i0} = 0$$

  - For $k = 1, 2, \cdots, N$:

* **Positive phase:** At starting state the visible units are in state representing a training pattern $\mathbf{x}_k$ and the hidden units are chosen random (0 or 1). Preform Gibbs sampling until a thermal equilibrium is reached. Store the statistics for the visible phase according the Hebbian learning rule:

$$pp_{ij}^{new} = \begin{cases} pp_{ij}^{old} + 1 & if \;\; x_i \cdot x_j = 1 \\ pp_{ij}^{old} & \text{otherwise.} \end{cases} \tag{15.57}$$

and for the bias

$$pp_{i0}^{new} = \begin{cases} pp_{i0}^{old} + 1 & if \;\; x_i = 1 \\ pp_{i0}^{old} & \text{otherwise.} \end{cases} \tag{15.58}$$

* **Negative phase:** At starting state the visible units are chosen random and the hidden units are chosen random (0 or 1). Preform Gibbs sampling until a thermal equilibrium is reached. Store the statistics for the negative phase according the anti Hebbian learning rule:

$$pn_{ij}^{new} = \begin{cases} pn_{ij}^{old} + 1 & if \;\; x_i \cdot x_j = 1 \\ pn_{ij}^{old} & \text{otherwise.} \end{cases} \tag{15.59}$$

and for the bias

$$pn_{i0}^{new} = \begin{cases} pn_{i0}^{old} + 1 & if \;\; x_i = 1 \\ pn_{i0}^{old} & \text{otherwise.} \end{cases} \tag{15.60}$$

Negative phase can be identified with unlearning and it was suggested that such reverse learning appears in REM sleep (Crick1983).

– Normalize

$$\overline{pp}_{ij}^{new} = \frac{pp_{ij}^{old}}{N}, \quad \overline{pp}_{i0}^{new} = \frac{pp_{i0}^{old}}{N},$$

$$\overline{pn}_{ij}^{new} = \frac{pn_{ij}^{old}}{N}, \quad \overline{pn}_{i0}^{new} = \frac{pn_{i0}^{old}}{N}$$

Adapt the weights and the bias

$$\Delta w_{ij} = \eta \cdot (\overline{pp}_{ij} - \overline{pn}_{ij}) \tag{15.61}$$

and the bias

$$\Delta b_i = \eta \cdot (\overline{pp}_{i0} - \overline{pn}_{i0}). \tag{15.62}$$

The learning process in the Boltzmann machine is very slow, particularly when the number of hidden neurons used in the machine is large.

After the training we start with some configuration $\mathbf{x}_{query}$ at the visible units (clamped for pattern completion) and the network will converge after several steps using the update rule to an attractor that represents the thermal equilibrium.

15.4.3 *Proof of learning in Boltzmann machine**

Energy of a Boltzmann machine is

$$H = -\frac{1}{2} \cdot \sum_{i=1}^{n} \sum_{j=1}^{n} w_{ij} \cdot x_i \cdot x_j - \sum_{i=1}^{n} b_i \cdot x_i \tag{15.63}$$

or simplified assuming bias is equal to w_{i0} and $x_0 = 1$

$$H = -\frac{1}{2} \cdot \sum_{i=1}^{n} \sum_{j=0}^{n} w_{ij} \cdot x_i \cdot x_j \tag{15.64}$$

is the same as for a Hopfield network with bias b_i. Usually the energy function has many local minima. If no hidden units are present, then the learning is related to of the for a Hopfield network

$$w_{ij} = \frac{1}{n} \cdot \sum_{k=1}^{N} x_{k,i} \cdot x_{k,j} \tag{15.65}$$

we divide by n and not N, since its storage capacity is lower than N, since N can be maximally $L = 0.138 \cdot n$.

A state of the Boltzmann machine is described by the random variable X, we preform a partition into visible sates V and hidden states H [Haykin (2008)]. Assuming the training sample is statistically independent with possible values $\mathbf{v}_k$, the overall probability is

$$p(V) = \prod_{k=1}^{N} p(\mathbf{v}_k) \tag{15.66}$$

Maximizing the likelihood (ML) is dependent on $\mathbf{w}$ is

$$\mathbf{w}_{ML} = \arg\max_{\mathbf{w}} p(V|\mathbf{w})) = \arg\max_{\mathbf{w}} \log(p(V) \tag{15.67}$$

since log is monotonic increasing function

$$\mathbf{w}_{ML} = \arg\max_{\mathbf{w}} \log\left(\prod_{k=1}^{N} p(\mathbf{v}_k)\right) = \arg\max_{\mathbf{w}} \sum_{k=1}^{N} (\log p(\mathbf{v}_k)) \tag{15.68}$$

and we can define a $E(\mathbf{w})$

$$E(\mathbf{w}) = \sum_{k=1}^{N} (\log p(\mathbf{v}_k)) \tag{15.69}$$

By the law of total probability

$$p(\mathbf{v}_k) = \sum_{\mathbf{h}} p(\mathbf{v}_k, \mathbf{h}) = \frac{1}{Z} \cdot \sum_{\mathbf{h}} e^{\left(-\frac{H(\mathbf{v}_k,\mathbf{h})}{T}\right)} \tag{15.70}$$

and

$$Z = \sum_{\mathbf{x}} e^{\left(-\frac{H(\mathbf{x})}{T}\right)} \tag{15.71}$$

and we get

$$E(\mathbf{w}) = \sum_{k=1}^{N} \left(\log \left(\frac{1}{Z} \cdot \sum_{\mathbf{h}} e^{\left(-\frac{H(\mathbf{v}_k,\mathbf{h})}{T}\right)} \right) \right) \tag{15.72}$$

$$E(\mathbf{w}) = \sum_{k=1}^{N} \left(\log \left(\sum_{\mathbf{h}} e^{\left(-\frac{H(\mathbf{v}_k,\mathbf{h})}{T}\right)} \right) - \log \left(\sum_{\mathbf{x}} e^{\left(-\frac{H(\mathbf{x})}{T}\right)} \right) \right) \tag{15.73}$$

differentiation $E(\mathbf{w})$

$$\frac{\partial E(\mathbf{w})}{\partial w_{ij}} = \sum_{k=1}^{N} \left(\frac{\partial}{\partial w_{ij}} \log \left(\sum_{\mathbf{h}} e^{\left(-\frac{H(\mathbf{v}_k,\mathbf{h})}{T}\right)} \right) - \frac{\partial}{\partial w_{ij}} \log \left(\sum_{\mathbf{x}} e^{\left(-\frac{H(\mathbf{x})}{T}\right)} \right) \right) \tag{15.74}$$

$$= \frac{1}{T} \cdot \sum_{k=1}^{N} \left(\frac{\left(\sum_{\mathbf{h}} e^{\left(-\frac{H(\mathbf{v}_k,\mathbf{h})}{T}\right)} \cdot \frac{\partial H(\mathbf{v}_k,\mathbf{h})}{\partial w_{ij}} \right)}{\sum_{\mathbf{h}} e^{\left(-\frac{H(\mathbf{v}_k,\mathbf{h})}{T}\right)}} - \frac{\left(\sum_{\mathbf{x}} e^{\left(-\frac{H(\mathbf{x})}{T}\right)} \cdot \frac{\partial H(\mathbf{x})}{\partial w_{ij}} \right)}{\sum_{\mathbf{x}} e^{\left(-\frac{H(\mathbf{x})}{T}\right)}} \right) \tag{15.75}$$

and we can simplify to

$$\frac{\partial E(\mathbf{w})}{\partial w_{ij}} = \frac{1}{T} \cdot \sum_{k=1}^{N} \left(\sum_{\mathbf{h}} p(\mathbf{v}_k, \mathbf{h}) \cdot x_i \cdot x_j - \sum_{\mathbf{x}} p(\mathbf{x}) \cdot x_i \cdot x_j \right). \tag{15.76}$$

We introduce two definitions

(1)

$$\langle x_i x_j \rangle_{data} = \sum_{k=1}^{N} \sum_{\mathbf{h}} p(\mathbf{v}_k, \mathbf{h}) \cdot x_i \cdot x_j$$

correlation when the network is clamped

(2)

$$\langle x_i x_j \rangle_{model} = \sum_{k=1}^{N} \sum_{\mathbf{x}} p(\mathbf{x}) \cdot x_i \cdot x_j$$

and

$$\frac{\partial E(\mathbf{w})}{\partial w_{ij}} = \frac{1}{T} \cdot \left(\langle x_i x_j \rangle_{data} - \langle x_i x_j \rangle_{model} \right)$$

and the gradient ascent rule is called the Boltzmann learning rule:

$$\Delta w_{ji} = \epsilon \cdot \frac{\partial E(\mathbf{w})}{\partial w_{ij}} = \eta \cdot \left(\langle x_i x_j \rangle_{data} - \langle x_i x_j \rangle_{model} \right)$$

with

$$\eta = \frac{\epsilon}{T}.$$

15.5 Harmonium - Restricted Boltzmann Machine

The learning process in the Boltzmann machine is very slow, particularly when the number of hidden units used in the machine is large. A restricted Boltzmann machine (RBM) has only connections between visible and hidden units to make inference and learning easier. It was initially invented under the name Harmonium by Paul Smolensky in 1986 [Smolensky (1986)], later it was renamed as a restricted Boltzmann machine [Salakhutdinov and Hinton (2012)], see Figure 15.3. There is only one layer of hidden units,

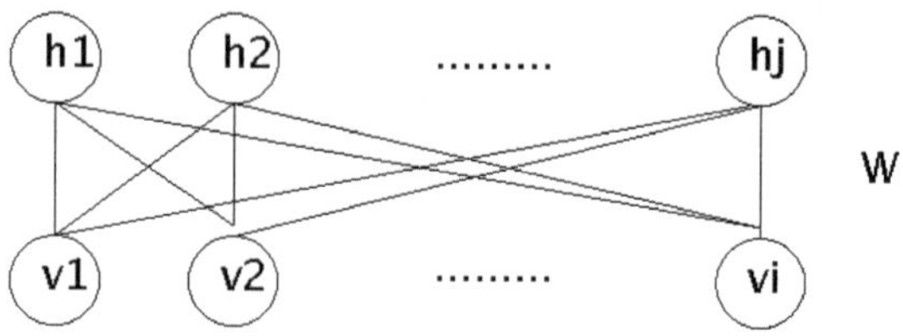

Fig. 15.3 A harmonium, renamed as a restricted Boltzmann machine.

there are no connections between hidden units. There is as well only one layer of visible units, there are no connections between visible units. Energy of a restricted Boltzmann machine can rewritten

$$H(\mathbf{v},\mathbf{h}) = -\sum_{i=1}^{H}\sum_{j=1}^{V} w_{ij}\cdot h_i\cdot v_j - \sum_{i=1}^{n} b_i\cdot h_i - \sum_{j=1}^{n} c_j\cdot v_j. \tag{15.77}$$

since there are no connections between units $h_i \cdot h_j$ or $v_i \cdot v_j$. Due to the constraints an RBM it only takes one step to reach thermal equilibrium when the visible units are clamped and the the hidden units are chosen random (0 or 1). One can quickly get the exact value of

$$\langle v_i h_j\rangle_{data}. \tag{15.78}$$

During the negative phase the units are chosen random random (0 or 1) one preforms Gibbs sampling until a thermal equilibrium is reached

$$\langle v_i h_j\rangle_{model} \tag{15.79}$$

and one preforms the update rule

$$\Delta w_{ij} = \eta\cdot(\langle v_i h_j\rangle_{data} - \langle v_i h_j\rangle_{model}). \tag{15.80}$$

After the training we start with some configuration $\mathbf{x}_{query}$ at the visible units (clamped for pattern completion) and the network will converge after several steps using the update rule to an attractor that represents the thermal equilibrium.

15.5.1 *Contrast divergence*

To avoid the long computing time of $\langle v_i h_j \rangle_{model}$ contrastive divergence (CD) based learning was proposed [Haykin (2008)], [Salakhutdinov and Hinton (2012)]. It does not directly use Gibbs sampling starting at random chosen units. Instead the training starts with a clamped vector $\mathbf{v}^0$ on the visible units and the hidden layer values $\mathbf{h}^0$ are computed with

$$p(h_i = 1|v) = \frac{1}{1 + e^{-(\sum_{j=1}^{n} w_{ij} v_j + c_i)}}, \tag{15.81}$$

that define

$$\langle v_i h_j \rangle_{data}^0. \tag{15.82}$$

Then a reconstruction of the visible layer $\mathbf{v}^1$ is computed with

$$p(v_i = 1|h) = \frac{1}{1 + e^{-(\sum_{j=1}^{n} w_{ij} h_j + b_i)}}, \tag{15.83}$$

with the clamped reconstructed vector $\mathbf{v}^1$ on the visible units and the hidden layer values $\mathbf{h}^1$ are computed using the Equation 15.81 again.

$$\langle v_i h_j \rangle_{recon}^1. \tag{15.84}$$

One alternate between updating all the hidden units in parallel and updating all the visible units in parallel repeating τ steps resulting in

$$\Delta w_{ij} = \epsilon \cdot (\langle v_i h_j \rangle_{data}^0 - \langle v_i h_j \rangle_{recon}^\tau) \tag{15.85}$$

It was shown (19) that if the process of forward sampling and reconstruction were repeated τ times, then (10) would converge to the true gradient as $\tau \to \infty$ although in practice the updates are computed using just a single-step reconstruction with $\tau = 1$. The single-step reconstruction wit $\tau = 1$ is not following the gradient of the log likelihood, sometimes CD may take many iterations with $1 \ll \tau$ to converge.

15.6 Deep Learning with Deep Belief Nets

A deep belief network (DBN) is a generative graphical model, or alternatively, a class of deep neural network, composed of multiple layers of latent variables (hidden units), with connections between the layers but not between units within each layer. It can be viewed as a composition of restricted Boltzmann machines. Deep belief networks [Hinton and Sejnowski (1986)] capture the higher-level representations of input features. In 2012, DBNs were renamed as deep neural networks (DNNs) [Salakhutdinov and Hinton (2012)].

- Then, the activations of the trained features are treated as if they are input features and the features of features in a second hidden layer are learned. Then, the activations of the trained features are used as input data to train a second trained RBM.
- The process of learning the features of features is continued until the number t of hidden layers, that is, until t RBMs have been trained, as shown in Figure 15.4.
- A restricted Boltzmann machine (RBM) is trained directly on the input data, thereby making it possible for the stochastic neurons in the hidden layer of the RBM to capture the important features that characterize the input data.

- Then, the activations of the trained features are treated as if they are input features and the features of features in a second hidden layer are learned. Then, the activations of the trained features are used as input data to train a second trained RBM.
- The process of learning the features of features is continued until the number t of hidden layers, that is, until t RBMs have been trained, as shown in Figure 15.4.

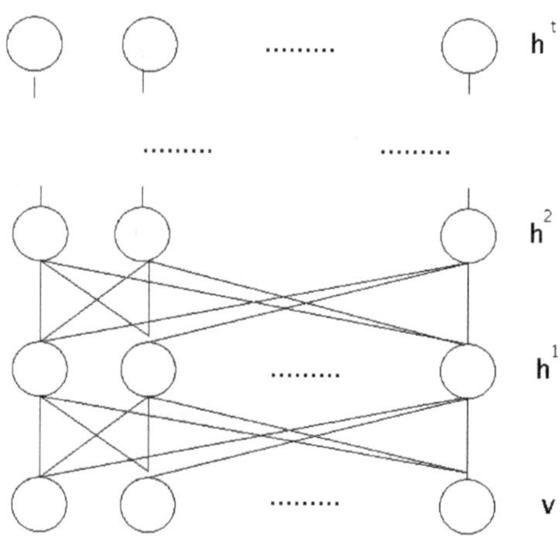

Fig. 15.4 A deep belief network.

A deep neural network was trained with the MNIST database (Modified National Institute of Standards and Technology database) consisting of 0 to 9 handwritten digits, as shown in Figure 15.5. The MNIST database contains 60, 000 training images and 10, 000 testing images. The images of the digits contain gray levels represented by a 28×28 matrix resulting in a 784-dimensional input vector. The architecture of the model is indicated

Fig. 15.5 Example of MNIST digits represented by gray images of the size 28×28.

in the Figure 15.6 The model learns to generate combinations of labels

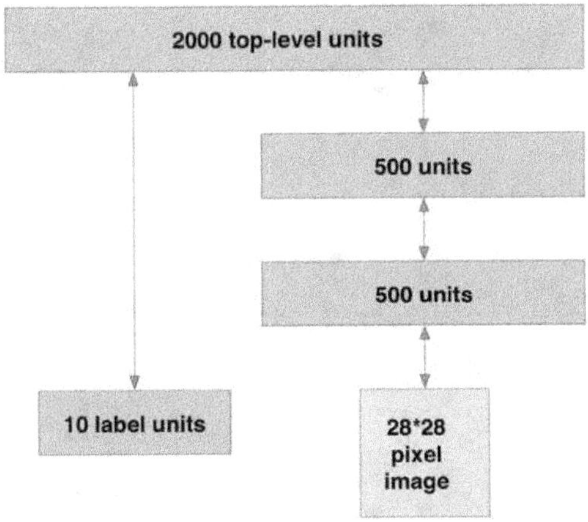

Fig. 15.6 The model learned to to generate combinations of labels and images. To perform recognition we start with a random state of the label units and clamp the input image. Then we do up-pass from the image followed by a few iterations of the top-level layers.

and images [Salakhutdinov and Hinton (2012)]. To perform recognition, we start with a random state of the label units and clamp the input image. Then, we do an uppass from the image followed by few iterations of the top-level layers. The results are comparable to the back-propagation algorithm. The process of learning may be viewed as one of learning the features of features. It can be confirmed that each time we add another layer of features we improve a variational lower bound on the log probability of the training data. A possible explanation for the success of deep belief networks is that each layer of the deep belief network represents a more abstract representation of the data. The deep belief network learns to disregard irrelevant features while simultaneously learning relevant features. Deep belief nets provide considerable freedom. An efficient sampling method, which is proposed by future quantum annealers, may extend this creativity to yet unknown frontiers.

Chapter 16

Adiabatic Quantum Computation and Quantum Annealing

16.1 Adiabatic Computation

Adiabatic quantum computation is an alternative approach to quantum computation. It is based on the time evolution of a quantum system. Adiabatic quantum computation is the polynomial equivalent to the quantum gate model. The main distinction between the two approaches is that the quantum gate model based on unitary operators is discrete with defined states, and adiabatic computation is analog. In the adiabatic computation, there are no unitary operators that change the discrete quantum states; instead, the quantum states gradually evolve, as described by the time-dependent Hamiltonian. The energy of a system can be described by a function represented by Hamiltonians [Farhi *et al.* (2000)], [Farhi *et al.* (2009)]. The lowest energy that the system can assume is called the ground state and corresponds to the global minima for the function. If the energy is dependent on two variables it can be represented by a two-dimensional function. Specifically, a ball that is left on the slope will descend until it reaches the lowest point in the valley and will stay there. The corresponding point is stationary. If the function describing the energy of the system changes very slowly, the ball will be resting in a location, which is the minimum point of the new equation. If one starts with a solution for the first simple function, one will end up with a solution to a complicated function. The initial Hamiltonian H_I is in the ground state, which corresponds to the solution of the initial simple problem. Then, the initial Hamiltonian changes very slowly until it becomes the final Hamiltonian H_F.

$$H_I \overset{slowly}{\longrightarrow} H_F. \tag{16.1}$$

As the Hamiltonian changes slowly, multiple qubits are close to the point representing the ground state. The addition of a slight amount of energy by slowly changing Hamiltonian keeps the system in the ground state. If we change the Hamiltonian too fast, the system may move out from the ground state. Therefore, the Hamiltonian is time-dependent

$$i \cdot h \cdot \frac{d}{dt}|x(t)\rangle = H(t) \cdot |x(t)\rangle \tag{16.2}$$

with h being the Planck's constant. $H(t)$ is the $n \times n$ Hermitian matrix with all real eigenvalues. The eigenvectors of $H(t)$ correspond to the observable states of the system. They are called the eigenstates (basis states) of the system. The eigenvalues of $H(t)$ correspond to the energies of their eigenstates. The spectral representation of $H(t)$ indicates all possible energies and eigenstates of the system

$$H(t) = \lambda(t)_1 \cdot |x(t)_1\rangle\langle x(t)_1| + \cdots + \lambda(t)_n \cdot |x(t)_n\rangle\langle x(t)_n|. \tag{16.3}$$

The set of all possible energies is the energy spectrum of size n

$$\{\lambda(t)_1, \lambda(t)_2, \cdots, \lambda(t)_n\}$$

Two or more states with the same energy are called degenerate $\lambda(t)_1 = \lambda(t)_2$,. The ground state is an observable state with the minimum energy over all eigenstates with

$$\min\{\lambda(t)_1, \lambda(t)_2, \cdots, \lambda(t)_n\}.$$

A state that is not a ground state is said to be excited. The second lowest energy in the system is called the first excited state. A Hamiltonian $H(t)$ can be considered as an operator that changes the state of the system in continuous time

$$H(t) \cdot |x(t)\rangle \rightarrow |x(t')\rangle \tag{16.4}$$

rather than in the discrete time of the unitary operator. A Hamiltonian $H(t)$ can also be considered to be observable. The eigenstates of $H(t)$ correspond to the observable states, which are the eigenvalues to the energies of those eigenstates. With eigenstate (eigenvector) $|x_k(t)\rangle$

$$H(t) \cdot |x_k(t)\rangle = \lambda_k(t) \cdot |x_k(t)\rangle \tag{16.5}$$

the energy $\lambda_k(t)$ is measured. In real quantum computation, the application of an operator and measuring by an observable are not the same despite the notational similarity [McGeoch (2014)].

16.1.1 *Adiabatic optimization*

Quantum adiabatic optimization is a class of procedures for solving combinatorial optimization problems [McGeoch (2014)]. The objective of combinatorial optimization is to minimize the cost function of a finite, discrete system characterized by a large number of possible solutions. The cost function is called an objective function or a loss function. We can convert any decision problem into an optimization problem. Frequently, the problem definition includes some constraints. For example, to factor integer M, it is necessary to identify a pair of integers with the constraint $x > 1$, $y > 1$ to minimize

$$f_M(x, y) = (M - x \cdot y)^2$$

The basic strategy for adiabatic optimization is as follows:

- Design final Hamiltonian H_F whose ground state encodes the solution of an optimization problem. The ground state is an eigenstate of H_F with a minimum eigenvalue.
- Prepare the known ground state of a simple initial Hamiltonian H_I that is easy to find.
- Slowly interpolate through the adiabatic evolution. The adiabatic evolution path (adiabat) is represented by a function $\alpha(t)$ that decreases from 1 to 0 with

  $$t : 0 \rightarrow t_{final}$$

  and

  $$\alpha(t) = 1 - \frac{t}{t_{final}}. \tag{16.6}$$

The resulting tome dependent Hamiltonian $H(t)$ is represented by a slow interpolation from H_I to H_F

$$H(t) = \alpha(t) \cdot H_I + (1 - \alpha(t)) \cdot H_F. \tag{16.7}$$

Usually the Hamiltonians are described by the Pauli operators σ^x, σ^y and σ^z in matrix notation by

$$\sigma^x = \begin{pmatrix} 0 & 1 \\ 1 & 0 \end{pmatrix}, \quad \sigma^y = \begin{pmatrix} 0 & -i \\ i & 0 \end{pmatrix}, \quad \sigma^z = \begin{pmatrix} 1 & 0 \\ 0 & -1 \end{pmatrix}.$$

16.1.1.1 *Example: two bit disagree problem*

In the two bit disagree problem the output is $|01\rangle$ or $|10\rangle$ but not $|0\rangle$ or $|11\rangle$ [Farhi *et al.* (2000)]. The cost/objective function is

$$f_{Dis}(x_1, x_2) = \begin{cases} 0 \; if \; x_1 \neq x_2 \\ 1 \; otherwise \end{cases} \tag{16.8}$$

The final Hamiltonian: For the eigenstates representing $|x_1\rangle$, $|x_2\rangle$ the Hamiltonian should have the eigenvalues that correspond to $f_{Dis}(|x_1, x_2\rangle)$. The final Hamiltonian is

$$H_F = \frac{I - \sigma_1^z \cdot \sigma_2^z}{2} = \frac{I_2 - (I \otimes \sigma^z) \cdot (\sigma^z \otimes I)}{2} \tag{16.9}$$

with subscript j in σ_j^z that the operator is applied only to the qubit x_j.

$$H_F = \frac{\begin{pmatrix} 1\,0\,0\,0 \\ 0\,1\,0\,0 \\ 0\,0\,1\,0 \\ 0\,0\,0\,1 \end{pmatrix} - \left(\begin{pmatrix} 1\,0 \\ 0\,1 \end{pmatrix} \otimes \begin{pmatrix} 1 & 0 \\ 0 & -1 \end{pmatrix}\right) \cdot \begin{pmatrix} 1 & 0 \\ 0 & -1 \end{pmatrix} \otimes \left(\begin{pmatrix} 1\,0 \\ 0\,1 \end{pmatrix}\right)}{2} \tag{16.10}$$

$$H_F = \frac{I - \sigma_1^z \cdot \sigma_2^z}{2} = \begin{pmatrix} 1\,0\,0\,0 \\ 0\,0\,0\,0 \\ 0\,0\,0\,0 \\ 0\,0\,0\,1 \end{pmatrix} \tag{16.11}$$

with the eigenstates (eigenvectors) and eigenvalues (energies)

$$H_F \cdot |00\rangle = 1 \cdot |00\rangle, \quad H_F \cdot |01\rangle = 0 \cdot |01\rangle,$$

$$H_F \cdot |10\rangle = 0 \cdot |10\rangle, \quad H_F \cdot |11\rangle = 1 \cdot |11\rangle.$$

The eigenstate and eigenvalues correspond to $f_{Dis}(|x_1, x_2\rangle)$ and the ground states with the minimal energy are $|01\rangle$ and $|10\rangle$.

The initial Hamiltonian: The ground state of initial Hamiltonian should be specified as a superposition of the eigenstates (basis states) of the final Hamiltonian, in our example

$$\frac{1}{2} \cdot |00\rangle + \frac{1}{2} \cdot |01\rangle + \frac{1}{2} \cdot |10\rangle + \frac{1}{2} \cdot |11\rangle.$$

To do it we will use the Pauli operator σ^x

$$\sigma^x = \begin{pmatrix} 0\,1 \\ 1\,0 \end{pmatrix}$$

with the eigenvectors and eigenvalues

$$\sigma^x \cdot \begin{pmatrix} \frac{1}{\sqrt{2}} \\ \frac{1}{\sqrt{2}} \end{pmatrix} = +1 \cdot \begin{pmatrix} \frac{1}{\sqrt{2}} \\ \frac{1}{\sqrt{2}} \end{pmatrix}, \qquad \sigma^x \cdot \begin{pmatrix} \frac{1}{\sqrt{2}} \\ -\frac{1}{\sqrt{2}} \end{pmatrix} = -1 \cdot \begin{pmatrix} \frac{1}{\sqrt{2}} \\ -\frac{1}{\sqrt{2}} \end{pmatrix}. \tag{16.12}$$

With

$$H_I^1 = \frac{1}{2} \cdot (I - \sigma^x) = \begin{pmatrix} \frac{1}{2} & -\frac{1}{2} \\ -\frac{1}{2} & \frac{1}{2} \end{pmatrix} \tag{16.13}$$

we get the eigenvectors and eigenvalues

$$H_I^1 \cdot \begin{pmatrix} \frac{1}{\sqrt{2}} \\ \frac{1}{\sqrt{2}} \end{pmatrix} = 0 \cdot \begin{pmatrix} \frac{1}{\sqrt{2}} \\ \frac{1}{\sqrt{2}} \end{pmatrix}, \quad H_I^1 \cdot \begin{pmatrix} \frac{1}{\sqrt{2}} \\ -\frac{1}{\sqrt{2}} \end{pmatrix} = +1 \cdot \begin{pmatrix} \frac{1}{\sqrt{2}} \\ -\frac{1}{\sqrt{2}} \end{pmatrix}. \quad (16.14)$$

We construct our initial Hamiltonian H_I with

$$H_I = H_I^2 = \sum_{j=1}^{2} \frac{1}{2} \cdot (I - \sigma_j^x) = \frac{1}{2} \cdot (I_2 - I \otimes \sigma^x) + (I_2 - \sigma^x \otimes I)) \quad (16.15)$$

$$H_I = \frac{\begin{pmatrix} 1\,0\,0\,0 \\ 0\,1\,0\,0 \\ 0\,0\,1\,0 \\ 0\,0\,0\,1 \end{pmatrix} - \left(\begin{pmatrix} 1\,0 \\ 0\,1 \end{pmatrix} \otimes \sigma^x \right) + \begin{pmatrix} 1\,0\,0\,0 \\ 0\,1\,0\,0 \\ 0\,0\,1\,0 \\ 0\,0\,0\,1 \end{pmatrix} - \left(\sigma^x \otimes \begin{pmatrix} 1\,0 \\ 0\,1 \end{pmatrix} \right)}{2} \quad (16.16)$$

$$H_I = \sum_{j=1}^{2} \frac{1}{2} \cdot (I - \sigma_j^x) = \begin{pmatrix} 1 & -\frac{1}{2} & -\frac{1}{2} & 0 \\ -\frac{1}{2} & 1 & 0 & -\frac{1}{2} \\ -\frac{1}{2} & 0 & 1 & -\frac{1}{2} \\ 0 & -\frac{1}{2} & -\frac{1}{2} & 1 \end{pmatrix} \quad (16.17)$$

with the eigenstates (eigenvectors) and eigenvalues (energies)

$$H_I \cdot \begin{pmatrix} \frac{1}{2} \\ -\frac{1}{2} \\ -\frac{1}{2} \\ \frac{1}{2} \end{pmatrix} = 2 \cdot \begin{pmatrix} \frac{1}{2} \\ -\frac{1}{2} \\ -\frac{1}{2} \\ \frac{1}{2} \end{pmatrix}, \quad H_I \cdot \begin{pmatrix} -\frac{1}{\sqrt{2}} \\ 0 \\ 0 \\ \frac{1}{\sqrt{2}} \end{pmatrix} = 1 \cdot \begin{pmatrix} -\frac{1}{\sqrt{2}} \\ 0 \\ 0 \\ \frac{1}{\sqrt{2}} \end{pmatrix}$$

$$H_I \cdot \begin{pmatrix} 0 \\ -\frac{1}{\sqrt{2}} \\ \frac{1}{\sqrt{2}} \\ 0 \end{pmatrix} = 1 \cdot \begin{pmatrix} 0 \\ -\frac{1}{\sqrt{2}} \\ \frac{1}{\sqrt{2}} \\ 0 \end{pmatrix}, \quad H_I \cdot \begin{pmatrix} \frac{1}{2} \\ \frac{1}{2} \\ \frac{1}{2} \\ \frac{1}{2} \end{pmatrix} = 0 \cdot \begin{pmatrix} \frac{1}{2} \\ \frac{1}{2} \\ \frac{1}{2} \\ \frac{1}{2} \end{pmatrix},$$

with the ground state (minimal energy/eigenvalue=0)

$$\frac{1}{2} \cdot |00\rangle + \frac{1}{2} \cdot |01\rangle + \frac{1}{2} \cdot |10\rangle + \frac{1}{2} \cdot |11\rangle$$

for which each eigenstate in the standard basis is equally probable.

Non Commuting Hamiltonians The initial Hamiltonian and the final Hamiltonian should not commute,

$$[H_I, H_F] \neq 0$$

If the Hamiltonians H_I and H_F commute they share the same set of eigenvectors, not necessary the same eigenvalues. If we prepare a ground state of the first Hamiltonian, then that will remain an eigenstate throughout the whole adiabatic evolution, and we get out what we put in [Farhi *et al.* (2000)].

The algorithm We will use the transition

$$\alpha(t) = 1 - \frac{t}{t_{final}}.$$

The algorithm is specified by

$$H(t) = \alpha(t) \cdot H_I + (1 - \alpha(t)) \cdot H_F.$$

At the end of the computation the register $|x_1\rangle$, $|x_2\rangle$ is in a low-energy superposition and the algorithm will return after measuring $|01\rangle$ or $|10\rangle$.

16.1.2 *Adiabatic theorem*

The adiabatic theorem describes certain properties that evolve according to the Schrödinger equation

$$i \cdot h \cdot \frac{d}{dt}|x(t)\rangle = H(t) \cdot |x(t)\rangle.$$

$H(t)$ describes the algorithm which evolves over time

$$t : 0 \rightarrow t_{final}.$$

Let $\tilde{H}(s)$ be an equivalent Hamiltonian on the time scale

$$s : 0 \rightarrow 1$$

with $s = \frac{t}{t_{final}}$ and let $\tau(s)$ determine the rate at which Hamiltonian changes as a function of s. Then we have

$$\frac{d}{ds}|x(s)\rangle = -i \cdot \tau(s) \cdot \tilde{H}(s) \cdot |x(s)\rangle. \tag{16.18}$$

If we assume that $\tilde{H}$ has a non-degenerated ground state (one eigenstate for minima energy/eigenvalue) and that the difference between the minimal eigenvalue of the ground state and the first excited state at time s is δ_s [Farhi *et al.* (2000)], [McGeoch (2014)]. The minimum spectral gap is

$$\delta_m = \min_s(\delta_s)$$

and we suppose that $\tau(s)$ is bounded by

$$\tau(s) \gg \frac{\left\| \frac{d}{s}\tilde{H}(s) \right\|_2}{(\delta_m)^2} \tag{16.19}$$

with the matrix norm $\|.\|_2$ induced by the l_2 metric, the spectral norm $\|H\|_2$ which is the square root of the maximum eigenvalue of $H^* \cdot H$

$$\|H\|_2 = (maximum\ eigenvalue\ of\ H^* \cdot H)^{1/2}.$$

Then the adiabatic theorem states that if for $s = 0$, $|x(s = 0)\rangle$ in the ground state and δ_m is strictly greater than 0 through time s and the process evolves slowly enough according to the Equation 16.19, then the process will finish in the ground state $|x(s = 1)\rangle$ with sufficiently high probability.

16.1.2.1 *Spectral gap*

For the theorem to hold, there must be a spectral gap δ_s between the ground state and the first excited state. The smaller the gap becomes, the slower one needs to interpolate to prevent mixing between the ground and first excited states. If the spectral gap δ_s is small, a too-quick transition time yields an increased probability that the system will jump from the ground state to the first excited state. For such a jump, an optimal solution cannot be reached. Figure 16.1 shows that the eigenvalues of the two-bit disagree problem move over time s [Farhi *et al.* (2000)]. The spectral gap δ_s is large. As s approaches 1, two ground states come together, and both of them represent a solution. Level crossing corresponds to $\delta_m = 0$, mixing

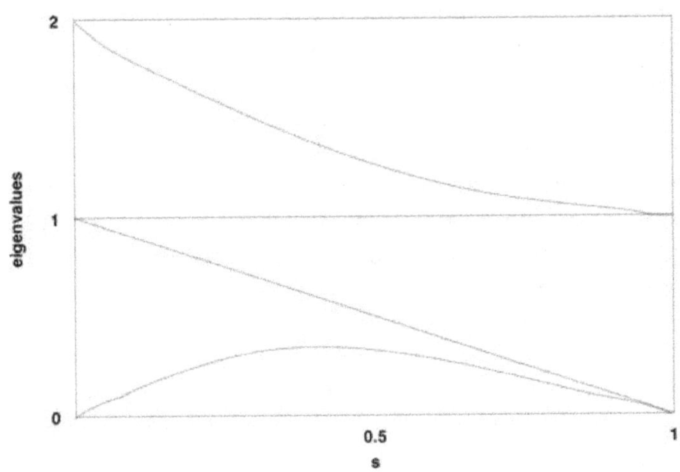

Fig. 16.1 The eigenvalues of the two-bit disagree problem move over time s. The spectral gap δ_s is large. As s approaches 1, two ground states come together, and both of them represent a solution.

cannot be prevented and therefore, the adiabatic theorem is not valid. The analysis of δ_m for a given algorithm is difficult. Therefore, the estimation of the upper bound of t_{final} is difficult.

16.2 Quantum Annealing

Frequently, adiabatic quantum computation and quantum annealing are used interchangeably; however there are some differences. Adiabatic quantum computation refers to a universal model to solve any Turing-compatible problem that runs in an adiabatically closed system without interference from the environment. Quantum annealing solves optimization problems. During computation, it is not assumed that the entire computation occurs in the ground state. The computation can run in an open system, and it does not need to be perfectly isolated from the environment. Energy from the environment creates noise that interferes with the computation so that the computation becomes heuristic. Therefore, the adiabatic theorem does not apply any more [McGeoch (2014)].

Quantum annealing is a method for finding the global minimum of a function [Brooke *et al.* (1999)], [Johnson *et al.* (2011)]. In quantum annealing, the quantum fluctuation parameter replaces a local minimum state with a randomly selected neighboring state in some fixed radius. The neighborhood extends in the entire search space at the beginning, and then, it is slowly reduced until the neighborhood shrinks to those few states that differ minimally from the current states. In a quantum system, quantum fluctuation can be performed directly by an adiabatic process rather than by needing to be simulated. These processes are based on quantum tunneling. In simulated annealing [Hertz *et al.* (1991)], temperature plays a role that is related to quantum fluctuation. In simulated annealing, the neighborhood stays the same throughout the search. The temperature determines the probability of moving out of a local minimum. At the beginning, the temperature is high, and the probability of moving out of a minimum is high. Then, the temperature is slowly reduced until the probability of moving out of a minimum is zero (see Figure 16.2). The disordering Hamiltonian H_D introduces quantum fluctuations in quantum annealing. The transverse field coefficient Γ, also called the tunneling coefficient, controls the passage of the solution landscape by tunneling. Like time temperature in simulated annealing, Γ starts at a high value and gradually decreases. With a final Hamiltonian H_F representing the objective function, the time-dependent Hamiltonian is represented with

$$H(t) = H_F + \Gamma(t) \cdot H_D \tag{16.20}$$

with

$$[H_F, H_D] \neq 0.$$

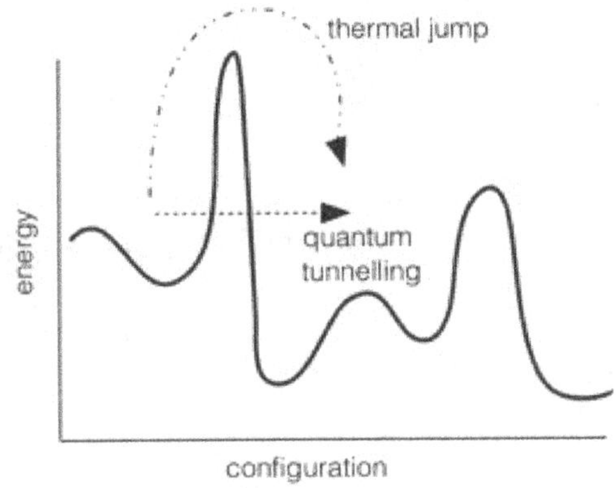

Fig. 16.2 Quantum annealing versus simulated annealing.

A decrease in $\Gamma(t)$ moves the system closer to H_F by reducing the tunneling effect. When $\Gamma(t)$ is large, H_D disorders the landscape of H_F, which represents an objective function. It allows the computation to escape the local minima of the objective function by tunneling through hills instead of climbing over them. Quantum annealing is similar to the adiabatic quantum computation, and the problem Hamiltonian H_F is the same. The disordering Hamiltonian H_D, which allows the heuristic search to escape local minima, is analogous to the initial Hamiltonian H_I, which ensures that the initial superposition states are equiprobable, and the transverse field coefficient Γ corresponds to the adiabatic path [McGeoch (2014)]. In adiabatic quantum computation, one finishes a ground state starting from the ground state. In quantum annealing one starts with an arbitrary state (random state) and converges with an error ϵ to the optimal solution. Unlike simulated annealing on a classical computer, a single state is not represented by moving across the energy landscape, but by several values that correspond to the superposition represented by the state.

16.2.1 *Problem Hamiltonian for Ising model*

Ising model describes a magnetic field consist of the internal field produced by the spins and varing external field h_i that influences the spins. The coefficient w_{ij} measures the strength of the influence of spin. The influence is symmetric $w_{ij} = w_{ji}$ with the Hamiltonian is

$$H_{Ising} = -\frac{1}{2} \cdot \sum_{i=1}^{n} \sum_{j=1}^{n} w_{ij} \cdot s_i \cdot s_j - \sum_{i=1}^{n} h_i \cdot s_i. \tag{16.21}$$

The quantum version of this Hamiltonian is with n qubits $|x_1, x_2, \cdots, x_n\rangle$ that are arranged in a grid where each qubit $|x_i\rangle$ interacts with its neighbor with the influence w_{ij} the Hamiltonian is

$$H_{Ising} = -\sum_{i=1}^{n} \sum_{j=1}^{n} w_{ij} \cdot \sigma_i^z \cdot \sigma_j^z - \sum_{i=1}^{n} h_i \cdot \sigma_i^z. \tag{16.22}$$

with subscript j in σ_j^z that the operator is applied only to the qubit x_j with the eigenstates (eigenvectors) and eigenvalues (energies)

$$\sigma^z \cdot |0\rangle = 1 \cdot |0\rangle, \quad \sigma^z \cdot |1\rangle = -1 \cdot |1\rangle,$$

with

$$\sigma_j^z \in \{-1, 1\}.$$

There is correspondence between $|x_i\rangle$ and s_i with

$$|1\rangle \to -1, \quad |0\rangle \to 1$$

$$\left(-\sum_{i=1}^{n} \sum_{j=1}^{n} w_{ij} \cdot \sigma_i^z \cdot \sigma_j^z - \sum_{i=1}^{n} h_i \cdot \sigma_i^z \right) |x\rangle$$

$$= -\sum_{i=1}^{n} \sum_{j=1}^{n} w_{ij} \cdot s_i \cdot s_j - \sum_{i=1}^{n} h_i \cdot s_i. \tag{16.23}$$

The time dependent Hamiltonian for quantum annealing is

$$H(t) = -\sum_{i=1}^{n} \sum_{j=1}^{n} w_{ij} \cdot \sigma_i^z \cdot \sigma_j^z - h \sum_{i=1}^{n} h_i \cdot \sigma_i^z - \Gamma(t) \sum_{i=1}^{n} \sigma_i^x \tag{16.24}$$

with disordering Hamiltonian $H_D = \sum_{i=1}^{n} \sigma_i^x$ which imposes a superposition of all states and

$$[H_{Ising}, H_D] \neq 0.$$

Usually on writes the strength of the influence of spin as J_{ij} instead of w_{ij} resulting in

$$H(t) = -\sum_{i<j} J_{ij} \cdot \sigma_i^z \cdot \sigma_j^z - \sum_{i} h_i \cdot \sigma_i^z - \Gamma(t) \sum_{i} \sigma_i^x. \tag{16.25}$$

16.2.2 *D-Wave*

The D-Wave [McGeoch (2014)] problem Hamiltonian is

$$H_P = \sum_{i<j} J_{ij} \cdot \sigma_i^z \cdot \sigma_j^z + \sum_i h_i \cdot \sigma_i^z \tag{16.26}$$

and the initial Hamiltonian (disordering Hamiltonian)

$$H_I = \sum_i \sigma_i^x. \tag{16.27}$$

The annealing evolution path is defined by a pair of envelope functions $A(s)$ and $B(s)$ (see Figure 16.3) with

$$s(t) : 0 \to 1, \qquad t : 0 \to t_{final}$$

and the time dependent Hamiltonian

$$H(t) = A(s(t)) \cdot H_I + B(s(t)) \cdot H_P \tag{16.28}$$

or

$$H(s) = A(s) \cdot H_I + B(s) \cdot H_P.$$

During the computation, the following tree steps occur: programming, annealing, and readout [McGeoch (2014)].

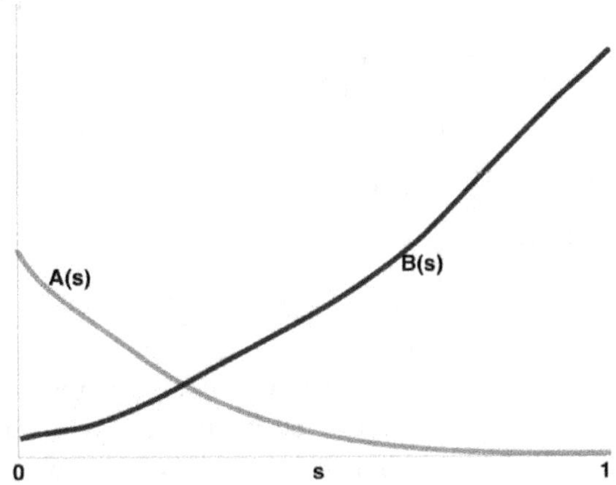

Fig. 16.3 The annealing evolution path is defined by a pair of envelope functions $A(s)$ and $B(s)$ with $s(t) : 0 \to 1, \quad t : 0 \to t_{final}$.

- Programming: The programmer specifies the weights J_{ij}, h_i, and t_{final}. The analog circuit has a fixed range and a limited precision. Then, the qubits are placed in superposition according to H_I. During the initialization, the qubits are in a superposition; however, they are not entangled. The qubits are represented by a loop of niobium controlled by Josephson junctions. When cooled, niobium loops exhibit a quantum mechanical behavior. By cooling the niobium loops to a very low temperature, the qubits are placed into superposition. The initialization time T_I, including the cooling time, dominates the computing time.
- Execution of the program:
  (1) Annealing: During annealing, the qubits change according to the annealing evolution path from the initial superposition to the problem Hamiltonian. A qubit can tunnel through the energy barrier and be entangled with other qubits. The anneal time T_A is negligible compared to the initialization time T_I.
  (2) Readout: At the end of the annealing process the qubits are in classical states and represent with some probability the ground states according to problem Hamiltonian. The computation does not need to finish in the ground state because the environment that creates noise infers with the computation. In addition, qubits are represented in a classical state to avoid the interaction with the environment during the read. The qubits are read, and the chip is cooled again for the next resampling phase with time T_R,
- Because the computation is heuristic, the anneal read out cycle is repeated $k = 1000$ to $k = 10000$ times to increase the probability of finding the correct solution. With

$$T_A < T_R \ll T_I$$

the computing costs are

$$T_k = T_I + k \cdot (T_A + T_R). \tag{16.29}$$

It is difficult to compare simulated annealing times with D-Wave quantum annealing times because the times are mostly dominated by T_I initialization times. The comparison becomes interesting for many qubits. D-Wave, which is the central processor, is made of loops of niobium surrounded by components designed to protect it from heat, vibration, and electromagnetic noise, see Figure 16.4. The D-Wave 2000Q architecture uses 2048 qubits, and the next-generation Pegasus chip uses 5000 qubits. The adiabatic theorem does not apply for the current D-Wave quantum annealer since the

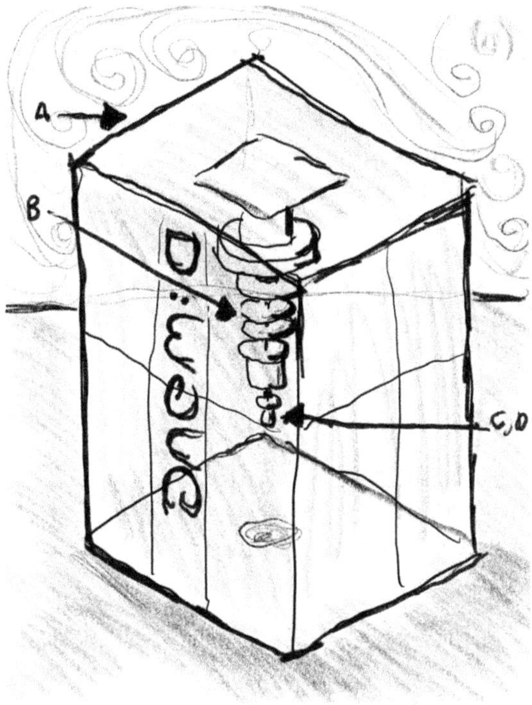

Fig. 16.4 A). Refrigeration system uses liquid helium to cool the D-Wave chip. B) Gold-plated copper disks draw heat up and away from the chip to keep vibration and other energy from disturbing the quantum state of the processor. C) A grid of hundreds of tiny niobium loops, which serve as qubits. When cooled, they exhibit a quantum mechanical behavior. D) Noise shields.

architecture is constrained. The D-Wave quantum annealer is not a general quantum computer. The current chips require problem Hamiltonians to be specified with reals on the diagonal and zeros on the off-diagonal. Furthermore, the structure of the graph is local, and not every qubit communicates with another qubit.

16.2.2.1 *Native form*

A general optimization problem is transformed into a a native instance in a two-step process. In the first step, the problem is translated into the Ising model and then mapped into the connectivity graph of the D-Wave quantum annealer. Fully connected graphs have to be encoded because the graph structure of the D-Wave quantum annealer is restricted, and not every qubit communicates with another qubit. Without any embedding, only sparse connected models can be used. For mapping, one binary variable in the quadratic optimization problem frequently needs to be represented by two (or more) qubits instead of one, which makes the number of physical qubits needed to solve the original problem larger than before [Dattani and Chancellor (2019)].

Chimera graph: In early devices, a chimera graph structure was used. The Chimera architecture comprises sets of connected unit cells, each with four horizontal qubits connected to four vertical qubits by couplers. Unit cells are tiled vertically and horizontally with adjacent qubits being connected, creating a lattice of sparsely connected qubits.

Pegasus graph: Pegasus is a graph that offers a considerably increased connectivity between the qubits of quantum annealing hardware compared to that in the Chimera graph (see Figure 16.5, Figure 16.6, Figure 16.7. [Dattani *et al.* (2019)].

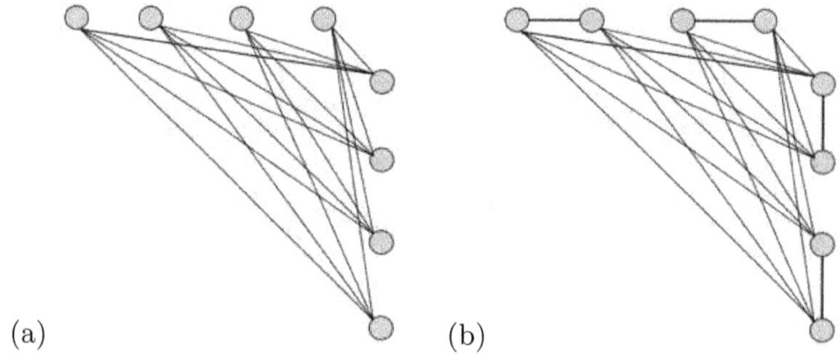

Fig. 16.5 (a) A single cell of a grid of a Chimera graph by triangle representation. (b) A single cell of a grid of a Pegasus graph by triangle representation, thick lines indicate the new connections.

16.2.2.2 *Boltzmann machine*

To apply the Boltzmann machine to machine learning for a training pattern, the parameters are assigned values so that the energy associated with the pattern within the training set is significantly lower than that for an arbitrary pattern. Then, when posed with a task of recognizing whether a particular unknown pattern resembles that from the training set, the en-

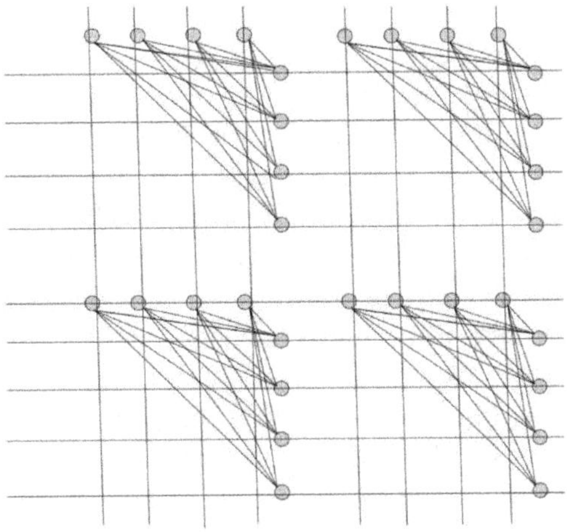

Fig. 16.6 Triangle sepiction of the Chimera graph, with open edges to show that the pattern repeats.

ergy for that pattern is calculated. A low value indicates a high likelihood of a positive answer. The model assumes that some given dataset is generated according to the Boltzmann distribution, and the goal of the training procedure is to identify a set of parameters that most closely match the input data distribution. The joint probability is described by the Boltzmann distribution

$$p_\alpha = \frac{1}{Z} \cdot e^{\left(-\frac{H_\alpha}{k \cdot T}\right)} = \frac{1}{Z} \cdot e^{(-\beta \cdot H_\alpha)} \tag{16.30}$$

where β is the inverse temperature of the system

$$\beta = \frac{1}{k \cdot T} \tag{16.31}$$

and Z is the normalizing constant or a partition function. While it is easy to compute the unnormalized probability $e^{(-\beta \cdot H_\alpha)}$, the exact calculation of the partition function Z is intractable for a large system. Therefore, approximate methods are usually employed by generating unbiased samples from the true Boltzmann distribution, which can then be used to estimate the partition function. In a quantum annealer, we approximate the Boltzmann distribution with

$$p_\alpha = \frac{1}{Z} \cdot e^{(-\beta_{eff} \cdot H_{P\alpha})}. \tag{16.32}$$

The scale factor β_{eff} between the problem Hamiltonian H_P is not the usual β [Amin *et al.* (2018)], [Schuld and Petruccione (2018)], [Ulanov *et al.* (2020)]. The dimensional scale factor β_{eff} has to be programmed and determined by empirical experiments. A quantum annealer with a linear annealing schedule does not return Boltzmann distribution and will deviate from the equilibrium distribution and soon after the dynamics will freeze. Experiments on the D-Wave annealer showed that distributions can deviate from the classical Boltzmann distribution; however, they work well for training the Boltzmann machine and reduce the number of training steps compared to the contrast divergence. In addition, compared to the contrast divergence algorithm, fully connected Boltzmann machines can be used [Ulanov *et al.* (2020)]. Moreover, if the dynamical slow-down and freeze-out happen within a short period of time during the annealing, then the final distribution will be close to the quantum Boltzmann distribution at a single point s^* called the freeze-out time. Thus, the quantum annealer with a linear annealing schedule will provide approximate samples from the Boltzmann distribution [Amin *et al.* (2018)]. If $A(s^*)$ happens to be sufficiently small, the resulting Boltzmann distribution will be close to the classical Boltzmann distribution. In such a case, the quantum annealer can be used as an approximate classical Boltzmann sampler to train the Boltzmann machine. If s^* is in the region where the evolution is still quasistatic (sufficiently slowly for the system to remain in internal equilibrium),

$$H(s^*) = A(s^*) \cdot H_I + B(s^*) \cdot H_P.$$

$$H(s^*) = A(s^*) \cdot \sum_i \sigma_i^x + B(s^*) \cdot \sum_{i<j} J_{ij} \cdot \sigma_i^z \cdot \sigma_j^z + \sum_i h_i \cdot \sigma_i^z. \tag{16.33}$$

the quantum annealer will provide samples with the Boltzmann distribution

$$w_{ij} = \beta_{eff} \cdot B(s^*) \cdot J_{ij}, \qquad b_i = \beta_{eff} \cdot B(s^*) \cdot h_i. \tag{16.34}$$

16.2.2.3 *Deep belief networks*

Deep neural networks or deep belief networks [Salakhutdinov and Hinton (2012)] capture higher level representations of input features. They are composed of multiple layers of restricted Boltzmann machines. Due to the constraints of RBM, only one step is required to reach thermal equilibrium when the visible units are clamped and the hidden units are chosen random (0 or 1). One can quickly obtain the exact value of

$$\langle v_i h_j \rangle_{data}. \tag{16.35}$$

During the negative phase to avoid the long computing time of model expectations

$$\langle v_i h_j \rangle_{model} \tag{16.36}$$

contrastive divergence (CD)-based learning has been proposed. It does not directly use Gibbs sampling starting at random chosen units. An alternative approach is to estimate model expectations by a quantum annealer [Wilson *et al.* (2019)]. This method was tested using a D-Wave annealer on a coarse-grained version of the MNIST data set [Adachi and Henderson (2015)]. During the tests of the quantum sampling-based training, the described approach achieved comparable or better accuracy with significantly fewer iterations of generative training than conventional CD-based training [Adachi and Henderson (2015)], [Wilson *et al.* (2019)].

16.3 Variational Algorithms

Variational algorithms are related to the adiabatic quantum computation, however they are based on discrete unitary evolution [Schuld and Petruccione (2018)], [Hidary (2019)]. The eigenvalues of a Hamiltonian H correspond to the energies of their eigenstates. The spectral representation of H indicates all possible energies and eigenstates of the system

$$H = \lambda_1 \cdot |x_1\rangle\langle x_1| + \cdots + \lambda_n \cdot |x_n\rangle\langle x_n|. \tag{16.37}$$

The set of all possible energies is the energy spectrum of the size n

$$\{\lambda_1, \lambda_2, \cdots, \lambda_n\}$$

the ground state is a state is an observable state having minimum energy over all eigenstates with

$$\min\{\lambda_1, \lambda_2, \cdots, \lambda_n\} \leq \langle H \rangle = \sum_{i=1}^{n} \lambda_i \cdot p(\lambda_i).$$

16.3.1 *Variational quantum eigensolvers*

The variational quantum eigensolver is a hybrid algorithm based on a quantum device and a classical algorithm to estimate the ground state of a system [Schuld and Petruccione (2018)], [Hidary (2019)]. A parametrized quantum state is prepared by parametrized quantum operator. For example the state $\psi(\theta)$ is generated by a rotation operator R_θ with

$$|\psi(\theta)\rangle = R_\theta \cdot |0\rangle = \begin{pmatrix} \cos\theta & -\sin\theta \\ \sin\theta & \cos\theta \end{pmatrix} \cdot \begin{pmatrix} 1 \\ 0 \end{pmatrix} \tag{16.38}$$

and the expected value is determined through several measurements with

$$C(\theta) = \langle \psi(\theta)|H|\psi(\theta)\rangle \tag{16.39}$$

For different parameter θ the expected values $C(\theta)$ are determined that describe a function $f(\theta)$

$$C(\theta) = f(\theta). \tag{16.40}$$

A classical algorithm tries to determine the next possible θ that minimizes the function $f(\theta)$. The goal is to estimate the minima of the unknown function $f(\theta)$ that represents the ground state of the Hamiltonian H. A high dimensional state $\psi(\tilde{\theta})$ is generated by al tensor product of several parametrized operators. A Hamiltonian can be decomposed leading to a quantum advantage compared to a classical approach. Many practical cases the hamiltonian H can be written as weighted sum of local 1-qubit or 2-qubit operators

$$H = \sum_{k=1}^{L} h_k \cdot H_k \tag{16.41}$$

with the expectation

$$C(\tilde{\theta}) = \sum_{k=1}^{L} h_k \cdot \langle \psi(\tilde{\theta}) | H_k | \psi(\tilde{\theta}) \rangle \tag{16.42}$$

over the local expectation values $\langle \psi(\tilde{\theta}) | H_k | \psi(\tilde{\theta}) \rangle$ that are much easier to estimate.

16.3.1.1 *Quantum chemistry*

Chemical reactions can be simulated by Hamiltonian simulation together with variational quantum Eigensolvers [Hidary (2019)]. An already programmable array of superconducting qubits was used to compute the energy surface of molecular hydrogen [O'Malley *et al.* (2016)].

16.3.2 *Quantum approximate optimization algorithms*

Quantum approximate optimization algorithms are used for optimization problems. The goal is to optimize a cost function represented by a Hamiltonian [Schuld and Petruccione (2018)], [Hidary (2019)]. The algorithm is motivated by quantum adiabatic computation; however, instead of a smooth continuous evolution, where the inititwo operators $U(I, \beta)$ and $U(P, \gamma)$. With the problem Hamiltonian al Hamiltonian H_I is slowly turned into the final Hamiltonian H_F without leaving the ground state, one uses alternating evolutions defined by two operators $U(I, \beta)$ and $U(P, \gamma)$. With the problem Hamiltonian

$$H_P = -\sum_{i<j} J_{ij} \cdot \sigma_i^z \cdot \sigma_j^z - \sum_i h_i \cdot \sigma_i^z \tag{16.43}$$

and the initial Hamiltonian (disordering Hamiltonian)

$$H_I = -\sum_i \sigma_i^x. \tag{16.44}$$

We define the unitary operators

$$U(P, \gamma) = e^{-i \cdot H_P \cdot \gamma} \tag{16.45}$$

with a parameter γ corresponding to an angle and

$$U(I, \beta) = e^{-i \cdot H_I \cdot \beta} \tag{16.46}$$

with a parameter β corresponding to an angle. Strat with an initial superposition of n qubits

$$|s\rangle = W_n \cdot |0^{\otimes n}\rangle = \frac{1}{\sqrt{2^n}} \sum_{x \in B^n} |x\rangle. \tag{16.47}$$

Alternately apply p times

$$|\psi(\theta)\rangle = \prod_{i=1}^{p} U(I, \beta_i) \cdot U(P, \gamma_i) \cdot |s\rangle \tag{16.48}$$

with different parameters β_i, γ_i at each step. The parameters θ consists of parameters $\beta_1, \beta_2, \cdots \beta_p, \gamma_1, \gamma_2 \cdots \gamma_p$. Estimate the expectation value of H_P

$$C(\theta) = \langle \psi(\theta) | H_P | \psi(\theta) \rangle. \tag{16.49}$$

We use then a classical optimization algorithm to compute the maximum or minimum value for $C(\theta)$. Repeat the procedure several times. Then later we can sample $|\psi(\theta)\rangle$ that encodes the approximate optima of H_P. It was shown using the adiabatic theorem that if we have enough different parameters β_i, γ_i with

$$\lim_{p \to \infty} \max_{\theta} C(\theta) = \max_{x} H_P. \tag{16.50}$$

We preform approximate optimization since p is finite [Schuld and Petruccione (2018)]. However, it has been reported that there are strong limitations in variational quantum approximate optimization [Akshay *et al.* (2020)]. The ability to approximate optimal solutions for any fixed depth quantum circuit is fundamentally dependent on the problem constraints to variable count. This is sometimes called clause density. The problematic instances of high density with optimal solutions cannot be approximated with a guaranteed success, regardless of the algorithm's run time.

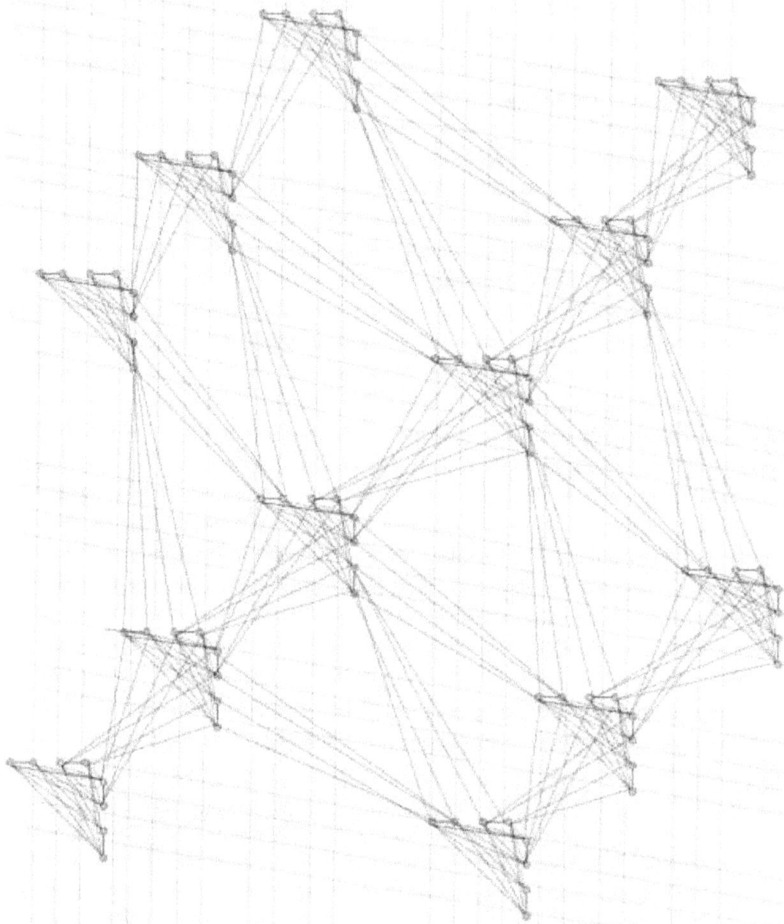

Fig. 16.7 A triangle description of a patch out of a Pegasus graph that connects different layers.

Chapter 17

Quantum Cognition

The wave function in quantum mechanics represents a superposition of states. If unobserved it evolves smoothly and continuously; however, during the measurement, it collapses into a definite state. According to most physical textbooks, the existence of the wave function and its collapse is only present in the microscopic world and is not present in the macroscopic world. More physical experiments indicate that wave functions are present in the macroscopic world [Vedral (2011)]. Physical experiments state that the size does not matter and that a very large number of atoms can be entangled [Ghosh *et al.* (2003)], [Amico *et al.* (2008)]. Clues from psychology indicate that human cognition is not only based on traditional probability theory as explained by Kolmogorov's axioms but additionally on quantum probability, see [Busemeyer *et al.* (2006b); Busemeyer and Trueblood (2009); Busemeyer *et al.* (2009, 2012); Busemeyer and Wang (2014); Khrennikov (2009)]. For example, humans when making decisions violate the law of total probability. The emerging field that studies the corresponding models is called Quantum Cognition. This approach would lead to the conclusion that a wave function can be present at the macro scale of our daily life.

17.1 Ordering Effects

Order effects represent the probability of asking question A followed by question B, which usually gives different results if we pose questions in a reverse order. Moore describes the violation of order effects [Moore (2002)]. One of the quantum approaches, which is used to explain order effects, is the quantum projection model, which is also known as the quantum geometric model [Pothos *et al.* (2013)], [Trueblood *et al.* (2014)]. In the quantum projection model, the quantum interference parameters do not play any role in the computation of final probabilities. To model a sequence of answers, we start by projecting this superposition state into the basis with the desired answer. From this basis, we perform a second projection to another basis, which represents the desired answer for the second question and corresponds to the rotation of the initial basis state. Person's beliefs correspond to the n-dimensional superposition state (for the case of binary questions, $n = 2$), which is represented by the real vector of the length one in the l_2 norm [Moreira and Wichert (2017)].. With a symmetrical real vector $\mathbf{x}$ of length one in l_2, for example

$$\mathbf{x} = \begin{pmatrix} x_1 \\ x_2 \end{pmatrix}$$

with

$$1 = |x_1|^2 + |x_2|^2.$$

Each dimension corresponds to a belief with the probability of

$$p(belief_1) = |x_1|^2, \quad p(belief_2) = |x_2|^2$$

A question is represented by an orthogonal matrix of dimension $n \times n$ with $A^T \cdot A = 1$. (For complex matrices the matrix is unitary). The vector is rotated

$$\mathbf{y} = A \cdot \mathbf{x}$$

Since multiplication with an orthogonal is norm preserving in l_2

$$1 = |y_1|^2 + |y_2|^2$$

The probability of beliefs is now

$$p(belief_1) = |y_1|^2, \quad p(belief_2) = |y_2|^2$$

A second question is represented a second orthogonal matrix of dimension $n \times n$ with $B^T \cdot B = 1$.

$$\mathbf{z} = A \cdot \mathbf{y}$$

The probability of beliefs is now

$$p(belief_1) = |z_1|^2, \quad p(belief_2) = |z_2|^2$$

We can summarize by

$$\mathbf{z} = B \cdot A \cdot \mathbf{x}.$$

Usually matrix multiplication is not commutative

$$A \cdot B \neq B \cdot A \Longleftrightarrow [A, B] \neq 0.$$

with

$$[A, B] := A \cdot B - B \cdot A$$

It follows

$$B \cdot A \cdot \mathbf{x} \neq A \cdot B \cdot \mathbf{x}.$$

The model is called quantum-like since the motivated by observables and it uses the l_2 norm that is norm preserving since the l_1 norm is not length preserving during rotation.

17.2 Quantum Probability

Until "recently" quantum physics was the only branch in science that evaluated a probability $p(x)$ of a state x as the squared magnitude of a probability amplitude $A(x)$, which is represented by a complex number

$$p(x) = |A(x)|^2 = A(x)^* \cdot A(x). \tag{17.1}$$

This is because the product of complex number with its conjugate is always a real number. With

$$A(x) = \alpha + \beta \cdot i \tag{17.2}$$

$$A(x)^* \cdot A(x) = (\alpha - \beta \cdot i) \cdot (\alpha + \beta \cdot i) \tag{17.3}$$

$$A(x)^* \cdot A(x) = \alpha^2 + \beta^2 = |A(x)|^2. \tag{17.4}$$

Quantum physics by itself does not offer any justification or explanation beside the statement that it just works fine, see [Binney and Skinner (2014)]. This quantum probabilities are as well called von Neumann probabilities.

17.2.1 *Two-slit interference*

Suppose there are two mutual exclusive events x and y. This means x and y do not occur together. The classical probability of an event x or event y is just

$$p(x \vee y) = p(x) + p(y). \tag{17.5}$$

This is the sum rule for probabilities for exclusive events. For probability amplitudes, it is as well

$$A(x \vee y) = A(x) + A(y). \tag{17.6}$$

However converting these amplitudes into probabilities according to Equation 17.1 leads to an interference term $2 \cdot \Re(A(x) \cdot A^*(y))$,

$$\begin{aligned} |A(x) + A(y)|^2 &= |A(x)|^2 + |A(y)|^2 + 2 \cdot \Re(A(x) \cdot A^*(y)) \\ |A(x) + A(y)|^2 &= p(x) + p(y) + 2 \cdot \Re(A(x) \cdot A^*(y)), \end{aligned} \tag{17.7}$$

making both approaches, in general, incompatible

$$|A(x) + A(y)|^2 \neq p(x) + p(y). \tag{17.8}$$

In other words, the summation rule of classical probability theory is violated, resulting in one of the most fundamental laws of quantum mechanics, see [Binney and Skinner (2014)]. Suppose that an unobserved state evolves smoothly and continuously. However, during the measurement, it collapses into a definite state with a probability $p(x) = |A(x)|^2$. For instance, let us imagine a gun that fires electrons and a screen with two narrow slits x and y and a photographic plate. An emitted electron can pass through slit x or slit y and reaches the photographic plate at the position z, which is equidistant from both slits. The electron detectors show from which slit the electron went through, and we find that the probability of the electron hitting the photographic plate is

$$p(z) = p(x) + p(y). \tag{17.9}$$

This probability means that, when measured, the electron behaved as a particle. On the other hand, if we remove the detectors, the electron is unobserved, not knowing through which slit it went through. Now, the electron is represented as a wave with the amplitudes

$$a(x, \theta_1) = \sqrt{p(x)} \cdot e^{i \cdot \theta_1} = A(x), \tag{17.10}$$

$$a(y, \theta_2) = \sqrt{p(y)} \cdot e^{i \cdot \theta_2} = A(y). \tag{17.11}$$

These amplitudes contain a parameter θ, which corresponds to the phase of the wave. The equation then becomes

$$|a(x, \theta_1) + a(y, \theta_2)|^2 = (a(x, \theta_1) + a(y, \theta_2)) \cdot (a(x, \theta_1) + a(y, \theta_2))^* \tag{17.12}$$

with

$$p(z) \neq |a(x, \theta_1) + a(y, \theta_2)|^2 \geq 0$$

for most values of θ_1, θ_2. Since the norm is being positive or more precisely non-negative, the value are always bigger equal zero. Then

$$|a(x,\theta_1) + a(y,\theta_2)|^2 =$$

$$\left(\sqrt{p(x)} \cdot e^{i\cdot\theta_1} + \sqrt{p(y)} \cdot e^{i\cdot\theta_2}\right) \cdot (\sqrt{p(x)} \cdot e^{-i\cdot\theta_1} + \sqrt{p(y)} \cdot e^{-i\cdot\theta_2}) =$$

$$\sqrt{p(y) \cdot p(x)} \cdot e^{i\cdot(\theta_2-\theta_1)} + \sqrt{p(x) \cdot p(y)} \cdot e^{i\cdot(\theta_1-\theta_2)}. =$$

$$p(x) + p(y) + \sqrt{p(x) \cdot p(y)} \cdot \left(e^{i\cdot(\theta_1-\theta_2)} + e^{-i\cdot(\theta_1-\theta_2)}\right). \tag{17.13}$$

With

$$\cos(\theta_1 - \theta_2) = \frac{\left(e^{i\cdot(\theta_1-\theta_2)} + e^{-i\cdot(\theta_1-\theta_2)}\right)}{2}. \tag{17.14}$$

we simplify to

$$p(x) + p(y) + 2 \cdot \sqrt{p(x) \cdot p(y)} \cdot \cos(\theta_1 - \theta_2). \tag{17.15}$$

The amplitude is the root of the belief multiplied with the corresponding phase with the phase $\theta \in [0, 2 \cdot \pi)$

$$A(x) = a(x,\theta) = \sqrt{p(x)} \cdot e^{i\cdot\theta}. \tag{17.16}$$

As stated before the numerical degree of belief can result from either from a frequentist approach or be determined from the nature of the universe, like for example the probability of throwing a six in a fair dice. Alternatively it can be seen as a subjective viewpoint. On the other hand it is difficult to attribute any meaning to the phase specified by the angle θ, see Figure 17.1. One way tp overcome this problem is to fit θ to some experimental data. In the following sections, rather than dealing with some binary events, we will introduce some states corresponding to some states of nature. Logical possibilities of events are usually called the elementary events or states of nature. Here we will address to them simply as states.

17.3 Decision Making

Humans when making decisions violate the law of total probability. The violation can be explained as a quantum interference resulting from the phase represented by the angle θ. In an experiment, the violation of the law of total probability was demonstrated by a categorization and decision experiment [Busemeyer *et al.* (2009)]. 26 participants preformed 51 trials

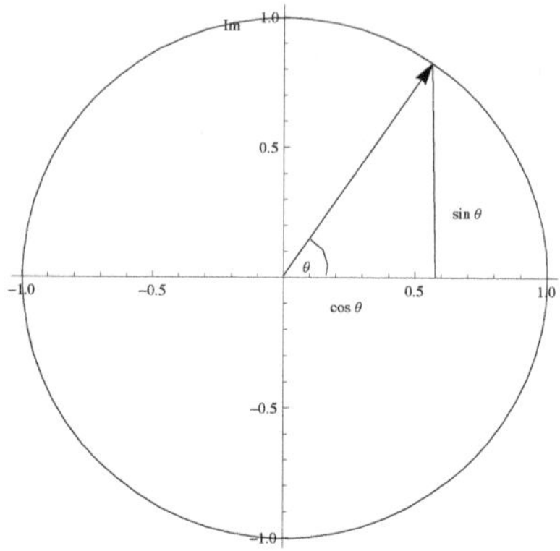

Fig. 17.1 The value of θ correspond to an angle, can take infinite many values describing a circle in the complex number plane of the radius one described by the equation $e^{i\cdot\theta} = \cos\theta + i \cdot \sin\theta$.

per condition. All together there were $26 \cdot 51 = 1326$ observation per condition. During the experiment the participants were shown pictures of faces. They should categorize the person represented on the pictures as good or bad and in the next step decide to act friendly or aggressive. There were two experimental conditions:

- Make a decision without reporting any categorization.
- Make a decision after categorizing a face.

In the second condition the conditional probabilities of categorization images of face were determined

$$p(good|face) = 0.17 \quad p(bad|face) = 0.83$$

mostly the faces were categorized as being bad. Then the conditional probabilities of acting friendly or aggressive were determined,

$$p(aggressive|good) = 0.42 \quad p(friendly|good) = 0.58$$

and

$$p(aggressive|bad) = 0.63 \quad p(friendly|bad) = 0.37.$$

We can represent the experiment by a simple graph with two nodes with the following simplification

$$p(good) = p(good|face) = 0.17$$

$$p(\neg good) = p(bad|face) = 0.83$$

and

$$p(\neg friendly|good) = 0.42 \;\; p(friendly|good) = 0.58$$

$$p(\neg friendly|\neg good) = 0.63 \;\; p(friendly|\neg good) = 0.37,$$

see Figure 17.2. For mutually exclusive events

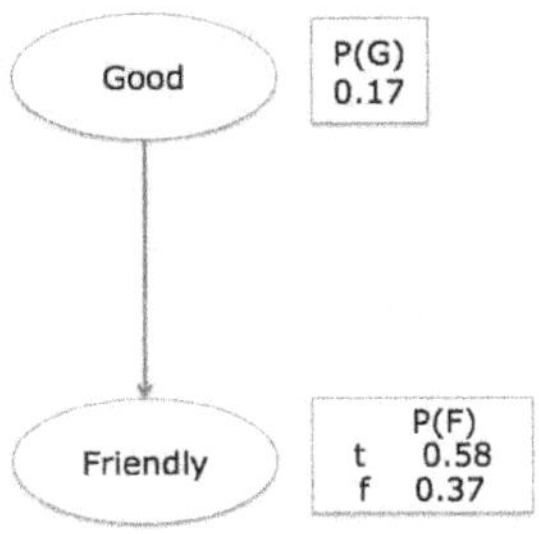

Fig. 17.2 A graph with two nodes and the corresponding conditional probability tables. Each row requires one number p for $p(X) = true$ ($p(X) = false$ is $1 - p$).

$$p(good) + p(\neg good) = 1$$

the law of total probability is

$$p(Friendly) = \sum_{good} p(Friendly|good) \cdot p(good) \tag{17.17}$$

$$p(Friendly|Good) = p(good) \cdot p(Friendly|good)$$

$$+ p(\neg good) \cdot p(Friendly|\neg good) \tag{17.18}$$

$$p(friendly) = 0.58 \cdot 0.17 + 0.37 \cdot 0.83 = 0.4057, \tag{17.19}$$

$$p(\neg friendly) = 0.42 \cdot 0.17 + 0.63 \cdot 0.83 = 0.5943. \tag{17.20}$$

In the first condition of the experiment a decision without reporting any categorization was determined. The value was

$$p(\neg friendly) = p(aggressive|face) = 0.69.$$

The value is incompatible with the classical probability theory, it does not correspond to the correct value as indicated by the law of total probability

$$0.69 > \sum_{good} p(\neg friendly|good) \cdot p(good) = 0.5943.$$

Why do human violate the law of total probability during decision making? A possible explanation is given by the quantum probabilities. In quantum probabilities the law of total probability is not valid

$$p(\neg friendly) \neq$$

$$\left| \sum_{i=1}^{2} e^{i \cdot \theta_{frendly|good}} \cdot \sqrt{p(\neg firendly|good)} \cdot e^{i \cdot \theta_{good}} \cdot \sqrt{p(good)} \right|^2 . \quad (17.21)$$

In quantum cognition the quantum probabilities are used to explain this violation, Usually the corresponding phase values are fitted to the data. We will indicate the solution for the Equation 17.21. We simplify the Equation 17.21 to the equivalent equation

$$\left| \sum_{i=1}^{2} e^{i \cdot \theta_{\alpha_i}} \cdot \sqrt{\alpha_i} \cdot e^{i \cdot \theta_{\beta_i}} \cdot \sqrt{\beta_i} \right|^2 = \quad (17.22)$$

$$\left| e^{i \cdot \theta_{\alpha 1}} \cdot \sqrt{\alpha_1} \cdot e^{i \cdot \theta_{\beta 1}} \cdot \sqrt{\beta_1} + e^{i \cdot \theta_{\alpha 2}} \cdot \sqrt{\alpha_2} \cdot e^{i \cdot \theta_{\beta 2}} \cdot \sqrt{\beta_2} \right|^2 =$$

with the complex conjugate representation

$$\left(e^{i \cdot \theta_{\alpha 1}} \cdot \sqrt{\alpha_1} \cdot e^{i \cdot \theta_{\beta 1}} \cdot \sqrt{\beta_1} + e^{i \cdot \theta_{\alpha 2}} \cdot \sqrt{\alpha_2} \cdot e^{i \cdot \theta_{\beta 2}} \cdot \sqrt{\beta_2} \right) \cdot$$

$$\left(e^{i \cdot \theta_{\alpha 1}} \cdot \sqrt{\alpha_1} \cdot e^{i \cdot \theta_{\beta 1}} \cdot \sqrt{\beta_1} + e^{i \cdot \theta_{\alpha 2}} \cdot \sqrt{\alpha_2} \cdot e^{i \cdot \theta_{\beta 2}} \cdot \sqrt{\beta_2} \right)^* = \quad (17.23)$$

$$\left(e^{i \cdot \theta_{\alpha 1}} \cdot \sqrt{\alpha_1} \cdot e^{i \cdot \theta_{\beta 1}} \cdot \sqrt{\beta_1} + e^{i \cdot \theta_{\alpha 2}} \cdot \sqrt{\alpha_2} \cdot e^{i \cdot \theta_{\beta 2}} \cdot \sqrt{\beta_2} \right) \cdot$$

$$\left(e^{-i \cdot \theta_{\alpha 1}} \cdot \sqrt{\alpha_1} \cdot e^{-i \cdot \theta_{\beta 1}} \cdot \sqrt{\beta_1} + e^{-i \cdot \theta_{\alpha 2}} \cdot \sqrt{\alpha_2} \cdot e^{-i \cdot \theta_{\beta 2}} \cdot \sqrt{\beta_2} \right) = \quad (17.24)$$

$$\alpha_1 \cdot \beta_1 + \alpha_2 \cdot \beta_2 + \sqrt{\alpha_1} \cdot \sqrt{\alpha_2} \cdot \sqrt{\beta_1} \cdot \sqrt{\beta_2} \cdot$$

$$\left(e^{i \cdot (\theta_{\alpha_1} - \theta_{\alpha_2} + \theta_{\beta_1} - \theta_{\beta_2})} + e^{-i \cdot (\theta_{\alpha_1} - \theta_{\alpha_2} + \theta_{\beta_1} - \theta_{\beta_2})} \right) =$$

$$\alpha_1 \cdot \beta_1 + \alpha_2 \cdot \beta_2 + \sqrt{\alpha_1} \cdot \sqrt{\alpha_2} \cdot \sqrt{\beta_1} \cdot \sqrt{\beta_2} \cdot 2 \cdot \cos(\theta_{\alpha_1} - \theta_{\alpha_2} + \theta_{\beta_1} - \theta_{\beta_2}) \quad (17.25)$$

with

$$\theta := \theta_{\alpha_1} - \theta_{\alpha_2} + \theta_{\beta_1} - \theta_{\beta_2}$$

we can simplify to

$$\alpha_1 \cdot \beta_1 + \alpha_2 \cdot \beta_2 + 2 \cdot \sqrt{\alpha_1} \cdot \sqrt{\alpha_2} \cdot \sqrt{\beta_1} \cdot \sqrt{\beta_2} \cdot \cos(\theta). \quad (17.26)$$

It should be noted that

$$-1 \leq \cos(\theta) \leq 1 \tag{17.27}$$

and

$$\frac{\alpha_1 \cdot \beta_1 + \alpha_2 \cdot \beta}{2} \geq \sqrt{\alpha_1} \cdot \sqrt{\alpha_2} \cdot \sqrt{\beta_1} \cdot \sqrt{\beta_2}. \tag{17.28}$$

If

$$0 \leq \alpha_1 \cdot \beta_1 + \alpha_2 \cdot \beta \leq 1 \tag{17.29}$$

then

$$0 \leq \alpha_1 \cdot \beta_1 + \alpha_2 \cdot \beta_2 + 2 \cdot \sqrt{\alpha_1} \cdot \sqrt{\alpha_2} \cdot \sqrt{\beta_1} \cdot \sqrt{\beta_2} \cdot \cos(\theta) \leq 2. \tag{17.30}$$

and we have to fit the parameter θ to the data so it becomes the desired probability value. The solution for the Equation 17.21 is

$$\left| \sum_{i=1}^{2} e^{i \cdot \theta_{frendly|good}} \cdot \sqrt{p(\neg firendly|good)} \cdot e^{i \cdot \theta_{good}} \cdot \sqrt{p(good)} \right|^2 =$$
$$p(\neg firendly|good) \cdot p(good) + p(\neg firendly|\neg good) \cdot p(\neg good) +$$
$$2 \cdot \sqrt{p(\neg firendly|good)} \cdot \sqrt{p(\neg firendly|\neg good)}$$
$$\cdot \sqrt{p(good)} \cdot \sqrt{p(\neg good)} \cdot \cos(\theta). \tag{17.31}$$

The Equation 17.31 is the quantum interpretation of probability. Quantum probabilities obey the law of total probability only in the case

$$\cos(\theta) = 0, \quad \theta = \frac{\pi}{2}$$

in which the interference part is canceled out. In our example with

$$\theta = \theta_{\neg friendly|good} - \theta_{\neg friendly|\neg good} + \theta_{good} - \theta_{\neg good}$$

the quantum probabilities obey the law of total probability in the case

$$\frac{\pi}{2} = \theta_{\neg friendly|good} - \theta_{\neg friendly|\neg good} + \theta_{good} - \theta_{\neg good}.$$

The quantum interpretation of probability can explain the incompatibility with the classical probability theory by the Equation 17.31. The value $p(\neg friendly)$ for a decision without reporting any categorization was 0.69. By Equation 17.31 we can determine the corresponding θ. We add the classical probability 0.5943 the interference term

$$0.69 = 0.42 \cdot 0.17 + 0.63 \cdot 0.83 + 2 \cdot \sqrt{0.42} \cdot \sqrt{0.63} \cdot \sqrt{0.17} \cdot \sqrt{0.83} \cdot \cos(\theta) \tag{17.32}$$

and the value of $\cos(\theta)$ is

$$0.247642 = \frac{0.69. - 0.5943}{0.386446} = \cos(\theta)$$

with

$$\theta = 1.32055 \approx 0.42 \cdot \pi = \frac{21}{50} \cdot \pi.$$

17.3.1 *Unpacking effects*

An event can be described in more or less detail. The unpacking effect is present when the whole is less than the sum of its parts [Boven and Epley (2003)]. With more details the unpacking effects appear. In the experiment by two conditions were present [Busemeyer *et al.* (2011)], [Busemeyer *et al.* (2012)].

- What is the probability that some one died from natural causes? This is the packed condition.
- What is the probability that some one died from cancer? After this what is the probability that some one died from natural causes other than cancer?

see Figure 17.3 for the graph representation. According to classical proba-

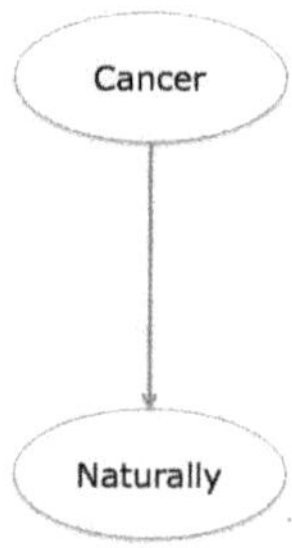

Fig. 17.3 A graph with two nodes.

bility theory

$$p(Naturally) = \sum_{cancer} p(Naturally|cancer) \cdot p(cancer). \tag{17.33}$$

It follows that

$$p(naturally) = p(naturally|cancer) \cdot p(cancer) + p(naturally|\neg cancer) \cdot p(\neg cancer). \tag{17.34}$$

However for packed condition

$$p(naturally) < p(naturally|cancer) \cdot p(cancer) + p(naturally|\neg cancer) \cdot p(\neg cancer). \tag{17.35}$$

According to the quantum interpretation of probability

$$\left| \sum_{i=1}^{2} e^{i \cdot \theta_{naturally|cancer}} \cdot \sqrt{p(\neg naturally|cancer)} \cdot e^{i \cdot \theta_{cancer}} \cdot \sqrt{p(cancer)} \right|^2$$

$$= p(\neg naturally|cancer) \cdot p(cancer) + p(\neg naturally|\neg cancer) \cdot$$

$$\cdot p(\neg cancer) + 2 \cdot \sqrt{p(\neg naturally|cancer} \cdot \sqrt{p(\neg naturally|\neg cancer)}$$

$$\cdot \sqrt{p(cancer)} \cdot \sqrt{p(\neg cancer)} \cdot \cos(\theta). \tag{17.36}$$

with

$$\cos(\theta) < 0.$$

A disadvantage of individual fitting is that is does not allow to do any predictions or generalizations. If we want to preform predictions the represented values have to represent probabilities for all θ values, see Equation 17.30.

17.4 Intensity Waves

The intensity wave is defined as

$$I(y, \theta_1, \theta_2) = |a(y, x, \theta_1) + a(y, \neg x, \theta_2)|^2 \tag{17.37}$$

$$I(y, \theta_1, \theta_2) = p(y, x) + p(y, \neg x) + 2 \cdot \sqrt{p(y, x) \cdot p(y, \neg x)} \cdot \cos(\theta_1 - \theta_2) \tag{17.38}$$

Note that for simplification we can replace $\theta_1 - \theta_2$ with θ,

$$\theta = \theta_1 - \theta_2$$

$$I(y, \theta) = p(y) + 2 \cdot \sqrt{p(y, x) \cdot p(y, \neg x)} \cdot \cos(\theta) \tag{17.39}$$

and

$$I(\neg y, \theta_{\neg 1}, \theta_{\neg 2}) = |a(\neg y, x, \theta_{\neg 1}) + a(\neg y, \neg x, \theta_{\neg 2})|^2 \tag{17.40}$$

with

$$\theta_{\neg} = \theta_{\neg 1} - \theta_{\neg 2}$$

$$I(\neg y, \theta_{\neg}) = p(\neg y) + 2 \cdot \sqrt{p(\neg y, x) \cdot p(\neg y, \neg x)} \cdot \cos(\theta_{\neg}) \tag{17.41}$$

and for certain phase values

$$I(y, \theta) + I(\neg y, \theta_{\neg}) \neq 1. \tag{17.42}$$

17.5 Probability Waves

Intensity waves $I(y, \theta)$ and $I(\neg y, \theta_\neg)$ are probability waves $p(y, \theta)$ and $p(\neg y, \theta_\neg)$ if:

(1) they sum to one

$$p(y, \theta) + p(\neg y, \theta_\neg) = p(y) + p(\neg y) = 1; \tag{17.43}$$

(2) they are smaller or equal to one

$$p(y, \theta) \leq 1, \quad p(\neg y, \theta_\neg) \leq 1. \tag{17.44}$$

17.5.1 *Normalized probability waves*

Often a normalization is done, see [Moreira and Wichert (2014, 2016a)], [Moreira and Wichert (2016b)], with

$$p(y, \theta) = \frac{I(y, \theta)}{I(y, \theta) + I(\neg y, \theta_\neg)}, \tag{17.45}$$

and

$$p(\neg y, \theta_\neg) = \frac{I(\neg y, \theta_\neg)}{I(y, \theta) + I(\neg y, \theta_\neg})) \tag{17.46}$$

with

$$p(y, \theta) + p_(\neg y, \theta_\neg) = 1 \tag{17.47}$$

and

$$p(y) = p\left(y, \pm\frac{\pi}{2}\right), p(\neg y) = p\left(\neg y, \pm\frac{\pi}{2}\right).$$

Usually is is assumed that

$$\theta = \theta_\neg \tag{17.48}$$

In Figure 17.4 b) we see two probability waves after normalization of the intensity waves with the parametrization as indicated in corresponding to the values of Figure 6.2 (Chapter 6) and $\theta = \theta_\neg$.

17.5.2 *Law of balance*

Instead of simple normalization of the intensity we propose the law of balance [Wichert and Moreira (2018); Wichert *et al.* (2020)]. The law is related

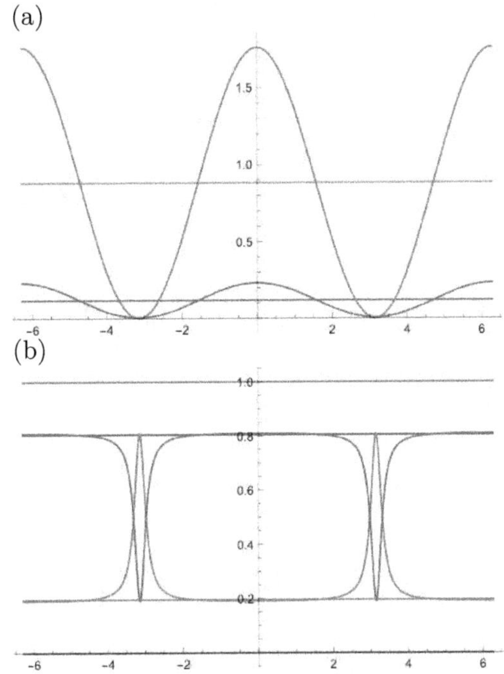

Fig. 17.4 (a) Two intensity waves $I(y,\theta)$, $I(\neg y,\theta_\neg)$ in relation to the phase $(-2\cdot\pi, 2\cdot\pi)$ with the parametrization as indicated in corresponding to the values of Figure 6.2. Note that the two waves oscillate around $p(y) = 0.1950$ and $p(\neg y) = 0.8050$ (the two lines). (b) Normalization of the two intensity waves $I(y,\theta)$, $I(\neg y,\theta_\neg)$. The two normalized waves do not oscillate around $p(y)$ and $p(\neg y)$.

to the alternation law proposed by [Yukalov and Sornette (2011)]. The interference is balanced, which means that the interference of $p(y,\theta)$ and $p(\neg y,\theta_\neg)$ cancel each out

$$\sqrt{p(y,x)\cdot p(y,\neg x)}\cdot\cos(\theta) = -\sqrt{p(\neg y,x)\cdot p(\neg y,\neg x)}\cdot\cos(\theta_\neg). \quad (17.49)$$

We can solve the Equation for the phase $\theta_\neg$ or θ resulting in three possible cases. For the constraint

$$\frac{p(y|x)\cdot p(y|\neg x)}{p(\neg y|x)\cdot p(\neg y|\neg x)} < 1. \quad (17.50)$$

we get

$$\theta_\neg = \cos^{-1}\left(-\sqrt{\frac{p(y|x)\cdot p(y|\neg x)}{p(\neg y|x)\cdot p(\neg y|\neg x)}}\cdot\cos(\theta)\right) \quad (17.51)$$

Since $\cos^{-1}(x)$ is only defined for $x \in [-1,1]$ the Equation 17.51 is valid for the constraint. The smaller probability wave determines the other probability wave as

$$p(\neg y, \theta_\neg) = 1 - p(y, \theta). \tag{17.52}$$

For the constraint

$$\frac{p(\neg y|x) \cdot p(\neg y|\neg x)}{p(y|x) \cdot p(y|\neg x)} < 1. \tag{17.53}$$

we get

$$\theta = \cos^{-1}\left(-\sqrt{\frac{p(\neg y|x) \cdot p(\neg y|\neg x)}{p(y|x) \cdot p(y|\neg x)}} \cdot \cos(\theta_\neg)\right) \tag{17.54}$$

Again, the smaller probability wave determines the other probability wave as

$$p(y, \theta) = 1 - p(\neg y, \theta_\neg). \tag{17.55}$$

For the constraint

$$\frac{p(y|x) \cdot p(y|\neg x)}{p(\neg y|x) \cdot p(\neg y|\neg x)} = \frac{p(\neg y|x) \cdot p(\neg y|\neg x)}{p(y|x) \cdot p(y|\neg x)} = 1. \tag{17.56}$$

we get

$$\theta_\neg = \cos^{-1}(-\cos(\theta)) \tag{17.57}$$

or

$$\theta = \cos^{-1}(-\cos(\theta_\neg)) \tag{17.58}$$

This case applies for double stochastic models [Busemeyer *et al.* (2006b)], [Busemeyer and Trueblood (2009)], [Busemeyer *et al.* (2009)], [Busemeyer *et al.* (2012)], [Busemeyer and Wang (2014)].

17.5.2.1 *Smaller equal one*

We assume without loss of generality

$$p(y) \leq p(\neg y) \tag{17.59}$$

it follows that

$$p(y) \leq 0.5. \tag{17.60}$$

By the inequality of arithmetic and geometric means

$$\sqrt{p(y,x) \cdot p(y,\neg x)} \leq \frac{p(y,x) + p(y,\neg x)}{2} \tag{17.61}$$

$$2 \cdot \sqrt{p(y,x) \cdot p(y,\neg x)} \leq p(y) = p(y,x) + p(y,\neg x) \tag{17.62}$$

$$p(y,\theta) = p(y) + 2 \cdot \sqrt{p(y|x) \cdot p(x) \cdot p(y|\neg x) \cdot p(\neg x)} \cdot \cos(\theta) \leq 2 \cdot p(y) \leq 1. \tag{17.63}$$

17.6 Balanced Probability Waves

The probability waves with $\overline{\theta}_\neg$ and $\overline{\theta}$ that are determined by the law of balance from the phases $\theta_\neg$ and θ are

$$p(\neg y, \overline{\theta}_\neg) = p(\neg y) + 2 \cdot \sqrt{p(\neg y|x) \cdot p(x) \cdot p(\neg y|\neg x) \cdot p(\neg x)} \cdot \cos(\overline{\theta}_\neg). \quad (17.64)$$

and

$$p(y, \overline{\theta}) = p(y) + 2 \cdot \sqrt{p(y|x) \cdot p(x) \cdot p(y|\neg x) \cdot p(\neg x)} \cdot \cos(\overline{\theta}). \quad (17.65)$$

They are called the balanced probability waves. In Figure 17.5 b) we see two balances probability waves with the parametrization as indicated in corresponding to the values of Figure 6.2 (Chapter 6) and $\theta = \theta_\neg$.

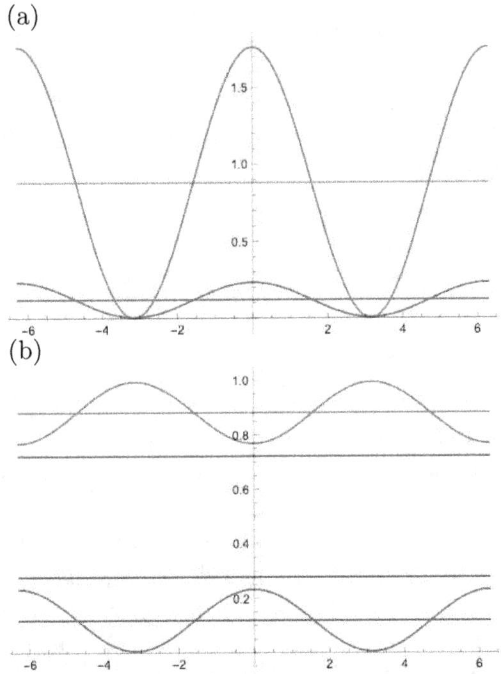

Fig. 17.5 (a) Two intensity waves $I(y, \theta)$, $I(\neg y, \theta_\neg)$ in relation to the phase $(-2 \cdot \pi, 2 \cdot \pi)$ with the parametrization as indicated in corresponding to the values of Figure 6.2. Note that the two waves oscillate around $p(y) = 0.1950$ and $p(\neg y) = 0.8050$ (the two lines). (b) The resulting probability waves as determined by the law of balance, the bigger wave is replaced by the negative smaller one.

17.6.1 *Prisoner's dilemma game and probability waves*

In the prisoner's dilemma game, there are two prisoners, prisoner x and prisoner y. They have no means of communicating with each other. Each prisoner is offered by the prosecutors a bargain: testifying against the other one she can betray the other one (Defect). On the other hand, the prisoner can refuse the deal and cooperate with the other one by remaining silent, for more information please consult [Moreira and Wichert (2016a)].

Several psychological experiments were made assuming that the probability of prisoner x cooperating is $p(x) = 0.5$ and the probability of defecting is $p(\neg x) = 0.5$. The participants of the experiment were asked three different questions.

- What is the probability that the prisoner y defects given x defects, $p(\neg y|\neg x)$.
- What is the probability that the prisoner y defects given x cooperates, $p(\neg y|x)$.
- What is the probability that the prisoner y defects given there is no information present about knowing if prisoner x cooperates or defects. This can be expressed by

$$p(\neg y) = p(\neg y, x) + p(\neg y, \neg x) =$$

$$p(\neg y|x) \cdot p(x) + p(\neg y|\neg x) \cdot p(\neg x). \tag{17.66}$$

  and is represented by a graph (see Figure 6.2) that indicates the influence between events x and y.

In Table 17.1, we summarize the results of several experiments of the literature concerned with the prisoner's dilemma experiment. Using the values of Table 17.1 , we can determine the balanced probability waves $p(\neg y, \overline{\theta_\neg})$, $p(y, , \overline{\theta})$ as indicated in Figure 17.6. Figure 17.6 indicates that the balanced probability waves do not overlap. Prisoner's Dilemma Game results are explained by the values of the balanced probability waves that are closest to the equal distribution. By doing so the uncertainty is maximized since the correct values for the phases are unknown. The principle of maximum entropy states that the probability distribution which best represents the current state of knowledge is the one with largest entropy [Jaynes (1957a,b, 1968)]. In the case of a binary event the highest entropy corresponds to an equal distribution. For $p(y) \leq p(\neg y)$ the closest values to the the equal distribution are for $\overline{\theta} = 0$ define the quantum probability value

$$p_q(y) = p(y) + 2 \cdot \sqrt{p(y,x) \cdot p(y,\neg x)}, \quad p_q(\neg y) = 1 - p_q(y). \tag{17.67}$$

Table 17.1 Experimental results obtained in four different works of the literature for the prisoner's dilemma game. The column $p(\neg y|\neg x)$ corresponds to the probability of *defecting* given that it is known that the other participant chose to *defect*. The column $p(\neg y|x)$ corresponds to the probability of *defecting* given that it is known that the other participant chose to *cooperate*. Finally, the column $p_{sub}(\neg y)$ corresponds to the subjective probability of the second participant choosing the *defect* action given there is no information present about knowing if prisoner x cooperates or defects. The column $p(\neg y)$ corresponds to the classical probability.

Experiment	$p(\neg y\|\neg x)$	$p(\neg y\|x)$	$p_{sub}(\neg y)$	$p(\neg y)$
(a) [Shafir and Tversky (1992)]	0.97	0.84	0.63	0.9050
(b) [Li and Taplin (2002)]	0.82	0.77	0.72	0.7950
(c) [Busemeyer *et al.* (2006a)]	0.91	0.84	0.66	0.8750
(d) [Hristova and Grinberg (2008)]	0.97	0.93	0.88	0.9500
(e) Average	0.92	0.85	0.72	0.8813

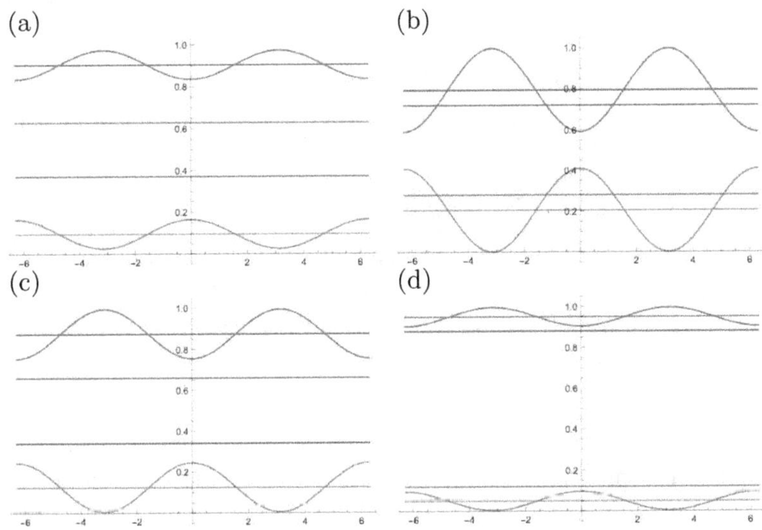

Fig. 17.6 Balanced probability waves for the experiments described in Table 17.1. In plots (a) - (d) the waves $p(\neg y, \overline{\theta}_\neg)$ oscillate are around $p(\neg y)$, (for (e) see Figure 17.5). Additionally the values $p_{sub}(\neg y)$ and $p_{sub}(y)$ are indicated by a line.

For $p(\neg y) \leq p(y)$ the closest values to the the equal distribution are for $\overline{\theta}_\neg = 0$

$$p_q(\neg y) = p(\neg y) + 2 \cdot \sqrt{p(\neg y, x) \cdot p(\neg y, \neg x)}, \quad p_q(y) = 1 - p_q(\neg y). \quad (17.68)$$

The resulting quantum probability values are indicated in the Table 17.2. Humans are not good in calculating, however balanced probability waves

Table 17.2 The column $p_{sub}(\neg y)$ corresponds to the subjective probability of the second participant choosing the *cooperate* action given there is no information present about knowing if prisoner x cooperates or defects. The column $p_q(y)$ indicates the values that are based on quantum probabilities. The column $p(y)$ corresponds to the classical probability.

Experiment	$p_{sub}(y)$	$p_q(y)$	$p(y)$
(a) [Shafir and Tversky (1992)]	0.37	0.16	0.095
(b) [Li and Taplin (2002)]	0.28	0.41	0.205
(c) [Busemeyer *et al.* (2006a)]	0.34	0.24	0.125
(d) [Hristova and Grinberg (2008)]	0.12	0.1	0.05
(e) Average	0.28	0.23	0.1187

that do not overlap indicate a simple heuristic to estimate the quantum probability value out of a classical probability value as can be seen in the Table 17.2,

$$p(y) \leq p(\neg y) \longrightarrow p_q(y) \approx 2 \cdot p(y),$$

it two times the value that results from the classical law of total probability.

17.6.2 *Two stage gambling game*

In the two stage gambling game the participants were asked whether they want to play a gamble that has an equal chance of winning $p(x) = 0.5$ or losing $p(\neg x) = 0.5$, see [Moreira and Wichert (2016a)]. The participants of the experiment were asked three different questions.

- What is the probability that they play the gamble y if they had lost the first gamble x, $p(y|\neg x)$
- What is the probability that they play the gamble y if they had won the first gamble x, $p(y|x)$
- What is the probability that they play the gamble y given there is no information present knowing if they had won the first gamble x. This would by by the law of total probability

$$p(y) = p(y|x) \cdot p(x) + p(y|\neg x) \cdot p(\neg x) \tag{17.69}$$

In Table 17.3, we summarize the results of several experiments of the literature concerned with the two stage gambling game. Using the values of Table 17.3 , we can determine the balanced probability waves $p(\neg y, \overline{\theta_\neg})$, $p(y, , \overline{\theta})$ as indicated in Figure 17.7. The Figure 17.7 indicates that the balanced probability waves do overlap. In this case the closest equal distribution is always 0.5 and all information about the balanced probability

Table 17.3 Experimental results obtained in three different works of the literature indicating the probability of a player choosing to make a second gamble for the two stage gambling game. The column $p(y|\neg x)$ corresponds to the probability when the outcome of the first gamble is known to be lost. The column $p(y|x)$ corresponds to the probability when the outcome of the first gamble is known to be win. Finally, the column $p_{sub}(y)$ corresponds to the subjective probability when the outcome of the first gamble is not known. The column $p(y)$ corresponds to the classical probability.

Experiment	$p(y\|\neg x)$	$p(y\|x)$	$p_{sub}(y)$	$p(y)$
(i) [Tversky and Shafir (1992)]	0.58	0.69	0.37	0.6350
(ii) [Kuhberger *et al.* (2001)]	0.47	0.72	0.48	0.5950
(iii) [Lambdin and Burdsal (2007)]	0.45	0.63	0.41	0.5400
(iv) Average	0.50	0.68	0.42	0.5900

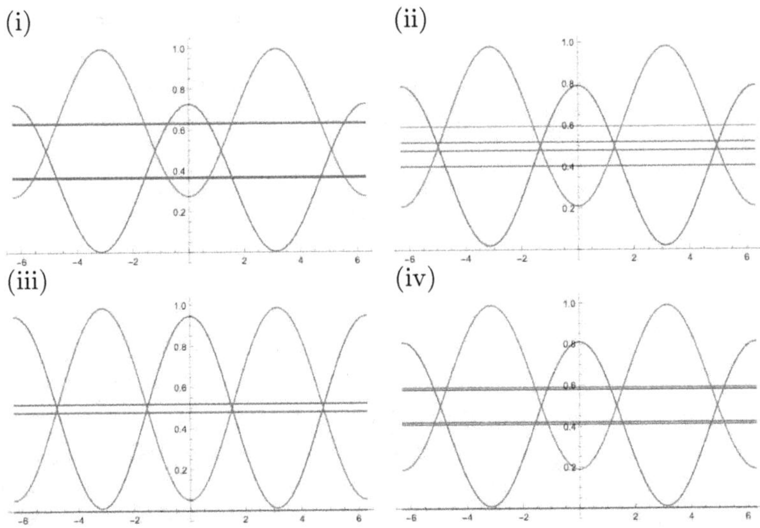

Fig. 17.7 Balanced probability waves for the experiments described in Table 17.3. In the plots (i) - (iv) the waves $p(y,\overline{\theta})$ oscillate are around $p(y)$. Additionally the values $p_{sub}(\neg y)$ and $p_{sub}(y)$ are indicated by a line. Note that the curves overlap.

wave is lost. We notice that for

$$p(y) \leq p(\neg y)$$

$$p(y) = p(y,x) + p(y,\neg x) \approx 2 \cdot \sqrt{p(y,x) \cdot p(y,\neg x)}. \tag{17.70}$$

We increase uncertainty by mirror the "probability values". For the case $p(y) \leq p(\neg y)$ we chose only the maximal interference

$$p_q(\neg y) = 2 \cdot \sqrt{p(y,x) \cdot p(y,\neg x)} \approx p(y) \tag{17.71}$$

and

$$p_q(y) = 1 - p_q(\neg y). \qquad (17.72)$$

The resulting quantum probability values are indicated in the table 17.4. Humans are not good in calculating, however balanced probability waves

Table 17.4 The column $p_{sub}(y)$ corresponds to the subjective probability when the outcome of the first gamble is not known. The column $p_q(y)$ indicates the values that are based on quantum probabilities. The column $p(y)$ corresponds to the classical probability.

Experiment	$p_{sub}(y)$	$p_q(y)$	$p(y)$
(i) [Tversky and Shafir (1992)]	0.37	0.36	0.0635
(ii) [Kuhberger *et al.* (2001)]	0.48	0.39	0.595
(iii) [Lambdin and Burdsal (2007)]	0.41	0.45	0.540
(iv) Average	0.42	0.40	0.590

that do not overlap indicate a simple heuristic to estimate the quantum probability value out of a classical probability value as can be seen in the Table 17.4,

$$p(y) \leq p(\neg y) \longrightarrow p_q(\neg y) \approx p(y),$$

it two times the value that results from the classical law of total probability.

17.6.3 *Comparison*

We compare the results that are based on balanced probability waves with previous works that deal with predictive quantum-like models for decision making, see Table 17.5. We compare it with two models, the Quantum Prospect Decision Theory [Yukalov and Sornette (2011)] and the quantum-like bayesian networks of [Moreira and Wichert (2016a)]. Both models preform a normalization. In Quantum Prospect Decision Theory the interference alternation law leads to interference quarter law by estimation. The interference value is estimated by the probability distribution in the interval [0, 1] as being 0.25. The quarter law states that the interference term of total probability is fixed to the value ± 0.25 [Yukalov and Sornette (2011)]. The alternation law states that we add 0.25 to smaller probability value and subtract 0.25 from the bigger one.

$$p(y) \leq p(\neg y) \longrightarrow p_q(y) = p(y) + 0.25, \quad p_q(\neg y) \approx p(\neg y) - 0.25 \qquad (17.73)$$

The dynamic heuristic as described by [Moreira and Wichert (2016a)] is used quantum-like bayesian networks. After the normalization the threshold parameters of the heuristic are determined by examples of a domain.

Table 17.5 Comparison between the Quantum Prospect Decision Theory (PT), see [Yukalov and Sornette (2011)] , the dynamic heuristic (DH), see [Moreira and Wichert (2016a)] and the law of balance (BL) The results of the dynamic heuristic (DH) and the law of maximal uncertainty (BL) are similar, however the the law of maximal uncertainty (BL) was not adapted to a domain.

Experiment	*classical*	*observed*	*PT*	*DH*	*BL*
(a)	0.91	0.63	0.65	0.64	0.84
(b)	0.79	0.72	0.54	0.71	0.59
(c)	0.88	0.66	0.63	0.80	0.76
(d)	0.95	0.88	0.70	0.90	0.90
(e) Average	0.88	0.72	0.63	0.76	0.77
(i)	0.64	0.37	0.39	0.36	0.36
(ii)	0.59	0.48	0.35	0.40	0.39
(iii)	0.54	0.41	0.29	0.41	0.45
(iv) Average	0.59	0.42	0.34	0.39	0.40

The results of the dynamic heuristic (DH) and the law of balance (BL) are similar, however the the law of balance was not adapted to a domain.

Does the law of balance make sense? For double stochastic models according to the law of balance

$$\theta_{\neg} = \cos^{-1}\left(\cos(\theta \pm \pi)\right) \tag{17.74}$$

or

$$\theta = \cos\left(\cos(\theta_{\neg} \pm \pi)\right) \tag{17.75}$$

for $\theta = 0$ it is $\theta_{\neg} = \pi$ with

$$e^{i \cdot 0} = 0, \quad e^{i \cdot \pi} = -1$$

we get a unitary matrix

$$\begin{pmatrix} \sqrt{p(y|x)} & \sqrt{p(y|\neg x)} \\ \sqrt{p(\neg y|x)} & -\sqrt{p(\neg y|\neg x)} \end{pmatrix} \cdot \begin{pmatrix} \sqrt{p(y|x)} & \sqrt{p(y|\neg x)} \\ \sqrt{p(\neg y|x)} & -\sqrt{p(\neg y|\neg x)} \end{pmatrix} = \begin{pmatrix} 1 & 0 \\ 0 & 1 \end{pmatrix} \tag{17.76}$$

and for $\theta \neg = \pm\pi$ it is $\theta = 0$ with the unitary matrix

$$\begin{pmatrix} \sqrt{p(y|x)} & -\sqrt{p(y|\neg x)} \\ \sqrt{p(\neg y|x)} & \sqrt{p(\neg y|\neg x)} \end{pmatrix} \cdot \begin{pmatrix} \sqrt{p(y|x)} & \sqrt{p(y|\neg x)} \\ -\sqrt{p(\neg y|x)} & \sqrt{p(\neg y|\neg x)} \end{pmatrix} = \begin{pmatrix} 1 & 0 \\ 0 & 1 \end{pmatrix} \tag{17.77}$$

The law of balance is conform with the unitary operators for double stochastic models.

17.6.4 *Quantum-like human decision making*

More physical experiments indicate that wave functions are present in the world, see [Vedral (2011)]. Physical experiments state that the size does not matter and that a very large number of atoms can be entangled, see [Ghosh *et al.* (2003); Amico *et al.* (2008)]. Clues from psychology indicate that human cognition is based on quantum probability rather than the traditional probability theory as explained by Kolmogorov's axioms, see [Busemeyer *et al.* (2006b); Busemeyer and Trueblood (2009); Busemeyer *et al.* (2009, 2012)]. This approach leads to the conclusion that a wave function can be present at the macro scale of our daily life.

A unified explanation of human interference using quantum probability and classical theories was proposed for the first time in [Trueblood *et al.* (2017)], [Wichert *et al.* (2020)]. The hierarchy of mental representations, from quantum-like to classical, is built and allows the combination of both Bayesian and non-Bayesian influences. In this model, classical representations provide a better account of data as individuals gain familiarity with it. Motivated by this model, we propose a distinction between unknown, which is considered as the truth value, and ignorance, which is considered as the lack of knowledge or as being unaware. An event can be true false or unknown.

- For unknown events, the law of total probabilities is applied
- For the events of which we are unaware, we apply quantum-like models in which the phase information is related to ignorance. We determine the possible value of the wave by the law of maximum uncertainty of quantum-like systems.

An unknown event is not known to us because we do not have enough information. Ignorance means that we cannot achieve this information. Ignorance is not a truth value at all. An ignorant event means that we do not know the value at all. The relation is equivalent as the relation between pseudo randomness and true randomness. Pseudo randomness appears to us as random due to our lack of information. True quantum randomness corresponds to ignorance. The distinction between unknown and ignorance can be explained by the two-slit interference of the experiment with an electron gun.

- With electron detectors showing through which slit the electron goes, the electron behaves as a particle. If we assume that the information about the detectors is unknown to us, we apply the law of total probability.

- Now, we remove the detectors. The electron is not unobserved and is represented as a wave. In this case, we apply the quantum-like law of total probability.

Ignorance corresponds to **prediction in the future**. It is assumed that if humans perform predictions, the future is predicted by the general heuristic approach, which results from the balanced probability waves and the maximization of uncertainty. The closest values to the equal distribution are avoided with

$$p(y) \leq p(\neg y) \;\; and \;\; p(y) < \frac{1}{4} \longrightarrow \begin{cases} p_q(y) \approx 2 \cdot p(y) \\ p_q(\neg y) = 1 - p_q(y) \end{cases} \tag{17.78}$$

and

$$p(y) \leq p(\neg y)) \;\; and \;\; p(y) \geq \frac{1}{4} \longrightarrow \begin{cases} p_q(\neg y) \approx p(y) \\ p_q(y) = 1 - p_q(\neg y). \end{cases} \tag{17.79}$$

17.7 Quantum-like Bayesian Network*

We apply the law of balance to Bayesian networks our next step. We apply the law of balance to several unknown variables and study the resulting consequences [Wichert *et al.* (2020)]. For binary event x and non binary event y

$$p(x) + p(\neg x) = 1, \quad \sum_{i=1}^{M} p(y_i) = 1 \tag{17.80}$$

the law of total probability is represented by

$$p(y) = \sum_{i=1}^{M} p(y, x_i) = \sum_{i=1}^{M} p(y|x_i) \cdot p(x_i) \tag{17.81}$$

and

$$p(\neg y) = \sum_{i=1}^{M} p(\neg y, x_i),$$

$$p(\neg y) = \sum_{i=1}^{M} p(\neg y|x_i) \cdot p(x_i). \tag{17.82}$$

The intensity wave is defined as

$$I(y, \theta_1, \cdots, \theta_M) = \left| \sum_{i=1}^{M} A(y, x_i) \right|^2 \tag{17.83}$$

$$I(y,\theta_1,\cdots,\theta_M) = p(y) + 2\cdot\sum_{i=1}^{M-1}\sum_{j=i+1}^{M}\sqrt{p(y,x_i)\cdot p(y,x_j)}\cdot\cos(\theta_i-\theta_j) \tag{17.84}$$

and

$$I(\neg y,\theta_{\neg 1},\cdots) = p(\neg y) + 2\cdot\sum_{i=1}^{M-1}\sum_{j=i+1}^{M}\sqrt{p(\neg y,x_i)\cdot p(\neg y,x_j)}\cos(\theta_{\neg i}-\theta_{\neg j}) \tag{17.85}$$

usually

$$I(y,\theta_1,\theta_2,\cdots,\theta_M) + I(\neg y,\theta_{\neg 1},\theta_{\neg 2},\cdots,\theta_{\neg M}) \neq 1. \tag{17.86}$$

$I(z,\theta_1,\theta_2,\cdots,\theta_M))$ is always non negative

$$0 \le I(y.\theta_1,\theta_2,\cdots,\theta_M) = \left|\sum_{i=1}^{M} a(y,x_i,\theta_i)\right|^2 = \left\|\sum_{i=1}^{M} a(y,x_i,\theta_i)\right\|^2 \tag{17.87}$$

since the norm is non-negative.

17.7.1 *Probability waves sum to one according by the law of balance*

The interference cancel each out

$$I(y,\theta_1,\theta_2,\cdots,\theta_M) + I(\neg y,\theta_{\neg 1},\theta_{\neg 2},\cdots,\theta_{\neg M}) = 1 \tag{17.88}$$

if

$$\sum_{i=1}^{M-1}\sum_{j=i+1}^{M}\sqrt{p(y,x_i)\cdot p(y,x_j)}\cdot\cos(\theta_i-\theta_j)$$

$$= -\sum_{i=1}^{M-1}\sum_{j=i+1}^{M}\sqrt{p(\neg y,x_i)\cdot p(\neg y,x_j)}\cdot\cos(\theta_{\neg i}-\theta_{\neg j}). \tag{17.89}$$

The relation between different combinations of phases $\theta_{\neg i}-\theta_{\neg j}$ cannot be simplified. It is not possible to define a $\theta_{\neg}$ as before. If we decompose the Equation 17.89 for each i and j we get

$$p = \frac{M!}{(M-2)!\cdot 2!} = \frac{M\cdot(M-1)}{2} \tag{17.90}$$

and sub-equations

$$\sqrt{p(y,x_i)\cdot p(y,x_j)}\cdot\cos(\theta_i-\theta_j) = -\sqrt{p(\neg y,x_i)\cdot p(\neg y,x_j)}\cdot\cos(\theta_{\neg i}-\theta_{\neg j}) \tag{17.91}$$

representing p subsystems that can be solved independently as before.

17.7.2 *Probability waves are smaller equal one only after normalization*

With

$$I(y,\theta_1,\cdots,\theta_M)=\sum_{i=1}^{M}p(y,x_i)+2\cdot\sum_{i=1}^{M-1}\sum_{j=i+1}^{M}\sqrt{p(y,x_i)\cdot p(y,x_j)}\cdot\cos(\theta_i-\theta_j) \tag{17.92}$$

by the inequality of arithmetic and geometric means

$$\sqrt{p(y,x_i)\cdot p(y,x_j)}\leq\frac{p(y,x_i)+p(y,\neg x_j)}{2}, \tag{17.93}$$

it follows

$$2\cdot\sqrt{p(y,x_i)\cdot p(y,\neg x_j)}\leq p(y,x_i)+p(y,\neg x_j). \tag{17.94}$$

There are $M/2$ pairs $p(y,x_i)+p(y,\neg x_j)$ since the summation goes over M. There are $p=\frac{M\cdot(M-1)}{2}$ interference sub-equations $2\cdot\sqrt{p(y,x_i)\cdot p(y,\neg x_j)}$. It means that there are $M-1$ more interference sub-equations. For M the intensity wave becomes a probability wave if we normalise the interference part by dividing through $M-1$. Note for $M=2$ we do not need to normalise since the value is one. The intensity wave is a probability wave by using the law of balance and by normalising the interference part by dividing through $M-1$.

$$p(y,\overline{\theta}_1,\cdots)=\sum_{i=1}^{M}p(y,x_i)+\frac{2}{M-1}\cdot\sum_{i=1}^{M-1}\sum_{j=i+1}^{M}\sqrt{p(y,x_i)\cdot p(y,x_j)}\cos(\overline{\theta}_i-\overline{\theta}_j) \tag{17.95}$$

The interference **not** symmetric,

$$Interference_{max}\neq -Interference_{max}$$

since it is composed out of a sum of sub-equations.

17.7.3 *Example of estimation of balanced phases*

In the following example

$$p(y,\overline{\theta}_1,\overline{\theta}_2,\overline{\theta}_3)=p(y,x_1)+p(y,x_2)+p(y,x_3)+\sqrt{p(y,x_1)\cdot p(y,x_2)}\cdot\cos(\overline{\theta}_1-\overline{\theta}_2)$$
$$+\sqrt{p(y,x_1)\cdot p(y,x_3)}\cdot\cos(\overline{\theta}_1-\overline{\theta}_3)+\sqrt{p(y,x_2)\cdot p(y,x_3)}\cdot\cos(\overline{\theta}_2-\overline{\theta}_3). \tag{17.96}$$

The relation between different combinotions of phases $\overline{\theta}_i-\overline{\theta}_j$ cannot be simplified. It is not possible to define a $\overline{\theta}$ as before since two out of three permutations exist. Having two different phases there is only one combinotion and we can project the two dimensional function onto one dimension function see Figure 17.8 (a). With three different phases a three dimensional function cannot be projected onto one dimension. Assuming the following values

$$p(x_1) = 0.2,\ p(x_2) = 0.5,\ p(x_3) = 0.3$$

and

$$p(y|x_1) = 0.13,\ p(y|x_2) = 0.33,\ p(y|x_3) = 0.23$$

in the Figures 17.8 (b), (c), (d) we assume that each of the three phases of $p(y, \overline{\theta}_1, \overline{\theta}_2, \overline{\theta}_3)$ is zero and get three different plots which approximate the three dimensional function by three projections onto two dimension.

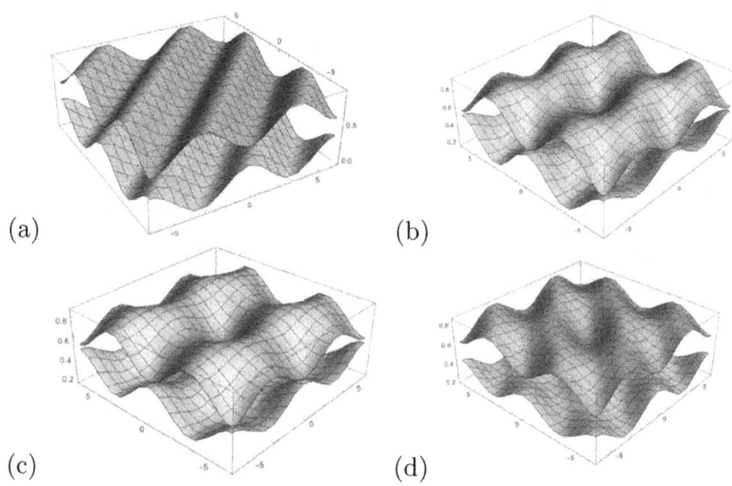

Fig. 17.8 (a) Having two different phases there is only one combination and we can project the two dimensional function onto one dimension function. The cos function in the relation $\overline{\theta}_1 - \overline{\theta}_2$. In (b), (c), (d) we assume that each of the three phases of $p(y, \overline{\theta}_1, \overline{\theta}_2, \overline{\theta}_3)$ and $p(\neg y, \overline{\theta}_{\neg 1}, \overline{\theta}_{\neg 2}, \overline{\theta}_{\neg 3})$ is zero and get three different plots which approximate the three dimensional function by three projections onto two dimension. In (b) we assume $\overline{\theta}_{\neg 3} = \overline{\theta}_3 = 0$. In (c) we assume $\overline{\theta}_{\neg 2} = \overline{\theta}_2 = 0$. In (d) we assume $\overline{\theta}_{\neg 1} = \overline{\theta}_1 = 0$.

We define the intervals that describe the probability waves as

$$I_y = [p(y) - Interference_{max}, p(y) + Interference_{max}] \tag{17.97}$$

and

$$I_{\neg y} = [p(\neg y) - Interference_{max}, p(\neg y) + Interference_{max}]. \tag{17.98}$$

We determine $\pm Interference_{max}$ of three or more dimensional wave numerically. We chose the balanced phases according to the Equation 17.91 and determine the minima and maxima of the three dimensional Equation 17.96 wave numerically by a numerical computing environment[1]. With

$$I_y \cap I_{\neg y} = \emptyset$$

and

$$p(y) = 0.26, \quad I_y = [0.13, 0.48], \quad p_q(y) = 0.48$$

and

$$p(\neg y) = 0.74, \quad I_{\neg y} = [0.52, 0.87], \quad p_q(\neg y) = 0.52.$$

17.7.4 *Example of Bayesian network*

For the Bayesian networks represented in Figure 6.3, for unknown variables like x_3 using the ignorance rule we get the Equation 17.99

$$p(x_4, \theta_i, \theta_{ii}|x_1, x_2) = \alpha \cdot p(x_2) \cdot p(x_4|x_1) \cdot (p(x_1|x_2, x_3) \cdot p(x_3) + p(x_1|x_2, \neg x_3) \cdot$$

$$\cdot p(\neg x_3) + 2 \cdot \sqrt{p(x_1|x_2, x_3) \cdot p(x_3) \cdot p(x_1|x_2, \neg x_3) \cdot p(\neg x_3)} \cdot \cos(\theta_i - \theta_{ii})) \tag{17.99}$$

We use the roman notation $i, ii, iii, vi, \cdots$ for the index of the phase to distinguish between the index of variables. Two solutions exist, with the constraint

$$\frac{p(\neg x_4|x_1)}{p(x_4|x_1)} \leq 1 \tag{17.100}$$

$$\theta_i - \theta_{ii} = \cos^{-1}\left(-\frac{p(\neg x_4|x_1)}{p(x_4|x_1)} \cdot \cos(\theta_{\neg i} - \theta_{\neg ii})\right) \tag{17.101}$$

With the constraint

$$\frac{p(x_4|x_1)}{p(\neg x_4|x_1)} \leq 1. \tag{17.102}$$

$$\theta_{\neg i} - \theta_{\neg ii} = \cos^{-1}\left(-\frac{p(x_4|x_1)}{p(\neg x_4|x_1)} \cdot \cos(\theta_i - \theta_{ii})\right) \tag{17.103}$$

Using the parameters of Figure 6.3 it is

$$p(x_4|x_1, x_2) = 0.9, \quad p(\neg x_4|x_1, x_2) = 0.1 \tag{17.104}$$

[1]In our case we use Mathematica using the build in functions *Maximize* and *Minimize*.

Since the parameter values are small, $Burglary(= x_2 = 0.001)$, $Earthquake(= x_3 = 0.002)$, the interference part becomes not noticeable, with

$$I_y \cap I_{\neg y} = \emptyset$$

and

$$p(x_4|x_1) = 0.9, \quad I_y = [0.899992, 0.900008], \quad p_q(x_4|x_1) = 0.899992,$$

and

$$p(\neg x_4|x_1) = 0.1, \quad I_{\neg y} = [0.099992, 0.100008], \quad p_q(\neg x_4|x_1) = 0.100008.$$

For unknown variables x_3, x_1 we get the four dimensional probability wave We get the Equation

$$p(x_4, \overline{\theta}_i, \overline{\theta}_{ii}, \overline{\theta}_{iii}, \overline{\theta}_{iv}|x_2) = \alpha \cdot p(x_2) \cdot ($$

$$p(x_4|x_1) \cdot p(x_1|x_2, x_3) \cdot p(x_3) + p(x_4|x_1) \cdot p(x_1|x_2, \neg x_3) \cdot p(\neg x_3) +$$

$$p(x_4|\neg x_1) \cdot p(\neg x_1|x_2, x_3) \cdot p(x_3) + p(x_4|\neg x_1) \cdot p(\neg x_1|x_2, \neg x_3) \cdot p(\neg x_3)) + 2/3 \cdot ($$

$$\sqrt{p(x_4|x_1) \cdot p(x_1|x_2, x_3) \cdot p(x_3) \cdot p(x_4|x_1) \cdot p(x_1|x_2, \neg x_3) \cdot p(\neg x_3)} \cdot \cos(\overline{\theta}_i - \overline{\theta}_{ii}) +$$

$$\sqrt{p(x_4|x_1) \cdot p(x_1|x_2, x_3) \cdot p(x_3) \cdot p(x_4|x_1) \cdot p(x_1|x_2, \neg x_3) \cdot p(\neg x_3)} \cdot \cos(\overline{\theta}_i - \overline{\theta}_{ii}) +$$

$$\cdots\cdots$$

$$\cdots\cdots$$

$$\sqrt{p(x_4|\neg x_1) \cdot p(\neg x_1|x_2, x_3) \cdot p(x_3) \cdot p(x_4|\neg x_1) \cdot p(\neg x_1|x_2, \neg x_3) \cdot p(\neg x_3)}$$

$$\cdot \cos(\overline{\theta}_{iii} - \overline{\theta}_{iv})).$$

One can clearly see that the interference value diminish since six we multiply for each interference part seven probability values. With

$$\alpha = \frac{1}{p(x_2)} = \frac{1}{p(X_1, x_2, X_3, x_4) + p(X_1, x_2, X_3, \neg x_4)}. \tag{17.105}$$

we get six sub-equations of which each has two solutions with constraints that are defined by three different equations and their symmetrical contra parts

$$\theta_i - \theta_{ii} = \cos^{-1}\left(-\frac{p(\neg x_4|x_1)}{p(x_4|x_1)} \cdot \cos(\theta_{\neg i} - \theta_{\neg ii})\right). \tag{17.106}$$

The second equation

$$\theta_i - \theta_{iii} = \cos^{-1}\left(-\frac{(p(\neg x_4|x_1) \cdot p(\neg x_4|\neg x_1)}{p(x_4|x_1) \cdot p(x_4|\neg x_1)} \cdot \cdot \cos(\theta_{\neg i} - \theta_{\neg iii})\right) \quad (17.107)$$

which is also valid for $\theta_i - \theta_{iv}$, $\theta_{ii} - \theta_{iii}$ and $\theta_{ii} - \theta_{iv}$.

$$\theta_{iii} - \theta_{iv} = \cos^{-1}\left(-\frac{p(\neg x_4|\neg x_1)}{p(x_4|\neg x_1)} \cdot \cos(\theta_{\neg iii} - \theta_{\neg iv})\right) \quad (17.108)$$

The balanced phases are computed as before. Using the parameters of Figure 6.3 we determine the balanced wave

$$p(x_4, \overline{\theta}_i, \overline{\theta}_{ii}, \overline{\theta}_{iii}, \theta_{iv}|x_2).$$

We have to determine the minima or maxima of the four dimensional wave numerically[2]. Since the parameter values are small $Burglary(= x_2 = 0.001)$, $Earthquake(= x_3 = 0.002)$, the interference part becomes nearly not noticeable as before with

$$I_y \cap I_{\neg y} = \emptyset$$

and

$$p(x_4|x_1) = 0.857072, \quad I_y = [0.857047, 0.857094], \quad p_q(x_4|x_1) = 0.857047,$$

and

$$p(\neg x_4|x_1) = 0.142928, \quad I_{\neg y} = [0.14288, 0.142979], \quad p_q(\neg x_4|x_1) = 0.142979.$$

It seems that the interference seem to diminish with the complexity of the decision scenario as indicated with the examples of balanced quantum-like Bayesian network.

The interference becomes too small to have any effect in human decision making. Since the interference value are negligible they cannot be observed during experiments.

[2]In our case we use Mathematica using the build in functions *Maximize* and *Minimize*

Chapter 18

Quantum like-Evolution

18.1 Evolutionary Dynamics

Evolutionary dynamics have traditionally been studied in the context of homogeneous populations. Population structures are modeled by arranging individuals on a graph in which each vertex represents an individual. Their evolutionary behavior is modeled by Markov chains described by a stochastic matrix. They represent a unifying framework for the emergence of cooperation, modeling global climate change, economics evolution, or cancer development. The evolution of stochastic matrix does not lead to a loss of information if the matrix is orthogonal. An example orthogonal stochastic matrix is the permutation matrix. A permutation matrix is a square binary matrix that has exactly one entry 1 in each row and each column and is 0 elsewhere. Thus, each state cannot be reached from another state. In other cases, the information about the initial condition is lost and cannot be reconstructed. The asymptotic behavior of Markov chains either converges to a fixed distribution or goes to a periodic sequence of distributions. In an ergodic Markov chain, there is a stationary distribution. A Markov chain is ergodic if there is a number n such that any state can be reached from any other state in any number of steps greater than or equal to number n. In the case of a fully connected transition matrix, where all transitions have a nonzero probability (all entries of the stochastic matrix are larger than zero), this condition is fulfilled with $n = 1$. The stationary distribution corresponds to the l_1 normalized eigenvector of the stochastic matrix with eigenvalue 1.

An important question is whether more generalizable probabilistic models can be found using quantum probabilities. These can potentially improve upon classical models of evolution in complex networks such as those making predictions in finance, economics, biology, sociology, and other fields.

18.2 Phase-Balanced Matrix

Quantum-like evolution is evolution that is l_2 norm-preserving but in which the matrix does not need to be unitary. Quantum-like evolution can simulate probability distribution [Wichert (2019)]. By coding the phase of the input vector into the phase of the balanced phase matrix, we can simulate unitary evolution. The phase that describes the matrix is dynamically updated. The resulting complex output vector of the length one differs from the corresponding vector, which is a result of the unitary evolution by phase. We can map any 2×2 stochastic matrix into the l_2 norm-preserving balanced phase matrix that maps real vectors of the length one into complex vectors of the length one. Using the tensor product, higher dimensional balanced phase matrices can be build. Quantum-like evolution can be simulated by coding the phase of the input vector into the phase of the balanced phase matrix, a Markov chain, or an alternative evolution that can lead to fixed, periodic, or chaotic behavior, resulting in strange oscillations.

18.2.1 *Hadamard product*

The Hadamard product for matrices (also known as the Schur product) [Davis (1962)] is defined as

$$\begin{pmatrix} a_{11} & a_{12} \\ a_{21} & a_{22} \end{pmatrix} \circ \begin{pmatrix} b_{11} & b_{12} \\ b_{21} & b_{22} \end{pmatrix} = \begin{pmatrix} a_{11} \cdot b_{11} & a_{12} \cdot b_{12} \\ a_{21} \cdot b_{21} & a_{22} \cdot b_{22} \end{pmatrix} \tag{18.1}$$

and for vectors

$$\begin{pmatrix} a_{11} \\ a_{21} \end{pmatrix} \circ \begin{pmatrix} b_{11} \\ b_{21} \end{pmatrix} = \begin{pmatrix} a_{11} \cdot b_{11} \\ a_{21} \cdot b_{21} \end{pmatrix}. \tag{18.2}$$

18.2.2 *Quantum law of total probability*

The law of total probability can be represented by a 2×2 stochastic matrix P with

$$\mathbf{y} = P \cdot \mathbf{x}, \tag{18.3}$$

$$\begin{pmatrix} p(y) \\ p(\neg y) \end{pmatrix} = \begin{pmatrix} p(y|x) & p(y|\neg x) \\ p(\neg y|x) & p(\neg y|\neg x) \end{pmatrix} \cdot \begin{pmatrix} p(x) \\ p(\neg x) \end{pmatrix}. \tag{18.4}$$

A stochastic matrix P can be decomposed into a Hadarmad product

$$\begin{pmatrix} p(y|x) & p(y|\neg x) \\ p(\neg y|x) & p(\neg y|\neg x) \end{pmatrix} = \begin{pmatrix} \sqrt{p(y|x)} \cdot e^{i \cdot \theta_1} & \sqrt{p(y|\neg x)} \cdot e^{i \cdot \theta_2} \\ \sqrt{p(\neg y|x)} \cdot e^{i \cdot \theta_{\neg 1}} & \sqrt{p(\neg y|\neg x)} \cdot e^{i \cdot \theta_{\neg 2}} \end{pmatrix}$$

$$\circ \begin{pmatrix} \sqrt{p(y|x)} \cdot e^{-i \cdot \theta_1} & \sqrt{p(y|\neg x)} \cdot e^{-i \cdot \theta_2} \\ \sqrt{p(\neg y|x)} \cdot e^{-i \cdot \theta_{\neg 1}} & \sqrt{p(\neg y|\neg x)} \cdot e^{-i \cdot \theta_{\neg 2}} \end{pmatrix}$$

$$= \begin{pmatrix} \sqrt{p(y|x)} \cdot e^{i \cdot \theta_1} & \sqrt{p(y|\neg x)} \cdot e^{i \cdot \theta_2} \\ \sqrt{p(\neg y|x)} \cdot e^{i \cdot \theta_{\neg 1}} & \sqrt{p(\neg y|\neg x)} \cdot e^{i \cdot \theta_{\neg 2}} \end{pmatrix}^{\bar{\circ} 2}$$

into infinite many matrices. To make the law of balance unambiguous we restrict the matrices to the left handed phase matrices and right handed phase matrices

$$\begin{pmatrix} p(y|x) & p(y|\neg x) \\ p(\neg y|x) & p(\neg y|\neg x) \end{pmatrix} = \begin{pmatrix} \sqrt{p(y|x)} \cdot e^{i \cdot \theta} & \sqrt{p(y|\neg x)} \\ \sqrt{p(\neg y|x)} \cdot e^{i \cdot \theta_{\neg}} & \sqrt{p(\neg y|\neg x)} \end{pmatrix}^{\bar{\circ} 2} = \left(\sqrt{P_\theta}\right)_L^{\bar{\circ} 2}$$

and right handed phase matrices

$$\begin{pmatrix} p(y|x) & p(y|\neg x) \\ p(\neg y|x) & p(\neg y|\neg x) \end{pmatrix} = \begin{pmatrix} \sqrt{p(y|x)} & \sqrt{p(y|\neg x)} \cdot e^{i \cdot \theta} \\ \sqrt{p(\neg y|x)} & \sqrt{p(\neg y|\neg x)} \cdot e^{i \cdot \theta_{\neg}} \end{pmatrix}^{\bar{\circ} 2} = \left(\sqrt{P_\theta}\right)_R^{\bar{\circ} 2}.$$

The quantum law of total probability with the probability wave representation with $\overline{\theta}_{\neg}$ and $\overline{\theta}$ that are determined according to the law of balance is

$$\begin{pmatrix} p(y,\overline{\theta}) \\ p(\neg y,\overline{\theta}_{\neg}) \end{pmatrix} = \left(\begin{pmatrix} \sqrt{p(y|x)} \cdot e^{i \cdot \overline{\theta}} & \sqrt{p(y|\neg x)} \\ \sqrt{p(\neg y|x)} \cdot e^{i \cdot \overline{\theta}_{\neg}} & \sqrt{p(\neg y|\neg x)} \end{pmatrix} \cdot \begin{pmatrix} \sqrt{p(x)} \\ \sqrt{p(\neg x)} \end{pmatrix} \right)^{\bar{\circ} 2} \tag{18.5}$$

or

$$\begin{pmatrix} p(y,\overline{\theta}) \\ p(\neg y,\overline{\theta}_{\neg}) \end{pmatrix} = \left(\begin{pmatrix} \sqrt{p(y|x)} & \sqrt{p(y|\neg x)} \cdot e^{i \cdot \overline{\theta}} \\ \sqrt{p(\neg y|x)} & \sqrt{p(\neg y|\neg x)} \cdot e^{i \cdot \overline{\theta}_{\neg}} \end{pmatrix} \cdot \begin{pmatrix} \sqrt{p(x)} \\ \sqrt{p(\neg x)} \end{pmatrix} \right)^{\bar{\circ} 2} \tag{18.6}$$

with

$$\begin{pmatrix} p_q(y,\overline{\theta}) \\ p_q(\neg y,\overline{\theta}_{\neg}) \end{pmatrix} = \begin{pmatrix} p(y) \\ p(\neg y) \end{pmatrix} + 2 \cdot \begin{pmatrix} \sqrt{p(y,x) \cdot p(y,\neg x)} \cdot \cos(\overline{\theta}) \\ \sqrt{p(\neg y,x) \cdot p(\neg y,\neg x)} \cdot \cos(\overline{\theta}_{\neg}) \end{pmatrix}. \tag{18.7}$$

18.2.2.1 *Norm preserving phase balance matrix*

For input vector with phase zero the balanced matrix preserves the l_2 norm of

$$\sqrt{\mathbf{y}_{\theta^R}} = (\sqrt{P_{\overline{\theta}}})_R \cdot \sqrt{\mathbf{x}} \tag{18.8}$$

$$\begin{pmatrix} \sqrt{p(y)} \cdot e^{i \cdot \theta^R} \\ \sqrt{p(\neg y)} \cdot e^{i \cdot \theta^R_{\neg}} \end{pmatrix} = \begin{pmatrix} \sqrt{p(y|x)} & \sqrt{p(y|\neg x)} \cdot e^{i \cdot \overline{\theta}} \\ \sqrt{p(\neg y|x)} & \sqrt{p(\neg y|\neg x)} \cdot e^{i \cdot \ \overline{\theta}_{\neg}} \end{pmatrix} \cdot \begin{pmatrix} \sqrt{p(x)} \\ \sqrt{p(\neg x)} \end{pmatrix} \tag{18.9}$$

with

$$\left\| \sqrt{\mathbf{y}_{\theta^R}} \right\| = \left\| \left(\sqrt{P_{\overline{\theta}}} \right)_R \cdot \sqrt{\mathbf{x}} \right\|, \quad \left\| \sqrt{\mathbf{y}_{\theta^L}} \right\| = \left\| \left(\sqrt{P_{\overline{\theta}}} \right)_L \cdot \sqrt{\mathbf{x}} \right\| \tag{18.10}$$

and

$$\begin{pmatrix} \sqrt{p(y)} \cdot e^{i \cdot \theta^R} \\ \sqrt{p(\neg y)} \cdot e^{i \cdot \theta^R_{\neg}} \end{pmatrix} \neq \begin{pmatrix} \sqrt{p(y)} \cdot e^{i \cdot \theta^L} \\ \sqrt{p(\neg y)} \cdot e^{i \cdot \theta^L_{\neg}} \end{pmatrix}. \tag{18.11}$$

18.2.2.2 *Unitary matrix*

A phase balance matrix can be unitary. A symmetric matrix P corresponds to a double stochastic models with the law of balance

$$\theta_{\neg} = \cos^{-1}\left(-\cos(\theta)\right) = \cos^{-1}\left(\cos(\theta \pm \pi)\right) \tag{18.12}$$

or

$$\theta = \cos^{-1}\left(-\cos(\theta_{\neg})\right) = \cos\left(\cos(\theta_{\neg}) \pm \pi\right) \tag{18.13}$$

For the the case $\theta = 0$ we get $\theta_{\neg} = \pi$ and the matrix $(\sqrt{P_{\overline{\theta}}})_R$ is unitary since

$$\begin{pmatrix} \sqrt{p(y|x)} & \sqrt{p(y|\neg x)} \\ \sqrt{p(\neg y|x)} & -\sqrt{p(\neg y|\neg x)} \end{pmatrix} \cdot \begin{pmatrix} \sqrt{p(y|x)} & \sqrt{p(y|\neg x)} \\ \sqrt{p(\neg y|x)} & -\sqrt{p(\neg y|\neg x)} \end{pmatrix} = \begin{pmatrix} 1 & 0 \\ 0 & 1 \end{pmatrix} \tag{18.14}$$

For the the case $\theta \neg = \pm\pi$ we get $\theta = 0$ and the matrix $(\sqrt{P_{\overline{\theta}}})_R$ is unitary since

$$\begin{pmatrix} \sqrt{p(y|x)} & -\sqrt{p(y|\neg x)} \\ \sqrt{p(\neg y|x)} & \sqrt{p(\neg y|\neg x)} \end{pmatrix} \cdot \begin{pmatrix} \sqrt{p(y|x)} & \sqrt{p(y|\neg x)} \\ -\sqrt{p(\neg y|x)} & \sqrt{p(\neg y|\neg x)} \end{pmatrix} = \begin{pmatrix} 1 & 0 \\ 0 & 1 \end{pmatrix} \tag{18.15}$$

For $(\sqrt{P_{\overline{\theta}}})_L$ the proof is symmetric.

18.2.2.3 *Tensor product of phase balanced matrices*

The product of two phase balance matrices that are not unitary is not a balanced matrix. However the tensor product phase balanced matrices is a phase balanced matrix. Suppose we have two phase balanced matrices either left or right

$$\sqrt{P_{\overline{\theta}}}, \sqrt{M_{\overline{\gamma}}}$$

snd two vectors

$$\sqrt{\mathbf{x}}, \sqrt{\mathbf{y}}$$

By definition of the tensor is follows

$$\left(\sqrt{P_{\overline{\theta}}} \otimes \sqrt{M_{\overline{\gamma}}}\right) \cdot (\sqrt{\mathbf{x}} \otimes \sqrt{\mathbf{y}}) = \left(\sqrt{P_{\overline{\theta}}} \cdot \sqrt{\mathbf{x}}\right) \otimes \left(\sqrt{M_{\overline{\gamma}}} \cdot \sqrt{\mathbf{x}}\right) \tag{18.16}$$

and

$$\left\| \left(\sqrt{P_{\overline{\theta}}} \otimes \sqrt{M_{\overline{\gamma}}}\right) \cdot (\sqrt{\mathbf{x}} \otimes \sqrt{\mathbf{y}}) \right\| = \left\| \sqrt{\mathbf{x}} \otimes \sqrt{\mathbf{y}} \right\|. \tag{18.17}$$

If we do not build a phase balanced matrix of size $M \times M$ by tensor product, then the interference is composed out of p interference parts

$$p = \frac{M!}{(M-2)! \cdot 2!} = \frac{M \cdot (M-1)}{2} \tag{18.18}$$

for each row of the matrix, since

$$\left| \sum_{i=1}^{M} \sqrt{p(y, x_i)} \cdot e^{i \cdot \theta_i} \right|^2 = p(y) + 2 \cdot \sum_{i=1}^{M-1} \sum_{j=i+1}^{M} \sqrt{p(y, x_i) \cdot p(y, x_j)} \cdot \cos(\theta_i - \theta_j) \tag{18.19}$$

Since we cannot simplify $\theta_i - \theta_j$ into one value the optimisation task concerns the cancelation of p interference parts.

18.3 Quantum Like Evolution

The discrete probabilistic time evolution represents a Markov chain that can be described by linear mapping

$$\mathbf{x}^{(t+1)} = P \cdot \mathbf{x}^{t}. \tag{18.20}$$

$$\begin{pmatrix} p(x^{(t+1)}) \\ p(\neg x^{(t+1)}) \end{pmatrix} = \begin{pmatrix} p(x_1|x_0) & p(x_1|\neg x_0) \\ p(\neg x_1|x_0) & p(\neg x_1|\neg x_0) \end{pmatrix} \cdot \begin{pmatrix} p(x^t) \\ p(\neg x^t) \end{pmatrix}. \tag{18.21}$$

The quantum like evolution with $\overline{\theta}_\neg$ and $\overline{\theta}$ that are determined according to the law of balance is represented as

$$\begin{pmatrix} \sqrt{p(x^{(t+1)})} \cdot e^{i \cdot \theta^R} \\ \sqrt{p(\neg x^{(t+1)})} \cdot e^{i \cdot \theta^R_\neg} \end{pmatrix} = \begin{pmatrix} \sqrt{p(y|x)} & \sqrt{p(y|\neg x)} \cdot e^{i \cdot \overline{\theta}} \\ \sqrt{p(\neg y|x)} & \sqrt{p(\neg y|\neg x)} \cdot e^{i \cdot \overline{\theta}_\neg} \end{pmatrix} \cdot \begin{pmatrix} \sqrt{p(x^t)} \\ \sqrt{p(\neg x^t)} \end{pmatrix} \tag{18.22}$$

in short notation

$$\sqrt{\mathbf{x}_{\theta^R}^{(t+1)}} = \left(\sqrt{P_{\overline{\theta}}}\right)_R \cdot \sqrt{\mathbf{x}^t}, \quad \sqrt{\mathbf{x}_{\theta^L}^{(t+1)}} = \left(\sqrt{P_{\overline{\theta}}}\right)_L \cdot \sqrt{\mathbf{x}^t} \tag{18.23}$$

During the quantum like evolution the phase information is eliminated from the vector $\sqrt{\mathbf{x}^t}$ since it required that the input vector has the phase zero. The evolution is determined by the phase of phase balanced matrix [Wichert (2019)]. There are two different categories of quantum like evolution with a constant phase and the dynamic one.

18.3.1 *Constant phase evolution*

In the constant phase evolution the phase of the balanced matrix is a value that is determined independent of the evolution. In this kind of evolution there is no distinction between right and left handed phase balanced matrix since the results that represent both probabilities are equal. For a symmetric stochastic matrix

$$P = \begin{pmatrix} 0.9 & 0.1 \\ 0.1 & 0.9 \end{pmatrix} \tag{18.24}$$

the quantum like evolution with the fixed phase with $\overline{\theta}_\neg = 0$ and $\overline{\theta} = \pi$ determined according to the law of balance resulting in the balanced phase matrix that is unitary matrix with

$$\begin{pmatrix} \sqrt{p(x^{(t+1)})} \cdot e^{i \cdot \theta'} \\ \sqrt{p(\neg x^{(t+1)})} \cdot e^{i \cdot \theta'_\neg} \end{pmatrix} = \begin{pmatrix} \sqrt{0.9} & -\sqrt{0.1} \\ \sqrt{0.1} & \sqrt{0.9} \end{pmatrix} \cdot \begin{pmatrix} \sqrt{p(x^t)} \\ \sqrt{p(\neg x^t)} \end{pmatrix}. \tag{18.25}$$

With $\sqrt{p(x^1)} = 0$ and $\sqrt{p(\neg x^1)} = 1$ the evolution of the probability values is an oscillation between two values, see Figure 18.1 (a). If the balanced phase matrix is not unitary the evolution converge to a fixed vector, the eigenvector of the balanced phase matrix. For a not symmetric stochastic matrix P' that is nearly symmetric

$$P' = \begin{pmatrix} 0.9 & 0.11 \\ 0.1 & 0.89 \end{pmatrix} \tag{18.26}$$

the quantum like evolution with the fixed phase with phase with $\overline{\theta}_\neg = 0$ and $\overline{\theta} = 2.81816$ that are determined according to the law of balance resulting in the balanced phase matrix that is not a unitary matrix with

$$\begin{pmatrix} \sqrt{p(x^{(t+1)})} \cdot e^{i \cdot \theta'} \\ \sqrt{p(\neg x^{(t+1)})} \cdot e^{i \cdot \theta'_\neg} \end{pmatrix} = \begin{pmatrix} \sqrt{0.9} & \sqrt{0.11} \cdot e^{i \cdot 2.81816} \\ \sqrt{0.1} & \sqrt{0.89} \end{pmatrix} \cdot \begin{pmatrix} \sqrt{p(x^t)} \\ \sqrt{p(\neg x^t)} \end{pmatrix} \tag{18.27}$$

With $\sqrt{p(x^1)} = 0$ and $\sqrt{p(\neg x^1)} = 1$ the evolution of the probability values converge after several steps as shown in the Figure 18.1 (b). Constant phase

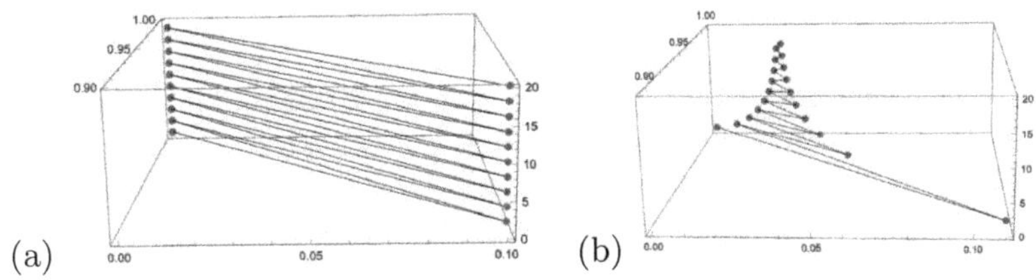

Fig. 18.1 (a) For a symmetric stochastic matrix with the fixed phase with $\overline{\theta}_\neg = 0$ and $\overline{\theta} = \pi$ the balanced phase matrix is unitary. With $\sqrt{p(x^1)} = 0$ and $\sqrt{p(\neg x^1)} = 1$ the evolution of the probability values is an oscillation between two values, (b) For a balanced phase matrix that is nearly unitary with $\sqrt{p(x^1)} = 0$ and $\sqrt{p(\neg x^1)} = 1$ the evolution of the probability values converge in several steps to a fixed value.

evolution is equal to Markov evolution for any stochastic matrix P with the fixed phase with $\overline{\theta}_\neg = \pi/2$ and $\overline{\theta} = \pi/2$ that are determined according to the law of balance resulting in the phase balanced matrix

$$\begin{pmatrix} \sqrt{p(y|x)} & i \cdot \sqrt{p(y|\neg x)} \\ \sqrt{p(\neg y|x)} & i \cdot \sqrt{p(\neg y|\neg x)} \end{pmatrix}. \tag{18.28}$$

18.3.2 *Dynamic quantum-like evolution*

In the dynamic evolution the phase of the balanced matrix is determined by the phase of the output vector so that no information is eliminated. In this kind of evolution there is the distinction between right and left handed phase balanced matrix since the phase information is dependent on the output. Dynamic evolution can describe a unitary evolution. The dynamic quantum-like evolution is defined as

$$\sqrt{\mathbf{x}^{(t+1)}_{\theta^{(t+1)}}} = \sqrt{P_{\overline{\Theta}^{(t)}}} \cdot \sqrt{\mathbf{x}^t} \tag{18.29}$$

$$\begin{pmatrix} \sqrt{p(x^{(t+1)})} \cdot e^{i \cdot \theta^{(t+1)}} \\ \sqrt{p(\neg x^{(t+1)})} \cdot e^{i \cdot \theta_{\neg}^{(t+1)}} \end{pmatrix} = \begin{pmatrix} \sqrt{p(y|x)} & \sqrt{p(y|\neg x)} \cdot e^{i \cdot \overline{\Theta}^{(t)}} \\ \sqrt{p(\neg y|x)} & \sqrt{p(\neg y|\neg x)} \cdot e^{i \cdot \overline{\Theta}_{\neg}^{(t)}} \end{pmatrix} \cdot \begin{pmatrix} \sqrt{p(x^t)} \\ \sqrt{p(\neg x^t)} \end{pmatrix} \tag{18.30}$$

with

$$\theta^{(1)} = \theta_{\neg}^{(1)} = 0, \qquad \Theta^{(t)} = \theta^{(t)} \pm \theta_{\neg}^{(t)} \tag{18.31}$$

and $\overline{\Theta}_{\neg}^{(t)}$, $\overline{\Theta}^{(t)}$ are determined by the law of balance. We either sum or subtract the phases $\theta^{(t)}$, $\theta_{\neg}^{(t)}$. In the next section we will investigate when to add or subtract the phases if we want to simulate a unitary evolution.

18.3.2.1 *Dynamic phase and unitary evolution*

If we P is symmetric the probability values of the dynamic quantum-like evolution are similar as in the unitary evolution. For unitary evolution with phases ϕ, $\phi_{\neg}$ and

$$\Phi^{(t)} = \phi^{(t)} - \phi_{\neg}^{(t)}$$

it follows

$$\left(\begin{pmatrix} \sqrt{p(y|x)} & -\sqrt{p(y|\neg x)} \\ \sqrt{p(\neg y|x)} & \sqrt{p(\neg y|\neg x)} \end{pmatrix} \cdot \begin{pmatrix} \sqrt{p(x^t)} \cdot e^{i \cdot \phi^{(t)}} \\ \sqrt{p(\neg x^t)} \cdot e^{i \cdot \phi_{\neg}^{(t)}} \end{pmatrix} \right)^{\bar{\circ} 2} = \tag{18.32}$$

$$\begin{pmatrix} \sqrt{p(y|x)} \cdot \sqrt{p(x^t)} \cdot e^{i \cdot \phi^{(t)}} & \sqrt{p(y|\neg x)} \cdot \sqrt{p(\neg x^t)} \cdot e^{i \cdot (\phi_{\neg}^{(t)} + \pi)} \\ \sqrt{p(\neg y|x)} \cdot \sqrt{p(x^t)} \cdot e^{i \cdot \phi^{(t)}} & \sqrt{p(\neg y|\neg x)} \cdot \sqrt{p(\neg x^t)} \cdot e^{i \cdot \phi_{\neg}^{(t)}} \end{pmatrix}^{\bar{\circ} 2} = \tag{18.33}$$

$$\begin{pmatrix} \sqrt{p(y|x)} \cdot \sqrt{p(x^t)} & \sqrt{p(y|\neg x)} \cdot \sqrt{p(\neg x^t)} \cdot e^{i \cdot (\Phi^{(t)} + \pi)} \\ \sqrt{p(\neg y|x)} \cdot \sqrt{p(x^t)} & \sqrt{p(\neg y|\neg x)} \cdot \sqrt{p(\neg x^t)} \cdot e^{i \cdot \Phi^{(t)}} \end{pmatrix}^{\bar{\circ} 2}. \tag{18.34}$$

With

$$\cos^{-1}(-\cos(\theta)) = \begin{cases} -\theta - \pi & -2 \cdot \pi \leq \theta \leq \pi \\ \theta + \pi & -\pi \leq \theta \leq 0 \\ -\theta + \pi & 0 \leq \theta \leq \pi \\ \theta - \pi & \pi \leq \theta \leq 2 \cdot \pi \end{cases} \tag{18.35}$$

the phase may differ by the sign. Using the complex argument function

$$arg(a + b \cdot i) = \tan^{-1}\left(\frac{a}{b}\right) \tag{18.36}$$

that indicates the phase θ of a complex number, we get the following equality

$$\left| arg\left(e^{i \cdot (\theta^{(t)} + \pi)}\right) \right| = \left| arg\left(e^{i \cdot \left(\cos^{-1}(-\cos(\theta^{(t)}))\right)}\right) \right|. \tag{18.37}$$

For two phases

$$\phi^{(t)} = \pm\theta^{(t)}, \quad \phi_{\neg}^{(t)} = \pm\theta_{\neg}^{t)}$$

for

$$\Phi^{(t)} = \phi^{(t)} - \phi_{\neg}^{(t)}$$

the equality

$$\left|arg\left(e^{i\cdot\left(\Phi^{(t)}+\pi\right)}\right)\right| = \left|arg\left(e^{i\cdot\left(\cos^{-1}(-\cos(\Theta^{(t)}))\right)}\right)\right| \tag{18.38}$$

is valid if we subtract for even distribution of the signs

$$\Theta^{(t)} = \theta^{(t)} - \theta_{\neg}^{(t)} \quad if \quad \phi^{(t)} \cdot \phi_{\neg}^{(t)} = \theta^{(t)} \cdot \theta_{\neg}^{(t)}$$

and sum for uneven signs distribution of the signs

$$\Theta^{(t)} = \theta^{(t)} + \theta_{\neg}^{(t)} \quad if \quad \phi^{(t)} \cdot \phi_{\neg}^{(t)} \neq \theta^{(t)} \cdot \theta_{\neg}^{(t)}$$

As a consequence the equality of the resulting probability values of the unitary matrix are equal to the quantum like evolution

$$\begin{pmatrix} \sqrt{p(y|x)} \cdot \sqrt{p(x^t)} & \sqrt{p(y|\neg x)} \cdot \sqrt{p(\neg x^t)} \cdot e^{i\cdot\left(\Phi^{(t)}+\pi\right)} \\ \sqrt{p(\neg y|x)} \cdot \sqrt{p(x^t)} & \sqrt{p(\neg y|\neg x)} \cdot \sqrt{p(\neg x^t)} \cdot e^{i\cdot\Phi^{(t)}} \end{pmatrix}^{\bar{\circ}2} =$$

$$\begin{pmatrix} \sqrt{p(y|x)} \cdot \sqrt{p(x^t)} & \sqrt{p(y|\neg x)} \cdot \sqrt{p(\neg x^t)} \cdot e^{i\cdot\left(\cos^{-1}(-\cos(\Theta^{(t)}))\right)} \\ \sqrt{p(\neg y|x)} \cdot \sqrt{p(x^t)} & \sqrt{p(\neg y|\neg x)} \cdot \sqrt{p(\neg x^t)} \cdot e^{i\cdot\Theta^{(t)}} \end{pmatrix}^{\bar{\circ}2}. \tag{18.39}$$

For most case we can either sum or subtract since one of the two phases is zero. If both phases are non zero and if we exchange the signs of the phases of the matrix, sum instead of subtracting or visa versa, the resulting dynamic evolution may be different from the unitary one. Due to four classes of unitary matrices that are phase balanced matrices we verified empirically that with

$$\theta^{(1)} = \theta_{\neg}^{(1)} = 0, \quad \Theta^{(t)} = \theta^{(t)} + \theta_{\neg}^{(t)} \tag{18.40}$$

it is

$$\left(\begin{pmatrix} \sqrt{p(y|x)} & -\sqrt{p(y|\neg x)} \\ \sqrt{p(\neg y|x)} & \sqrt{p(\neg y|\neg x)} \end{pmatrix} \cdot \begin{pmatrix} \sqrt{p(x^t)} \cdot e^{i\cdot\theta^{(t)}} \\ \sqrt{p(\neg x^t)} \cdot e^{i\cdot\theta_{\neg}^{(t)}} \end{pmatrix}\right)^{\bar{\circ}2} = \tag{18.41}$$

$$\left(\begin{pmatrix} \sqrt{p(y|x)} & \sqrt{p(y|\neg x)} \cdot e^{i\cdot\left(\cos^{-1}(-\cos(\Theta^{(t)}))\right)} \\ \sqrt{p(\neg y|x)} & \sqrt{p(\neg y|\neg x)} \cdot e^{i\cdot\Theta^{(t)}} \end{pmatrix} \cdot \begin{pmatrix} \sqrt{p(x^t)} \\ \sqrt{p(\neg x^t)} \end{pmatrix}\right)^{\bar{\circ}2} \tag{18.42}$$

and

$$\left(\begin{pmatrix} \sqrt{p(y|x)} & \sqrt{p(y|\neg x)} \\ \sqrt{p(\neg y|x)} & -\sqrt{p(\neg y|\neg x)} \end{pmatrix} \cdot \begin{pmatrix} \sqrt{p(x^t)} \cdot e^{i\cdot\theta^{(t)}} \\ \sqrt{p(\neg x^t)} \cdot e^{i\cdot\theta_\neg^{(t)}} \end{pmatrix}\right)^{\bar{\circ}2} = \tag{18.43}$$

$$\left(\begin{pmatrix} \sqrt{p(y|x)} & \sqrt{p(y|\neg x)} \cdot e^{i\cdot\Theta^{(t)}} \\ \sqrt{p(\neg y|x)} & \sqrt{p(\neg y|\neg x)} \cdot e^{i\cdot\left(\cos^{-1}(-\cos(\Theta^{(t)}))\right)} \end{pmatrix} \cdot \begin{pmatrix} \sqrt{p(x^t)} \\ \sqrt{p(\neg x^t)} \end{pmatrix}\right)^{\bar{\circ}2} \tag{18.44}$$

With

$$\theta^{(1)} = \theta_\neg^{(1)} = 0, \qquad \Theta^{(t)} = \theta^{(t)} - \theta_\neg^{(t)} \tag{18.45}$$

it is

$$\left(\begin{pmatrix} -\sqrt{p(y|x)} & \sqrt{p(y|\neg x)} \\ \sqrt{p(\neg y|x)} & \sqrt{p(\neg y|\neg x)} \end{pmatrix} \cdot \begin{pmatrix} \sqrt{p(x^t)} \cdot e^{i\cdot\theta^{(t)}} \\ \sqrt{p(\neg x^t)} \cdot e^{i\cdot\theta_\neg^{(t)}} \end{pmatrix}\right)^{\bar{\circ}2} = \tag{18.46}$$

$$\left(\begin{pmatrix} \sqrt{p(y|x)} \cdot e^{i\cdot\left(\cos^{-1}(-\cos(\Theta^{(t)}))\right)} & \sqrt{p(y|\neg x)} \\ \sqrt{p(\neg y|x)} \cdot e^{i\cdot\Theta^{(t)}} & \sqrt{p(\neg y|\neg x)} \end{pmatrix} \cdot \begin{pmatrix} \sqrt{p(x^t)} \\ \sqrt{p(\neg x^t)} \end{pmatrix}\right)^{\bar{\circ}2} \tag{18.47}$$

and

$$\left(\begin{pmatrix} \sqrt{p(y|x)} & \sqrt{p(y|\neg x)} \\ -\sqrt{p(\neg y|x)} & \sqrt{p(\neg y|\neg x)} \end{pmatrix} \cdot \begin{pmatrix} \sqrt{p(x^t)} \cdot e^{i\cdot\theta^{(t)}} \\ \sqrt{p(\neg x^t)} \cdot e^{i\cdot\theta_\neg^{(t)}} \end{pmatrix}\right)^{\bar{\circ}2} = \tag{18.48}$$

$$\left(\begin{pmatrix} \sqrt{p(y|x)} \cdot e^{i\cdot\Theta^{(t)}} & \sqrt{p(y|\neg x)} \\ \sqrt{p(\neg y|x)} \cdot e^{i\cdot\left(\cos^{-1}(-\cos(\Theta^{(t)}))\right)} & \sqrt{p(\neg y|\neg x)} \end{pmatrix} \cdot \begin{pmatrix} \sqrt{p(x^t)} \\ \sqrt{p(\neg x^t)} \end{pmatrix}\right)^{\bar{\circ}2}. \tag{18.49}$$

The equations are only valid for the unitary versus dynamic evolution. For non unitary evolution or quasi unitary evolution the summation or subtraction of the phases has to be determined for each case. If we exchange the signs of the phases of the matrix, sum instead of subtracting or visa versa the resulting evolution starts with chaotic oscillations behaviour followed by a periodic behaviour or it results in strange oscillations as will be shown in next sections.

18.3.2.2 *Example of unitary and dynamic evolution*

For a symmetric stochastic matrix

$$P = \begin{pmatrix} 0.1 \; 0.9 \\ 0.9 \; 0.1 \end{pmatrix} \tag{18.50}$$

the quantum like evolution with the fixed phase with $\overline{\theta}_\neg = \pi$ and $\overline{\theta} = 0$ determined according to the law of balance resulting in the balanced phase matrix that is unitary matrix with the unitary evolution

$$\begin{pmatrix} \sqrt{p(x^{(t+1)})} \cdot e^{i \cdot \theta^{(t+1)}} \\ \sqrt{p(\neg x^{(t+1)})} \cdot e^{i \cdot \theta_\neg^{(t+1)}} \end{pmatrix} = \begin{pmatrix} \sqrt{0.1} & \sqrt{0.9} \\ -\sqrt{0.9} & \sqrt{0.1} \end{pmatrix} \cdot \begin{pmatrix} \sqrt{p(x^{(t)})} \cdot e^{i \cdot \theta^{(t)}} \\ \sqrt{p(\neg x^{(t)})} \cdot e^{i \cdot \theta_\neg^{(t)}} \end{pmatrix} \tag{18.51}$$

With $\sqrt{p(x^1)} = 1$ and $\sqrt{p(\neg x^1)} = 0$ the evolution indicating the two amplitudes values $\pm\sqrt{p(x^{(t)})}$, $\pm\sqrt{p(\neg x^{(t)})}$ forming a unit circle represented in Figure 18.3.2.2 a), since the phase is either 0 or π. In Figure 18.3.2.2 a) we ad the time axes for 200 time steps and in 18.3.2.2 b) we indicate the transitions between the time steps. Figure 18.4 a) represent the projection of the two amplitude values the unitary evolution into two probability values that evolve in time and Figure 18.4 b) represents the two probability values as two functions in dependence of time.

The corresponding dynamic quantum-like evolution is defined as

$$\begin{pmatrix} \sqrt{p(x^{(t+1)})} \cdot e^{i \cdot \theta^{(t+1)}} \\ \sqrt{p(\neg x^{(t+1)})} \cdot e^{i \cdot \theta_\neg^{(t+1)}} \end{pmatrix} =$$

$$\begin{pmatrix} \sqrt{0.1} \cdot e^{i \cdot \Theta^{(t)}} & \sqrt{0.9} \\ \sqrt{0.9} \cdot e^{i \cdot \left(\cos^{-1}(-\cos(\Theta^{(t)}))\right)} & \sqrt{0.1} \end{pmatrix} \cdot \begin{pmatrix} \sqrt{p(x^t)} \\ \sqrt{p(\neg x^t)} \end{pmatrix} \tag{18.52}$$

with

$$\theta^{(1)} = \theta_\neg^{(1)} = 0, \qquad \Theta^{(t)} = \theta^{(t)} - \theta_\neg^{(t)} \tag{18.53}$$

and $\overline{\Theta}_\neg^{(t)}$, $\overline{\Theta}^{(t)}$ are determined by the law of balance. With $\sqrt{p(x^1)} = 1$ and $\sqrt{p(\neg x^1)} = 0$ the evolution indicating the two amplitudes values $\pm\sqrt{p(x^{(t)})}$, $\pm\sqrt{p(\neg x^{(t)})}$ forming a half unit circle represented in Figure 18.3.2.2 b), since the phase is either 0 or π. In Figure 18.3.2.2 c) we ad the time axes for 200 time steps and in 18.3.2.2 d) we indicate the transitions between the time steps. Figure 18.4 b) represents the two probability values as two functions in dependence of time for dynamic quantum-like evolution that are identical to the unitary evolution.

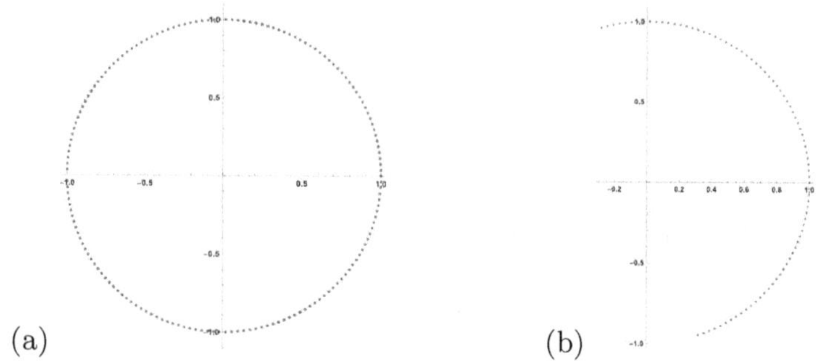

Fig. 18.2 (a) With $\sqrt{p(x^1)} = 1$ and $\sqrt{p(\neg x^1)} = 0$ the evolution indicating the two amplitudes values $\pm\sqrt{p(x^{(t)})}$, $\pm\sqrt{p(\neg x^{(t)})}$ forming a unit circle since the phase is either 0 or π. (b) With $\sqrt{p(x^1)} = 1$ and $\sqrt{p(\neg x^1)} = 0$ the evolution indicating the two amplitudes values $\pm\sqrt{p(x^{(t)})}$, $\pm\sqrt{p(\neg x^{(t)})}$ forming a half unit circle.

18.4 Quasi Unitary Evolution*

For a stochastic matrix

$$P = \begin{pmatrix} 0.1 & 0.89999 \\ 0.9 & 0.10001 \end{pmatrix} \tag{18.54}$$

that is not symmetric but nearly symmetric, a unitary evolution can be not described since the resulting evolution is not norm preserving. The evolution with the fixed phase with $\overline{\theta}_\neg = \pi$ and $\overline{\theta} = 0$ determined according to the law of balance resulting in the balanced phase matrix that iescribes the evolution

$$\begin{pmatrix} \sqrt{p(x^{(t+1)})} \cdot e^{i \cdot \theta^{(t+1)}} \\ \sqrt{p(\neg x^{(t+1)})} \cdot e^{i \cdot \theta_\neg^{(t+1)}} \end{pmatrix} = \begin{pmatrix} \sqrt{0.1} & \sqrt{0.89999} \\ -\sqrt{0.9} & \sqrt{0.10001} \end{pmatrix} \cdot \begin{pmatrix} \sqrt{p(x^{(t)})} \cdot e^{i \cdot \theta^{(t)}} \\ \sqrt{p(\neg x^{(t)})} \cdot e^{i \cdot \theta_\neg^{(t)}} \end{pmatrix} \tag{18.55}$$

With $\sqrt{p(x^1)} = 1$ and $\sqrt{p(\neg x^1)} = 0$ Figure 18.5 a) represents the two values as two functions in dependence of time that are not norm preserving, the values cannot be interpreted as probabilities any more.

However the corresponding dynamic quantum-like evolution defined as

$$\begin{pmatrix} \sqrt{p(x^{(t+1)})} \cdot e^{i \cdot \theta^{(t+1)}} \\ \sqrt{p(\neg x^{(t+1)})} \cdot e^{i \cdot \theta_\neg^{(t+1)}} \end{pmatrix} =$$

$$\begin{pmatrix} \sqrt{0.1} \cdot e^{i \cdot \Theta^{(t)}} & \sqrt{0.89999} \\ \sqrt{0.9} \cdot e^{i \cdot \left(\cos^{-1}(-\cos(\Theta^{(t)}))\right)} & \sqrt{0.10001} \end{pmatrix} \cdot \begin{pmatrix} \sqrt{p(x^t)} \\ \sqrt{p(\neg x^t)} \end{pmatrix} \tag{18.56}$$

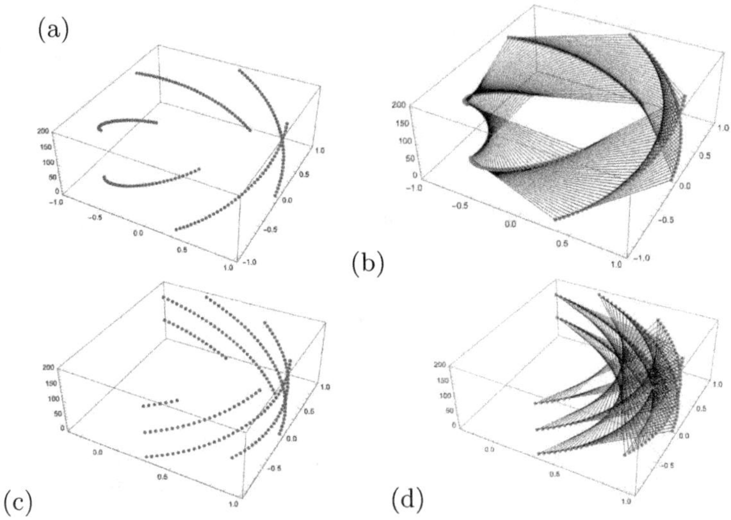

Fig. 18.3 (a) The time axes for 200 time steps is added of the unitary evolution. (b) The transitions (connections) between the time steps of the unitary evolution. (c) The time axes for 200 time steps is added of the dynamic quantum-like evolution. (d) The transitions between the time steps of dynamic quantum-like evolution.

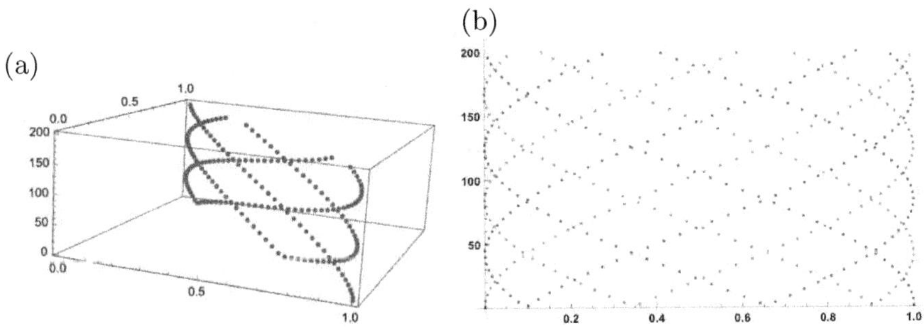

Fig. 18.4 (a) Projection of the two amplitude values representing the unitary evolution into two probability values that evolve in time (b) The two probability values as two functions in dependence of time. They are identical for the unitary evolution and the dynamic quantum-like evolution.

with

$$\theta^{(1)} = \theta_{\neg}^{(1)} = 0, \qquad \Theta^{(t)} = \theta^{(t)} + \theta_{\neg}^{(t)} \tag{18.57}$$

and $\overline{\Theta}_{\neg}^{(t)}$, $\overline{\Theta}^{(t)}$ are determined by the law of balance is norm preserving. With $\sqrt{p(x^1)} = 1$ and $\sqrt{p(\neg x^1)} = 0$ the evolution of the probability values as indicated in Figure 18.5 b) for 600 time steps and in Figure 18.6 a) for 6000 steps. In Figure 18.6 b) we describe the same evolution for 6000 steps

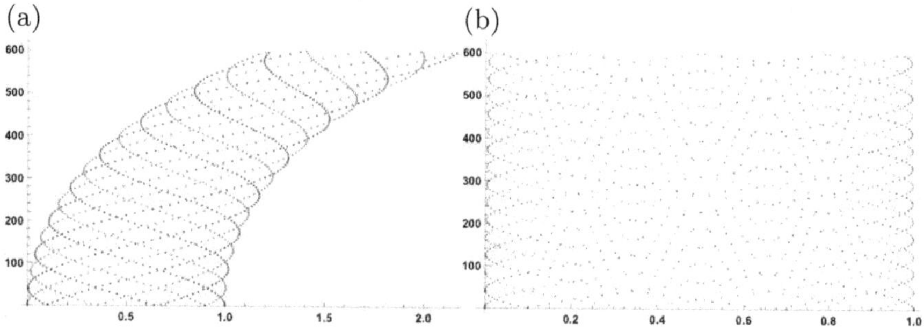

Fig. 18.5 (a) Two values as two functions in dependence of time that are not norm preserving, the values cannot be interpreted as probabilities any more. (b) The corresponding dynamic quantum-like evolution is norm preserving and can be interpreted as probabilities.

however we change the way we compute $\Theta^{(t)}$ to

$$\theta^{(1)} = \theta_{\neg}^{(1)} = 0, \qquad \Theta^{(t)} = \theta^{(t)} - \theta_{\neg}^{(t)} \tag{18.58}$$

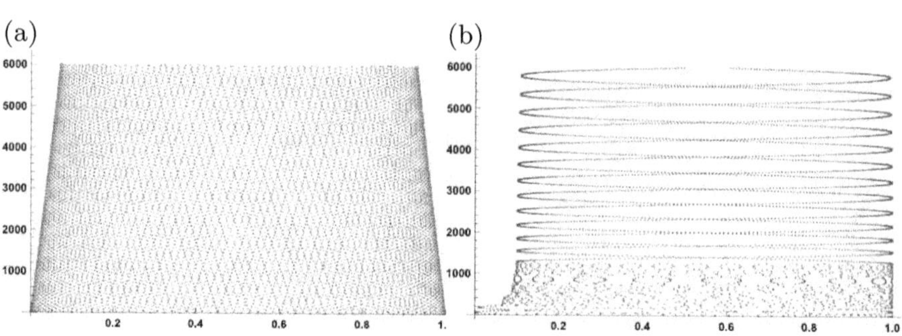

Fig. 18.6 (a) The corresponding dynamic quantum-like evolution is norm preserving and can be interpreted as probabilities. For 6000 times steps the amplitude of the oscillations slowly diminishes. (b) The corresponding dynamic quantum-like evolution for $\Theta^{(t)} = \theta^{(t)} - \theta_{\neg}^{(t)}$.

In another experiments the dynamic quantum-like evolution is defined as

$$\begin{pmatrix} \sqrt{p(x^{(t+1)})} \cdot e^{i \cdot \theta^{(t+1)}} \\ \sqrt{p(\neg x^{(t+1)})} \cdot e^{i \cdot \theta_{\neg}^{(t+1)}} \end{pmatrix} =$$

$$\begin{pmatrix} \sqrt{0.7}\cdot e^{i\cdot\Theta^{(t)}} & \sqrt{0.29999} \\ \sqrt{0.3}\cdot e^{i\cdot\left(\cos^{-1}(-\cos(\Theta^{(t)}))\right)} & \sqrt{0.70001} \end{pmatrix}\cdot\begin{pmatrix} \sqrt{p(x^t)} \\ \sqrt{p(\neg x^t)} \end{pmatrix} \tag{18.59}$$

with

$$\theta^{(1)} = \theta_{\neg}^{(1)} = 0, \qquad \Theta^{(t)} = \theta^{(t)} + \theta_{\neg}^{(t)} \tag{18.60}$$

and $\overline{\Theta}_{\neg}^{(t)}$, $\overline{\Theta}^{(t)}$ are determined by the law of balance. With $\sqrt{p(x^1)} = 0.5$ and $\sqrt{p(\neg x^1)} = 0.5$ the evolution of the probability values as indicated in n Figure 18.7 a) and with

$$\theta^{(1)} = \theta_{\neg}^{(1)} = 0, \qquad \Theta^{(t)} = \theta^{(t)} - \theta_{\neg}^{(t)} \tag{18.61}$$

in Figure 18.7 b). For a stochastic matrix that is not similar to a symmetric

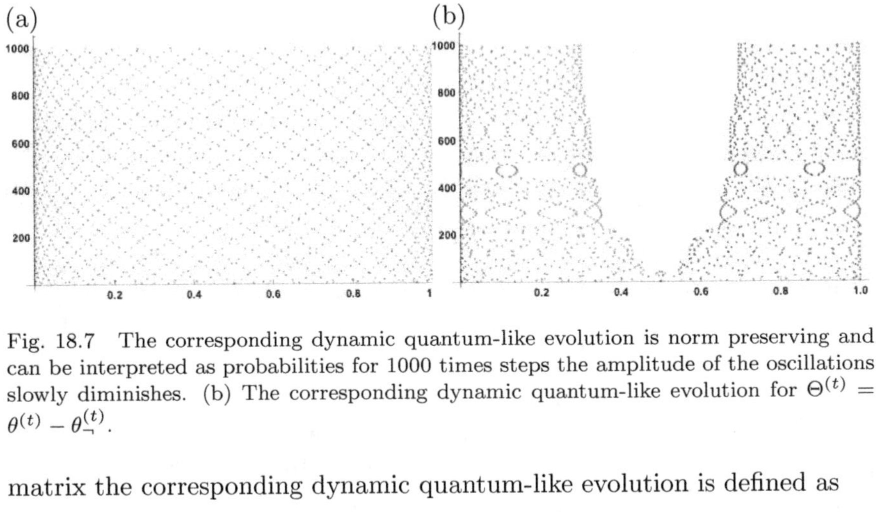

Fig. 18.7 The corresponding dynamic quantum-like evolution is norm preserving and can be interpreted as probabilities for 1000 times steps the amplitude of the oscillations slowly diminishes. (b) The corresponding dynamic quantum-like evolution for $\Theta^{(t)} = \theta^{(t)} - \theta_{\neg}^{(t)}$.

matrix the corresponding dynamic quantum-like evolution is defined as

$$\begin{pmatrix} \sqrt{p(x^{(t+1)})}\cdot e^{i\cdot\theta^{(t+1)}} \\ \sqrt{p(\neg x^{(t+1)})}\cdot e^{i\cdot\theta_{\neg}^{(t+1)}} \end{pmatrix} =$$

$$\begin{pmatrix} \sqrt{0.16}\cdot e^{i\cdot\Theta^{(t)}} & \sqrt{0.08} \\ \sqrt{0.84}\cdot e^{i\cdot\left(\cos^{-1}(-\cos(\Theta^{(t)}))\right)} & \sqrt{0.92} \end{pmatrix}\cdot\begin{pmatrix} \sqrt{p(x^t)} \\ \sqrt{p(\neg x^t)} \end{pmatrix} \tag{18.62}$$

with

$$\theta^{(1)} = \theta_{\neg}^{(1)} = 0, \qquad \Theta^{(t)} = \theta^{(t)} + \theta_{\neg}^{(t)} \tag{18.63}$$

and $\overline{\Theta}_{\neg}^{(t)}$, $\overline{\Theta}^{(t)}$ are determined by the law of balance. With $\sqrt{p(x^1)} = 0.5$ and $\sqrt{p(\neg x^1)} = 0.5$ the evolution of the probability values as indicated in Figure 18.8, there are no oscillations.

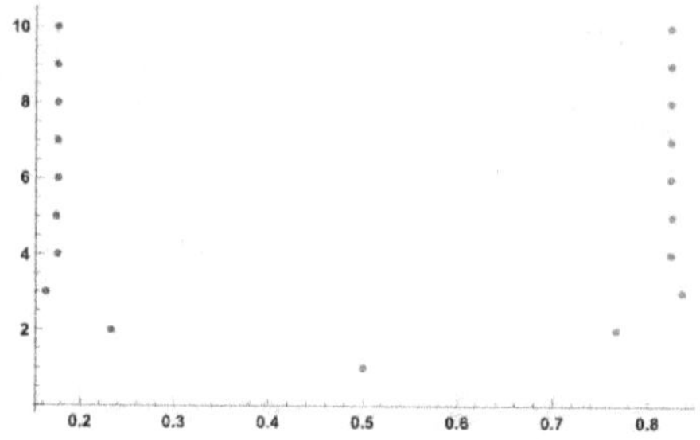

Fig. 18.8 The stochastic matrix is not similar to a symmetric matrix, during the evolution there are no oscillations.

18.4.1 *Strange oscillations**

The corresponding dynamic quantum-like evolution is defined as

$$\begin{pmatrix} \sqrt{p(x^{(t+1)})} \cdot e^{i \cdot \theta^{(t+1)}} \\ \sqrt{p(\neg x^{(t+1)})} \cdot e^{i \cdot \theta_{\neg}^{(t+1)}} \end{pmatrix} =$$

$$\begin{pmatrix} \sqrt{0.6} \cdot e^{i \cdot \Theta^{(t)}} & \sqrt{0.5} \\ \sqrt{0.4} \cdot e^{i \cdot \left(\cos^{-1}(-\cos(\Theta^{(t)}))\right)} & \sqrt{0.5} \end{pmatrix} \cdot \begin{pmatrix} \sqrt{p(x^t)} \\ \sqrt{p(\neg x^t)} \end{pmatrix} \tag{18.64}$$

with

$$\theta^{(1)} = \theta_{\neg}^{(1)} = 0, \qquad \Theta^{(t)} = \theta^{(t)} - \theta_{\neg}^{(t)} \tag{18.65}$$

and $\overline{\Theta}_{\neg}^{(t)}$, $\overline{\Theta}^{(t)}$ are determined by the law of balance. With $\sqrt{p(x^1)} = 0.5$ and $\sqrt{p(\neg x^1)} = 0.5$ the evolution of the probability values as indicated in Figure 18.9 a), they converge after some steps to fixed values. However with

$$\theta^{(1)} = \theta_{\neg}^{(1)} = 0, \qquad \Theta^{(t)} = \theta^{(t)} + \theta_{\neg}^{(t)} \tag{18.66}$$

the evolution of the probability values as indicated in Figure 18.9 b) is chaotic resulting in strange oscillations.

Another example with the dynamic quantum-like evolution is defined as

$$\begin{pmatrix} \sqrt{p(x^{(t+1)})} \cdot e^{i \cdot \theta^{(t+1)}} \\ \sqrt{p(\neg x^{(t+1)})} \cdot e^{i \cdot \theta_{\neg}^{(t+1)}} \end{pmatrix} =$$

$$\begin{pmatrix} \sqrt{0.514} \cdot e^{i \cdot \Theta^{(t)}} & \sqrt{0.49} \\ \sqrt{0.486} \cdot e^{i \cdot \left(\cos^{-1}(-\cos(\Theta^{(t)}))\right)} & \sqrt{0.51} \end{pmatrix} \cdot \begin{pmatrix} \sqrt{p(x^t)} \\ \sqrt{p(\neg x^t)} \end{pmatrix} \tag{18.67}$$

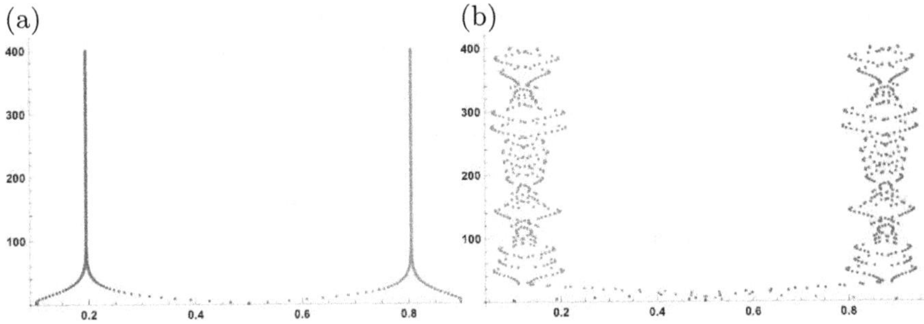

Fig. 18.9 (a) With $\Theta^{(t)} = \theta^{(t)} - \theta_{\neg}^{(t)}$ the evolution of the probability values converges after some steps to fixed values. (b) With $\Theta^{(t)} = \theta^{(t)} + \theta_{\neg}^{(t)}$ the evolution of the probability values is chaotic resulting in strange oscillations.

with

$$\theta^{(1)} = \theta_{\neg}^{(1)} = 0, \qquad \Theta^{(t)} = \theta^{(t)} + \theta_{\neg}^{(t)} \tag{18.68}$$

and $\overline{\Theta}_{\neg}^{(t)}$, $\overline{\Theta}^{(t)}$ are determined by the law of balance. With $\sqrt{p(x^1)} = 0.5$ and $\sqrt{p(\neg x^1)} = 0.5$ the evolution of the probability values as indicated in Figure 18.10 a) is chaotic resulting in strange oscillations. We increase the number of steps from 8000 til 50000 and strange oscillations remain aperiodic, see Figure 18.10 b). In another experiment we increased the number of steps till 100000 not shown in a Figure and they remained aperiodic. A mathematical proof that indeed the evolution of the dynamic quantum-like evolution can lead to deterministic chaos has yet to be done.

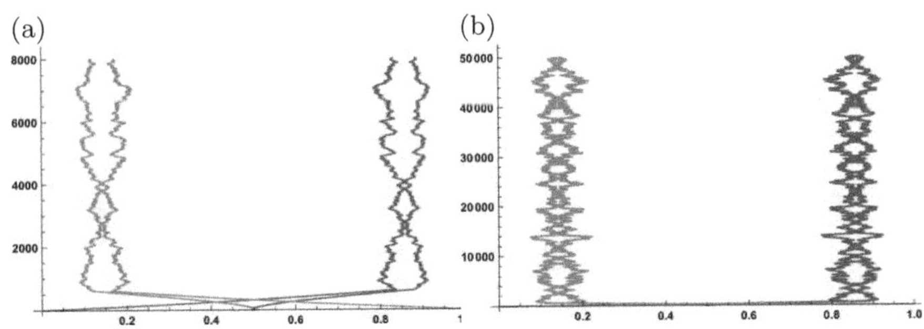

Fig. 18.10 (a) The evolution of the probability values is chaotic resulting in strange oscillations. (b) We increase the number of steps from 8000 til 50000 and strange oscillations remain aperiodic.

Dynamic quantum like evolution can also be applied to non symmetric matrices that are nearly symmetric. In such an evolution instead of having periodic waves with a constant amplitude, the waves have the same period however their amplitude diminishes slowly. The reduction of the amplitude during the steps of the evolution may be modeled as some kind of friction that is related to the the dissimilarity from the symmetric matrix. If we exchange the signs of the phases of the matrix the resulting evolution starts with chaotic oscillations behaviors that are followed by a periodic behaviors. If however the stochastic matrix P is closed to a matrix of the form

$$P = \begin{pmatrix} 0.5 & 0.5 \\ 0.5 & 0.5 \end{pmatrix} \tag{18.69}$$

the resulting dynamic quantum-like evolution can results in strange oscillations which seem to result in deterministic chaos.

Chapter 19

Quantum Computation and the Multiverse

19.1 Many-worlds

The laws of quantum mechanics also apply to the measuring device. We have to consider the entire system, including the measuring device, as a single quantum system [Bousso and Susskind (2012)]. In this case, the Schrödinger's cat paradox [Schrödinger (1935)] has a trivial solution. We represent the measuring device together with us as $|We\rangle$,

$$(|Cat_{alive}\rangle + |Cat_{death}\rangle)\cdot|We\rangle = |Cat_{alive}\rangle\cdot|We\rangle + |Cat_{death}\rangle\cdot|We\rangle \quad (19.1)$$

with

$$|Cat_{alive}\rangle \cdot |We\rangle \neq |Cat_{death}\rangle \cdot |We\rangle$$

which leads to the many-worlds theory (multiverse) [Everett (1959)], [Byrne (2007)]. $|We\rangle$ define the observable by being in a basis state. The explanation is simple, but

$$|Cat_{alive}\rangle \cdot |We\rangle \neq |Cat_{death}\rangle \cdot |We\rangle.$$

leads to some philosophical questions that, for some scientists, create an uncomfortable feeling. However, there is another strong argument for the multiverse by David Deutsch. In his book "The Fabric of Reality? [Deutsch (1997)], David Deutsch poses a question: "*To those who still cling to a single-universe world-view, I issue this challenge: explain how Shor's algorithm works. I do not merely mean predict that it will work, which is merely a matter of solving a few uncontroversial equations. I mean provide an explanation. When Shor's algorithm has factorized a number, using* 10^{500} *or so times the computational resources than can be seen to be present, where was the number factorized? There are only about* 10^{80} *atoms in the entire visible universe, an utterly minuscule number compared with* 10^{500}*. So if* *the visible universe were the extent of physical reality, physical reality would not even remotely contain the resources required to factorize such a large number. Who did factorize it, then? How, and where, was the computation performed?*" In the year 2001, Shor's algorithm was demonstrated by a group at IBM that factored 15 into 3×5 using the NMR implementation of a quantum computer with 7 qubits [Vandersypen *et al.* (2001)]. Where were the 128 states represented?

The Everett many-worlds theory views reality as a many-branched tree in which every possible quantum outcome is realized [Everett (1959)], [Wheeler (1957)], [Dewitt and Graham (1973)], [Deutsch (1997)], [Deutsch (2002)], [Wallace (2002)], [Wallace (2003a)], [Wallace (2003a)], [Byrne (2007)]. The modern version of the wavefunction collapse is based on decoherence and leads to the multiverse interpretation of quantum mechanics [Bousso and Susskind (2012)]. Every time a quantum experiment with different possible outcomes is performed, all outcomes are obtained. If a quantum experiment is performed with two outcomes with a quantum mechanical probability $1/100$ for outcome A and $99/100$ for outcome B, then both the world with outcome A and the world with outcome B will exist. A person should not expect any difference between the experience in worlds A and B. The open question is as follows. Due to the deterministic nature of branching, why should a rational person care about the corresponding probabilities? Why not simply assume that the probabilities are equally probable due to the deterministic nature of branching [Greaves (2007)]? How can we solve this problem without introducing additional structure into the many-worlds theory?

David Deutsch suggested that decision theory can solve this problem [Deutsch (1999)], [Wallace (2003b)], [Wallace (2007)]. A person identifies the consequences of decision theory with things that happen to its individual future copies on particular branches. A person who does not care in receiving 1 on the first branch A and 99 on the second branch B labels them with a probability $1/2$. A rational person that cares assigns the probability $1/100$ for outcome A and $99/100$ for outcome B.

19.2 Deutsch's Decision-theoretic Argument

Decision theory according to Savage is a theory designed for the analysis of rational decision-making under conditions of uncertainty [Deutsch (1999)],[Wichert and Moreira (2016)]. A rational person faces a choice of acts as a function from the set of possible states to the set of consequences. There are some constraints on the acts of the rational person, as for example the preferences must be transitive. It can be then shown that there exists a probability measure p on states s and a utility function U on the set of consequences of an act A so that the expected utility is defined as

$$EU(A) := \sum_{s} p(s) \cdot U(A(s)). \tag{19.2}$$

It follows that a rational person prefers act A to act B if the expected utility of A is greater than that of B. The behaviour corresponds to the maximisation of the expected utility with respect to some probability measure [Russell and Norvig (2003)].

19.2.1 *Decision-theoretic argument*

In the context of the many-worlds the rational person is able to describe each of its acts as a function from the set of possible future branches that will result from a given quantum measurement to the set of consequences [Deutsch (1999)]. Consequences are the things that happen to individual future copies of the person on particular branch. Act is a function from states to consequences, the preferences must be transitive. If a rational person prefers act A to act B, and prefers act B to act C, then the same person must prefer act A to act C. This can be summarised by assigning a real number to each possible outcome in such a way that the preferences are transitive. The corresponding number is called the utility or value. The deterministic process of branching is identified as a chance setup for the rational person by a quantum game with a payoff function P associating a consequence with each eigenvalue of the observable $\hat{X}$. When the measurement is performed the state vector collapses into one or the other eigenstate of the observable being measured, a projection into a eigenstate is preformed. For observable $\hat{X}$ and the state $|y\rangle$ in which the expression for the probability reduces to $|\langle x|y\rangle|^2$ in which x is an eigenvector of $\hat{X}$. A quantum game is specified by the triple

$$(|y\rangle, \hat{X}, P).$$

It is assumed that the utilities of the possible payoffs have an additivity property [Deutsch (1999)]. The approach is based on two non-probabilistic axioms of decision theory. The principle of substitutibility, constrains the values of sub-games. If any of the sub-games is replaced by a game of equal value then the value of the composite game is unchanged. The other axiom concerns two-player zero sum games. If there are two possible acts A and B with payoff c for A and $-c$ for B then playing A and B results in zero. The expected utility or value for playing A and B is

$$EU(A) + EU(B) = c - c = 0.$$

For any two acts A, B, the rational person prefers A to B if

$$EU(A) > EU(B).$$

The person acts if she regarded her multiple future branches as multiple possible futures. In classical decision theory two rational persons may be represented by different probability measures on the set of states. Not so in David Deutsch suggested approach that deals with many-worlds theory [Greaves (2007)]. Expected value with an observable $\hat{X}$ is

$$EU(|y\rangle) = \langle y|\hat{X}|y\rangle \tag{19.3}$$

and since

$$\langle y|\hat{X}|y\rangle = \sum_i |\langle x_i|y\rangle|^2 \cdot x_i = \sum_i p(x_i) \cdot x_i \tag{19.4}$$

representing the weighted mean over the eigenvalues of $\hat{X}$. IA rational person that makes decision about outcomes of measurement believes that each possible eigenvalue x_i had the probability $|\langle x_i|y\rangle|^2 = p(x_i)$ due to the process of maximizing the probabilistic expectation value of the payoff [Deutsch (1999)].

19.2.1.1 *The derivation of probabilities for real amplitudes*

We sketch the proof by David Elieser Deutsch, see [Deutsch (1999)]. If $|y\rangle$ is an eigenstate $|x\rangle$ of $\hat{X}$ it follows that

$$EU(|y\rangle) = x$$

is equal to the eigenvalue x. By appealing twice to the additivity of utilities for eigenvectors $|x_i\rangle$ and adding a constant k we arrive at

$$EU\left(\sum_i \omega_i \cdot |x_i + k\rangle\right) = EU\left(\sum_i \omega_i \cdot |x_i\rangle\right) + k. \tag{19.5}$$

The rational person is indifferent in receiving the separate payoffs with utilities x_1 and x_2 or receiving a single payoff with utility $x_1 + x_2$. The expected utility of $|x_i + k\rangle$ has by additivity the same value as the expected utility of $|x_i\rangle$ followed by k. This is the central equation on which the proof of David Deutsch is based. The constant k on the left side corresponds to a combination of eigenstates. This is because it is required that for each branch the payoffs are present. The constant k on the right side corresponds to a combination of the corresponding eigenvalues.

According to additivity the left side of equation has the same expected utility as the superposition of possible branches and the payoffs represented by a corresponding combination of eigenvalues is on the right side. The other equation follows from the axiom concerns two-player zero- sum games

$$EU\left(\sum_i \omega_i \cdot |x_i\rangle\right) + EU\left(\sum_i \omega_i \cdot |-x_i\rangle\right) = 0. \tag{19.6}$$

If $|y\rangle$ is in a superposition

$$|y\rangle = \frac{1}{\sqrt{2}} \cdot |x_1\rangle + \frac{1}{\sqrt{2}} \cdot |x_2\rangle. \tag{19.7}$$

and with

$$k = -x_1 - x_2 \tag{19.8}$$

it follows

$$EU\left(\frac{1}{\sqrt{2}}\left(|x_1 - x_1 - x_2\rangle + |x_2 - x_1 - x_2\rangle\right)\right) = EU\left(\frac{1}{\sqrt{2}}\left(|-x_2\rangle - |x_1\rangle\right)\right) = \tag{19.9}$$

$$-EU\left(\frac{1}{\sqrt{2}}\left(|x_1\rangle + |x_2\rangle\right)\right) = EU\left(\frac{1}{\sqrt{2}}\left(|x_1\rangle + |x_2\rangle\right)\right) - x_1 - x_2 \tag{19.10}$$

and by the Equation the value of the expected utility is derived as

$$\frac{1}{2}\left(x_1 + x_2\right) = EU\left(\frac{1}{\sqrt{2}}\left(|x_1\rangle + |x_2\rangle\right)\right). \tag{19.11}$$

For a superposition of n eigenstates

$$\frac{1}{n}\left(x_1 + x_2 + \cdots + x_n\right) = EU\left(\frac{1}{\sqrt{n}}\left(|x_1\rangle + |x_2\rangle + \cdots + |x_n\rangle\right)\right) \tag{19.12}$$

the proof is based on induction from the principle of substitutibility and additivity. For $n = 2^m$ the proof follows from substitutibility by inserting a two equal amplitude game into remaining 2^{m-1} equal-amplitude outcomes. Otherwise the proof follows inductive hypothesis and additivity by replacing $n-1$ by n, for details see [Deutsch (1999)]. For unequal amplitudes

$$\frac{m}{n} \cdot x_1 + \frac{n-m}{n} \cdot x_2 = EU\left(\sqrt{\frac{m}{n}} \cdot |x_1\rangle + \sqrt{\frac{n-m}{n}} \cdot |x_2\rangle\right). \tag{19.13}$$

we introduce auxiliary system that can be in two states different states, either

$$\sqrt{\frac{1}{n}} \cdot \sum_{a=1}^{m} |z_a\rangle \tag{19.14}$$

or

$$\sqrt{\frac{1}{n-m}} \cdot \sum_{a=m+1}^{n} |z_a\rangle \tag{19.15}$$

with eigenstates $|z_a\rangle$ and eigenvalues z_a of the observable $\hat{Z}$ that are all distinct. Then the joint state is given by

$$\sqrt{\frac{1}{n}} \cdot \left(\sum_{a=1}^{m} |x_1\rangle|z_a\rangle + \sum_{a=m+1}^{n} |x_2\rangle|z_a\rangle \right). \tag{19.16}$$

When we measure the observable $\hat{Z}$ depending on the index a of the eigenvalues z_a we know that $\hat{X}$ is x_1 if $a < m+1$ or x_2 otherwise. With additional properties of the eigenvalues

$$\sum_{a=1}^{m} z_a = \sum_{a=m+1}^{n} z_a = 0 \tag{19.17}$$

and all n values

$$x_1 + z_a, \ 1 \leq a \leq m \tag{19.18}$$

and

$$x_2 + z_a, \ m+1 \leq a \leq n \tag{19.19}$$

are all distinct, the composite measurement with observable $\hat{X}$ and $\hat{Z}$ has the same value as the one with observable $\hat{X}$ alone. Because of the additivity the state is equivalent to the amplitude superposition

$$\sqrt{\frac{1}{n}} \cdot \left(\sum_{a=1}^{m} |x_1\rangle|z_a\rangle + \sum_{a=m+1}^{n} |x_2\rangle|z_a\rangle \right) \tag{19.20}$$

and it follows

$$\frac{1}{n} \cdot \left(\sum_{a=1}^{m} |x_1\rangle|z_a\rangle + \sum_{a=m+1}^{n} |x_2\rangle|z_a\rangle \right) = \frac{m}{n} \cdot x_1 + \frac{n-m}{n} \cdot x_2. \tag{19.21}$$

A rational person would choose the expected value of $|y\rangle$ with an observable $\hat{X}$

$$EU(|y\rangle) = \langle y|\hat{X}|y\rangle \tag{19.22}$$

and since

$$\langle y|\hat{X}|y\rangle = \sum_i |\langle x_i|y\rangle|^2 \cdot x_i = \sum_i p(x_i) \cdot x_i \tag{19.23}$$

represents the weighted mean over the eigenvalues of $\hat{X}$, the rational person interprets p_i as probabilities. For complex amplitudes it is assumed that the unitary transformation

$$|x_a\rangle \rightarrow e^{i \cdot \theta_a}|x_a\rangle \tag{19.24}$$

with a corresponding phase θ_a does not alter the payoff, the player is indifferent as to whether it occurs or not. The proof can be extended to irrational numbers, it is based on the idea that the state undergoes some unitary evolution before the measurement [Deutsch (1999)]. The unitary evolution leads to real amplitudes with eigenvalues that exceeds the original state. Each game played after the unitary transformation is as valuable as the original game, and the values of such games have a lower bound of the original game.

19.3 Expected Utility and Entropy

A fundamental property of rational persons is that they prefer certainty to uncertainty. Humans prefer to choose an action that brings them a certain, but lower utility instead of an action that is uncertain, but can bring a higher utility [Epstein (1999)], [Wichert and Moreira (2016)].

We measure the uncertainty by the entropy of the experiment. The experiment starts at t_0 and ends at t_1. At t_0, we have no information about the results of the experiment, and at t_1, we have all of the information, so that the entropy of the experiment is 0. We can describe an experiment by probabilities. For the outcome of the flip of a fair coin, the probability for a head or tail is 0.5, $p = (0.5, 0.5)$. A person A knows the outcome, but person B does not. Person B could ask A about the outcome of the experiment. If the question is of the most basic nature, then we could measure the minimal number of optimally required questions B must pose to know the result of the experiment. A most basic question corresponds to the smallest information unit that could correspond to a yes or no answer. For a fair coin, we pose just one question, for example, is it a tail? For a card game, to determine if a card is either red, clubs or spades, we have a different number of possible questions. If the card is red, then we need only one question. However, in the case in which the card is not red, we need another question to determine whether it is a spade or a club. The probability of being red is 0.5, of clubs 0.25 and spades 0.25, $p = (0.5, 0.25, 0.25)$. For clubs and spades, we need two questions. In the meantime, we must ask $1 \cdot 0.5 + 2 \cdot 0.25 + 2 \cdot 0.25$ questions, which would result in 1.5 questions. The entropy is represented by Shannon's entropy H for an experiment A

$$H(A) = -\sum_i p_i \log_2 p_i. \tag{19.25}$$

It indicates the minimal number of optimal binary yes/no questions that a rational person must pose to know the result of an experiment [Shannon (1948)], [Topsoe (1974)]. We can describe the process of measuring a state by an observable as measuring the entropy of the experiment. Before the measurement of a state $|x\rangle$ by an observable we are uncertain about the outcome. We measure the uncertainty by Shannon's entropy. After the measurement the state is in eigenstate, the entropy is zero, Shannon's entropy is defined for any observable and any probability distribution, according to Leslie Ballentin [Ballentine (2012)], page 617 "It measures the maximum amount of information that may be gained by measuring that observable."

Assuming that a Hilbert space H_n can be represented as a collection of orthogonal subspaces

$$H_n = E_1 \oplus E_2 \oplus \ldots \oplus E_f \tag{19.26}$$

with $f \leq n$. A state $|y\rangle$ can be represented with $|x_i\rangle \in E_i$ as

$$|y\rangle = \omega_1 \cdot |x_1\rangle + \omega_2 \cdot |x_2\rangle + \cdots + \omega_f \cdot |x_f\rangle.$$

For one dimensional subspaces $f = n$ and the value $|x_k\rangle$ is observed with a probability $\| \omega_k \cdot |x_k\rangle \|^2 = |\omega_k|^2$. Shannon's entropy is defined as

$$E(|y\rangle) = -\sum_{i=1}^{n} (|\omega_i|^2 \cdot \log_2 |\omega_i|^2) = -\sum_i p_i \log_2 p_i. \tag{19.27}$$

19.3.1 *Weighted sum of surprisals*

We say that events that seldom happen, for example, the letter x in a message, have a higher surprise. Some letters are more frequent than others; an e is more frequent than an x. The larger the probability that we receive a character, the less surprised we are. Surprise is inversely related to probability.

$$s_i = \frac{1}{p_i}$$

The logarithm of surprise

$$I_i = -\log_2 \frac{1}{|\omega_i|^2} = 2 \cdot \log_2 |\omega_i| = -\log_{\sqrt{2}} |\omega_i| = \log_2 s_i \tag{19.28}$$

is the self-information or surprisal I_i. The Shannon's entropy H represents the wighted sum of surprisals.

$$H(A) = \sum_i^n p_i \cdot \log_2 s_i = \sum_i^n p_i \cdot I_i. \tag{19.29}$$

It can be interpreted as an expected utility

$$EU(A) := \sum_i p_i \cdot U(A(i)) = \sum_i^n p_i \cdot I_i. \tag{19.30}$$

with the utility function $U(A(i))$

$$U(A(i)) = I_i. \tag{19.31}$$

For acts the expected utility is identified with the representation of the entropy of an action, represented by H

$$H(A) := EU(A).$$

That the rewards are determined by the negative information content is already known and is used for the utility representation problems in economics [Candeal *et al.* (2001)], [Ortega and Braun (2009)], [Robert *et al.* (2009)]. If there are two possible acts A and B with payoff c for A and $-c$ for B then playing A and B results in zero. The expected utility or value for playing A and B is

$$H(A) + H(B) = c - c = 0,$$

but for any two acts A, B, the rational person prefers A to B if

$$H(A) < H(B)$$

because the uncertainty is lower. The theoretic proof David Deutsch can be applied, for example

$$|y\rangle = \frac{1}{\sqrt{2}} \cdot |x_1\rangle + \frac{1}{\sqrt{2}} \cdot |x_2\rangle. \tag{19.32}$$

and with

$$k = -x_1 - x_2 \tag{19.33}$$

the right side of the equation with eigenvalues $x_1 = 1$ and $x_2 = 1$

$$k = -x_1 - x_2 = -2 \tag{19.34}$$

or $U(A(i)) = I_i = \log_2 2 = 1$. Therfore

$$\frac{1}{2}(1+1) = \frac{1}{2}(x_1 + x_2) = EU\left(\frac{1}{\sqrt{2}}(|x_1\rangle + |x_2\rangle)\right) \tag{19.35}$$

and

$$1 = 0.5 \cdot 1 + 0.5 \cdot 1. \tag{19.36}$$

However we can as well recover the probabilities from the definition of Shannon's entropy. This strengthens idea even more.

19.3.2 Recovering probabilities from entropy

The entropy or the uncertainty is maximal in the case in which all probabilities are equal, which means that $p = (1/n, 1/n..., 1/n)$. In this case

$$H(F) = -\sum_i p_i \log_2 p_i = -\log_2 1/n = \log_2 n. \tag{19.37}$$

the surprisal I_i is equal to the entropy

$$H(F) = \log_2 n = I_i. \tag{19.38}$$

If $|y\rangle$ is in a superposition of n eigenstates

$$|y\rangle = \frac{1}{\sqrt{n}} (|x_1\rangle + |x_2\rangle + \cdots + |x_n\rangle) \tag{19.39}$$

it follows that a surprisal I_i^* of each state represented by amplitude $\omega_i = \frac{1}{\sqrt{n}}$ is

$$I_i^* = \log_2 \sqrt{n} = \frac{1}{2} \cdot \log_2 n. \tag{19.40}$$

We know that in the case of equal amplitudes $\log n$ yes/no questions have to be asked with $H(F) = I_i$ so the function $f(I^*)$ is equal to multiply by two

$$H(|y\rangle) = I_i = f(I_i^*) = 2 \cdot \log_2 \sqrt{n} = \log_2 n = -\log_2 \left(\frac{1}{\sqrt{n}}\right)^2 \tag{19.41}$$

that is equivalent to

$$p_i = 2^{I_i} = \left(\frac{1}{\sqrt{n}}\right)^2. \tag{19.42}$$

In the case of complex amplitudes with phase θ_a

$$\omega_i = e^{i \cdot \theta_a} \frac{1}{\sqrt{n}} \tag{19.43}$$

$$I_i^* = \log_2 e^{i \cdot \theta_a} \sqrt{n} = \frac{i \cdot \theta_a}{\log 2} + \frac{1}{2} \cdot \log_2 n, \tag{19.44}$$

the operations described by $f(I^*)$ would be, first get rid of the complex number $i \cdot \theta_a / \log 2$ by subtracting $-i \cdot \theta_a / \log 2$ and then multiply by 2. Or

$$p_i = 2^{I_i} = \left(\frac{1}{e^{-i \cdot \theta_a} e^{i \cdot \theta_a} \cdot \sqrt{n}}\right)^2 = \left(\frac{1}{\sqrt{n}}\right)^2. \tag{19.45}$$

For unequal amplitudes for each surprisal I_i^* of each state we multiply it by two and recover from I_i the value $p_i = 2^{I_i}$. This operation leads to the minimal number of optimal binary yes/no questions. For example for

$$|y\rangle = \sqrt{\frac{m}{n}} \cdot |x_1\rangle + \sqrt{\frac{n-m}{n}} \cdot |x_2\rangle \tag{19.46}$$

we get by operations described by $f(I^*)$

$$H(|y\rangle) = -\frac{m}{n} \cdot \log_2 \frac{m}{m} - \left(\frac{n-m}{n}\right) \cdot log_2 \left(\frac{n-m}{n}\right), \tag{19.47}$$

the correct value of Shannon's entropy. We assume

$$p_i = \left(\frac{1}{|\omega_i|}\right)^2. \tag{19.48}$$

19.3.3 *Biological principle of energy minimization*

Identity is a concept that defines the properties of a rational person over time [Pöppel (2010)]. It is a unifying concept based on the biological principles of homeostasis [Bernard (1957)], [Gross (1998)]. Organisms have to be kept stable to guarantee the maintenance of life, like for example the regulation of body temperature. This principle was extended by allostasis [Sterling (2004)] for regulation of bodily functions over time. To preform this task efficient mechanisms for the prediction of future states are needed to anticipate future environmental constellations [von Holst and Mittelstaedt (1950)], [Bao *et al.* (2014)]. This is done, because the homeostatic state may be violated by unexpected changes in the future. It means as well that every organism implies a kind of self identity over time [Zhou *et al.* (2014)]. This identity requires a time interval of finite duration within which sensory information is integrated. Different sensor information arrives at different time stamps. The fusion process has to be done over some time window. Similar problems are present during a sensor fusion task in a mobile robot. For example in visual and auditory perception in humans the transduction of the acoustic information is much shorter then the visual [Pöppel *et al.* (1990)]. In it is suggested that in humans a temporal window with the duration of 3 s is created [Pöppel (2009)]. This window represents the psychological concept of "now" [Zhou *et al.* (2014)]. The consciousness concept of "now " represented by the temporal window is shifted backward in time of the consciousness itself, since a subconsciousness mechanism is required to preform the integration task [Wichert and Moreira (2016)].

19.3.3.1 *Prediction of events*

David's Deutsch probability rule within unitary quantum mechanics is based on rationality. Instead of rationality we introduced the biological principle of homeostasis.

One of the brain functions is to provide a casual consistent explanation of events to maintain self identity over time leading to the psychological concept of "now". Split brain research and stimulation or brain regions during awake operation suggest that the brain generates an explanation of effects that were not initiated by consciousness [Libet (2004)], [Coon and Mitterers (2012)]. Before an event happens an explanation has to be incited by the subconsciousness parts of the brain so that it is possible to integrate it into the temporal window of the self when the event happens. As well other organism functions need be put in alert due to some predicted possible events.

Organisms must maintain stability, e.g., the regulation of body temperature, to guarantee the maintenance of life. This principle is extended by allostasis [Sterling (2004)] for the regulation of bodily functions over time. To perform this task, efficient mechanisms for the prediction of future states are necessary to anticipate future environmental constellations [von Holst and Mittelstaedt (1950)], [Bao *et al.* (2014)].

Events with higher surprise are more difficult to explain than events with low surprise values. An explanation has to be possible. When the surprise is too high, an explanation may be impossible and the identity of self could break. The idea is related to the general constructor theory of David Elieser Deutsch, see [Deutsch (2013)]. The metabolic cost of neural information processing of explaining higher surprise events require higher energy levels than lower surprise events. Fechner's law states that there is a logarithmic relation between the stimulus and its intensity [Frisby and Stone (2010)]. We assume as well that there is a logarithmic relation between the cost of initiation an explanation of an event and its surprise value s_i, that is $\log s_i$. Neuronal computation is energetically expensive [Laughlin *et al.* (1998)]. Consequently, the brain's limited energy supply imposes constraints on its information processing capability. The costs should be fair divided into the explanation of all predicted possible branches since the organism will be deterministic present in all of them. A possible solution is given by the Shannon's entropy. The corresponding value I_i is weighted in relation

$$p_i = 2^{I_i} \tag{19.49}$$

and the resulting costs are $p_i \cdot I_i$. The resulting costs of initiating n explanations for action A of n predicted branches before a split are

$$H(A) = \sum_i^n p_i \cdot \log_2 s_i = \sum_i^n p_i \cdot I_i \tag{19.50}$$

For the human (subconsciousness) brain it makes sense to choose A to B if

$$H(A) < H(B).$$

since it requires less energy.

19.4 Free Will

Incompatibilism states that a deterministic universe is logically incompatible with the notion that people have free will. Then again, it is supposed that non-deterministic quantum mechanics plays an essential role in the understanding of the human mind and free will. It is assumed that the mind is non-algorithmic and thus incapable of being modeled by a computer. We follow the idea of Descartes that the mind and the brain are two different things. We assume, first, that the universe is deterministic and, second, that the mind interacts with the brain only in one direction: The mind senses the brain but does not make decision known to the brain. Despite these two major constraints, we indicate how free will can be present [Wichert (2016a)].

19.4.1 *Computer metaphor*

Among many brain researchers and computer scientists, there is the strong belief that artificial intelligence can provide an answer to the problem of the mind and consciousness. The main task of artificial intelligence is the development of artificial intelligence systems that are as intelligent as humans or maybe even more so. It is speculated that the mind is an emergent property of complex systems simulated by a computer. The brain is viewed as being such a complex system that can be simulated on a computer. Some scientists even speculate that it is possible to achieve cybernetic immortality by downloading the information describing our brain onto a computer. Since a computer is a deterministic and executes algorithms, free will does not exist, and only one course of events is possible. Free will is an illusion, and the mind is generated as part of the process of computation. These are metaphysical speculations; however, their metaphysical nature is often denied by corresponding scientists. Related to this denouement is the intermixture of the terms cognition and mind. The word cognition comes from the Latin cognoscere, which means "to know", "to conceptualise" or "to recognise". Cognition is closely related to human intelligence and can be simulated by machines such as computers. On the other hand, mind has a vague definition; it has some consciousness, a combination of cognition and emotion, including an unconscious cognitive process. It manifests itself as a stream of consciousness, as described in the literary masterpiece Ulysses by James Joyce. It seems that cognition and the mind are closely related, but is this actually the case?

19.4.2 *Explanation as a function of the brain*

One of the cognitive brain functions is to provide a causally consistent explanation of events to maintain self-identity over time, leading to the psychological concept of "now". Identity is a concept that defines the properties of a rational person over time. It is a unifying concept based on the biological principles of homeostasis [Bernard (1957)], [Gross (1998)]. Organisms must maintain stability, e.g., the regulation of body temperature, to guarantee the maintenance of life. This principle is extended by allostasis [Sterling (2004)] for the regulation of bodily functions over time. To perform this task, efficient mechanisms for the prediction of future states are necessary to anticipate future environmental constellations [von Holst and Mittelstaedt (1950)], [Bao *et al.* (2014)].

This is done, because the homeostatic state may be violated by unexpected changes in the future. It means as well that every organism implies a kind of self identity over time [Zhou *et al.* (2014)]. This identity requires a time interval of finite duration within which sensory information is integrated. Before an event occurs, an explanation must be incited by the subconscious parts of the brain so that it is possible to integrate it into the temporal window of the self when the event occurs. Additionally, other organic functions must be put on alert due to some predicted possible events. If an explanation is not possible due to a lack of causality, the identity of the self may break. In this context, the mind defines the psychological concept of "now", and identity is more related to human senses than to an algorithmic device. From this perspective, artificial intelligence models human cognition but not the mind or consciousness. It is a window of our consciousness into the quantum reality. In the next section, we attempt to establish a relationship with quantum physics.

19.5 Quantum Reality

If one assumes that quantum effects are only present at the microscopic scale, as suggested by the Copenhagen interpretation, then it would follow that the corresponding probabilities are rarely observed at the macroscopic scale. The corresponding statistics are near to certainty at the macroscopic scale, resulting in classical deterministic mechanics, as proposed by adequate determinism. However, it seems that our organism and our subconscious brain are aware of the quantum nature of the universe. Clues from psychology indicate that human cognition is based on quantum probability rather than the theory of traditional probability, as explained by Kolmogorov's axioms [Busemeyer *et al.* (2006b)], [Busemeyer and Trueblood (2009)], [Busemeyer *et al.* (2009)], [Busemeyer *et al.* (2012)]. This approach would lead to the conclusion that a wave function can be present at the macro scale of our everyday life. The modern version of the wave-function collapse in quantum mechanics is based on decoherence and leads to the multiverse interpretation of quantum mechanics [Bousso and Susskind (2012)]. Every time a quantum experiment with different possible outcomes is performed, all outcomes are obtained. If a quantum experiment is performed with two outcomes, i.e., with outcome A and outcome B, then both the world with outcome A and the world with outcome B will exist.

A person should not expect any difference between the experience in a world A and B. This corresponds to the Everett many-worlds theory, it views reality as a many-branched tree in which every possible quantum outcome is realised [Everett (1959)], [Wheeler (1957)], [Dewitt and Graham (1973)], [Deutsch (1997)], [Deutsch (2002)], [Wallace (2002)], [Wallace (2003a)], [Wallace (2003a)], [Byrne (2007)]. A person should not expect any difference between the experience in world A and world B, but a person in world A is a different person in world B. We are one person described by the path in the multiverse that is correlated with our free choices.

19.5.1 *Multiverse metaphor: Library of Babel metaphor*

Someone is reading a book about a certain hero and his adventures. uring the process of reading, he identifies with the hero and lives through his ups and downs. Reading is a complex cognitive process, and it cannot be described by a simple function. It requires high cognitive functions for textual interpretation and decoding into a cognitive representation and comprehension. The brain preforms these functions; it decodes and interprets the story, but it does not create it. However, an illusion that the reader is the hero described in the book and that the reader is making the decisions may exist. Let us perform a thought experiment. A human being's life, with all of his decisions, is recorded and transcribed into an enormous book called the book of life. A demon allows the human being to live again; however, he would erase all of his memories. The new life of the human consists of reading the previously recorded book of life. Does this mean that, during the reading, the human being is making his free choices or not? One can argue that the person makes free choices because the book describes free choices in a free world and these choices are those of the person. One can argue that, to write such a book, one must live in a free world. The book is a description of a real free life. By reading it, one cannot distinguish between the moment in which one is making choices and reading the book of life.

What if some demon knew about the person's free choices and wrote the book of life without the person actually having lived and having made the choices at all? Is it possible that a demon can predict free choices?

In Borges' story, the universe consists of an enormous library of an indefinite and perhaps infinite number of books. The books contain every possible ordering of just a few basic characters. Most of the books are completely useless to the reader and have no meaning. However, among all of these meaningless books, there are all the books that are or ever will be written. These meaningful books define causality; in other words, causality is represented by a meaningful book. These include all possible biographies of any person and translations of every book into every language. By chance, a person will find his book. By reading some noise, we become nothing. We are defined by our book of life, as we are defined by our human body. Do we make free choices? Yes, we do because we cannot make any distinction between reading our book of life and living in a free world.

A person should not expect any difference between reading book A and book B, but the person reading book A is a different person from the person reading book B. We are one person described by the book that we are reading or, in the language of quantum physics, by the path in the multiverse that is correlated with our free choices.

There are billions similar persons, but they are not us. Our choices are a part of the multiverse, they are not created and they do not disappear, they are forever the part of static deterministic multiverse. Our choices are defined by our personality. The multiverse corresponds to some Platonic world of ideas that is explained to us by our mind, our consciousness is the unchangeable part of us. It is nonphysical and it senses the world. It does not interact with the brain in the other way beside it [Wichert (2016a)].

19.5.2 *Conclusion*

We redefined free will as the concept of identity in a deterministic universe. Causality is related to a meaningful explanation. For impossible explanations, causality does not exist, and the identity of the self breaks. Only in meaningful causal worlds may personal identities exist. We are one person described by the meaningful path in the multiverse that is correlated with our free choices.

Chapter 20

Conclusion

20.1 Quantum Brain

Neuroimaging indicates how information processing is implemented in the brain and when specific structures and processes are invoked. For example, fMRI measures local properties of the cerebral blood flow and is based on blood oxygen level dependence. Changes of activity associated with various stimulus conditions are correlated with brain activity. However: "It is unclear that we will come to a better understanding of mental processes simply by observing which neural loci are active while subjects perform a task ", [Kosslyn (1999)]. In this section, we will describe the relationship between quantum computation principles that speed up the computation and the human brain. Human vision is based on information integration and is non-reversible. Hubel and Wiesel's discoveries provided a large amount of influence on the ways that neuroscientists think about the brain [Hubel (1988)]. They have inspired several models for pattern recognition. In these models, the neural units have a local view, unlike the common fully-connected networks [Fukushima (1980)], [Wichert (1993)], [Riesenhuber and Poggio (1999)], [Fukushima (1989)], [Cardoso and Wichert (2010)]. They gradually reduce the information from the input layer through the output layer. This task is accomplished by integrating local features into more global features in sequential transformations. Its purpose is to classify topological data by gradually reducing the information from the input layer through the output layer. Each of these transformations is composed of two different steps. The first step reduces the information by representing it with previously learned templates. The second step blurs the information to allow positional shifts, giving the model some invariance under shifts and distortions. A quantum neural model should perform a reversible

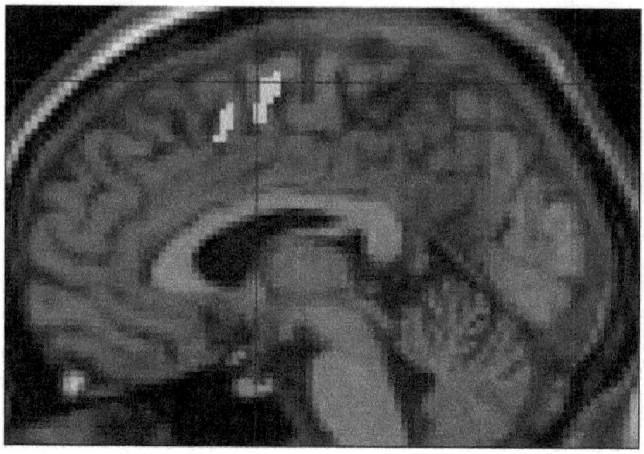

Fig. 20.1 Changes of activity associated with various stimulus conditions are correlated with the brain activity. A cluster indicates a brain activity during an experiment [Wichert *et al.* (2002)].

computation. Neurons do not perform a reversible computation, neither do neural networks.

A noncomputable process involves the possibility of generating true randomness [Penrose (1991)]. Classical physics leads to the paradox of free will in a deterministic world. We redefined free will as the concept of identity in a deterministic universe. Causality is related to a meaningful explanation. For impossible explanations, causality does not exist, and the identity of the self breaks. Only in meaningful causal worlds may personal identities exist. We are one person described by the meaningful path in the multiverse that is correlated with our free choices. The consciousness concept of "now ? is represented by the temporal window that is shifted backward in time of the consciousness itself since a subconsciousness mechanism is required to perform the integration task. Does the concept of "now? also include the integration of different possible events of the multiverse by the brain? Is time just an event in the multiverse? Many questions besides the computational nature of the brain are still unexplored. Why does the illusion of motion result when a series of film images are displayed in quick succession? The proposed persistence of vision is now considered to be a myth. Why do we dream, why do we have consciousness?

The question concerning randomness is highly metaphysical. In classical physics, randomness does not exist; in quantum physics, it cannot be explained. In addition to randomness, quantum computation cannot offer any noncomputable schema such as that claimed by the quantum mind or the quantum consciousness hypothesis [Nunn *et al.* (1994)]. However, quantum cognition assumes that the brain is a classical computer in a quantum world. Because the wave function can be present at the macro scale, predictions, such as the hidden inference, are based on von Neumann probabilities and not on the classical probability theory.

20.2 Epilogue

Adiabatic quantum computation is an alternative approach to quantum computation. It is based on the time evolution of a quantum system. Adiabatic quantum computation is the polynomial equivalent to the quantum gate model. Quantum annealing solves optimization problems. It allows the computation to escape local minima of the objective function by tunneling through hills instead of climbing over them.

Quantum computation with the quantum gate model is based on two principles to speed up the computation:

- The QFT can determine the period of a wave.
- Grover's algorithm can speed up the search quadratically for a given number of possible solutions.

Linear-algebra based quantum machine learning is based on the HHL quantum algorithm for solving linear equations and qPCA founded on first principle (Kitaev's phase estimation algorithm). The two principles can be combined together in a quantum counting algorithm to estimate the number of possible solutions. A symbolical artificial intelligence framework allows an elegant description of a possible universal quantum computer model that is capable of faster execution of programs.

The geometrical structure of the world can be used to speed up problem solving. This structure is present in simple Euclidian geometry as experienced by humans. It is also present in the geometrical structure of the world, as described by the quantum physics results with Grover's algorithm, which is based on the Householder reflection.

Bibliography

Aaronson, S. (2004). Is quantum mechanics an island in theoryspace? in A. Khrennikov (ed.), *Proceedings of the Växjö Conference Quantum Theory: Reconsideration of Foundations*, Vol. 10, pp. 15–28.

Aaronson, S. (2015). Quantum machine learning algorithms: Read the fine print, *Nature Physics* **11**, pp. 291–293.

Ackley, D. H., E., H. G. and Sejnowski, T. J. (1985). A learning algorithm for boltzmann machines, *Cognitive Science* **9**, 1, pp. 147–169.

Adachi, S. H. and Henderson, M. P. (2015). Application of quantum annealing to training of deep neural networks, *ArXiv Quantum Physics e-prints* **abs/1510.06356**.

Aharonov, D. (1999). *Noisy Quantum Computation*, Ph.D. thesis, Hebrew University.

Aharonov, D., Ambainis, A., Kempe, J. and Vazirani, U. (2001). Quantum walks on graphs, in *Proceedings of ACM Symposium on Theory of Computation (STOC'01)*, pp. 50–59.

Aikins, J. (1986). Prototypical knowledge for expert systems, *Artificial Intelligence* **20**, pp. 163–210.

Aïmeur, E., Brassard, B. and Gambs, S. (2013). Quantum speed-up for unsupervised learning, *Machine Learning* **90**, pp. 261–287.

Akshay, V., Philathong, H., Morales, M. E. S. and Biamonte, J. D. (2020). Reachability deficits in quantum approximate optimization, *Physical Review Letters* **124**, p. 090504.

Ambainis, A. (2003). Quantum walks and their algorithmic applications, *International Journal of Quantum Information* **1**, p. 507, URL `http://www.citebase.org/abstract?id=oai:arXiv.org:quant-ph/0403120`.

Ambainis, A. (2004). Quantum search algorithms, *SIGACT News* **35**, 2, pp. 22–35, doi:http://doi.acm.org/10.1145/992287.992296.

Ambainis, A. (2007). A nearly optimal discrete query quantum algorithm for evaluating NAND formulas, *ArXiv e-prints* .

Ambainis, A., Childs, A. and Reichardt, B. (2007). Any and-or formula of size n can be evaluated in time $n^{\frac{1}{2}+o(1)}$ on a quantum computer, in *Foundations of Computer Science, 2007. FOCS '07. 48th Annual IEEE Symposium on*, pp. 363 -372, doi:10.1109/FOCS.2007.57.

Amico, L., Fazio, R., Osterloh, A. and Vedral, V. (2008). Entanglement in many-body systems, *Reviews of Modern Physics* **80**, 2, pp. 517–576.

Amin, M. H., Andriyas, E., Rolfe, J., Kulchytskyy, B. and Melko, R. (2018). Quantum boltzmann machine, *Physical Review X* **8**, 021050.

Anderson, J. (1983). *The Architecture of Cognition* (Harvard University Press).

Anderson, J. A. (1995a). *An Introduction to Neural Networks* (The MIT Press).

Anderson, J. R. (1995b). *Cognitive Psychology and its Implications*, 4th edn. (W. H. Freeman and Company).

Aspray, W. (1990). *John von Neumann and the origins of modern computing*, History of computing (MIT Press), ISBN 9780262011211.

Ballard, D. H. (1997). *An Introduction to Natural Computation* (The MIT Press).

Ballentine, L. E. (2012). *Quantum Mechanics A Modern Development 2nd Edition* (World Scientific).

Bao, Y., Pöppel, E., Liang, W. and Yang, T. (2014). When is the right time? a little later! – delayed responses show better temporal control, *Procedia - Social and Behavioral Sciences* **126**, pp. 199–200.

Bebis, G. and Georgiopoulos, M. (1994). Feed-forward neural networks, *IEEE Potentials* **13**, 4, pp. 27–31.

Bennett, C. (1973). Logical reversibility of computation, *IBM Journal of Research and Development* **17**, pp. 525–532.

Bennett, C. H. (1982). The thermodynamics of computation–a review, *International Journal of Theoretical Physics* **21**, 12, pp. 905–940.

Bennett, C. H. (1988). Notes on the history of reversible computation, *IBM J. Res. Dev.* **32**, 1, pp. 16–23.

Bennett, C. H. (1989). Time/space trade-offs for reversible computation, *SIAM Journal on Computing* **18**, 4, pp. 766–776, doi:10.1137/0218053, URL `http://link.aip.org/link/?SMJ/18/766/1`.

Bennett, C. H. (2003). Notes on landauer's principle, reversible computation, and maxwell's demon, *Studies In History and Philosophy of Science Part B: Studies In History and Philosophy of Modern Physics* **34**, 3, pp. 501 – 510, doi:DOI:10.1016/S1355-2198(03)00039-X.

Bennett, C. H., Bernstein, E., Brassard, G. and Vazirani, U. (1997). Strengths and weaknesses of quantum computing, URL `http://www.citebase.org/abstract?id=oai:arXiv.org:quant-ph/9701001`.

Bennett, C. H., Brassard, G., Crépeau, C., Jozsa, R., Peres, A. and Wootters, W. K. (1993). Teleporting an unknown quantum state via dual classical and einstein-podolsky-rosen channels, *Phys. Rev. Lett.* **70**, 13, pp. 1895–1899, doi:10.1103/PhysRevLett.70.1895.

Bentz, H. J., Hagstroem, M. and Palm, G. (1989). Information storage and effective data retrieval in sparse matrices, *Neural Networks* **2**, 4, pp. 289–293.

Bernard, C. (1957). *An Introduction to the Study of Experimental Medicine* (New York, NY: Dover).

Bernstein, E. and Vazirani, U. (1993). Quantum complexity theory, in *STOC '93: Proceedings of the twenty-fifth annual ACM symposium on Theory of computing* (ACM, New York, NY, USA), ISBN 0-89791-591-7, pp. 11–20, doi:http://doi.acm.org/10.1145/167088.167097.

Berry, D. W., Ahokas, G., Cleve, R. and Sanders, B. C. (2006). Efficient quantum algorithms for simulating sparse hamiltonians, *Communications in Mathematical Physics* **270**, 2, p. 359371.

Biamonte, J., Wittek, P., Pancotti, N., Rebentrost, P., Wiebe, N., and Lloyd, S. (2017). Quantum machine learning, *Nature* **549**, pp. 195–202.

Biederman, I. and Ju, G. (1988). Surface vs. edge-based determinants of visual recognition, *Cognitive Psychology* **20**, pp. 38–6.

Binney, J. and Skinner, D. (2014). *The Physics of Quantum Mechanics* (Oxford University Press).

Bishop, C. (2006). *Pattern Recognition and Machine Learning* (Springer).

Boltzman, L. (1995). *Lectures on Gas Theory* (Dover Books on Physics).

Bousso, R. and Susskind, L. (2012). Multiverse interpretation of quantum mechanics, *Physical Reviewd D* **85**, 4, p. 045007.

Boven, L. V. and Epley, N. (2003). The unpacking effect in evaluative judgments: When the whole is less than the sum of its parts, *Journal of Experimental Social Psychology* **39**, pp. 263–269.

Boyer, M., Brassard, G., Hoeyer, P. and Tapp, A. (1998). Tight bounds on quantum searching, *Fortschritte der Physik* **46**, p. 493, URL `http://www.citebase.org/abstract?id=oai:arXiv.org:quant-ph/9605034`.

Brassard, G., Hoyer, P., Mosca, M. and Tapp, A. (2000). Quantum Amplitude Amplification and Estimation, *eprint arXiv:quant-ph/0005055* .

Brassard, G., Hoyer, P. and Tapp, A. (1998). Quantum counting, URL `http://www.citebase.org/abstract?id=oai:arXiv.org:quant-ph/9805082`.

Brooke, J., Bitko, D., Rosenbaum, T. and Aeppli, G. (1999). Quantum annealing of a disordered magnet, *Science* **284**, 5415, pp. 779–781.

Brownston, L., Farell, R., Kant, E. and Martin, N. (1985). *Programming Expert Systems in OPS5: An Introduction to Rule-Based Programming* (Addison-Wesley).

Brunak, S. and Lautrup, B. (1990). *Neural Networks Computers with Intuition* (World Scientific).

Busemeyer, J., Matthew, M. and Wang, Z. (2006a). A quantum information processing explanation of disjunction effects, in *Proceedings of the 28th Annual Conference of the Cognitive Science Society*, pp. 131–135.

Busemeyer, J., Pothos, E., Franco, R. and Trueblood, J. (2011). A quantum theoretical explanation for probability judgment errors, *Journal of Psychology Review* **118**, pp. 193–218.

Busemeyer, J. and Wang, Z. (2014). Quantum cognition: Key issues and discussion. *Topics in Cognitive Science* **6**, pp. 43–46.

Busemeyer, J., Wang, Z. and Trueblood, J. (2012). Hierarchical bayesian estimation of quantum decision model parameters, in *Proceedings of the 6th International Symposium on Quantum Interactions*, pp. 80–89.

Busemeyer, J. R. and Trueblood, J. (2009). Comparison of quantum and bayesian inference models, in P. Bruza, D. Sofge, W. Lawless, K. van Rijsbergen and M. Klusch (eds.), *Quantum Interaction, Lecture Notes in Computer*

Science, Vol. 5494 (Springer Berlin / Heidelberg), pp. 29–43, URL `http://dx.doi.org/10.1007/978-3-642-00834-4-5`.

Busemeyer, J. R., Wang, Z. and Lambert-Mogiliansky, A. (2009). Empirical comparison of markov and quantum models of decision making, *Journal of Mathematical Psychology* **53**, 5, pp. 423 – 433, doi:DOI:10.1016/j.jmp.2009.03.002.

Busemeyer, J. R., Wang, Z. and Townsend, J. T. (2006b). Quantum dynamics of human decision-making, *Journal of Mathematical Psychology* **50**, 3, pp. 220 – 241, doi:DOI:10.1016/j.jmp.2006.01.003.

Byrne, P. (2007). The many worlds of hugh everett, *Scientific American Magazine* , pp. 98–105.

Candeal, J. C., De Miguel, J. R., Indura, E. and Mehta, G. B. (2001). Utility and entropy, *Economic Theory* **17**, pp. 233–238.

Cardoso, A. and Wichert, A. (2010). Neocognitron and the map transformation cascade, *Neural Networks* **23**, 1, pp. 74–88.

Childs, A. M. (2011). *LECTURE 14: Discrete-time quantum walk*, University of Waterloo, URL `http://www.math.uwaterloo.ca/~amchilds/teaching/w11/l14.pdf`.

Childs, A. M., Reichardt, B. W., Spalek, R. and Zhang, S. (2007). Every NAND formula of size N can be evaluated in time $N^{\frac{1}{2}+o(1)}$ on a quantum computer, *eprint arXiv:quant-ph/0703015* .

Church, A. (1936a). A note on the entscheidungsproblem, *Journal of Symbolic Logic* **1**, 1, pp. 40–41.

Church, A. (1936b). An unsolvable problem of elementary number theory, *American Journal of Mathematics* **58**, 2, pp. 345–363.

Church, A. (1941). *The Calculi of Lambda-Conversion*, Annals of Mathematics Studies (Princeton University Press, Princeton, New Jersey, USA).

Churchland, P. S. and Sejnowski, T. J. (1994). *The Computational Brain* (The MIT Press).

Cleve, R., Gavinsky, D. and Yonge-Mallo, D. (2008). Quantum algorithms for evaluating min-max trees, in Y. Kawano and M. Mosca (eds.), *Proceedings of Theory of Quantum Computation, Communication, and Cryptography (TQC 2008)*, Vol. 5106 (Springer Berlin / Heidelberg), pp. 11–15.

Coon, D. and Mitterers, J. O. (2012). *Introduction to Psychology Gateways to Mind and Behavior, 13th Edition* (Wadsworth Publishing).

Cormen, T. H., Leiserson, C. E., Rivest, R. L. and Stein, C. (2001). *Introduction to Algorithms, 2/e* (MIT Press).

Cortes, C. and Vapnik, V. (1995). Support-vector networks, *Machine Learning* **20**, pp. 273–297.

Cybenko, G. (1989). Approximations by superpositions of sigmoidal functions, *Mathematics of Control, Signals, and Systems* **2**, 4, pp. 303–314.

Dattani, N. and Chancellor, N. (2019). Embedding quadratization gadgets on chimera and pegasus graphs, *ArXiv Quantum Physics e-prints* **abs/1901.07676**.

Dattani, N., Szalay, S. and Chancellor, N. (2019). Pegasus: The second connectivity graph for large-scale quantum annealing hardware, *ArXiv Quantum Physics e-prints* **abs/1901.07636**.

Davis, C. (1962). The norm of the schur product operation, *Numerische Mathematik* **4**, 1, pp. 343–344.

de Sá, J. P. M. (2001). *Pattern Recognition: Concepts, Methods and Applications* (Springer-Verlag).

Deutsch, D. (1985). Quantum theory, the church-turing principle and the universal quantum computer, in *Proceedings of the Royal Society of London-Series A, Mathematical and Physical Sciences*, Vol. 400, pp. 97–117.

Deutsch, D. (1997). *The Fabric of Reality* (Penguin Group).

Deutsch, D. (1999). Quantum theory of probability and decisions, *Proceedings of the Royal Society A* **455**, pp. 3129–97.

Deutsch, D. (2002). The structure of the multiverse, *Proceedings of the Royal Society A* **458**, 2028, pp. 2911–23.

Deutsch, D. (2013). Constructor theory, *Synthese* **190**, 18.

Deutsch, D. and Jozsa, R. (1992). Rapid Solution of Problems by Quantum Computation, *Royal Society of London Proceedings Series A* **439**, pp. 553–558.

Dewitt, B. S. and Graham, N. (eds.) (1973). *The Many-Worlds Interpretation of Quantum Mechanics* (Princeton University Press).

Duda, R. O., Hart, P. E. and Stork, D. G. (2000). *Pattern Classification (2nd Edition)* (Wiley-Interscience), ISBN 0471056693.

Epstein, L. G. (1999). A definition of uncertainty aversion, *The Review of Economic Studies* **66**, 3, pp. 579–608.

Everett, H. (1959). "relative state" formulation of quantum mechanics, *Reviews of Modern Physics* **29**, pp. 454–462.

Farhi, E., Goldstone, J., Gosset, D., Gutmann, S., Meyer, H. B. and Shor, P. (2009). Quantum adiabatic algorithms, small gaps, and different paths, URL `http://www.citebase.org/abstract?id=oai:arXiv.org:0909.4766`.

Farhi, E., Goldstone, J. and Gutmann, S. (2008). A quantum algorithm for the hamiltonian nand tree, *Theory of Computing* **4**, 1, pp. 169–190, doi:10.4086/toc.2008.v004a008.

Farhi, E., Goldstone, J., Gutmann, S. and Sipser, M. (2000). Quantum Computation by Adiabatic Evolution, *ArXiv Quantum Physics e-prints* .

Farhi, E. and Gutmann, S. (1998). Quantum computation and decision trees, *Phys. Rev. A* **58**, 2, pp. 915–928, doi:10.1103/PhysRevA.58.915.

Feldman, J. (1985). Four frames suffice: A provisional model of vision and space, *Behavioral and Brain Sciences* **8**, pp. 265–289.

Fikes, R. E. and Nilsson, N. J. (1971). Strips: A new approach to the application of theorem proving, *Artificial Intelligence* **2**.

Forgy, C. (1981). Ops5 user's manual cmu-cs-81-135, Tech. rep., Computer Science Department, Carnegie-Mellon University, Pittsburgh, Pensilvania USA.

Franklin, S. (1997). *Artificial Minds* (MIT Press).

Freeman, J. A. (1994). *Simulating Neural Networks with Mathematica* (Addison-Wesley).

Frisby, J. P. and Stone, J. V. (2010). *Seeing, The Computational Approach to Biological Vision, 2nd Edition* (MIT Press).

Fukushima, K. (1980). Neocognitron: a self organizing neural network model for a mechanism of pattern recognition unaffected by shift in position. *Biol Cybern* **36**, 4, pp. 193–202.

Fukushima, K. (1989). Analisys of the process of visual pattern recognition by the neocognitron, *Neural Networks* **2**, pp. 413–420.

Fuster, J. (1995). *Memory in the Cerebral Cortex* (The MIT Press).

Gardner, M. (1979). Mathematical games: Mathematical games: The random number omega bids fair to hold the mzsteries of the universe, *Scientific American* , pp. 20–30.

Gaylord, R. J. and Wellin, P. R. (1995). *Computer Simulations with Mathematica* (Spriner Verlag).

Ghosh, S., Rosenbaum, T. F., Aeppli, G. and Coppersmith, S. N. (2003). Entangled quantum state of magnetic dipoles, *Nature* **425**, pp. 48–51.

Gilovich, T. (1999). Tversky, in *The MIT Encyclopedia of the Cognitive Sciences* (The MIT Press), pp. 849–850.

Giovannetti, V., Lloyd, S., and Maccone, L. (2008). Quantum random access memory, *Physical Review Letters* **100**, p. 160501.

Givan, R. and Dean, T. (1997). Model minimization, regression, and propositional strips planning, in *15th International Joint Conference on Artificial Intelligence*, pp. 1163–8.

Glauber, R. J. (1963). Timedependent statistics of the ising model, *Journal of Mathematical Physics* **4**, 294.

Goldstone, R. (1999). Similarity, in *The MIT Encyclopedia of the Cognitive Sciences* (The MIT Press), pp. 763–765.

Goodfellow, I., Bengio, Y. and Courville, A. (2016). *Deep Learning* (MIT Press).

Greaves, H. (2007). Probability in the everett interpretation, *Philosophy Compass* **1**, 109-128.

Gross, C. and Mishkin (1977). The neural basis of stimulus equivalence across retinal translation, in S. Harnad, R. Dorty, J. Jaynes, L. Goldstein and Krauthamer (eds.), *Lateralization in the nervous system* (Academic Press, New York), pp. 109–122.

Gross, C. G. (1998). Claude bernard and the constancy of the internal environment, *Neuroscientist* **4**, pp. 380–385.

Grover, L. K. (1996). A fast quantum mechanical algorithm for database search, in *STOC '96: Proceedings of the twenty-eighth annual ACM symposium on Theory of computing* (ACM, New York, NY, USA), ISBN 0-89791-785-5, pp. 212–219, doi:http://doi.acm.org/10.1145/237814.237866.

Grover, L. K. (1997). Quantum mechanics helps in searching for a needle in a haystack, *Physical Review Letters* **79**, p. 325, URL `doi:10.1103/PhysRevLett.79.325`.

Grover, L. K. (1998a). A framework for fast quantum mechanical algorithms, in *STOC '98: Proceedings of the thirtieth annual ACM symposium on Theory of computing* (ACM, New York, NY, USA), ISBN 0-89791-962-9, pp. 53–62, doi:http://doi.acm.org/10.1145/276698.276712.

Grover, L. K. (1998b). Quantum computers can search rapidly by using almost any transformation, *Phys. Rev. Lett.* **80**, 19, pp. 4329–4332, doi:10.1103/PhysRevLett.80.4329.

Haines, T. (1999). *Walking with Dinosaurs - a Natural History* (BBC Worldwide Limited).

Halpern, J. Y. (2003). *Reasoning about Uncertainty* (MIT Press).

Harrow, A., Hassidim, A. and Lloyd, S. (2009). Quantum algorithm for solving linear systems of equations, *Physical Review Letters* **103**, p. 150502.

Haykin, S. O. (2008). *Neural Networks and Learning Machines (3rd Edition)* (Prentice Hall).

Hecht-Nielsen, R. (1989). *Neurocomputing* (Addison-Wesley).

Heisenberg, W. (1949). *The Physical Principles of the Quantum Theory* (Courier Dover Publications).

Hertz, J., Krogh, A. and Palmer, R. G. (1991). *Introduction to the Theory of Neural Computation* (Addison-Wesley).

Hey, A. and Walters, P. (2003). *The New Quantum Universe* (Cambridge University Press).

Hidary, J. D. (2019). *Quantum Computing: An Applied Approach* (Springer).

Hinton, G. E. and Sejnowski, T. J. (1983). Optimal perceptual inference, in *Proceedings of the IEEE conference on Computer Vision and Pattern Recognition*, pp. 448–453.

Hinton, G. E. and Sejnowski, T. J. (1986). Learning and relearning in boltzmann machines, in D. E. Rumelhart and J. L. McClelland (eds.), *Parallel Distributed Processing: Explorations in the Microstructure of Cognition. Volume 1: Foundations* (The MIT Press), pp. 282–317.

Hirvensalo, M. (2004). *Quantum Computing* (Springer-Verlag, Berlin Heidelberg).

Hogg, T. (2008). Quantum random walk from the wolfram demonstrations project, http://demonstrations.wolfram.com/QuantumRandomWalk/.

Hopfield, J. J. (1982). Neural networks and physical systems with emergent collective computational abilities, *Proceedings of the National Academy of Sciences of the USA* **79**, 8, pp. 2554–2558.

Hornik, K. (1991). Approximation capabilities of multilayer feedforward networks, *Neural Networks* **4**, 2, pp. 251–257.

Hornik, K., Stinchcombe, M. and White, H. (1989). Multilayer feedforward networks are universal approximators, *Neural Networks* **2**, 5, pp. 359–366.

Hristova, E. and Grinberg, M. (2008). Disjunction effect in prisonner's dilemma: Evidences from an eye-tracking study, in *Proceedings of the 30th Annual Conference of the Cognitive Science Society*, pp. 1225–1230.

Hubel, D. H. (1988). *Eye, Brain, and Vision* (Scientific Ammerican Library, Oxford, England).

Hummel, J. (1999). Binding problem, in R. A. Wilson and F. C. Keil (eds.), *The MIT Encyclopedia of the Cognitive Sciences* (The MIT Press), pp. 85–86.

Hyman, A. (1985). *Charles Babbage: Pioneer of the Computer* (Princeton University Press).

Islam, M., Rahman, M., Begum, Z. and Hafiz, M. (2009). Low cost quantum realization of reversible multiplier circuit, *Information Technology Journal* **8**, 2, pp. 208–213.

Jackson, P. (1999). *Introduction to Expert Systems*, 3rd edn. (Addison-Wesley).

Jaynes, E. T. (1957a). Information theory and statistical mechanics, *Physical Review. Series II* **106**, 4, pp. 620–630.

Jaynes, E. T. (1957b). Information theory and statistical mechanics ii, *Physical Review. Series II* **108**, 2, pp. 171–190.

Jaynes, E. T. (1968). Prior probabilities, *IEEE Transactions on Systems Science and Cybernetics.* **4**, 3, pp. 227–241.

Johnson, M. W., Amin, M. H. S., Gildert, S., Lanting, T., Hamze, F., Dickson, N., Harris, R., Berkley, A. J., Johansson, J., Bunyk, P., Chapple, E. M., Enderud, C., Hilton, J. P., Karimi, K., Ladizinsky, E., Ladizinsky, N., Oh, T., Perminov, I., Rich, C., Thom, M. C., Tolkacheva, E., Truncik, C. J. S., Uchaikin, S., Wang, J., Wilson, B. and Rose, G. (2011). Quantum annealing with manufactured spins, *Nature* **473**, 7346, pp. 194–198, URL `http://dx.doi.org/10.1038/nature10012`.

Kahn, G., Kepner, A. and Pepper, J. (1987). Test: a model-driven application shell, in *National Conference on Artificial Intelligence*, pp. 814–18.

Kaye, P. R., Laflamme, R. and Mosca, M. (2007). *An Introduction to Quantum Computing* (Oxford University Press, USA).

Kempe, J. (2003). Quantum random walks - an introductory overview, *Contemporary Physics* **44**, pp. 307–327, URL `http://www.citebase.org/abstract?id=oai:arXiv.org:quant-ph/0303081`.

Khrennikov, A. (2009). Quantum-like model of cognitive decision making and information processing, *Journal of BioSystems* **95**, pp. 179–187.

Kitaev, A. (1996). Quantum measurements and the abelian stabilizer problem, *Electronic Colloquium on Computational Complexity* **3**, TR96-003.

Klahr, P. and Waterman, D. (1986). *Expert Systems: Techniques, Tools and Applications* (Addison-Wesley).

Knoblauch, A., Palm, G. and Sommer, F. (2010). Memory capacities for synaptic and structural plasticity, *Neural Computation* **22**, pp. 289–341.

Kohonen, T. (1989). *Self-Organization and Associative Memory*, 3rd edn. (Springer-Verlag).

Kolda, T. G. and Bader, B. W. (2009). Tensor decompositions and applications, *SIAM Review* **51**, 3, pp. 455–500.

Kolmogorov, A. (1933). *Grundbegriffe der Wahrscheinlichkeitsrechnung* (Springer-Verlag).

Korf, R. E. (1985). Depth-first iterative-deepening : An optimal admissible tree search, *Artificial Intelligence* **27**, 1, pp. 97 – 109, doi:DOI:10.1016/0004-3702(85)90084-0.

Kosko, B. (1992). *Neural Networks and Fuzzy Systems: A Dynamical Systems Approach to Machine Intelligence* (Prentice-Hall).

Kosslyn, S. M. (1994). *Image and Brain, The Resolution of the Imagery Debate* (The MIT Press).

Kosslyn, S. M. (1999). If neuroimaging is the answer, what is the question? *Philosophical Transactions of the Royal Society of London B Biological Sciences* **354**, pp. 1283–1294.

Kropff, E. and Treves, A. (2005). The storage capacity of potts models for semantic memory retrieval, *Journal of Statistical Mechanics: Theory and Experiment* .

Kuhberger, A., Komunska, D. and Josef, P. (2001). The disjunction effect: Does it exist for two-step gambles? *Organizational Behavior and Human Decision Processes* **85**, pp. 250–264.

Kurbat, M., Smith, E. and Medin, D. (1994). Categorization, typicality, and shape similarity, in A. Ram and K. Eiselt (eds.), *Proceedings of the Cognitive Science Meeting* (Atlanta, GA), pp. 520–530.

Kurfess, F. J. (1997). Neural networks and structured knowledge, in C. Hermann, F. Reine and A. Strohmaier (eds.), *Knowledge in Neural Networks* (Logos Verlag, Berlin), pp. 5–22.

Kurzweil, R. (1990). *The Age of Intelligent Machines* (The MIT Press).

Laird, J. E., Rosenbloom, P. S. and Newell, A. (1986). Chunking in soar: The anatomy of a general learning mechanism, *Machine Learning* **1**, 1, pp. 11–46.

Laird, J. F., Newell, A. and Rosenbloom, P. S. (1987). SOAR: An architecture for general intelligence, *Artificial Intelligence* **40**.

Lakeoff, G. (1987). *Women, Fire, and Dangerous Things* (The University of Chicago Press).

Lambdin, C. and Burdsal, C. (2007). The disjunction effect reexamined: Relevant methodological issues and the fallacy of unspecified percentage comparisons, *Organizational Behavior and Human Decision Processes* **103**, pp. 268–276.

Lambert, D. (1983). *Collins Guide to Dinosaurs* (Diagram Visual Information Ltd).

Lambert, D. (1993). *The Ultimate Dinosaur Book* (Dorling Kindersley).

Lancy, D. (1983). *Cross-Cultural Studies in Cognition and Mathematics* (Academic Press, New York).

Landauer, R. (1961). Irreversibility and heat generation in the computing process, *IBM Journal of Research and Development* **5**, pp. 183–191.

Landauer, R. (1992). Information is physical, in *Physics and Computation, 1992. PhysComp '92., Workshop on*, pp. 1–4.

Laughlin, S. B., de Ruyter van Steveninck, R. R. and Anderson, J. C. (1998). The metabolic cost of neural information, *Nature neuroscience* **1**, 1, pp. 36–41.

Lewis, H. R. and Papadimitriou, C. H. (1981). *Elements of the Theory of Computation* (Prentice Hall PTR, Upper Saddle River, NJ, USA), ISBN 0132624788.

Li, S. and Taplin, J. (2002). Examining whether there is a disjunction effect in prisoner's dilemma game, *Chinese Journal of Psychology* **44**, pp. 25–46.

Libet, B. (2004). *Mind Time - The Temporal Factor in Consciousness* (Harvard University Press).

Lloyd, S. (1996). Universal quantum simulators, *Science* **273**, 5278, pp. 1073–1078.

Lloyd, S., Mohseni, M. and Rebentrost, P. (2014). Quantum principal component analysis, *Nature Physics* **10**, pp. 631–633.

Luger, G. F. and Stubblefield, W. A. (1993). *Artificial Intelligence: Structures and Strategies for Complex Problem Solving: Second Edition* (The Benjamin/Cummings Publishing Company, Inc, Menlo Park, CA, USA).

Luger, G. F. and Stubblefield, W. A. (1998). *Artificial Intelligence, Structures and Strategies for Complex Problem Solving*, 3rd edn. (Addison-Wesley).

Marcinowski, M. (1987). *Codierungsprobleme beim Assoziativen Speichern*, Master's thesis, Fakultät für Physik der Eberhard-Karls-Universität Tübingen.

Markov, A. (1954). *The theory of algorithms* (National Academy of Sciences, USSR).

Maxwell, J. C. (2001). *Theory of Heat (9ed)* (Courier Dover Publications).

McClelland, J. and Kawamoto, A. (1986). Mechanisms of sentence processing: Assigning roles to constituents of sentences, in J. McClelland and D. Rumelhart (eds.), *Parallel Distributed Processing* (The MIT Press), pp. 272–325.

McClelland, J. and Rumelhart, D. (1985). Distributed memory and the representation of general and specific memory, *Journal of Experimental Psychology: General* **114**, pp. 159–188.

McGeoch, C. C. (2014). *Adiabatic Quantum Computation and Quantum Annealing: Theory and Practice* (Morgan & Claypool).

Metropolis, N., Rosenbluth, A., Rosenbluth, M., Teller, A. and Teller, E. (1953). Equation of state calculations by fast computing machines, *Journal of Chemical Physics* **21**, pp. 1087–1092.

Miikkulainen, R. (1993). *Subsymbolic Natural Language Processing: An Integrated Model of Scripts, Lexicon and Memory* (The MIT Press).

Minsky, M. (1975). A framework for representing knowledge, in P. Winston (ed.), *The Psychology of Computer Vision* (McGraw-Hill, New York), pp. 211–77.

Minsky, M. (1986). *The Society of Mind* (Simon and Schuster, New York).

Minsky, M. and Papert, S. (1972). *Perceptrons: An Introduction to Computational Geometry* (MIT Press).

Mitchell, T. (1997). *Machine Learning* (McGraw-Hill).

Moore, C. and Russell, A. (2001). Quantum Walks on the Hypercube, *eprint arXiv:quant-ph/0104137* .

Moore, D. (2002). Measuring new types of question-order effects: Additive and subtractive, *Public Opinion Quarterly* **66**, pp. 80–91.

Moreira, C. and Wichert, A. (2014). Interference effects in quantum belief networks, *Applied Soft Computing* **25**, pp. 64–85.

Moreira, C. and Wichert, A. (2016a). Quantum-like bayesian networks for modeling decision making, *Frontiers in Psychology* **7**.

Moreira, C. and Wichert, A. (2016b). Quantum probabilistic models revisited: the case of disjunction effects in cognition, *Frontiers in Physics: Interdisciplinary Physics* **4**, 26.

Moreira, C. and Wichert, A. (2017). Are quantum models for order effects quantum? *International Journal of Theoretical Physics* **82:**, pp. 73–83.

Murphy, G. and Brownell, H. (1985). Category differentiation in object recognition: Typicality constraints on the basic category advantage, *Journal of Experimental Psychology* **11**, p. 70ff.

Myers, J. M. (1997). Can a universal quantum computer be fully quantum? *Phys. Rev. Lett.* **78**, 9, pp. 1823–1824, doi:10.1103/PhysRevLett.78.1823.

Newell, A. (1990). *Unified Theories of Cognition* (Harvard University Press).

Newell, A. and Simon, H. (1972). *Human Problem Solving* (Prentice-Hall).

Newell, A. and Simon, H. (1976). Computer science as empirical inquiry: symbols and search. *Communication of the ACM* **19**, 3, pp. 113–126.

Nielsen, M. A. and Chuang, I. L. (2000). *Quantum Computation and Quantum Information* (Cambridge University Press, Cambridge, MA, USA).

Nilsson, N. J. (1982). *Principles of Artificial Intelligence* (Springer-Verlag).

Nunn, C. M., Clarke, C. and Blott, B. (1994). Collapse of a quantum field may affect brain function, *Journal of Consciousness Studies* **1**, 1, pp. 127–139.

OFTA (1991). *Les Réseaux de Neurones* (Masson).

O'Malley, P. J. J., Babbush, R., Kivlichan, I. D., Romero, J., McClean, J. R., Kelly, R. B. J., Roushan, P., Tranter, A., Ding, N., Campbell, B., Chen, Y., Chen, Z., Chiaro, B., Dunsworth, A., Fowler, A. G., Jeffrey, E., Lucero, E., Megrant, A., Mutus, J. Y., Neeley, M., Neill, C., Quintana, C., Sank, D., Vainsencher, A., Wenner, J., White, T. C., Coveney, P. V., Love, P. J., Neven, H., Aspuru-Guzik, A. and Martinis, J. M. (2016). Scalable quantum simulation of molecular energies, *Physical Review X* **6**, p. 031007.

Opwis, K. and Plötzner, R. (1996). *Kognitive Psychologie mit dem Computer* (Spektrum Akademischer Verlag, Heidelberg Berlin Oxford).

Ortega, P. A. and Braun, D. A. (2009). A conversion between utility and information, in *roceedings of the Third Conference on Artificial General Intelligence*, pp. 115–120.

Osherson, D. N. (1987). New axioms for the contrast model of similarity, *Journal of Mathematical Psychology* **31**, pp. 93–103.

Osherson, D. N. (1995). Probability judgment, in E. E. Smith and D. N. Osherson (eds.), *Thinking*, Vol. 3, 2nd edn., chap. two (MIT Press), pp. 35–75.

Palm, G. (1982). *Neural Assemblies, an Alternative Approach to Artificial Intelligence* (Springer-Verlag).

Palm, G. (1990). Assoziatives Gedächtnis und Gehirntheorie, in *Gehirn und Kognition* (Spektrum der Wissenschaft), pp. 164–174.

Palm, G., Schwenker, F. and Bibbig, A. (1992). Theorie Neuronaler Netze 1, Skript zur Vorlesung, university of Ulm, Department of Neural Information Processing.

Pan, J., Cao, Y., Yao, X., Li, Z., Ju, C., Peng, X., Kais, S., Du, J. and Du, J. (2014). Experimental realization of quantum algorithm for solving linear systems of equations, *Physical Review A.* **89**, 2, p. 022313.

Pearl, J. (1984). *Heuristics: Intelligent Strategies for Computer Problem Solving* (Addison-Wesley).

Pearl, J. (1989). *Probabilistic Reasoning in Intelligent Systems: Networks of Plausible Inference* (Morgan Kaufmann, Palo Alto, CA).

Penrose, R. (1991). *The Emperor's New Mind* (Penguin).

Pöppel, E. (2009). Pre-semantically defined temporal windows for cognitive processing, *Philos. Trans. R. Soc. Lond. B Biol. Sci.* .

Pöppel, E. (2010). Perceptual identity and personal self: neurobiological reflections, in M. Fajkowska and M. M. Eysenck (eds.), *Personality From Biological, Cognitive, and Social Perspectives* (Clinton Corners, NY: Eliot Werner Public), pp. 75–82.

Pöppel, E., Schill, K. and von Steinbüchel, N. (1990). Sensory integration within temporally neutral system states: a hypothesis, *Naturwissenschaftem* **77**, pp. 89–91.

Posner, M. I. and Raichle, M. E. (1994). *Images of Mind* (Scientific American Library, New York).

Post, E. (1943). Formal reductions of the general combinatorial problem, *American Journal of Mathematics* **65**, pp. 197–268.

Pothos, E., Busemeyer, J. and Trueblood, J. (2013). A quantum geometric model of similarity, *Psychological Review* **120**, pp. 679–696.

Quillian, R. (1968). Semantic memory, in M. Minsky (ed.), *Semantic Information Processing* (MIT Press), pp. 227–270.

Rao, C. R. (1973). *Linear Statistical Inference and its Applications: Second Editon* (John Wiley and Sons).

Reid, C. (1996). *Hilbert* (Spriner Verlag).

Reif, J. H. (1998). Efficient approximate solution of sparselinear systems, *Computers Mathematical Applications* **36**, 9, pp. 37–58.

Resnikoff, H. L. (1989). *The Illusion of Reality* (Springer-Verlag).

Richardson, M. and Domingos, P. (2006). Markov logic networks, *Machine learning* **62**, 1-2, pp. 107–136.

Rieffel, E. and Polak, W. (2011). *Quantum Computing - A Gentle Introduction* (The MIT Press).

Riesenhuber, M. and Poggio, T. (1999). Hierarchical models of object recognition in cortex, *Nature Neuroscience* **2**, pp. 1019–1025.

Riley, K. F., Hobson, M. P. and Bence, S. J. (2006). *Mathematical methods for physics and engineering* (Cambridge University Press).

Robert, F. N., Jose, V. R. R. and Winkler, R. L. (2009). Duality between maximization of expected utility and minimization of relative entropy when probabilities are imprecise, in *6th International Symposium on Imprecise Probability: Theories and Applications*, pp. 337–346.

Rosenbaum, D. and Perkowski, M. (2009). Extended superposed quantum-state initialization using disjoint prime implicants, *Physical Review A* **79**, 6, p. 052310.

Rosenblatt, F. (1962). *Principles of neurodynamics: Perceptrons and the theory of brain mechanisms* (Spartan Books).

Ross, S. M. (2009). *Introduction to probability and statistics for engineers and scientists*, 4th edn. (Academic Press).

Rumelhart, D. and McClelland (1986). On learning the past tense of english verbs, in J. McClelland and D. Rumelhart (eds.), *Parallel Distributed Processing* (MIT Press), pp. 216–271.

Russell, S. and Norvig, P. (2010). *Artificial intelligence: a modern approach*, Prentice Hall series in artificial intelligence (Prentice Hall), ISBN 9780136042594, URL `http://books.google.pt/books?id=8jZBksh-bUMC`.

Russell, S. J. and Norvig, P. (1995). *Artificial intelligemce: a modern approach* (Prentice-Hall).

Russell, S. J. and Norvig, P. (2003). *Artificial intelligemce: a modern approach*, 2nd edn. (Prentice-Hall).

Sacramento, J. and Wichert, A. (2012). Binary willshaw learning yields high synaptic capacity for long-term familiarity memory, *Biological Cybernetics* **106**, 2, pp. 123–133.

Salakhutdinov, R. and Hinton, G. (2012). An efficient learning procedure for deep boltzmann machines, *Neural Computation* **24**, pp. 1967–2006.

Schrödinger, E. (1935). Die gegenwärtige situation in der quantenmechanik, *Naturwissenschaften* **23**, 807.

Schuld, M. and Killoran, N. (2019). Quantum machine learning in feature hilbert spaces, *Physical Review Letters* **122**.

Schuld, M. and Petruccione, F. (2018). *Supervised Learning with Quantum Computers* (Springer).

Schwenker, F. (1996). Küntliche Neuronale Netze: Ein Überblick über die theoretischen Grundlagen, in G. Bol, G. Nakhaeizadeh and K. Vollmer (eds.), *Finanzmarktanalyse und -prognose mit innovativen und quantitativen Verfahren* (Physica-Verlag), pp. 1–14.

Shafir, E. and Tversky, A. (1992). Thinking through uncertainty: nonconsequential reasoning and choice, *Cognitive Psychology* **24**, pp. 449–474.

Shannon, C. E. (1948). A mathematical theory of communication, *Bell System Technical Journal* , pp. 1–54.

Shannon, C. E. (1953). Computers and automata, *Proceedings of the I.R.E.* **41**, pp. 1253–1241.

Shastri, L. (1988). *Semantic Networks: An Evidential Formulation and its Connectionistic Realization* (Morgan Kaufmann, London).

Shenvi, N., Kempe, J. and Whaley, K. B. (2003). Quantum random-walk search algorithm, *Phys. Rev. A* **67**, 5, p. 052307, doi:10.1103/PhysRevA.67.052307.

Shim, G. M., Kim, D. and Choi, M. Y. (1990). Statistical-mechanical formulation of the wiiishaw model with local inhibition, *Physical Review A A* **43**, 12, pp. 7012–7018.

Shor, P. (1994). Algorithms for quantum computation: discrete logarithms and factoring, in *Proceedings 35th Annual Symposium on Foundations of Computer Science*, pp. 124–134, doi:10.1109/SFCS.1994.365700.

Shor, P. W. (1995). Polynomial-Time Algorithms for Prime Factorization and Discrete Logarithms on a Quantum Computer, *ArXiv Quantum Physics e-prints* .

Simon, H. A. (1991). *Models of my Life* (Basic Books, New York).

Smith, E., Balzano, G. and Walker, J. (1978). Nominal, perceptual, and semantic codes in picture categorization, in J. Cotton and R. Klatzky (eds.), *Semantic factors in cognition* (Hillsdale, NJ: Erlbaum Associates), pp. 137–168.

Smith, E. and Sloman, S. (1994). Similarity vs. rule-based categorization, *Memory Cognition* **22**, pp. 377–386.

Smith, E. E. (1995). Concepts and categorization, in E. E. Smith and D. N. Osherson (eds.), *Thinking*, Vol. 3, 2nd edn., chap. one (MIT Press), pp. 3–33.

Smolensky, P. (1986). Information processing in dynamical systems: Foundations of harmony theory, in D. E. Rumelhart and J. L. McClelland (eds.), *Parallel*

Distributed Processing: Explorations in the Microstructure of Cognition. Volume 1: Foundations (The MIT Press), pp. 194–281.

Sommer, F. T. (1993). *Theorie neuronaler Assoziativspeicher*, Ph.D. thesis, Heinrich-Heine-Universität Düsseldorf, Düsseldorf.

Squire, L. R. and Kandel, E. R. (1999). *Memory. From Mind to Moleculus* (Scientific American Library).

Steinbuch, K. (1961). Die Lernmatrix, *Kybernetik* **1**, pp. 36–45.

Steinbuch, K. (1971). *Automat und Mensch*, 4th edn. (Springer-Verlag).

Sterling, P. (2004). Principles of allostasis: optimal design, predictive regulation, pathophysiology and rational therapeutics, in J. Schulkin (ed.), *Allostasis, Homeostasis, and the Costs of Adaptation* (Cambridge: University Press), pp. 17–64.

Stonier, T. (1990). *Information and the Internal Structure of Universe* (Springer-Verlag).

Sun, R. (1995). A two-level hybrid architecture for structuring knowledge for commonsense reasoning, in R. Sun and L. A. Bookman (eds.), *Computational Architectures Integrating Neural and Symbolic Processing*, chap. 8 (Kluwer Academic Publishers), pp. 247–182.

Sussman, G. (1975). *A Computer Model of Skill Acquisition* (MIT, Cambridge).

Suzuki, M. (1985). Decomposition formulas of exponential operators and lie exponentials with some applications to quantum mechanics and statistical physics, *Journal of Mathematical Physics* **206**, 601.

Szilárd, L. (1929). Über die entropieverminderung in einem thermodynamischen system bei eingriffen intelligenter wesen, *Zeitschrift für Physik* **53**, pp. 840–856.

Tarrataca, L. and Wichert, A. (2011a). Problem-solving and quantum computation, *Cognitive Computation* **3**, pp. 510–524, URL `http://dx.doi.org/10.1007/s12559-011-9103-6`.

Tarrataca, L. and Wichert, A. (2011b). Tree search and quantum computation, *Quantum Information Processing* **10**, 4, pp. 475–500, 10.1007/s11128-010-0212-z.

Tarrataca, L. and Wichert, A. (2012a). Iterative quantum tree search, CiE 2012 - How the World Computes, 2012.

Tarrataca, L. and Wichert, A. (2012b). A quantum production model, *Quantum Information Processing* **11**, 1, pp. 189–209, URL `http://dx.doi.org/10.1007/s11128-011-0241-2`, 10.1007/s11128-011-0231-4.

Tarrataca, L. and Wichert, A. (2013a). Intricacies of quantum computational paths, *Quantum Information Processing* **12**, pp. 1365–1378, doi:10.1007/s11128-012-0475-7.

Tarrataca, L. and Wichert, A. (2013b). Quantum iterative deepening with an application to the halting problem, *PLOS ONE* **8**, 3.

Tarski, A. (1944). The semantic conception of truth and foundations of semantics, *Philos. and Phenom. Res.* **4**, pp. 241–376.

Tarski, A. (1956). *Logic, Semantics,Metamathematics* (Oxford University Press, London).

Tarski, A. (1995). *Pisma logiczno-filozoficzne. Prawda*, Vol. 1 (Wydawnictwo Naukowe PWN, Warszawa).

Tay, N., Loo, C. and Perus, M. (2010). Face recognition with quantum associative networks using overcomplete gabor wavelet, *Cognitive Computation* , pp. 1–6URL `http://dx.doi.org/10.1007/s12559-010-9047-2`, 10.1007/s12559-010-9047-2.

Toffoli, T. (1980a). Reversible computing, in *Proceedings of the 7th Colloquium on Automata, Languages and Programming* (Springer-Verlag, London, UK), ISBN 3-540-10003-2, pp. 632–644.

Toffoli, T. (1980b). Reversible computing, Tech. rep., Massschusetts Institute of Technology, Laboratory for Computer Science, Massachusetts, MA, USA.

Toffoli, T. (1980c). Reversible computing, in J. de Bakker and J. van Leeuwen (eds.), *Automata, Languages and Programming, Lecture Notes in Computer Science*, Vol. 85 (Springer Berlin / Heidelberg), pp. 632–644, URL `http://dx.doi.org/10.1007/3-540-10003-2$_$104`.

Topsoe, F. (1974). *Informationstheorie* (Teubner Sudienbucher).

Trueblood, J., Pothos, E. and Busemeyer, J. (2014). Quantum probability theory as a common framework for reasoning and similarity, *Frontiers in Psychology* **5**.

Trueblood, J. S., Yearsley, J. M. and Pothos, E. M. (2017). A quantum probability framework for human probabilistic inference, *Journal of Experimental Psychology: General* **146**, 9, p. 1307.

Turing, A. (1936). On computable numbers, with an application to the entscheidungsproblem, in *Proceedings of the London Mathematical Society*, Vol. 2, pp. 260–265.

Turing, A. M. (1950). Computing machinery and intelligence, *Mind* **59**.

Tversky, A. (1977). Feature of similarity, *Psychological Review* **84**, pp. 327–352.

Tversky, A. and Shafir, E. (1992). The disjunction effect in choice under uncertainty, *Journal of Psychological Science* **3**, pp. 305–309.

Ulanov, A. E., Tiunov, E. S. and Lvovsky, A. I. (2020). Quantum-inspired annealers as boltzmann generators for machine learning and statistical physics, *ArXiv Quantum Physics e-prints* **abs/1912.08480**.

Vandersypen, L. M. K., Steffen, M., Breyta, G., Yannoni, C. S., Sherwood, M. H. and Chuang, I. L. (2001). Experimental realization of shor's quantum factoring algorithm using nuclear magnetic resonance, *Nature* **414**, pp. 883–887.

Vedral, V. (2011). Living in a quantum world, *Scientific American* **304**, 6, pp. 38–43.

Ventura, D. and Martinez, T. (1988). Quantum associative memory with exponential capacity, in *Neural Networks Proceedings, 1998. IEEE World Congress on Computational Intelligence.*, Vol. 1, pp. 509–513.

Ventura, D. and Martinez, T. (1999). Initializing the amplitude distribution of a quantum state, *Foundations of Physics Letters* **12**, 6, pp. 547–559.

Ventura, D. and Martinez, T. (2000). Quantum associative memory, *Information Sciences* **124**, 1, pp. 273–296.

von Holst, E. and Mittelstaedt, H. (1950). Das reafferenzprinzip (wechselwirkungen zwischen zentralnervensystem und peripherie, *Naturwissenschaften* **37**, pp. 464–476.

von Neumann, J. (1945). First draft of a report on the edvac, Tech. rep., University of Pennsylvania.

Wallace, D. (2002). Worlds in the everett interpretation, *Studies in History and Philosophy of Modern Physics* **33**, pp. 637–661.

Wallace, D. (2003a). Everett and structure, *Studies in History and Philosophy of Modern Physics* **34**, pp. 87–105.

Wallace, D. (2003b). Everettian rationality: defending deutsch's approach to probability in the everett interpretation, *Studies in History and Philosophy of Modern Physics* **24**, pp. 415–439.

Wallace, D. (2007). Quantum probability from subjective likelihood: Improving on deutsch's proof of the probability rule, *Studies in History and Philosophy of Modern Physics* **38**, pp. 311–332.

Watrous, J. (1998). Quantum simulations of classical random walks and undirected graph connectivity, *CoRR* **cs.CC/9812012**.

Wennekers, T. (1999). *Synchronisation und Assoziation in Neuronalen Netzen* (Shaker Verlag, Aachen).

Wheeler, J. (1957). Assessment of everett's "relative state", *Reviews of Modern Physics* **29**, pp. 463–465.

White, H. (1992). *Artificial Neural Networks - Approximation and Learning Theorz* (Blackwell).

Wichert, A. (1993). MTCn-nets, in *Proceedings World Congres on Neural Networks* (Lawrence Erlbaum), pp. 59–62.

Wichert, A. (1998). Hierarchical categorization, in M. W. Evens (ed.), *Ninth Midwest Artificial Intelligence and Cognitive Science Conference* (AAAI Press), pp. 141–148.

Wichert, A. (2000). A categorical expert system "jurassic", *Expert Systems with Application* **19**, 3, pp. 149–158.

Wichert, A. (2001). Pictorial reasoning with cell assemblies, *Connection Science* **13**, 1.

Wichert, A. (2002). Learning of associative prediction by experience, *Neurocomputing* **48**, 1-4, pp. 741–42.

Wichert, A. (2004). Categorial expert systems, *Expert Systems* **21**, 1, pp. 34–47.

Wichert, A. (2005a). Associative computer: a hybrid connectionistic production system, *Cognitive Systems Research* **6**, 2, pp. 111–144.

Wichert, A. (2005b). Associative diagnose, *Expert Systems* **22**, 1, pp. 26–39.

Wichert, A. (2006). Cell assemblies for diagnostic problem-solving, *Neurocomputing* **69**, 7-9, pp. 810–824.

Wichert, A. (2009). Sub-symbols and icons, *Cognitive Computation* **1**, 4, pp. 342–347.

Wichert, A. (2011). The role of attention in the context of associative memory, *Cognitive Computation* **3**, 1.

Wichert, A. (2012). Inference, ontologies and the pump of though, in E. Davelaar (ed.), *Connectionist Models of Neurocognition and Emergent Behavior* (World Scientific), pp. 227 –224.

Wichert, A. (2013). Proto logic and neural subsymbolic reasoning, *Journal of Logic and Computation* **23**, 3, pp. 627–643.

Wichert, A. (2016a). Brain and mind in everett many-worlds, *Journal of Consciousness Exploration and Research,* **7**, 19, pp. 817–822.

Wichert, A. (2016b). The quantum binding problem in the context of associative memory, *PLOS ONE* **11**, 9, p. e0162312.

Wichert, A. (2019). Principles of quantum-like evolution, *Open Systems & Information Dynamics* **26**, 2, p. 1950007.

Wichert, A., Abler, B., Grothe, J., Walter, H. and Sommer, F. T. (2002). Exploratory analysis of event-related fmri demonstrated in a working memory study, in F. Sommer and A. Wichert (eds.), *Exploratory analysis and data modeling in functional neuroimaging*, chap. 5 (MIT Press, Boston, MA), pp. 77–108.

Wichert, A. and Moreira, C. (2016). Probabilities and shannon's entropy in the everett many-worlds theory, *Frontiers in Physics: Interdisciplinary Physics* **4**, 47.

Wichert, A. and Moreira, C. (2018). Balanced quantum-like model for decision making, in Springer (ed.), *Proceedings of 11th International Conference on Quantum Interaction*, pp. 79–90.

Wichert, A., Moreira, C. and Bruza, P. (2020). Quantum-like bayesian networks, *Entropy* **22**, 2, p. 170.

Wichert, A., Pereira, J. D. and Carreira, P. (2008). Visual search light model for mental problem solving, *Neurocomputing* **71**, 13-15, pp. 2806–2822.

Wickelgren, W. A. (1969). Context-sensitive coding, associative memory, and serial order in (speech)behavior, *Psychological Review* **76**, pp. 1–15.

Wickelgren, W. A. (1977). *Cognitive Psychology* (Prentice-Hall).

Williams, C. P. and Clearwatter, S. H. (1997). *Explorations in Quantum Computing* (Springer-Verlag).

Willshaw, D., Buneman, O. and Longuet-Higgins, H. (1969). Nonholgraphic associative memory, *Nature* **222**, pp. 960–962.

Wilson, M., Vandal, T., ad Hogg and Rieffel, E. G. (2019). Quantum-assisted associative adversarial network: Applying quantum annealing in deep learning, *ArXiv Quantum Physics e-prints* **abs/1904.10573**.

Winston, P. H. (1992). *Artificial Intelligence*, 3rd edn. (Addison-Wesley).

Wittek, P. (2014). *Quantum Machine Learning, What Quantum Computing Means to Data Mining*, Elsevier Insights (Academic Press).

Yukalov, V. and Sornette, D. (2011). Decision theory with prospect interference and entanglement, *Theory and Decision* **70**, pp. 283–328.

Zalka, C. (1999). Grover's quantum searching algorithm is optimal, *Physical Review A* **60**, p. 2746, URL `http://www.citebase.org/abstract?id=oai:arXiv.org:quant-ph/9711070`.

Zhou, B., Pöppel, E. and Bao, Y. (2014). In the jungle of time: the concept of identity as a way out, *Frontiers in Psychology* **5**, p. 844.

Index

www.ingramcontent.com/pod-product-compliance
Lightning Source LLC
LaVergne TN
LVHW011656200926
848484LV00004B/960
* 9 7 8 9 8 1 1 2 2 4 3 0 0 *